W9-AYF-191

TUSCANY & UMBRIA

VIRGINIA MAXWELL
ALEX LEVITON, LEIF PETTERSEN

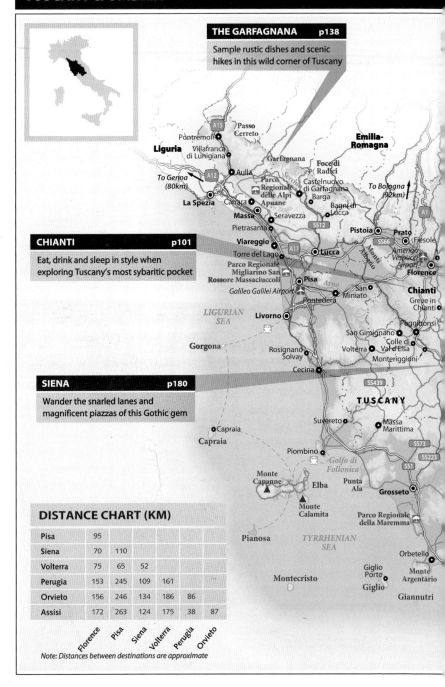

THE GARFAGNANA p138

Sample rustic dishes and scenic hikes in this wild corner of Tuscany

CHIANTI p101

Eat, drink and sleep in style when exploring Tuscany's most sybaritic pocket

SIENA p180

Wander the snarled lanes and magnificent piazzas of this Gothic gem

DISTANCE CHART (KM)

	Florence	Pisa	Siena	Volterra	Perugia	Orvieto
Pisa	95					
Siena	70	110				
Volterra	75	65	52			
Perugia	153	245	109	161		
Orvieto	156	246	134	186	86	
Assisi	172	263	124	175	38	87

Note: Distances between destinations are approximate

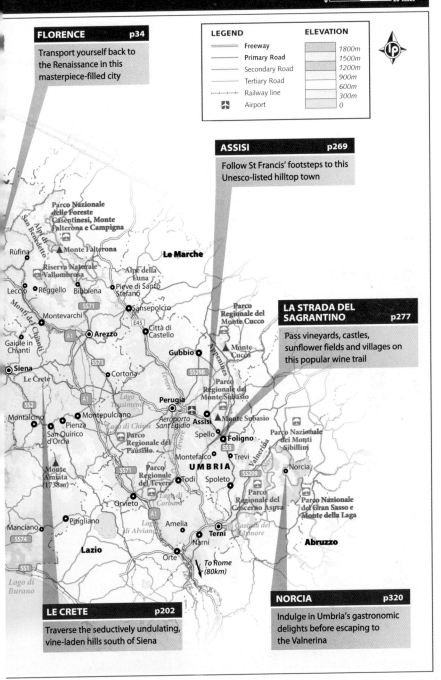

0 — 40 km
0 — 20 miles

FLORENCE p34

Transport yourself back to the Renaissance in this masterpiece-filled city

LEGEND

Freeway
Primary Road
Secondary Road
Tertiary Road
Railway line
Airport

ELEVATION

1800m
1500m
1200m
900m
600m
300m
0

ASSISI p269

Follow St Francis' footsteps to this Unesco-listed hilltop town

LA STRADA DEL SAGRANTINO p277

Pass vineyards, castles, sunflower fields and villages on this popular wine trail

Parco Nazionale delle Foreste Casentinesi, Monte Falterona e Campigna

Monte Falterona

Le Marche

Rùfina

Riserva Naturale Vallombrosa

Alpe di San Benedetto

Alpe della Luna

Lecco   Reggello   Bibbiena

Pieve di Santo Stefano

Parco Regionale del Monte Cucco

Sansepolcro

Montevarchi

SS71

E45

Città di Castello

Monte Cucco

Gaiole in Chianti

Monti del Chianti

Arezzo

A1

Gubbio

Appennines

Siena

Le Crete

SS571

Cortona

Tevere

SS298

Parco Regionale del Monte Subasio

Lago Trasimeno

A1

Perugia

SS52

Montepulciano

Montalcino

Lago di Chiusi

Aeroporto Sant'Egidio

Assisi   Monte Subasio

Pienza

Parco Regionale del Pausillo

Spello   Foligno

Parco Nazionale dei Monti Sibillini

San Quirico d'Orcia

Tevere

SS3

Valnerina

Nera

Montefalco   Trevi

Monte Amiata (1738m)

SS71

Parco Regionale del Tevere

UMBRIA

Todi   Spoleto

SS209

Norcia

Lago di Corbara

Parco Regionale del Coscerno Aspra

Parco Nazionale del Gran Sasso e Monte della Laga

Orvieto

A1

Amelia

Lago di Alviano

Manciano

Pitigliano

Cascata del Marmore

Abruzzo

SS74

Lazio

Narni   Terni

Orte

SS1

To Rome (80km)

Lago di Burano

LE CRETE p202

Traverse the seductively undulating, vine-laden hills south of Siena

NORCIA p320

Indulge in Umbria's gastronomic delights before escaping to the Valnerina

INTRODUCING TUSCANY & UMBRIA

LADEN WITH GRAND-SLAM SIGHTS AND EXPERIENCES, THIS PART OF ITALY OFFERS THE PERFECT INTRODUCTION TO THE COUNTRY'S FAMED DOLCE VITA.

Despite incessant praise, the beauty and charm of Tuscany and Umbria continue to defy description. They truly do have it all: extraordinary art and architecture; colourful festivals; season-driven cuisines emulated the world over; and never-ending, picture-perfect landscapes of olive groves, vineyards and poplars. And let's not forget the locals – this may be the land of Dante and Michelangelo, but it's also the home of the Ferragamo and Gucci fashion houses, and celebrity chefs such as Fabio Picchi and Gianfranco Vissani. Here, food, fashion, art and nature intermingle effortlessly and to magnificent effect.

There's an overabundance of things to do and see because Tuscany and Umbria have been value-adding since Etruscan times. You can visit a World Heritage Site in the morning (there are seven), drive through a national park in the afternoon (there are four) and bunk down in stylish vineyard accommodation at night (we wouldn't dare hazard a guess at how many of these there are). Medieval fortresses, Renaissance masterpieces and Gothic cathedrals? Check. Spectacular hiking and sensational Slow Food? Yep. Hills laden with vines, ancient olive groves? You've got the picture.

FLORENCE

CHIANTI

TOP Mingling after dark in Piazza della Signoria (p50), Florence BOTTOM LEFT Autumnal landscape, Chianti (p101) BOTTOM Sunflowers brighten the wine route through Montefalco (p280)

LA STRADA DEL SAGRANTINO

SIME/SIMEONE GIOVANNI

SIENA

THE GARFAGNANA

MARKA / ALAMY

NORCIA

TOP LEFT Piazza del Campo (p181), Siena's civic centre **TOP RIGHT** Butcher's shop in Norcia (p320), a town famous for its meat products **BOTTOM LEFT** Horse trekking through the Garfagnana (p138) **BOTTOM CENTRE** Winery on the fertile hills of Le Crete (p202), south of Siena **BOTTOM RIGHT** The upper church of Basilica di San Francesco (p270), Assisi

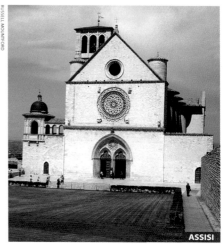
LE CRETE

ASSISI

GETTING STARTED

WHAT'S NEW?

★ Exciting exhibitions at Florence's Palazzo Strozzi (p62)

★ An opulent refurbishment of Brufa's best hotel restaurant (p268)

★ Sagrantino tastings at the Arnaldo Caprai vineyard, Montefalco (p281)

★ The meticulously restored Palazzo Blu in Pisa (p117)

★ A purpose-built outdoor theatre in Narni (p328)

★ The unique dining experience of Umbria Grill (p309)

CLIMATE: FLORENCE

Average Max/Min

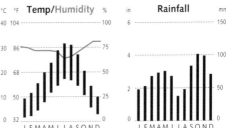

PRICE GUIDE

	BUDGET	MIDRANGE	TOP END
SLEEPING	<€80	€80-180	>€180
MEALS	<€25	€25-45	>€45
250ML WINE	€2	€3	€8

TOP Chianti wine display in Florence **BOTTOM LEFT** Piazza and Basilica di Santa Croce (p69), Florence **BOTTOM RIGHT** Fashionable Via de' Tornabuoni (p60), Florence **FAR RIGHT** Beachside bliss, Elba (p166)

ACCOMMODATION

Tuscany and Umbria are blessed with accommodation styles and options to suit every taste and budget, with comfortable midrange choices predominating. In cities and large towns there are plenty of family-run *pensioni* (guest houses) and B&Bs; in rural areas the *agriturismo* (farm-stay accommodation) reigns supreme. These rural retreats inject money into small local communities, provide much-needed employment and allow visitors to explore the countryside slowly and in great style. For more information on accommodation in the region, see p391.

MAIN POINTS OF ENTRY

PISA INTERNATIONAL AIRPORT (PSA; ☎ 050 84 93 00; www.pisa-airport.com) Known as Galileo Galilei, this is Tuscany's major hub for international arrivals.

FLORENCE AIRPORT (FLR; ☎ 055 306 13 00; www.aeroporto.firenze.it) Also known as Amerigo Vespucci; hosts flights from Rome, Sicily, Sardinia and some European destinations.

STAZIONE DI SANTA MARIA NOVELLA (Piazza della Stazione, Florence) Trains from European and Italian destinations arrive here, including Eurostar and Alta Velocità Eurostar Italia (fast train) services.

THINGS TO TAKE

★ Detailed driving map

★ Mosquito repellent (mossies can be a pest in summer)

★ Picnic-friendly pocket knife with corkscrew

★ Sunglasses, hat and something to cover shoulders when visiting churches

★ Sturdy walking shoes to combat cobbles and country paths

JON DAVISON

WEBLINKS

ANGLOINFO TUSCANY (http://tuscany.angloinfo.com) Useful English-language website.

BELLA UMBRIA (www.bellaumbria.net) Comprehensive guide to Umbria.

THE GREEN HEART OF ITALY (www.umbria-turismo.it) Umbrian tourist-board website.

TURISMO IN TOSCANA (www.turismo.intoscana.it) Tuscany tourist-board website.

TUSCANY & WINE (www.tuscany-wine.com) Wine website with useful links.

DALLAS STRIBLEY

FESTIVALS & EVENTS

FEBRUARY/MARCH

CARNEVALE

VIAREGGIO
Fireworks, floats, parades and parties galore from February to early March (p143).

MARCH/APRIL

SETTIMANA SANTA

ASSISI
Easter Week in this famous pilgrimage town is celebrated with processions and performances.

APRIL/MAY/JUNE

CORSA ALL'ANELLO

NARNI
Held over three weekends in April and May, the Corsa all'Anello (Race for the Ring) features medieval costumes, sombre processions and neighbourhood feasts.

MAGGIO MUSICALE FIORENTINO

FLORENCE
The oldest arts festival in Italy stages world-class performances of theatre, classical music, jazz and dance between late April and June (www.maggiofiorentino.com, in Italian).

LA GIOSTRA DELLA QUINTANA

FOLIGNO
This medieval tournament sees neighbourhoods challenging each other in a friendly jousting competition at the start of June and in September (www.quintana.it).

GIOSTRA DELL'ARCHIDADO

CORTONA
Coinciding with Ascension Day (40 days after Easter), this week-long festival includes trumpeting, parades and a crossbow competition.

LUMINARIA

PISA
Streets along the Arno are illuminated with 70,000 candles on the night of 16 June to honour the city's patron saint, St Ranieri.

FESTA DI SAN GIOVANNI

FLORENCE
Florence celebrates its patron saint on 24 June with a *calcio storico* (medieval football) match and fireworks.

TOP Confetti-strewn children at Viareggio's Carnevale (p143), northwestern Tuscany **RIGHT** The spectacular pageantry of Il Palio (p185), Siena

FESTIVAL DEI DUE MONDI

SPOLETO

This internationally renowned festival sees opera, theatre, ballet and art performances taking place around town during late June to early July (www.spoletofestival .it; p318).

www.spoletofestival.it; p318

JULY/AUGUST

UMBRIA JAZZ

PERUGIA

One of Italy's top music festivals and a major event on the international jazz circuit (www.umbriajazz.com, in Italian; p262).

PUCCINI FESTIVAL

TORRE DEL LAGO

Staged in a lakeside open-air theatre, this is a must for all opera fans (www.puccini festival.it; p135).

IL PALIO

SIENA

The most spectacular event on the Tuscan calendar, held in July and August (p185).

SEPTEMBER

SAGRA MUSICALE UMBRA

PERUGIA

This renowned holy-music festival is held in the second half of the month (www .perugiamusicaclassica.com, in Italian; p263).

OCTOBER

FESTA DI SAN FRANCESCO

ASSISI

The life of Assisi's most famous son is celebrated on 3 and 4 October with religious services, folk dancing and song.

DALLAS STRIBLEY

CULTURE

RUSSELL MOUNTFORD

TUSCAN FILM

A ROOM WITH A VIEW
(Merchant Ivory, 1986) A
homage to EM Forster's
novel and the visual beauty of
Florence.

LIFE IS BEAUTIFUL
(Roberto Benigni, 1997) Part of
this uplifting Holocaust film is
set in Arezzo.

STEALING BEAUTY
(Bernaldo Bertolucci, 1996) A
young American girl grapples
with her grief and burgeoning
sexuality in the lush Tuscan
countryside.

TEA WITH MUSSOLINI
(Franco Zeffirelli, 1999)
The great director's semi-
autobiographical film is
set in Florence and San
Gimignano.

THE ENGLISH PATIENT
(Anthony Minghella, 1996)
Features stunning scenes shot
in a monastery just outside
Pienza.

RENAISSANCE ART

This region constitutes the world's biggest (and
most important) showcase of Renaissance art. In
the 14th and 15th centuries it was home to innova-
tors and geniuses the likes of which the world had
never seen before – and probably never will again.
Artists such as Nicola Pisano and Cimabue set the
stage for the Renaissance (Rebirth) of classical art
and architecture, and practitioners such as Giotto
and Brunelleschi supplied bravura performances
with masterpieces such as the frescos in the Basilica di San Francesco at Assisi (p270) and the
dome of Florence's Duomo (p44). Even the smallest towns have churches adorned with important
works of art, and the major museums in Florence,
Siena and Perugia are crammed with so many
masterpieces that even three or four visits are inadequate – one can almost seem criminally negligent.
For more on art and architecture, see p351.

4CORNERS/BORCHI MASSIMO

TOP Interior view of Florence's Duomo (p44) **BOTTOM** A *passeggiata* through luminous Perugia (p253)
RIGHT Historic Caffè Rivoire (p51), Florence **FAR RIGHT** Orvieto's ornate cathedral (p302)

TOP CATHEDRALS

DUOMO (FLORENCE) A facade and dome beyond compare (p44).

DUOMO (PISA) One of the extraordinary structures on Piazza dei Miracoli (p113).

CATHEDRAL (ORVIETO) Known as the 'golden lily'; a stunning building that blends the Romanesque and Gothic styles (p302).

CATHEDRAL (SIENA) One of Italy's greatest Gothic structures (p185).

CHIESA DI SANTA MARIA DELLA CONSOLAZIONE (TODI) A 16th-century architectural masterpiece (p312).

JULIET COOMBE

DAMIEN SIMONIS

DON'T MISS EXPERIENCES

* *Aperitivo* – Kick back in the company of good wine, food and friends (p347).

* Historic cafes – Sip cappuccino in the morning and espresso in the afternoon (p348).

* Open-air concerts – Take to amphitheatres and piazzas on sultry summer evenings (p97, p83).

* Medieval and religious festivals – Watch the locals play dress-ups (p10).

* *Passeggiata* – Join the traditional evening promenade (p276).

* Wine tasting – Sniff, sip and swill your way around Chianti (p101), Montepulciano (p211) and Torgiano (p266).

TUSCAN READS

A TABERNACLE FOR THE SUN (Linda Proud, 1997) Book One of the Botticelli Trilogy.

THE DECAMERON (Giovanni Boccaccio, 1353) A bawdy masterpiece.

THE DIVINE COMEDY (Dante Alighieri, 1321) Italian literature's supreme achievement.

UNDER THE TUSCAN SUN (Frances Mayes, 1996) Best-selling memoir.

WHERE ANGELS FEAR TO TREAD (EM Forster, 1905) Predates *A Room with a View*.

DALLAS STRIBLEY

CULTURE

UMBRIAN TALES

AFTER HANNIBAL (Barry Unsworth, 1996) Novel set in rural Umbria.

BROTHER SUN, SISTER MOON (Franco Zeffirelli, 1972) Feature film about the lives of St Francis and St Clare of Assisi.

LADY IN THE PALAZZO (Marlena de Blasi, 2006) Memoir set in Orvieto.

MY HOUSE IN UMBRIA (Richard Loncraine, 2003) Feature film based on the novel by Richard Trevor.

DOS & DON'TS

Observe local codes of behaviour and etiquette:

DRESSING Flip-flops and singlets are reserved for the beach.

GREETING Strangers and acquaintances shake hands; friends kiss two cheeks.

SIGHTSEEING Never intrude on a mass or service in a church.

SUNBATHING Topless sunbathing is considered unacceptable.

VISITING Take *dolcetti* (sweet biscuits or cakes) for your host.

WORSHIPPING Cover your shoulders, décolletage and thighs when entering a church.

AN ITALIAN ICON

At the end of WWII, manufacturer Enrico Piaggio gave his employee Corradino d'Ascanio the task of designing a simple motorcycle that was tough, economical and elegant. He specified that it should be easy to drive for both men and women, be able to carry a passenger, and not get its driver's clothes dirty. The result was one of Italy's great design icons: the Vespa MP6. On being presented with the prototype, Piaggio exclaimed 'It looks like a wasp!', so giving the famous scooter its nickname. Today, Vespas are produced by the Piaggio plant in Pontedera, southeast of Pisa, and are exported throughout the world. For more information on Italian design, see p350.

TOP The Vespa (above): an Italian design icon RIGHT The Medicis continue to make an impact in Pisa (p112)

THE MEDICI

Few Italian dynasties were as illustrious as the Medici. From the 14th to 18th centuries, members of this mercantile and banking family dominated Florence and many nearby cities, controlling business and government, and functioning as influential patrons of the arts, sciences and humanities. Three popes came from the Medici ranks, as did two queens of France. Names such as Cosimo the Elder, Cosimo I and Lorenzo the Magnificent are synonymous with the city of Florence, and the list of architects, artists and scientists whom they nurtured and supported – Michelangelo, Masaccio, Galileo, Brunelleschi, Botticelli, Fra' Angelico and Donatello to name but a few – couldn't be more exalted. For more on the family's enduring influence, see p35 and p338.

TUSCAN & UMBRIAN MAESTROS

* Giacomo Puccini (born Lucca, 1858; died Brussels, 1924) – The great opera composer (see p135).

* Pietro Mascagni (born Livorno, 1863; died Rome, 1945) – Best known for his opera *Cavalleria Rusticana*.

* Guido d'Arrezzo (born and died Arrezzo, 11th century) – Invented musical notation and the doh-ray-me scale.

* Heinrich Isaac (15th century) – Prolific composer of masses, songs and instrumental music for the Medici.

DAMIEN SIMONIS

FOOD & DRINK

© CARO / ALAMY

FESTIVALS

MOSTRA MERCATO DEL TARTUFO NERO (Norcia; p321) Celebrates the black truffle in late February and early March.

SAGRA DEL FUNGO PORCINO (Cortona) This festival in mid-August honours the delectable *porcino* mushroom.

JAZZ & WINE FESTIVAL (Montalcino) Jazz-loving oenophiles savour this event in the second and third weeks of July.

MOSTRA MERCATO NAZIONALE DEL TARTUFO BIANCO DI SAN MINIATO (San Miniato; p130) This Tuscan hilltop town celebrates the white truffle on the last three weekends of November.

BANCO D'ASSAGGIO DEI VINI (Torgiano) A dedicated wine-tasting demonstration and major wine competition in November that's an important event on the international calendar.

REGIONAL CUISINE

'To cook like your mother is good; to cook like your grandmother is better', says the Tuscan proverb. Indeed, it's the age-old recipes passed between generations that form the backbone of contemporary Tuscan and Umbrian cuisine. This peasant fare based on beans, bread and other cheap, abundant essentials has led to Tuscans being dubbed *mangiafagioli* (bean eaters) – something they and their neighbours have no problem with. The age-old *cucina povera* (cooking of the poor) they enjoy is dictated by the season, uses local produce or leftovers, and is savoured around a shared table with locally produced wine and lots of conversation. To discover more about the Tuscan and Umbrian table, see p381.

GIORGIO COSULICH

TOP Mixing it up at a *porcino* festival, Tuscany BOTTOM Nerbone food stall in Florence's Mercato Centrale (p66) RIGHT Preparing *bistecca alla fiorentina* (p83) FAR RIGHT The acclaimed black truffle (p307)

TOP FOODIE WEBSITES

CHOWHOUND (http://chowhound.chow.com/boards/58) Well-regarded foodie website.

DELICIOUS ITALY (www.deliciousitaly.com) For the traveller who likes to eat well.

DIVINA CUCINA (www.divinacucina.com) Cooking teacher Judy Francini gives recipes and restaurant tips for Florence and Chianti, plus a link to her popular blog.

FAITH WILLINGER (www.faithwillinger.com) Florence is home to author, food critic and chef Faith Willinger.

LUCILLIAN DELIGHTS (http://lucullian.blogspot.com) Excellent blog with regional recipes.

DON'T MISS EXPERIENCES

- ★ Almond *cantucci* and Vin Santo – Hard, sweet biscuits and Tuscan dessert wine is a marriage truly made in heaven.
- ★ Brunello di Montalcino– Drink this magnificent wine anywhere, any time (p196).
- ★ *Cinghiale* – Local wild boar served in a rich, peppery stew or in salami.
- ★ *Taglierini* with *porcini* mushrooms – Try this exquisite pasta dish when *porcini* are in season (late August to October).
- ★ Truffles – Freshly sourced and shaved over pasta. For white truffles head to San Miniato (p129); for black, Norcia (p320).
- ★ Vernaccia – Aromatic white wine preferably drunk before dinner on a San Gimignano terrace (p196).

LOOK OUT FOR

CHIANINA BEEF Tender, flavoursome meat from white oxen raised near Arezzo and Siena.

FAGIOLO DI SORANA Delicate white beans from the hills around Pescia.

FARRO DELLA GARFAGNANA Intensely flavoured, firm and slightly crunchy spelt from northwestern Tuscany.

LENTICCHIA DI CASTELLUCCIO DI NORCIA Small, thin-skinned lentils from southern Umbria.

ZAFFERANO DI SAN GIMIGNANO Strongly scented local saffron.

STEFANO SCATA

FOOD & DRINK

TOP SPOTS

NORCIA For butchers so famous they've entered the lexicon (p321).

SIENA Home to sweet delights including panforte (a rich cake of almonds, honey and candied fruit) and *ricciarelli* (small almond cakes; p180).

SPOLETO Famous for its black truffles (p315).

THE GARFAGNANA The place to feast on fruits of the forest (p138).

THE LUNIGIANA Authentic *cucina rustica* (rustic cuisine) for everyone to savour (p146).

LE STRADE DEL VINO

Wine routes are an enjoyable way to explore the region. See p375 for a full list.

STRADA DEI VINI CHIANTI RÙFINA E POMINO (www.chiantirufina.com) East of Florence.

STRADA DEI VINI DEL CANTICO (www.stradadeivinidelcantico.it) Incorporates Assisi, Spello, Todi and Torgiano in Umbria.

STRADA DEL SAGRANTINO (www.stradadelsagrantino.it) Around Bevagna and Montefalco in Umbria.

STRADA DEL VINO NOBILE DI MONTEPULCIANO (www.stradavinonobile.it) Montepulciano and the Val d'Orcia in Tuscany.

STRADA DEL VINO TERRE DI AREZZO (www.stradadelvino.arezzo.it) Around Arezzo and Cortona in Tuscany.

DOCG WINES

The prestigious appellation DOCG (Denominazione d'Origine Controllata e Garantita) is awarded to Italian wines that meet strict requirements regarding quality, production area, grape varietals, and viticultural and bottling techniques. There are currently 44 DOCGs in Italy, including eight from Tuscany and two from Umbria. The Tuscan denominations are Brunello di Montalcino; Carmignano; Chianti; Chianti Classico; Morellino di Scansano; Vernaccia di San Gimignano; Vino Nobile di Montepulciano; and Elba Aleatico Passito. The Umbrian denominations are Montefalco Sagrantino and Torgiano Rosso Riserva. For more on the region's wonderful tipples, see p375.

TOP *Lardo di colonnata* (p146) is cut after seasoning **RIGHT** A delicious display of panforte

THE ARK OF TASTE

A project born and headquartered in Florence, the Ark of Taste is an international catalogue of endangered food products drawn up by the Slow Food Foundation for Biodiversity in partnership with the region of Tuscany. It aims to protect indigenous edibles threatened with extinction by industrialisation, globalisation, hygiene laws and environmental dangers, and actively encourages their cultivation for consumption. Foods included in the list must be culturally or historically linked to a specific region, locality, ethnicity or traditional production practice, and must also be rare. There are 31 Tuscan and three Umbrian foods listed. For more details on the Ark, go to www.fondazioneslowfood.com/eng/arca/lista.lasso; for more on Slow Food, see p385.

WHY NOT TRY...

★ *Biroldo* – Local version of haggis; best sampled in Castelnuovo di Garfagnana (p141)

★ *Lardo di colonnata* – Wafer-thin pig fat marinated in olive oil and herbs (p146)

★ *Lumache* – Snails; scoff the slimy stuff in Bevagna (p280)

★ *Mallegato* – San Miniato's Slow Food–accredited blood sausage (p129)

★ *Maltagliati* – Random leftover bits after other pasta has been cut; literally 'bad pasta' and somewhat rudely called *lasagna bastarde* in the Lunigiana (p148)

★ Tripe sandwich – Florence's favourite fast food (p84)

ROBERTO GEROMETTA

OUTDOORS

HIKING SPOTS

APUANE ALPS Spectacular marble mountains located between the Apennines and the Versilian coast (p144).

LAGO TRASIMENO Wildlife, olive groves, sunflowers and glorious water views in a tranquil lake area (p290).

MONTI SIBILLINI Mountainous national park with red deer and plains of wildflowers (p322).

PARCO REGIONALE DELLA MAREMMA Sandy beaches, reclaimed marshland, wide plains where the famous Maremma cattle graze, and the wildlife-rich Monti dell'Uccellina (p225).

THE CASENTINO REGION Monasteries, botanical gardens and waterfalls in the heavily treed Parco Nazionale delle Foreste Casentinesi (p247).

THE GARFAGNANA Chestnuts and *porcini* mushrooms in the forests and hills (p138).

NATIONAL PARKS

The region's national parks cover large areas and protect a diverse collection of land, river, lake and marine ecosystems. There are three national parks in Tuscany: the Parco Nazionale dell'Arcipelago Toscana (p165), Europe's largest marine park; the Parco Nazionale delle Foreste Casentinesi, Monte Falterona e Campigna (p247), Italy's most extensive and best-preserved forest; and the Parco Nazionale de'Appennino Tosco-Emiliano, covering the fragile mountain environment of the Apennines. In Umbria, there is only one – the Parco Nazionale dei Monti Sibillini (p322), which takes its name from the principal mountain range in the area. The combined offerings of these parks provide many opportunities for hikes, day walks, bike riding, hang-gliding, horse riding and wildlife- and bird-watching. For more information, go to www.parks.it and see p369 of this book.

TOP Picnic on the Piano Grande, Monti Sibillini (p322) **BOTTOM** Still waters at Lago Trasimeno (p290) **RIGHT** Cattle herding in the Maremma (p225) **FAR RIGHT** Cycling through Chianti (p101)

TOP OUTDOOR ACTIVITIES

* Bird-watch in the Parco San Rossore and Riserva Naturale Lago di Burano (p118, p228).
* Canoe along the coastline in the Parco Regionale della Maremma (p225).
* Fish for eel, trout, perch, tench and carp in Lago Trasimeno (p291).
* Hang-glide or paraglide the skies over Monti Sibillini (p323).
* Take a bicycle tour of the Etruscan Coast (p164).

© DANITA DELIMONT / ALAMY

4CORNERS/AMANTINI STEFANO

DON'T MISS EXPERIENCES

* Discover the source of the Arno – Hike through the Parco Nazionale delle Foreste Casentinesi, Monte Falterona e Campigna (p247).
* Emulate Venus – Swim the protected waters of the Parco Nazionale dell'Arcipelago Toscana (p165), where the goddess rose from the waves.
* Explore the enigmatic Vie Cave – These Etruscan sunken roads are found in the valleys below Pitigliano (p232).
* Follow in St Francis' footsteps – Take a walk outside Assisi (p273).
* Ride a horse through fields of wildflowers – Visit the magnificent Piano Grande (p322).
* Trace the foundations of a Roman aqueduct – Traverse Spoleto's Via del Ponte (p317).

BIKE RIDES

CHIANTI Pedal through vineyards and olive groves (p101).

ETRUSCAN COAST Take in coastal views and nature reserves (p164).

LAGO TRASIMENO Enjoy the flat terrain and fish dinners (p290).

MAREMMA (www.maremma bike.it, in Italian) Tour gentle hills, thick woods and archaeological sites.

TUSCAN ARCHIPELAGO (www.aptelba.it) Explore Elba and six other islands on two wheels.

OUTDOORS

REGIONAL PARKS

PARCO ALPI APUANE (www .parcapuane.it) In northwestern Tuscany.

PARCO DI MIGLIARINO, SAN ROSSORE, MASSACIUCCOLI (www .parcosanrossore.org, in Italian) Runs between Viareggio and Livorno (p118).

PARCO DEL LAGO TRASIMENO (www.parco trasimeno.it) Around Lago Trasimeno.

PARCO NATURALE DELLA MAREMMA (www.parco -maremma.it) South of Grosseto (p225).

WALKING GUIDES

Useful books about walking in Tuscany and Umbria:

50 HIKES IN & AROUND TUSCANY (Jeff Taylor)

ITALY'S SIBILLINI NATIONAL PARK (Gillian Price) Walking and hiking guide.

THE ALPS OF TUSCANY (Francesco Greco) Selected hikes in the Apuane Alps.

TREADING GRAPES (Rosemary George) Walking through the vineyards of Tuscany.

WALKING & EATING IN TUSCANY & UMBRIA (James Lasdun and Pia Davis)

WALKING IN TUSCANY (Gillian Price)

GETTING AROUND ON TWO WHEELS

Although most historic town and city centres are closed to cars, cyclists are free to enter at will. There are plenty of places where you can rent a bike, buy colour-coordinated lycra and obtain advice on routes and itineraries – many of the latter are mentioned in this book. In May and early June the international cycling community descends upon Italy to see and compete in one of the world's great long-distance races, the Giro d'Italia. Its route, which changes each year, often traverses part of Tuscany (in 2009 Florence was an official stage). For more information on cycling in the region, see p369.

TOP Walking in the Apuane Alps (p144) RIGHT Wildflowers blanket the Piano Grande beneath Casteluccio (p322)

WHEN TO GO?

If you're keen to take to the outdoors while you're here, try to visit in spring or autumn (fall). Spring is the prettiest time, while the colours of autumn have their own mellow appeal and since summertime lingers into late October, you'll have plenty of daylight for your activities. If possible, avoid the busy Easter week. If you're planning to walk in the Apuane Alps or other mountain areas, the most pleasant time is in summer. Remember, though, that August is the month when most Italians take their holidays and the trails get very busy. Lower terrain, including cycling routes, is best left untrodden or un-cycled in high summer as both the crowds and the heat can be oppressive. For more information, see p369.

DRIVING TOURS

Tour through striking landscapes and discover the very best of regional wine and food:

* Abbazia di San Galgano to Pretoio – Into the hills of Le Crete (p202)

* Livorno to Piombino – Along the Tuscan coast (p160)

* Monte Argentario to Manciano – Amidst Tuscany's Etruscan heritage (p229)

* Sansepolcro to Arezzo – The Piero della Francesca trail (p246)

* The Valnerina – Steep valleys and jagged mountains (p323)

* The Via Francigena – A medieval pilgrimage route in the untamed Lunigiana (p148)

© GUIDO BAVIERA/GRAND TOUR/CORBIS

FAMILY TRAVEL

TOP ACTIVITIES

FUNIVIA COLLE ELETTO
Take the kids for a steep ride on Gubbio's birdcage funicular (p284).

LEANING TOWER Clamber up the 294 steps of Pisa's world-famous tower (p113).

PALAZZO VECCHIO Let actors impersonating Medici family members show you around this important building in Florence (p53).

DON'T MISS EXPERIENCES

★ Bike riding in Lucca – Pedal around the city's monumental city walls (p131).

★ Farm-stay accommodation – Enjoy animals, swimming pools and lots of space in an *agriturismo* (p391).

★ Gelato – Kids of all sizes love the local ice cream (p89).

★ *Passeggiata* – Search out carousels, cafes and convivial company of every age on a traditional evening stroll (p276).

★ Sculpture parks – Frolic between site-specific sculptures in these outdoor art galleries (p361).

★ The original Narnia – Visit Narni, the original world within the wardrobe (p325).

TRAVEL WITH CHILDREN

Families with children are welcomed in this part of Italy. Restaurants and cafes are extremely family friendly, as are museums and galleries. Family passes are available for many high-profile attractions, and admission to many galleries and museums is free for under 10s or under 18s (particularly EU citizens). Cities and large towns often lack green spaces and playgrounds, though, so head to the hills or the coast for running room. In restaurants it's perfectly acceptable to order a *mezza porzione* (half serve), and on trains the *offerte familia* gives a 20% discount to family groups of three to five people. Many hotels and *pensione* (guest houses) have family rooms sleeping up to five.

TOP Choose your favourite flavour of gelato from the delectable selection at Grom, Florence (p89)

CONTENTS

THE AUTHORS

VIRGINIA MAXWELL

Coordinating Author, Florence, Northwestern Tuscany
After working for many years as a publishing manager
at Lonely Planet's Melbourne headquarters, Virginia
decided that she'd be happier writing guidebooks than
commissioning them. Since making this decision she's
written or contributed to Lonely Planet books covering
nine countries, eight of which are on the Mediterranean. Italy is a favourite destination – as well as working
on this title, Virginia has covered Rome for *Italy* and
the north of the country for *Western Europe*.

ALEX LEVITON

Northern Umbria, Southern Umbria
Alex updated her original Northern and Southern
Umbria chapters for the fourth edition in a row. As a
frequent visitor to Umbria since 1998, she considers
the region to be a home. Alex lives mostly in San Fran-
cisco and sometimes in Durham, North Carolina, but
has dreams of one day buying a farmhouse near Lago
Trasimeno or Bevagna.

LONELY PLANET AUTHORS

Why is our travel information the best in the world? It's simple: our authors are passionate, dedicated travellers. They don't take freebies in exchange for positive coverage so
you can be sure the advice you're given is impartial. They travel widely to all the popular
spots, and off the beaten track. They don't research using just the internet or phone.
They discover new places not included in any other guidebook. They personally visit
thousands of hotels, restaurants, palaces, trails, galleries, temples and more. They speak
with dozens of locals every day to make sure you get the kind of insider knowledge only
a local could tell you. They take pride in getting all the details right, and in telling it how it
is. Think you can do it? Find out how at lonelyplanet.com.

LEIF PETTERSEN

Central Coast & Elba, Central Tuscany, Southern Tuscany, Eastern Tuscany

In 2003 Leif was 'Kramered' by an unbalanced friend into abandoning an idiotproof career with the Federal Reserve Bank of Minneapolis and embarking on an odyssey of travel writing. Good coffee, phenomenal food and cheap wine have fuelled him through more than 100 Italian cities and 300 restaurants since then. He writes an almost-award-winning, 'slightly caustic' blog at KillingBatteries.com.

ITINERARIES

ONLY THE BEST

10 DAYS // FLORENCE ROUND TRIP // 800KM

Florence (p34) anchors any 'best of' tour. Squeeze in three days of highlights before moving on to **Lucca** (p130), light on heavyweight museums but loaded with important

churches and top-notch restaurants. Next day, pop into **Pisa** (p112) to scale its Leaning Tower, leaving after lunch to arrive at a Tuscan farmhouse in **Chianti** (p101) before dusk. Check in for two nights and day trip the next morning to **San Gimignano** (p192). On day seven, your destination is **Siena** (p180), full of museums and charm. Then step into Umbria and follow the pilgrims to **Assisi** (p269). On day nine, visit **Spoleto** (p315) and **Todi** (p310) before taking the A1 back to Florence.

GOTHIC GEMS

EIGHT DAYS // LUCCA TO GUBBIO // 500KM

Start your Gothic gyration in lovely Lucca (p130), visiting its Cattedrale di San Martino (p131) and spending the night in a luxurious villa on its outskirts (p398). Proceed

to Pisa (p112), spending at least two days admiring the marble pulpits in the Baptistry (p115) and Duomo (p115), the paintings and sculpture in the Museo Nazionale di San Matteo (p117) and the exquisite Chiesa di Santa Maria della Spina (p118). The next day, make your way to gloriously Gothic Siena (p180) and spend three days ogling its architecture and art. Onwards to Umbria, visiting the magnificent Abbazia di San Galgano (p202) en route. Spend the night in Orvieto (p302) and visit its cathedral (p302) before finishing in Gubbio (p283), an imposing hill-town packed with Gothic buildings.

WORLD HERITAGE SITES

SEVEN DAYS // FLORENCE TO ASSISI // 470KM

The region has more than its fair share of cultural gems. Start with a serious slug of Renaissance splendour by spending three days in Florence (p34). Decamp to Pisa (p112) to

visit the Piazza dei Miracoli, sampling the city's delectable seafood-dominated cuisine while you're at it (p119). Next day, head towards the fairytale-like medieval towers of San Gimignano (p192). Stay as long as you can bear the crowds before hightailing it to the historic centre of Siena (p180), where extraordinary Gothic architecture and delectable dining at Antica Osteria da Divo (p190) await. Scale down the pace a little on day six, making a slow procession to jewel-like Pienza (p209), where you should overnight. On your final day, cross into Umbria to marvel at Giotto's frescos in Assisi (p269).

CONTEMPORARY CONTEMPLATIONS

SEVEN DAYS // FLORENCE TO SIENA // 530KM

Embrace the contemporary in this weeklong jaunt around Tuscany. Book in advance to visit **Fattoria di Celle** (p100), a huge estate filled with world-class site-specific installation

art. Come here on a day trip from master-piece-packed **Florence** (p34), where you should spend at least three days wandering; check out the **Palazzo Strozzi** (p62) and **Palazzo Medici-Riccardi** (p65) for temporary exhibitions. Then head south along the coastal highway to Niki de Saint Phalle's whimsical **Il Giardino dei Tarocchi** (p228), staying overnight in **Montemerano** (p407) or **Sorano** (p408). Next day, contemplate the cutting-edge at **Galleria Continua** (p196) in **San Gimignano** (p192), over-nighting both here and **Siena** (p180) before ending your tour at the nearby **Parco Sculture del Chianti** (p106).

HILLTOP HOP

FOUR DAYS // SAN MINIATO TO PERUGIA // 480KM

This region is full of pretty medieval hilltop fortresses. Start your tour at the gourmet destination of **San Miniato** (p129), where you can pick up provisions and enjoy a picnic be-

fore heading to spectacularly sited **Volterra** (p198) for the afternoon. Crowd favourite **San Gimignano** (p192) should be your overnight stop. In the morning, visit wine mecca **Montalcino** (p204) then lunch at Ristorante la Porta in pretty **Monticchiello** (p210) and overnight in **Montepulciano** (p211). Next day, work off the indulgences of the night before by climbing the wickedly steep streets of **Cortona** (p248) and then cross into Umbria, where ancient stone town walls and arches slumber in the sun at **Amelia** (p330) and **Narni** (p325). Your last day sees you paying a call to cosmopolitan hilltop city **Perugia** (p253).

DELICIOUS UMBRIA

FOUR DAYS // LAGO TRASIMENO TO NORCIA // 170KM

Kick off at Lago Trasimeno, lunching on local specialities at Castiglione del Lago's **La Cantina** (p295). In the afternoon, visit Umbria's most famous winemaking family in

Torgiano (p266), where the aromatic Rubesco Riserva is produced, and check in for two nights at **Relais Borgo Brufa** (p268), with its sybaritic spa and sensational restaurant. Swill, sniff and spit the next day away in **Montefalco** (p280), sampling the stock in its *enoteche* (wine bars) and at **Arnaldo Caprai** (p281) winery in search of the perfect Sagrantino. On day three, enjoy a leisurely lunch at **Il Bacco Felice** (p279) in Foligno and spend the remaining smidgen of afternoon savouring Italy's best olive oil in Slow City **Trevi** (p282) . Have the final course in **Norcia** (p320), famous for its *cinghiale* (wild boar) and black truffles.

TUSCAN WINE TRAIL

FOUR DAYS // FLORENCE TO MONTALCINO // 200KM

Florence (p34) has a plethora of *enoteche* and *fiaschetterie* (small taverns serving wine and snacks), with places such as **Le Volpe e L'uva** (p88) pouring top tipples from around

the country. For tasting in and around the vineyards, follow the **Strada dei Vini Chianti Rùfina** (p105) east of Florence, staying overnight at the stylish **Podere Castellare** (p396), then bear south to **Chianti Fiorentino** (p101) to taste the full complement of regional wines at **Le Cantine di Greve in Chianti** (p102). While in Chianti, stay two nights at **Fattoria di Rignana** (p396), tour the historic wine cellars at **Badia di Passignano** (p103), dine at the Antinori estate's **Osteria di Passignano** (p104) and visit the **Castello di Brolio** (p106) estate near Siena. Finish in **Montalcino** (p204), home of Tuscany's best wine, Brunello.

FLORENCE

3 PERFECT DAYS

♥ DAY 1 // A DAVID TOUR
Follow a naked man around the city: start with Michelangelo's original in the Galleria dell'Accademia (p66), saunter past the famous copy on Piazza della Signoria (p50) and make your way to the Museo Nazionale del Bargello (p72) to see versions by Donatello and Andrea Verrocchio. Later, watch the sun set over Florence from Piazzale Michelangelo (p81), home to yet another copy of this famous statue. For a souvenir of your day, buy a replica in chocolate from Scudieri (p45).

♥ DAY 2 // FABULOUS FRESCOS
Kick-start your day with a quick coffee at Caffè Gilli (p50) before visiting Domenico Ghirlandaio's vibrant frescos in the Basilica di Santa Maria Novella (p57). Grab a casual lunch at Trattoria Mario (p86) or La Mescita (p86) before spending a contemplative hour or so admiring Fra' Angelico's religious reliefs at the Museo di San Marco (p67) and Benozzo Gozzoli's gorgeous Cappella dei Magi at the Palazzo Medici-Riccardi (p65). In the evening, dine under 13th-century frescos at Alle Murate (p86).

♥ DAY 3 // BOTH SIDES OF THE ARNO
Spend the morning at the Uffizi (p53), then grab a midday snack at Cantinetta dei Verrazzano (p83) or La Canova di Gustavino (p84). Refreshed, you'll be ready to embark on our Walking Tour (p41); make sure you detour along Via de' Tornabuoni (p60) for some upmarket retail therapy and a truffle panino at Procacci (p85). At night, cross the Arno for a drink at Le Volpe e L'uva (p88) before dinner at Ristorante Il Guscio (p89) or Trattoria Cammillo (p89).

INTRODUCING FLORENCE

pop 364,700

It may be home to the world's greatest concentration of Renaissance art, but there's more to this riverside city than priceless masterpieces. Strolling its narrow streets evokes a thousand tales of the past: medieval dyers changed the colour of wool in *caldaie* (vats) on Via delle Caldaie; Renaissance *calzaiuoli* (hosiers) hand-crafted fine shoes in workshops on Via dei Calzaiuoli; and tanners made a stink in *conce* (tanneries) on Via delle Conce. Here, living history is a reality rather than a marketing ploy. Today, workshops proliferate in the streets around Via delle Caldaie, shoes are still sold on Via dei Calzaiuoli and leathergoods are fashioned in ateliers around Via delle Conce.

Plush, decadent and just as exotic as the city's Medici-dominated history is contemporary Florence's flamboyant line-up of designer boutiques on and around Via de' Tornabuoni. Gucci was born here, as was fashion designer Roberto Cavalli who, like many a smart Florentine, hangs out in the wine-rich hills around Florence today. After a little while in this intensely absorbing city, you might just want to do the same.

Florence's history stretches to the time of the Etruscans, who based themselves in Fiesole. Julius Caesar founded the Roman colony of Florentia around 59 BC, making it a strategic garrison on the narrowest crossing of the Arno in order to control the Via Flaminia linking Rome to northern Italy and Gaul.

After the collapse of the Roman Empire, Florence fell to invading Goths, followed by Lombards and Franks. The year AD 1000 marked a crucial turning point in the city's fortunes, when Margrave Ugo of Tuscany moved his capital from Lucca to Florence. In 1110 Florence became a free *comune* (city-state) and by 1138 it was ruled by 12 consuls, assisted by the Consiglio di Cento (Council of One Hundred), whose members were drawn mainly from the prosperous merchant class. Agitation among differing factions in the city led to the appointment in 1207 of a foreign head of state called the *podestà,* aloof in principle from the plotting and wheeler-dealing of local cliques and alliances.

Medieval Florence was a wealthy, dynamic *comune,* one of Europe's leading financial, banking and cultural centres, and a major player in the international wool, silk and leather trades. The sizeable population of moneyed merchants and artisans began forming guilds and patronising the growing number of artists who found lucrative commissions in this burgeoning city. But a political crisis was on the horizon.

Struggles between the pro-papal Guelphs (Guelfi) and the pro-Holy Roman Empire Ghibellines (Ghibellini) started in the mid-13th century, with power yo-yoing between the two for almost a century. Into this fractious atmosphere were born revolutionary artist Giotto and outspoken poet Dante Alighieri, whose family belonged to the Guelph camp. After the Guelphs split into two factions, the Neri (Blacks) and Bianchi (Whites), Dante went with the Bianchi – the wrong side – and was expelled from his beloved city in 1302, never to return.

In 1348 the Black Death spirited away almost half the population. This dark period was used as a backdrop by Boccaccio for his *Decameron.*

(Continued on page 40)

FLORENCE

FLORENCE

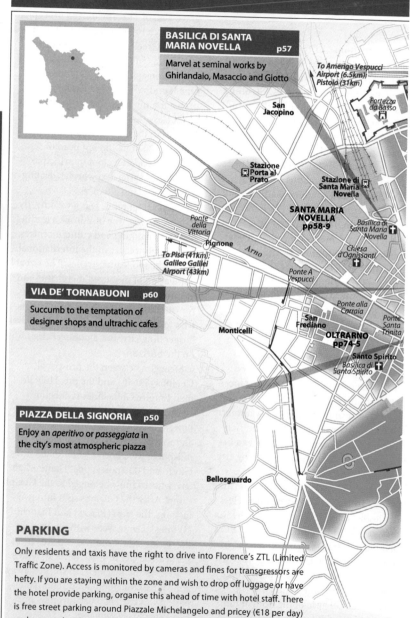

BASILICA DI SANTA MARIA NOVELLA   p57

Marvel at seminal works by Ghirlandaio, Masaccio and Giotto

VIA DE' TORNABUONI   p60

Succumb to the temptation of designer shops and ultrachic cafes

PIAZZA DELLA SIGNORIA   p50

Enjoy an *aperitivo* or *passeggiata* in the city's most atmospheric piazza

To Amerigo Vespucci Airport (6.5km); Pistoia (31km)

Fortezza da Basso

San Jacopino

Stazione Porta al Prato

Stazione di Santa Maria Novella

SANTA MARIA NOVELLA pp58-9

Basilica di Santa Maria Novella

Ponte della Vittoria

Pignone

Arno

To Pisa (41km); Galileo Galilei Airport (43km)

Chiesa d'Ognissanti

Ponte A Vespucci

Ponte alla Carraia

Ponte Santa Trinita

San Frediano

Monticelli

OLTRARNO pp74-5

Santo Spirito

Basilica di Santo Spirito

Bellosguardo

PARKING

Only residents and taxis have the right to drive into Florence's ZTL (Limited Traffic Zone). Access is monitored by cameras and fines for transgressors are hefty. If you are staying within the zone and wish to drop off luggage or have the hotel provide parking, organise this ahead of time with hotel staff. There is free street parking around Piazzale Michelangelo and pricey (€18 per day) underground parking around the Fortezza da Basso and in the Oltrarno.

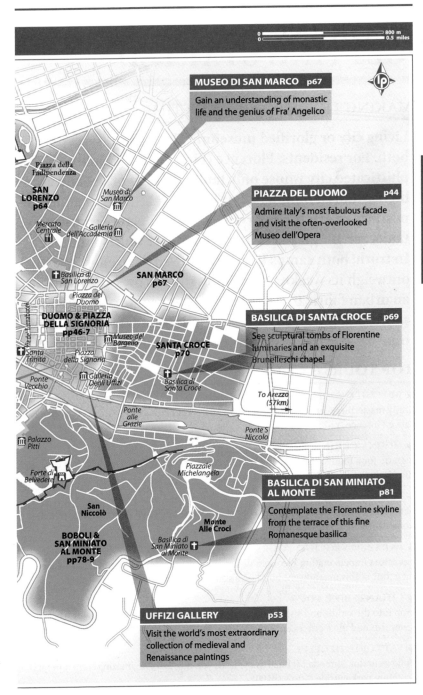

MUSEO DI SAN MARCO p67

Gain an understanding of monastic life and the genius of Fra' Angelico

PIAZZA DEL DUOMO p44

Admire Italy's most fabulous facade and visit the often-overlooked Museo dell'Opera

BASILICA DI SANTA CROCE p69

See sculptural tombs of Florentine luminaries and an exquisite Brunelleschi chapel

BASILICA DI SAN MINIATO AL MONTE p81

Contemplate the Florentine skyline from the terrace of this fine Romanesque basilica

UFFIZI GALLERY p53

Visit the world's most extraordinary collection of medieval and Renaissance paintings

FLORENCE GETTING STARTED

FLORENCE

MAKING THE MOST OF YOUR TIME

Living city or glorified museum? The answer is 'yes' to both. For residents, Florence (Firenze) is a friendly, sophisticated city whose only faults are high prices and even higher tourist numbers. For tourists, the city is a gilded repository of extraordinary art and architecture whose only faults are…high prices and even higher tourist numbers. In truth, both camps know that the city's strengths vastly outweigh its weaknesses. Think sunsets over the Arno, an urban fabric that has hardly changed since the Renaissance, and food and wine so wonderful that the tag 'fiorentina' has become a worldwide form of quality assurance.

TOP TOURS & COURSES

❧ BRITISH INSTITUTE OF FLORENCE
Study masterpieces in situ by enrolling in an expert five-day course on Art in Renaissance Florence (p62).

❧ DIVINA CUCINA
Sign up for a food lover's walking tour or cooking class with self-proclaimed cooking diva Judy Francini (p66).

❧ FREYA'S FLORENCE
Set off on a walk around Florence with this infectiously enthusiastic and extremely knowledgeable tour guide (p41).

❧ PALAZZO VECCHIO TOURS
Let actors impersonating Eleonora di Toledo, Cosimo I and Giorgio Vasari take you on a tour of this magnificent building's secret passageways and rooms (p51).

❧ CHIANTI BIKE TOUR
Hop into the saddle and spend a full day biking along Chianti's back roads, visiting vineyards and olive groves en route (p101).

❧ FATTORIA DI CELLE
Follow curator Miranda McPhail as she leads you through this amazing contemporary sculpture park outside Pistoia (p100).

GETTING AWAY FROM IT ALL

Florence can be overwhelming; if you need peace and quiet, here are some options:

* **Escape to the Florentine hills** Enjoy a leisurely lunch and spectacular views in Fiesole (p95).
* **Relax in a Chianti agriturismo** Put all of that museum-going behind you and chill out on a historic wine estate (p395).
* **Take tea in the Giardino Bardini** The peaceful belvedere in these manicured gardens offers a spectacular view of the Florentine skyline (p80).
* **Visit Pistoia for the day** Appreciate Gothic churches, Renaissance art and tourist-free streets in this city to the north of Florence (p98).

ADVANCE PLANNING

* **Uffizi & Galleria dell'Accademia** Queues for these major attractions can stretch to five hours, but can be avoided by booking ahead (see p44).
* **Maggio Musicale Fiorentino** Tickets to this month-long arts festival are highly prized – book at least one month in advance (see p82).
* **Memorable Meals** If you're keen to eat at high-profile restaurants such as Ristorante Cibrèo or Enoteca Pinchiorri, make a reservation at least one week in advance (p83).
* **Fattoria di Celle** Access to this extraordinary sculpture garden (p100) outside Pistoia is highly sought after; put in a request a few months before your trip.

TOP EATING EXPERIENCES

* **ENOTECA PINCHIORRI**
The only Tuscan restaurant with three Michelin stars (p87)

* **L'OSTERIA DI GIOVANNI**
A wonderfully welcoming *osteria* with great food (p85)

* **LE VOLPE E L'UVA**
Boutique cheeses, brilliant wine list (p88)

* **RISTORANTE CIBRÈO**
Fabio Picchi's innovative and elegant restaurant (p88)

* **RISTORANTE IL GUSCIO**
Affordable and delicious modern Florentine cooking (p89)

* **TRATTORIA LE CAVE DI MAIANO**
A rustic delight outside Fiesole (p97)

* **OSTERIA DI PASSIGNANO**
Refined cuisine in an 11th-century abbey (p104) in Badia di Passignano

RESOURCES

* **APT Firenze** (www.firenzeturismo.it) Official Florence tourism website
* **Firenze Musei** (www.firenzemusei.it) Online booking site for Florentine museums
* **Firenze Spettacolo** (www.firenzespettacolo .it) Definitive entertainment publication
* **Maggio Musicale Fiorentina** (www .maggiofiorentino.com) Booking page for the city's premier music festival
* **The Florentine** (www.theflorentine.net) Useful English-language magazine

FLORENCE

(Continued from page 35)

The history of Medici Florence begins in 1434, when Cosimo the Elder (also known simply as Cosimo de' Medici), a patron of the arts, assumed power. His eye for talent and tact in dealing with artists saw the likes of Alberti, Brunelleschi, Luca della Robbia, Fra' Angelico, Donatello and Fra' Filippo Lippi flourish under his patronage.

In 1439 the Church Council of Florence, aimed at reconciling the Catholic and Eastern churches, brought to the city Byzantine scholars and craftsmen, whom they hoped would impart the knowledge and culture of classical antiquity. The Council, attended by the pope, achieved nothing in the end, but it did influence what was later known as the Renaissance. Under the rule of Cosimo's popular and cultured grandson, Lorenzo il Magnifico (1469–92), Florence became the epicentre of this 'Rebirth', with artists such as Michelangelo, Botticelli and Domenico Ghirlandaio at work. Lorenzo's court, which was filled with Humanists (a school of thought begun in Florence in the late 14th century affirming the dignity and potential of mankind and embracing Latin and Greek literary texts), fostered a flowering of art, music and poetry, turning Florence into Italy's cultural capital.

Florence's golden age was not to last though, effectively dying (along with Lorenzo) in 1492. Just before his death, the Medici bank had failed and two years later the Medici were driven out of Florence. In a reaction against the splendour and excess of the Medici court, the city fell under the control of Girolamo Savonarola, a humourless Dominican monk who led a stern, puritanical republic. In 1497 the likes of Botticelli gladly consigned their 'immoral' works and finery to the flames of the infamous 'Bonfire of the Vanities'. The following year Savonarola fell from public favour and was burned as a heretic.

The pro-French leanings of the subsequent republican government brought it into conflict with the pope and his Spanish allies. In 1512 a Spanish force defeated Florence and the Medici were reinstated. Their tyrannical rule endeared them to few and when Rome, ruled by the Medici pope Clement VII, fell to the emperor Charles V in 1527, the Florentines took advantage of this low point in the Medici fortunes to kick the family out again. Two years later though, imperial and papal forces besieged Florence, forcing the city to accept Lorenzo's great-grandson, Alessandro de' Medici, a ruthless transvestite whom Charles made Duke of Florence. Medici rule continued for another 200 years, during which time they gained control of all of Tuscany, though after the reign of Cosimo I (1537–74), Florence drifted into steep decline.

The last male Medici, Gian Gastone, died in 1737, after which his sister, Anna Maria, signed the grand duchy of Tuscany over to the House of Habsburg-Lorraine (at the time effectively under Austrian control). This situation remained unchanged, apart from a brief interruption under Napoleon from 1799 to 1814, until the duchy was incorporated into the Kingdom of Italy in 1860. Florence briefly became the national capital a year later, but Rome assumed the mantle permanently in 1871.

Florence was badly damaged during WWII by the retreating Germans, who blew up all of its bridges except the Ponte Vecchio. Devastating floods ravaged the city in 1966, causing inestimable damage to its buildings and artworks. However, the salvage operation led to the widespread use of modern restoration techniques that have saved artworks throughout the country. In 1993 the Mafia exploded a massive car bomb, killing five, injuring 37 and destroying a part of the Uffizi. Just over a decade later and amid a fair amount of controversy, this world-class gallery embarked on its biggest-ever expansion, set to double its exhibition area by 2013.

ESSENTIAL INFORMATION

EMERGENCIES // **Doctor Stephen Kerr** (Map pp46-7; ☎ 055 28 80 55; www.dr-kerr.com; Piazza Mercato Nuovo 1; ☾ 3-5pm Mon-Fri) Resident British doctor, by appointment or open clinic weekday afternoons between 3pm and 5pm. **Emergency Doctor** (Guardia Medica; ☎ 055 233 94 56 north of the Arno, ☎ 055 21 56 16 south of the Arno) For a doctor at night, on weekends or on public holidays. **Hospital** (Ospedale di Santa Maria Nuova; Map p67; ☎ 055 2 75 81; Piazza di Santa Maria Nuova 1) **Police station** (Questura; Map p64; ☎ 055 4 97 71; Via Zara 2; ☾ 24hr) Report thefts at the foreigners' office here. **SOS Turista phoneline** (☎ 055 276 03 82) For tourists involved in disputes over hotel bills, taxi fares etc. **Tourist police** (Polizia Assistenza Turistica; Map p70; ☎ 055 20 39 11; Via Pietrapiana 50r, Piazza dei Ciompi; ☾ 8.30am-6.30pm Mon-Fri, to 1pm Sat).
TOURIST OFFICES // **APT Florence** (www .firenzeturismo.it); Piazza Beccaria (Map p70; ☎ 055 233 20; Via Manzoni 16; ☾ 9am-1pm Mon-Fri); Amerigo Vespucci airport (☎ 055 31 58 74; ☾ 8.30am-8.30pm); San Lorenzo (Map p64; ☎ 055 29 08 32; Via Cavour 1r; ☾ 8.30am-6.30pm Mon-Sat, to 1.30pm Sun) **Comune di Firenze Tourist Office** (Map p70; ☎ 055 234 04 44; www.comune.fi.it, in Italian; Borgo Santa Croce 29r; ☾ 9am-7pm Mon-Sat, to 2pm Sun).

ORIENTATION

Central train station Stazione di Santa Maria Novella is a good reference point. The main route to the city centre (a 10-minute walk) is Via de' Panzani then Via de' Cerretani. Spot the Duomo and you're there.

Most major sights are within easy walking distance. From Piazza di San Giovanni around the baptistry, Via Roma leads to Piazza della Repubblica and beyond to the Ponte Vecchio. From Piazza del Duomo follow Via de' Calzaiuoli for Piazza della Signoria, the historic seat of government. The Uffizi is on the piazza's southern edge, near the Arno. The less touristy area south of the river is known as Oltrarno.

We have divided our coverage into seven geographical areas: Santa Maria Novella, Duomo and Piazza della Signoria, San Lorenzo, San Marco, Santa Croce, Oltrarno, and Boboli and San Miniato al Monte. Most of these owe their names to the significant basilicas located within their borders, which make excellent navigational landmarks.

WALKING TOUR

Distance: 2km
Duration: two hours
Florence is perfectly suited to exploration on foot. All major sights are within or right on the boundaries of the *centro storico* (historic city centre) and the terrain is flat (Boboli and San Miniato al Monte being the only exceptions). The walk outlined here follows a tour offered by **Freya Middleton** (Freya's Florence; ☎ 349 0748907; freyasflorence@yahoo.com), one of the city's most successful private tour guides. An expat Aussie who studied art history in Venice before settling in Florence and marrying a local, she knows the streets and buildings of the city like the back of her hand.

Have a preparatory caffeine charge at one of the historic cafes on **Piazza**

FLORENCE

della Repubblica (1; p49) before walking one block south along Via Calimala and turning left (east) into Via Orsanmichele, where you'll find the **Chiesa di Orsanmichele** (2; p50) with its ornate statuary. Backtrack to Via Calimala and continue walking south until you see a huge loggia. This is the **Mercato Nuovo** (3; New Market), a 16th-century market building commissioned by Cosimo I and called the New Market to differentiate it from the Mercato Vecchio (Old Market), which had occupied the site since the 11th century. In Cosimo's day it was used primarily for the sale of wool, silk and gold, so its current incarnation as an emporium for tacky merchandise is something of an affront. Florentines know the market as 'Il Porcellino' (The Piglet) after the bronze statue of a wild boar on its southern side. Local legend has it that

rubbing its snout will ensure your return to Florence.

Walk past the market and down Via Porta Rossa until you come to the magnificent **Museo di Palazzo Davanzati** (4; ☎ 055 27 76 461; www.polomuseale.firenze.it/davanzati; Via Porta Rossa 13; admission free; ⏰ 8.15am-1.50pm, closed 2nd & 4th Sun, 1st, 3rd & 5th Mon of month), a warehouse and residence built in the mid-14th century and occupied by the wealthy Davanzati merchant family from 1578. The piazza in front of the building was once edged with heavily fortified tower houses such as this one, but many were demolished in a controversial 19th-century urban renovation of the city. Inside, don't miss the carved faces of the original owners on the pillars in the inner courtyard, the 1st-floor reception room with its painted wooden ceiling and the exquisitely decorated Sala dei Pappagalli

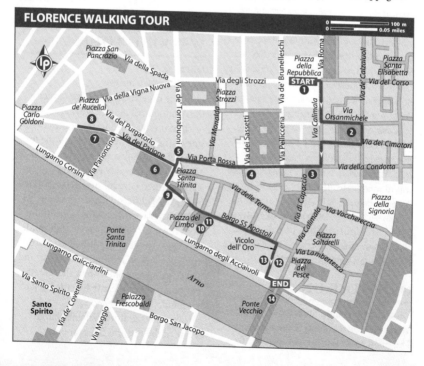

FLORENCE WALKING TOUR

(Parrot Room) and Camera dei Pavoni (Peacock Bedroom).

Continue along Via Porta Rossa until you reach fashionable **Via de' Tornabuoni** (5; p60) and the church of **Santa Trìnita** (6; p62). From here, wander down Via del Parione to visit the workshops of artisans including **Alberto Cozzi** (7; p92) and **Letizia Fiorini** (8; p93).

Retrace your steps to Via de' Tornabuoni, cross the road and pass the 13th-century **Palazzo Spini-Feroni** (9; p62), home of Salvatore Ferragamo's flagship store, and enter Borgo Santissimi Apostoli. A short way ahead is the Romanesque **Chiesa dei Santissimi Apostoli** (10; Piazza del Limbo 1), hidden in a sunken square that was once a cemetery for unbaptised babies (hence its name of Piazza del Limbo). In the piazza, a plaque indicates the incredible height to which the 1966 floodwaters rose – this church, one of the oldest in Florence, was badly damaged as a result.

After having a browse in **La Bottega dell' Olio** (11; p91), continue east and turn right into Vicolo dell' Oro, home to the ultrachic **Continentale hotel** (12; p392) and **Gallery-Hotel Art** (13; ☎ 055 2 72 63; Vicolo dell' Oro 5), both run by the Ferragamo company. The **Fusion Bar** (☎ 055 2 72 63; Vicolo dell' Oro 3; ☯ noon-midnight) on the ground floor of the Gallery-Hotel Art is one of the city's sleekest watering holes.

The Arno is now directly in front of you. Look left and you will see the **Ponte Vecchio** (14; p73), where this tour ends.

If you're keen to continue walking, follow the tour through San Niccolò on p81.

EXPLORING FLORENCE

Florence seriously overwhelms. Its wealth of museums and galleries house many of the world's most important and exquisite examples of Renaissance art,

and its architecture is unrivalled. Yet the secret is not to feel pressured to see and do everything on offer here: combine your personal pick of the major sights with ample meandering through the city's warren of narrow streets.

In true Italian fashion, state museums and monuments (the Uffizi and Galleria dell'Accademia included) close on Mondays. But Florence is a year-round destination and there are plenty of major sights open whichever days you are in town. Note that museum ticket offices usually shut 30 minutes before closing time.

Most churches enforce a strict dress code for visitors: no shorts, sleeveless shirts or plunging necklines.

FREE ENTRY & DISCOUNTS

European Union (EU) passport holders aged under 18 and over 65 get into Florence's state museums for free, while EU citizens aged between 18 and 25 pay half-price. Have your ID with you at all times.

For one week of the year (usually some time in spring), admission to state museums is free of charge; dates change, making it impossible to plan a trip around this, so keep your eyes open.

One date that doesn't shift is 18 February, the day Anna Maria Louisa de' Medici (1667–1743) died. In honour of the last of the Medici family, who bequeathed the city its vast cultural heritage, admission to all state museums is free on this day.

DUOMO & PIAZZA DELLA SIGNORIA

The tight grid of streets between Piazza del Duomo and Piazza della Signoria is the heart of the city geographically, historically and artistically.

FLORENCE

PREBOOKING MUSEUM TICKETS

In summer and in busy periods such as Easter, ridiculously long queues are a fact of life at Florence's major museums, leading to waits of up to four or five hours if you haven't booked a ticket in advance.

For a fee of €3 per ticket (€4 for the Uffizi and Galleria dell'Accademia), tickets to all 13 *musei statali* (state museums) can be reserved, including the Uffizi, Galleria dell'Accademia (where *David* lives), Palazzo Pitti, Museo Nazionale del Bargello and the Medici chapels (Cappelle Medicee). In reality, the only museums where prebooking is necessary are the Uffizi and the Accademia – for these, prebooking is a *really* good idea. To organise your ticket, phone **Firenze Musei** (Florence Museums; ☎ 055 29 48 83, 055 265 4321; ⊗ booking line 8.30am-6.30pm Mon-Fri, to 12.30pm Sat) or use the online booking facility at www.firenzemusei.it.

At the Uffizi, signs point prebooked ticket holders to the building opposite the gallery where prebooked tickets can be collected; once you've got the ticket you go to Door One of the museum (for prebooked tickets only) and queue again to enter the gallery. It's annoying, but you'll still save hours of queuing time overall.

In Florence, tickets can easily be prebooked a day or two ahead of time at **Firenze Musei information desks** (⊗ 8.30am-7pm Tue-Sun) at the Uffizi (p53), Palazzo Pitti (p77) or the ticket window at the rear of the Chiesa di Orsanmichele (p50) – if you're in town for a few days, this is the savvy thing to do.

Many hotels and B&Bs also prebook museum tickets for guests.

☙ PIAZZA DEL DUOMO // CONTEMPLATE A PICTURE-PERFECT CATHEDRAL CLUSTER

Duomo

Not only is Florence's **Duomo** (Cattedrale di Santa Maria del Fiore or St Mary of the Flower; Map pp46-7; ☎ 055 21 53 80; www.duomofirenze.it; ⊗ 10am-5pm Mon-Wed & Fri, 10am-3.30pm Thu, 10am-4.45pm Sat, 10am-3.30pm 1st Sat of month, 1.30-4.45pm Sun, mass in English 5pm Sat) the city's most iconic landmark, it's also one of Italy's 'Big Three' (with Pisa's Leaning Tower and Rome's Colosseum). Its famous red-tiled dome, graceful bell tower and breathtaking pink, white and green marble facade have the wow factor in spades.

Begun in 1296 by Sienese architect Arnolfo di Cambio, the cathedral took almost 150 years to complete. Its neo-Gothic facade was designed in the 19th century by architect Emilio de Fabris to replace the uncompleted original, torn down in the 16th century. The oldest and most clearly Gothic part of the cathedral is its south flank, pierced by Porta dei Canonici (Canons' Door), a mid-14th-century High Gothic creation (you enter here to climb up inside the dome).

When Michelangelo went to work on St Peter's in Rome, he reportedly said: 'I go to build a greater dome, but not a fairer one'. One of the finest masterpieces of the Renaissance, Florence's famous cathedral **dome** (adult/under 6yr €8/free; ⊗ 8.30am-7pm Mon-Fri, to 5.40pm Sat) is indeed a feat of engineering and one that cannot be fully appreciated without climbing its 463 interior stone steps.

The dome was built between 1420 and 1436 to a design by Filippo Brunelleschi. Taking his inspiration from Rome's Pantheon, Brunelleschi arrived at an innovative engineering solution of a distinctive octagonal shape of inner and outer concentric domes resting on the drum of the cathedral rather than the roof itself, allowing artisans to build from the ground up without needing a wooden support frame. Over four million bricks were used in the construction, all of them laid in consecutive rings in horizontal courses using a vertical herringbone pattern. The final product is 91m high and 45.5m wide.

The climb up the spiral staircase is relatively steep, and should not be attempted if you are claustrophobic. Make sure to pause when you reach the balustrade at the base of the dome, which gives an aerial view of the octagonal *coro* (choir) of the cathedral below and the seven round stained-glass windows (by Donatello, Andrea del Castagno, Paolo Uccello and Lorenzo Ghiberti) that pierce the octagonal drum.

Look up and you'll see flamboyant late-16th-century frescos by Giorgio Vasari and Federico Zuccari, depicting the *Giudizio Universale* (Last Judgment).

As you climb, snapshots of Florence can be spied through small windows. The final leg – a straight flight up the curve of the inner dome – rewards with an unforgettable 360-degree panorama of one of Europe's most beautiful cities.

After the visual wham-bam of the facade and dome, the sparse decoration of the cathedral's vast interior, 155m long and 90m wide, comes as a surprise – most of its artistic treasures have been removed over centuries according to the vagaries of ecclesiastical fashion, and many are now on show in the Museo dell'Opera del Duomo (p48). The interior is also unexpectedly secular in places (a reflection of the sizeable chunk of the cathedral not paid for by the church): down the left aisle two immense frescos of equestrian statues portray two *condot-*

tieri (mercenaries) – on the left Niccolò da Tolentino by Andrea del Castagno (1456) and on the right Sir John Hawkwood by Uccello (1436) – who fought in the service of Florence in the 14th century.

Between the left (north) arm of the transept and the apse is the Sagrestia delle Messe (Mass Sacristy), its panelling a marvel of inlaid wood carved by Benedetto and Giuliano da Maiano. The fine bronze doors were executed by Luca della Robbia – his only known work in the material. Above the doorway is his glazed terracotta *Resurrezione* (Resurrection).

A stairway near the main entrance of the cathedral leads down to the **crypt** (admission €3; ⏰ 10am-5pm Mon-Wed & Fri, to 4.45pm Sat), where excavations between 1965 and 1974 unearthed parts of the 5th-century Chiesa di Santa Reparata that originally stood on the site.

The steep 414-step climb up the 85m-high **campanile** (bell tower; adult/under 6yr €6.50/free; ⏰ 8.30am-6.50pm), designed by Giotto, offers the reward of a view nearly as impressive as that from the dome. The queues here are usually much shorter, too.

The first tier of bas-reliefs around the base of the campanile are copies of those carved by Pisano, but possibly designed by Giotto, depicting the Creation of Man and the *attività umane* (arts and industries). Those on the second tier depict the planets, the cardinal virtues, the arts and the seven sacraments. The sculptures of the Prophets and Sibyls in the niches of the upper storeys are copies of works by Donatello and others; see the originals in the Museo dell'Opera del Duomo.

If you're in need of a coffee break before moving onto the Baptistry and museum, **Scudieri** (☎ 055 21 07 33; Piazza di San Giovanni 21r; ⏰ 7.30am-9pm) is known for its Duomo view, *schiaccata alla fiorentina* (a traditional

FLORENCE

DUOMO & PIAZZA DELLA SIGNORIA

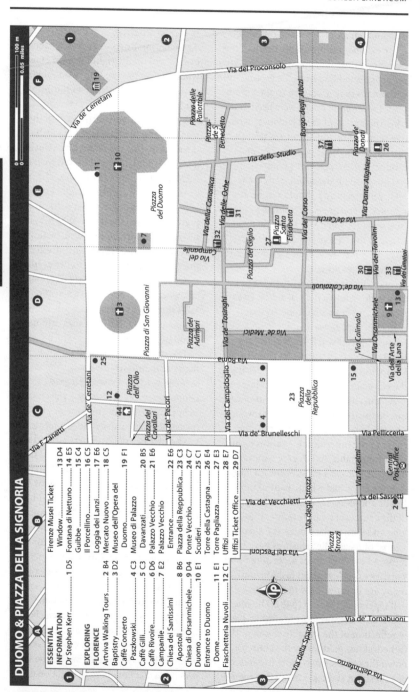

FLORENCE

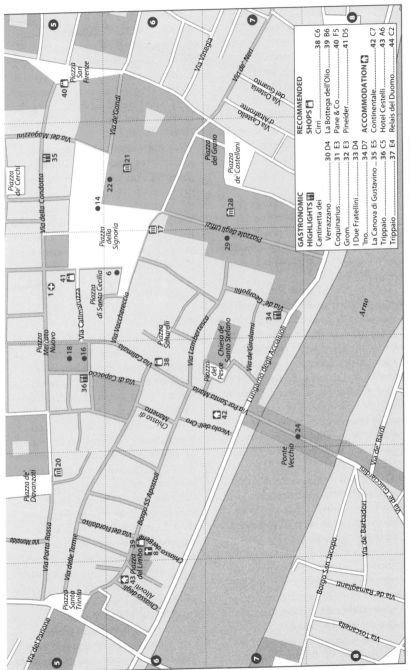

flat cake dusted with sugar) and chocolate replicas of Michelangelo's *David*.

Museo dell'Opera del Duomo

Surprisingly overlooked by the crowds, the **Museo dell'Opera del Duomo** (Cathedral Museum; Map pp46-7; Piazza del Duomo 9; www .operaduomo.firenze.it; admission €6; 9am-6.50pm Mon-Sat, to 1pm Sun) on the northern (street) side of the cathedral safeguards treasures that once adorned the Duomo, Baptistry and campanile and is one of the city's most impressive museums.

Make a beeline for the glass-topped courtyard with its awe-inspiring display of seven of the original 10 panels from Ghiberti's glorious masterpiece the *Porta del Paradiso* (Door of Paradise), designed for the Baptistry.

The nearby large room is devoted to statuary from Arnolfo di Cambio's original never-to-be-completed Gothic facade. Pieces include several by Arnolfo – *Pope Boniface VIII, The Virgin and Child* (with its somewhat strange glass eyes) and *Santa Reparata* – as well as Donatello's 1408 statue of *St John*, which was the sculptor's first large-scale work. Next door, the smaller space is home to exquisite marble panels from the Duomo's *coro* carved by Baccio Bandinelli and Giovanni Bandini in 1547.

On the stair landing is the museum's best-known piece, Michelangelo's *Pietà*, a work he intended for his own tomb. Vasari recorded in his *Lives of the Artists* that, dissatisfied with both the quality of the marble and of his own work, Michelangelo broke up the unfinished sculpture, destroying the arm and left leg of the figure of Christ. A student of Michelangelo's later restored the arm and completed the figure.

Continue upstairs, where a pair of exquisitely carved *cantorie* (singing galleries) or organ lofts – one by Donatello, the other by Luca della Robbia – face each other. Originally in the cathedral's sacristy, their scenes of musicians and children at play add a refreshingly frivolous touch amid so much sombre piety. There are also several carvings by Donatello here, including his *Prophet Habakkuk*, originally in the bell tower, which has always been known as '*lo zuccone*' (big head). Vasari wrote that he visited Donatello in his studio one day to find him looking intensely at this extremely life-like statue and commanding it to talk (he'd obviously been working far too hard!). Don't miss the same sculptor's wooden representation of a gaunt, desperately desolate *Mary Magdalene* in the same room, a work completed late in his career.

Baptistry

The gilded bronze bas-reliefs adorning the doors at the eastern entrance of this wonderful, 11th-century Romanesque **baptistry** (admission €4; 12.15-6.30pm Mon-Sat, 8.30am-1.30pm Sun & 1st Sat of month) were designed by Lorenzo Ghiberti, who jointly won a 1401 competition involving the greatest artists of the day for the honour of undertaking this task. His co-winner was Filippo Brunelleschi, who was so annoyed at not winning outright that he withdrew from the project. Looking at their entries, both of which are now in the collection of the Museo Nazionale del Bargello (p72), Brunelleschi's tantrum seems providential: Ghiberti's graceful panel, which was cast in a single piece and is clearly more unified in conception and execution, is much more impressive.

Ghiberti's finished product – which depicts assorted scriptural subjects, comprises 10 panels and took over two decades to complete – was so extraordinary that, many years later, Michelangelo stood before the doors in awe and declared them fit to be the *Porta del Paradiso* (Gate of Paradise), hence their name. What we see today are copies; most of the originals are on display in the Museo dell'Opera del Duomo.

The Gate of Paradise is one of the Baptistry's three sets of doors, conceived as a series of panels in which the story of humanity and the Redemption would be told. The earliest (now south) door is by Andrea Pisano (1336) and illustrates the life of St John the Baptist in 28 panels. Ghiberti sculpted the panels for both the east (1425–52) and north (1403–24) doors. The top 20 panels of the north door recount episodes from the New Testament, and the eight lower ones show the four Evangelists and four fathers of the Church.

The building itself is an octagonal striped structure of white and green marble that was built on the site of a Roman temple. The earliest documentation in existence dates from 897, although the building is thought to be much older than that and incorporates Roman columns with Corinthian capitals. The interior is encrusted in magnificent mosaics, the oldest of which (c 1250) covers the apse. The glittering (and wonderfully lit) dome mosaics date from the end of the 13th century and took many decades to complete. Look for the *Christ in Majesty* and *Last Judgment*.

To the right of the apse lies the magnificent tomb of Baldassare Cossa (1370–1419) sculpted by Donatello. Better known as the antipope John XXIII, Cossa was hardly a saint, but as antipope he had helped Giovanni di Bicci de' Medici (1360–1429) – the Medici credited with making the Medici rich – break into papal banking. So when Cossa asked

in his will to be buried in the Baptistry, it was the least Giovanni could do. The tomb is remarkable for its elegant carving and for the fact that it is squeezed into the narrow space between two Roman columns but still seems perfectly proportioned.

❦ FIASCHETTERIA NUVOLI // INDULGE IN AN OLD-STYLE DRINK OR TWO

Not too many decades ago, it was common to see a '*Vinaio*' or '*Fiaschetteria*' sign on every second street in the city. These small, unpretentious places served wine and simple snacks all day and were the Florentine equivalent of the corner bar or pub – albeit with Tuscan wine instead of beer and *crostini* taking the place of crisps or peanuts. This fiaschetteria (☎ 055 239 66 16; Piazza dell'Olio 15r; ☼ 7am-9pm Mon-Sat) a street away from the Duomo is one of the few survivors, and is greatly loved by locals as a consequence. Pull up a stool on the street and strike up a conversation with one of the regulars over a glass of the decent *vino della casa* (house wine), or squeeze inside to enjoy a glass of *prosecco* (a type of sparkling wine) and a tasty snack. Don't even *think* about asking to use a credit card.

❦ PIAZZA DELLA REPUBBLICA // SAMPLE THE CITY'S BEST COFFEE AND CAKES

Originally the site of a Roman forum and the heart of medieval Florence, this busy civic space was created in the late 1880s as part of a controversial plan of 'civic improvements' involving the demolition of the old market, Jewish ghetto and surrounding slums, and the relocation of nearly 6000 residents. Fortunately, Vasari's lovely *Loggia del Pesce* (Fish Market; Map p70) was saved and re-erected

FLORENCE

on Via Pietrapiana. Today, the piazza is known for its concentration of historic cafes, the bars of which are filled day and night with Florentines catching up with friends and family, recovering after shopping exertions or grabbing a caffeine fix on the way to or from work (the terraces tend to be tourist-only territory).

The most famous of these cafes is **Caffè Gilli** (Map pp46-7; ☎ 055 21 38 96; www .gilli.it; Via Roma 1r; ⏳ 8am-midnight Wed-Mon Mar-Oct, 8am-9pm Nov-Feb), which has been serving utterly delectable cakes and excellent coffee in Florence since 1733 (it moved to this site in 1910 and sports a beautifully preserved Liberty-style (art nouveau) interior). Its *millefoglie* (sheets of puff pastry filled with rich vanilla or chocolate chantilly cream) and fresh-fruit tartlets are beyond compare. The sweet temptations and coffee are equally good at **Caffè Concerto Paszkowski** (Map pp46-7; ☎ 055 21 02 36; Piazza della Repubblica 31-35r; ⏳ 7am-1am Tue-Sun), which dates from 1846; and though the sweet treats aren't of the same quality at **Giubbe** (Map pp46-7; ☎ 055 21 22 80; Piazza della Repubblica 13-14r; ⏳ 8am-1am) on the opposite side of the piazza, the coffee is excellent and the interior is worth seeing, having changed little from its heyday in the early 20th century, when die-hard members of the Futurist artistic movement used to drink and debate here. Note that a coffee will be three to four times more expensive than its bar price if you sit and order at a table at any of these cafes.

♥ CHIESA DI ORSANMICHELE // ADMIRE A POSSE OF PATRON SAINTS
The arcades of an old grain market were walled in during the 14th century to create the unusual **Chiesa di Orsanmichele** (Map pp46-7; ☎ 055 2 38 85; Via dell'Arte della Lana;

⏳ 10am-5pm Tue-Sun). The *signoria* (city government) ordered the city's guilds to finance the church's decoration and commissioned sculptors to erect statues of the guild's patron saints in niches and tabernacles around the building's exterior.

These statues, commissioned over the 15th and 16th centuries, represent the work of some of the greatest Renaissance artists; many are now kept in the rarely open museum above the church and only copies adorn the building's exterior. Some have made it into the collections of museums around the city: Andrea Pisano's *St Stephen* is in the Museo dell'Opera del Duomo (p48); Lamberti's *St John the Evangelist* is in the Spedale degli Innocenti (p68) and his *St Luke* is in the Museo Nazionale del Bargello (p72); and Donatello has one work in the Bargello *(St George)* and another, *Saint Louis of Toulouse,* in the Museo dell'Opera di Santa Croce (p71). The main feature of the interior is the splendid Gothic tabernacle by Andrea Orcagna.

♥ PIAZZA DELLA SIGNORIA // JOIN THE PASSEGGIATA AROUND THE CITY'S SYMBOLIC HEART
Edged by historic cafes, crammed with Renaissance sculptures and presided over by the magnificent bulk of Palazzo Vecchio (opposite), this photogenic piazza (Map pp46–7) is the hub of Florentine life, and has been so for centuries.

Whenever the city entered one of its innumerable political crises, the people would be called here as a *parlamento* (people's plebiscite) to rubber-stamp decisions that frequently meant ruin for some ruling families and victory for others. Scenes of great pomp and circumstance alternated with those of terrible suffering: it was here that vehemently pious preacher-leader Savonarola set light to the city's art – books, paintings, musical instruments, mirrors, fine clothes and so on – during his famous 'Bonfire of the Vanities' in 1497, and where he was hung in chains and burnt as a heretic, along with two other supporters, a year later.

The same spot where both fires burned is marked by a bronze plaque embedded in the ground in front of Ammannati's **Fontana di Nettuno** (Neptune Fountain; Map pp46-7). With its pin-headed bronze satyrs and divinities frolicking at its edges, this huge fountain is hardly pretty and is much mocked as *il biancone* (the big white thing), not to mention a waste of good marble, by many a Florentine. Far more impressive are the equestrian statue of Cosimo I by Giambologna in the centre of the piazza, the much-photographed copy of Michelangelo's David that has guarded the western entrance to the Palazzo Vecchio since 1910 (the original stood here until 1873 but is now in the Galleria dell'Accademia; p66) and two copies of important Donatello works – Marzocco, the heraldic Florentine lion (for the original see the Museo Nazionale del Bargello; p72) and Giuditta e Oloferne (Judith and Holofernes, c 1455; original inside Palazzo Vecchio). Facing this line-up is the 14th-century **Loggia dei Lanzi** (Map pp46–7), where works such as Giambologna's *Rape of the Sabine Women* (c 1583), Benvenuto Cellini's bronze *Perseus* (1554) and Agnolo Gaddi's *Seven Virtues* (1384–89) are displayed. The loggia owes its name to the *Lanzichenecchi* (Swiss bodyguards) of Cosimo I, who were stationed here, and the present day guards live up to this heritage, sternly monitoring crowd behaviour and promptly banishing anyone carrying food or drink.

The piazza is a favourite *passeggiata* choice for Florentines, who saunter around it and surrounding streets in the early evening and all day on the weekend, dodging herds of camera-toting tourists before stopping for a coffee, hot chocolate or *aperitivo* at the city's most famous cafe, **Caffè Rivoire** (Map pp46-7; ☎ 055 21 44 12; Piazza della Signoria 4; ☷ 8am-midnight Tue-Sun). Grab a table on its terrace facing Palazzo Vecchio and settle into a long people-watching session – tourists and locals alike have been doing so since 1872, when Enrico Rivoire left the service of the Dukes of Savoy and first began to seduce Florentines with his exquisite chocolate creations.

❦ PALAZZO VECCHIO // APPRECIATE ART AND POLITICS IN SPLENDID SURROUNDS

The traditional seat of government, Florence's imposing fortress palace with its striking crenellations and 94m-high **Torre d'Arnolfo** was designed by Arnolfo di Cambio between 1298 and 1314 for the *signoria* that ruled medieval and Renaissance Florence, hence its original name, Palazzo della Signoria. During their short time in office the nine *priori* (consuls) – guild members picked at random – of the *signoria* lived in the palace. Every two months nine new names were pulled out of the hat, ensuring ample comings and goings.

In 1540 Cosimo I made the palace his ducal residence and centre of government, commissioning Vasari to renovate and decorate the interior. Not too long after the renovation, he and his wife Eleonora di Toledo (famously immortalised in Bronzino's portrait in the Uffizi collection) decided that the newly renovated apartments were too uncomfortable for their large family to live in year-round

FLORENCE

and he purchased Palazzo Pitti as a summer residence. After the death of Eleonora and her sons Giovanni and Garzia from malaria in 1562, Cosimo moved the rest of his family to Palazzo Pitti permanently. At this time, the building became known as **Palazzo Vecchio** (Old Palace; Map pp46-7; ☎ 055 276 82 24; www.palazzovecchio-museoragazzi.it; Piazza della Signoria; adult/3-17yr/18-25yr €6/2/4.50; ⊗ 9am-7pm Fri-Wed, to 2pm Thu). It remains the seat of the city's power, home to the mayor's office and the municipal council.

The best way to discover this den of political drama and intrigue is by thematic guided tour (see the boxed text, opposite). Highlights of the interior include the magnificent 53m-long, 22m-wide **Salone dei Cinquecento** (aka La Sala Grande), created within the original building in the 1490s to accommodate the Consiglio dei Cinquecento (Council of 500) that ruled Florence at the end of the 15th century. Star of the show at floor level is Michelangelo's sculpture *Genio della Vittoria* (Genius of Victory), destined for Rome and Pope Julius II's tomb, but left unfinished in the artist's studio when he died.

Sheer size aside, what impresses most about this room are the swirling battle scenes, painted floor to ceiling by Vasari and his apprentices. These glorify Florentine victories by Cosimo I over arch-rivals Pisa and Siena: unlike the Sienese, the Pisans are depicted bare of armour (play 'Spot the Leaning Tower'). To top off this unabashed celebration of his own power, Cosimo had himself portrayed as a god in the centre of the exquisite panelled ceiling – but not before commissioning Vasari to raise the original ceiling 7m in height. It took Vasari and his school, in consultation with Michelangelo, just two years

(1563–65) to construct the ceiling and paint the 34 gold-leafed panels, which rest simply on a wooden frame. The effect is mesmerising.

Off this huge space is the **Chapel of SS Cosmas and Damian**, home to Vasari's 1557–58 triptych panels of the two saints depicting Cosimo the Elder as Cosmas (on the right) and Cosimo I as Damian (on the left). Next to the chapel is the **Sala di Leo X**, the private suite of apartments of Cardinal Giovanni de' Medici, the son of Lorenzo Il Magnifico, who became pope in 1513.

Up the stairs and across the balcony (from where you can enjoy wonderful views of the Salone dei Cinquecento), are the **Quartiere di Eleonora di Toledo**, the private apartments for both Eleonora and her ladies-in-waiting. These bear the same heavy-handed decor blaring the glory of the Medici as the rest of the palace. Of note is the ceiling in the Camera Verde (Green Room) by Ridolfo del Ghirlandaio, inspired by designs from Nero's Domus Aurea in Rome, and the vibrant frescos by Bronzino in the chapel.

Also on the 2nd floor, the **Sala dei Gigli**, named after its frieze of fleur-de-lys, representing the Florentine Republic, is home to Donatello's original *Judith and Holofernes*. Domenico Ghirlandaio's fresco on the far wall in this room, depicting figures from Roman history, was meant to be one of a series by other artists, including Botticelli.

A small study off the hall is the **chancery**, once Niccolò Machiavelli's office. Another room, the **Sala delle Carte Geografiche** (Map Room), houses Cosimo I's fascinating collection of 16th-century maps charting everywhere in the known world at the time, from the polar regions to the Caribbean.

PALAZZO VECCHIO TOURS

Once you have purchased your entrance ticket to **Palazzo Vecchio** (p51), you have the option of joining a **guided tour** (extra charge adult/concession & child €2/1 for 1st tour, each additional tour €1; 9.30am, 12.30pm, 3.30pm & 6.30pm Mon-Wed & Fri, 9.30pm & 12.30pm Thu, 10am, 1.30pm, 3pm & 6.30pm Sat & Sun). These are highly recommended, as they often take you into parts of the building that are not otherwise accessible. The tours are around one hour long and are conducted by English-speaking guides.

The best of the adult bunch is probably the 'Secret Passages' tour, in which groups of 12 are led along the secret staircase built between the palace's super-thick walls in 1342 as an escape route for French Duke of Athens Walter de Brienne, who seized the palace and nominated himself Lord of Florence only to be sent packing back to France by the Florentines a year later. It follows this staircase to the **tesoretto** (treasury) of Cosimo I – a tiny room no larger than a cupboard for his private collection, entered by one carefully concealed door and exited by another – and the equally intimate but substantially more sumptuous **studiolo** (study) of his introverted, alchemy-mad son Francesco I. Cosimo commissioned Vasari and a team of top Florentine Mannerist artists to decorate the study, Francesco appearing in one of the 34 emblematic paintings covering the walls not as a prince, but as an inconsequential scientist experimenting with gunpowder. The lower paintings concealed 20 cabinets in which the young prince hid his shells, stones, crystals and other curious treasures. The tour ends in the **roof** above the Salone dei Cinquecento, where you can see the huge wooden trusses that hold up Vasari's ornate ceiling.

The children's tours are wonderful, involving actors dressed in Renaissance costume who rope young participants into the performance. A sumptuously attired Eleonora of Toledo, clearly shocked by the casual attire of today's children, has been known to give advice about proper grooming for young ladies, and Cosimo I is happy to lay down the law about the proper age for a Medici to take on duties as a cardinal (the answer is 14, the age of his son Ferdinando when he became a cardinal).

It is highly advisable to book the tours in advance by visiting the desk behind the ticket office on the day before your visit, by emailing info.museoragazzi@comune.fi.it (children's tours only) or by telephoning ☎ 055 276 82 24. Note that discounts for family groups apply.

For details about the special cumulative ticket for Palazzo Vecchio and the Cappella Brancacci, see p76.

❦ THE UFFIZI // RENAISSANCE ART TO TAKE YOUR BREATH AWAY

There are some museums that tower over all others in terms of the quality of their collections – think MoMA, the Egyptian Museum, the Hermitage, the Louvre, the Prado and the Vatican. But this list wouldn't be complete without adding Florence's jewel in the crown, the **Uffizi Gallery** (Galleria degli Uffizi; Map pp46-7; Piazzale degli Uffizi 6; ☎ 055 238 86 51; adult/concession €6.50/3.25, 85min audio guide for 1/2 €5.50/8; 8.15am-6.35pm Tue-Sun, to 9pm Tue Jul-Sep). Filling the vast, oversized U-shaped **Palazzo degli Uffizi**, the collection comprises 50-odd rooms and 1555 masterpieces. Allow at least four hours for your visit.

If you are in need of a break between viewing the works, the gallery has a pleasant **rooftop cafe** (only accessible once you're inside) serving light snacks (pizza/panino €4.50/6.50, beer €6, cappuccino standing up/sitting down €1.60/4.50) and fabulous views. During the grand old days of the Medici, the clan often gathered here to listen to music performances on the square below.

To beat the queue, which can sometimes involve a three- or four-hour wait, prebook your ticket through Firenze Musei (see p44).

The Palace

Cosimo I commissioned Vasari to design and build this gargantuan U-shaped palace in 1560 – a government office building (*uffizi* means offices) for the city's administrators, judiciary and guilds.

Vasari was also the design brain behind the **Corridoio Vasariano**, a covered elevated passageway begun a year later than the Uffizi to link Palazzo Vecchio and Palazzo Pitti, cutting through the Uffizi and across Ponte Vecchio en route. It is currently closed for restoration.

Following Vasari's death in 1564, architects Alfonso Parigi and Bernando Buontalenti took over the Uffizi project, Buontalenti modifying the upper floor of the palace to house the works of art keenly collected by Francesco I, a passion inherited from his father. In 1580 the building was finally complete. By the time the last of the Medici family died in 1743, the family's private art collection was enormous. Fortunately, it was bequeathed to the City of Florence on the strict proviso that it never leave the city.

Over the years, sections of the collection have been moved to the Museo Nazionale del Bargello and the Museo Archeologico, and other collections in turn have been

moved here. Several artworks were destroyed or badly damaged in 1993 when a car bomb planted by the Mafia exploded outside the gallery's west wing, killing five people. Documents cataloguing the collection were also destroyed.

An ongoing and vastly overdue €60 million refurbishment and redevelopment project will see the addition of a new exit loggia designed by Japanese architect Arato Isozaki and the doubling of exhibition space. The estimated completion date is 2013 and some rooms are likely to be temporarily closed and the contents of others changed in the meantime.

The Collection

Arranged in chronological order by school, the collection spans the whole gamut of art history from ancient Greek sculpture to 18th-century Venetian paintings, but its core is the masterpiece-rich Renaissance collection. We mention highlights in the following paragraphs.

Works are displayed on the 3rd floor in a series of numbered rooms off two dramatically long corridors – the first (*primo corridoio*) and third (*terzo corridoio*). They are linked at one end by a loggia (*secondo corridoio*), from where you can enjoy the finest view in Florence of the crowded Ponte Vecchio and mysterious Corridoio Vasariano.

Upon arrival at the gallery, boards at the ticket booth and at the main entrance say what's closed that day. For an updated room-by-room breakdown, visit www.polomuseale.firenze.it/English; search the gallery catalogue online at www.virtualuffizi.com.

Tuscan Masters: 13th Century to 14th Century

The first room to the left of the staircase highlights 13th-century Sienese Art and is dominated by three large altarpieces from Florentine churches viewed in chronological order – *Madonna Enthroned* by Tuscan masters Duccio di Buoninsegna, Cimabue and Giotto. These clearly reflect the transition from the Gothic to the nascent Renaissance style. Note the overtly naturalistic realism overtones in Giotto's portrayal of the Madonna and child among angels and saints, painted some 25 years after that of Duccio and Cimabue (c 1306–10).

The next room stays in Siena but moves into the 14th century. The highlight is Simone Martini's shimmering *Annunciation* (1333), which was painted with Lippo Memmi and sets the Madonna in a sea of gold. Also of note is the *Madonna with Child and Saints* triptych (1340) by Pietro Lorenzetti, which demonstrates a realism similar to Giotto's; unfortunately both Pietro and his artistic brother Ambrogio died from the plague in Siena in 1348.

Masters in 14th-century Florence paid as much attention to detail as their Sienese counterparts, as works in the next room demonstrate: savour the depth of realism and extraordinary gold-leaf work of *San Reminio Pietà* (1360–65) by gifted Giotto pupil, Giottino (otherwise known as Giotto di Stefano).

International Gothic

Rooms 5 and 6 (actually one large room) are dedicated to works of the International Gothic style, with the knockout piece being Gentile da Fabriano's *Adoration of the Magi* (1423), originally commissioned by Palla Strozzi for Santa Trìnita.

Renaissance Pioneers

A concern for perspective was a hallmark of the early-15th-century Florentine school (room 7) that pioneered the Renaissance. One panel (the other two are in the Louvre and London's National Gallery) from Paolo Uccello's striking *Battle of San Romano,* which celebrates Florence's victory over Siena, shows the artist's efforts to create perspective with amusing effect as he directs the lances, horses and soldiers to a central disappearing point.

In room 8, Piero della Francesca's famous profile portraits (1465) of the crooked-nosed, red-robed Duke and Duchess of Urbino are wholly humanist in spirit: the former painted from the left side as he'd lost his right eye in a jousting accident, and the latter painted a deathly white, reflecting the fact that the portrait was painted posthumously.

Carmelite monk Fra' Filippo Lippi had an unfortunate soft spot for earthly pleasures, eloping with a nun from Prato and causing a huge scandal. Search out the artist's self-portrait as a podgy friar in *Coronation of the Virgin* (1439–47) and don't miss his later *Madonna and Child with Two Angels* (1460–65), an exquisite work that clearly influenced his pupil, Sandro Botticelli.

Another related pair, brothers Antonio and Piero del Pollaiolo, fill room 9, where their seven cardinal and theological values of 15th-century Florence – commissioned for the merchant's tribunal in Piazza della Signoria – burst forth with fantastic energy. More restrained are Piero's *Portrait of Galeazzo Maria Sforza* and Antonio's *Portrait of a Lady in Profile.*

The only canvas in the theological and cardinal virtues series not to be painted by the Pollaiolos was *Strength* (1470), the first documented work by Botticelli.

Botticelli Room

The spectacular Sala del Botticelli, numbered 10 to 14 but in fact one large hall,

FLORENCE

is one of the Uffizi's most popular rooms and is always packed. Of the 15 works by the Renaissance master known for his ethereal figures, *Birth of Venus* (c 1484), *Primavera* (Spring; c 1478), the deeply spiritual *Cestello Annunciation* (1489–90), the *Adoration of the Magi* (1475, featuring the artist's self-portrait on the extreme right) and *The Madonna of the Magnificat* (1483) are the best known, but true aficionados rate his twin set of miniatures depicting a sword-bearing Judith returning from the camp of Holofernes and the discovery of the decapitated Holofernes in his tent (1495–1500) as being among his finest works.

Leonardo Room
Room 15 displays two early Florentine works by Leonardo da Vinci: the incomplete *Adoration of the Magi* (1481–2), drawn in red earth pigment, and his *Annunciation* (c 1472).

La Tribuna
The Medici clan stashed away their most precious masterpieces in this exquisite octagonal-shaped treasure trove (room 18) created by Francesco I. Today their family portraits hang on the red upholstered walls and a walkway leads visitors around the edge. The popular favourites here are the Bronzino portraits of the family of Cosimo I, including his wife Eleonora di Toledo (painted with their son Giovanni), the duke himself, young Giovanni holding a bird, daughter Bia and son Francesco.

Flemish and German Masters
Rooms 20 to 23 house works by Northern Renaissance painters including Dürer (*Adoration of the Magi;* 1504), Lucas Cranach the Elder (*Adam and Eve;* 1528) and Hans Memling (*Madonna and Child Enthroned With Two Angels;* 1480).

High Renaissance to Mannerism
Passing through the loggia, the first room (25) in the third corridor is home to Michelangelo's dazzling *Tondo Doni,* a depiction of the Holy Family. The composition is unusual and the colours as vibrant as when they were first applied in 1504–06. It was painted for wealthy Florentine merchant Agnolo Doni (who hung it above his bed) and bought by the Medici for Palazzo Pitti in 1594.

Raphael and Andrea del Sarto works rub shoulders in room 26, where Raphael's charming *Madonna of the Goldfinch* (1505–06) holds centre stage, though his striking portrait of *Pope Leo X with Giulio de' Medici and Luigi de' Rossi* is just as impressive.

The work of Venetian masters graces room 28, where 11 Titians are displayed. Masterpieces include the sensual nude *Venus of Urbino* (1538), the seductive *Flora* (1515) and the striking portrait of *Eleonora Gonzaga, Duchess of Urbino* (1536–37).

Room 29 is notable for Parmigianino's oddly elongated *Madonna of the Long Neck* (1534–40), and subsequent rooms feature works by Paolo Veronese, Tintoretto, Rubens and Rembrandt. Don't miss room 42, known as the Niobe Room, which was built to house a group of statues representing Niobe and her children. Discovered in a Roman vineyard in 1583 and brought to Florence in 1775, the works are 4th century BC Roman copies of Greek originals.

Baroque & Neoclassicism
Downstairs on the 1st floor (something of a building site as the Uffizi revamps itself) are an intense and dramatic group of works by Caravaggio and his admirers. These include the artist's *Bacchus* (1595–97) and *Medusa* (1595–98) as

well as Artemisia Gentileschi's gruesome *Judith Slaying Holofernes* (1620–21). One of the first female artists to be acclaimed in post-Renaissance Italy, Gentileschi (1593–1653), the victim in a highly scandalous seven-month rape trial, painted strong women seeking revenge on evil males. Like Caravaggio, she used *chiaroscuro* (contrast of light and dark) to full dramatic effect.

☙ ARTVIVA WALKING TOURS // LET THE EXPERTS SHOW YOU THEIR CITY

Of the many outfits specialising in walking tours of this pedestrian-friendly city, **Artviva** (Map pp46-7; ☎ 055 264 5033; www.italy .artviva.com; Via Sassetti 1; ☙ 8am-6pm Mon-Sat, to 1.30pm Sun) – which describes itself as 'the original and the best' – is the best known. It offers group and private tours including a 'Classic Walk' covering the most famous sights (€25, three hours), a 'Masterpieces of the Uffizi Gallery' tour (€39, two hours) and an 'Evening Walk/Murder Mystery Tour' (€30, two hours). All are led by English-speaking art history graduates. Private tours start at €250.

SANTA MARIA NOVELLA

Radiating west and south from the venerable basilica, the neighbourhood of Santa Maria Novella is blessed with chic boutiques, impressive palaces and art-adorned churches.

☙ BASILICA DI SANTA MARIA NOVELLA // VISIT A REPOSITORY OF FABULOUS FLORENTINE FRESCOS

Just south of Stazione di Santa Maria Novella, this **church** (Map pp58-9; ☎ 055 21 59 18; Piazza di Santa Maria Novella; admission €2.50; ☙ 9am-5pm Mon-Thu, 1-5pm Fri) was begun in the mid-13th century as the Dominican order's Florentine base. Although it was mostly completed by 1360, work on the facade and embellishment of the interior continued well into the 15th century.

The lower section of the green-and-white marble facade is transitional from Romanesque to Gothic, while the upper section and the main doorway were designed by Leon Battista Alberti and completed between 1456 and 1470.

The interior is full of artistic masterpieces. As you enter, look straight ahead and you will see Masaccio's superb fresco *Trinity* (1424–25), one of the first artworks to use the then newly discovered techniques of perspective and proportion. Close by, hanging in the nave, is a luminous painted *Crucifix* by Giotto (c 1290).

The first chapel to the right of the altar, **Cappella di Filippo Strozzi**, features spirited late 15th-century frescos by Filippino Lippi (son of Fra' Filippo Lippi) depicting the lives of St John the Evangelist and St Philip the Apostle. Behind the main altar itself are the highlights of the interior – Domenico Ghirlandaio's series of frescos in the **Sanctuary**. Relating the lives of the Virgin Mary, St John the Baptist and others, these vibrant frescos were painted in the late 15th century and are notable for their depiction of Florentine life during the Renaissance. They feature portraits of Ghirlandaio's contemporaries and members of the Tornabuoni family, who commissioned them. To the far left of the altar is the **Cappella Strozzi**, covered in wonderful frescos by Narno di Cione; the fine altarpiece here was painted by his brother Andrea, better known as Andrea Orcagna.

Museo di Santa Maria Novella

To reach this **museum** (Map pp58-9; ☎ 055 28 21 87; adult/child/concession €2.70/1/2; ☙ 9am-5pm

FLORENCE

FLORENCE

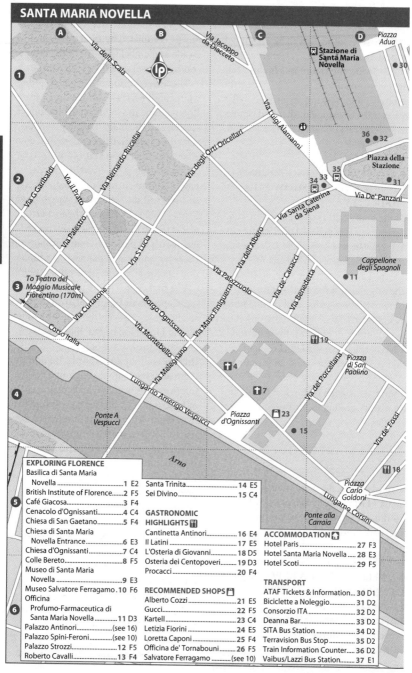

SANTA MARIA NOVELLA

FLORENCE

Mon-Thu & Sat), exit the church and follow signs for the *museo*.

Arranged around the monastery's tranquil **Chiostro Verde** (Green Cloister; 1332–62), which takes its name from the green earth base used for the frescos on three of the cloister's four walls, the museum's indisputable highlight is the spectacular **Cappellone degli Spagnoli** (Spanish Chapel) on the north side of the cloister, which is covered in extraordinary frescos (c 1365–67) by Andrea di Bonaiuto. The vault features depictions of the *Resurrection, Ascension* and *Pentecost* and on the altar wall are scenes of the *Via Dolorosa, Crucifixion* and *Descent into Limbo*. On the right wall is a huge fresco of *The Militant and Triumphant Church* – look in the foreground (right) for a portrait of Cimabue, Giotto, Boccaccio, Petrarch and Dante. Other frescos in the chapels depict the *Triumph of Christian Doctrine,* 14 figures symbolising the Arts and Sciences and the *Life of St Peter.*

On the west side of the cloister, a passage leads to the **Chiostro Grande** (Big Cloister; not open to visitors), the 14th-century **Cappella degli Ubriachi** and a large **refectory** featuring ecclesiastical relics and a 1583 *Last Supper* by Alessandro Allori.

❤ **OFFICINA PROFUMO-FARMACEUTICA DI SANTA MARIA NOVELLA // FOLLOW YOUR NOSE TO THIS HISTORIC PERFUMERY**
In business since 1612, this **perfumery-pharmacy** (Map pp58-9; ☎ 055 21 62 76; Via della Scala 16; ⏰ 9.30am-7.30pm Mon-Sat, 10.30am-8.30pm Sun, museum 10am-5.30pm Mon-Fri) began its life when the Dominican friars of Santa Maria Novella began to concoct cures and sweet-smelling unguents using medicinal herbs cultivated in the monastery

garden. The shop is an absolute treasure, having changed little over centuries, and its palatial salesrooms stock a wide range of fragrances, remedies, herbal teas and skincare products. After a day battling crowds at the Uffizi or Accademia, you may want to come here to source some Aqua di Santa Maria Novella, which is said to cure hysterics.

♥ BORGO OGNISSANTI // EXPLORE BOTTICELLI'S CHILDHOOD STAMPING GROUND

This long street runs from Piazza Carlo Goldoni towards the Porta al Prato, one of the city's ancient gates. As you walk west you'll pass antiques shops, designer boutiques such as **Kartell** (p91) and the 13th-century **Chiesa d'Ognissanti** (Map pp58-9; ☽ 7am-12.30pm & 4-8pm Mon-Sat, 4-8pm Sun), built as part of a Benedictine monastery. Much altered in the 17th century and given a new facade in the 19th century, this church possesses a number of significant paintings, including Domenico Ghirlandaio's fresco of the Madonna della Misericordia protecting members of the Vespucci family, who were the church's main patrons. Amerigo Vespucci, the Florentine navigator who gave his name to the American continent, is supposed to be the young boy whose head peeks between the Madonna and the old man. Also here are a *Crucifixion* by Taddeo Gaddi, Ghirlandaio's *St Jerome* (1480) and Botticelli's pensive *St Augustine* (also 1480). Botticelli, who grew up in a house on Borgo Ognissanti, is buried here (look for the simple round tombstone marked 'Sandro Filipepe' in the south transept). After exiting the church, turn right and enter the cloister to see Ghirlandaio's *Last Supper,* which covers most of a wall in the former monastery's **Cenacolo** (Refectory; Map pp58-9; ☎ 348 645 03

90; 42 Borgo Ognissanti; donation requested; ☽ 9am-noon Mon, Tue & Sat).

If you're here around lunchtime, stylish **Sei Divino** (Map pp58-9; ☎ 055 21 77 91; Borgo Ognissanti 42r; ☽ 8am-2am) offers simple daily plates for around €10. After 7pm it hosts one of the city's most happening *aperitivo* scenes, complete with ultra-smooth music, the odd exhibition opening and plenty of pavement action.

♥ VIA DE' TORNABUONI // GIVE YOUR CREDIT CARD A WORKOUT

Renaissance palaces and the flagship stores of Italian fashion houses border Via de' Tornabuoni, the city's most expensive shopping strip. Named after a wealthy Florentine noble family (which died out in the 17th century), it is sometimes referred to as the 'Salotto di Firenze' (Florence's Drawing Room).

From the Duomo, walk west along Via de' Pecori and its extension, Via degli Agli, crossing three streets before coming to Via de' Tornabuoni. Straight ahead, at the T-intersection, is the **Palazzo Antinori** (Map pp58–9), owned by the Antinori family since 1506 (the *palazzo* itself dates from 1461–69). One of Florence's most aristocratic families, the Antinori are known for the wines they produce on their Tuscan estates, which can be sampled at **Cantinetta Antinori** (p84), their elegant *enoteca*-restaurant on the *palazzo*'s ground floor. To the left of the *palazzo* is the street's most beautiful shop, **Loretta Caponi** (p90). Opposite, huge stone steps lead up to the 17th-century **Chiesa di San Gaetano** (Map pp58–9). A bit further down is the utterly irresistible **Procacci** (p85), where you should consider refuelling over a truffle panino and glass of *prosecco*.

Continuing towards the Arno, you will pass the most impressive of the street's

Renaissance mansions, **Palazzo Strozzi** (p62), and then hit the main concentration of designer fashion stores, which are strung along both sides of the street like jewels on a particularly precious necklace. Prada, Gucci, Ferragamo, Gianfranco Ferre, Armani and Pucci are all represented, as are many other international luxury labels. Two streets radiating west off Tornabuoni – Via della Spada and Via Della Vigna Nuova – are where the more edgy boutiques are found. After some serious retail therapy, you might want to join the city's fully-fledged fashionistas at **Café Giacosa** (Map pp58-9; ☎ 055 211 656; Via della Spada 10; 9am-11pm Mon-Sat). Owned by local fashion designer Roberto Cavalli, who has his flagship store next door, it's a great spot for a coffee, drink or snack.

Heading towards the **Ponte Santa Trìnita**, built over the Arno in 1567 and painstakingly restored after being blown up by the Nazis in 1944, you will pass the church of **Santa Trìnita** (p62) and, opposite, the splendid **Palazzo**

INTERVIEW: MICHELE GIUTTARI

Why do you set your crime novels in Florence? Florence is a city with a double face. It has a beautiful side, but there's also a dark side. I know this because I worked with this dark side for many years…I saw what the tourists don't see.

How did you become familiar with this 'dark side'? I spent eight years as the head of Florence's Squadra Mobile (elite police investigative unit) and four years as the head of a special taskforce investigating the Monster of Florence case.

What was that? Between 1974 and 1985, seven couples were murdered while making love in cars parked in the hills around Florence. Despite our best efforts, the killer was never found; the case is now closed.

The main character in your novels, Michele Ferrara, is also the head of the Squadra Mobile. Are you and he one and the same? We're very similar in terms of character, so I suppose you could call him my alter ego. He can do things I couldn't, though…he gets his evidence together and solves cases quickly. It's easy to do this in a novel, but not so easy in real life!

The plot in A Florentine Death is about a serial killer on the loose in Florence and A Death in Tuscany is about a high-level conspiracy surrounding the murder of a girl just outside the city. Were you inspired by your work on the Monster case? I started writing as a release valve when I was working on the Monster case, so it must have had an influence.

Did you work on other high-profile cases? I was head of Florence's anti-Mafia squad when the Cosa Nostra bombed the Uffizi in 1993. It's still fresh in my mind, and I put it into my latest book, La Donna della 'ndrangheta (published in English as Death of a Mafia Don).

And what about the beautiful side of Florence? I love to walk across the Ponte Vecchio (p73), along the lungarno and up to Piazzale Michelangelo (p81) where I sit on the terrace at La Loggia and enjoy the view. I will never get tired of how beautiful this city is.

Michele Giuttari is the author of the bestselling crime novels Scarabeo *(published in English as* A Florentine Death*),* La Loggia degli Innocenti *(A Death in Tuscany) and* La Donna della 'ndrangheta *(Death of a Mafia Don).*

Spini-Feroni (Map pp58-9; Piazza Santa Trinita 2), a palace dating from the 13th century. Built for Geri Spini, a rich cloth merchant and banker, it has been the home of the Ferragamo fashion empire since 1938 and the ground floor is a showcase for its classy shoes, handbags, clothes and accessories. Anyone with even the faintest tendency towards shoe addiction (or fetishism) should be sure to visit the **Museo Salvatore Ferragamo** (opposite) in the basement.

♥ PALAZZO STROZZI // FEEL THE ENERGY AT FLORENCE'S MOST EXCITING MUSEUM

Built for wealthy merchant Filippo Strozzi, one of the Medicis' major political and commercial rivals, this impressive 15th-century **palace** (Map pp58-9; cnr Via de' Tornabuoni & Via degli Strozzi; admission prices & opening hours vary according to exhibition) has been reimagined over recent years and is now home to the city's most exciting exhibition spaces. The building – half palace/half fortress as befits its era and the Strozzi family history (Filippo's entire family was banished from Florence in 1434 and didn't return until 1466) – is built over three levels from large stone blocks. The design, in which Strozzi is thought to have been heavily involved, is incomplete, as he died two years after building commenced and his son soon ran out of money. Today it hosts blockbuster exhibitions in its upstairs spaces and contemporary work in both its basement gallery and imposing internal courtyard. There's always a buzz around this place, with young Florentines congregating in the courtyard cafe and on the benches built into the *palazzo*'s eastern facade, which fronts Piazza Strozzi. Also on the piazza is the local fashion scene's bar of choice,

the uberstylish **Colle Bereto** (Map pp58-9; ☎ 055 28 31 56; www.collebereto.com; Piazza Strozzi 5; ✉ 11am-3am Tue-Sun). Its *aperitivo* hour is when the bold and the beautiful (or should that be the botoxed and the blinged?) come to see or be seen.

♥ THE BRITISH INSTITUTE OF FLORENCE // SIGN UP FOR AN ART HISTORY COURSE

This well-regarded **cultural institute** (Map pp58-9; ☎ 055 267 78 200; www.british institute.it; Piazza Strozzi 2) runs a number of art history courses, including 'Art in Renaissance Florence' (€450, five days), 'Florentine Frescos' (€450, five days) and 'Madonna and Child in Renaissance Art' (€725, 10 days). The courses are run by experts in the field and include illustrated lectures and plenty of site visits.

♥ SANTA TRÌNITA // BE OVERWHELMED BY THIS OFT-OVERLOOKED GEM

This 14th-century **church** (Map pp58-9; Piazza Santa Trinità), which was built in Gothic style and later given a Mannerist facade of indifferent taste, is home to some of the best frescos in the city. The church interior has little natural light, so you'll need to spring for a few coins to illuminate the chapels. Don't miss Lorenzo Monaco's *Annunciation* (1422) in the **Cappella Salimbenes/Bartholini**, which was badly damaged by the 1966 flood but subsequently restored. During the restoration process, another fresco was found underneath, and this was removed and placed in the chapel next door. Look out for the crest of the Salimbenes/Bartholini family on the floor of the chapel – it features poppies and the motto 'Per Non Dormire' (For Those Who Don't Sleep), a reference to the fact that the family fortune resulted from the acquisition of an important cargo of wool from Northern Europe, a deal sealed unbeknownst to their business rivals, who had been doped with opium-laced wine at a lavish party the night before the cargo was due to arrive in Florence.

Even more eye-catching are the wonderfully preserved frescos in the **Cappella Sassetti** to the right of the altar, which were painted by Ghirlandaio from 1483 to 1485. These depict the life of St Francis of Assisi and include the portraits of many prominent Florentines of the time – Lorenzo the Magnificent is portrayed with Francesco Sassetti, the merchant who commissioned the work, in *St Francis Receiving the Rule of the Order from Pope Honorius,* which is set in Piazza della Signoria; and Ghirlandaio portrayed himself in the *Miracle of the Boy Brought Back to Life,* which takes place on Piazza Santa Trìnita (he's on the far right, wearing a red cloak).

❦ MUSEO SALVATORE FERRAGAMO // OGLE MARILYN'S RED RHINESTONE COURT SHOES

Those who are serious about their footwear or are interested in the socio-historical context of fashion will adore this esoteric but oddly compelling **shoe museum** (Map pp58-9; ☎ 055 336 04 56; Via de' Tornabuoni 2; adult/under 10yr or over 65yr €5/free; ⊗ 10am-6pm Wed-Mon). Housed in the basement of the Palazzo Spini-Feroni, it showcases classic Ferragamo shoes, many worn by Hollywood stars such as Marilyn Monroe, Judy Garland, Greta Garbo and Sofia Loren. An interesting audio guide tells the story of the Ferragamo empire and the shoes on display, and is included in the price. Those seduced by the shoes on show here can purchase reproductions in the upstairs museum shop (€500 to €1000 per pair).

SAN LORENZO

This is Medici territory – come here to see their palace, church, library and mausoleum, all of which are decorated with extraordinary works of art.

❦ BASILICA DI SAN LORENZO // SEE WHERE THE MEDICI FAMILY WORSHIPPED

In 1425, Cosimo the Elder, who lived nearby, commissioned Brunelleschi to rebuild the basilica on this site, which dated to the 4th century. The new building would become the Medici parish church and mausoleum – many members of the family are buried here. Considered one of the most harmonious examples of Renaissance architecture, the **basilica** (Map p64; Piazza San Lorenzo; admission €3.50, incl basilica & biblioteca €6; ⊗ 10am-5pm Mon-Sat, 1.30-5pm Sun) has never been finished – Michelangelo was commissioned to design the facade in 1518 but his design in white Carrara marble was never executed, hence the building's rough unfinished appearance.

In the austere interior, columns of *pietra serena* (soft grey stone) crowned with Corinthian capitals separate the nave from the two aisles. Donatello, who was still sculpting the two bronze pulpits (1460–67) adorned with panels of the Crucifixion when he died, is buried in the chapel featuring Fra' Filippo Lippi's *Annunciation* (c 1450). Left of the altar is the **Sagrestia Vecchia** (Old Sacristy), designed by Brunelleschi and decorated in the main by Donatello.

❦ BIBLIOTECA LAURENZIANA MEDICEA // MAKE A GRAND ENTRANCE VIA MICHELANGELO'S FAMOUS STAIRCASE

To the left of the basilica's entrance are peaceful cloisters, off which an

FLORENCE

FLORENCE

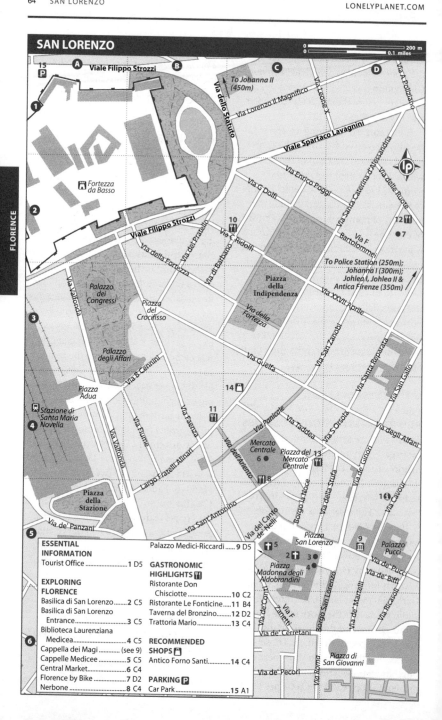

SAN LORENZO

extraordinary staircase designed by Michelangelo leads to the **Biblioteca Laurenziana Medicea** (Map p64; ☎ 055 21 15 90; www.bml.firenze.sbn.it; Piazza San Lorenzo 9; admission €3, incl basilica & biblioteca €6; ⏰ 9.30am-1pm Sun-Fri), commissioned by Guilio de' Medici (Pope Clement VII) in 1524 to house the extensive Medici library that had been started by Cosimo the Elder and greatly added to by Lorenzo the Magnificent. The real attraction here is Michelangelo's magnificent vestibule and staircase, designed in walnut but subsequently executed in grey *pietra serena*. Its curvaceous steps are a sign of the master's move towards Mannerism from the stricter bounds of Renaissance architecture and design.

❦ CAPPELLE MEDICEE // BEHOLD SELF-AGGRANDISEMENT IN SCULPTURAL FORM

Nowhere is Medici conceit expressed so explicitly as in their mausoleum, the **Cappelle Medicee** (Medicean Chapels; Map p64; ☎ 055 238 86 02; Piazza Madonna degli Aldobrandini; adult/concession €6/3; ⏰ 8.15am-4.50pm Tue-Sat & 1st & 3rd Sun & 2nd & 4th Mon of month). Sumptuously adorned with granite, the most precious marble, semiprecious stones and some of Michelangelo's most beautiful sculptures, it is the burial place of 49 members of the dynasty. Francesco I lies in the grandiose **Cappella dei Principi** (Princes' Chapel) alongside Ferdinando I and II and Cosimo I, II and III. Lorenzo il Magnifico is buried in the stark but graceful **Sagrestia Nuova** (New Sacristy), Michelangelo's first architectural work and showcase for three of his most haunting sculptures: *Dawn and Dusk* on the sarcophagus of Lorenzo, Duke of Urbino; *Night and Day* on the sarcophagus of Lorenzo's son Giuliano; and *Madonna and Child,* which adorns Lorenzo's tomb.

❦ PALAZZO MEDICI-RICCARDI // MARVEL AT A SUPREME EXAMPLE OF RENAISSANCE PAINTING

Cosimo the Elder entrusted Michelozzo with the design of the family's townhouse in 1444. The result was this **palace** (Map p64; ☎ 055 276 03 40; www.palazzo-medici.it; Via Cavour 3; adult/concession €7/4; ⏰ 9am-7pm Thu-Tue), a blueprint that influenced the construction of Florentine family residences such as Palazzo Pitti and Palazzo Strozzi for years to come.

Confident that his power base was solid, Cosimo determined that it wasn't necessary to build a fortress townhouse and allowed Michelozzo to create a self-assured, stout but not inelegant pile on three storeys. The rusticated facade of the ground floor gives a rather stern aspect to the building, though the upper two storeys are less aggressive, maintaining restrained classical lines – already a feature of the emerging Renaissance canon. The heavy timber roof has broad eaves protruding over the street below.

The Medici lived here until 1540, making way for the Riccardi family a century later, who gave the palace a comprehensive remodelling and built the sumptuously decorated **Sala Lucca Giordano** on the 2nd floor. Giordano adorned the ceiling with his complex *Allegory of Divine Wisdom* (1685), a rather overblown example of late baroque dripping with gold leaf and bursting with colour. The *palazzo* now houses the offices of the Florence Provincial Authority and hosts temporary exhibitions in its public rooms.

Cappella dei Magi

This upstairs chapel is the main reason to visit the *palazzo*. It houses one of the supreme achievements of Renaissance painting and is an absolute must-see

FLORENCE

for art lovers. The tiny space is covered in a series of wonderfully detailed and recently restored frescos (c 1459–63) by Benozzo Gozzoli, a pupil of Fra' Angelico. His ostensible theme of *Procession of the Magi to Bethlehem* is but a slender pretext for portraying members of the Medici clan in their best light; try to spy Lorenzo il Magnifico and Cosimo the Elder in the crowd. The chapel was reconfigured to accommodate a baroque staircase – hence the oddly split fresco of a Patriarch on a grey horse. The mid-15th-century altarpiece of the *Adoration of the Child* is a copy of the original (originally here) by Fra' Filippo Lippi.

Only 10 visitors are allowed in at a time for a maximum of just five minutes; reserve your slot in advance at the palace ticket desk.

❦ CENTRAL MARKET // STOCK UP ON ARTICHOKES, ASPARAGUS AND ATMOSPHERE

To research what produce is in season (and therefore what you should be ordering for dinner), take a stroll through the oldest and largest fresh-produce market in the city, the **Mercato Centrale** (Map p64; Piazza del Mercato Centrale; ⏱ 7am-2pm Mon-Fri, to 5pm Sat). Housed in a 19th-century iron-and-glass structure, it's noisy, smelly and full of wonderful stuff to cook and eat. For a snack while you're here, follow the steady stream of stallholders making their way to **Nerbone** (primi/secondi €4/7; ⏱ 7am-2pm Mon-Sat), which supplies lunchtime platters of *trippa alla fiorentina* (tripe and tomato stew), tripe panini and – should tripe simply be too offal (!) for you to stomach – *panini con bollito,* a boiled beef bun. Dine standing up or around a handful of tables.

Judy Francini of **Divina Cucina** (www.divinacucina.com) conducts highly regarded food-lovers' walking tours (€125) of the market on Mondays. The three-hour experience includes tastings and lunch at a nearby trattoria. The American chef, who is married to a Florentine and has lived in Florence since 1984, also offers a three-day program (€770) including the tour, a day in Chianti and a one-day Tuscan cooking course.

SAN MARCO

Most visitors leave this pocket of the city after visiting its most famous resident, one Sig. David, but we suggest staying to visit the superb frescos at the Museo di San Marco, and one of Brunelleschi's earliest architectural triumphs, the Spedale degli Innocenti.

❦ GALLERIA DELL'ACCADEMIA // PAY A CALL ON A NAKED MAN

A lengthy queue marks the door to this **gallery** (Map p67; ☎ 055 294 883; Via Ricasoli 60; adult/concession €6.50/3.25; ⏱ 8.15am-6.50pm Tue-Sun) where Michelangelo's *David* is displayed. Fortunately, the most famous statue in the world is worth the long wait. Carved from a single block of marble already worked on by two sculptors before him (both of whom had given up), the statue of the nude warrior assumed its pedestal in front of Palazzo Vecchio on Piazza della Signoria in 1504, providing Florentines with a powerful emblem of power, liberty and civic pride.

Michelangelo was also the master behind the unfinished *San Matteo* (St Matthew; 1504–08) and four *Prigioni* ('Prisoners' or 'Slaves'; 1521–30) on display here. The Prisoners seem to be writhing and struggling to free themselves from the marble; they were meant for the tomb of Pope Julius II, itself never completed.

SAN MARCO

Adjacent rooms contain paintings by Andrea Orcagna, Taddeo Gaddi, Domenico Ghirlandaio, Filippino Lippi and Sandro Botticelli.

♥ MUSEO DI SAN MARCO // APPRECIATE FRA' ANGELICO'S PAINTERLY DEVOTIONS

At the heart of Florence's university area sits the Chiesa di San Marco and adjoining 15th-century Dominican monastery where both gifted painter Fra' Angelico (c 1400–55) and the sharp-tongued Savonarola piously served God. Today,

the monastery is home to the **Museo di San Marco** (Map p67; ☎ 055 238 86 08; Piazza San Marco 1; adult/concession €4/2; ☼ 8.15am-1.50pm Tue-Fri, to 4.50pm Sat, to 4.50pm 2nd & 4th Sun & 1st, 3rd & 5th Mon of month), a showcase of the work of Fra' Angelico and one of Florence's most spiritually uplifting museums.

Enter via Michelozzo's **Cloister of Saint Antoninus** (1440). Turn immediately right to enter the **Sala dell'Ospizio** (Pilgrims' Hospital), where Fra' Angelico's attention to perspective and the realistic portrayal of nature comes to life in a number of major paintings, including the *Deposition of Christ* (1432), originally commissioned for the church of Santa Trìnita.

Giovanni Antonio Sogliani's fresco *The Miraculous Supper of St Domenic* (1536) dominates the former monks' **refectory** in the cloister; and Fra' Angelico's huge *Crucifixion and Saints* fresco (1441–42) decorates the former **chapterhouse**. But it is the 44 **monastic cells** on the 1st floor that are the most haunting: At the top of the stairs, Fra' Angelico's most famous work, *Annunciation* (c 1440), commands all eyes. A stroll around each of the cells reveals snippets of many more fine religious reliefs by the Tuscan-born friar, who decorated the cells between 1440 and 1441 with deeply devotional frescos to guide the meditation of his fellow friars. Most were executed by Fra' Angelico himself; others are by aides under his supervision, including Benozzo Gozzoli. Among several masterpieces is the magnificent *Adoration of the Magi* in the cell used by Cosimo the Elder as a meditation retreat (No 38-39). Quite a few of the frescos are extremely gruesome – check out the cell of San Antonino Arcivescovo, which features a depiction of Jesus pushing open the door of his sepulchre, squashing a nasty-looking devil in the process. After centuries of being known as 'Il Beato Angelico' (literally 'the blessed angelic one') or simply 'Il Beato' (the blessed), the Renaissance's most blessed religious painter was made a saint by Pope John Paul II in 1984.

Contrasting with the pure beauty of these frescos are the plain rooms that Savonarola called home from 1489. Rising to the position of prior at the Dominican convent, it was from here that the fanatical monk railed against luxury, greed and corruption of the clergy. Kept as a kind of shrine to the turbulent priest, they house a portrait, a few personal items, the linen banner Savonarola carried in processions and a grand marble monument erected by admirers in 1873.

❦ **PIAZZA DELLA SANTISSIMA ANNUNZIATA // ESCAPE THE TOURIST HOARDS FOR A CHANGE**
Giambologna's equestrian statue of Grand Duke Ferdinando I de' Medici commands the scene from the centre of this square, which teems with students rather than tourists and hosts the popular Jazz & Co festival in summer (see p83).

The church that gives the square its name, **Chiesa della Santissima Annunziata** (Map p67; Piazza della Santissima Annunziata; ⏱7.30am-12.30pm & 4-6.30pm), was established in 1250 by the founders of the Servite order, and rebuilt by Michelozzo and others in the mid-15th century. It is dedicated to the Virgin Mary and has frescos by Perugino (in the fifth chapel) and Andrea del Sarto (in the atrium). Be warned that visitors often find it hard to squeeze in between the seven masses held each morning.

The **Spedale degli Innocenti** (Hospital of the Innocents; Map p67) was founded on the southeastern side of the piazza in 1421 as Europe's first orphanage, hence the 'Innocents' in its name. Brunelleschi designed the classically influenced portico, which Andrea della Robbia (1435–1525) famously decorated with terracotta medallions of babies in swaddling clothes. At the north end of the portico, the false door surrounded by railings was once a revolving door where unwanted children were left. Inside, the **Museo dello Spedale degli Innocenti** (☎ 055 203 73 08; www.istitutodeglinnocenti.it; Piazza della Santissima Annunziata 12; adult/concession €4/2.50; ⏱8.30am-7pm Mon-Sat, to 2pm Sun) on the 2nd floor displays works by Florentine artists, including Domenico Ghirlandaio's striking *Adoration of the Magi* (1488), two wonderfully serene wooden sculptures of the *Madonna* and *St Joseph* by Marco della Robbia (c 1505), a *Madonna with Holy Child and Angel* (1465–66) by Botticelli and a charming *Madonna of the Innocents* (c 1440) by Domenico di Michelino. Less valuable, but even more moving, is the display case of 19th-century markers left on the clothing of abandoned babies to allow for eventual reunification with their mothers.

About 200m southeast of the piazza is the **Museo Archeologico** (Map p67; ☎ 055 23 57 50; Via della Colonna 38; adult/concession €4/2; ⏰ 2-7pm Mon, 8.30am-7pm Tue & Thu, 8.30am-2pm Wed & Fri-Sun), whose rich collection of finds, including most of the Medici hoard of antiquities, plunges you deep into the past and offers an alternative to Renaissance splendour. On the 1st floor you can either head left into the ancient Egyptian collection or right for the smaller section on Etruscan and Graeco-Roman art.

If you're in need of a refuel over coffee and cake after your exploration of this area, **Robiglio** (Via dei Servi 112; ⏰ 8am-8pm Mon-Sat) is one of the city's most famous cafes.

SANTA CROCE

Presided over by the massive Franciscan basilica of the same name, this neighbourhood has a slightly rough veneer that is slowly being polished by the opening of a number of top-end restaurants.

❦ PIAZZA DI SANTA CROCE // MAKE AN APPEARANCE ON AN ANCIENT FOOTBALL FIELD

This square was initially cleared in the Middle Ages, primarily to allow hordes of the faithful to gather when the church itself was full. In Savonarola's day, heretics were executed here.

Such an open space inevitably found other uses, and from the 14th century it was often the colourful scene of jousts, festivals and *calcio storico* matches. Still played in this square in the third week of June each year, *calcio storico* (www .calciostorico.it) is like a combination of football and rugby with few rules (head-butting, punching, elbowing and choking are allowed, but sucker-punching and kicks to the head are forbidden). Look for the marble stone embedded in the wall below the gaily frescoed facade of **Palazzo dell'Antella** (Map p70), on the south side of the piazza; it marks the halfway line on this, one of the oldest football pitches in the world.

Curiously enough, the Romans used to have fun in much the same area centuries before. The city's 2nd-century amphitheatre took up the area facing the western end of Piazza di Santa Croce. To this day, Piazza dei Peruzzi, Via de' Bentaccordi and Via Torta mark the oval outline of the north, west and south sides of its course.

❦ BASILICA DI SANTA CROCE // CHURCH, CLOISTERS AND CHAPELS GALORE

When Lucy Honeychurch, the heroine of EM Forster's *A Room With a View*, is stranded in Santa Croce without a Baedeker, she first panics and then, looking around, wonders why it's thought to be such an important building. After all, doesn't it look just like a barn?

On entering, many visitors to this massive Franciscan **basilica** (Map p70; ☎ 055 246 61 05; adult/concession incl Museo dell'Opera €5/3; ⏰ 9.30am-5.30pm Mon-Sat, 1-5.30pm Sun) share the same reaction. The austere

FLORENCE

SANTA CROCE

ESSENTIAL INFORMATION
Tourist Office.................................1 C3
Tourist Office.................................2 F1
Tourist Police................................3 D1

EXPLORING FLORENCE
Basilica di Santa Croce...................4 C3
Café Cibrèo...................................5 E2
Cappella de' Pazzi.........................6 C3
Loggia del Pesce............................7 D1
Museo dell'Opera di Santa
   Croce.......................................8 C3
Museo Nazionale del
   Bargello....................................9 A2
Palazzo del Bargello....................(see 9)
Palazzo dell'Antella.....................10 C3
Teatro del Sale............................11 D2

GASTRONOMIC HIGHLIGHTS
Alle Murate.................................12 A2
Antico Noè..................................13 C1

Caffè Italiano Sud.........................14 B2
Enoteca Pinchiorri........................15 C2
Gelateria dei Neri.........................16 B3
Gelateria Vivoli............................17 B2
Il Pizzaiuolo..................................18 D1
La Pentola dell' Oro......................19 D1
Osteria del Caffè Italiano...............20 B4
Pizzeria del Caffè Italiano...........(see 20)
Ristorante Cibrèo..........................21 E1
Ristorante del Fagioli....................22 B4
Trattoria Cibrèo.........................(see 21)
Vestri...23 C1

RECOMMENDED SHOPS
La Bottega del Cioccolato............24 D2
Maestri di Fabbrica.......................25 B2
Scuola del Cuoio..........................26 C4

ACCOMMODATION
Borghese Palace Art Hotel............27 B2
Hotel Orchidea.............................28 B1

interior can come as something of a shock after the magnificent neo-Gothic facade, which is enlivened by varying shades of coloured marble (both it and the *campanile*, or bell tower, are 19th-century additions). The church itself was designed by Arnolfo di Cambio between 1294 and 1385 and owes its name to a splinter of the Holy Cross donated by King Louis of France in 1258.

Though most visitors come to see the tombs of famous Florentines buried inside this church – including Michelangelo, Galileo, Ghiberti and Machiavelli – it's the frescos by Giotto and his school in the chapels to the right of the altar that are the real highlights. Some of these are substantially better preserved than others – Giotto's murals in the **Capella Peruzzi** are in particularly poor condition. Fortunately, those in the **Capella Bardi** (1315–20) depicting scenes from the life of St Francis have fared better. Giotto's assistant and most loyal pupil, Taddeo Gaddi, frescoed the neighbouring **Chapelle Majeure** and nearby **Capella Baroncelli** (1332–38); the latter takes as its subject the life of the Virgin.

Taddeo's son Agnolo painted the **Cappella Castellani** (1385) with delightful frescos depicting the life of St Nicholas (later transformed into 'Santa Claus') and was also responsible for the frescos above the altar.

From the transept chapels a doorway designed by Michelozzo leads into a corridor, off which is the **Sagrestia**, an enchanting 14th-century room dominated on the left by Taddeo Gaddi's fresco of the Crucifixion. There are also a few relics of St Francis on show, including his cowl and belt. Through the next room, the church bookshop, you can access the **Scuola del Cuoio** (p92), a leather school and shop, where you can see the goods

being fashioned and also buy the finished products. At the end of the corridor is a Medici chapel with a fine two-tone altarpiece in glazed terracotta by Andrea della Robbia.

Cloisters & Cappella de' Pazzi

Brunelleschi designed the second of Santa Croce's two serene **cloisters** just before his death in 1446. His unfinished **Cappella de' Pazzi** at the end of the first cloister is notable for its harmonious lines and restrained terracotta medallions of the Apostles by Luca della Robbia, and is a masterpiece of Renaissance architecture. It was built for, but never used by, the wealthy banking family destroyed in the 1468 Pazzi Conspiracy – when papal sympathisers sought to overthrow Lorenzo il Magnifico and the Medici dynasty.

Museo dell'Opera di Santa Croce

Santa Croce's **museum** (Map p70; admission incl basilica adult/concession €5/3; 9.30am-5.30pm Mon-Sat, 1-5.30pm Sun) is located off the first cloister. It features a *Crucifixion* by Cimabue, restored to the best degree possible after flood damage in 1966, when more than 4m of water inundated the Santa Croce area. Other highlights include Donatello's gilded bronze statue *St Louis of Toulouse* (1424), originally placed in a tabernacle on the Orsanmichele facade; a wonderful terracotta bust of St Francis receiving the stigmata by the della Robbia workshop; and frescos by Taddeo Gaddi, including *The Last Supper* (1333).

❦ PALAZZO DEL BARGELLO // ADMIRE RENAISSANCE SCULPTURE FROM DONATELLO TO MICHELANGELO

It was behind the stark exterior of the Palazzo del Bargello, Florence's earliest public building, that the *podestà* meted out justice from the late 13th century until 1502. Today the building is home to the **Museo Nazionale del Bargello** (Map p70; ☎ 055 238 86 06; Via del Proconsolo 4; adult/EU citizen 18-25yr €7/3.50; ⏰ 8.15am-5pm Tue-Sun & 1st & 3rd Mon of month), Italy's most comprehensive collection of Tuscan Renaissance sculpture.

Crowds clamour to see *David* but few rush to see his creator's early works, many of which are on display in the Bargello's downstairs Sala di Michelangelo. The artist was just 21 when a cardinal commissioned him to create the drunken grape-adorned *Bacchus* (1496–97) displayed here. Unfortunately the cardinal didn't like the result and sold it to a banker. Other Michelangelo works to look out for here include the marble bust of *Brutus* (c 1539–40), the *David/Apollo* from 1530–32 and the large, uncompleted roundel of the Madonna and Child with the infant St John (1503–05, aka the *Tondo Pitti)*.

After Michelangelo left Florence for the final time in 1534, sculpture was dominated by Baccio Bandinelli (his 1551 *Adam & Eve,* created for the Duomo, is displayed in the Sala di Michelangelo) and Benvenuto Cellini (look for his playful 1548–50 marble *Ganimede* in the same room).

On the 1st floor, to the right of the staircase, is the Sala di Donatello. Here, in the majestic Salone del Consiglio Generale where the city's general council met, works by Donatello and other early-15th-century sculptors can be admired. Originally on the facade of Chiesa di Orsanmichele (p50) and now within a tabernacle at the hall's far end, Donatello's wonderful *St George* (1416–17) brought a new sense of perspective and movement to Italian sculpture. Also look for the bronze bas-reliefs created for the

Baptistry doors competition by Brunelleschi and Ghiberti (see p48).

Yet it is Donatello's two versions of *David,* a favourite subject for sculptors, which really fascinate: Donatello fashioned his slender, youthful dressed image in marble in 1408 and his fabled bronze between 1440 and 1450. The latter is extraordinary – the more so when you consider it was the first freestanding naked statue to be sculpted since classical times.

Criminals received their last rites before execution in the palace's 1st-floor Capella del Podestà, also known as the Mary Magdalene Chapel, where *Hell* and *Paradise* are frescoed on the walls, as are stories from the lives of Mary of Egypt, Mary Magdalene and John the Baptist. These remnants of frescos by Giotto were not discovered until 1840, when the chapel was turned into a storeroom and prison.

The 2nd floor moves into the 16th century with a superb collection of terracotta pieces by the prolific della Robbia family, including some of their best-known works, such as Andrea's *Ritratto Idealizia di Fanciullo* (Bust of a Boy; c 1475) and Giovanni's *Pietà* (1514). Instantly recognisable, Giovanni's works are more elaborate and flamboyant than either father Luca's or cousin Andrea's, using a larger palette of colours.

☙ FABIO PICCHI'S EMPIRE // EAT, DRINK AND BE MERRY – FLORENTINE STYLE

Larger-than-life chef Fabio Picchi is one of Florence's living treasures. Having colonised almost an entire block near the Mercato Sant'Ambrogio with his trio of the Cibrèo restaurant, trattoria and cafe, he went on to open one of the city's most unique institutions in 2002, the eccentric **Teatro del Sale** (Map p70; ☎ 055 200 14 92; www.teatrodelsale.com; Via dei Macci 111r;

breakfast/lunch/dinner €7/20/30; ⊙ 9-11am, 12.30-2.15pm & 7-11pm Tue-Sat Sep-Jul). Occupying an old theatre, this members-only club (tourists welcome, annual membership fee €5) is open for breakfast, lunch and dinner, culminating at 9.30pm in a live performance of drama, music or comedy arranged by artistic director Maria Cassi, a famous Florentine actress (and Picchi's wife). Dinners are hectic affairs – you grab a chair, serve yourself water, wine and antipasti and then wait for Picchi to yell out what's just about to be served before queuing at the glass hatch for your *primo* and *secondo*. Dessert and coffee are laid out buffet-style just prior to the performance. Come during the day to join the club and make a reservation for that evening, and then enjoy a coffee and sugar-dusted *ciambella* (doughnut ring) at charming **Café Cibrèo** (Map p70; ☎ 055 234 58 53; Via Andrea del Verrocchio 5; ⊙ 8am-1am Tue-Sat Sep-Jul), in the street opposite. For reviews of Ristorante and Trattoria Cibrèo, see p88 and p88.

OLTRARNO

Literally 'other side of the Arno', atmospheric Oltrarno is the traditional home of the city's artisanal workshops. It takes in the area south of the river and west of Ponte Vecchio and its backbone is busy Borgo San Jacopo, home to restaurants, shops and two 12th-century towers –Torre dei Marsili and Torre de' Belfredelli.

✤ PONTE VECCHIO // CROSS THE ARNO'S ONLY ORIGINAL BRIDGE

The first documentation of a stone bridge here, at the narrowest crossing point along the entire length of the Arno, dates from 972. The Arno looks placid enough, but when it gets mean, it gets very mean. Floods in 1177 and 1333 destroyed the bridge, and in 1966 it came close to being destroyed again. Many of the jewellers with shops on the bridge were convinced the floodwaters would sweep away their livelihoods; however – fortunately – the bridge held.

They're still here. Indeed, the bridge has twinkled with the glittering wares of jewellers, their trade often passed down from generation to generation, ever since the 16th century, when Ferdinando I de' Medici ordered them here to replace the often malodorous presence of the town butchers, who used to toss unwanted leftovers into the river.

The bridge as it stands was built in 1345 and was the only one saved from destruction at the hands of the retreating Germans in 1944. Look above the shops on the eastern side and you'll see the **Corridoio Vasariano**, an elevated covered passageway joining the Palazzo Vecchio, Uffizi and Palazzo Pitti, designed by Vasari for Cosimo I in 1565. Its original design incorporated small windows to ensure the privacy of the Medici family members who used it, but when Hitler visited Florence in 1941, his mate and fellow dictator Benito Mussolini had new windows punched into the corridor walls over the bridge so that his guest could enjoy an expansive view down the Arno when walking between the Ufizzi and Palazzo Pitti.

At the southern end of the bridge is the medieval **Torre dei Mannelli** (Map pp74–5), which looks rather odd as the Corridoio Vasariano was built around it, not simply straight through it, as the Medici would have preferred.

✤ PIAZZA SANTO SPIRITO // MAKE YOUR WAY TO THE OLTRARNO'S BUSIEST PIAZZA

This somewhat grungy square appears to best advantage on summer nights, when the striking facade of Brunelleschi's

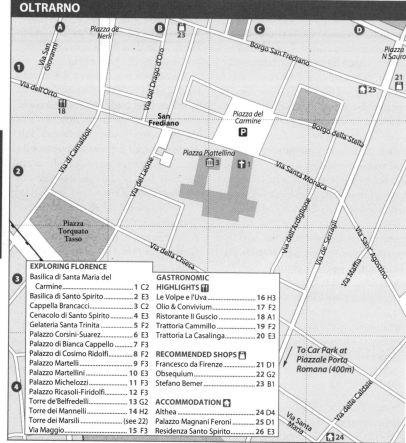

OLTRARNO

EXPLORING FLORENCE

Basilica di Santa Maria del Carmine	1 C2
Basilica di Santo Spirito	2 E3
Cappella Brancacci	3 C2
Cenacolo di Santo Spirito	4 E3
Gelateria Santa Trinita	5 F2
Palazzo Corsini-Suarez	6 E3
Palazzo di Bianca Cappello	7 F3
Palazzo di Cosimo Ridolfi	8 F2
Palazzo Martelli	9 F3
Palazzo Martellini	10 E3
Palazzo Michelozzi	11 F3
Palazzo Ricasoli-Firidolfi	12 F3
Torre de'Belfredelli	13 G2
Torre dei Mannelli	14 H2
Torre dei Marsili	(see 22)
Via Maggio	15 F3

GASTRONOMIC HIGHLIGHTS

Le Volpe e l'Uva	16 H3
Olio & Convivium	17 F2
Ristorante Il Guscio	18 A1
Trattoria Cammillo	19 F2
Trattoria La Casalinga	20 E3

RECOMMENDED SHOPS

Francesco da Firenze	21 D1
Obsequium	22 G2
Stefano Bemer	23 B1

ACCOMMODATION

Althea	24 D4
Palazzo Magnani Feroni	25 D1
Residenza Santo Spirito	26 E3

Basilica di Santo Spirito (Map pp74–5; ⏰ 9.30am–12.30pm & 4-5.30pm Thu-Tue) forms a backdrop to open-air concerts and a busy outdoor social scene.

Inside the basilica, the entire length of the building is lined by a series of semicircular chapels, and the colonnade of grey *pietra forte* Corinthian columns lends an air of monumental grandeur. Artworks to look out for include Domenico di Zanobi's *Madonna of the Relief* (1485) in the Cappella Velutti, in which the Madonna wards off a little red devil with a club, and Filippino Lip-pi's poorly lit *Madonna with Child and Saints* (1493–94) in the Cappella Nerli in the right transept. The main altar, beneath the central dome, is a voluptuous baroque flourish, rather out of place in Brunelleschi's characteristically spare interior. Ask an attendant to show you the sacristy, where you'll find a poignant wooden crucifix attributed by some experts to Michelangelo.

Next door to the church is the **Cenacolo di Santo Spirito** (Map pp74–5; ☎ 055 28 70 43; Piazza Santo Spirito 29; admission €2.20; ⏰ 9am-5pm Sat Apr-Oct, 10.30am-1.30pm Sat Nov-Mar).

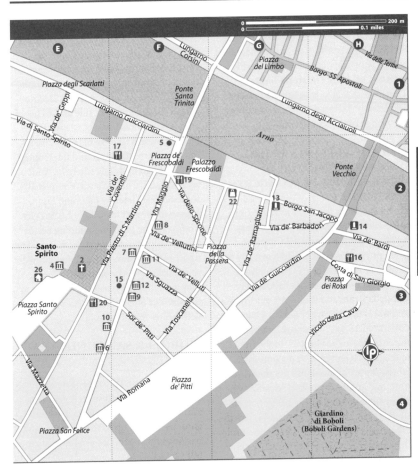

Andrea Orcagna decorated this refectory with a grand fresco depicting the *Last Supper* and the *Crucifixion* (c 1370). Also on display is a collection of rare pre-Romanesque sculptures.

♥ VIA MAGGIO // MEANDER ALONG A STREET OF RENAISSANCE MANSIONS

This was a posh address in the 16th century, as the line-up of fine Renaissance mansions duly attests. These days it's home to high-end antiques shops. The sumptuously decorated **Palazzo**

di Bianca Cappello (Map pp74–5), at No 26, is named after Bianca Cappello, Francesco I de' Medici's lover, who eventually became his wife. Across the street, a series of mansions, more or less following the same Renaissance style, include **Palazzo Ricasoli-Firidolfi** (Map pp74–5) at No 7, **Palazzo Martellini** (Map pp74–5) at No 9, **Palazzo Michelozzi** (Map pp74–5) at No 11, **Palazzo Martelli** (Map pp74–5) at No 13 and **Palazzo di Cosimo Ridolfi** (Map pp74–5) at No 15. All were built and/or renovated over the 14th, 15th and 16th

FLORENCE

centuries. Over the road, take a glance at the squarely imposing **Palazzo Corsini-Suarez** (Map pp74–5) at No 42. At the end of your viewing, stop for a freshly churned gelato at **Gelateria Santa Trinita** (Map pp74-5; cnr Via Maggio & Lungarno Guicciardini; ☺ 11.30am-midnight), overlooking the bridge of the same name.

♥ BASILICA DI SANTA MARIA DEL CARMINE // CATCH A QUICK GLIMPSE OF MASACCIO'S MASTERPIECES

On the southern flank of Piazza del Carmine, now a car park, the 13th-century **Basilica di Santa Maria del Carmine** (Map pp74–5) was all but destroyed by fire in the late 18th century. Fortunately the fire spared the magnificent frescos in its **Cappella Brancacci** (Map pp74-5; ☎ reservations 055 276 82 24, 055 76 85 58; admission €4; ☺ 10am-4.30pm Wed-Sat & Mon, 1-4.30pm Sun), entered via the entrance to the cloisters, to the right of the church entrance. A maximum of 30 visitors are allowed into the chapel at a time, and you *must* book in advance. Visits are often marred by the belligerent attitude taken by the attendants, who strictly enforce the ridiculous 15-minute-visit rule that applies here. How the church authorities think that this is enough time to appreciate the magnificent frescos on show is an absolute mystery.

This chapel is a treasure of paintings by Masolino da Panicale, Masaccio and Filippino Lippi; see p364 for an in-depth look. Masaccio's fresco cycle illustrating the life

MONEY SAVER

Visiting the **Cappella Brancacci** (above) and **Palazzo Vecchio** (p51)? Buy a com-bined ticket (adult/3-17yr/18-25yr €8/3/6, fam-ily of 4/5 €21/24), which covers both sights and is valid for three months.

of St Peter is considered among his greatest works, representing a definitive break with Gothic art and a plunge into new worlds of expression in the early stages of the Renaissance. *The Expulsion of Adam and Eve from Paradise* and *The Tribute Money,* both on the left side of the chapel, are his best-known works. Masaccio painted these frescos in his early 20s, taking over from Masolino, and interrupted the task to go to Rome, where he died, aged only 27. The cycle was completed some 60 years later by Filippino Lippi. Masaccio himself features in his *St Peter Enthroned;* he's the one standing beside the Apostle, staring out at the viewer. The figures around him have been identified as Brunelleschi, Masolino and Alberti. Filippino Lippi also painted himself into the scene of *St Peter's Crucifixion,* along with his teacher, Botticelli.

BOBOLI & SAN MINIATO AL MONTE

When you reach the stage of museum overload and need to stretch your legs and see some sky, this tier of parks and gardens leading up to the Romanesque basilica of San Miniato al Monte fits the bill perfectly.

♥ PALAZZO PITTI // BE OVERWHELMED BY THE MEDICI FAMILY PILE

Wealthy banker Luca Pitti commissioned Brunelleschi to design this forbidding-looking **palace** (Map pp78-9; ☎ 055 94 48 83; Piazza de' Pitti 1) in 1457, but by the time it was completed the family fortunes were on the wane, forcing them to sell it to arch-rivals, the Medici, in 1549.

Following the demise of the Medici dynasty, the *palazzo* remained the residence of the city's rulers, the Habsburg-Lorraine grand dukes of Tuscany. When

TICKETING

There are two types of tickets to **Palazzo Pitti** (opposite), on sale at the office to the far right of the main entrance. The first (adult/concession €6/3) gives you entrance to the **Galleria del Costume, Giardino di Boboli, Museo degli Argenti, Porcelain Museum** and **Giardino Bardini**. The second (€8.50/4.25) covers the **Royal Apartments, Palatine Gallery** and **Galleria d'Arte Moderna**.

Note that tickets are more expensive if temporary exhibitions are being staged. If there are no temporary exhibitions, you may purchase a **combined ticket** (€11.50, valid 3 days), which gives access to all sights. To do everything here justice, you'll need a full day.

Florence was made capital of the nascent Kingdom of Italy in 1865, it became a residence of the Savoy royal family, who presented it to the state in 1919.

Museo degli Argenti

Our recent stroll around the ground-floor **Museo degli Argenti** (Silver Museum; Map pp78–9; 8.15am-7.30pm Jun-Aug, to 6.30pm Mar-May & Sep, to 5.30pm Oct, to 4.30pm Nov-Feb; closed 1st & last Mon of month) was notable for the fact that no silver was on display. Go figure. Come instead to see the elaborately frescoed audience chambers, which host temporary exhibitions. These include the Sala di Giovanni da San Giovanni, which sports lavish head-to-toe frescos (1635–42) celebrating the life of Lorenzo the Magnificent – spot Michelangelo giving Lorenzo a statue. 'Talk little, be brief and witty' is the curt motto above the painted staircase in the next room, the public audience chamber, where the grand duke received visitors in the presence of his court.

Palatine Gallery & Royal Apartments

Raphaels and Rubens vie for centre stage in the enviable collection of 16th- to 18th-century art amassed by the Medici and Habsburg-Lorraine dukes in the 1st-floor **Galleria Palatina** (Map pp78–9; 8.15am-6.50pm Tue-Sun), reached by a staircase from the palace's central courtyard. This gallery has retained the original display arrangement of paintings (squeezed in, often on top of each other) so can be visually overwhelming – go slow and focus on the works one by one.

Highlights include Fra' Filippo Lippi's *Madonna and Child with Stories from the Life of St Anne* (aka the Tondo Bartolini; 1452–53) and Botticelli's *Madonna with Child and a Young Saint John the Baptist* (c 1490–95) in the Sala di Prometeo; Raphael's *Madonna of the Window* (1513–14) in the Sala di Ulisse; and Caravaggio's *Sleeping Cupid* (1608) in the Sala dell'Educazione di Giove. Don't miss the Sala di Saturno, which is full of magnificent works by Raphael, including the *Madonna of the Chair* (1511) and portraits of Anolo Doni and Maddalena Strozzi (c 1506). Nearby, in the Sala di Giove, the same artist's *Lady with a Veil* (aka *La Velata*; c 1516) holds court alongside Giorgione's *Three Ages of Man* (c 1500). The sentimental favourite, Tiberio Titi's charming portrait of the young Prince Leopoldo de' Medici, hangs in the Sala di Apollo, and the Sala di Venere shines with Titian's *Portrait of a Lady* (c 1536).

Past the Sala di Venere is the **Appartamenti Reali** (8.15am-6.50pm Tue-Sun Feb-Dec), a series of rooms presented as they were c 1880–91, when they were occupied by members of the House of Savoy. The style and division of tasks assigned to each room is reminiscent of Spanish royal palaces, all heavily bedecked with

FLORENCE

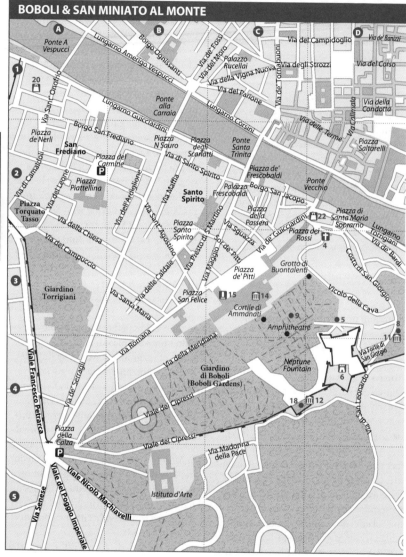

BOBOLI & SAN MINIATO AL MONTE

drapes, silk and chandeliers. Each room has a colour theme, ranging from aqua green to deep-wine red.

Galleria d'Arte Moderna

By modern, the Pitti's curators mean 18th and 19th century (again, go figure).

So forget about Marini, Mertz or Clemente – the collection of the 2nd-floor **Galleria d'Arte Moderna** (Map pp78-9; 8.15am-6.50pm Tue-Sun) is dominated by late-19th-century works by artists of the Florentine Macchiaioli school (the local equivalent of Impressionism), including

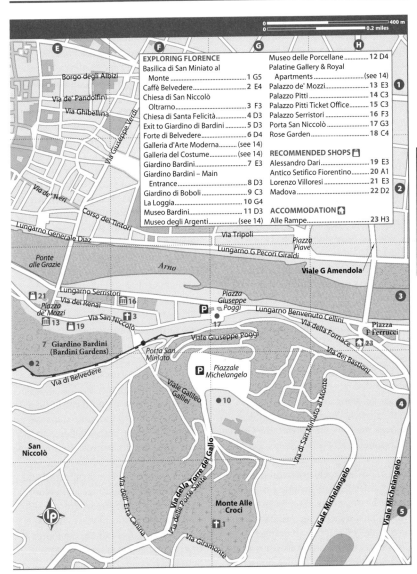

FLORENCE

Telemaco Signorini (1835–1901) and
Giovanni Fattori (1825–1908).

Galleria del Costume

Few visitors make the effort to visit the
Pitti's **Galleria del Costume** (Map pp78-
9; 8.15am-7.30pm Jun-Aug, to 6.30pm Mar-May &

Sep, to 5.30pm Oct, to 4.30pm Nov-Feb; closed 1st & last
Mon of month), thus missing its absolutely
fascinating, if somewhat macabre, display
of the semidecomposed burial clothes of
Cosimo I, his wife Eleonora di Toledo and
their son Don Garzia. Considering their
age and the fact that they were buried for

FLORENCE

centuries, Eleanora's gown and silk stockings are remarkably preserved, as are Cosimo's satin doublet and wool breeches and Garzia's doublet, beret and short cape.

In contrast, the sculptural 1990s haute couture pieces by Maurizio Galante look as if they've just been created – they're guaranteed to impress.

ꙮ GIARDINO DI BOBOLI // PICK UP SOME RENAISSANCE GARDENING TIPS

The palace's expansive **Giardino di Boboli** (Map pp78-9; 🕙 8.15am-7.30pm Jun-Aug, to 6.30pm Mar-May & Sep, to 5.30pm Oct, to 4.30pm Nov-Feb; closed 1st & last Mon of month) was laid out in the mid-16th century according to a design by architect Niccolò Pericoli, aka Il Tribolo.

Boboli is a prime example of a formal Tuscan garden and it's fun to explore: skip along the **Cypress Alley**; let the imagination rip with a gallant frolic in the walled **Giardino del Cavaliere** (Knights' Garden); dance around 170-odd statues; meditate next to the **Isoletto**, a gorgeous ornamental pool; discover birdsong and species in the garden along the signposted **nature trail**; or watch *Venere* (Venus) by Giambologna rise from the waves in the **Grotta del Buontalenti** (🕙 visits 11am, 1pm, 3pm, 4pm & 5pm), a fanciful grotto designed by the eponymous artist. Other typical Renaissance garden features include a six-tier **amphitheatre**, originally embellished with 24 niches sheltering classical statues surrounded by animals; an **orangery** (*limonaia*; 1777), which stills keeps around 500 citrus trees snug in winter; and a **botanical garden**. The 17th-century maze, a Tuscan horticultural standard, was razed in the 1830s to make way for a driveway for carriages. Don't miss the monumental 'face' sculpture (1998) by Polish sculptor Igor Mitoraj (b 1944), at home in Pietrasanta near Carrara today.

At the upper, southern limit of the gardens, fantastic views over the Florentine countryside fan out beyond the box-hedged **rose garden** where the **Museo delle Porcellane** (Porcelain Museum; Map pp78–9) is located. This is home to Sèvres, Vincennes, Meissen, Wedgwood and other porcelain pieces collected by Palazzo Pitti's wealthy tenants.

ꙮ GIARDINO BARDINI // TAKE TEA IN A RENAISSANCE BELVEDERE

Florence's little-known **Giardino Bardini** (Map pp78-9; ☎ 055 29 48 83; www .bardinipeyron.it; entrances at Via de' Bardi 1r and Costa San Giorgio 2; adult/concession incl Giardino di Boboli & Museo delle Porcellane €6/3; 🕙 8.15am-sunset) was named after art collector Stefano Bardini (1836–1922), who bought the villa in 1913, restored much of its medieval garden and created new garden elements. Smaller and more manicured than the Boboli, it has all the features of a quintessential Tuscan garden – artificial grottos, orangery, marble statues, fountains, loggia, amphitheatre and a monumental baroque stone staircase staggering up the beautiful tiered gardens – but not the crowds. A springtime stroll is an extra-special joy when its azaleas, peonies, wisteria (all April and May) and irises (June) are all in bloom. Its charming **Caffè Belevdere** (coffee €3, Twinings tea with biscotti €5, panino €3) which is set in a loggia overlooking the Florentine skyline, is a wonderful spot for a light lunch or afternoon tea.

Inside the villa is the **Museo Bardini** (☎ 055 263 85 99; www.bardinipeyron.it, in Italian; adult/concession €6/4; 🕙 10am-6pm Wed-Sun Apr-Sep, to 4pm Wed-Fri, to 6pm Sat & Sun Oct-Mar), home to a collection of Roberto Capucci-designed haute couture and host to other temporary exhibitions.

From here, you can return to the Giardino di Boboli via the Costa San Giorgo exit or exit at Via de' Bardi.

☙ A WALK THROUGH SAN NICCOLÒ // EXPLORE A QUIET POCKET OF TOWN

Walking east from the Ponte Vecchio, the first stretch of Via de' Bardi shows clear signs of its recent history. This entire area was flattened by German mines in 1944, and hastily rebuilt in questionable taste after the war.

The street spills into Piazza di Santa Maria Soprarno. Follow the narrow Via de' Bardi (the right fork) away from the square and you enter a pleasantly quieter corner of Florence. The powerful Bardi family once owned all the houses along this street, but by the time Cosimo the Elder wed Contessina de' Bardi in 1415, the latter's family was on the decline.

Via de' Bardi expires in Piazza de' Mozzi, surrounded by the sturdy facades of grand residences. Pope Gregory X stayed at **Palazzo de' Mozzi** (Map pp78-9; Piazza de' Mozzi 2) when brokering peace between the Guelphs and Ghibellines.

Next, turn east down Via dei Renai, past leafy Piazza Nicola Demidoff, dedicated to the 19th-century Russian philanthropist who lived nearby in Via San Niccolò. At the end of Via dei Renai, 16th-century **Palazzo Serristori** (Map pp78-9) was home to Joseph Bonaparte in the last years of his life until his death in 1844; a humble end to the man who, at the height of his career, had been appointed king of Spain by his brother Napoleon.

Turn right and you end up on Via San Niccolò; walk east along this street to emerge at the tower marking **Porta San Niccolò** (Map pp78-9), all that is left of the city walls. To get an idea of what the walls were once like, walk south from Chiesa di San Niccolò Oltrarno through **Porta San Miniato** (Map pp78-9). The wall extends a short way to the east and for a stretch further west, up a steep hill that leads you to **Forte di Belvedere** (Map pp78-9), a rambling fort designed by Bernardo Buontalenti for Grand Duke Ferdinando I at the end of the 16th century. From this massive bulwark soldiers kept watch on four fronts – as much for internal security to protect the Palazzo Pitti as against foreign attack. The fort is currently closed for restoration.

☙ PIAZZALE MICHELANGELO // STAGE A PHOTO SHOOT WHERE THE FLORENTINE SKYLINE UNFOLDS

Turn your back on the bevy of ticky-tacky souvenir stalls flogging David statues and take in the spectacular city panorama from this vast **piazza** (Map pp78-9), which is inevitably full of tour buses. It's a 10-minute uphill walk along the serpentine road, paths and steps that scale the hillside from the river and Piazza Giuseppe Poggi. After your photo session, consider having a sunset *aperitivo* at **La Loggia** (Map pp78-9; ☎ 234 28 32; Piazzale Michelangelo 1; ⏱ noon-11pm Thu-Tue), the terrace bar-cafe overlooking all of the action.

Bus 13 links Stazione di Santa Maria Novella with Piazzale Michelangelo.

☙ BASILICA DI SAN MINIATO AL MONTE // VISIT THE FINEST OF ALL TUSCAN ROMANESQUE BASILICAS

The view of the city skyline is even better from the terrace of this superb **Romanesque basilica** (Map pp78-9; Via Monte alle Croce; ⏱ 8am-7pm May-Oct, 8am-noon & 3-6pm Nov-Apr).

The church is dedicated to St Minias, an early Christian martyr in Florence who is said to have flown to this spot after his death down in the town (or, if you care to believe an alternative version, to have walked up the hill with his head tucked underneath his arm).

The church dates from the early 11th century. Its typically Tuscan multicoloured marble facade, which features a mosaic depicting Christ between the Virgin and St Minias, was added a couple of centuries later and is one of the most beautiful in all Italy. Inside, 13th- to 15th-century frescos adorn the south wall and intricate inlaid marble designs line the length of the nave, leading to a fine Romanesque crypt. The raised choir and presbytery have an intricate marble pulpit and screen, rich in complex geometrical designs. The **Sacristy** (admission €1) in the southeast corner features frescos by Spinello Aretino depicting the life of St Benedict.

Slap bang in the middle of the nave is the bijou **Capella del Crocefisso**, a 15th-century tabernacle designed by Michelozzo and decorated by artists including Agnolo Gaddi and Luca della Robbia.

The 15th-century **Cappella del Cardinale del Portogallo**, beside the north aisle, features a tomb by Antonio Rossellino and a tabernacle ceiling in terracotta by Luca della Robbia.

FESTIVALS & EVENTS

Festa di Anna Maria Medici (Feast of Anna Maria Medici) Marks the death in 1743 of the last Medici, Anna Maria, with a costumed parade from Palazzo Vecchio to her tomb in the Cappelle Medicee; 18 February.

Scoppio del Carro (Explosion of the Cart) A cart of fireworks is exploded in front of the cathedral at 11am on Easter Sunday – get there at least two hours early to grab a good position.

Maggio Musicale Fiorentino (www .maggiofiorentino.com, in Italian) This month-long arts festival held in Florence's Teatro del Maggio Musicale Fiorentino is the oldest in Italy; it stages world-class

ACCOMMODATION

You're spoiled for choice when it comes to sourcing a room in Florence, as there are plenty of *pensioni*, B&Bs, hotels and apartments on offer. In Chianti we suggest booking into an *agriturismo* (working farm or country villa offering rooms). Here are our some of our favourites.

* **Continentale** (p392) As hip as Florence gets; stylish surrounds and a location next to the Arno

* **Hotel Morandi alla Crocetta** (p393) A medieval convent turned into a charming boutique hotel

* **Hotel Santa Maria Novella** (p392) Luxurious but well-priced option overlooking the Basilica di Santa Maria Novella

* **Johanna & Johlea** (p393) Attractive and well-equipped apartments dotted around the historic centre

* **Rignana** (p396) Two styles of room in a gorgeous *agriturismo* overlooking the vine-laden hills of Chianti

For B&B ideas, check the **Associazione Bed & Breakfast Affittacamere** (www.abba-firenze.it); for more accommodation options, see p391.

performances of theatre, classical music, jazz and dance between late-April and June.

Festa di San Giovanni (Feast of St John) Florence celebrates its patron saint with a *calcio storico* match on Piazza di Santa Croce and fireworks over Piazzale Michelangelo; 24 June.

Sant'Ambrogio Summer Festival (www .firenzejazz.it, in Italian) The streets between Borgo La Croce and Piazza Beccaria become an evening stage for art, dance, jazz and theatre; June and July.

Jazz & Co (www.santissima.it, in Italian) On summer nights, Piazza della Santissima Annunziata is filled with tables of people enjoying an *aperitivo* or dinner catered by Slow Food International while listening to jazz musicians from Italy and overseas perform; late June to September.

Festival Firenze Classica The month of July sees Florence's highly regarded Orchestra da Camera Toscana (www.orcafi.it) performing classical music in the atmospheric settings of the Oratorio di San Michele a Castello and Palazzo Strozzi; between April and October, the orchestra performs in the Chiesa di Orsanmichele and in the courtyard of the Museo Nazionale del Bargello.

Festa delle Rificolone (Festival of the Paper Lanterns) A procession of children carrying lanterns, accompanied by drummers, *sbandieratori* (flag throwers), musicians and others in medieval dress, winds its way from Piazza di Santa Croce to Piazza della Santissima Annunziata to celebrate the Virgin Mary's birthday; 7 September.

GASTRONOMIC HIGHLIGHTS

The best-known local dish is the juicy *bistecca alla fiorentina,* a slab of prime T-bone steak rubbed with olive oil, seared on the char grill, garnished with salt and pepper and served *al sangue* (bloody). Other dishes that you will regularly see on menus include *crostini* (toasts topped with chicken-liver pâté), *ribollita* (a thick vegetable, bread and bean soup), *pappa al pomodoro* (soup made with bread and tomatoes) and *trippa alla fiorentina* (tripe cooked in a rich tomato sauce).

DUOMO & PIAZZA DELLA SIGNORIA

❧ CANTINETTA DEI VERRAZZANO €

Map pp46-7; ☎ 055 26 85 90; Via dei Tavolini 18-20; platters €4.50-12, focaccia €3-3.50, panini €1.70-3.90; ⏱ noon-9pm Mon-Sat

Together, a *forno* (baker's oven) and *cantinetta* (small cellar) equal a match made in heaven. Come here for focaccia fresh from the oven, perhaps topped with caramelised radicchio or *porcini* mushrooms, washed down with a glass of wine (€2.50 to €8) from the Verrazzano estate in Chianti (p102). Other plates on offer include cheese and meat platters, panini filled with truffle or prosciutto, salads and bruschetta.

❧ COQUINARIUS €€

Map pp46-7; ☎ 055 230 21 53; www .coquinarius.com; Via delle Oche 15r; meals €30; ⏱ noon-10.30pm

Nestled within the shadow of the Duomo, this *enoteca* (wine bar) is extremely popular with tourists, who respond well to its casually stylish decor and friendly vibe. The menu ranges from salads and *crostini* (a huge choice of both) to an unusual array of pastas – try the justly famous ravioli with cheese and pear. There's a good range of wines by the glass, the multilingual staff is extremely efficient and a delicious finale to the meal can be found only a few doors away at Grom (see p89). Bookings are essential.

❧ I DUE FRATELLINI €

Map pp46-7; ☎ 055 239 60 96; www.iduefratellini .com; Via dei Cimatori 38r; panini €2.50; ⏱ 9am-8pm Mon-Sat, closed Fri & Sat 2nd half of Jun & all Aug

A legend in its own time and in business since 1875, this hole in the wall whips out imaginative panini (sun-dried

FLORENCE

tomato with goat cheese, wild boar salami, truffled *pecorino* cheese and rocket etc), freshly filled as you order. Wash your choice down with a shot, glass or beaker of wine – it's the perfect pavement lunch. Etiquette requires you leave your empty on a wooden shelf outside.

♥ 'INO €

Map pp46–7; ☎ 055 21 92 08; Via dei Georgofili 3r-7r; panini €5-8; ☽ 11am-8pm Mon-Sat, noon-5pm Sun

Short for 'panino', this stylish sandwich shop near the Uffizi sources its artisan gourmet ingredients locally and uses them in inventive and delicious ways. Choose your own combination or select from the always-delectable house specials. Scoff on the spot with a glass of wine (included in the price of the sandwich) or take away to picnic on the banks of the Arno.

♥ LA CANOVA DI GUSTAVINO €

Map pp46–7; ☎ 055 239 98 06; Via della Condotta 29r; meals €22; ☽ noon-midnight

The rear dining room of this atmospheric *enoteca* is lined with shelves full of Tuscan wine – the perfect accompaniment to a bowl of soup, pasta dish or hearty main. The emphasis here is on Tuscan classics – *ribollita, trippa alla fiorentina, baccalà alla livornese* (salted cod in a tomato sauce) – but it's perfectly fine if you choose to limit yourself to a simple cheese and meat platter or a bruschetta topped with *lardo* (wafer-thin slices of pork fat marinated in a mix of herbs and oils) and cherry tomato.

SANTA MARIA NOVELLA

♥ CANTINETTA ANTINORI €€€

Map pp58–9; Via de' Tornabuoni 7; meals €56; ☽ lunch & dinner Mon-Fri

This *enoteca* is a 1960s creation of the city's most famous winemaking dynasty (www.antinori.it). Located in a *palazzo* dating to 1502, it's a *molto simpatico* spot to sample fine wine accompanied by classic Tuscan cuisine. Pull up a bar stool and enjoy a glass of wine (the Cabernet Sauvignon-dominated Solaia and Marchese Antinori Chianti Classico DOCG Riserva are particularly highly regarded) with cheese plate, or colonise a table and order from a limited but alluring menu.

♥ IL LATINI €€

Map pp58–9; ☎ 055 21 09 16; www.illatini.com; Via dei Palchetti 6r; meals €40; ☽ lunch & dinner Tue-Sun

TRIPE: A FAST-FOOD FAVOURITE

When Florentines fancy a fast munch-on-the-move rather than a slow, full lunch, they flit by a *trippaio* – a cart on wheels or mobile stand – for a juicy plate or sandwich of tripe. Think cow's stomach chopped up, boiled, sliced and served with seasoning. Yum! Or is it…yuk?

Much loved by the Slow Food Movement (see the boxed text, p385) as a bastion of good old-fashioned Florentine tradition, *trippai* are increasingly few and far between these days. Two old faithfuls still going strong are found on the southwest corner of the Mercato Nuovo (Map pp46–7) and near Via Dante Alighieri close to Piazza della Signoria (Map pp46–7). Pay under €3 for tripe doused in *salsa verde* (pea-green sauce of smashed parsley, garlic, capers and anchovies) or garnished with salt, pepper and ground chilli. Alternatively, opt for a bowl of *lampredotto* (cow's fourth stomach chopped and simmered for hours).

You have two choices at this Florentine favourite: request a menu (as a tourist, you might not be offered one) or put yourself in the hands of the exuberant waiters and feast on a mixed antipasto of melt-in-your-mouth *crostini* and mixed Tuscan meats followed by a bowl of (indifferent) pasta and a hunk of roasted meat – rabbit, lamb, chicken or veal with white beans (the rabbit is particularly tasty). The wine and water flows and if you're lucky you might get a complimentary plate of *cantucci* (hard, sweet biscuits) and glass of *moscato* (an Italian dessert wine) with the bill. There are two dinner seatings (7.30pm and 9pm); seating is shared and bookings are mandatory.

♥ L'OSTERIA DI GIOVANNI €€

Map pp58-9; ☎ 055 28 48 97; Via del Moro 22; meals €45; ⏰ lunch & dinner Wed-Mon

Our number one choice for Florentine dining is – insert drum roll – this wonderfully friendly neighbourhood eatery, where everything is delicious and where the final reckoning will be within most budgets. Many opt to start with the house antipasto (a plate of salami, fresh ricotta and *crostini* with liver pâté and *lardo*), move onto a plate of homemade pasta with *porcini* mushrooms and black truffles and then forge ahead with a milk-fed veal chop with roasted cherry tomatoes or a sensational *bistecca alla fiorentina*. Make sure you ask about daily specials, particularly desserts.

♥ OSTERIA DEI CENTOPOVERI €€

Map pp58-9; ☎ 055 21 88 46; Via Palazzuolo 31r; meals €30; ⏰ lunch & dinner

The 'hostel of the hundred poor people' is far from being a soup kitchen. It's a modern dining option serving creative variations on traditional Tuscan cuisine.

Choose from decent pizzas, excellent pasta (the lasagnette of fresh *porcini* mushrooms is delicious) and a range of daily specials. The set menu of antipasto (Tuscan salami, cheese and honey), *bistecca alla fiorentina* with roast potatoes, a dessert, water and coffee for €28 is excellent value.

♥ PROCACCI €

Map pp58-9; ☎ 055 21 16 56; Via de' Tornabuoni 64r; ⏰ 10am-8pm Mon-Sat

The last remaining bastion of genteel old Florence on Via de' Tornabuoni, this tiny cafe was born in 1885 opposite the English pharmacy as a delicatessen serving truffles in its repertoire of tasty morsels. Bite-sized *panini tartufati* (truffle pâté rolls, €1.80) remain the thing to order, best accompanied by a glass of *prosecco* (€4.50).

SAN LORENZO

♥ RISTORANTE DON CHISCIOTTE €€€

Map p64; ☎ 055 47 54 30; www.ristorante donchisciotte.it; Via Cosimo Ridolfi 4r; meals €55; ⏰ lunch & dinner Tue-Sat, dinner Mon

It can be difficult to find good seafood in this meat-obsessed city, so locals and tourists alike regularly give praise for the existence of this upmarket restaurant near Piazza della Independenza. The highly professional waiters will outline the day's menu, which might start with seafood in a tomato-based soup and move onto oven-roasted sea bream with a tomato and bread puree and slices of eggplant.

♥ RISTORANTE LE FONTICINE €€

Map p64; ☎ 055 28 21 06; www.lefonticine .com; Via Nazionale 79r; meals €35; ⏰ lunch & dinner Tue-Sat

Named for the 16th-century fountain by Luca della Robbia that is just to the right of the entrance, this popular eatery features the same checked tablecloths, painting-filled walls, serving trollies and (dare we say it) waiters that have been here since it opened in 1959. The huge menu features excellent homemade pasta and the best *crema di mascarpone* (mascarpone cream) in town.

❦ TAVERNA DEL BRONZINO €€€

Map p64; ☎ 055 49 52 20; Via delle Ruote 27r; meals €58; ⊗ lunch & dinner Mon-Sat

Built in 1580 for one of Bronzino's pupils, this building is named in the great painter's honour; a copy of his famous portrait of Eleonora di Toledo presides over the first of two formal dining rooms. When Florentines celebrate special occasions this is one of their venues of choice, and after sampling delectable dishes such as the ravioli of spinach and ricotta with a saffron and lemon butter sauce, Slow Food–branded *antipasto toscana* and perfectly cooked beef fillet, you'll understand why.

❦ TRATTORIA MARIO €

Map p64; ☎ 055 21 85 50; www.trattoriamario .com; Via Rosina 2; meals €20; ⊗ noon-3.30pm Mon-Sat, closed 3 weeks Aug

Despite being in every guidebook, this jam-packed place retains its soul and allure with locals. A 100% family affair since opening in 1953, its chefs shop at the nearby Mercato Centrale (p66) and dish up tasty, dirt-cheap dishes with speed and skill. Get here right on the dot of noon to score a stool (tables are shared) and be aware that credit cards aren't accepted. Monday and Thursday are tripe days and Friday is fish day.

SAN MARCO

❦ ACCADEMIA RISTORANTE €€

Map p67; ☎ 055 21 73 43; www.ristorante accademia.it; Piazza San Marco 7r; meals €30; ⊗ lunch & dinner

There aren't too many decent eateries in this area, which is one of the reasons why this family-run restaurant is perennially packed. Factors such as friendly staff, cheerful decor and consistently good food help too. The pasta is just like mamma makes and the coffee could stand up and be counted on Piazza della Repubblica. The set menu of *antipasto toscana*, a raviolo with *porcini* mushrooms or truffles, spaghetti in a spicy sauce, and *bistecca alla fiorentina* with oven-roasted potatoes (€30) is excellent value.

❦ LA MESCITA €

Map p67; Via degli Alfani 70r; plates €4-7, panini €1.60-3.50; ⊗ 10.30am-4pm Mon-Sat, closed Aug

Part *enoteca* and part *fiaschetteria*, this unapologetically old-fashioned place (it opened in 1927) serves up Tuscan specialities such as *maccheroni* with sausage and *insalata di farro* (farro salad). Noontime tipplers and all-day drinkers mingle at the old marble-topped bar, where you'll find tasty panini and *crostini* to go with the daily pouring of Chianti.

SANTA CROCE

❦ ALLE MURATE €€€

Map p70; ☎ 055 24 06 18; www.artenotai.org; Via del Proconsolo 16r; meals €85, tasting menu €90; ⊗ dinner Tue-Sat

Feast on 13th-century frescos and contemporary Tuscan cuisine at this unique restaurant near the Palazzo del Bargello. The decor is stunning, wine list superb and menu, which takes its inspiration from the seasons, extremely refined. Unfortunately, the 15% service charge (probably the steepest in Florence) was certainly not deserved on the night we visited. Owner Umberto Montano has one of the most successful restaurant empires in the city, including Osteria del Caffè Italiano (opposite) and Caffè Italiano Sud (opposite).

❦ ANTICO NOÈ €

Map p70; ☎ 055 234 08 38; Volta di San Piero 6r; meals €24; ☺ noon-midnight Mon-Sat

Don't be put off by the dank, rough-and-ready alley in which this legendary place (an old butcher's shop with white marble-clad walls and wrought-iron meat hooks) is found. The drunks loitering outside are generally harmless and the down-to-the-earth Tuscan fodder served in the *osteria* (casual tavern or eatery) is a real joy. For a quick bite, choose from the 18 different types of imaginatively stuffed panini (€2.50 to €5) served at the adjoining *fiaschetteria*. No credit cards.

❦ CAFFÈ ITALIANO SUD €€

Map p70; ☎ 055 28 93 68; Via della Vigna Vecchia; meals €28; ☺ 7.30-11pm Tue-Sun

Chef Umberto Montano's ode to southern Italy brings a breathe of fresh air into a local food scene that can suffer from being too inward-looking. Loads of homemade pasta – including unusual dishes from his native Puglia – and other typical dishes from the south can be eaten in or taken away. There are also plenty of vegetarian options (unusual in this meat-obsessed region) and pizzas from Osteria del Caffè Italiano's pizzeria (see right). The house wines are displayed in 58L straw-cushioned glass flasks, from which quarter-, half- and one-litre pitchers are drawn.

❦ ENOTECA PINCHIORRI €€€

Map p70; ☎ 055 24 27 77; www.enotecapinchiorri .com; Via Ghibellina 87r; meals €270, degustation & tasting menus €250-300; ☺ lunch & dinner Thu-Sat, dinner Wed, closed Aug

Chef Annie Féolde applies French techniques to her versions of refined Tuscan cuisine and does it so well that this is one of only six Italian restaurants to possess three Michelin stars (and the only one in Tuscany). The setting is a 16th-century palace, the wine list is mind-boggling in its extent and excellence and the prices reach the stratosphere. A once-in-a-lifetime experience.

❦ IL PIZZAIUOLO €

Map p70; ☎ 055 24 11 71; Via dei Macci 113r; pizzas €5-10, pastas €6.50-12; ☺ lunch & dinner Mon-Sat, closed Aug

Bar Sant'Ambrogio in the piazza of the same name is a popular drinking spot for young Florentines, who often kick on here to nosh on Neapolitan thick-crust pizzas hot from the wood-fired oven. Simplicity is the rule of thumb, from the name ('The Pizza Maker') to the house speciality, *pizza Margherita* (pizza with tomato, mozzarella and oregano). Bookings are essential for dinner (and even then you'll probably have to queue).

❦ LA PENTOLA DELL'ORO €€

Map p70; ☎ 055 24 18 08; www.lapentoladelloro .it; Via di Mezzo 24-26r; meals €40; ☺ lunch & dinner Mon-Sat

Long a jealously guarded secret among Florentine gourmands, Florence's old-style Golden Pot doesn't need to advertise. Word of mouth draws the culinary curious here to sample Renaissance dishes reinvented for modern tastes by culinary artist Giuseppe Alessi. Dine at sub-street level or at the street-level offshoot with marble-topped tables, wooden benches and 25 place settings.

❦ OSTERIA DEL CAFFÈ ITALIANO €€

Map p70; ☎ 055 28 90 20; www.caffeitaliano.it; Via dell'Isola delle Stinche 11-13r; meals €40, 5-course set menu €50; ☺ lunch & dinner Tue-Sun

The menu here holds no surprises – it's full of simple classics such as *mozzarella di bufala* with Parma ham, ravioli stuffed with ricotta and *cavolo nero* (black cabbage) and succulent skewered meats – and the service on our recent visits has been spectacularly bad – but there's still something satisfying about dining in this old-fashioned *osteria* occupying the ground floor of the 14th-century Palazzo Salviati. It's an excellent spot to try the city's famous *bistecca alla fiorentina* (per kg €50). Next door, the **Pizzeria del Caffè Italiano** has a simple dining space and offers a limited menu of three types of pizzas – *Margherita, Napoli* and *Marinara*.

❤ RISTORANTE CIBRÈO €€€

Map p70; ☎ 055 234 11 00; Via Andrea del Verrocchio 8r; meals €80; ⏰ 1-2.30pm & 7pm-midnight Tue-Sat Sep-Jul

The flagship of Fabio Picchi's food and entertainment empire (see p72), this elegant restaurant is an essential stop for anyone interested in modern Tuscan cuisine. Service is personable – waiters sit down with you to discuss the daily menu and construct a perfectly balanced meal – and the food is magnificent. Knock-out choices on our most recent visit were a *primo* of spicy fish soup and a *secondo* of roast pigeon with mustard fruits. The wine list is equally impressive.

❤ RISTORANTE DEL FAGIOLI €

Map p70; ☎ 055 24 42 85; Corso del Tintori 47r; meal €23; ⏰ lunch & dinner Mon-Fri

This Slow Food favourite near the Basilica di Santa Croce is the archetypical Tuscan trattoria. It opened in 1966 and has been serving well-priced bean dishes, soups and roasted meats to throngs of appreciative local workers and residents ever since. Try the oven-roasted pork, any of the soups or the *involtini di Gigi* (pan-fried beef slices stuffed with cheese, ham and artichokes). No credit cards.

❤ TRATTORIA CIBRÈO €€

Map p70; Via dei Macci 122r; meals €28; ⏰ 12.50-2.30pm & 6.50-11.15pm Tue-Sat Sep-Jul

Dine here and you'll instantly understand why a queue gathers outside each evening before it opens. Once in, revel in top-notch Tuscan cuisine: perhaps ricotta and potato flan with a rich meat sauce, puddle of olive oil and grated parmesan (divine!) or a simple plate of polenta, followed by homemade sausages, beans in a spicy tomato sauce and braised celery. Arrive before 7pm to snag one of the eight tables and remember – no advance reservations, no credit cards, no pasta and no coffee.

OLTRARNO

❤ LE VOLPE E L'UVA €

Map pp74-5; ☎ 055 239 81 32; Piazza dei Rossi 1; cheese or meat platters €7; ⏰ 11am-9pm Mon-Sat

Florence's best *enoteca* – bar none. Just over the Ponte Vecchio, this intimate place has an extraordinarily impressive list of wines by the glass and serves a delectable array of accompanying antipasti, including juicy prosciutto di Parma, *lardo*-topped *crostini* and boutique Tuscan cheeses (try the Rocco made by Fattoria Corzano e Paterno and you will attain true bliss). Go.

❤ OLIO & CONVIVIUM €€

Map pp74-5; ☎ 055 265 81 98; www.convivium firenze.it, in Italian; Via di Santo Spirito 4; meals €35; ⏰ l0am-3pm Mon, 10am-3pm & 5.30-10.30pm Tue-Sat

A key address on any gastronomy agenda: your tastebuds will tingle at the sight of the legs of ham, conserved truffles, wheels of cheese, artisan-made bread and other delectable delicatessen products sold in its shop. You can order a sandwich to go, or take advantage of the bargain lunchtime menu (cold mixed platter, wine, water and dessert for €15). Come dusk, try veal-stuffed fresh artichokes or *taglierini* (a narrower type of tagliatelle) with tiger prawns and black cabbage.

❦ RISTORANTE IL GUSCIO €€

Map pp74-5; ☎ 055 22 44 21; Via dell'Orto 49; meals €37; ⏱ lunch & dinner Mon-Fri, dinner Sat

This family-run gem in San Frediano used to be one of the city's best-kept secrets, but recently the local foodie grapevine has been running hot with raves about the exceptional dishes coming out of its kitchen. Meat and fish are given joint billing, with triumphs such as white bean soup with prawns and fish joining superbly executed mains including guinea fowl breast in balsamic vinegar on the sophisticated menu. The lunchtime deal of a daily plate, wine, water and coffee costs a ludicrously low €12.

❦ TRATTORIA CAMMILLO €€

Map pp74-5; ☎ 055 21 24 27; Borgo San Jacopo 57r; meals €43; ⏱ lunch & dinner Thu-Mon

Crostini topped with aphrodisiacal white-truffle shavings, deep-fried battered green tomatoes or zucchini flowers and home-made walnut liqueur are but a few of the seasonal highlights gracing the menu of this staunchly traditional trattoria (check the menu of daily specials). The quality of products used is exceptional and service is endearingly old-fashioned.

❦ TRATTORIA LA CASALINGA €

Map pp74-5; ☎ 055 21 86 24; Via de' Michelozzi 9r; meals €18; ⏱ lunch & dinner Mon-Sat

Family run and much loved by locals, this unpretentious and always busy place is one of the city's cheapest trattorias. You'll be relegated behind locals in the

FLORENCE

TOP **FIVE**

GELATERIE

Florentines take their gelato seriously. There's a healthy rivalry among the local *gelaterie artigianale* (makers of handmade gelato), who all strive to create the creamiest, most flavourful and freshest product in the city. Flavours change according to what fruit is in season, and a serve costs around €2/3/4/5 per small/medium/large/maxi. After extensive on-the-ground-research, we have narrowed down our favourites:

★ **Carabé** (Map p67; www.gelatocarabe.com; Via Ricasoli 60r; ⏱ 10am-midnight, closed mid-Dec–mid-Jan) Traditional Sicilian gelato, granita (sorbet) and brioche (a Sicilian ice-cream sandwich).

★ **Gelateria dei Neri** (Map p70; 22r Via de' Neri; ⏱ 9am-midnight) Semifreddo-style gelato that is cheaper than its competitors; known for its coconut, gorgonzola (yes, you read that correctly) and ricotta and fig flavours.

★ **Gelateria Vivoli** (Map p70; Via dell'Isola delle Stinche 7; ⏱ 9am-1am Tue-Sat) Choose a flavour from the huge choice on offer (both pistachio and chocolate with orange are crowd favourites) and scoff it in the pretty piazza opposite; tubs only.

★ **Grom** (Map pp46-7; www.grom.it; cnr Via del Campanile & Via delle Oche; ⏱ 10.30am-11pm, to midnight Apr-Sep) This relative newcomer has taken the city by storm; the flavours are all delectable and many ingredients are organic.

★ **Vestri** (Map p70; www.vestri.it; Borgo degli Albizi 11r; ⏱ 10.30am-8pm Mon-Sat) Specialises in chocolate; go for the decadent white chocolate with wild strawberries or the chocolate with pepper.

queue – it's a fact of life and not worth protesting – with the eventual reward being hearty peasant dishes such as *bollito misto con salsa verde* (mixed boiled meats with green sauce).

RECOMMENDED SHOPS

Florence has been synonymous with craftsmanship since medieval times, when goldsmiths, silversmiths and shoemakers were as *alta moda* as sculptors and artists. Modern Florentines are just as enamoured of design and artisanship, and are all keen to *fare la bella figura* (cut a fine figure) – appearances are important here, and high-end shops are patronised by people across the income scale. Some may purchase full wardrobes, others the occasional accessory, but all will be very conscious of the labels they and other people are wearing.

Those keen to take a distinctively Florentine treat home should consider leather goods, jewellery, hand-embroidered linens, designer fashion, natural pharmaceuticals, handmade paper, wine, puppets or gourmet foods.

For a useful and authoritative guide to the city's fashion ateliers, go to www .florenceartfashion.com, a website put together by the City of Florence's Department of Tourism and Fashion. It lists ateliers creating fashion (men's, women's and children's), jewellery, footwear, leatherwear, textiles, jewellery and perfume. It also shows the ateliers' locations on maps and advertises occasional free guided tours in its 'news' section.

For a review of the 17th-century Officina Profumo-Farmaceutica di Santa Maria Novella go to p59, and for information about Salvatore Ferragamo's flagship store see p60.

FABRIC & FASHION

❦ ANTICO SETIFICO FIORENTINO
Map pp78-9; ☎ 055 21 38 61; Via L Bartoini 4; ☽ Mon-Fri
Precious silks, velvets and other luxurious fabrics are woven on 18th- and 19th-century looms at this world-famous fabric house, where opulent damasks and brocades in Renaissance styles have been made since 1786.

❦ CIRRI
Map pp46-7; ☎ 055 239 65 93; Via Por Santa Maria 38-40r; ☽ Mon-Fri & Sat morning Mar-Oct, closed Mon morning Nov-Feb
Hand embroidery galore, with table linen, handkerchiefs and lingerie in cotton, silk and linen, as well as classic ensembles for babies and children.

❦ GUCCI
Map pp58-9; ☎ 055 26 40 11; www.gucci.com; Via de' Tornabuoni 73-81r
This indisputable icon of Florentine fashion dates back to 1921, when Guccio Gucci opened a saddlery shop selling leather goods on Via della Vigna Nuova. Two years later the shop moved to Via del Parione and in 1967 this flagship store arrived in the city's best-dressed street. It sells leather goods, jewellery, watches, accessories and designer fashion for both men and women.

❦ LORETTA CAPONI
Map pp58-9; ☎ 055 21 36 68; www.lorettacaponi .com; Piazza Antinori 4r; ☽ Mon-Fri & Sat morning Mar-Oct, closed Mon afternoon Nov-Feb
Occupying the ground floor of a restored *palazzo*, this utterly gorgeous shop sells hand-embroidered sleepwear, bed linen and table linen, as well as slippers, bathrobes, cushions and exquisitely smocked children's clothes.

FLORENCE

FOOD & WINE

ANTICO FORNO SANTI
Map p64; ☎ 055 28 35 66; www.biscottisanti
.com; Via Nazionale 121r; 9.30am-1.30pm & 3.30-
7.30pm Tue-Sat, 11am-7pm Sun
Stock up on *cantucci* studded with almonds, chocolate, figs or apricots at this
artisan bakery. You can also buy bottles
of the biscuit's traditional accompaniment, Vin Santo, here.

LA BOTTEGA DEL CIOCCOLATO
Map p70; ☎ 055 200 16 09; www.bottegadelcioc
colato.it; Via dei Macci 50; 10am-1pm & 3-7.30pm
Mon-Fri, closed Aug
Andrea Bianchini makes his prize-
winning chocolates on the premises of
his chic side-street shop. Unafraid to
experiment, he marries the finest chocolate with flavours such as mango with
coriander and ginger, lemon with violet,
rosemary with sea salt and passionfruit
with Szechuan pepper.

LA BOTTEGA DELL'OLIO
Map pp46-7; ☎ 055 267 04 68; Piazza del Limbo 2r;
10am-1pm & 2-7pm Mon-Sat
Owner Andrea Trambusti takes great care
with the displays in this pretty boutique
next to the 11th-century Chiesa dei Santissimi Apostoli. There's a huge array of
olive oils to choose from, as well as olive
oil soaps, platters made from olive wood
and skincare products made with olive oil
(the Lepo range is particularly good).

OBSEQUIUM
Map pp74-5; ☎ 055 21 68 49; www.obsequium.it;
Borgo San Jacopo 17-39r
Occupying the ground floor of one of the
city's best-preserved medieval towers,
this shop offers a wide range of fine Tuscan wines, wine accessories and gourmet
foods, including truffles.

PANE & CO
Map pp46-7; ☎ 055 21 30 63; Piazza San Firenze 5r;
9am-8pm Mon-Sat
This veritable cornucopia of a shop is full
of wine and food products handmade by
small Tuscan producers, including pasta,
cheese, *biscotti* (biscuits), panforte, olive
oil, *lardo*, truffles, vinegars, bread and
olives. You can also buy meals to go.

HOMEWARES

KARTELL
Map pp58-9; ☎ 055 28 89 21; Borgo Ognissanti
50-52r; Tue-Sat
Over its 60-year history, this Italian furniture company has worked with designers including Ron Arad, Anna Castelli
Ferrieri and Phillipe Stark. Its distinctive clear plastic furniture and lamps in
lolly-like colours can be found in stylish
restaurants, bars and hotels throughout
the city and make for a colourful display
at this showroom.

MAESTRI DI FABBRICA
Map p70; ☎ 055 24 23 21; www.maestridifabbrica
.it; Borgo degli Albizi 68r
Occupying four rooms in the
Renaissance-era Palazzo Albizzi, this
high-end factory outlet offers stylish
blown glass, carved alabaster, kitchen-
ware and sleek contemporary furniture.

JEWELLERY

ALESSANDRO DARI
Map pp78-9; ☎ 055 24 47 47; www.alessandro
dari.com; Via San Niccolò 115r
Flamboyant jeweller and classical guitar-
ist Alessandro Dari creates unique and
extremely beautiful pieces in his atmospheric 15th-century workshop-showroom
in San Niccolò. He describes his pieces as
'sculpture that you can wear' and presents
them in thematic collections.

FLORENCE

FLORENCE

LEATHER

❦ FRANCESCO DA FIRENZE

Map pp74–5; ☎ 055 21 24 28; Via di Santo Spirito 62r; ❧ closed 2 weeks Aug

Hand-stitched leather is the cornerstone of this tiny family business. You can buy ready-to-wear men's and women's shoes or order a pair made to measure. Wallets and purses are also available.

❦ MADOVA

Map pp78–9; ☎ 055 239 65 26; Via de' Guicciardini 1r

Forget the fact that this shop is on a particularly touristy stretch – instead of hawking tourist tat like most of its neighbours, it sells gorgeous gloves in supple leather of every colour, most produced in the adjacent workshop. It will make to order and ship free of charge anywhere in the world.

❦ SCUOLA DEL CUOIO

Map p70; ☎ 055 24 45 33; www.scuoladelcuoio .com; Via San Giuseppe 5r; ❧ 10am-6pm

Watch leatherworkers fashioning goods and buy their creations at this atmospheric workshop in a courtyard behind the cloisters of the Basilica di Santa Croce. You can access it from the church (with ticket) or via the shop entrance on Via San Giuseppe.

❦ STEFANO BEMER

Map pp74–5; ☎ 055 22 25 58; www.bemers.it; Borgo San Frediano 143r

The finest men's shoes that money can buy, these ready-to-wear and made-to-measure numbers combine classic designs with modern flair, and are made from all types of leather (including crocodile, ostrich, stingray and toad); all are packaged in beautiful wooden shoeboxes.

PAPER

❦ ALBERTO COZZI

Map pp58–9; ☎ 055 29 49 68; Via del Parione 35r; ❧ Mon-Fri

Florence is famous for its exquisite marbled paper and this family-run shop has been making sheets of the stuff by hand since 1908. Come here to buy paper, leather-bound journals and colourful cards. It's also a well-known bookbinder and restorer, with clients in museums and galleries around the world.

❦ PINEIDER

Map pp46–7; ☎ 055 28 46 55; www.pineider.com; Piazza della Signoria 13-14r; ❧ 10am-7pm

Florence's most exclusive stationer opened here in 1774 and once designed calling cards for Napoleon. You can order your own, or choose from a tempting range of paper products and elegant leather office accessories.

PERFUME

❦ LORENZO VILLORESI

Map pp78–9; ☎ 055 234 11 87; www.lorenzo villoresi.it; Via de' Bardi 14; ❧ 9am-1pm & 2-5pm Mon-Fri

Villoresi's perfumes and potpourris meld distinctively Tuscan elements such as laurel, olive, cypress and iris with essential oils and essences from around the world. His bespoke fragrances are highly sought after. Visiting his showroom, which occupies his family's 15th-century *palazzo*, is quite an experience.

❦ OFFICINA DE' TORNABUONI

Map pp58–9; ☎ 055 21 10 06; www.officina detornabuoni.com; Via de' Tornabuoni 19, ❧ Mon afternoon-Sun

Once at the gorgeous premises at No 97, this famous retailer of health and beauty products is now in a much smaller but

DESIGNER OUTLET STORES

Prices at the high-end fashion boutiques on and around Via de' Tornabuoni are beyond the reach of many shoppers. If you're keen to replenish your wardrobe with a few designer pieces while in town but don't want to break the bank, a visit to Florence's outlet malls may be the answer. Most offer a 30% to 50% discount on retail prices. The two most popular:

- ★ **Barberino Designer Outlet** (☎ 055 84 21 61; barberino.mcarthurglen.it, in Italian; A1 Florence-Bologna, exit Barberino di Mugello; 🕓 10am-8pm Tue-Fri, 10am-9pm Sat & Sun, 2-8pm Mon Jan, Jun-Sep & Dec) Polo Ralph Lauren, D&G, Prada, Class Roberto Cavalli, Missoni, Furla, Benetton and Bruno Magli are just a few of the 100 labels with stores here. Outlet shuttle buses (return €12) leave Fortezza da Basso and Piazza Stazione in Florence at 10am daily, and depart from the outlet, which is 40km north in Barberino di Mugello, at 1.30pm.
- ★ **The Mall** (☎ 055 865 77 75; www.themall.it; Via Europa 8, Leccio; 🕓 10am-7pm) Gucci, Ferragamo, Burberry, Ermenegildo Zegna, Yves Saint Laurent, Tod's, Fendi, Giorgio Armani, Marni, Valentino et al are represented in this mall, which is 35km from Florence. Buses (€3.10, two daily on weekends, four daily on weekdays) leave from the SITA bus station; make sure you check the timetable for details of return services (12.45pm and 7.05pm daily plus 4pm Monday to Saturday at time of research). By car, take the Incisa exit off the northbound A1 and follow signs for Leccio.

Long-established tour company **CAF** (☎ 055 21 06 12; www.caftours.com; Via Sant'Antonino 6r) runs daily tours to the Prada Outlet in Montevarchi and The Mall (€28, six hours) on Mondays, Tuesdays, Fridays and Saturdays departing from Piazza Stazione.

equally beautiful shop (part of a 16th-century palace) down the street. It has been selling sweet-smelling potions and lotions for every ailment or cosmetic need since 1843, and only uses natural products.

TOYS

LETIZIA FIORINI

Map pp58-9; ☎ 055 21 65 04; Via del Parione 60r; 🕓 Tue-Sat 10.30am-7.30pm

This charming shop is a one-woman affair – Letizia Fiorini sits at the counter and makes her distinctive puppets by hand in between assisting customers. You'll find Pulchinella (Punch), Arlecchino the clown, beautiful servant girl Colombina, Doctor Peste (complete with plague mask), cheeky Brighella, swashbuckling Il Capitano and many other characters from traditional Italian puppetry. An inexpensive and adorable gift for the little ones in your life.

TRANSPORT

TO/FROM THE AIRPORT

AIRPORT // Amerigo Vespucci airport (Map p96; FLR; ☎ 055 306 13 00; www.aeroporto.firenze.it), 5km northwest of the city centre, caters for domestic and a handful of European flights. The much larger **Galileo Galilei** (PSA; ☎ 050 84 93 00; www.pisa-airport.com) is one of northern Italy's main international and domestic airports. It is closer to Pisa (p120), but is well linked with Florence by public transport (see p94).

TAXI // A taxi between Amerigo Vespucci airport and central Florence costs a flat rate of €20, plus surcharges of €2 on Sundays and holidays, €3.30 between 10pm and 6am and €1 per bag. As you exit the terminal building, walk right and you will come to the taxi rank.

BUS // A Volainbus shuttle (€4.50, 25 minutes) travels between Amerigo Vespucci airport and Florence's Stazione di Santa Maria Novella train station/SITA bus station (Map pp58–9) every 30 minutes between 6am and 11.30pm. Terravision (www.terravision.eu) runs daily services (adult single/return €10/16, child single/return €5/9, 1¼ hours, 13 daily) between the bus stop outside Florence's Stazione di Santa Maria Novella on Via Alamanni (Map pp58–9) and Pisa's Galileo Galilei airport. In Florence tickets are sold at the Consorzio ITA counter inside Stazione di Santa Maria Novella and at the Terravision desk (Via Alamanni 9r; ⏱ 6am-7pm) inside Deanna Bar opposite the Terravision bus stop; at Galileo Galilei airport, the Terravision ticket desk dominates the arrival hall.

TRAIN // Regular trains link Florence's Stazione di Santa Maria Novella with Galileo Galilei airport (€5.60, 1½ hours, at least hourly from 4.30am to 10.25pm).

GETTING AROUND

BUS // From the SITA bus station (Map pp58–9; ☎ 800 37 37 60; www.sitabus.it, in Italian; Via Santa Caterina da Siena 17r; ⏱ information office 8.30am-12.30pm & 3-6pm Mon-Fri, 8.30am-12.30pm Sat), situated just west of Piazza della Stazione, there are *corse rapide* (express services) to/from Siena (€6.80, 1¼ hours, at least hourly between 6.10am and 9.15pm). To get to San Gimignano (€6), you need to go to Poggibonsi (50 minutes, at least hourly between 6.10am and 7.50pm) and catch a connecting service (30 minutes, at least hourly between 6.05am and 8.35pm). Direct buses also serve Castellina in Chianti, Greve in Chianti and other smaller cities throughout Tuscany. Vaibus/Lazzi (Map pp58–9; ☎ 055 21 51 55; www.vaibus.it, in Italian; Piazza Adua) runs buses to/from Pistoia (€3, 50 minutes, four daily), Lucca (€5.10, 1½ hours, frequent) and Pisa (€6.10, two hours, hourly).

CAR & MOTORCYCLE // Nonresident traffic is banned from the centre of Florence for most of the week. See the boxed text, opposite, for more information. Florence is connected by the A1 northwards to Bologna and Milan, and southwards to Rome and Naples. The Autostrada del Mare (A11) links Florence with Pistoia, Lucca, Pisa and the coast, but most locals use the FI-PI-LI – a *superstrada* (dual carriageway, hence no tolls); look for blue signs saying FI-PI-LI (as in Firenze-Pisa-Livorno). Another dual carriageway, the S2, links Florence with Siena. The much more picturesque SS67 connects the city with Pisa to the west, and Forli and Ravenna to the east.

TRAIN // Florence's central train station is Stazione di Santa Maria Novella (Map pp58-9; Piazza della Stazione). The train information counter (Map pp58-9; ⏱ 7am-7pm) faces the tracks in the main foyer, as does Consorzio ITA (signposted Informazioni Turistiche Alberghiere), which makes hotel reservations (€3) and sells tickets for guided tours and shuttle buses to/from Galileo Galilei airport (p93). The left-luggage department (⏱ 6am-11.50pm) is located on platform 16 and the *Assistenza Disabili* (Disabled Assistance) office is on platform 5. International train tickets are sold in the ticketing hall (⏱ 6am-9pm); No 19 has a ramp suitable for wheelchairs. For domestic tickets, skip the queue and buy your tickets from the touch-screen automatic ticket-vending machines next to the train information counter or on the concourse; machines have an English option and accept cash and credit cards. Florence is on the Rome–Milan line. There are regular trains to/from Rome (€16 to €39.90, 1¾ hours to 4¼ hours), Bologna (€5.40 to €24.70, one hour to 1¾ hours), Milan (€22.50 to €44.70, 2¼ hours to 3½ hours) and Venice (€19 to €53.20, 2¾ hours to 4½ hours). Frequent regional trains run to Pistoia (€2.90, 45 minutes to one hour, half-hourly), Pisa (€5.60 to €11.40, one hour to 1½ hours, frequent) and Lucca (€5, 1½ hours to 1¾ hours, half-hourly).

BICYCLES & SCOOTERS // Bike-tour operator Florence by Bike (Map p64; ☎ 055 48 89 92; www.florencebybike; Via San Zanobi 120r; ⏱ 9am-7.30pm) rents wheels (city bike €14.50 per day, scooter €68 per day), as does the open-air rental outlet Biciclette a Noleggio (Map pp58-9; Piazza della Stazione; per hr/day €1.50/8; ⏱ 7.30am-7pm Mon-Sat,

FLORENCE

PARKING IN FLORENCE

There is a strict Limited Traffic Zone (Zona Traffico Limitato; ZTL) in Florence's historic centre between 7.30am and 7.30pm Monday to Friday and 7.30am to 6pm Saturday for all nonresidents, monitored by cyclopean cameras positioned at all entry points. The exclusion also applies on Friday, Saturday and Sunday between midnight and 4am mid-May to the end of October. Motorists staying in hotels within the ZTL are allowed to drive to their hotel to drop off luggage, but must tell reception their car registration number and the time they were in no-cars-land (there's a two-hour window) so that the hotel can inform the authority and organise a temporary access permit. Disabled permit holders who need to enter the ZTL with their vehicle should call the toll-free number ☎ 800 339891.

If you transgress, a fine of around €150 will be sent to you (or the car-hire company you have used). Many travellers have written to us to complain about credit-card charges from car-hire companies being levied months after their unknowing infraction of the ZTL occurred, often with administrative costs of up to €100 added to the fine. For a map of the ZTL, go to www.comune.fi.it/opencms/export/sites/retecivica/materi ali/turismo/ztlnov.JPG.

There is free street parking around Piazzale Michelangelo (park within blue lines; white lines are for residents only). Pricey (€18 per day) underground parking can be found in the area around the Fortezza da Basso (Map p64) and in the Oltrarno beneath Piazzale di Porta Romana (off Map pp74–5). Otherwise, many hotels can arrange parking for guests.

9am-7pm Sun May-Sep, shorter hours Oct-Apr), in front of Stazione di Santa Maria Novella.

PUBLIC TRANSPORT // Buses and electric *bussini* (minibuses) run by **ATAF** (Azienda Trasporti Area Fiorentina; Map pp58-9; ☎ 800 42 45 00; www .ataf.net, in Italian) serve the city and its periphery. Most – including bus 7 to Fiesole and bus 13 to Piazzale Michelangelo – start/terminate at the ATAF bus stops opposite the southeastern exit of Stazione di Santa Maria Novella. Tickets cost €1.20 (on board €2) and are sold at kiosks, tobacconists and the **ATAF ticket & information office** (Map pp58-9; Piazza Adua; ⏰ 7am-8pm), next to the bus stops opposite the station. A carnet of 10/21 tickets costs €10/20, a handy *biglietto multiplo* (four-journey ticket) is €4.50 and a one-/three-day pass is €5/12. Only one child shorter than 1m in height can travel for free per adult (additional children pay full fare) and passengers caught travelling without a time-stamped ticket (punch it on board) are fined €40.

TAXI // For a taxi, call ☎ 055 42 42 or ☎ 055 43 90.

AROUND FLORENCE
· · · · · ·

One of the joys of Florence is leaving it behind. Be it admiring the views in Fiesole or tracking down perfect wine in the hilly region of Chianti, there is no shortage of places to go and pleasures to savour.

FIESOLE

pop 14,100

This bijou village perched in hills 9km northeast of Florence is the city's traditional getaway. Its cooler air, olive groves, scattering of Renaissance-styled villas and spectacular views of the plain below have seduced for centuries (victims include

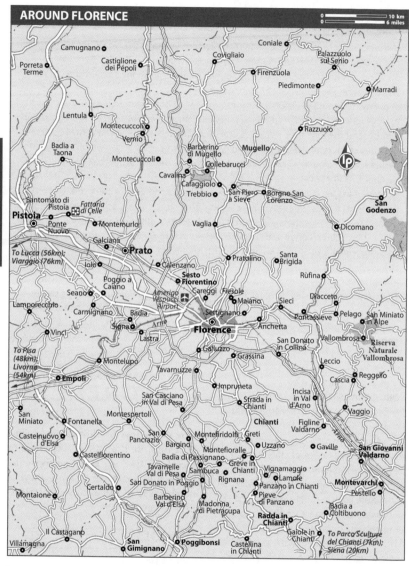

AROUND FLORENCE

Boccaccio, Marcel Proust, Gertrude Stein and Frank Lloyd Wright) – and still do.

Founded in the 7th century BC by the Etruscans, Fiesole was the most important city in northern Etruria and makes a delightful foray of a few hours from Florence. Its main square, Piazza Mino di Fiesole, hosts an antiques market on the first Sunday of each month. The **tourist office** (☎ 055 597 83 73; www.comune .fiesole.fi.it; Via Portigiani 3; ⏰ 9.30am-6.30pm Mon-Fri, 10am-1pm & 2-6pm Sat & Sun Mar-Oct, 9.30am-6pm Mon-Sat, 10am-4pm Sun Nov-Feb) is just off the main square, a couple of doors down from the archaeological site. It can supply maps and information about walks in the area.

EXPLORING FIESOLE

♥ AREA ARCHEOLOGICA // HEAR WORLD-CLASS PERFORMANCES IN A ROMAN AMPHITHEATRE

This **archaeological site** (☎ 055 59 47 77; www.fiesolemusei.it; Via Portigiani 1; adult/under 6yr/concession €12/free/8; ☷ 10am-7pm Wed-Mon Apr-Sep, to 6pm Wed-Mon Oct & Mar, to 4pm Thu-Mon Nov-Feb) ensnares a small Etruscan temple, Roman baths, an archaeological museum with exhibits from the Bronze Age to the Roman period, and a 1st-century-BC Roman amphitheatre where musicians and actors take to the stage during the oldest open-air arts festival in Italy, the famous **Estate Fiesolana** (☷ Jun-Aug). In mid-July, the theatre hosts the **Vivere Jazz Festival** (www.viverejazz.it).

♥ A WALK AROUND TOWN // SEEK OUT FINE ART AND EVEN FINER PANORAMAS

Entrance to the tiny **Museo Bandini** (☎ 055 59 47 77; Via Dupré; ☷ 9.30am-7pm Apr-Sep, 9.30am-6pm Oct & Mar, 10am-5pm Wed-Mon Nov-Dec, 11am-5pm Thu-Mon Jan & Feb) next to the archaeological site is included in its admission price. The collection of early Tuscan Renaissance works inside includes fine medallions (c 1505–20) by Giovanni della Robbia and Taddeo Gaddi's luminous *Annunciation* (1340–45).

From the museum, a 300m walk along Via Giovanni Dupré will bring you to the **Museo Primo Conti** (☎ 055 59 70 95; www.fondazioneprimoconti.org; Via Dupré 18; admission €3; ☷ 9.30am-1.30pm Mon-Sat), where the eponymous avant-garde 20th-century artist lived and worked. The views from the garden here are lovely and there are more than 60 of his paintings inside. Ring to enter.

Backtrack to Piazza Mino di Fiesole, presided over by the **Cattedrale di San Romolo** (Piazza della Cattedrale 1; ☷ 7.30am-noon & 3-5pm), and make your way up steep Via San Francesco. Your reward will be the staggeringly beautiful views of Florence from a terrace next to the 15th-century **Basilica di Sant'Alessandro**, which hosts temporary exhibitions – and has irregular opening hours). Further up the hill, you can also pay a visit to the 14th-century **Chiesa di San Francesco** (☷ 9am-noon & 3-6pm).

GASTRONOMIC HIGHLIGHTS

♥ RISTORANTE LA REGGIA DEGLI ETRUSCHI €€

☎ 055 5 93 85; www.lareggia.org; Via San Francesco; meals €35; ☷ 11am-3pm & 6-11pm
The cuisine – which features dishes such as homemade tagliatelle with guinea-hen sauce or risotto with *porcini* mushrooms and local pecorino cheese – plays second fiddle to a stunning view at this terrace restaurant tucked up high in an old stone wall. If you don't feel like a large meal, platters of cheese or salami (€10 to €12) are available. On weekends, bookings are essential.

♥ TRATTORIA LE CAVE DI MAIANO €€

☎ 055 5 91 33; www.trattoriacavedimaiano.it; Via Cave di Maiano 16, Maiano; meals €34; ☷ lunch & dinner, closed Mon winter
Florentines adore this terrace restaurant in Maiano, a neighbouring village five minutes from Fiesole by car, and flock here every fine weekend to enjoy leisurely lunches on the outdoor terrace. The food here is memorable – huge servings are the rule of thumb and everything is homemade, with pastas and vegetable

dishes being particularly impressive. The rustic inclination of the chef is reflected in the number of dishes featuring rabbit, boar and suckling pig, all of which go wonderfully well with the quaffable house wine. A taxi from Fiesole costs approximately €9 and the trip back will be double that (the meter starts ticking when the taxi leaves its base in Fiesole to collect you).

TRANSPORT

BUS // Take ATAF (www.ataf.net, in Italian) bus 7 (€1.20, 30 minutes) from Florence. If you want to be sure of a seat, it's best to get on the bus at Piazza dell'Unità Italiana, which is located one stop east of Stazione di Santa Maria Novella. The bus travels via the station and Piazza San Marco, winds its way up the hilly and winding road to Fiesole and terminates at Piazza Mino da Fiesole.

CAR // If you're driving, Fiesole is signed from Florence's Piazza della Libertà, north of the cathedral.

PISTOIA

pop 89,400
Pleasant Pistoia sits snugly at the foot of the Apennines. Only 45 minutes northwest of Florence by train, it deserves more attention than it normally gets. Although it has grown well beyond its medieval ramparts, its historic centre is well preserved and extremely pedestrian-friendly.

On Wednesday and Saturday mornings, the main square Piazza del Duomo and its surrounding streets become a sea of blue awnings and jostling shoppers as Pistoia hosts a lively **market**. The town's **fresh produce market** (Mon-Sat) occupies Piazza della Sala, west of the cathedral, and is situated close to the helpful **tourist office** (☎ 0573 2 16 22; www.pistoia.turismo.toscana.it, in Italian; 9am-1pm & 3-6pm).

MONEY SAVER

When in Pistoia, consider purchasing a **cumulative ticket** (€6.50), which gives entrance to the Museo Civico, the Museo Rospigliosi e Museo Diocesano and the Centro Documentazione e Fondazione Marino Marini. You can purchase it at the tourist office or any of these museums.

On 25 July each year, a medieval equestrian and jousting festival known as **Giostra dell'Orso** (Joust of the Bear) fills Piazza del Duomo in honour of Pistoia's patron saint, San Giacomo.

EXPLORING PISTOIA

♥ PIAZZA DEL DUOMO // SEARCH FOR BONES AND A FAMOUS MOSQUITO
Pistoia's visual wealth is concentrated on this central square. The Pisan-Romanesque facade of **Cattedrale di San Zeno** (Piazza del Duomo; ☎ 0573 2 50 95; 8.30am-12.30pm & 3.30-7pm) boasts a lunette of the Madonna and Child between two Angels by Andrea della Robbia. The cathedral's other highlight – the silver **Dossale di San Giacomo** (Altarpiece of St James; adult/child €4/2) begun in 1287 and finished off by Brunelleschi two centuries later – is in the gloomy **Cappella di San Jacopo** off the north aisle. To visit, track down a church official.

Next to the cathedral is the **Museo Rospigliosi e Museo Diocesano** (adult/concession €4/2; guided tours 10am, 11.30am & 3pm Mon, Wed & Fri), guardian of a wealth of artefacts that were discovered during restoration work of this former bishop's palace undertaken by the Casa di Risparmio di Pistoia e Pescia, the bank that now owns the building. Many treasures from the cathedral's collection are also on show here, including a 15th-century reliquary by Lorenzo Ghiberti supposedly housing a bone of St James and parts of his mother's and the Virgin's pelvic bones. Visits are strictly by guided tour (1¼ hours).

Across Via Roma is the 14th-century octagonal **baptistry** (Piazza del Duomo; admission free; ☼ varies, check with tourist office), elegantly banded in green-and-white marble to a design by Andrea Pisano. An ornate square marble font and soaring dome enlivens the otherwise bare, red-brick interior.

The Gothic **Palazzo Comunale** that sits on the eastern flank of the square is home to the **Museo Civico** (☎ 0573 37 12 96; www.commune.pistoia.it/museocivico, in Italian; Piazza del Duomo 1; adult/concession €3.50/2; ☼ 10am-5pm or 6pm Tue & Thu-Sat, 3-6pm or 7pm Wed, 11am-5pm or 6pm Sun), which holds works by Tuscan artists from the 13th to 20th centuries. Don't miss Bernardino di Antonio Detti's *Madonna della Pergola* (1498), with its extraordinarily modern treatment of St James, the Madonna and Baby Jesus; look out for the mosquito on Jesus' arm.

FLORENCE

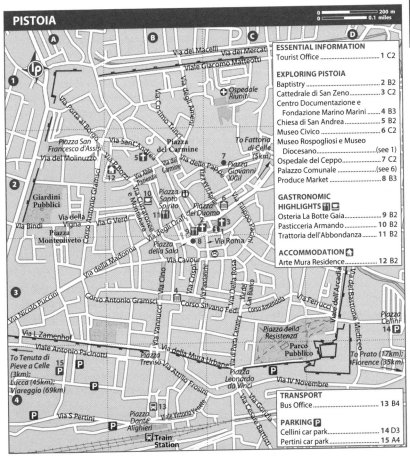

FLORENCE

♥ ARTISTIC TREASURES // ADMIRE SCULPTURES FROM THREE ARTISTIC ERAS

The rich portico of the nearby **Ospedale del Ceppo** (Piazza Giovanni XXIII), with its detailed 16th-century polychrome terracotta frieze by Giovanni della Robbia, will stop even the most monument-weary in their tracks. It depicts the *Sette Opere di Misericordia* (Seven Works of Mercy), while the five medallions represent the *Virtù Teologali* (Theological Virtues), including a beautiful Annunciation.

The 12th-century **Chiesa di San Andrea** (☎ 0573 2 19 12; Via San Andrea; 🕑 8.30am-12.30pm & 3-6pm) was built outside the original city walls, which explains its windowless state (it needed to be fortified). The facade is enlivened by a relief of the *Journey and Adoration of the Magi* (1166) and inside is a magnificent marble pulpit carved by Giovanni Pisano (1298–1301).

A short distance and a half millennium away is the **Centro Documentazione e Fondazione Marino Marini** (☎ 0573 3 02 85; www.fondazionemarinomarini.it; Corso Silvano Fedi; adult/concession €3.50/2; 🕑 10am-5pm Mon-Sat), a museum-gallery devoted to Pistoia's most famous modern son, the eponymous sculptor and painter (1901–80).

GASTRONOMIC HIGHLIGHTS

Local specialities include *carcerato* (a type of offal), *frittata con rigatino* (omelette with salt-cured bacon), *farinata con cavalo* (chickpea pancake with cabbage), *migliacci* (fritters made with pig's blood) and *berlingozzo* (a traditional sweet served with a glass of local Vin Santo). To drink, try the local Sangiovese- or Trebbiano-dominated Carmignano DOCG, the Barco Reale di Carmignano DOC or the Bianco della Valdinievole DOC.

♥ OSTERIA LA BOTTEGAIA €€

☎ 0573 36 56 02; www.labottegaia.it; Via del Lastrone 17; meals €25; 🕑 lunch & dinner Tue-Sat, dinner Sun & Mon

Dishes range from the staunchly traditional (egg pasta with duck sauce and aromatic herbs) to experimental (vegetable flan dipped in a *pecorino* cheese fondue) at this Slow Food-hailed *osteria*, known for its finely butchered cured meats and interesting wine list. It's popular, so book ahead.

♥ TRATTORIA DELL'ABBONDANZA €

☎ 0573 36 80 37; Via dell'Abbondanza 10; meals €20; 🕑 lunch & dinner Fri-Tue, dinner Thu

---

∼ WORTH A TRIP ∼

A tea house, aviary and other romantic 19th-century follies mingle with cutting-edge art installations created in situ by the world's top contemporary artists at the **Fattoria di Celle** (off Map p99; ☎ 0573 47 94 86, 0573 47 99 07; www.goricoll.it, in Italian; Via Montalese 7, Santomato di Pistoia; 🕑 visits by appointment only Mon-Fri May-Sep), 5km from Pistoia. The extraordinary private collection and passion of local businessman Giuliano Gori, this unique sculpture park showcases 70 site-specific installations sprinkled around his vast family estate. Visits – reserved for serious art lovers – require forward planning (apply in writing at least five weeks in advance) and entail a three- to four-hour hike around the art-rich estate, led by the collection's curator, Miranda McPhail.

If you plan to stay overnight in the area, consider the excellent *agriturismo* Tenuta di Pieve a Celle (see p395).

Ask a local where they eat, and the answer will often be this unassuming place behind the Duomo. The simple Tuscan dishes on its menu are extremely well priced and absolutely delicious. You can choose between indoor or outdoor tables.

♥ PASTICCERIA ARMANDO €

☎ 0573 2 31 28; Via Curtatone Montanara 38; ⏰ 6.30am-1pm & 3-8.30pm Tue-Fri, till 8pm Sat & Sun

Pistoia's best cafe-bar has been plying appreciative locals with delicious cakes, cocktails and coffees since 1947. It's a great place to relax and refuel between museum and church visits.

TRANSPORT

TRAIN // Services link the city with Florence (€2.70, 35 to 50 minutes, frequent), Lucca (€3.50, 45 minutes to one hour, half-hourly) and Pisa (€4.50 to €6.50, 1¾ hours, one daily or change at Lucca).

CAR // The city is on the A11 and the SS64 and SS66, which head northeast for Bologna and northwest for Parma respectively.

PARKING // Most hotels provide motoring guests with a pass ensuring free street parking in the centre; otherwise there is free parking in the Cellini car park on the city's eastern edge and cheap parking (€1 per day) at the Pertini car park near the train station.

BUS // Blubus (☎ 800 57 05 30, www.blubus.it) services connect Pistoia with Florence (€3, four daily) and local towns in Tuscany; buy tickets, get schedules and hop aboard at the **bus office** (☎ 0573 363 243; Via XX Settembre 71; ⏰ 6.15am-8.15pm Mon-Sat, 7am-8.10pm Sun) opposite the train station. Local buses 1 and 10 (€1) connect the train station with the cathedral, but it's easier to walk (15 minutes).

CHIANTI

When people imagine classic Tuscan countryside, they usually conjure up images of Chianti – olive groves, gentle hills, sun-baked red farmhouses and vines, lots of them. Post WWII, the region suffered severe economic hardship and depopulation. But in the 1960s, waves of sun-hungry foreigners started discovering these beautiful valleys enviably wedged between Florence and Siena. They snapped up holiday homes or moved in permanently to what, by 1989, had been dubbed 'Chiantishire' by playwright John Mortimer in his TV adaptation of *Summer Lease* – set in Tuscany.

The ruby-red, violet-scented Chianti and Chianti Classico DOCGs, blends of red grapes with a minimum of 75% (Chianti) or 80% (Chianti Classico) Sangiovese, are the region's oldest, most famous wines, but other DOCs also hail from the region: Colli dell'Etruria Centrale, Pomino, Vin Santo del Chianti and Vin Santo del Chianti Classico. The biggest wine-producing estates have shops where you can taste and buy wine, but few vineyards – big or small – can be visited without an advance reservation; most only open their doors to tour groups.

The lovely Monti del Chianti rising into the Apennines mark the area's eastern boundary and the scenic Strada Chiantigiana (SS222) snakes from Florence to Siena. Bus hopping is feasible, but your own wheels – two or four – are the only real way to discover the region. Keen walkers can pick up a copy of *Chianti Classico: Val di Pesa-Val d'Elsa*, a map at 1:25,000 with hiking trails superimposed.

CHIANTI FIORENTINO

This is the northern half of Chianti in the province of Florence. To get around by pedal or scooter power, rent wheels from **Ramuzzi** (☎ 055 85 30 37; www.ramuzzi .com; Via Italo Stecchi 23; bike/50cc scooter per day €20/30; ⏰ 9am-1pm & 3-7pm Mon-Fri, 9am-1pm Sat) in Greve in Chianti, its main town. **Florence by Bike** (Map p64; ☎ 055 48 89 92;

www.florencebybike.it; Via San Zanobi 120r; 9am-7.30pm) offers a 32km-long day tour of northern Chianti (including lunch & wine tasting €76) leaving Florence at 9.30am and returning by 4pm. Other companies offering guided bike tours of the region include **I Bike Italy** (055 234 23 71; www.ibikeitaly.com) and **I Bike Tuscany** (335 812 07 69; www.ibiketuscany.com).

EXPLORING CHIANTI FIORENTINO

❦ GREVE IN CHIANTI // EAT, DRINK AND WALK OFF THE CALORIES

This small town (population 14,100), 20km south of Florence on the SS222 and the only one in Chianti easily accessible from Florence by SITA bus (€3.10, one hour, half-hourly), has two claims to fame. They are local *macelleria* (butcher shop) **Antica Macelleria Falorni** (055 85 30 29; www.falorni.it; Piazza Matteotti 71; closed Wed pm & 1-4pm daily), known for its mean cuts since 1729; and Giovanni da Verrazzano (1485–1528). Local-boy-made-good and discoverer of New York harbour, Verrazzano, was commemorated there by the Verrazano Narrows bridge (the good captain lost a 'z' from his name somewhere in the mid-Atlantic), linking Staten Island to Brooklyn and indelibly printed on the soles of every runner who's done the New York marathon.

In the first or second week of September, the town's main square, Piazza Matteotti, hosts Greve's annual wine fair. The **tourist office** (055 854 62 87; Piazza Matteotti 11; 9am-1pm & 2-6pm Mon-Sat May-Sep) has little documentation to browse but stocks a mine of electronic info on vineyards to visit and trails to cycle or stroll. Particularly popular is the 3km-long walk west (1½ to two hours) it suggests to **Castello di Montefioralle**, a medieval fortified hilltop village with a 10th-century Romanesque church and a couple of restaurants to lunch at.

Note that a popular open-air market is held in Piazza Matteotti every Saturday morning – do not leave your car there the night before as it may be towed away. If you're driving into Greve on a Saturday, you'll find that many of the streets are closed to traffic because of the market – park on the outskirts of town.

❦ LE CANTINE DI GREVE IN CHIANTI // TASTE-TEST THE REGION'S LIQUID GOLD

For a one-stop wine taste and shop in Chianti, there is no better place than this vast commercial **enoteca** (055 854 64 04; www.lecantine.it; Piazza delle Cantine 2; 10am-7pm) in Greve, which stocks more than 1200 varieties of wine. To indulge in some of the 140 different wines available for tasting (including Super Tuscans, top DOCs and DOCGs, Vin Santo and grappa), buy a prepaid wine card costing €10 to €25 from the central bar, stick it into one of the many taps and out will trickle your tipple of choice. Any unused credit will be refunded when you return the card. It's fabulous fun, though somewhat distressing for designated drivers. To find it, look for the supermarket on the main road – it's down a staircase opposite the supermarket entrance.

❦ CASTELLO DI VERRAZZANO // WINE AND DINE IN AN HISTORIC WINERY

Three kilometres north of Greve, on the SS222, is the **Castello di Verrazzano** (055 85 42 43; www.verrazzano.com; guided tours 10am & 11am Mon-Fri), ancestral home of Greve's New York pioneer. This estate has been producing Chianti Classico, Vin Santo, grappa, honey, olive oil and balsamic vinegar for centuries. You can tour its historic wine cellar and gardens and enjoy a tasting of its wines (1½ hours, €14, Monday to Friday only) or go the whole hog and lunch on five estate-produced courses in the company of five different wines (three hours, €48, Monday to Friday only). On Saturdays, there's a 2½-hour 'Chianti Tradition' option including a tour, tasting and light repast (€28).

♥ WINE TOURS AND TASTINGS // GO BEHIND THE SCENES AT A WINE ESTATE

Founded in 1049 by Benedictine monks of the Vallombrosan order, Badia di Passignano is a massive, towered castle-abbey encircled by cypresses. It sits in a magnificent setting of olive groves and vineyards about 8km west of Greve. Its church safeguards 17th-century frescos by Passignano (so called because he was born here) and its refectory is graced by Domenico and Davide Ghirlandaio's *Last Supper* (1476). Given monks still live here, neither can be visited.

Today, though, the centuries-old cellars of this mighty abbey contain the viticulture stash of the Antinori family, one of Tuscany's oldest (think 600 years) and most prestigious winemaking families. Guided **wine tours** (2hr visit €25; ⏱ 3.30pm Mon-Wed, Fri & Sat) visit the estate's cellar and vineyard and taste four Antinori wines;

DRIVING MAPS

Chianti's roads can be impossibly narrow and frustratingly difficult to navigate – to cut down on driving stress, grab a copy of the detailed road map *Le Strade del Gallo Nero* (The Road of the Black Cock; 1:80,000), which is marked up with wineries and every last back road. Buy it for €3 at the Greve in Chianti tourist office.

bookings must be made in advance at the **Osteria di Passignano** (☎ 055 807 12 78; www.osteriadipassignano.com; Via Passignano 31; ⏱ wine shop 10am-11pm Mon-Sat), the Antinori wine shop and restaurant situated below the abbey. You don't need to make a reservation to enjoy a **wine tasting** (€15, €20 & €30 for three wines depending on what you taste) in the *osteria*.

♥ ANTICA MACELLERÌA CECCHINI // EAT THE BEST BURGER IN THE WORLD

The sleepy, medieval village of Panzano in Chianti's claim to fame is its **macellerìa** (☎ 055 85 20 20; http://dariocecchini.blogspot .com; Via XX Luglio 11; ⏱ 9am-2pm Mon, Tue, Thu & Sun, to 6pm Fri & Sat), owned and run by exuberant butcher Dario Cecchini. This Tuscan celebrity has carved out a niche for himself as guardian of the *bistecca* and knife-wielding performer of poetry recitals. He's even opened a burger joint, **Mac Dario**, above the shop, where he serves what guest Jack Nicholson allegedly described as the 'best burger in the world' (€10 for burger, potatoes and vegetables). Panzano is 7km south of Greve on the SS222 to Castellina in Chianti.

GASTRONOMIC HIGHLIGHTS
♥ LA CANTINETTA DI RIGNANA // BADIA DI PASSIGNANO €€

☎ 055 85 26 01; www.lacantinettadirignana.it; Rignana; meals €30; ⏱ lunch & dinner Wed-Mon

Idyllically nestled in the old oil mill on the Rignana estate (p396), this eatery offers quintessential Tuscan views from its large terrace. Rustic dishes on offer include wild boar *carpaccio*, truffle-stuffed ravioli, warm gooey oven-baked *tomino* (a type of cheese) with locally gathered mushrooms or a simple grilled slab of meat. Service is friendly, but we were perplexed by the fact that the *cantinetta*

FLORENCE

doesn't serve wine by the glass – a real problem for diners who need to get back behind the wheel. It's a 15-minute drive from Badia di Passignano, between Panzano and Mercatale Val di Pesa.

❤ LA LOCANDA DI PIETRACUPA // PIETRACUPA €€

☎ 055 807 24 00; www.locandapietracupa.it; Via Madonna di Pietracupa 31; meals €45; 🕑 lunch & dinner Wed-Mon

You'll find this innovative restaurant in the tiny village of Madonna di Pietracupa, just outside picturesque San Donato in Poggio. Occupying a charming villa on the main road, it serves sophisticated cuisine in an extremely elegant dining room and on a garden terrace. Choose between decadent dishes such as tagliatelle topped with zucchini flowers and shaved truffles or simple, perfectly executed Tuscan favourites including rabbit sirloin in a creamy fennel sauce. Finish off with an array of hard-to-source local cheeses. From Panzano, take the SS222 south and then veer west onto the SP76b (Strada Provinciale di San Donato).

❤ OSTERIA DI PASSIGNANO // BADIA DI PASSIGNANO €€€

☎ 055 807 12 78; www.osteriadipassignano.com; Via di Passignano 33; meals €65, degustazion menus €60 & €100; 🕑 lunch & dinner Mon-Sat

This is one of Tuscany's most impressive restaurants. An elegant dining room on the Antinori Estate, it offers sophisticated cuisine, an impressive wine list and professional service – without a hint of pretension. The food utilises local produce and is decidedly Tuscan in inspiration, but its execution is refined rather than rustic. Knock-your-socks-off dishes on a recent visit included fresh thyme-flavoured taglierine in a red mullet and tomato broth, and slices of beef

tenderloin that were meltingly tender and fantastically flavoursome.

❤ OSTERIA LE PAZANELLE // PANZANO IN CHIANTI €

☎ 0577 73 35 11; Lucarelli; meals €23; 🕑 lunch & dinner Tue-Sun

Perfect for a light lunch beneath trees, this roadside inn makes a great lunch stop en route to Siena. Swiss-born chef Angelo cooks up a straightforward choice of around six dishes per course. Don't miss his *crostini* topped with *lardo* and orange peel, or his pasta dressed in a *pecorino* cheese and pear sauce. He also does a mean Tuscan-style burger, and the wine list is particularly well suited to those wanting to taste different Chianti wines. Find it 5km south of Panzano on the SP2 to Radda in Chianti.

❤ RISTORO L'ANTICA SCUDERIA // BADIA DI PASSIGNANO €€

☎ 055 807 16 23; www.risterolanticascuderia.com; Via di Passignano 17; meals €41; 🕑 lunch & dinner Wed-Mon

If you fancy the idea of lunching on a pretty terrace overlooking one of the Antinori vineyards, this casual eatery may well fit the bill. Lunch features antipasti, pastas and traditional grilled meats, while dinner sees plenty of pizza-oven action and liberal pourings of red wine.

❤ SOLOCICCIA // PANZANO IN CHIANTI €€

☎ 055 85 27 27; Via XX Luglio 11r; macelleria cecchini@tin.it; fixed menu incl wine €30; 🕑 reservation only 7pm & 9pm Thu-Sat, 1pm Sun Mar-Jan

Share a meal with Chianti's charismatic butcher *chez Dario*. Offering a chance to share his family recipes passed down between generations and show off his meat-cutting and -cooking prowess, Dario (who speaks fluent French and a spot of

English) cooks up a six-course feast in his apartment restaurant near the post office.

🌩 TRATTORIA DELLA FONTE // BADIA DI PASSIGNANO €€

☎ 055 824 47 00; www.fontedemedici.it; Via Santa Maria a Macerata 31; meals €40; ⊗ lunch & dinner Tue-Sun

A must for wine buffs, this trattoria in a 15th-century *borgo* (hamlet) where pilgrims en route from Florence to Siena once stopped is wedged between Solaia and Tignanello vineyards owned by the Antinori family. The menu is traditionally Tuscan, featuring meat platters, fresh pasta, Chianina beef, beef stewed in Chianti and fresh *pecorino*. You can also stay here overnight in apartments.

CHIANTI SENESE

South of Panzano, Chianti dips into the province of Siena. Castellina is a great place to pick up information and hire a car if you need to.

🌩 CASTELLINA IN CHIANTI // ETRUSCAN ARTEFACTS AND MEDIEVAL WARRENS

The huge cylindrical silos at the entry to this town (population 2850) brim with Chianti Classico, the classic nectar that, together with tourism, brings wealth to this small community.

From the southern car park, take Via Ferruccio, then turn right almost immediately to walk into town beneath the tunnel-like Via del Volte. This medieval street, originally open to the elements, then encroached upon by shops and houses, is now a long, vaulted, shady tunnel, particularly welcoming in summer. Wine shops are rife here and there are plenty of places to taste and buy, among them **Antica Fattoria la Castellina** (☎ 0577 74 04 54; Via Ferruccio 26). The nearby **tourist office** (☎ 0577 74 13 92; www .essenceoftuscany.com; Via Ferruccio 40; ⊗ 10am-1pm & 2-6pm daily Mar-Nov, 10am-1pm & 2-4pm Mon-Sat Dec & Feb), which is privately run, can help with maps, tours, accommodation and information.

The town's well-preserved *rocca* (fortress) is home to the **Museo Archeologico del Chianti Senese** (☎ 055 74 20 90; www.museoarcheologicochianti.it; Piazza del Comune 18; adult/concession €3/2; ⊗ 10am-1pm & 3.30-6.30pm Thu-Tue), which showcases Chianti's Etruscan roots. The museum uses multimedia technology to highlight finds from archaeological digs around Castellina, Radda, Castelnuovo Berardenga and Gaiole.

CHIANTI RÙFINA

Forget Chianti Classico. Instead, why not blaze a wine-tasting trail through the territory of **Chianti Rùfina**, the smallest of the Chianti appellations, covering a privileged pocket of 12,482 hectares in the high hills east of Florence. Dry and red with hints of violets, the wine produced in this region has been overshadowed by its Classico big sister for centuries; nevertheless, international wine critics constantly rank Chianti Rùfina's best-known estates – **Fattoria Selvapiana** (☎ 055 836 98 48; www.selvapiana.it; Via Selvapiana, Rùfina) and **Castello di Nipozzano** (☎ 055 27 141; www.frescobaldi.it; Nipozzano, Pelago) – among the best of the Tuscan producers. The Nipozzano estate is owned by Florence's famous Frescobaldi wine family, which also owns the nearby **Castello di Pomino**, where it produces the well-regarded Cassafonte and Pomino Rosso DOCs (Denominazione d'Origine Controllata).

For more information about the Chianti Rùfina trail, go to www.chiantirufina.com.

FLORENCE

♥ RADDA IN CHIANTI // WHERE THE LOCAL PHILOSOPHY IS 'IN VINO VERITAS'

Shields and escutcheons add a dash of drama to the facade of 16th-century **Palazzo del Podestà** (Piazza Ferrucci) on the main square in Radda in Chianti (population 1750), a popular tourist spot 11km east of Castellina. The volunteer-staffed **Ufficio Pro Loco** (☎ 0577 73 84 94; Piazza Castello 6; ☺ 10am-1pm & 3-7pm Mon-Sat, 10.30am-1pm Sun mid-Apr–mid-Oct, 10.30am-12.30pm & 3.30-6.30pm Mon-Sat mid-Oct–mid-Apr) supplies tourist information, including ample information on walking in the area, including several pretty half-day walks. **Enoteca Toscana** (☎ 0577 73 88 45; Via Roma 29) is the place to taste and buy local wine and olive oil.

Alternatively, head 6km north to the gorgeous old-stone hilltop hamlet of **Castello di Volpaia** (☎ 0577 73 80 66; www .volpaia.it; Piazza della Cisterna 1, Volpaia), where particularly lovely wines, olive oils and vinegars have been made for aeons. Book ahead to enjoy a tour or take a cooking class, or pop into the *enoteca,* which is inside the main tower of the castle, to stock up on a few bottles.

♥ GAIOLE IN CHIANTI & AROUND // APERITIVO AND ART INSTALLATIONS ON THE ROAD TO SIENA

There's little to do in this postcard-pretty village except make your way to the magnificent nearby **Castello di Brolio** (☎ 0577 73 19 19; www.ricasoli.it; admission €5; ☺ 10am-5.30pm Mar-Nov), owned by the Ricasoli family since the 12th century. Wander through the park and Italian garden, walk the battlements and peep into the burial chapel of the Ricasoli family before adjourning to the estate's *osteria* for lunch. On Tuesday evenings in sum-

mer there are special wine cellar tours including *aperitivi* and a four-course dinner with matched wines (€40), and on Wednesday and Thursday evenings there are guided castle tours including a four-course dinner with matched wines (€35). For guided tours at other times contact the castle.

Continuing south to Siena on the SS408, take a walk on the wild art side at the **Parco Sculture del Chianti** (☎ 0577 35 71 51; www.chiantisculpturepark.it; adult/child €7.50/5; ☺ 10am-sunset Apr-Oct, by appointment Nov-Mar), a vast green wooded area studded with contemporary sculptures and art installations in Pieve Asciata, 20km south of Gaiole and 13km north of Siena.

NORTHWESTERN TUSCANY

3 PERFECT DAYS

🌿 DAY 1 // LUCCA BY BIKE

The Lucchesi version of the Giro d'Italia is shorter and considerably less strenuous. Hire a bike (p136), provision yourself with a selection of Forno Giusti's fresh-from-the-oven focaccia and pizza (p134), and free-wheel along the city's cobbled medieval streets. Enjoy your lunch atop the monumental city walls (p131), or pedal east to picnic in the grounds of a Renaissance villa (p136). At day's end, attend a Puccini recital in the medieval church of SS Giovanni e Reparata (p133).

🌿 DAY 2 // THE VALDO PISANO

Visit the monuments in Pisa's picture-perfect Piazza dei Miracoli (p113), before leaving the city and making your way to the hilltop town of San Miniato (p129). Visit shops that have been selling the region's unique wines, meats and sweets for generations, and sample some of their wares over lunch. As the afternoon wanes, watch the sun set from the tower of a medieval fortress or settle down for the night at the Fattoria di Stibbio (p398), a 15th-century villa built for members of the Medici family.

🌿 DAY 3 // ART IN THE APUANES

For a day of monumental proportions, start in Carrara (p145), home of the famous white marble. Visit a marble studio (p145), and then drive up to Cava di Fantiscritti, (p146), a quarry since Roman times. After sampling the local speciality of *lardo di colonnata* (pork fat) at lunch (p146), head down to refined Pietrasanta (p143), where museums and galleries exhibit modern sculpture and other art.

NORTHWESTERN TUSCANY

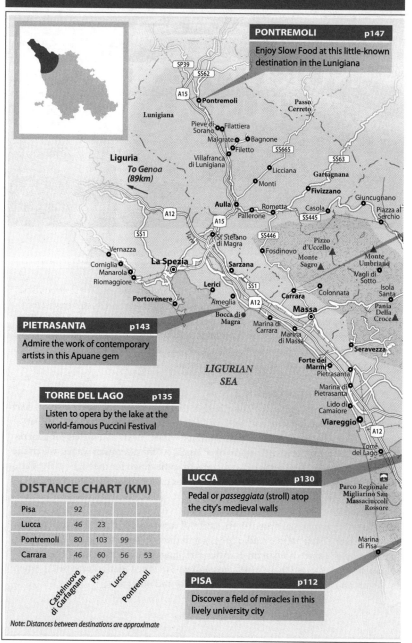

PONTREMOLI p147

Enjoy Slow Food at this little-known destination in the Lunigiana

SP39
SS62
A15 Pontremoli
Lunigiana
Passo Cerreto
Pieve di Sorano Filattiera
Malgrate Bagnone
Filetto SS665
Villafranca di Lunigiana SS63
Liguria Licciana Garfagnana
To Genoa (89km) Monti Fivizzano Giuncugnano
Aulla Rometta Casola Piazza al Serchio
A12 A15 Pallerone SS445
SS1 St Stefano di Magra SS446 Pizzo d'Uccello
Vernazza Fosdinovo Monte Sagro Monte Umbriano
Corniglia La Spezia Sarzana Vagli di Sotto
Manarola Lerici SS1 Isola Santa
Riomaggiore Carrara Colonnata Pania Della Croce
Portovenere Ameglia A12 Massa
Bocca di Magra Marina di Carrara Seravezza
Marina di Massa Forte dei Marmi
Pietrasanta
Marina di Pietrasanta
LIGURIAN SEA Lido di Camaiore
Viareggio A12
Torre del Lago

PIETRASANTA p143

Admire the work of contemporary artists in this Apuane gem

TORRE DEL LAGO p135

Listen to opera by the lake at the world-famous Puccini Festival

Parco Regionale Migliarino San Massaciuccoli Rossore

Marina di Pisa

DISTANCE CHART (KM)

	Castelnuovo di Garfagnana	Pisa	Lucca	Pontremoli
Pisa	92			
Lucca	46	23		
Pontremoli	80	103	99	
Carrara	46	60	56	53

Note: Distances between destinations are approximate

LUCCA p130

Pedal or *passeggiata* (stroll) atop the city's medieval walls

PISA p112

Discover a field of miracles in this lively university city

GETTING AROUND

The major towns and cities in this part of Tuscany are well connected by the A11 and A12, but it's far more fun to veer off the motorways and onto scenic secondary roads and narrow rural routes, particularly in the Lunigiana and Garfagnana. Both Pisa and Lucca have strictly enforced Limited Traffic Zones in their historic centres, so be careful where you park. Regular and reliable trains run between Florence, Lucca, Pisa and Viareggio.

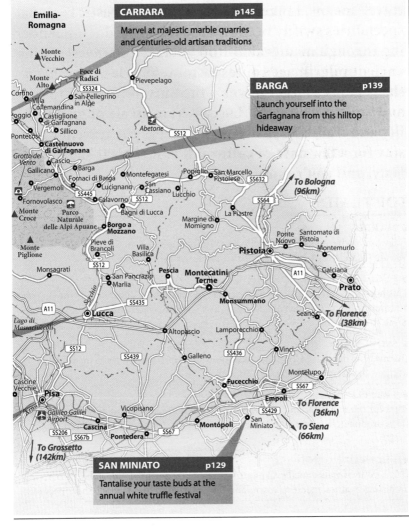

CARRARA p145
Marvel at majestic marble quarries and centuries-old artisan traditions

BARGA p139
Launch yourself into the Garfagnana from this hilltop hideaway

SAN MINIATO p129
Tantalise your taste buds at the annual white truffle festival

NORTHWESTERN TUSCANY

NORTHWESTERN TUSCANY GETTING STARTED

MAKING THE MOST OF YOUR TIME

Travel through this corner of Tuscany and you will be left with a true understanding of what the term 'slow travel' means. Lingering over a lunch of rustic regional specialities swiftly becomes the norm, as does meandering through medieval hilltop villages and investigating ancient pilgrimage routes by foot, bicycle or car. Even the regions's larger towns – the university hub of Pisa and 'love at first sight' Lucca – have an air of tranquillity and tradition that positively begs the traveller to stay for a few days of cultural R & R. This is snail-paced Italy, and you're sure to love it.

TOP TRAILS

❦ MARBLE

Follow in Michelangelo's footsteps when visiting Carrara's marble quarries, Museo del Marmo (Marble Museum) and historic marble workshops (p145).

❦ PUCCINI

This homage to the great composer starts in his birthplace, Lucca, before moving on to his home at Torre del Lago and finishing at Viareggio, where his favourite cafe is still going strong (p135).

❦ SLOW FOOD

Discover the delights of local food traditions, products and dishes in the wild and wonderful Garfagnana region (p138).

❦ TRUFFLES

Hunt for *tuber magnatum pico* (white truffle) in the woods before sampling the precious product in San Miniato, a hilltop town famous for its annual white truffle festival (p129).

❦ VIA FRANCIGENA

Drive, cycle or walk a medieval pilgrimage route through the Lunigiana, discovering prehistoric statues, medieval towns and Romanesque churches along the way (p148).

GETTING AWAY FROM IT ALL

★ **Trek the Garfagnana** Challenge yourself on a guided or self-guided hike through these rugged and magnificent mountains, sleeping in isolated farmhouses, medieval hermitages and hilltop villages along the way (p138).

★ **Explore Pietrasanta** Discover the artistic delights of this diminutive city hidden in the Versilian hinterland (p143).

★ **Tour Lucchesi villas** Bicycle or drive through the hills east of Lucca and take in the magnificent gardens of three historic villas (p136).

ADVANCE PLANNING

This corner of Tuscany suits slow and spontaneous travel but some sights and events require planning in advance.

★ **Carnevale, Viareggio** Book your tickets and hotel in advance if you're keen to join this famous street party (p143), held from mid-February to early March.

★ **Festival Puccini** Tickets to this renowned open-air opera festival (p135) held in July and August fly out of the box office as soon as sales open; book ahead online.

★ **Leaning Tower, Pisa** In summer, beat the queues and ensure a ticket by using the online booking system at least 15 days in advance (p113).

★ **San Miniato National White Truffle Market** Hotels in and around this truffle-obsessed town are in great demand on the last three weekends in November; book if you want to stay overnight (p398).

TOP EATING EXPERIENCES

☙ **LARDO DI COLONNATA**
Why not try a hunk of fat (p146), Tuscan style?

☙ **OSTERIA VECCHIO MOLINO**
A genial host will ply you with local food and wine (p141) in Castelnuovo di Garfagnana.

☙ **RISTORO AL VECCHIO TEATRO**
This Pisa restaurant's justifiably famous set menu features local seafood specialities (p119).

☙ **TADDEUCCI**
Buccellato (ring-shaped loaf with sultanas, aniseed and sugar) was first baked in this Lucca cafe in 1881 (p133).

☙ **TRATTORIA DA BUSSÈ**
Fresh *porcini* mushrooms feature at this rustic eatery (p148) in Pontremoli.

RESOURCES

★ **APT Lucca** (www.luccaturismo.it) Official Lucca tourism website

★ **APT Massa Carrara** (www.aptmassa carrara.it) Information on the marble quarries, Pietrasanta and the Lunigiana

★ **APT Pisa** (www.pisaturismo.it) Official Pisa tourism website

★ **Fondazione Festival Pucciniano** (www.puccinifestival.it) Ticket sales for the Puccini Festival (p135) at Torre del Lago

★ **Parco Apuane** (www.parcapuane.it/turismo /default_ing.htm) Info about the Parco Regionale delle Alpi Apuane

NORTHWESTERN TUSCANY

PISA

· · · · · ·

pop 87,500

Most people know Pisa as the home of an architectural project gone terribly wrong, but the Leaning Tower is just one of many noteworthy sights in this compact and compelling city. Education has fuelled the local economy since the 1400s, and students from across Italy still compete for places in Pisa's elite university and research schools. This endows the centre of town with a vibrant and affordable cafe and bar scene, and balances what is an enviable portfolio of well-maintained Romanesque buildings, Gothic churches and Renaissance piazzas with a lively street life dominated by locals rather than tourists.

Pisa became an important naval base and commercial port under Rome and remained a significant port for centuries. The city's golden days began late in the 10th century, when it became an independent maritime republic and a formidable rival of Genoa and Venice. A century on, the Pisan fleet was sailing far beyond the Mediterranean, successfully trading with the Orient and bringing home new ideas in art, architecture and science. At the peak of its power (the 12th and 13th centuries), Pisa controlled Corsica, Sardinia and the Tuscan coast. Most of the city's finest buildings date from this period, when the distinctive Pisan-Romanesque architectural style with its use of coloured marbles and subtle references to Andalucian architectural styles flourished. Many of these buildings sported decoration by the great father-and-son sculptural team of Nicola and Giovanni Pisano.

Pisa's support for the imperial Ghibellines during the tussles between the Holy Roman Emperor and the pope brought the city into conflict with its mostly Guelph Tuscan neighbours, including Siena, Lucca and Florence. The real blow came when Genoa's fleet inflicted a devastating defeat on Pisa at the Battle of Meloria in 1284. After the city fell to Florence in 1406, the Medici court encouraged great artistic, literary and scientific endeavours and reestablished Pisa's university, where the city's most famous son, Galileo Galilei, taught in the late 16th century.

The form of the medieval city changed in the 18th century under the Habsburg-Lorraine grand dukes of Tuscany, who began a process of demolition to make way for wider boulevards to ease traffic problems. During WWII about 40% of old Pisa was destroyed, and significant buildings including the Camposanto (opposite) were damaged. The slow-paced restoration of historic buildings and precincts that started after the war continues today. At the same time, city authorities are planning major new civic developments such as a redevelopment of the Santa Chiara hospital to a design by internationally renowned, British-based architect David Chipperfield.

ESSENTIAL INFORMATION

EMERGENCIES // **Police** (☎ 050 9 71 81; Via Guido da Pisa 1; ☯ 8am-8pm) **Santa Chiara Hospital** (☎ 050 99 21 11; Via Roma 67)
TOURIST OFFICES // **APT Pisa** (www.pisa turismo.it); Airport (☎ 050 50 25 18; ☯ 11am-11pm); Piazza dei Miracoli (☎ 050 4 22 91; entrance foyer of the Museo dell'Opera del Duomo; ☯ 10am-7pm); Piazza Vittorio Emanuele II (☎ 050 4 22 91; ☯ 9am-7pm Mon-Fri, to 1.30pm Sat)

EXPLORING PISA

Many visitors to Pisa limit their sightseeing to the Piazza dei Miracoli monuments, but those in the know tend to stay an extra day or two to explore the historic centre. This inclination to linger will become even more pronounced when the Museo Navi Antiche Romane di Pisa (Museum of the Ancient Ships of Pisa) on Lungarno Simonelli opens in early 2010. The museum will display a remarkable collection of nine Roman cargo ships excavated from Pisa's silted up harbour in 1998 and restored over the past decade. See www.cantierenavipisa.it, in Italian, for more details.

❦ PIAZZA DEI MIRACOLI // EXQUISITE ROMANESQUE ARCHITECTURE…AND WONKY ENGINEERING

No Tuscan sight is more immortalised in kitsch souvenirs than the iconic tower teetering on the edge of this famous piazza, which is also known as the Campo dei Miracoli (Field of Miracles) or Piazza del Duomo (Cathedral Square). The piazza's expansive green lawns provide an urban carpet on which Europe's most extraordinary concentration of Romanesque buildings – in the form of cathedral, baptistry and tower – are arranged. With two million visitors every year, crowds are the norm, many arriving by tour bus from Florence for a whirlwind visit.

Leaning Tower

Yes, it's true: the **Leaning Tower** (Torre Pendente; ☎ ticket reservations 050 387 22 10; www .opapisa.it/boxoffice/index; admission adult ticket office/online €15/17, under 10yr free; ☉ 8.30am-8.30pm Apr–mid-Jun & last 2 weeks Sep, 8.30am-11pm mid-Jun–mid-Sep, 9am-7pm Oct, 10am-5pm Nov-Feb, 9am-6pm or 7pm Mar) really *does* lean. See the boxed text, p117, for some background on how it ended up in its sorry state.

In 1160 Pisa boasted 10,000-odd towers – but had no *campanile* (bell tower) for its cathedral. Loyal Pisan Berta di Bernardo righted this in 1172 when she died, by leaving a legacy for construction of a *campanile*. Work began in 1173 but ground to a halt a decade later when the structure's first three tiers were observed to be tilting. In 1272 work started again, with artisans and masons attempting to bolster the foundations but failing miserably. Despite this, they kept going,

PIAZZA DEI MIRACOLI TICKETING

Ticket pricing for **Piazza dei Miracoli** (above) sights is a little complicated. Tickets to the **Leaning Tower** (ticket office/online €15/17) and the **Duomo** (Mar-Oct €2, Nov-Feb free) are sold individually, but the remaining sights are accessed through combined tickets. These cost €5/6/8/10 for one/two/three/five sights and cover the Duomo, Baptistry, Camposanto, Museo dell'Opera del Duomo and Museo delle Sinópie. Children aged under 10 years gain free entrance to all sights except the tower. All tickets also allow access to the multimedia and information areas located in the Museo dell'Opera del Duomo and Museo delle Sinópie.

Tickets are sold at two **ticket offices** (www.opapisa.it) on the piazza: the central ticket office is located behind the Tower and a second office is located in the entrance foyer of the Museo delle Sinópie. To guarantee your visit to the Tower, we recommend you book tickets via the website at least 15 days in advance.

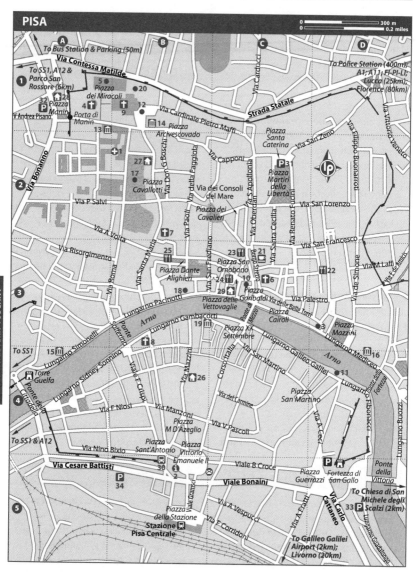

PISA

0   300 m
0   0.2 miles

To Bus Station & Parking (50m)
Via Contessa Matilde
To SS1, A12 &
Parco San
Rossore (6km)
To Police Station (400m);
A1; A11; FI-PI-LI;
Lucca (25km);
Florence (80km)

compensating for the lean by gradually
building straight up from the lower storeys and creating a subtle banana curve.

Over the centuries, the tower has tilted
an extra 1mm each year. By 1993 it was
4.47m out of plumb, more than five degrees from the vertical. The most recent

solution saw steel braces slung around the
third storey that were then joined to steel
cables attached to neighbouring buildings.
This held the tower in place as engineers
began gingerly removing soil from below
the northern foundations. After some 70
tonnes of earth had been extracted from

the northern side, the tower sank to its 18th-century level and, in the process, rectified the lean by 43.8cm. Experts believe that this will guarantee the tower's future (and a fat tourist income) for the next three centuries.

Access to the tower is limited to 40 people at one time, and children aged under eight are not admitted. If you don't want to wait for hours, book in advance (online or by telephone); otherwise go straight to a ticket office when you arrive at the piazza and book the first available slot.

Visits involve a steep climb up 294 occasionally slippy steps and last 30 minutes; late evening visits in summer proffer enchanting views of Pisa by night. All bags, including handbags, must be deposited at the free left-luggage desk next to the central ticket office.

Duomo

Construction of Pisa's **Duomo** (☺ 10am-8pm Apr-Sep, to 7pm Oct, 10am-1pm & 2-5pm 1 Nov-24 Dec & 8 Jan-24 Feb, 9am-6pm 25 Dec-7 Jan, 10am-6pm or 7pm Mar) began in 1063 and continued until the 13th century, when the main facade was added. The elliptical dome, the first of its kind in Europe, dates from 1380. The building's striking cladding of alternating bands of green and cream marble became the blueprint for Romanesque churches throughout Tuscany.

The cathedral was the largest in Europe when it was constructed; its breathtaking proportions were designed to demonstrate Pisa's domination of the Mediterranean. The main facade has four exquisite tiers of columns diminishing skywards, while the vast interior is propped up by 68 hefty granite columns. The wooden ceiling decorated with 24-carat gold is a legacy from the period of Medici rule.

Inside, don't miss the extraordinary early-14th-century octagonal **pulpit** in the north aisle. Sculpted from Carrara marble by Giovanni Pisano and featuring nude and heroic figures, its depth of detail and heightening of feeling brought a new pictorial expressionism and life to Gothic sculpture. Pisano's work forms a striking contrast to the modern pulpit and altar by Italian sculptor Giuliano Vangi, which were controversially installed in 2001.

The **Cappella Ranieri** in the south transept is home to a preserved skeleton of St Ranieri, the patron saint of Pisa. A former wandering minstrel and party boy, Ranieri saw the error of his ways and became a poor and penitential monk. On the night of 16 June each year, 70,000 candles illuminate the streets running along the Arno to honour the saint.

Baptistry

The unusual round **Baptistry** (Battistero; ☺ 8am-8pm Apr-Sep, 9am-6pm or 7pm Mar & Oct,

NORTHWESTERN TUSCANY

10am-5pm Nov-Feb) has one dome piled on top of another, each roofed half in lead, half in tiles. Construction began in 1152, but it was notably remodelled and continued by Nicola and Giovanni Pisano more than a century later and was finally completed in the 14th century – hence its hybrid architectural style.

Inside, the beautiful hexagonal marble **pulpit** carved by Nicola Pisano between 1259 and 1260 is the undisputed highlight. Inspired by the Roman sarcophagi in the Camposanto (see below), Pisano used powerful classical models to enact scenes from biblical legend. His figure of Daniel, who supports one of the corners of the pulpit on his shoulders, was clearly modelled on an ancient statue of Hercules and is one of the earliest heroic nude figures in Italian art, often cited as the inauguration of a tradition that would reach perfection with Michelangelo's *David*.

Every 30 minutes, a custodian demonstrates the double dome's remarkable acoustics and echo effects.

Camposanto & Museo delle Sinópie

Soil shipped from Calvary during the Crusades is said to lie within the white walls of the hauntingly beautiful **Camposanto** (8am-8pm Apr-Sep, 9am-6pm or 7pm Mar & Oct, 10am-5pm Nov-Feb), a cloistered quadrangle where prominent Pisans were once buried. Some of the sarcophagi here are of Graeco-Roman origin, recycled in the Middle Ages.

During WWII, Allied artillery destroyed many of the precious 14th- and 15th-century frescos that covered the cloister walls. Among the few to survive was the *Triumph of Death* – a remarkable illustration of Hell attributed to 14th-century painter Buonamico Buffalmacco. A program of restoration of those frescos damaged but not destroyed by the bombs

is currently underway and the *sinópie* (preliminary sketches) drawn by the artists in red earth pigment on the walls of the Camposanto before the frescos were overpainted are now on display in the **Museo delle Sinópie** (8am-8pm Apr-Sep, 9am-6pm or 7pm Mar & Oct, 10am-5pm Nov-Feb), on the opposite side of the square.

Museo dell'Opera del Duomo

Housed in the cathedral's former chapter house, the **Museo dell'Opera del Duomo** (8am-8pm Apr-Sep, 9am-6pm or 7pm Mar & Oct, 10am-5pm Nov-Feb) is a repository for works of art once displayed in the cathedral and baptistry. Highlights include Giovanni Pisano's ivory carving of the *Madonna and Child* (1299), made for the cathedral's high altar, and his mid-13th-century *Madonna del colloquio*, originally from a gate of the Duomo. Legendary booty includes various pieces of Islamic art including the griffin that once topped the cathedral and a 10th-century Moorish hippogriff.

♥ BORGO STRETTO // MEDIEVAL GRAFFITI MEETS MODERN MERCANTILE ACTIVITY

From Piazza dei Miracoli, head south along Via Santa Maria and turn left at Piazza Cavallotti to reach **Piazza dei Cavalieri**, the historic civic centre. After admiring the piazza's magnificent *palazzi* (palaces; large buildings), wander southwards down Borgo Stretto, the city's medieval heart. Investigate the shops and cafes tucked under the monumental arcades, and marvel at the survival of the graffiti on the facade of **Chiesa di San Michele in Borgo**, which dates all the way back to a 15th-century election for the rector of a local school. A daily **fresh-produce market** is held in adjoining **Piazza delle Vettovaglie**, which is ringed with 15th-century porticoes. In

NORTHWESTERN TUSCANY

THE LEANING CITY OF ITALY

Most people know that Pisa's famous tower leans, but not too many realise that a number of other historic buildings in the city follow its lead. The reason? The soil on which the city is founded is barely 2m above sea level; it's made up of a treacherous sand-and-clay mix atop a series of alternate strata of clay, moisture and sand that reaches a depth of more than 40m.

Unfortunately the city's medieval architects didn't realise that this was the case and failed to compensate with adequate calculations to match the density and mass of structures with the city's precarious ground. If architect Bonanno Pisano had designed his tower to have a wider circumference, it probably wouldn't have tilted to the degree we now observe.

Bonanno wasn't the only one to fudge his calculations. In the Piazza dei Miracoli, the Duomo tilts 25cm to the north and the baptistry inclines a considerable 51cm north. The grand Palazzo Agostini on the Lungarno Pacinotti also displays a decided lean.

Additional tilting towers in town include the octagonal bell tower of Chiesa di San Nicola on Via Santa Maria and the tower of Chiesa di San Michele degli Scalzi on Via San Michele degli Scalzi.

the evening, the piazza's bars are popular spots for an *aperitivo* (predinner drink).

From Piazza Garibaldi, veer east along the waterfront boulevard, Lungarno Mediceo, to visit the **Museo Nazionale di San Matteo** (☎ 050 54 18 65; Piazza San Matteo in Soarta, Lungarno Mediceo; adult/concession €5/2.50; ☯ 8.30am-7pm Tue-Sat, to 1.30pm Sun), a repository of medieval masterpieces housed in a 13th-century former Benedictine convent. This fine gallery has a notable collection of 14th- and 15th-century Pisan sculptures, including pieces by Nicola and Giovanni Pisano, Andrea and Nino Pisano, Francesco di Valdambrino, Donatello, Michelozzo and Andrea della Robbia, but its collection of paintings from the Tuscan school (c 12th to 14th centuries) is even better, with works by Berlinghiero, Lippo Memmi, Taddeo Gaddi, Gentile da Fabriano and Ghirlandaio on show. Don't miss Masaccio's *St Paul*, Fra Angelico's *Madonna of Humility* and Simone Martini's *Polyptych of Saint Catherine*.

To view art from a different era, make your way to the nearby **Babette Food & Art Café** (☎ 050 991 33 02; Lungarno Mediceo 15; ☯ 9am-11pm Tue-Sun; ☞), a favourite haunt of the local bohemian set. Its exposed brick walls play host to a changing program of works by local artists and its casual vibe encourages coffee-fuelled conversation.

♥ SOUTH OF THE ARNO // AN ORNATE RIVERSIDE RESIDENCE AND A GOTHIC GEM

From the *lungarno*, cross the Ponte di Mezzo to reach Pisa's major shopping boulevard, **Corso Italia**. West of the *corso*, facing the river, is the **Palazzo Blu** (☎ 050 2 85 15; www.palazzoblu.it; Lungarno Gambacorti 9; ☯ 10am-6pm Tue-Sun), a magnificently restored 14th-century building that sports over-the-top 19th-century interior decoration. Home to the Foundation CariPisa art collection, which comprises predominantly Pisan works from the 14th to the 20th century, the *palazzo* also hosts temporary exhibitions. Access is via a free 20-minute guided tour (at 4pm, 4.30pm and 5pm daily) in Italian, or by prebooked one-hour tour in English or French (€17 for up to five people).

Continuing west, one of Pisa's architectural gems, the **Chiesa di Santa Maria della Spina** (Lungarno Gambacorti; adult/concession €2/1.50; ☺ 10am-1.45pm & 3-5.45pm Tue-Fri, 10am-1.45pm & 3-6.45pm Sat Mar-Oct, 10am-2pm Tue-Sun Nov-Feb), is on the river side of the *lungarno*. A fine example of Pisan-Gothic style, this now-deconsecrated church was built between 1230 and 1223 to house a reliquary of a *spina* (thorn) from Christ's crown and is refreshingly intimate after the heavyweights of Piazza dei Miracoli. Its ornately spired exterior is encrusted with tabernacles and statues but the interior is simple and perfectly suited to quiet reflection. The focal point inside is Andrea and Nino Pisano's *Madonna and Child* (aka Madonna of the Rose; 1345–48), a masterpiece of Gothic sculpture that still bears traces of its original colours and gilding. At the other end of the church is a copy of the graceful *Madonna del latte* (Our Lady of Milk; 1343–47), sculpted by either Nino or Andrea Pisano, now occupying pride of place in the collection of the Museo Nazionale di San Matteo (p117).

❦ NATURAL LANDSCAPES // COMMUNE WITH NATURE INSIDE OR OUTSIDE THE CITY

Those wanting to escape the tour-group crush around Piazza dei Miracoli will find their needs perfectly met by the nearby **Orto Botanico** (☎ 050 221 53 74; Via Luca Ghini 5; adult/concession €2.50/1.50; ☺ 8.30am-1pm Mon-Sat Sep-Jun), founded by the botanist and physician Luca Ghini in 1543 to cultivate and display plants with medicinal and pharmacological properties. The botanical gardens have been on this site since 1591.

For a back-to-nature experience outside the city limits, **Il Navicello** (☎ 050 50 31 01; www.ilnavicello.it) runs boats between Pisa's San Paolo Pier and the visitors centre at **Tenuta di San Rossore** (☎ 050 53 01 01; www.parks.it/parco.migliarino.san.rossore, visitsr@tin.it), an entry point to the **Parco San Rossore** (www.parcosanrossore.org, in Italian; admission free; ☺ 8am-7pm Sun & holidays daylight saving time, 8.30am-5pm Sun & holidays rest of year), part of the 23,000-hectare Parco Regionale Migliarino San Rossore Massaciuccoli. The sand dunes, coastal woods and wetland of this coastal nature reserve, which runs between Livorno and Viareggio, attract a rich variety of bird life. The boats run on Sundays and holidays

ACCOMMODATION

This part of Tuscany is rich in outstanding *agriturismi* (farm-stay accommodation). See the Accommodation chapter, p391, for a full listing of accommodation options in the area. Here are some of our favourites:

★ **Costa d'Orsola** (p400) Charming farm conversion near the foodie destination of Pontremoli

★ **Fattoria di Pietrabuona** (p398) Spectacularly sited farmhouse rentals in a green valley outside Pescia

★ **Fattoria di Stibbio** (p398) A stunning 15th-century Medici villa near San Miniato

★ **Il Benefizio** (p399) Well-equipped apartments overlooking the picturesque hilltop town of Barga

★ **Pradaccio di Sopra** (p399) Cheap, cheerful and comfortable rooms in the Garfagnana

★ **Villa Michaela** (p399) Luxurious accommodation in a villa on Lucca's outskirts

between May and September, departing at 10am and 1pm. The trip costs €8 for adults and €7 for children aged between three and 10 years; children under three years are free. This section of the park can only be explored on a guided tour (by foot, bicycle, coach or miniature train), which must be booked ahead by phone or email.

GASTRONOMIC HIGHLIGHTS

Pisa has an excellent range of eateries, many offering impressive seafood-based menus. Local specialities include fresh *pecorino* cheese from San Rossore, *zuppe di cavolo* (cabbage soup), fresh pasta, and delectable desserts such as *pan ficato* (fig cake) and *castagnaccio* (chestnut-flour cake enriched by nuts). The local DOCG is Chianti delle Colline Pisane and though there's no Pisan DOC, Bianco Pisano di San Torpè, a Trebbiano-dominated wine with a delicate, dry flavour, is a popular substitute. For more on wine, see p375.

❦ BAR PASTICCERIA SALZA €
☎ 050 58 02 44; Borgo Stretto 44; ☺ 8am-8.30pm Apr-Oct, variable hours Tue-Sun Nov-Mar

Salza has been tempting patrons off Borgo Stretto and into sugar-induced wickedness ever since the 1920s. Claim one of the tables in the arcade, or save some money by standing at the bar – the excellent coffee and dangerously delicious cakes and chocolates will satisfy regardless of where you sample them.

❦ ENOTECA OSTERIA IL COLONNINO €€
☎ 050 313 84 30; Via Sant'Andrea 37-41; meals €29; ☺ lunch & dinner Tue-Sun

Located in the warren of medieval streets between Piazza San Francesco and the river, Il Colonnino is a great spot for

lunch, *aperitivo* or dinner. Modern-accented Italian dishes such as fillet of pork with a balsamic vinegar and pink peppercorn sauce provide perfect accompaniments to an impressive wine list. The weekday lunch deal of a daily plate, water and glass of 'good wine' (€10) is a steal.

❦ IL MONTINO €
Vicolo del Monte 1; pizza slice €1.20-1.50, full pizza €3.80-7.20; ☺ 10.30am-3pm & 5-10pm Mon-Sat

Students and sophisticates alike adore the *cecina* (chickpea pizza) and *spuma* (sweet, nonalcoholic drink) that are the specialities of this famous pizzeria. You can follow their lead or instead opt for a *foccacine* (flat roll) filled with salami, pancetta or *porchetta* (suckling pig). Order to take away or claim one of the outdoor tables. You'll find it in the laneway behind Caffetiera Ginostra.

❦ OSTERIA DEL PORTON ROSSO €€
☎ 050 58 05 66; Vicolo del Porton Rosso 11; meals €30; ☺ lunch & dinner Mon-Sat

Two menus – one from the land and one from the sea – tempt at this old-fashioned but excellent *osteria* (casual tavern or eatery) in a laneway behind the Hotel Victoria. Here, Pisan specialities such as fresh ravioli with salted cod and chickpeas happily coexist with Tuscan classics such as grilled fillet steak. If you're lucky, unusual dishes such as *ribollita di mare* (rustic bread and fish soup) may grace the menu.

❦ RISTORO AL VECCHIO TEATRO €€
☎ 050 2 02 10; Piazza Dante Alighieri; set menu €35; ☺ lunch Mon-Sat, dinner Tue-Sat)

The Vecchio Teatro's genial host is proud of his set menu, and for good reason. The four courses are dominated by local seafood specialities and diners will encounter delights such as *torta di ceci*

DRIVING & PARKING RESTRICTIONS

There is a strict Limited Traffic Zone (ZTL) in Pisa's historic centre that applies to all nonresidents, and this is rigorously enforced. If you drive into the zone, your car will be photographed and a fine of €76 will be sent to you (or to the car-hire company you are renting from). Many travellers have written to us to complain about credit-card charges from car-hire companies being levied months after their unknowing infraction of the ZTL has occurred, often with administrative costs of up to €100 added to the fine. If you are staying at a hotel in the zone, you must supply the car's registration details to hotel staff as soon as you check in so that they can register you for a temporary permit. People with disabilities should call ☎ 800 08 65 40 to organise a free temporary permit. To obtain maps of the ZTL, go to https://secure.comune.pisa.it/tzi/info.jsp.

infranti con le arselle (an unusual savoury cake of smashed chickpeas with mussels) and risotto with prawns and orange. The dessert finale includes a *castagnaccio* (cake baked with chestnut flour, studded with raisins and topped with a rosemary sprig) that has been known to prompt diners to spontaneous applause.

TRANSPORT

TO/FROM THE AIRPORT

AIRPORT // Galileo Galilei airport (PSA; ☎ 050 84 93 00; www.pisa-airport.com) Located 2km south of town, this is Tuscany's main international airport and it handles flights to most major European cities. The airport is linked to the city centre, and to Florence (p93), by both train and bus.

TRAIN // Services run to/from Stazione Pisa Centrale (€1.10, five minutes, 33 per day); be sure to purchase and validate your ticket before you get on the train.

BUS // The LAM Rossa (red) bus line (€1, 10 minutes, every 10 to 20 minutes) operated by local company CPT (see right) passes through the city centre and the train station on its way to/from the airport. If you purchase your ticket on board the bus rather than from the airport information office or a newsstand, it will cost an extra €0.50.

TAXI // A taxi between the airport and the city centre will cost between €8 and €10. To book, call ☎ 050 54 16 00 (airport), 050 4 12 52 (Pisa railway station) or 050 561 878 (Piazza dei Miracoli).

GETTING AROUND

TRAIN // Pisa is connected by rail to Florence and is also on the Rome–La Spezia train line. Destinations include Florence (€5.60, 1¼ hours, frequent), Rome (€17.65 to €37.10, 2½ to four hours, 16 daily), Livorno (€1.80, 15 minutes, frequent) and Lucca (€2.40, 30 minutes, every 30 minutes).

BUS // From its hub on Piazza Sant'Antonio, Pisan bus company CPT (Compagnia Pisana Trasporti; ☎ 800 012773; www.cpt.pisa.it, in Italian) runs buses to/from Volterra (€5, two hours, up to 10 daily) and Livorno (€2.50, 55 minutes, half-hourly to hourly). To get to Florence or Lucca take the train.

CAR // Pisa is close to the A11 and A12. The SCG FI-PI-LI (SS67) is a toll-free alternative for Florence and Livorno, while the north–south SS1, the Via Aurelia, connects the city with La Spezia and Rome. See the boxed text, above, for information on driving into the city centre.

PARKING // Parking costs between €0.50 and €2 per hour, but you must be careful that the car park you choose is not in the city's exclusion zone (see the boxed text, above). There's a free car park outside the zone on Lungarno Guadalongo near the Fortezza di San Gallo on the south side of the Arno; there's well-located pay parking to the west of the Piazza dei Miracoli just outside the Porta di Manin; at the bus station north of the Piazza dei Miracoli; in Piazza San Caterina (access this via Porta San Zeno); and on Via Cesare Battisti near the train station on the south side of the river.

(Continued on page 129)

NORTHWESTERN TUSCANY

THE BEST OF
TUSCANY
& UMBRIA

Whether you're unravelling a thousand Tuscan tales in the devilishly steep streets of a hilltop town; revelling in Florence's city-sophisticate pageant of Renaissance master-pieces; or committing yourself truly, madly, deeply to Umbria's sacred and savage soul, you'll discover the regions of Tuscany and Umbria are disproportionately rich – in art, in food and in passion.

ABOVE Fertile fields near San Gimignano (p192), Tuscany

THE BEST AGRITURISMI

1 AGRITURISMO LA CERRETA
Nature's the draw at this bucolic *agriturismo* (farm-stay accommodation; p401) in central coastal Tuscany. Don't be surprised if an antlered deer or a wild boar scampers by while you're at the restaurant or hiking the dozens of nearby trails. Kids will love the games and horse-riding lessons.

2 AGRITURISMO SAN LORENZO
If the 12th-century chapel isn't enough to entice you to this central Tuscan farm-stay (p404), perhaps the swimming pool fed by mountain spring water, cooking classes or organic home-grown olive oil will do the trick. Pick up ingredients at the local farmers market and cook in your own kitchen.

ENRICO CARACCIOLO

❸ FATTORIA DI RIGNANA

Who doesn't want to stay in a 17th-century noble villa in Tuscany (p396)? If you can tear yourself away from the ceiling frescos for long enough, you can enjoy the infinity pool with views of the countryside or dine at the on-site *cantinetta* (small cellar where wine is served; p103).

❹ FATTORIA DI VIBIO

Far from the rat race, this is an upmarket romantic oasis in southern Umbria where one can luxuriate in spa services in the morning, hike the trails in the afternoon, and down truffles and Sagrantino in the restaurant each night. Don't miss the view from the indoor swimming pool (p414).

❺ TORRE COLOMBAIA

The hand-built, fairy-tale-like main building of Torre Colombaia (p410) is surrounded by idyllic organic farmlands and a yoga studio. Seemingly isolated yet just 15 minutes from Perugia and the wine region, this rural swath of land invites relaxation and contemplation.

3

TOP Horse riding at Agriturismo la Cerreta BOTTOM LEFT Olive trees in blossom at Fattoria di Rignana
BOTTOM RIGHT Sleep in comfort at Fattoria di Rignana

THE BEST ART

1 **THE UFFIZI**

Arguably one of the best art museums on the planet, Florence's Uffizi Gallery (p53) has been stunning visitors for more than 400 years. Every major Italian artist and style of Italian art is represented here, from Giotto and Michelangelo to Botticelli and da Vinci.

2 **PINACOTECA NAZIONALE**

Witness the transformation of Tuscan art from the flat, gilded Gothic style to the dimensional and emotional style of the Renaissance. Dating back around 800 years, the works in the National Gallery of Siena (p188) are from both the Sienese and Florentine schools.

FORD-E-GAUTIER/SAGAPHOTO.COM / ALAMY

3 PALAZZO COMUNALE

The building itself (p181) is a Gothic architectural masterpiece anchoring Siena's Piazza del Campo, and the frescos and masterpieces inside are known for their secular themes of wisdom, justice and peace.

4 BASILICA DI SAN FRANCESCO

St Francis of Assisi is known for changing the world of religion, but his life (and death) also transformed the world of art. Gone were flat, iconic images and in their place arose natural backgrounds, animals and true emotion. Don't miss Giotto's fresco cycle in the upper church (p270).

5 PINACOTECA COMUNALE

The Alta Valle del Tevere in the far north of Umbria is known as Museum Valley for the richness of its historic treasures. This 15th-century palace (p287) in Città di Castello houses works from masters such as Signorelli, Raphael and Cristofano Gherardi, artists who lived here when Città was one of Umbria's most important artistic cities.

4

TOP Siena's Pinacoteca Nazionale is full of artistic riches **BOTTOM LEFT** Dramatic sculptures draw the eye in Florence's Uffizi Gallery **BOTTOM RIGHT** Giotto's stunning fresco, Basilica di San Francesco, Assisi

THE BEST RESTAURANTS

---

1 OSTERIA DI PASSIGNANO
Everything is memorable at this upmarket *osteria* (casual eatery; p104) in Badia di Passignano: the delectable dishes, professional service, tempting wine list and idyllic setting in an 11th-century Benedictine monastery on the Antinori wine estate. The menu is refined; lunch here is truly an affair to remember.

---

2 RISTORANTE CIBRÈO
The flagship of Fabio Picchi's food empire, this elegant restaurant (p88) in Florence treats diners to the city's most confident and creative Tuscan cuisine. Once you've eaten here, you're sure to join the ranks of the many adoring regulars.

© RICCARDO SPILA/GRAND TOUR/CORBIS

3 ANTICA OSTERIA DA DIVO

Fancy an Etruscan ruin with your guinea fowl and cherry millefeuille potatoes? Against a backdrop of a 2500-year-old subterranean grotto in Siena, you'll find fresh, seasonal cuisine, slow jazz and inventive fusion creations (p190).

4 HOTEL RISTORANTE LA BASTIGLIA

Although Umbrian food is known for its peasant roots, the cuisine can spruce up rather nicely. Set in the postcard-perfect village of Spello, La Bastiglia (p277) is known as much for its sommelier-crafted 800-bottle wine cellar as it is for its daring seasonal menu – fried egg yolk, blood gnocchi and the local Chianina beef.

5 RISTORANTE PIERMARINI

Whenever there's a gravy boat filled with truffle sauce, you know a restaurant is doing something right. Signore Piermarini serves dishes filled with truffles, freshly picked herbs, wild asparagus and other locally sourced ingredients in Ferentillo (p325).

TOP Picturesque Badia di Passignano (p103) is an ideal location for a memorable meal BOTTOM LEFT Freshly picked truffles feature at the best restaurants BOTTOM RIGHT Join the locals for a bite at Cibrèo

TOP Tour through the soft hues of the Valnerina landscape RIGHT Medieval architecture features along the Via Francigena in the Lunigiana region

THE BEST DRIVING TOURS

1 PIERO DELLA FRANCESCA TRAIL

This scenic route (p246) follows the art of the 15th-century Arezzo-based painter. While Piero della Francesca has famed paintings in Rome and Florence, many of his 'serene humanism' pieces can be found near his home town. Of particular note is his *Madonna del Parto* (Pregnant Madonna) fresco near Monterchi.

2 THE VALNERINA

Start your day with a Roman waterfall that has its own on/off switch. Next up, a village church where you can commune with mummified remains. For dinner, stop in at Ristorante Piermarini, where the truffles may have been freshly picked (p323).

3 ABBAZIA DI SAN GALGANO TO PETROIO

With a striking Gothic abbey as its starting point, the journey moves from Cistercian ruins to a Romanesque church and a 14th-century abbey covered in Luca Signorelli frescos, and finally stops in a medieval town for a visit to a terracotta museum (p202).

4 THE VIA FRANCIGENA

A pilgrimage route since the 7th century, the Via Francigena has a sacred beauty perfect for those looking for a more spiritual peregrination. Traversing the ancient Lunigiana region of Tuscany, the drive takes in castles, a medieval hilltop fortress and a 9th-century hermitage (p148).

(Continued from page 120)

SAN MINIATO

• • • • • •

pop 27,800
The *tuber magnatum pico* (**white truf-fle**) **reigns supreme at this medieval hilltop town located roughly halfway between Pisa and Florence. Here, the precious product is sourced, celebrated and scoffed by locals and aficionados from around the world.**

EXPLORING SAN MINIATO

San Miniato is a great weekend destination; many sights are only open on weekends and Sunday is the best day to visit.

❧ HIGH TOWN ARCHITECTURE // ADMIRE BUILDINGS OF ALL AGES AND STYLES

The cobbled streets of San Miniato Alto (the high town) are home to an impressive Romanesque cathedral, a reconstructed medieval fortress tower, magnificent palaces and a clutch of significant church buildings dating from the 14th to 18th centuries. A combined ticket to visit eight of these monuments is available (adults €4, under 14 years and over 65 years free) and can be purchased at the helpful **tourist office** (☎ 0571 4 27 45; www.cittadisanminiato .it; Via del Bastione 1, San Miniato Alto; 9am-1pm & 3-6.30pm Mon-Sat, 10am-1pm & 3-7pm Sun), which is obscurely located down a set of stairs off the modern piazza where the elevator from the lower car park terminates.

❧ LOCAL PRODUCE // GIVE YOUR TASTE BUDS A REGIONAL WORKOUT

San Miniato offers treats galore for gastronomes. **Sergio Falaschi** (☎ 0571 4 31 90;

www.sergiofalaschi.it; Via Augusto Conti 18-20) is a *macellaria* (butcher shop) specialising in products made from *cinta senese* (indigenous Tuscan pig from the area around Siena), including the Slow Food favourite, *mallegato* (blood sausage). Other local products worth searching out are *carciofo san miniatese* (locally grown artichokes) in April and May; chestnuts and wild mushrooms in autumn (fall); *formaggio di capra delle colline di san miniato* (the local goat's cheese); and locally raised Chianina beef. Excellent local bread and sweet specialities including *cantuccio san miniato* (aniseed-flavoured biscuits) can be sampled at **Pasticceria Il Cantuccio di Federigo** (☎ 0571 41 83 44; Via P Maioli 67).

These products join truffles on the menus of many of the town's eateries, including the much-lauded **Ristorate Pepenero** (☎ 0571 41 95 23; www.pepenerocucina .it; Via IV Novembre 13; set menu €30-50; dinner Mon-Sat, lunch & dinner Sun). Chef Gilberto Rossi is one of the new breed of innovative Tuscan chefs using traditional products to create modern, seasonally driven dishes. To share some of his secrets, consider signing up for one of his Wednesday-morning **cooking classes** (laura@pepenerocucina.it; classes per person incl lunch & wine €60), which are followed by an informal lunch on the restaurant's terrace.

TRANSPORT

TRAIN // Take the regional service from Pisa (€2.90, 30 minutes, hourly) or Florence (€3.50, 45 minutes, hourly) to San Miniato Fucecchio in the lower town and then hop on to the local shuttle bus (€1, every 20 minutes) to reach San Miniato Alto.

CAR // To drive here from Pisa or Florence, take the SCG FI-PI-LI (SS67).

PARKING // The best place to park is in Piazza del Popolo, in San Miniato Alto.

THE WHITE TRUFFLE

The dank sandy-soil woods around **San Miniato** (p129) are famed throughout Italy as hunting grounds for the white truffle, and one third of the country's annual crop is sourced here. Snouting out the precious fungus, which is pale ochre in colour, has been an integral part of local culture since the Middle Ages. Truffle paths and trails are closely guarded family secrets, passed between generations, and well-trained dogs with a good nose are highly prized.

The period from mid-September to December is when all of the action occurs. The best time to savour the mystique of this cloak-and-dagger truffle trade is during San Miniato's **Mostra Mercato Nazionale del Tartufo Bianco di San Miniato** (San Miniato National White Truffle Market), held on the last three weekends of November. During the festival, restaurateurs and truffle tragics come from every corner of the globe to purchase supplies, sample truffle-based delicacies in the town's shops and restaurants and breathe in one of the world's most distinctive aromas.

To see a truffle hunter and his dog in action, sign up for a two-hour early-morning **truffle hunt** (1 to 6 people incl aperitif & truffle tasting €300; mid-Sep–Dec) at Barbialla Nuovo Fattoria (see p398), a heavily wooded working farm and *agriturismo* (farm-stay accommodation) outside Montaione. Barbialla Nuovo Fattoria supplies international restaurants including London's River Café and has an enviable success rate when it comes to uncovering these nuggets of white gold.

LUCCA & AROUND

. . . . . .

Lucca is a gem of a city that endears itself to all who visit. Hidden behind imposing Renaissance walls, its cobbled streets, handsome piazzas and shady promenades make it a perfect destination to explore by foot. At day's end, historic cafes and restaurants tempt visitors to relax over a glass or two of Lucchesi wine and a slow progression of rustic dishes prepared with produce from the nearby Garfagnana. If you have a car, the hills to the east of Lucca reward exploration. Home to historic villas and a belle époque spa resort, they are easy and attractive day-trip destinations from Lucca.

LUCCA

pop 83,200

Founded by the Etruscans, Lucca became a Roman colony in 180 BC and a free *comune* (self-governing city) during the 12th century, when it enjoyed a period of prosperity based on the silk trade. In 1314 it briefly fell to Pisa but regained its independence under the leadership of local adventurer Castruccio Castracani degli Anterminelli, and began to amass territories in western Tuscany, including marble-rich Carrara. Castruccio died in 1328 but Lucca remained an independent republic for almost 500 years.

Napoleon ended all this in 1805 when he created the principality of Lucca and placed one of the seemingly countless members of his family in need of an Italian fiefdom (this time his sister Elisa) in control of all of Tuscany. Ten years later the city became a Bourbon duchy before being incorporated into the Kingdom of Italy. It miraculously escaped being bombed during WWII, so the fabric of the historic centre has remained unchanged for centuries.

ESSENTIAL INFORMATION

EMERGENCIES // Hospital (☎ 0583 97 01 11; Via dell'Ospedale) Police (☎ 0583 4 55 11; Viale Cavour 38)

TOURIST OFFICES // APT Lucca (www .luccatourist.it); Città di Lucca Info Point Piazzale Verdi (☎ 0583 58 31 50; ☺ 9am-7pm daily); Piazza Napoleone (☎ 0583 91 99 41; ☺ 10am-1pm & 2-6pm Mon-Sat); Piazza Santa Maria 35 (☎ 0583 91 99 31; ☺ 9am-8pm Mon-Sat Apr-Oct, 9am-12.30pm & 3-6.30pm Mon-Sat 1st 2 weeks Nov, 9am-12.30pm & 3-6.30pm daily mid-Nov-mid Dec, 9am-12.30pm & 3-6.30pm Mon-Sat mid-Dec-Mar)

EXPLORING LUCCA

❦ CITY WALLS // CIRCLE THE CITY ON WHEELS OR BY FOOT

Lucca's monumental **mura** (walls) were built around the old city in the 16th and 17th centuries and remain in almost perfect condition due to the long periods of peace the city has enjoyed over its history. Twelve metres high and 4km in length, the ramparts are crowned with a wide tree-lined footpath that looks down on the historic centre and out toward the Apuane Alps. This path is the favourite Lucchesi location for a *passeggiata* (traditional evening stroll), be it on foot, bicycle or inline skate. Children's playgrounds, swings and picnic tables beneath shady plane trees add a buzz of activity to Baluardo San Regolo, Baluardo San Salvatore and Baluardo Santa Croce – three of the 11 bastions studding the way – and older kids kick balls around on the vast green lawns of Balu-

ardo San Donato. The stylish **Caffetiera San Colombano** (☺ Tue-Sun) at Baluardo San Colombano provides the perfect caffeine pit stop.

For bicycle hire, see p136.

❦ PIAZZA SAN MARTINO // AN UNUSUAL CRUCIFIX AND A POIGNANT MEMORIAL

This attractive square is lined with palaces, a tower house and buildings associated with the predominantly Romanesque **Cattedrale di San Martino** (☎ 0583 95 70 68; www.museocattedralelucca.it, in Italian; Piazza San Martino; ☺ 9.30am-5.45pm Mon-Fri, to 6.45pm Sat, 9.30-10.45am & noon-6pm Sun mid-Mar–Oct, 9.30am-4.45pm Mon-Fri, to 6.45pm Sat, 9.30-10.45am & noon-5pm Sun Nov–mid-Mar), which dates to the start of the 11th century. The stunning facade was constructed in the prevailing Lucca-Pisan style and designed to accommodate the preexisting *campanile*. The reliefs over the left doorway of the portico are believed to be by Nicola Pisano.

The interior of the cathedral was rebuilt in the 14th and 15th centuries with a Gothic flourish. The **Volto Santo** (literally, Holy Countenance) is not to be missed. Legend has it that this simply fashioned image of a dark-skinned, life-sized Christ on a wooden crucifix was carved by Nicodemus, who witnessed the crucifixion. In fact, the Volto Santo has recently been dated to the 13th century. A major object of pilgrimage, the sculpture is carried in procession through the streets on 13 September each year at dusk during the Luminaria di Santa Croce, a solemn torchlit procession marking its miraculous arrival in Lucca.

The cathedral's many other works of art include a magnificent *Last Supper* by Tintoretto above the third altar of the south aisle and Domenico Ghirlandaio's

NORTHWESTERN TUSCANY

NORTHWESTERN TUSCANY

LUCCA

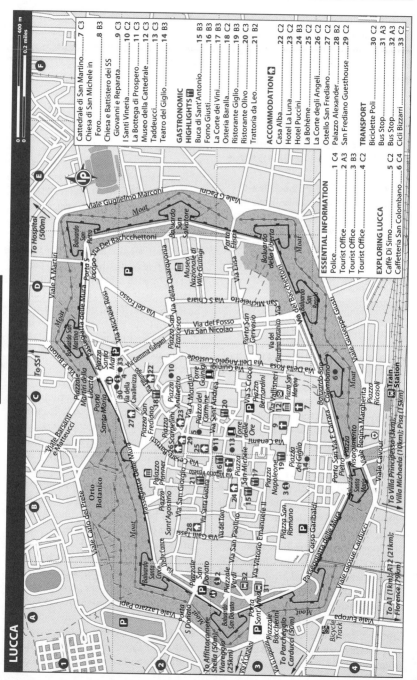

Cattedrale di San Martino	7	C3
Chiesa di San Michele in Foro	8	B3
Chiesa e Battistero dei SS Giovanni e Reparata	9	C3
I Santi Vineria	10	C3
La Bottega di Prospero	11	C3
Museo della Cattedrale	12	C3
Taddeucci	13	C3
Teatro del Giglio	14	B3

GASTRONOMIC HIGHLIGHTS 🍴

Buca di Sant'Antonio	15	B3
Forno Giusti	16	B3
La Corte dei Vini	17	B3
Osteria Baralla	18	C2
Ristorante Giglio	19	B3
Ristorante Olivo	20	C3
Trattoria da Leo	21	B2

ACCOMMODATION 🛏

Casa Alba	22	C2
Hotel La Luna	23	C2
Hotel Puccini	24	B3
La Bohème	25	C2
La Corte degli Angeli	26	C2
Ostello San Frediano	27	C2
Palazzo Alexander	28	B2
San Frediano Guesthouse	29	C2

TRANSPORT

Biciclette Poli	30	C2
Bus Stop	31	A3
Bus Stop	32	A3
Cicli Bizzari	33	C2

ESSENTIAL INFORMATION

Police	1	C4
Tourist Office	2	A3
Tourist Office	3	B3
Tourist Office	4	C2

EXPLORING LUCCA

Caffè Di Simo	5	C2
Caffetteria San Colombano	6	C4

1479 *Madonna Enthroned with Saints*. This impressive work by Michelangelo's master is currently located in the sacristy (adult/concession €2/1.50), opposite the exquisite marble memorial to Ilaria del Carretto carved by Jacopo della Quercia in 1407. The young second wife of the 15th-century lord of Lucca, Paolo Guinigi, Ilaria died in childbirth aged only 24.

The adjacent **Museo della Cattedrale** (☎ 0583 49 05 30; adult/concession €4/2.50; ✆ 10am-6pm mid-Mar–Oct, 10am-2pm Mon-Fri, to 5pm Sat & Sun Nov–mid-Mar) is home to elaborate gold and silver decorations made for the Volto Santo, including a 17th-century crown and a 19th-century sceptre.

♥ CHIESA E BATTISTERO DEI SS GIOVANNI E REPARATA // HEAR PUCCINI'S ARIAS SOAR TO THE HEAVENS

The 12th-century interior of the deconsecrated **Chiesa e Battistero dei SS Giovanni e Reparata** is a hauntingly atmospheric setting for early-evening opera recitals staged by **Puccini e la sua Lucca** (☎ 340 8106042; www.puccinielasualucca .com; adult/concession €15/10), which are held at 7pm every evening from mid-March to October, and on every evening except Thursdays from November to mid-March. Professional singers present a one-hour program of arias and duets dominated by the music of Puccini but also featuring works by Verdi, Mozart, Mascagni and Cilea. Tickets are available from the church between 10am and 6pm.

In the north transept of the church is a **baptistry** (☎ 0583 49 05 30; Piazza San Giovanni; adult/concession €2.50/1.50; ✆ 10am-6pm mid-Mar–Oct, 10am-5pm Sat, Sun & religious holidays Nov–mid-Mar), which crowns an archaeological area comprising five building levels going back to the Roman period.

MONEY SAVER

Those choosing to visit the **Cattedrale di San Martino sacristy** (left), the **Museo della Cattedrale** (left) and the baptistry of the nearby **SS Giovanni e Reparata** (left) can save money by purchasing a combined ticket (adult/child €6/4) at any of the venues.

♥ PIAZZA SAN MICHELE // A TREAT FOR BOTH BODY AND SOUL

Once the site of a Roman forum, this prominent piazza is home to the Romanesque **Chiesa di San Michele in Foro** (☎ 0583 4 84 59; Piazza San Michele; ✆ 7.40am-noon & 3-6pm Apr-Oct, 9am-noon & 3-5pm Nov-Mar), one of Lucca's many architecturally significant churches. The present building with its exquisite wedding-cake facade was constructed on the site of its 8th-century precursor over a period of nearly 300 years, beginning in the 11th century. Crowning the structure is a figure of the archangel Michael slaying a dragon. Inside, don't miss Filippino Lippi's 1479 painting of Sts Helen, Jerome, Sebastian and Roch (complete with plague sore) in the south transept.

There are a number of provedores worth investigating on the eastern side of the piazza, including the wildly popular **Forno Giusti** (see p134) and the historic **La Bottega di Prospero** (13 Via Santa Lucia; ✆ 9am-1pm & 4-7.30pm), which stocks a wide range of Lucchesi wines and olive oils, local *porcini* mushrooms and Garfagnese *biscotti al farro* (wheat biscuits). Most famous of all, though, is **Taddeucci** (☎ 0583 49 49 33; www.taddeucci .com; Piazza San Michele 34; ✆ 8.30am-7.45pm, closed Thu in winter), a *pasticceria* (pastry shop) where the traditional Lucchesi treat of *buccellato* was created in 1881. A ring-shaped loaf made with flour, sultanas, aniseed and sugar, it's the perfect accompaniment to a midmorning or midafternoon espresso – coffee and a slice of *buccellato* costs €3.50.

♥ VIA FILLUNGO // JOIN THE LOCALS ON LUCCA'S BUSIEST THOROUGHFARE

Threading its way through the medieval heart of the old city, this cobbled street is full of sleek, modern boutiques housed in buildings of great charm and antiquity – make sure you regularly cast your eyes above the street-level bustle to appreciate ancient awnings and architectural details. For a respite from the crowds, consider a coffee or *aperitivo* stop at **Caffè Di Simo** (☎ 0583 49 62 34; Via Fillungo 58; ☻ 9am-8pm & 8.30pm-1am), which is known for its charming Liberty (art nouveau) interior and excellent coffee and cakes.

East of Via Fillungo is one of Tuscany's loveliest piazzas, oval-shaped **Piazza Anfiteatro**, so-called after the amphitheatre that was located here in Roman times. Today it houses pavement cafes, restaurants and popular wine bars such as **I Santi Vineria** (☎ 0583 49 61 24; Via Anfiteatro 29a; ☻ Tue-Sun). If you look closely, you will be able to see remnants of the amphitheatre's brick arches and masonry on the exterior walls of the medieval houses ringing the piazza.

GASTRONOMIC HIGHLIGHTS

Lucca is known for its traditional cuisine and highly prized local olive oil. The city's proximity to the Garfagnana means that regional products such as chestnuts, *porcini* mushrooms, honey, *farro* (spelt), sheep's-milk cheese and *formenton* (ground corn) are widely used. The lo-

cal DOC wines are Colline Lucchesi and Montecarlo di Lucca – try the red varietals of the former and the delicate whites of the latter.

♥ BUCA DI SANT'ANTONIO €€

☎ 0583 5 58 81; www.bucadisantantonio.com; Via della Cervia 3; meals €38; ☻ Tue-Sat, lunch Sun

This atmosphere-laden restaurant dates to 1782 and is an outstanding spot for tasting top-notch Italian wines. Its flattering lighting and banquette seating make it a favourite destination for romantic dinners, and its standards of service are unmatched in the city. The food doesn't quite live up to all of these attributes, alas, the rustic dishes on offer being similar to the fare served up in many other, less-expensive eateries around the region. Bookings essential.

♥ FORNO GIUSTI €

☎ 0583 49 62 85; Via Santa Lucia 20; pizza & filled focaccia per kg €7-16; ☻ 7am-1pm & 4.30-7.45pm, closed Sat & Sun Jun-Aug & Wed afternoons in winter

Join the crowd queuing in front of this excellent bakery to purchase fresh-from-the-oven pizza and focaccia with a variety of fillings and toppings. Forno Giusti is the perfect place to buy picnic provisions.

♥ LA CORTE DEI VINI €

☎ 0583 58 44 60; Corte Campana 6; €22, platters €7-12; ☻ lunch & dinner Mon-Sat

Strategically placed between Piazza Napoleone and Piazza San Michele, this friendly '*enoteca e picola cucina*' (wine bar and small kitchen) is a great choice for an *aperitivo* or casual meal. It specialises in rustic dishes including *tortelli lucchesi* (meat ravioli) and *minestra di farro della garbagnana* (soup made with spelt), and also offers platters of local *pecorino* cheese, mushroom *torte* (savoury

THE PUCCINI TRAIL

Lucca has a particular lure for opera buffs, for it was here that the great Giacomo Puccini was born. The maestro, who came from a long line of Lucchesi musicians, was baptised in the **Chiesa e Battistero dei SS Giovanni e Reparata** (p133) the day after his birth in 1858 and grew up in an apartment at Corte San Lorenzo 9. During his teenage years, Puccini played the organ in the **Cattedrale di San Martino** (p131) and performed as a piano accompanist at the **Teatro del Giglio** (☎ 0583 4 65 31; www.teatrodelgiglio.it; Piazza del Giglio 13-15), the 17th-century theatre where the curtain later rose on his best-known operas: *La Bohème* (1896), *Tosca* (1900) and *Madame Butterfly* (1907).

Puccini left Lucca in 1880 to study at Milan's music conservatory. After his studies he returned to Tuscany and rented a house in **Torre del Lago**, on Lago Massaciuccoli, 15km west of Lucca. In 1899, after the successes of *Manon Lescaut* (1893) and *La Bohème*, he had a villa built on the shore of the lake and undertook the Liberty-style interior decoration himself. Puccini lived here with his wife, Elvira, for 24 years, spending his time working, hunting on the lake and carousing with a diverse group of hunters, fishermen and bohemian artists. *Madame Butterfly, La fanciulla del West* (1910), *La Rondine* (1917) and *Il Trittico* (1918) were composed on the Forster piano in his front study, and he wrote his scores on the specially made walnut table in the same room. The villa has been preserved almost exactly as it was during Puccini's residence, and now functions as the **Museo Villa Puccini** (☎ 0584 34 14 45; www.giacomopuccini.it; adult/child 6-13yr €7/2; ☷ 10am-12.40pm & 3-5.40pm Apr-Oct, 10am-12.40pm & 2.30-4.30pm Nov-Jan, 10am-12.40pm & 2.30-5.10pm Feb-Mar). The museum is closed on Monday mornings and open in the afternoon from 4pm to 8pm on the days of Puccini Festival performances. To visit, you must join one of the guided tours in Italian (audio guides in English are available), conducted every 40 minutes.

If you're planning to be in Tuscany in July or August, make sure you prebook tickets to the world-famous **Puccini Festival** (www.puccinifestival.it), which each year stages three or four of the great man's operas in a huge purpose-built outdoor theatre on the shore of the lake close to the villa. For details about getting to and from the festival by public transport, contact the tourist offices in Viareggio (p143) or Lucca (p131).

In 1921 Puccini and Elvira moved to a villa in the nearby coastal town of Viareggio, where the composer became a regular fixture at the **Gran Caffè Margherita** (p143). He worked on his last opera, the unfinished *Turandot* (1926), during this period. After Puccini's death in 1924, Elvira and son Antonio added a chapel to the Torre del Lago villa; Puccini's remains were interred there in 1926.

pie) and prosciutto to share. Get there early to score a choice table on the front terrace.

♥ OSTERIA BARALLA €€
☎ 0583 44 02 40; www.osteriabaralla.it; Via Anfiteatro 5; meals €32; ☷ Mon-Sat

Dine beneath magnificent red-brick vaults at this busy *osteria*, which inevitably will be packed to the rafters by noon. Rich in tradition (the place dates to 1860) and local specialities, its menu highlights include soup with new-season olive oil, salt cod and chickpeas, *bolito misto* (mixed boiled meat) on Thursdays and roast pork on Saturdays.

♥ RISTORANTE GIGLIO €€€

☎ 0583 49 40 58; www.ristorantegiglio.com; Piazza del Giglio 2; meals €45; ☽ lunch & dinner

Set in the frescoed splendour of the 18th-century Palazzo Arnolfini, this elegant restaurant serves refined versions of local specialities such as fresh spelt pasta with rabbit sauce, polenta with *porcini* mushrooms, and *bucellato* filled with ice cream and berries.

♥ RISTORANTE OLIVO €€

☎ 0583 49 62 64; www.ristoranteolivo.it/inglese; Piazza San Quirico 1; meals €45; ☽ lunch & dinner Thu-Tue Dec-Mar, daily Apr-Nov

Known for its fresh fish, which is brought in every day from Viareggio, the Olivo epitomises old-fashioned Lucchesi dining. The wine list is excellent (with Tuscan drops dominating). The menu balances classic Tuscan choices such as duck breast in grappa sauce with seafood specialities that include flat pasta with shellfish, seafood and basil.

♥ TRATTORIA DA LEO €

☎ 0583 49 22 36; Via Tegrimi 1; meals €15; ☽ Mon-Sat

Ask a local to recommend a lunch spot and inevitably they will nominate this bustling trattoria. The clientele of tourists, students, workers and ladies taking a break from shopping have one thing in common – an appreciation for the cheap food and friendly ambience on offer. The food ranges from acceptable to delicious, with stand-out dishes including the *vitello tonnato* (cold veal with a tuna and caper sauce) and fig and walnut tart. Note: no credit cards.

TRANSPORT

BICYCLE // Hire bikes from **Cicli Bizzarri** (☎ 0583 49 66 82; www.ciclibizzarri.net, in Italian; Piazza Santa Maria 32) and **Biciclette Poli** (☎ 0583 49 37 87; www.biciclettepoli.com, in Italian; Piazza Santa Maria 42), located on either side of the tourist information office on Piazza Santa Maria. Both are open from 9am to 7pm daily and charge €2.50 per hour. You'll need to leave ID.

TRAIN // The station is south of the city walls, but only a short walk away – take the path across the moat and through the tunnel under Baluardo San Colombano. Regional train services connect Lucca with surrounding cities and towns. Destinations include Florence (€5, 1¼ to 1¾ hours, hourly), Pisa (€2.40, 30 minutes, every 30 minutes) and Viareggio (€2.40, 25 minutes, hourly).

BUS // From the bus stops around Piazzale Verdi, **Vaibus** (www.vaibus.it) runs services throughout the region, including to destinations in the Garfagnana such as Castelnuovo (€4, 1½ hours, eight daily) and Bagni di Lucca (€3.20, one hour, eight daily). It also runs buses to/from Florence (€5.10, 1½ hours, hourly), Pisa and Galileo Galilei airport (€2.80, 45 minutes to one hour, 30 daily), and Viareggio (€3.20, 50 minutes, five daily) via Torre del Lago (€2.80, 30 minutes, six daily).

CAR // The A11 runs westwards to Pisa and Viareggio and eastwards to Florence. To access the Garfagnana, take the SS12 and continue on the SS445.

PARKING // Most car parks within the city walls are for residents only, and are indicated by yellow lines. Blue lines indicate pay parks (€1 to €1.50 per hour) that are available to all motorists, but these are few and far between. If you are staying within the city walls, contact your hotel ahead of your arrival and enquire about the possibility of getting a temporary resident permit during your stay. The parks just outside the city walls have a time limit of one to two hours and are closely monitored. The easiest option is to park at Parcheggio Carducci, just outside Porta Sant'Anna.

AROUND LUCCA

♥ VILLA TOUR // VISIT GLORIOUS GARDENS IN THE LUCCHESI HILLS

Between the 15th and 19th centuries, successful Lucchesi merchants often chose to announce their success to the world by building opulent summer residences. Some 300 of these villas were built on the hills around the city, and though a few have crumbled away or been abandoned, many are still private residences and some have opened their ornate gates to paying visitors (see www.villelucchesi.net).

Elisa Bonaparte, Napoleon's sister and short-lived ruler of Tuscany, once lived in the handsome **Villa Reale** (☎ 0583 3 01 08; Via Fraga Alta; garden tours €7; ☺ 10am-1pm & 3-7pm Tue-Sun Jul-Sep, 10am-1pm & 2-6pm Tue-Sun Oct & Apr-Jun), located 7km north of Lucca in Marlia. The house isn't open to the public, but the statuary-filled gardens can be visited by hourly guided tour.

The neoclassical **Villa Grabau** (☎ 0583 40 60 98, 349 601 36 52; www.villagrabau.it; Via di Matraia 269; villa €5, incl park €7; ☺ 10am-1pm & 3-7pm Tue-Sun Jul-Aug, 10am-1pm & 2-6pm Tue-Sun Easter-Jun, Sep & Oct, 11am-1pm & 2.30-5.30pm Sun & holidays Nov-Easter), located just north in San Pancrazio, is framed by a vast 9 hectares of parkland with sweeping traditional English- and Italian-styled gardens, splashing fountains, more than 100 terracotta pots with lemon trees and a postcard-pretty lemon house dating from the 17th century.

In the same village, the grounds of **Villa Oliva** (☎ 0583 40 64 62; www.villaoliva.it; gardens €6; ☺ 9.30am-12.30pm & 2-6pm mid-Mar–mid-Nov, by appointment rest of year), a 15th-century country residence designed by Lucchesi architect Matteo Civitali, are worth a peep. Retaining its original design, the fountain-rich park staggers across three levels and includes a romantic cypress alley and stables reckoned to be even more beautiful that those at Versailles.

To reach these villas, take the SS12 northeast from Lucca (direction Abetone) and exit onto the SP29 to Marlia. From Marlia, San Pancrazio is a mere 1.2km north.

♥ MONTECATINI TERME // UNWIND IN STYLE AT THIS SYBARITIC SPA TOWN

Verdi and Puccini are among the many high-profile names to have undergone spa treatments and sampled the mineral-rich waters at this charming resort. It has six functioning *terme* (thermal baths) occupying grand buildings arranged around a beautifully maintained park. The oldest, Leopoldine, dates back to 1773 and the most impressive, Tettuccio, was built in 1928. All are open from May to October and offer a wide range of health, relaxation and beauty treatments. The town's extremely helpful **tourist office** (☎ 0573 77 22 44; www.montecatiniturismo.it; Viale Verdi 66-68; ☺ 9am-12.30pm & 3-6pm Mon-Sat year-round, 9am-noon Sun Easter-Oct) can supply more information, and for lists of treatments and prices go to www.termemon tecatini.it/attesa_en.html.

You don't need to book treatments to visit. The park is open to the public, as is Tettuccio's wonderfully atmospheric cafe-bar. In summer locals and visitors gravitate towards Viale Verde, the boulevard linking Piazza del Popolo with the *terme* complex, to ride the historic carousel, buy gelato from **Desideri** (Viale Verdi 84-86; ☺ 9am-2am daily summer & spring, Sat afternoon & all day Sun autumn & winter), listen to the open-air orchestras and inspect the merchandise in a swath of upmarket boutiques.

If you're travelling by public transport, Montecatini Terme is easily accessed by train from Florence (€3.50, 50 minutes, every 30 minutes) or Lucca (€2.90, 30 minutes, every 30 minutes). Alight at Stazione Montecatini Centro – Piazza del Popolo is directly in front of the station exit.

NORTHWESTERN TUSCANY

THE GARFAGNANA

· · · · · ·

Nestled between the Apuane Alps and the Apennines are three stunning valleys formed by the Serchio and its tributaries: the low-lying Lima and Serchio Valleys and the higher Garfagnana Valley. These are often collectively referred to as the Garfagnana.

Many visitors to this relatively undiscovered area come to enjoy its hiking and biking. Others are attracted by the region's rustic cuisine, which utilises local fruits of the forest including chestnuts (often ground into flour), *porcini* mushrooms and honey. Enthusiasts for military history come to the area around Borgo a Mozzano to see remnants of fortifications from the Linea Gotica (Gothic Line), the last major line of defence mounted by the retreating German army in the final stages of WWII.

BAGNI DI LUCCA

pop 6540

In the early 19th century, Lucchesi aristocrats and members of the international literary set (including Byron, Shelley, Browning and Heine) came to this thermal spa in the Lima Valley to take the waters by day, carouse in its casino and theatre by night and repent in the town's unusually ornate Anglican church every Sunday. These days, it's a popular lunch stop for day-trippers to the area.

❦ CASINO // SEE WHERE VISITORS ONCE GAMBLED THE NIGHT AWAY

Strauss, Puccini and Liszt all played in the music room of this neoclassical build-

ing, which dates from 1837. After their performances, they no doubt dallied at the handsome bar or squandered their performance fee over the gaming tables. Lovers of trivia will be interested to know that this was the first licensed casino in Europe, and that one of its first managers, a Frenchman, went on to open the Monte Carlo Casino. These days the beautifully restored building is home to the **tourist office** (☎ 0583 80 57 45; Via del Casinò; ⏱ 10am-12pm & 4-7pm Mon-Sat, 10am-1pm Sun mid-May–Oct, 10am-1pm Wed-Mon Nov–mid-May).

❦ CIRCOLO DEI FORESTIERI // DINE LIKE A PRINCE ON A PAUPER'S BUDGET

The former home of the Foreigners' Club, this elegant belle époque building is located on the river side of Viale Umberto I, southeast of the casino. It now functions as a **restaurant** (☎ 0583 8 60 38; Piazza Jean Varraud 10; à la carte €30; ⏱ lunch & dinner Tue-Sun), and its grand dining room (complete with chandeliers) provides a splendid setting in which to enjoy what could well be the cheapest tourist menu in Tuscany (€11 for three courses and a side dish).

❦ BAGNI DI LUCCA TERME // REST AND REVITALISE IN A THERMAL SPA

The thermal springs in this area have been popular spots for relaxation and revitalisation ever since Roman times. These days there's only one in operation: the **Bagni di Lucca Terme** (☎ 0583 8 72 21; www.termebagnidilucca.it; Piazza San Martino 11; ⏱ 7am-12.30pm & 2.30-6pm summer & holidays, 7am-12.30pm rest of year), which has two geothermal caves and a wellness centre. It offers a range of steam and/or thermal mud baths (€20 to €40), massages (€34 to €84), beauty treatments (€20 to €126)

NORTHWESTERN TUSCANY

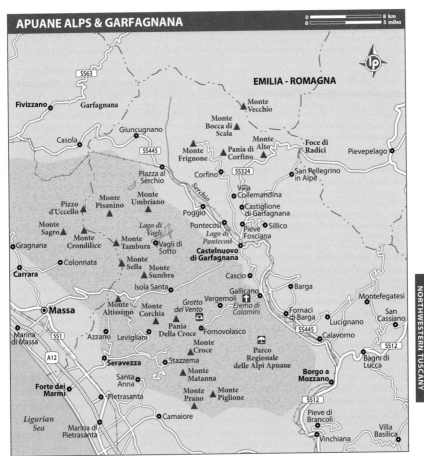

APUANE ALPS & GARFAGNANA

0 _____ 8 km
0 _____ 5 miles

EMILIA - ROMAGNA

NORTHWESTERN TUSCANY

and day packages (€82). You can also stay overnight in the comfortable spa **hotel** (r €40-48; ☾ closed mid-Feb–early Jan; 🅿 ✕ 🖥 🛜), which has its own thermal pool.

TRANSPORT

TRAIN // There are services to/from Lucca (€2.40, 30 minutes, seven per day) and Pisa (€3.50, one hour, five daily).

BUS // Vaibus (www.vaibus.it) runs services between Lucca and Bagni di Lucca (€3.20, one hour, eight daily).

CAR // Take the SS12 from Lucca (direction Abetone).

BARGA

pop 10,200

Barga is one of those irresistibly slow Tuscan hilltop towns with a disproportionately large and dynamic English-speaking community; it even has its own English-language website (www .barganews.com). The streets of Barga Vecchia (the walled Old Town on the hilltop) are full of churches, attractive stone houses and palaces built by rich merchants between the 15th and 17th centuries. The town's patron saint,

HIKING & BIKING

Hardy souls keen to see the Garfagnana by bike should check out **Le Vie della Cantera** (www.panterabike.com), a comprehensive site that suggests 10 cycling itineraries ranging in length from an easy 18km to a tougher 231km. Those wishing to hike should check out Barga-based **Tuscany Walking** (www.tuscanywalking.com), an English-speaking set-up that offers guided and self-guided hikes; or **Sherpa Expeditions** (www.sherpa-walking-holidays .co.uk), a UK-based outfit that has worked with a local expert to design an eight-day self-guided hike through the Apuane Alps starting from Fornaci di Barga in the Garfagnana. On the ground, pick up a copy of *Trekking in Garfagnana* from any of the local tourist offices. This free booklet devised by the Communità Montana della Garfagnana (www .turismo.garfagnana.eu, in Italian) outlines a nine-day loop that starts in Castelnuovo di Garfagnana and traverses the entire area, including two mountain peaks.

St Christopher, is honoured on 25 July with events including a torchlight procession through the streets of Barga Vecchia and performances in the beautifully restored late-18th-century **Teatro dei Differenti**. Also of note is July's **Sagra del Pesce e Patate** (Fish and Chip Festival), an event that doffs its cap to the many Barghigiani who emigrated to Scotland in search of a better life in the 19th century. For information on these and other cultural events in the area, contact the **tourist office** (☎ 0583 72 47 45, 800 02 84 97; www.comune.barga.lu.it, in Italian; Via di Mezzo 47; ☺ 9am-1pm Mon-Fri, 9am-1pm & 3-5pm Sat, 10am-noon & 3-5pm Sun), which is located in Barga Vecchia.

❦ **LA COLLEGIATA DI SAN CRISTOFORO // CLIMB TO THE TOWN'S ROMANESQUE CROWN**
The Old Town's lovely patchwork of narrow streets, archways, ancient walls and small piazzas tumbles downhill at the foot of this Romanesque **cathedral**, constructed in four stages between the 9th and 17th centuries. Its facade features local white Alberese stone that changes tone with the light, and the views of the Apuane and Apennine Alps from the terrace are quite breathtaking. Inside the cathedral, the

Romanesque fittings and decorations include a baptismal font, a stoup for holy water, an arresting polychrome wooden statue of St Christopher dating from 1100 and an exquisite marble pulpit. Later decorative additions include the baroque painting of *St Joseph, St Roche & St Anthony* (1500) in the chapel to the left of the main altar, which shows Barga and the cathedral in the background.

At the end of your visit, wander back down the hill and enjoy a coffee or homemade gelato at **La Gelateria** (☎ 0583 7 54 51; Piazza SS Annunziata; cones €1-3; ☺ 7.30am-8.30pm, to 3am in summer); for something more substantial, try **L'Osteria** (☎ 0583 72 45 47; Piazza Angelio 13-14; meals €19; ☺ Fri-Wed).

TRANSPORT

TRAIN // Trains run between Lucca and Barga-Gallicano (€2.90, 50 minutes, eight daily). Note that the train station is a few kilometres below Barga Vecchia. Most people walk from the station but you can prebook a (pricey) taxi service through **Taxi Barga** (☎ 348 810 61 12; taxibarga@libero.it).

BUS // **Vaibus** (www.vaibus.it) runs services between Lucca and Barga (€3.60, 70 minutes, 10 daily). The buses stop at Piazzale del Fosso by Porta Mancianella.

CAR // Take the SS12 from Lucca (direction: Abetone), veer left onto the SS445 and then turn right onto the

SP7 at Fornacci di Barga. Barga is 5km further on. Park at Piazzale del Fosso or in the car and campervan park on nearby Via Hayange.

CASTELNUOVO DI GARFAGNANA

pop 6130

The medieval eyrie of Castelnuovo crowns the confluence of the Serchio and its smaller tributary, the Turrite. Castelnuovo is the best spot in the Garfagnana to source information about the Apuane Alps. The extremely helpful **Centro Visite Parco Alpi Apuane** (☎ 0583 6 51 69; garfagnana@tin.it; Piazza delle Erbe 1; ⏱ 9.30am-1pm & 3-7pm Jun-Sep, 9.30am-1pm & 3-5.30pm Oct-May) can supply loads of information on walking, mountain biking, horse riding and other activities as well as lists of local guides. It also has plenty of information about *agriturismi* (farm-stay accommodation) and *rifugi* (mountain huts) off any beaten track and sells hiking maps.

❧ THE ROCCA // PEEK INTO A MEDIEVAL FORTRESS

At the town's centre is the formidable **Rocca Ariostesca** (Ariosto's Castle) built in the 12th century and enlarged by Castruccio Castracani in the following one. It takes its name from the Italian poet, who resided here between 1522 and 1525 when he was governor of the Garfagnana for the House of Este. Ariosto is best known as the author of the romantic epic poem *Orlando Furioso* (1516). The castle now functions as the town hall. On the ground floor, an **archaeological museum** (admission free; ⏱ 10am-noon & 4-6pm Sun), staffed by volunteers, sports a modest collection of artefacts. After peeking into the *rocca*'s courtyard and visiting the museum, follow Via Fulvio Testi to

the nearby **duomo**, home to a lovely *Madonna and Two Saints* by Michele di Ridolfo del Ghirlandaio.

❧ OSTERIA VECCHIA MULINO // SAMPLE GARFAGNESE SPECIALITIES AT AN HISTORIC OSTERIA

Locals and visitors alike have been noshing on local specialities at **Osteria Vecchia Mulino** (☎ 0583 6 21 92; www.ilvecchio mulino.com, in Italian; Via Vittorio Emanuele 12; ⏱ Tue-Sun 7.30am-8.30pm; tasting menu incl wine €15-20) for over a century. When we lunched here recently, our fellow diners included members of a cycling club from Barga, two restaurateurs from Florence, an English family from Essex and two local tradesmen. Everyone sat at communal tables and tucked into a tasting menu comprising locally cured prosciutto, *biroldo* (the local equivalent of haggis), *pecorino* drizzled with honey, a *torte* made with just-gathered *porcini* mushrooms and a wonderfully flavoursome chestnut cake. Served by a genial host, washed down with the eminently quaffable local wine and accompanied by shared laughter and conversation, it was about as memorable as Tuscany gets (and that's saying a lot). You can also purchase provisions here to take home.

TRANSPORT

TRAIN // Trains run between Lucca and Castelnuovo di Garfagnana (€3.50, one hour, nine daily).

BUS // **Vaibus** (www.vaibus.it) runs services between Lucca and Borgo a Mozzano and then another bus to Castelnuovo – but it's much easier to go by train.

CAR // Take the SS12 from Lucca (direction Abetone) and turn off onto the SS445.

PARKING // There's a car park at Piazza del Genio, off Via Roma on the opposite side of the river to the walled *centro storico* (historic city centre).

AROUND CASTELNUOVO DI GARFAGNANA

❦ SAN PELLEGRINO IN ALPE // TAKE A SCENIC ROAD TRIP

Several scenic roads fan out from Castelnuovo. If you've a car and steady nerves, try the concertina of hairpin bends that lifts you, via Castiglione di Garfagnana, to the scenic Foce di Radici pass across the Apennines and into Emilia-Romagna. The minor parallel road to the south leads you to **San Pellegrino in Alpe**, the site of a fine monastery and a well-regarded **ethnographic museum** (☎ 0583 64 90 72; Via del Voltone 4; adult/concession €2.50/1.50; ⏰ 10am-1pm & 2-6.30pm daily Jul & Aug, 10am-1pm & 2-6.30pm Tue-Sun Jun & Sep, 10am-1pm & 2-4.30pm Tue-Sun April-May, 9.30am-1pm Mon-Fri, 10am-1pm & 2-4.30pm Sat & Sun Oct-Mar).

❦ GROTTO DEL VENTO // EXPLORE SUBTERRANEAN CAVERNS

The SS445 follows the Serchio Valley to the east of the Apuane Alps and bores into the Lunigiana (see p146) at Tuscany's northern limit. It's a pretty, twisting route that leads you through lush green hills that are home to an astounding 1300 caves, nearly all requiring a guide and special tackle. The most accessible and spectacular of these is the **Grotta del Vento** (Wind Cave; ☎ 0583 72 20 24; www.grottadelvento.com; ⏰ 10am-noon & 2-6pm), 9km west of the SS445. Here, the wonders of the underground abysses, lakes and caverns contrast with the bleak landscape above. From April to October, you can take a one-hour guided tour (adult/under 11 years €7.50/5, eight times daily), a two-hour option (adult/child €12/8.50, four times daily) or a three-hour full monty (adult/child €17/11.50, at 10am and 2pm). From November to March only the one-hour tour is offered. Bring your woollies; it can feel chilly down there, even in high summer.

❦ EREMO DI CALOMINI // DETOUR TO A MEDIEVAL HERMITAGE

On the way to the Grotta del Vento, consider visiting the **Eremo di Calomini** (☎ 0583 76 70 03; www.eremocalomini.it/agriturismo .php, in Italian; ⏰ 9am-12.30pm & 3-6pm Jun-Sep, 9am-12.30 & 3-6pm Sat & Sun Oct-May), a medieval monastery spectacularly situated at the bottom of a huge protruding rock face. Masses are held at 11am and 5pm and during summer there's a popular **restaurant** (☎ 0583 76 70 20) nearby where you can have lunch. Don't miss the sacristy, ancient kitchen and monks' quarters, all of which are hewn out of the rock. You can also overnight here (€25 to €38 per person).

VERSILIA

· · · · · ·

The beaches from Viareggio northwards to Liguria are popular with local holidaymakers and some tourists, but have been blighted by beachfront strip development and get unpleasantly packed with Italy's beach-loving hoi polloi during the summer months. We suggest steering clear of this coastal strip and instead heading inland to explore the hinterland town of Pietrasanta, known for its vibrant arts culture and historic city centre.

Versilia is a major gateway to both the Apuane Alps and the Lunigiana, with roads from the coastal towns snaking their way deep into the heart of the mountains and connecting with small villages and walking tracks.

Trekking Bike: The Tuscan Coast details 12 walking and cycling itineraries along the coast and into the hinterland, split into 12 easy one-day legs (each three to four hours); pick it up at tourist offices. Online, see www.tuscancoast .com and www.rivieratoscana.com for more info.

VIAREGGIO

pop 63,800
This hugely popular sun-and-sand resort on the Versilian coastal strip is known as much for its flamboyant Mardi Gras Carnevale as for its once grand, now dishevelled, line-up of seafront Liberty-style facades.

💗 PIAZZA SHELLEY & THE WATERFRONT // STROLLING IN ARTISTIC COMPANY
It's a short walk from the train station to the waterfront, Viale Margherita, and the **central tourist office** (☎ 0584 96 22 33; www .aptversilia.it; Viale Carducci 10; ⏰ 9am-2pm & 3-7pm Mon-Sat, 9am-2pm Sun). The best place for a coffee or lunch stop is **Gran Caffè Margherita** (☎ 0584 58 11 43; www.ristorantemarg herita.it, in Italian; Viale Margherita 30; set menu €20-34; ⏰ 9am-midnight), which dates from 1929 and was once frequented by the great Puccini.

Literature lovers might like to pass by dishevelled Piazza Shelley, the only tangible reference to the Romantic poet who drowned in Viareggio; his body was washed up on the beach and his comrade-in-arts, Lord Byron, had him cremated on the beach in Viareggio.

💗 CARNEVALE // KICK UP YOUR HEELS, ITALIAN-STYLE
Viareggio's annual moment of glory lasts a good four weeks in February to early March when the city goes wild at

Carnevale (www.viareggio.ilcarnevale.com). This festival of floats, many featuring giant satirical effigies of political and other topical figures, includes fireworks and a decidedly dusk-to-dawn spirit. Tickets for the Sunday processions cost adult/under 10 years €15/free and can be bought at the Fondazione Carnevale on Piazza Mazzini or at ticket kiosks on the procession circuit.

TRANSPORT
TRAIN // Local trains run to Livorno (€3.50, 35 minutes, 16 daily), Pisa (€2.40, every 30 minutes), and La Spezia (€4.10 to €11.40, 40 minutes, 36 daily) via Massa and Carrara. Other services run to Florence (€6.50, one hour and 40 minutes) via Lucca (€2.40, 20 minutes).
BUS // **Vaibus** (www.vaibus.it) runs bus services from Piazza d'Azeglio to local destinations including Pietrasanta (€2.20, 30 minutes) and destinations around Tuscany including Galileo Galilei airport (€3.20, one hour, 30 daily) and Florence (€6.10, 1½ hours, 16 daily).
CAR // Take the A12 from Pisa or the A11/A12 from Lucca.
BOAT // **Consorzio Marittimo Turistico** (☎ 0187 73 29 87; www.navigazionegolfodeipoeti .it; Via Don Minzoni 13, La Spezia) Runs one passenger boat daily from late June to mid-September (adult €28 to €30, children 6 to 11 years €15) connecting Viareggio (and also Forte dei Marmi, Marina di Carrara and Marina di Massa) with Porto Venere and the Cinque Terre villages.

PIETRASANTA

pop 24,600
Often overlooked by Tuscan travellers, this refined town is a perfect base for explorations into the Apuane Alps. Founded by Guiscardo da Pietrasanta, *podestà* (governing magistrate) of Lucca in 1255, it was seen as a prize by Genoa, Lucca, Pisa and Florence, all of whom jostled for possession of its marble quarries and bronze foundries. As was

so often the case, Florence won out and Leo X (Giovanni de' Medici) took control in 1513. Leo put the town's famous quarries at the disposal of Michelangelo, who came here in 1518 to source marble for the facade of San Lorenzo in Florence (p63). The artistic inclination of Pietrasanta dates from this time, and today it is the home of many artists and artisans, including internationally lauded Colombian-born sculptor Fernando Botero.

The town was originally walled, and the *centro storico* is now a Limited Traffic Zone.

There's a **tourist information point** (☎ 0584 28 32 84; info@pietrasantamarina.it; ☺ 9am-1pm & 4.30-7pm Mon-Wed, Fri & Sat, 4.30-7pm Thu, 9am-1pm & 4-7.30pm Sun) in nearby Piazza Statuto.

☙ **A TOUR OF THE TOWN //
CHURCHES, MUSEUMS AND
SWEET TREATS**
From the tourist office, walk down the main shopping strip, Via Mazzini, which is bookended by contemporary street sculptures. The **Chiesa della Misericordia** on this strip is home to frescos of the *Gate of Paradise* and *Gate of Hell* by Botero (the artist portrays himself in hell). Nearby **Pasticceria Dazzi** (☎ 0584 7 01 74; Via Mazzini 64) is known for its excellent coffee and sweet treats, including the local favourite, marzipan.

Arriving at sculpture-filled Piazza del Duomo, you can walk straight ahead into Via Garibaldi, home to commercial art galleries and a 17th-century baptistry with two beautiful marble fonts dating from 1389 and 1509–1612 respectively. Here you'll also find Pietrasanta's best-loved *enoteca* (wine bar), the atmospheric **L'Enoteca Marcucci** (☎ 0584 79 19 62; Via Garibaldi 40; ☺ 10am-1pm & 5pm-1am Tue-Sun).

On the other side of the attractive **Duomo di San Martino**, which dates from 1256 and is notable for its fine interior marble carving, is the deconsecrated 13th-century **Chiesa di Sant'Agostino** (☺ 4pm-7pm Tue-Sun), now a wonderfully evocative venue for art exhibitions. The adjoining former convent dates from 1515 to 1579 and houses a cultural centre and the **Museo dei Bozzetti** (☎ 0584 79 55 00; www.museodei bozzetti.it; Via S Agostino 1; admission free; ☺ 2pm-7pm Tue-Sat, 4pm-7pm Sun), which exhibits moulds of famous sculptures cast or carved in Pietrasanta.

TRANSPORT

TRAIN // Local trains run to/from Viareggio (€1.80, 10 minutes, frequent) and Pisa (€2.90, 35 minutes, frequent).

BUS // Vaibus (www.vaibus.it) runs bus services between Pietrasanta and Lucca (€3.60, one hour, three daily). It also runs a service to/from Galileo Galilei airport (€3.20, 75 minutes, 15 daily) via Viareggio (€2.20, 30 minutes).

CAR // From Marina di Pietrasanta on the A12, turn inland 3.5km to reach the town.

PARKING // There's parking in front of the town hall on Piazza Matteotti.

APUANE ALPS

• • • • • •

Rearing up between the Versilian Riviera and the vast inland valley of the Garfagnana is this mountain range protected by the Parco Regionale delle Alpi Apuane.

You'll find a good network of marked walking trails and *rifugi* in the park. To guide your steps, pick up *Alpi Apuane Settentrionali* (1:25,000) published by the Massa Carrara APT; or Edizione Multigraphic Firenze's *Parco delle Alpi*

Apuane, (1:25,000; €7) or *Versilia: Parco delle Alpi Apuane* (1:50,000, €7). *The Alps of Tuscany* by Francesco Greco contains many enjoyable multiday routes.

The main gateways into the Parco Regionale delle Alpi Apuane (www .parcapuane.it) are Seravezza and Castelnuovo di Garfagnana. Both the **information centre** (☎ 0584 7 58 21; Via Corrado del Greco 11; ⏰ 9am-1pm & 3.30-7.30pm daily Jun-Sep, 9.30am-12.30pm & 3-6pm Wed-Mon Oct-May) in Seravezza and the **Centro Visite Parco Alpi Apuane** in Castelnuovo di Garfagnana (p141) can supply plenty of information.

CARRARA

pop 65,400

Many first-time visitors assume that the snowy-white mountain peaks forming Carrara's backdrop are capped with snow. In fact, the vista provides a breathtaking illusion – the white is 2000 hectares of marble gouged out of the foothills of the Apuane Alps in vast quarries that have been worked since Roman times.

The texture and purity of Carrara's white marble (the word is derived from the Greek *marmaros,* meaning shining stone) is unrivalled and it was here that Michelangelo selected marble for masterpieces including *David* (actually sculpted from a dud veined block). These days it's a multibillion-euro industry.

The quarries, which are 5km north of town in Colonnata and Fantiscritti, have long been the area's biggest employers. It's hard, dangerous work and on Carrara's central Piazza XXVII Aprile a monument remembers workers who have lost their lives up on the hills. These tough men formed the backbone of a strong leftist and anarchist tradition in Carrara,

something that won them no friends among the Fascists or, later, the occupying German forces.

Bar the thrill of seeing its mosaic marble pavements, marble street benches, decorative marble putti and marble everything else, the old centre of Carrara doesn't offer much to the visitor. The exception to this rule is from July to September in even-numbered years, when a contemporary sculpture biennale is staged here.

Opposite the stadium, halfway between Carrara and Marina di Carrara, there's a **tourist office** (☎ 0585 84 41 36; Viale XX Settembre; ⏰ 8.30am-5.30pm Jun-Aug, 9am-4pm Sep-May) that offers maps and brochures detailing local attractions.

❦ STUDI DI SCULTURA CARLO // UNCOVER THE SECRETS OF MARBLE ARTISTRY

If you're interested in the techniques that artisans use to transform slabs of marble into works of art, make an appointment to visit the dust-filled **Studi di Scultura Carlo Nicoli** (☎ 0585 7 00 79; www.nicoli-sculptures.com; Piazza XXVII Aprile 8), the most atmospheric of Carrara's five marble workshops. This is where internationally acclaimed artists such as Louise Bourgeois and Anish Kapoor instruct the marble *laboratory* (workshop) on how they want their work executed, thus taking advantage of a centuries-old tradition of artisanship that has often been handed down from generation to generation. Serious artists (as opposed to novices) can also apply to base themselves here for months at a time, learning techniques in situ. After visiting, make your way to the area around the Romanesque cathedral for a coffee at **Café Pasticceria Luzio Caflisch** (☎ 0585 7 16 76; Via Roma 2; ⏰ 7am-7.30pm Mon, Tue & Thu-Sat, 2-7.30pm Sun).

LARDO DI COLONNATA

The hamlet of Colonnata, 2km from Fantiscritti, is famous for more than its marble quarry. This is the home of *lardo di colonnata* (thinner-than-wafer-thin slices of local pig fat marinated in a mix of herbs and olive oil), one of Tuscany's gastronomic treats. Even those who initially find the idea of noshing on a hunk of fat off-putting are bound to be won over when sampling it melted over piping-hot *focaccette* (small, flat buns made of wheat flour and cornmeal). This is best tried at **Locanda Apuana** (☎ 0585 76 80 17; www.locandaapuana.com; Via Communale 1, Colonnata; meals €34; ☼ lunch & dinner Tue-Sat, lunch Sun) or **Ristorante Venanzio** (☎ 0585 75 80 62; Piazza Palestro 3, Colonnata; meals €34; ☼ closed Thu & dinner Sun). Once you're hooked, you can also purchase a vacuum-packed slab to take home from one of the many *larderia* (shops that sell *lardo*) in the village.

❦ **MUSEO DEL MARMO & THE MARBLE QUARRIES // MARBLE FROM MUSEUM TO MOUNTAINSIDE**

Opposite the tourist office is the **Museo del Marmo** (Marble Museum; ☎ 0585 84 57 46; Viale XX Settembre; adult/child/concession €4.50/free/2.50; ☼ 9.30am-1pm & 3.30-6pm Mon-Sat May-Sep, 9am-12.30pm & 2.30-5pm Mon-Sat Oct-Apr), which describes extraction from chisel-and-hammer days to the 21st-century's high-powered industrial quarrying. It also has a fascinating audiovisual oral history presentation documenting the lives of quarry workers in the 20th century.

After visiting the museum and Studi di Scultura Carlo Nicoli, make your way up the mountain to any of the three major marble quarries: **Cava di Colonnata, Cava di Torano** and **Cava di Fantiscritti**, all located roughly 5km north of town – follow the signs '*cave de marmo*' (marble quarries). Cava di Fantiscritti is the quarry best geared toward tourism; here, the hard graft is done in the morning, leaving the afternoons free for **tours** (Marmo Tour; ☎ 339 7657470; www.marmotour.com; 35min guided tour adult/under 10yr €7/3; ☼ noon-5pm Mon-Fri Mar, Apr, Sep & Oct, 11am-6.30pm Mon-Fri May-Aug, 11am-6.30pm Sat Mar-Oct) of the cathedral-like quarry hollowed out of the mountainside.

TRANSPORT

TRAIN // The Carrara-Avenza train station is between Marina di Carrara and Carrara; local buses connect it with both. Services arrive from Pisa (€3.50, 45 minutes, every 30 minutes) via Viareggio (€2.40, 25 minutes) and Pietrasanta (€1.80, 15 minutes).

BUS // CAT (☎ 800 223010; www.catspa.it, in Italian) runs frequent bus services between Carrara's bus station on Via del Cavatore and Marina di Carrara (€1.20, 30 minutes) via the Avenza train station (€1.20, 13 minutes). There are also services to Colonnata (€1.20, 27 minutes, nine daily) and to destinations around the Lunigiana.

CAR // From Marina di Massa on the A12, take Viale XX Settembre (direction Carrara).

THE LUNIGIANA
· · · · · ·

This landlocked enclave of territory is bordered to the north and east by the Apennines, to the west by Liguria and to the south by the Apuane Alps and the Garfagnana. The few tourists who make their way here tend to be following the Via Francigena, a medieval pilgrimage route, or visiting the charming town of Pontremoli, which is developing a growing reputation as an off-the-beaten-track gastronomic gem.

PONTREMOLI

pop 7930

It may be small, but this out-of-the-way town has a decidedly grand air, a legacy of its strategic location along the pilgrimage and trading route of Via Francigena (see p148). Its merchants made fortunes in medieval times, and adorned the town with palaces, piazzas and graceful stone bridges. A meander through its charming cobbled streets will take you under colonnaded arches, through former strongholds of opposing Guelph and Ghibelline factions, and past a 17th-century cathedral and an 18th-century theatre.

The Old Town is a long sliver stretching north to south between the Magra and Verde rivers, which have historically served as natural defensive barriers. Presiding over everything is the impressive bulk of the Castello del Piagnaro.

ESSENTIAL INFORMATION

TOURIST OFFICES // Tourist Office
(☎ 0187 83 20 00; infopontremoli@aptmassacarrara.it; Piazza della Repubblica 33; ☼ 10am-1pm & 3-6.30pm) Operates during summer only.

EXPLORING PONTREMOLI

❦ **CASTELLO DEL PIAGNARO //** PONDER ENIGMATIC SIGNS FROM PREHISTORIC TIMES

From central Piazza della Repubblica and adjacent Piazza del Duomo, walk along Via Garibaldi then bear left along Vietata l'Affissione, a pretty alley that continues uphill to Castello del Piagnaro (☎ 0187 83 14 39; www.statuestele.org; adult/6-16yr €4/2; ☼ 9am-12.30pm & 3-6pm Tue-Sun May-Sep, 9am-12.30pm &

2.30-5.30pm Tue-Sun Oct-Apr), a former military barracks that takes its name from the *piagnaro* (stone slabs) that were once widely used to roof Lunigianese buildings. Views across town from the castle are impressive and inside is a small museum showcasing primitive stelae statues found nearby. No-one knows exactly what these stelae, which have been found throughout the Lunigiana, were for – most depict male and female idols and date from around 3000 BC.

❦ **LOCAL SPECIALITIES //** STOCK UP ON LOCAL DELICACIES AND HISTORIC HANDICRAFTS

Pontremoli is surrounded by fecund woods and hills where intensely scented *porcini* mushrooms sprout under heavily loaded chestnut trees. Wild herbs cover nearby fields, and 5000 scattered hives produce the Lunigiana's famous chestnut and acacia honey. These fruits of the forest and other regional delicacies, including Zeri lamb, freshly baked *focaccette* (small flat buns made of wheat flour and cornmeal), crisp and sweet *rotella* apples, boiled pork shoulder, *caciotta* (a delicate cow's-milk cheese), *bigliolo* beans, local olive oil and Colli di Luni wines (the local DOC), are available in the town's enticing produce shops. Look out in particular for Il Castagneto della Manganella (☎ 0187 85 07 07; Via Garibaldi 3; ☼ daily) just off Piazza del Duomo, which specialises in dried *porcini* mushrooms (€8 to €15 per kilogram), and neighbouring Salumeria Angela (Via Garibaldi 11; ☼ Mon-Sat), which specialises in locally produced smallgoods.

For an unusual souvenir or gift, you can't beat a leather-bound pilgrimage journal from Legatoria Artigiana (☎ 0187 83 15 34; Via Garibaldi 8; journals €8-45; ☼ Tue-Sun). Pontremoli has been a famous bookbinding centre since the Middle

Ages, and this shop makes its notebooks by hand using medieval techniques.

GASTRONOMIC HIGHLIGHTS

☙ CAFFÈ DEGLI SVIZZERI €

☎ 0187 83 01 60; Piazza della Repubblica 21-22; ⏱ 7am-8pm Tue-Sun in summer, 7am-1.30pm & 2-8pmTue-Sun rest of year

This historic cafe overlooking Pontremoli's central square opened in 1842 and was given an art nouveau makeover in 1910 that has been lovingly restored. Make sure you sample the cakes here – the *spongata degli svizzeri* (almond cake) and *biscotti della salute* (aniseed biscuits) are exceptionally fine, but pale into insignificance when contrasted with the utter delight of the *amor* (wafer filled with zabaglione-style cream).

☙ OSTERIA DELLA BIETOLA €

☎ 0187 83 19 49; Via Bietola 4; meals €24; ⏱ closed Thu

Seating only 25 and adhering to a somewhat capricious serving policy (if staff feel like closing early or leaving tables empty, that's what happens), this neighbourhood *osteria* is the place to come for *porcini* mushrooms in season and a very tasty rabbit cooked with herbs. In case you're wondering, *bietola* is a type of chard.

☙ TRATTORIA DA BUSSÈ €

☎ 0187 83 13 71; Piazza del Duomo 32; meals €22; ⏱ dinner Mon-Thu, lunch & dinner Sat & Sun

This simple place has been run by the same family since the 1930s, and brands itself as being 'predominantly for Pontremolese'. It serves an almost exclusively regional menu, with treats such as *testaroli al pesto* (crepes served with pesto), *torta d'erbe della lunigiana* (herb pie cooked over coals in a cast-iron pan lined with chestnut leaves to keep the mixture from sticking) and *lasagna bastarde* (broken lasagne sheets made with

wheat and chestnut flour and served with olive oil and *pecorino*) joining plenty of meat dishes on the menu.

TRANSPORT

TRAIN // One direct train per day runs between Pisa and Pontremoli (€6.10, 90 minutes).There are also frequent services to La Spezia (€3.60 to €5.40, 40 to 55 minutes).
BUS // CAT (☎ 800 223010; www.catspa.it, in Italian) runs services to Carrara (€2.50, one hour and 40 minutes, eight daily) via Aulla (€2.50, 40 minutes).
CAR // Take the A15 and SP31 or SS62 from Aulla.

DRIVING TOUR: THE VIA FRANCIGENA

Distance: 32km
Duration: six hours (including lunch)
This medieval pilgrimage route connected Canterbury with Rome. Dating from the second half of the 7th century, it became so popular with pilgrims making their way from Great Britain to the tomb of St Peter in Rome that in the 8th century the Lombard kings commenced a building program along its Lunigiana length, erecting churches, hospices and monasteries offering shelter, succour and protection for pilgrims. This tour explores some of them.

In AD 990 Sigaric, the archbishop of Canterbury, followed the route home after his investiture in Rome, recording his journey in a travelling diary. His journey averaged 20km per day, covering 1700km in total, and took around 80 days. Modern-day pilgrims in cars, on foot and on bicycles make slightly better time, and many opt to limit their pilgrimage to the stages through Tuscany. For information about the route, including route maps and GPS coordinates, go to www.francigenalibrari.beniculturali.it.

From **Pontremoli**, head east to access the SS62 (direction Villafranca and Aulla).

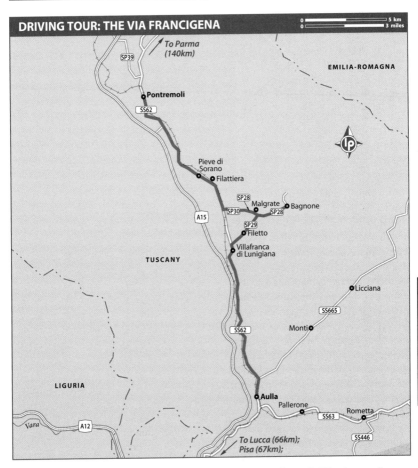

DRIVING TOUR: THE VIA FRANCIGENA

After 8km (around 15 minutes) you will encounter a turn-off (direction Viale della Vittoria) to Filattiera. The Romanesque **Pieve di Sorano** (Pieve di Santo Stefano; 9.30am-12.30pm), a parish church first mentioned in official papal records in 1148, is in the fields just before the town. Built in stone with a traditional *piagnaro* roof and arched architectural details on the exterior, the church incorporates a watchtower, signalling that this was once a fortified stop on the pilgrimage route. Inside, look out for the two prehistoric stellae statues found in the surrounding woods.

Continue through **Filattiera** and continue on the SS62 for approximately 2.5km until you see a turn-off on the left signposted SP30. Turn left here and follow the road for 2.3km; you will notice the hilltop fortress of **Malgrate** on your left. The road soon veers left into the SP28, and after another 2km you will come to **Bagnone**, once an important trading stop on the Via Francigena and now distinctive for its Malnido Castle, parochial church of San Nicolò and excellent eatery **Locanda La Lina** (☎ 0187 42 90 69; Piazza G Marconi 1; meals €40; lunch & dinner

NORTHWESTERN TUSCANY

NORTHWESTERN TUSCANY

Sat-Thu), which specialises in Lunigianese dishes.

From Bagnone, backtrack to the SP28, veer left after 2km (staying on the SP28) and then veer slightly left again after 1.2km onto the SP29 to reach **Filetto**. This tiny, walled medieval town takes its name from the Greek word *filakterion* (fortified place). Park outside the monumental gate and have a wander through the town's piazzas and narrow lanes. In mid-August, visitors flock here from throughout Tuscany for the town's medieval market.

Rejoin the SP29, turn left into the SS62 and drive 1km to reach **Villafranca in Lunigiana**. An important stop on the pilgrim route, it is picturesquely situated on the Magra river and is home to the impressive **Museo Etnografico della Lunigiana** (☎ 0187 49 34 17; Via dei Mulini 1; adult/6-14yr €2.50/1.50; ☼ 9.30am-12.30pm & 3-6pm Jun-Sep, 9.30am-12.30pm Tue-Sat Oct-May, 2.30-5.30pm Sun Oct-May), housed in an old flour mill. A short walk from the museum is **Locanda all'Antico Mulino** (☎ 0187 49 50 00; Piazza S Giovanni 1; meals €22; ☼ lunch & dinner Wed-Mon), an excellent place to sample local specialities including *testaroli, lasagna bastarde* and *torta d'erbe della lunigiana*.

Continue on the SS62 and after 15 or minutes or so you will reach **Aulla**, the largest town in the Lunigiana. Its **Abbazia di San Caprasio** (☼ 9am-12.30pm & 2.30-7pm) was founded in AD 884 and houses the remains of St Caprasio, the hermit monk who inspired the spread of monastic life in Provence from the 5th century.

CENTRAL COAST & ELBA

3 PERFECT DAYS

❦ DAY 1 // DIVE INTO GREAT SEAFOOD

Livorno (p156) does seafood like nowhere else in Tuscany. The raw specimens can be examined bright and early in the cavernous Mercato Centrale (p157). Though it's tempting to buy on the spot and commandeer the nearest kitchen, bide your time until lunch and dinner for perfectly prepared treats such as mussels, crustaceans and the city's famed *cacciucco,* a traditional seafood stew. Memorable Livorno eateries include Cantina Senese, Osteria Buatino, L'Ancora and Osteria La Barrocciaia (p158).

❦ DAY 2 // HINTERLAND CRUISE

Though the coast offers many idle resort and beach options, there are myriad offerings slightly inland. Here you'll find scenic roads, small but worthwhile walled and cliffside towns such as Bolgheri (p160), Suvereto (p161) and Sassetta (p161), and a few exceptional eating options such as Enoteca Tognoni (p161) and Osteria di Suvereto da I'Ciocio (p161).

❦ DAY 3 // THE ELBA EXPERIENCE

Truthfully Elba (p166) can satisfactorily fill several days of idleness at fine campsites and beaches, though activities abound. Inland hike and bike trails cleave through the island, dive sites pepper the coast, some with millennia-old shipwrecks, and there are several sea kayaking sites. A meandering circumnavigation of the island by car, with stops at Strada del Vino cellars and any number of outstanding restaurants like Osteria del Piano (p173), Il Ristorante Scaraboci (p169) and finally Cafescondido (p172) in Portoferraio, is a nice middling option.

CENTRAL COAST & ELBA

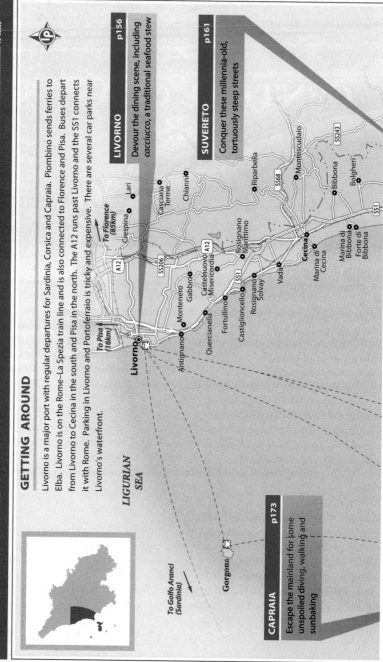

GETTING AROUND

Livorno is a major port with regular departures for Sardinia, Corsica and Capraia. Piombino sends ferries to Elba. Livorno is on the Rome–La Spezia train line and is also connected to Florence and Pisa. Buses depart from Livorno to Cecina in the south and Pisa in the north. The A12 runs past Livorno and the SS1 connects it with Rome. Parking in Livorno and Portoferraio is tricky and expensive. There are several car parks near Livorno's waterfront.

LIVORNO p156
Devour the dining scene, including *cacciucco*, a traditional seafood stew

SUVERETO p161
Conquer these millennia-old, tortuously steep streets

CAPRAIA p173
Escape the mainland for some unspoiled diving, walking and sunbaking

LIGURIAN SEA

To Florence (85km)

To Pisa (16km)

To Golfo Aranci (Sardinia)

Gorgona

Livorno

Lari
Crespina
Casciana Terme
Chianni
Antignano
Montenero
Gabbro
Castelnuovo
Misericordia
Quercianella
Fortullino
Castiglioncello
Rosignano Solvay
Rosignano Marittimo
Vada
Cecina
Marina di Cecina
Marina di Bibbona
Forte di Bibbona
Riparbella
Montescudaio
Bibbona
Bolgheri

A12
SS206
SS1
SS568
SS551
SS243

20 km
10 miles

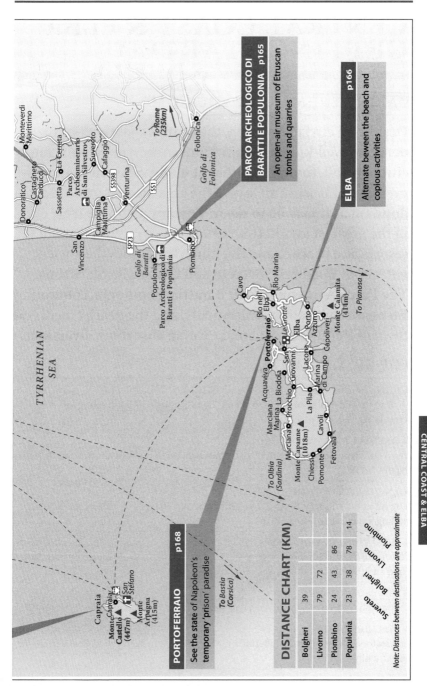

TYRRHENIAN SEA

Monteverdi Marittimo
Castagneto Carducci
La Cerreta
Parco Archeominerario di San Silvestro
Cafaggio
Donoratico
Sassetta
Campiglia Marittima
Venturina
San Vincenzo
Populonia
Piombino
SS398
SS1
SP23
To Rome (235km)
Follonica
Golfo di Follonica
Golfo di Baratti
Parco Archeologico di Baratti e Populonia

PARCO ARCHEOLOGICO DI BARATTI E POPULONIA   p165

An open-air museum of Etruscan tombs and quarries

ELBA   p166

Alternate beween the beach and copious activities

Cavo
Rio Marina
Bio nell'Elba
Rio nell'
Elba
To Pianosa
Monte Calamita (414m)
Porto Azzurro
Capoliveri
Le Grotte
San Giovanni
Portoferraio
Acquaviva
Marciana
Marina La Biodola
Procchio
Marina di Campo
Lacona
La Pila
Cavoli
Monte Capanne (1018m)
Fetovaia
Chiessi
Pomonte
Marciana
Elba
To Olbia (Sardinia)

PORTOFERRAIO   p168

See the state of Napoleon's temporary prison' paradise

To Bastia (Corsica)

Capraia
Monte Castello (447m)
Capraia
San Stefano
Monte Arpagna (415m)

DISTANCE CHART (KM)

	Suvereto	Bolgheri	Livorno	Piombino
Bolgheri	39			
Livorno	79	72		
Piombino	24	43	86	
Populonia	23	38	78	14

Note: Distances between destinations are approximate

CENTRAL COAST & ELBA
GETTING STARTED

MAKING THE MOST OF YOUR TIME

Despite an enviable setting, the central coast isn't burdened by well-known destinations. Anonymous working cities prevail, though significant medieval towns and well-preserved Etruscan sites give the area modest pride. Redundant as it may be to say in Tuscany, eating is truly one of the greatest joys in this region. The coast offers modest resorts and beaches and the hinterland hides the ancient villages of Bolgheri, Suvereto and Campiglia Marittima. The Parco Archeologico di Baratti e Populonia, containing Etruscan civilisation enticements, and the nearby medieval town of Populonia Alta make for an absorbing diversion.

TOP RESTAURANTS

❦ **CANTINA SENESE**
Livorno's wonderfully unpretentious and friendly neighbourhood eatery serves up sensational mussels (p159).

❦ **OSTERIA LA BARROCCIAIA**
The worst-kept dining secret in Livorno may be hard to find but it is well worth seeking out (p159).

❦ **ENOTECA TOGNONI**
Stop off in the village of Bolghieri for wild boar and 40 types of wine by the glass, including a star Super Tuscan (p161).

❦ **IL GARIBALDI INNAMORATO**
The creative fish-centric offerings of Il Garibaldi Innamorato are touted by both Slow Food and the Italian Celiac Association (p162).

❦ **CAFESCONDIDO**
The raucous cafe gives no sign of the delicious food that's served in the back room (p172).

❦ **LA LIBERTARIA**
The seafood dished up at La Libertaria may be enough to keep you in Portoferraio for an extra night (p173).

GETTING AWAY FROM IT ALL

Even in the off-season, the coast is a busy place. Retreat to the hinterlands or consider the shoulder seasons (April, May, September and October).

★ **Agriturismi stays at Le Fornacine and La Cerreta** Quiet, great value and within striking distance of the entire coast (p401).

★ **Road between Sassetta and Suvereto** This undulating road has been declared the 'second best for cycling and motor-cycling' in the country by Italian cycling journalist Enrico Caracciolo.

★ **Trekking tours of Gorgona** It takes some planning, but the effort pays off with some of the least tramped terrain in Tuscany (p174).

TOP EXPERIENCES

❦ **PARCO ARCHEOLOGICO DI BARATTI E POPULONIA**
A guided tour will reveal the park's excellent Etruscan ruins (p165).

❦ **AGRITURISMO LA CERRETA**
Discover Tuscan lifestyle philosophy at an educational biodynamic farm-stay (p401).

❦ **EAT, DRINK LIVORNO**
Even by Tuscan standards, eating here is both superb and affordable (p158).

❦ **CENTRO TREKKING ISOLA D'ELBA**
This outfit leads hiking, biking and kayaking excursions around Elba, Capraia, Giglio and Pianosa (p169).

CENTRAL COAST BEACH TOWNS

There are coastal towns that have decent beaches, then there are clumps of resorts masquerading as 'towns'. Here are a few of the more satisfying beach towns:

★ **Castiglioncello** (p162) Agreeably unpre-tentious and home to one of our favourite sleeping options on the coast, Pensione Bartoli (p402). The small sandy beaches on the north side of town are the best, although sunbed rental is expensive.

★ **San Vincenzo** (p163) Popular in sum-mer with Italian visitors. There's not much to do, but sandy beaches stretch to the north and south of town. Getting a room in summer is challenging and getting one inexpensively even more so.

★ **Golfo di Baratti** (p163) This is one of the prettiest mainland beaches, though it's often windy and so a favourite with windsurfers.

RESOURCES

★ **Costa degli Etruschi** (www.costadegli etruschi.it) Comprehensive guide to the Etruscan Coast

★ **Provincia di Livorno** (www.provincia .livorno.it in Italian) Official website of Livorno Province

★ **Isola di Capraia** (www.isoladicapraia.it, in Italian) Information for Capraia Island

★ **Isola d'Elba** (www.elbalink.it) Poorly organ-ised, yet voluminous information for Elba

★ **Tuscany Island** (www.aptelba.it) The Tuscan Archipelago's website for Elba

LIVORNO

. . . . . .

pop 161,000

Tuscany's second-largest city is a quintessential port town. Though first impressions are rarely kind, this is a 'real' city where one can buy socks (try that in San Gimignano!) and meet genuinely curious, warm locals. It really does grow on you. Low-impact diversions such as the seafood, reputedly the best on the Tyrrhenian coast, and the popular beaches that start south of the city make a pre/postferry layover agreeable. Leg stretching can be done in the worthwhile, if ambitiously labelled, 'Little Venice' district.

The earliest references to Livorno date from 1017. The port was in the hands of Pisa and then Genoa for centuries, until Florence took control in 1421. It was still tiny – by the 1550s it boasted a grand total of 480 permanent residents. All that changed under Cosimo I de' Medici, who converted the scrawny settlement into a heavily fortified coastal bastion.

It was declared a free port in the 17th century, sparking swift development. By the end of the 18th century it was a vital, cosmopolitan city, functioning as one of the main staging posts for British and Dutch merchants who were then operating between Western Europe and the Middle East, with a permanent population of around 80,000. The 19th century again saw the city swell with notable development in the economy, arts and culture.

As one of Fascist Italy's main naval bases, the city was heavily bombed during WWII then rebuilt with a largely unimaginative face that only a sea captain could love. Its bizarre anglicised name, Leghorn, is rarely used – and only then by impish guidebooks.

ESSENTIAL INFORMATION

EMERGENCIES // Hospital (☎ 0586 22 31 11; Viale Alfieri 36)
TOURIST OFFICES // Tourist Kiosk (☎ 0586 20 46 11; www.costadeglietruschi.it; Piazza del Municipio; ☷ 9am-5pm Apr-Oct, 9.30am-12.30pm & 2pm-5pm Mon-Sat Nov-Mar) Tourist Office (☎ 0586 89 53 20; ☷ Jun-Sep) Near the main ferry terminal at Stazione Marittima.

ORIENTATION

From the main train station on Piazza Dante walk westwards along Viale Carducci, Via de Larderel, then Via Grande into central Piazza Grande, Livorno's main square.

EXPLORING LIVORNO

After exhausting Livorno's offerings, consider a beach flop on the Etruscan Coast (Costa degli Etruschi). Pebbly but popular beaches stretch for some way south of town. A few grand old seaside villas along the way merit more than a glance. Bus 1 from the main train station heads down the coast road.

♥ PICCOLA VENEZIA // SAVOUR A LITTLE TASTE OF VENICE

The area known as Piccola Venezia (Little Venice) contains small canals built using Venetian methods of reclaiming land from the sea. What this area lacks in gondolas and tourists, it makes up with a certain shabby charm. The waterways here are flanked by faded, peeling apartments that are brightly decorated with strings of washing hanging out to dry. The area's primary attraction is the Fortezza Nuova (New Fort; admission free), built for the Medici court in the late 16th century. The interior of the fort is now a park and little else remains except the sturdy outer walls. **Fortezza Vecchia** (Old Fort), constructed 60 years earlier on the site of an 11th-century building, is on the waterfront. Deeply cracked and crumbling, it looks as though it might give up and slide into the sea at any moment. Admission is free.

❦ MERCATO CENTRALE // FOOD APPRECIATION WITHOUT ACTUALLY EATING

The **Mercato Centrale** (Via Buontalenti; 🕙 6am-2pm Mon-Sat), Livorno's magnificent late-19th-century, 95m-long neoclassical food market, miraculously survived Allied WWII bombing intact. The market is arresting both gastronomically and architecturally, though scaffolding from a plodding restoration makes it difficult to fully appreciate the structure's beauty. Market stalls sell food and beverages to satisfy any self-catering need, though mere browsing is agreeable enough, particularly in the fish section, which should charge admission to view its oddities.

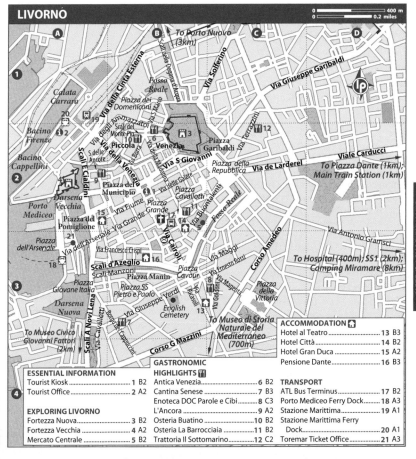

LIVORNO

CENTRAL COAST & ELBA

ESSENTIAL INFORMATION	
Tourist Kiosk	1 B2
Tourist Office	2 A2

EXPLORING LIVORNO	
Fortezza Nuova	3 B2
Fortezza Vecchia	4 A2
Mercato Centrale	5 B2

GASTRONOMIC HIGHLIGHTS 🍴	
Antica Venezia	6 B2
Cantina Senese	7 B3
Enoteca DOC Parole e Cibi	8 C3
L'Ancora	9 A2
Osteria Buatino	10 B2
Osteria La Barrocciaia	11 B2
Trattoria Il Sottomarino	12 C2

ACCOMMODATION 🏠	
Hotel al Teatro	13 B3
Hotel Città	14 B2
Hotel Gran Duca	15 A2
Pensione Dante	16 B3

TRANSPORT	
ATL Bus Terminus	17 B2
Porto Mediceo Ferry Dock	18 A3
Stazione Marittima	19 A1
Stazione Marittima Ferry Dock	20 A1
Toremar Ticket Office	21 A3

ACCOMMODATION

Unfortunately, the region is not well endowed with high-value accommodation. A full listing can be found in the Accommodation chapter, p391. Livorno, the resorts on the coast and Elba (in high season) have a particularly dispiriting price-to-value incongruity. If you have your own wheels, consider an off-the-beaten-track *agriturismo* (farm-stay accommodation), which can be a far more memorable experience.

★ **Agriturismo La Cerreta** (p401) A few kilometres east of Sassetta, La Cerreta strongly promotes the classic Tuscan lifestyle philosophy.

★ **Pensione Bartoli** (p402) Located in the unpretentious seaside town of Castiglioncello, this guest house offers unbeatable value.

★ **Agriturismo Le Fornacine** (p401) Situated outside Bibbona, this *agriturismo*'s nearby sights and activities include thermal pools, walks, beaches, mountain biking and day trips, all meticulously researched by the affable hostess.

♥ MUSEO DI STORIA NATURALE DEL MEDITERRANEO // LAY HANDS ON THE NATURAL SCIENCES

Livorno's friendly and hands-on **Museo di Storia Naturale del Mediterraneo** (☎ 0586 26 67 11; www.provincia.livorno.it, in Italian; Via Roma 234; adult/child €10/5; ☻ 9am-1pm Tue-Fri, 3-7pm Tue, Thu, Sat & Sun) is an exhaustive, first-rate museum experience for the natural sciences. Temporary exhibits rotate continually, while the highlight of the permanent collection is a 20m-long common whale skeleton called Annie.

♥ MUSEO CIVICO GIOVANNI FATTORI // STUDY ITALIAN IMPRESSIONISTS OF THE 19TH CENTURY

The **Museo Civico Giovanni Fattori** (☎ 0586 80 80 01; museofattori@comune.livorno.it; Via San Jacopo in Acquaviva 65; admission €4; ☻ 10am-1pm & 4-7pm Tue-Sun), in a pretty park, features works by the 19th-century Italian Impressionist Macchiaioli school, led by Livorno-born Giovanni Fattori. The group, inspired by the Parisian Barbizon school, flouted stringent academic art conventions and worked directly from

nature, emphasising immediacy and freshness through patches, or 'stains' *(macchia)*, of colour. Though the style was both noted and criticised for its 'lack of finish', it did not go nearly as far dissolving form into light as the simultaneous work done by French Impressionists. The museum often hosts temporary exhibitions.

GASTRONOMIC HIGHLIGHTS

Livorno's primary 'activity' is touring its abundance of affordable and exceptional restaurants. Be sure to tuck into a *cacciucco*, a remarkable mixed seafood stew and the pride of many local eateries. For self-catering nirvana, visit Livorno's magnificent Mercato Centrale (p157) to load up on all necessities, including produce, sandwich makings and seafood so fresh they think they're still swimming.

♥ ANTICA VENEZIA €€
☎ 0586 88 73 53; Piazza dei Domenicani; meals €19-23; ☻ Mon-Sat

A dog-eared, pen-written menu filled with tempting dishes can be produced, with difficulty, if requested, but servers prefer to launch straight into the catch-of-the-day specials, usually negating the need for further consideration. A giant *cacciucco* costs €16. The atmosphere is attractively upbeat and lunches get hectic.

☙ CANTINA SENESE €

☎ 0586 89 02 39; Borgo dei Cappuccini 95; meals €17-20; ☺ Mon-Sat

Food- and value-conscious harbour workers are the first to fill the long wooden tables at this wonderfully un-pretentious and friendly eatery, with neighbourhood families arriving later. Ordering is frequently done via faith in one's server, rather than by menu. The mussels are exceptional, as is the *cacciucco di pesce,* both served with piquant garlic bread.

☙ ENOTECA DOC PAROLE E CIBI €€

☎ 0586 88 75 83; Via Goldoni 40-44; meals €30-35; ☺ Tue-Sun

Changes its menu weekly; you can enjoy fresh pasta dishes, superb seafood and a variety of carpaccio served with bread that – for once – is entirely worth that vexing *coperto* (cover charge in restaurants). The wines are excellent; it styles itself as an *enoteca* (wine bar), *olioteca* (oil) and *whiskyteca* so you can be confident of getting top-quality lubricants, whatever your preference. For dessert, a sugary, chocolate pastry with vanilla cream is only €3.60.

☙ L'ANCORA €€

☎ 0586 88 14 01; Scali delle Ancore 10; meals €28-35; ☺ Wed-Mon

Though the canal-side terrace is a white-hot ticket in good weather, settling for a table in the elegantly simple 17th-century, Medici-built, barrel-ceilinged,

brick boat house isn't exactly a hardship. You can get *cacciucco* here, but the *carbonara di mare* (seafood and pasta in white sauce) is the family's pride and joy. Though reasonably priced, this is where locals send visitors looking for a 'nice' meal.

☙ OSTERIA BUATINO €€

☎ 338 4540190; Scali del Monte Pio 11; meals €28-32; ☺ Mon-Sat

The short, handwritten menu fixates on typical Tuscan and Livorno cuisine. Hold off on ordering your *secondo* (second course) until you've seen the pasta servings, which are especially generous. The Impressionist art on the walls and blue fish light fixtures will drive conversation during the added wait, should you have the stomach capacity to continue.

☙ OSTERIA LA BARROCCIAIA €

☎ 0586 88 26 37; Piazza Cavallotti 13; meals €20; ☺ Tue-Sat

Worst-kept dining secret in Livorno it may be, but locating Barrocciaia still takes a careful eye what with it being the most inconspicuous facade and well-hidden sign in Piazza Cavallotti. Big sandwiches (€5) are sold out of the tiny front room, but with luck and timing you can score a table and enjoy the real reason every local speaks of La Barrocciaia with reverence. The menu fluctuates continually, as does the art on the walls, with the exception of Grandpa's picture, quietly supervising the third generation of management.

☙ TRATTORIA IL SOTTOMARINO €€

☎ 0586 88 70 25; Via Terrazzini 48; meals €33-38; ☺ Wed-Sun

Another neighbourhood affair, the service borders on sibling familiarity and the possibly satirical decor of dated

Livornese tourism pictures, battleships and navel knick-knackery underscores the casualness of it all. Appropriate of a place calling itself 'the submarine', very little on the menu is not enriched by marine life, including the immense *cacciucco di mamma Vinicia* (€14).

TRANSPORT

BOAT // Livorno is a major port. Regular departures for Sardinia and Corsica leave from Calata Carrara, beside the **Stazione Marittima**. Ticket prices vary wildly depending on date and time of travel. Ferries to Capraia and Gorgona depart from **Porto Mediceo**, a smaller terminal near Piazza dell'Arsenale. Some services to Sardinia depart from **Porto Nuovo**, about 3km north of the city along Via Sant'Orlando. Ferry companies operating from Porto Mediceo include **Toremar** (☎ 199 123199; www.toremar.it, in Italian), with daily services to Capraia (€14.20, 2½ hours), and **Lloyd Sardegna** (☎ 0565 22 23 00; www.lloydsardegna.it) with daily ferries to Sardinia (Olbia; €15 to €45, 11 hours). From Stazione Marittima **Corsica Ferries/Sardinia Ferries** (☎ 019 215511; www.corsicaferries.com, www.sardiniaferries.com) offers two or three services per week (daily in summer) to Bastia, Corsica (deck-class €28 to €36, four hours), and four services per week (daily in summer) to Golfo Aranci, Sardinia (deck-class €32 to €40, six hours express, nine hours regular). **Moby** (☎ 199 30 30 40; www.moby.it) has services to Bastia, Corsica (€19 to €46, three to four hours) and Olbia, Sardinia (€16 to €83, eight to 12 hours).

BUS // **ATL** (☎ 0586 84 74 08; www.atl.livorno.it) Buses depart from cathedral for Cecina (€2.90, one hour, about hourly) **CPT** (www.cpt.pisa.it, in Italian) Buses to Pisa (€2.50, 55 minutes, half-hourly to hourly). ATL bus 1 runs from the main train station to Porto Medicedo. To reach Stazione Marittima, take bus 7 or electric bus PB1, PB2 or PB3. All of these bus services pass through Piazza Grande.

CAR // The A12 runs past the city and the SS1 connects Livorno with Rome.

PARKING // There are several car parks near the waterfront. There's free parking south and east of the centre, but it's elusive and a good hike.

TRAIN // Livorno is on the Rome–La Spezia line and is also connected to Florence and Pisa. Sample destinations and fares include Rome (€16.65 to €29.90, three to four hours, 12 daily), Florence (€6.50, 1½ hours, 16 daily) and Pisa (€1.80, 15 minutes, frequent). Trains are a lot less frequent to Stazione Marittima, the station for the ports, but buses to/from the main station run quite regularly.

THE ETRUSCAN COAST

· · · · · ·

The province of Livorno stretches down the coast to just beyond Piombino and the ferry to the island of Elba. Several attractive small towns are scattered within the hilly hinterland, while the slender plain between coast and hills offers the possibility of discovering some of Tuscany's lesser-known, but often very good, wines.

Overall, Tuscany's beaches are basic bucket-and-spade, though some have pebbles rather than sand. Watch out for the prices: you can fork out plenty for the privilege of a sunbed and brolly (around €8).

DRIVING TOUR: LIVORNO TO PIOMBINO

Distance: 116km
Duration: six to eight hours
It'll take nearly an hour to fight traffic out of Livorno and speed past legions of beachgoers to **Bolgheri**. Its castle, taking in the city gate and Romanesque Chiesa di SS Giacomo e Cristoro, was restructured towards the end of the 19th century. The village itself has been over-heritaged with pricey shops, though the house specialities of pork and wild boar

DRIVING TOUR: LIVORNO TO PIOMBINO

Gherardesca clan that once controlled the surrounding area. (The stronghold was turned into a mansion in the 18th century.) The 19th-century poet Giosuè Carducci spent much of his childhood here.

A winding, forested hill road leads to the tiny hamlet of **Sassetta**. Approaching from Castagneto, the houses here seem to be hanging on to their perches for dear life. There is a large map at the village entrance showing the main hikes in the area. Just east is the biodynamic 'harmonic project' and educational farmstay **Agriturismo La Cerreta** (p401).

Italian cycling journalist Enrico Caracciolo has declared the undulating road between Sasetta and **Suvereto** as the second best for cycling and motorcycling in the country, with the Amalfi Coast road (during low season!) being number one. Even a short walk on Suvereto's tortuous streets and steep stairways will quicken one's breathing. If that doesn't do it, then perhaps the accolades of being a 'Slow Food town' (p385), 'wine town' and 'oil town' will quicken the metabolic functions. It has been a busy centre since well before the year 1000. For a while it was the seat of a bishopric, only incorporated into the Tuscan grand duchy in 1815. Today, it's a well-tended place where flowers and plants contrast with the soft tones of brick and stone. There's a **tourist office** (☎ 0565 82 93 04; ☽ 10am-12.30pm & 5-10pm Mon-Sat, 5-10pm Sun Jun-Sep, closed Oct-May) on Piazza Gramsci, though if you haven't already eaten, you may want to proceed directly to **Osteria di Suvereto da l'Ciocio** (☎ 0565 82 99 47; www.osteriadisuvereto.it, in Italian; Loc Colombaia 31; meals €32-38), about 500m outside the historic centre on the road to the sport centre, for a meal passionately endorsed by locals and Slow Food. Or settle for a drink and snacks at

at **Enoteca Tognoni** (☎ 0565 76 20 01; www.enotecatognoni.it; Via Lauretta 5; meals €25-35; ☽ Thu-Tue) are worth a stop. It also serves 40 types of wine by the glass, including the locally produced and internationally famous 'Super Tuscan' Sassicaia at €20 per glass!

A densely wooded minor road south of Bolgheri rolls between vineyards and olive groves, then climbs up into the hills to reach **Castagneto Carducci**. Behind its town walls lies a web of steep, narrow lanes crowded in by brooding houses and dominated by the castle of the

CENTRAL COAST & ELBA

Enoteca dei Difficili (☎ 0565 82 80 18; Via San Leonardo; meals €15), an atmospheric brick-and-beam spot with a blockbuster selection of wines.

From Suvereto, drop down onto the plains along the SS398, signed Piombino, for about 5km, then turn off right to head back into the hills. Aim for the dun-coloured stone houses of **Campiglia Marittima**, another near-intact medieval town, with its roots in Etruscan times. The one building of special interest is the **Palazzo Pretorio**, up steep Via Cavour, which, these days, is also a wine information centre. Long the seat of government, its main facade, plastered with an assortment of coats of arms, resembles the bulky medalled chest of some banana-republic general.

There's precious little in **Piombino** to divert you from getting straight onto the ferry to Elba (p166), but should it be mealtime, seek out **Il Garibaldi Innamorato** (☎ 0565 4 94 10; Via Guiseppe Garibaldi 5; meals €28-33; ☽ Tue-Sun) on a tiny street near Piazza Bovio. Adorned with a variety of Garibaldi portraits and leftover equipment from its former incarnation as a butcher's shop, the day's creative fish-centric offerings are related orally by an attentive server, severely testing your Italian, and rewarding you with cuisine touted by both Slow Food and the Italian Celiac Association.

CASTIGLIONCELLO

This small seaside resort is agreeably unpretentious. In the late 19th century

INTERVIEW: ENRICO CARACCIOLO

Can you offer some tips for a memorable cycling holiday in Tuscany? Go slow, eat well and drink better. Many foreign cyclists arrive in Italy equipped with hydration backpacks. It's totally unnecessary. There are many bars in each village where it is possible to stop for a light meal, drink, good coffee, fresh water, sodas or fruit juice. Finally, go slow, look around, and be ready for hilly roads. There are also many excellent organised tours, like ex-pro American racer Andy Hampsten, who runs bike tours from Castagneto Carducci (www.cinghiale.com), including farm visits and cooking classes.

Many cyclists bring their own bikes to Tuscany. How good is breakdown support in the towns/villages? Bike racing has always been very popular in Italy, though travelling by bike is a recent trend. It's very easy to find a bike shop or mechanic in the villages and towns. In my town, Donoratico, there is a fantastic bike shop called **Ciclosport** (☎ 0565 77 71 49; www.goodbiketours.com; Via Aurelia 25) that is very popular with touring cyclists.

Are there road etiquette rules and general tips that foreign cyclists should know when riding in Tuscany? Car drivers are usually accustomed to sharing the road with cyclists, but keep to the right and ride in single file. Obviously, it's better to ride on country roads than in towns, where the traffic is sometimes chaotic. Don't plan your itinerary by only studying a map. You must ask people about road conditions. The map will not tell you if that road is good for cyclists or busy with speeding trucks and cars. For example, the Cecina–Volterra (SS68) and Siena–Grosseto (SS223) roads can be very dangerous. One last tip: on Saturdays and Sundays there aren't any trucks on the roads.

Enrico Caracciolo is a journalist, avid cyclist, occasional bike tour guide and the designer of over 20 Etruscan Coast cycling tours (p164). He lives in Donoratico, on the Tuscan coast.

Digo Martelli, the Italian critic and patron of the arts, held court here. He would play host to the Florentine Impressionist artists of the period, giving birth to the artistic movement known as La Scuola di Castiglioncello. The small sandy beaches on the north side of town are the best, although sunbed rental is expensive (from €8 per day).

There are frequent trains to/from Livorno (€2.40, 25 minutes) and you'll find the **tourist office** (☎ 0586 75 48 90; Via Aurelia 632; ☼ 9.30am-12.30pm & 4-6pm) within the station.

❤ CAFFÈ GINORI // PEOPLE-WATCH ON THE PIAZZA

With its large, shaded terrace, redolent of the best of the 1950s, **Caffè Ginori** (☎ 0586 75 90 55; Piazza della Vittoria; ☼ daily Mar-Oct, Fri-Wed Nov-Feb) is where locals drop by to jaw at the bar. Apart from the imprudently aged gelato, snacks here are delish. You can see why it was a favourite hangout of Italian heart-throb Marcello Mastroianni, who had a summer villa in town.

SAN VINCENZO

The moderately attractive seaside town of San Vincenzo is popular in summer with Italian visitors. There is a small **tourist office** (☎ 0565 70 15 33; Via B Alliata) here. Yachties can park their vessels in the marina, but there's not much to do after that. Sandy beaches stretch to the north and south of town; to the south beaches are backed by *macchia* (scrubland) and pine plantations.

❤ PARCO ARCHEOMINERARIO DI SAN SILVESTRO // PONDER 3000 YEARS OF MINING HISTORY

The **Parco Archeominerario di San Silvestro** (☎ 0565 83 86 80; admission €15; ☼ 10.30am-5.30pm Tue-Sun Jun-Sep, 10am-6pm Sat & Sun Mar-May & Oct, 10am-4pm Sun Nov-Feb) is just a few kilometres inland from San Vincenzo. Around 50m before the turn-off to the park entrance, a sunken lane on the right, signed *forni fusori,* leads to the remains of some Etruscan smelting ovens, once used for copper production.

The park tells the story of the area's 3000-year mining history. The highlight for most is **Rocca di San Silvestro,** a medieval mining town abandoned in the 14th century. The surrounding Temperino mines produced copper and lead, some used for the mints of Lucca and later Pisa.

There are two guided tours, one of Rocca di San Silvestro, the other to the Temperino mine and museum. The latter is in the same building as the ticket office near the entrance, while Rocca di San Silvestro is accessible via a new underground train that ferries visitors through the mines on the way. Extreme claustrophobics can opt for the half-hour walk. Tours leave approximately every hour.

❤ RISTORANTE LA BARCACCINA // EAT SEAFOOD BEACHSIDE

If you want to enjoy seafood with a view, drop in to **Ristorante La Barcaccina** (☎ 0565 70 19 11; www.barcaccina.it; Via Tridentina; meals €40-50; ☼ Thu-Tue) where the food matches the fine views over a great stretch of pale golden sand. On the smart side, it's not the kind of place where you stroll in wearing your beachwear. From the coast road (not the SS1), follow signs to the parking area near the Parco Comunale.

GOLFO DI BARATTI

A minor road leads off the SP23 and heads southwest for 5km to the Golfo di Baratti, one of the Tuscan coast's prettiest mainland beaches. Although, as the weird and wonderful postures of the trees attest, it's often windy – and so a favourite with windsurfers.

❦ POPULONIA // WANDER A PRIVATELY OWNED HAMLET
Populonia Alta is a three-street hamlet still owned by a single family. Walled in and protected by its 15th-century castle, the settlement grew up on the site of a Pisan watchtower. Its small, privately owned **Etruscan Museum** (adult/child €1.50/1) has a few local finds; opening times are sporadic. For superb views south along the coast, climb the **Torre di Populonia**

CYCLING THE ETRUSCAN COAST

The central coast is a favourite for cyclists, particularly along parts of the Strada del Vino (wine route), as opposed to the relatively drab coastal flats. Those not willing or able to haul their bikes from home can rent bikes through www.ecorent.net or, in some cases, through *agriturismi* (a partial list of such places is available at www.tuscanyaccommodation.com). A wonderfully conceived and detailed list of routes with maps can be found at www.costadeglietruschi.it, including accommodation options that cater to cyclists. Some of the more appealing, easy-to-moderate routes on this list:

★ **Full immersion in nature** – An entirely dirt-route affair, this 13.2km loop starts in the car park of Agriturismo La Cerreta (p401), east of Sassetta, and undulates through Casetta Fiorentina, past Podere I Colli and Podere La Pieve, where the landscape scenery peaks. Proceed downhill to the Lodano river valley and a small lake and back around towards Podere I Colli again. The signage gets pretty bad, but you'll eventually find a stony, tree-lined road heading down to Pian delle Vigne then left again towards Podere La Cerreta.

★ **Montenero: in the silence of the Livorno hills** – Requiring slightly more fitness, this is a convenient 20.5km lasso-loop route, starting at the Sanctuary of Montenero (about 10km south of Livorno), initially heading along Via del Poggio, then climbing past the small town of Castello. After transferring to a dirt road, proceed downhill, then ford a stream which you then follow along a flat road, curving along the picturesque Botro Quarata and Chioma valleys. After Palazzine, a rise leads to a wide firebreak, then a descent on a wide gravel road. The following climb ends with a view of Livorno and the coast. Going downhill, you reach an asphalt road heading back to Via del Poggio, then your starting point at the Sanctuary of Montenero.

★ **From the coast to the Val di Cornia** – A moderately difficult, 63.5km loop that includes the sensational run between Sassetta and Suvereto. Starting in Donoratico, an easy warm-up through Il Bambolo, San Giusto and Castagneto Carducci leads to the climb to Sassetta. Soon after, the bending drop into the Val di Cornia begins. Passing scrubland then into the valley itself, you sail past a series of olive grove–lined bends and into Suvereto. It's a gentle ride from here into San Lorenzo, then after passing the Petra wine cellar, a short climb and descent lead past Casalappi then Cafaggio. Next an unrelenting 4km climb leads to Campiglia Marittima. An exhilarating downhill takes you the remaining distance to the coast and San Vincenzo where it's a further, flat stretch back to Donoratico.

CENTRAL COAST & ELBA

(adult/child €2/1; ⊙ 9.30am-noon & 2.30-7pm), north of the museum. Among several craft workshops along the main street, the gallery at No 19 has a permanent exhibition of glass sculptures and creative lamps by artist Laura Pescae and her daughter.

Next to the car park is the **Etruscan acropolis** (⊙ 9am-7pm) of ancient Populonia. If your Italian is up to it, join a guided tour (every half-hour). The digs have revealed the foundations of an Etruscan temple dating to the 2nd century BC, along with its adjacent buildings.

❦ **PARCO ARCHEOLOGICO DI BARATTI E POPULONIA // STEP BACK IN TIME AMID ETRUSCAN TOMBS**

Inland from Populonia is the **Parco Archeologico di Baratti e Populonia** (☎ 0565 2 90 02; www.parchivaldicornia.it; Populonia; whole park adult/child/family €15/10/39, 1 sector adult/child €9/5; ⊙ 10am-6pm Jul & Aug, to 6pm Tue-Sun Mar-Jun & Sep-Oct, to 4pm Sat & Sun Nov-Feb) where several Etruscan tombs have been unearthed. Most interesting are the circular tombs in the Necropoli di San Cerbone, between the coast road and the visitors centre, which sells an excellent guidebook in English (€12). The Via delle Cave is a signed trail through shady woodland that passes by the quarries from which the soft ochre sandstone was extracted and into which tombs were later cut. Allow one to two hours to see the visitors centre and the Necropoli or as much as five hours to thoroughly wander the full grounds, including the hands-on pottery exhibit in the Centre of Experimental Archaeology. Good shoes and a sun hat are a must. Between March and October, there are guided tours (included in the admission fee) for each area or you can wander at will.

PARCO NAZIONALE DELL' ARCIPELAGO TOSCANO

· · · · · ·

A local legend tells, when Venus rose from the waves, seven precious stones fell from her tiara, creating seven islands off the Tuscan coast. They range in size from the 224 sq km of Elba, the largest, to tiny Gorgona, at just 2.23 sq km. A national park protects the delicate ecosystems of the islands as well as the 600 sq km of sea that washes around them, making it Europe's largest protected marine area.

Here, typical Mediterranean fish abound and rare species, such as the wonderfully named Neptune's shaving brush seaweed, unique to the archipelago, cling to life. The monk seal, driven from the other islands by human presence, still gambols in the deep underwater ravines off Montecristo. The islands serve as an essential rest stop for birds migrating between Europe and Africa. The shy red partridge survives on Elba and Pianosa and the archipelago supports over a third of the world's population of the equally uncommon Corsican seagull, adopted as the national park's symbol.

Toremar (p160) operates boats to the islands of Capraia and Gorgona from Livorno.

TRANSPORT

BOAT // A daily Toremar boat to Capraia sails from Livorno (see p160). On most days there is also a return trip but triple-check before you go. The one-way fare is €14.20. In summer, there are excursions from Elba to Capraia. Elba is an easy ferry journey from Piombino. If you arrive in Piombino by train, take a connecting train on to the port. Boats to Portoferraio are most frequent, while some call in at Rio Marina. Boats are run by **Moby** and **Toremar**. Unless it's a summer weekend or the middle of August, when queues can form, simply buy a ticket at the port. Fares (€10 to €18 per person, €35 to €49 per small car) vary according to season. Toremar also operates a passenger-only hydrofoil service (€14 to €17, 40 minutes) year-round and, between June and August, a fast vehicle and passenger service (car with two passengers from €69.20 return) to Portoferraio.

AIR // Most folk opt for the ferry to Elba, but there's a small **airport** (☎ 0565 97 60 11) at La Pila, just outside Marina di Campo. **Elbafly** (☎ 0565 9 19 61; www.elbafly.it) flies to and from Pisa, Bologna, Bastia, Cuneo and Milan (Malpensa), mid-June to mid-September.

ELBA

pop 31,000

Napoleon would think twice about fleeing from Elba (Isola d'Elba) had he been exiled here today. Though it's a bit more congested now than when he was charitably dumped here in 1814 (he managed to engineer an escape in less than a year; see the boxed text, p170), Elba is an ever-glorious setting of beaches, blue waters, mountain hiking and mind-bending views, all supplemented by some very fine cuisine.

Elba has been inhabited since the Iron Age and the extraction of iron ore and metallurgy were the island's principal sources of economic wellbeing until well into the second half of the 20th century. In 1917 some 840,000 tonnes of iron were produced, but in WWII the Allies bombed the industry to bits. By the beginning of the 1980s production was down to 100,000 tonnes. You can still

fossick around to your heart's content in museums dedicated to rocks.

Ligurian tribes people were the island's first inhabitants, followed by Etruscans and Greeks from Magna Graecia. Centuries of peace under the Pax Romana gave way to more uncertain times during the barbarian invasions, when Elba became a refuge for those fleeing mainland marauders. By the 11th century, Pisa (and later Piombino) was in control and built fortresses to help ward off attacks by Muslim raiders and pirates operating out of North Africa.

In the 16th century, Cosimo I de' Medici grabbed territory in the north of the island, where he founded the port town of Cosmopolis (today's Portoferraio).

ESSENTIAL INFORMATION

TOURIST OFFICES // Associazione Albergatori Isola d'Elba (☎ 0565 91 55 55; www .elbapromotion.it, in Italian; 2nd fl, Calata Italia 26, Portoferraio) The island's professional hotel association can reserve accommodation. **Info Park Are@** (☎ 0565 91 88 09; infoparkare@gmail.com; cnr Viale Elba & Calata Italia, Portoferraio; ☺ 9.30am-1.30pm & 3.30-7.30pm daily Easter to Oct, Mon-Sat rest of year) Provides information for the Parco Nazionale dell'Arcipelago Toscano. **Tourist Office** (Agenzia per il Turismo dell'Archipelago Toscano; ☎ 0565 91 46 71; www.aptelba.it; Calata Italia 43, Portoferraio; ☺ 9am-7pm daily Jun-Sep, to 7pm Mon-Fri, to 1pm Sat Apr-May, to 1pm Mon, Wed & Fri, to 1pm & 3pm-5pm Tue & Thu Feb-Mar) Near the ferry port; has volumes of information, including the island's limited internet log-on options.

EXPLORING ELBA

Over a million visitors a year take the one-hour ferry trip to Elba, the largest and most heavily populated island of the Tuscan archipelago. Yet this 28km-long,

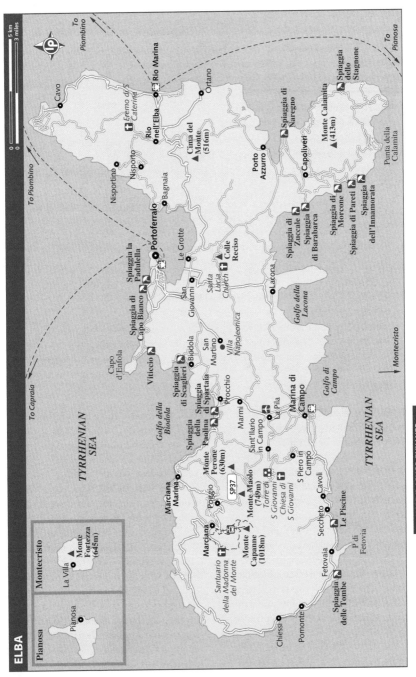

CENTRAL COAST & ELBA

ELBA ON LEG POWER

A dizzying network of walking and mountain-biking trails blankets Elba. Though some start right at Portoferraio, walkers can easily get to/from better, far-flung trailheads using the island's robust bus network. A few suggested outings are listed at www.elbalink.it, though the tourist office, Info Park Are@ and Il Libraio in Portoferraio have excellent trail maps for custom expedition planning.

A few of the more appealing outings:

★ **San Lucia to San Martino** A low-impact, 90-minute walking trail, starting just outside Portoferraio at the church of San Lucia, traversing meadows and former farmland being repossessed by nature for about 2.2km and terminating at Napoleon's villa in San Martino.

★ **Colle Reciso to San Martino and return** A 15km (round-trip), medium-difficulty mountain bike trail that peaks at about 280m. The trail continues past San Martino, descending into Marmi, but save some breath for the return trip as circling back to Portoferraio from Marmi on the main road is neither pleasant nor particularly safe in high season.

★ **Marciana to Chiessi** A 12km hike starting high up in Marciana, dribbling downhill past ancient churches, sea vistas and granite boulders for about six hours to the seaside in Chiessi.

★ **The Great Elba Crossing** A three- to four-day, 60km east–west island crossing, including Monte Capanne, Elba's highest point (1018m), overnighting down on the coast as camping is not allowed on the paths. The highlight is the final 19km leg from Poggio to Pomonte, passing the Santuario della Madonna del Monte and the Masso dell'Aquila rock formation.

CENTRAL COAST & ELBA

19km-wide island has plenty of quiet nooks, particularly if you visit in April, May, September or October.

♥ **PORTOFERRAIO OLD TOWN //**
FORTIFY YOUR NAPOLEONIC
KNOWLEDGE
Known to the Romans as Fabricia and later Ferraia (since it was a port for iron exports), this small harbour was acquired by Cosimo I de' Medici in the mid-16th century, when the fortifications took shape. The walls link two forts (Stella and Falcone) on high points and a third tower (Linguella) at the port entrance. In 1814 Napoleon was 'imprisoned' here at the start of his fleeting exile on Elba. From the ferry terminal, it's a bit less

than a kilometre along the foreshore to the Old Town.

Up on the bastions, between the two forts, is **Villa dei Mulini** (☎ 0565 91 58 46; Piazzale Napoleone; adult/child €3/1.50; ⏰ 9am-7pm Mon & Wed-Sat, to 1pm Sun), Napoleon's home while he was emperor of this small isle, with its splendid terraced garden and his library. During his brief Elban exile, the emperor certainly didn't want for creature comforts – contrast his Elba lifestyle with the simplicity of his camp bed and travelling trunk when he was on the campaign trail. It's a great history lesson, though there are no actual Napoleonic artefacts. Nearby is the city's defining **Forte Stella** (Via della Stella; adult/child €1.50/1.20; ⏰ 9am-7pm Easter-Sep). If you cross over to the Linguella fortifications, you'll find the modest **Museo Civico Archeologico** (☎ 0565 91 73 38; adult/child €2/1.50; 9am-2pm & 6pm-midnight mid-Jun–mid-Sep, 9am-8.30pm mid-Sep–Oct, 10am-1pm & 3.30-7.30pm Apr–mid-Jun, closed Nov-Mar), with a collection generally focused on ancient seafarers.

VILLA NAPOLEONICA DI SAN MARTINO // SEE NAPOLEON'S SUMMER RETREAT

Though he never even slept here, **Villa Napoleonica di San Martino** (☎ 0565 91 46 88; adult/child €3/1.50; 9am-7pm Wed-Sat, to 1pm Sun), set in hills about 5km southwest of town, was meant to be Napoleon's 'summer home'. Modest by Napoleonic standards, it's dominated by the overbearing mid-19th-century gallery built to house his memorabilia. A combined ticket for both of his villas costs €5.

OUTDOOR ELBA // CRUISE THE ISLAND BY FOOT, BIKE OR BOAT

If you're here for an active time, pick up the multilingual tourist office leaflet *Lo Sport Emerge dal Mare*. It has a useful map and summarises walking and cycling trails, plus lists where to sign on for scuba diving, windsurfing and other watery activities. Alternatively, you can spend a sedentary but nonetheless enjoyable two hours out on a glass-bottom boat with **Aquavision** (☎ 328 7095470; Portoferraio harbour; adult/child €15/8; Easter–mid-Oct)

The **Centro Trekking Isola d'Elba** (☎ 0565 93 08 37; www.geniodelbosco.it, in Italian), run by Il Genio del Bosco, leads hiking, biking and kayaking excursions around Elba, Capraia, Giglio and Pianosa.

Il Libraio (☎ 0565 91 71 35; Calata Mazzini 10), on the Portoferraio waterfront beside the Old Town, stocks a variety of walking and biking maps for the island starting at €7.

MARCIANA MARINA // ENJOY FINE FOOD AT THIS EXCEPTIONAL MARINA

Marciana Marina, 17km west of Portoferraio, unlike typical cookie-cutter marinas, has character and history to complement its pleasant pebble beaches. **Il Ristorante Scaraboci** (☎ 0565 99 68 68; Via XX Settembre 29; meals €38; Thu-Tue) is a promising fish and seafood venue where all pastas and desserts are homemade. **Terezina** (☎ 0565 9 90 49; Piazza della Vittoria 16; meals €25-32; closed Tue Oct-Mar) is suited for informal meals and families. The short menu is largely fish and fish in pasta.

MARCIANA // SCALE THE TINY STREETS OF THE HIGHEST TOWN ON ELBA

Marciana, both the highest (355m) and oldest town on the island, is an engaging, peaceful, tightly packed place. Puff up the town's pitiless streets and stairs, past arches, flower boxes and petite balconies to drop-offs revealing views of Marciana Marina and Poggio below. The much knocked-about **Fortezza Pisana** (Apr-Sep), above the village, is a reminder of the old medieval days. Down a cobbled lane below it is the modest **Museo Archeologico** (☎ 0565 90 12 15; Via del Pretorio; admission €2; Wed-Mon). A 40-or-so-minute walk west out of town brings you to the **Santuario della Madonna del Monte**, the most important site of pilgrimage on the island. A much-altered 11th-century church houses a stone upon which a divine hand is said to have painted an image of the Virgin. Some 750m south of Marciana, a **cable lift** (☎ 0565 90 10 20; one way/return €10/15; Easter-Nov) with open, barred cabins like parrot cages operates in summer and whisks you almost to the summit of **Monte Capanne** (1018m), the island's highest point with views as far as Corsica on a clear day.

CENTRAL COAST & ELBA

🌳 **POGGIO // EXPLORE THIS ENCHANTING VILLAGE WITH STUPENDOUS VIEWS**

A twisting 4km ascent into the mountains from Marciana Marina brings you to the attractive inland village of **Poggio**, famous for its spring water. It's an enchanting little place with steep, cobblestone alleys and stunning views of Marciana Marina and the coast. **Publius** (☎ 0565 9 92 08; meals €33-38; 🕙 Tue-Sun Easter-Oct), at the northern entrance to the village, is the place to spill money on a great meal, though the plunging views

THE EMPEROR NAPOLEON TAKES EARLY RETIREMENT

At precisely 6pm on 3 May 1814, the English frigate *Undaunted* dropped anchor in the harbour of Portoferraio on the island of Elba. It bore an unusual cargo. Under the Treaty of Fontainebleau, the emperor Napoleon was exiled to this seemingly safe open prison, some 15km from the Tuscan coast.

It could have been so much worse for the emperor, but the irony for someone who hailed from Corsica, just over the water, must have been bitter. Napoleon, the conqueror who had stridden across all of Europe and taken Egypt, was awarded this little island as his private fiefdom, to hold until the end of his days.

Elba would never quite be the same again. Napoleon, ever hyperactive, threw himself into frenetic activity in his new, humbler domain. He prescribed a mass of public works, which included improving the operations of the island's iron-ore mines – whose revenue, it is pertinent to note, now went his way. He also went about boosting agriculture, initiating a road-building program, draining marshes and overhauling the legal and education systems.

Some weeks after his arrival, his mother Letizia and sister Paolina rolled up. But he remained separated from his wife, Maria Luisa, and was visited for just two (no doubt hectic) days by his lover, Maria Walewska.

At the Congress of Vienna, the new regime in France called for Napoleon's removal to a more distant location. Austria, too, was nervous. Some participants favoured a shift to Malta, but Britain objected and suggested the remote South Atlantic islet of St Helena. The Congress broke up with no agreed decision.

Napoleon was well aware of the debate. Under no circumstances would he allow himself to be shipped off to some rocky speck in the furthest reaches of the Atlantic Ocean. A lifelong risk taker, he decided to have another roll of the dice. For months he had sent out on 'routine' trips around the Mediterranean a couple of vessels flying the flag of his little empire, Elba. When one, the *Incostante*, set sail early in the morning of 26 February 1815, no one suspected that the conqueror of Europe was stowed away on board. Sir Neil Campbell, his English jail warden, had returned to Livorno the previous day, confident that Napoleon was, as ever, fully immersed in the business of the island.

Napoleon made his way to France, reassumed power and embarked on the Hundred Days, the last of his expansionist campaigns that would culminate in defeat at Waterloo, after which he got his Atlantic exile after all, dying on St Helena in 1821, from arsenic poisoning – contracted, according to the most accepted contemporary theory, probably from the hair tonic he applied to keep that famous quiff glistening.

CENTRAL COAST & ELBA

down to the coast might distract from unmitigated food appreciation.

❤ MONTE PERONE & MONTE MAOLO // GET OUT OF THE CAR AND CLIMB TO SOME EXCELLENT VISTAS

If you follow the SP37 out of Poggio, park at the picnic site at the foot of **Monte Perone** (630m) – you can't miss it. To the left (east) you can wander up the mountain, with spectacular views across much of the island. To the right (west) you can scramble fairly quickly to a height that affords broad vistas down to Poggio, Marciana and Marciana Marina. From there you could press on to **Monte Maolo** (749m). The road then descends into the southern flank of the island. On the way, you pass the granite shell of the Romanesque **Chiesa di San Giovanni** and, shortly after, a ruined tower, the **Torre di San Giovanni.** Two small hamlets, **Sant'Ilario in Campo** and **San Piero in Campo**, are short on sights but still pleasant enough and little affected by tourism.

❤ MARINA DI CAMPO // EXPLORE THE HARBOUR IN ELBA'S SECOND-LARGEST TOWN

Marina di Campo, on the south side of the island, is Elba's second-largest town. Curling around a picturesque bay, its small fishing harbour adds personality to what is otherwise very much a holiday-oriented town. Its beach of bright, white sand pulls in vacationers by the thousands; coves further west, though less spectacular, are more tranquil. Just northeast of town in the Lacona/Porto Azzurro direction, over 150 Mediterranean species swim, crawl and wave about in the **Acquario dell'Elba** (☎ 0565 97 78 85; www.acquarioelba.com; adult/child €6/3; ☉ 9am-

11.30pm Jun–mid-Sep, to 7.30pm mid-Mar–May & mid-Sep–Nov).

❤ SOUTHCOAST SAUNTER // SPEND TIME IN ENCHANTING CAPOLIVERI AND BUSTLING PORTO AZZURRO

It's a comparatively long but not unpleasant drive along the south coast before climbing up a precipitous ridgeback in the southeastern pocket of the island to **Capoliveri**. This village is flirting with too-enchanting-for-its-own-good designation. The steep, narrow alleys and sandwiched houses are certainly pretty, though in high season the tourist mob is especially bad. **Il Chiasso** (☎ 0565 96 87 09; Via Cavour 32; meals €38; ☉ Easter-Oct) is one of the best restaurants in town, with a classy set menu and an excellent wine list. **Fandango** (☎ 0565 93 54 24; Via Cardenti 1; ☉ Tue-Sun), right beneath the main square, serves fine Tuscan wines in pleasant surroundings.

Backtrack down the ridge and head east to **Porto Azzurro**, a pleasant resort town, close to some good beaches and overlooked by a fort, built in 1603 by Philip III of Spain and now a prison. **Osteria La Botte Gaia** (☎ 0565 9 56 07; www.labottegaia.com; Via Europa 5-7; meals €34-38; ☉ dinner, closed Mon in winter) is Slow Food–featured and deservedly so. Homemade pasta supplements the ever-changing daily menu that runneth over with just-caught fish and a few vegie plates.

❤ NISPORTINO & NISPORTO // CRUISE THE BEAUTIFUL ROAD CONNECTING THESE TWO BEACH TOWNS

Time and energy permitting, a final bit of gorgeous driving can be done in the northeast corner of the island. Sail to and through the slightly gloomy, but

CENTRAL COAST & ELBA

THE COUNT OF MONTECRISTO

This feel-good swashbuckling tale was born from author Alexandre Dumas' acquaintance with Jérome Bonaparte, Napoleon Bonaparte's brother, whom he accompanied on a trip to Elba. Dumas became aware of another island, deserted Montecristo, deeper in the Mediterranean, and determined to write a novel in remembrance of the trip. In the person of the swashbuckling Dantes, Dumas takes a dig at the corruption of the bourgeois world. The dashing officer is imprisoned for a crime he hasn't committed and vows to get even. He escapes and, after a tip-off, searches for treasure on the island of Montecristo where, after much adventure and jolly japes, our man wins all the prizes – getting rich, becoming the Count of Montecristo and exacting a full measure of revenge on those who framed him.

Of course, it's all a tall tale (and no one has ever found any treasure on Montecristo) but this particular story has made a lot of loot for a lot of people. At least 25 film and TV versions of the story have been made, with greater or lesser skill. Among the better ones are the oldies: Rowland Lee's 1935 film and the 1943 version by Robert Vernay were equally good celluloid yarns. In Italy, Andrea Giordana had women swooning at their TV sets in the 1966 series by Edmo Fenoglio. Richard Chamberlain had a go at the lead role in David Greene's 1975 *The Count of Montecristo*, as, more recently, did Gérard Depardieu in *Montecristo* (1997).

refreshingly tourist-free **Rio nell'Elba**, the heart of the island's remaining iron-mining operation. Continue north out of town, stopping for a short stroll through what's left of **Eremo di Santa Caterina**, a tiny stone hermitage with great views. Then head for **Nisportino** and **Nisporto**. Both have small beaches and, in summer, snack stands and restaurants, but the spectacular views along the road connecting them is why you're here. A 3km dirt track south of Nisporto leads to lush, green **Bagnaia**, where you'll connect with the main road leading around the bay past **Le Grotte**, where a few stones still managing to stand on top of each other are all that remain of a Roman villa. Minutes later you'll be back in the traffic crawl of Portoferraio.

GASTRONOMIC HIGHLIGHTS

♥ CAFESCONDIDO €€

☎ 340 3400881; Via del Carmine 65, Portoferraio; meals €25-28; ☽ Mon-Sat

Way up the hill, toward Fortezza Falcone, the raucous cafe up front gives no sign of the delicious food served in the Impressionist art–festooned back room. Servers deftly explain Elba-centric culinary permutations on the chalkboard menu. The table wine is better than average and there's plenty of *crostata* (fruit tart) to choose from for dessert.

♥ DA LIDO €€€

☎ 0565 91 46 50; Salita del Falcone 2, Portoferraio; meals €30-43; ☽ Tue-Sun

The swanky appearance and almost hilariously slow service notwithstanding, this place is widely known and revered, both in Portoferraio and by anyone who's ever been to Portoferraio. Presentation is grand and food quality equally so. The black risotto with squid and the chocolate torte are both show-stoppers. The shrimp with brandy may elicit tears of joy, then tears of sorrow, as the small portion is too quickly gone.

❦ IL CASTAGNACCIAO PIZZERIA €

☎ 0565 91 58 45; Via del Mercato Vecchio 5, Portoferraio; half/whole pizzas €3/6; ✆ daily

Down a very narrow street from Piazza Cavour in the historic centre, this is a local institution for takeaway or sit-down pizza bliss. A bunch of friendly guys taking orders, prepping and baking pizzas, are squashed behind an impossibly cramped counter. Yet somehow, from this mayhem, more than 20 different types of wood-fired pizza appear.

❦ LA LIBERTARIA €€

☎ 0565 91 49 78; Calata Matteotti 12, Portoferraio; meals €28; ✆ Apr-Oct

In the unlikely event that nothing on the menu turns your crank, the kitchen is open to requests. Seating capacity and backdrops are meagre (a tent in the alley or out on the footpath, 5cm from speeding traffic), but the food is divine. The *linguine sarde e finocchietto* (pasta with sardines and fennel) is an unlikely treat and the cooked-to-perfection *tonno in crosta di pistacchi* (tuna fillet with pistachio crust) may actually keep you in Portoferraio an extra night for a second helping.

CAPRAIA

The elliptical, volcanic island of **Capraia**, 8km long by 4km wide, lies 65km from Livorno. Its highest point is Monte Castello at 447m and is covered mainly in *macchia*. Tuscany's third-largest island after Elba and Giglio, it has changed hands several times over the course of its

---

∼ WORTH A TRIP ∼

If it's the beach you want, Elba unsurprisingly has innumerable choices. West of Portoferraio, narrow and shelly though still nice, are **Spiaggia la Padulella** and its counterpart **Spiaggia di Capo Bianco**. Similar beaches dot the coast along the 7km stretch out to **Capo d'Enfola**. Or head south a few kilometres to **Viticcio** for the sandy strands lining **Golfo della Biodola**.

Or head further south still to **Procchio**, a small bustling beach town, home to the wonderful **Osteria del Piano** (☎ 0565 90 72 92; Via Provinciale 24; meals €29; ✆ Apr-Oct), whipping up dishes like black-and-white spaghetti served with a crab sauce. West from Procchio, the road hugs the cliffs above **Spiaggia di Spartaia** and **Spiaggia della Paolina**, beautiful little beaches requiring a steep clamber down.

The road along western Elba passes **Chiessi** and **Pomonte**, with pebbly beaches and beautiful water. Sandy **Spiaggia delle Tombe** is one of the few spots on the island with a nude-bathing scene.

At **Fetovaia**, **Seccheto** and **Cavoli** you'll find more protected sandy beaches and restaurants. West of Seccheto, **Le Piscine** is another mostly nudist stretch.

In southeast Elba, west of **Capoliveri** (on the road to Portoferraio, watch for signs), are the beaches of **Spiaggia di Zuccale** and **Spiaggia di Barabarca**. The road south from Capoliveri leads to three additional charming coves – **Morcone**, **Pareti** and **Innamorata**. East of Capoliveri is the comparatively long stretch of beach at **Naregno**. Another 5km and you reach a path down to **Spiaggia dello Stagnone**, which even in summer shouldn't be too crowded, due to the effort required to rattle down this far.

history, belonging to Genoa, Sardinia, the Saracens from North Africa and Napoleon. You can join boat trips (€12) around the coastline or hike across the island. The most popular walk is to the Stagnone, a small lake in the south.

Agenzia Viaggi e Turismo Parco (☎ 0586 90 50 71; www.isoladicapraia.it, in Italian; Via Assunzione 42) on Capraia can advise on activities, such as hiking and boat trips. It shares the same space as the **tourist office** (☎ 0586 90 51 38; Via Assunzione 42; ☼ 9am-12.30pm & 4.30-7pm Fri-Wed Apr-Sep).

❦ OUTDOOR CAPRAIA // HIKE AND DIVE AN EXTINCT VOLCANO

A variety of independent hikes can be done on the island, ranging from 30 minutes to seven hours. It takes some digging, but descriptions of island excursions and pictures can be found at www.isoladicapraia.it. There are seven popular dive sites off the coast. **Capraia Diving** (☎ 0586 90 51 37; www.capraiadiving.it; Via Assunzione 72) visits them all and has courses.

GORGONA

The tiny island of **Gorgona**, a mere 2.23 sq km, is the greenest and northernmost of the islands and cannot be visited without a guide. Its two towers were built respectively by the Pisans and the Medicis of Florence. Part of the island is off-limits as a low-security prison.

❦ TREK GORGONA // GET OFF THE BEATEN TREK

It's worth the scheduling dance to get out and see Gorgona's plunging coastline and beautiful interior, largely untouched since the penal colony opened in 1869, effectively closing the island to visitors. Both **Atelier del Viaggio** (☎ 0586 88 41 54;

www.atelierdelviaggio.it, in Italian) and **Toscana Trekking** (☎ 347 7922453; www.toscanatrekking.it, in Italian) lead hikes in high season.

CENTRAL COAST & ELBA

CENTRAL TUSCANY

3 PERFECT DAYS

❦ DAY 1 // SIENA

Siena has all the makings of a top-shelf Italian city: unforgettable museums, art, architecture, incredible dining and a massive and lavishly decorated cathedral (p185). Pick your sights carefully (and consider the time spent queuing that they entail). Save time and energy for an aimless wander of Siena's incredible conglomeration of streets, lined with looming Gothic buildings and as vehicle-free as a city of its size can be.

❦ DAY 2 // SAN GIMIGNANO & VOLTERRA

Owing to their relative compactness, San Gimignano and Volterra may seem congested in high season, which is all the more reason to spend the night and see their tranquil sides. Both cities are often mentioned in the same reverent breath, but their differences far outweigh their similarities. San Gimignano's distinguishing towers and medieval squares and streets win for sheer beauty, while Volterra's edgier rendering connotes an atmosphere where stone gargoyles spontaneously animating and swooping through the night isn't entirely out of the question. Both have worthwhile museums and galleries, but exploration and singular photo opportunities are what's likely to leave lasting memories.

❦ DAY 3 // LE CRETE

This pocket, south of Siena, rapidly transforms into a comparatively uncrowded yet still edifying landscape, peppered with far-flung abbeys and retiring, compact, fortified hill towns. Proximate, yet still seemingly remote, many of these sights can be admired in a single full-day driving tour (p202). For even more unaffected serenity, consider dipping further south to villages such as Monticchiello and Montefollonico (p210), both within easy striking distance of Pienza and Montepulciano.

CENTRAL TUSCANY

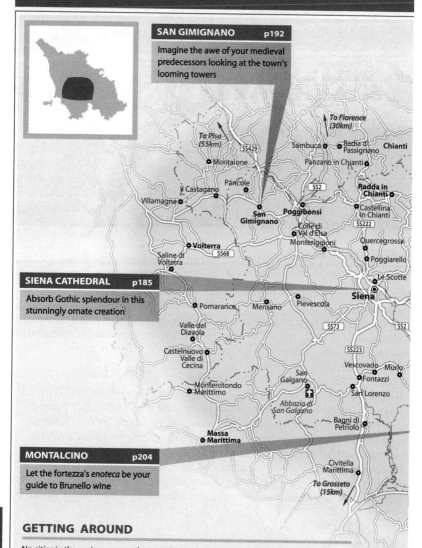

SAN GIMIGNANO   p192

Imagine the awe of your medieval predecessors looking at the town's looming towers

To Florence (30km)

To Pisa (55km)

SS429

Montaione

Sambuca

Badia di Passignano   **Chianti**

Panzano in Chianti

Pàncole

Il Castagano

SS2

Radda in Chianti

Villamagna

San Gimignano   **Poggibonsi**

Castellina in Chianti

Colle di Val d'Elsa

SS222

Monteriggioni

Quercegrossa

Volterra   SS68

Poggiarello

Saline di Volterra

Le Scotte

Siena

SIENA CATHEDRAL   p185

Absorb Gothic splendour in this stunningly ornate creation

Pomarance   Mensano   Pievescola

Valle del Diavola

SS73

SS2

Castelnuovo Valle di Cecina

SS223

Vescovado   Murlo

Fontazzi

Monterotondo Marittimo

San Galgano

San Lorenzo

Abbazia di San Galgano

Bagni di Petriolo

Massa Marittima

MONTALCINO   p204

Let the fortezza's *enoteca* be your guide to Brunello wine

Civitella Marittima

To Grosseto (15km)

GETTING AROUND

No cities in the region are on primary train routes. Siena and Volterra (Saline) have services to the Rome–Florence and Coast train lines respectively. San Gimignano's nearest train station is at Poggibonsi. There are direct bus connections to major cities from Siena, San Gimignano and Volterra. Bus service to cities south of Siena is less frequent to rare. The SS2 superstrada (expressway) and the SS222 and SS223 run roughly north–south. Parking around cities is challenging; costly car parks abound.

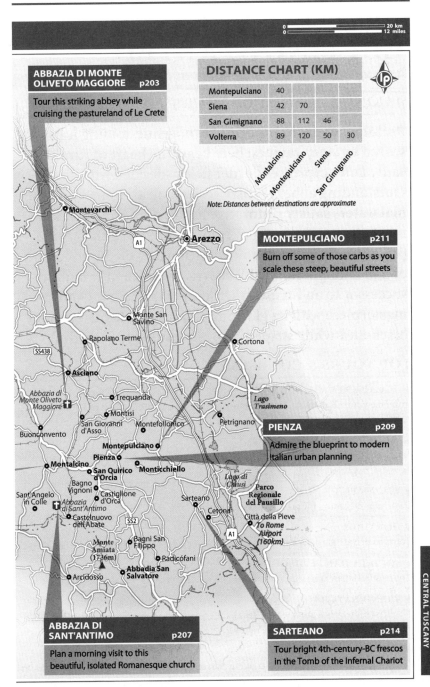

ABBAZIA DI MONTE OLIVETO MAGGIORE   p203

Tour this striking abbey while cruising the pastureland of Le Crete

DISTANCE CHART (KM)

	Montalcino	Montepulciano	Siena	San Gimignano
Montepulciano	40			
Siena	42	70		
San Gimignano	88	112	46	
Volterra	89	120	50	30

Note: Distances between destinations are approximate

MONTEPULCIANO   p211

Burn off some of those carbs as you scale these steep, beautiful streets

PIENZA   p209

Admire the blueprint to modern Italian urban planning

ABBAZIA DI SANT'ANTIMO   p207

Plan a morning visit to this beautiful, isolated Romanesque church

SARTEANO   p214

Tour bright 4th-century-BC frescos in the Tomb of the Infernal Chariot

CENTRAL TUSCANY

CENTRAL TUSCANY GETTING STARTED

MAKING THE MOST OF YOUR TIME

Buildings the colour of ripe corn, gentle-folding hills scored by steep ravines: here beats the heart of rural Tuscany. Lofty cypresses border fields speckled with sheep. Outstanding abbeys satisfy ecclesiastical wonder and thermal waters satisfy restorative needs. Some of Tuscany's most attractive towns poke up: steep, straggling Montepulciano; the pilgrim-route bastion and medieval towers of San Gimignano; and Volterra, the ancient brooding successor to an Etruscan settlement. Siena is a Gothic masterpiece with its glorious piazza, cobbled streets and black-and-white striped, marble-festooned cathedral.

TOP TOURS & COURSES

♥ **ACCADEMIA MUSICALE CHIGIANA**
Immerse yourself in Siena's tradition of classical music by enrolling in a summer course. (Map pp182-3; ☎ 0577 2 20 91; www.chigiana.it; Via di Città 89)

♥ **ASSOCIAZIONE SIENA JAZZ**
Courses with one of Europe's foremost jazz institutions. (Map pp182-3; ☎ 0577 27 14 01; www.sienajazz.it; Piazza Libertà)

♥ **ECCO SIENA**
Two-hour city tours for groups and individuals. (☎ 0577 4 32 73)

♥ **HORTIBUS**
Tours to private gardens and villas around Siena. (☎ 348 910 07 83; www.hortibus.com, in French)

♥ **SOCIETÀ DANTE ALIGHIERI**
Courses in Italian language and culture. (Map pp182-3; ☎ 0577 4 95 33; www.dantealighieri.com)

♥ **TRENO NATURA**
A tourist railway is a great way to see the scenery of the Crete Senese. (☎ 0577 20 74 13; www.ferrovieturistiche.it; ☙ May, early Jun, Sep & Oct)

♥ **WINERY AVIGNONESI**
Tempting wine-tasting tours and cooking classes. (☎ 0578 72 43 04; www.avignonesi.it; Montepulciano)

CENTRAL TUSCANY

GETTING AWAY FROM IT ALL

- ★ **Montisi & Petroio** So retiring they're almost comatose, these villages offer low-key medieval ambiance (p202).

- ★ **Agriturismo San Lorenzo** Just 3km from Volterra, this farm-stay offers a giddying fusion of sustainable tourism, countryside vistas, mod-cons and wonderful food (p404).

- ★ **Hotelito Lupaia** A captivatingly restored, remote luxury farmhouse with befitting comfort, food and vistas (p406).

- ★ **Monticchiello & Montefollonico** Offering reclusive, hilltop-town cultural immersion, similarly uncomplicated food, peace and little else (p210).

FESTIVALS

- ★ **Il Palio** (2 July and 16 August) This ancient horse race is the most spectacular event on the Sienese calendar (p185).

- ★ **Jazz & Wine Festival** (second and third weeks of July) Jazz-loving oenophiles will savour this event in Montalcino.

- ★ **Siena Jazz** (July and August) International festival promoted by the Associazione Siena Jazz (opposite).

- ★ **Volterra AD 1398** (third and fourth Sundays in August) Volterra rolls back the calendar some 600 years, taking to the streets in period costume.

- ★ **Bravio delle Botti** (last Sunday in August) Montepulciano's *contrade* (districts) continue a centuries-old spirit of fervent competition by racing giant barrels up the steep streets to Piazza Grande.

TOP EATING EXPERIENCES

ANTICA OSTERIA DA DIVO
This is the place for dining on inventive dishes amid Etruscan tombs (p190).

ENOTECA A GAMBE DI GATTO
Boasts exacting standards for the best products from organic producers (p191).

IL PINO
The menu includes massive pasta plates and several truffle-based specialities (p197).

RISTORANTE LA PORTA
This restaurant has a reputation for food and service that behoves a reservation (p210).

RISTORANTE DON BETA
Sample four truffle-based *primi* and five *secondi* that are enhanced by the truffles' fragrance (p201).

RESOURCES

- ★ **Terre di Siena** (www.terresiena.it) An excellent regional website

- ★ **San Gimignano** (www.sangimignano.com) Website for the city

- ★ **Volterra and the Cecine & Era Valleys** (www.volterratur.it) Useful regional site

- ★ **Proloco di Montalcino** (www.prolocomontalcino.it) Montalcino's tourism site

- ★ **Strada del Vino Nobile di Montepulciano** (www.stradavinonobile.it) Regional wine and tourism information

- ★ **Proloco Montepulciano** (www.prolocomontepulciano.it) Montepulciano's tourism site

SIENA

· · · · · ·

pop 53,900

Among Italy's most distinctive cities, Siena continues its rivalry with historic adversary Florence to this day. Every traveller seems to strongly identify with one over the other. It often boils down to aesthetic preference: while Florence saw its greatest flourishing during the Renaissance, Siena's enduring artistic glories are largely Gothic. The city's medieval centre bristles with majestic buildings, such as the Palazzo Comunale on Piazza del Campo, the main square, and its stupefyingly ornamented cathedral. A profusion of churches and small museums harbour a wealth of artwork. Your day can be filled by simply wandering the snarled lanes of the historic centre, itself a Unesco World Heritage Site.

According to legend Siena was founded by Senius, son of Remus; the symbol of the wolf feeding the twins Romulus and Remus is as ubiquitous in Siena as it is in Rome. The city was probably of Etruscan origin, although it wasn't until the 1st century BC, when the Romans established a military colony here called Sena Julia, that it began to grow into a proper town. Even so, it remained a minor outpost until the arrival of the Lombards in the 6th century. Under them, Siena became a key point along the main route from northern Italy to Rome, the Via Francigena. The medieval town was an amalgamation of three areas (Città, Camollia and San Martino) that would come to be known as the *terzi* (thirds). The city was next under the control of local bishops before power passed to locally elected administrators, the *consoli* (consuls).

By the 13th century Siena had become a wealthy trading city, producing textiles, saffron, wine, spices and wax, and its traders and bankers did deals all over Western Europe. Its rivalry with neighbouring Florence also grew proportionately, leading to numerous wars between Guelph Florence and Ghibelline Siena, each intent upon controlling ever more Tuscan territory. In 1230 Florence besieged Siena and catapulted dung and rotting donkey flesh over its walls in an attempt to spread the plague. Siena's revenge came at the Battle of Montaperti in 1260 – but victory was short-lived. Nine years later the Tuscan Ghibellines were defeated by Charles of Anjou and, for almost a century, Siena was obliged to toe the Florentine line.

Siena reached its peak under the republican rule of the Consiglio dei Nove (Council of Nine), an elected executive committee dominated by the rising mercantile class. Many of the finest buildings in the Sienese Gothic style were constructed during this period, including the cathedral, the Palazzo Comunale and the Piazza del Campo. The Sienese school of painting was born at this time, with Guido da Siena, and flowered in the early 14th century, when artists such as Duccio di Buoninsegna and Ambrogio Lorenzetti were at work.

A plague outbreak in 1348 killed two-thirds of the city's 100,000 inhabitants and led to a period of decline.

At the end of the 14th century, Siena came under the control of Milan's Visconti family, followed in the next century by the autocratic patrician Pandolfo Petrucci. Under Petrucci the city's fortunes improved, until the Holy Roman Emperor Charles V conquered it in 1555 after a two-year siege that left thousands dead. He handed the city over to Cosimo I de' Medici, who barred the inhabitants from operating banks, thus severely curtailing Siena's power.

Though the hapless residents who endured it may not agree, Siena's centuries-long economic downturn in the wake of the Medici takeover was a blessing that resulted in the city's present-day, matchless allure. Its predominantly Gothic surroundings have survived largely intact as no one could be bothered to undertake (or fund) demolition or new construction. Furthermore, unlike the poundings endured by neighbouring cities in WWII, the French took Siena virtually unopposed, sparing it discernible damage.

The city today relies for its prosperity on tourism and the success of its Monte dei Paschi di Siena bank, founded in 1472 and now one of the city's largest employers.

Siena was the first European city to banish motor traffic from its heart (in 1966). Strolling its historic centre without fear of flattened toes or side-view mirror contusions (scooters notwithstanding) is not the least of the town's pleasures.

ESSENTIAL INFORMATION

EMERGENCIES // Hospital (☎ 0577 58 51 11; Viale Bracci) Just north of Siena at Le Scotte. Police station (☎ 0577 20 11 11; Via del Castoro)

TOURIST OFFICES // Tourist office (☎ 0577 28 05 51; www.terresiena.it; Piazza del Campo 56; ⏰ 9am-7pm) Reserves accommodation and sells direct bus tickets to Pisa Airport (one way/return €14/26).

EXPLORING SIENA

♥ **PIAZZA DEL CAMPO & PALAZZO COMUNALE //** SAVOUR CENTRAL SIENA

On the Square

Piazza del Campo has been Siena's civic and social centre ever since it was staked out by the Consiglio dei Nove (Council of Nine) in the mid-14th century. The piazza was the site of a former Roman marketplace, and its pie-piece paving design is divided into nine sectors to represent the number of members of the ruling council. In 1346 water first bubbled forth from the **Fonte Gaia** (Happy Fountain) in the upper part of the square.

48 HOURS IN SIENA

RAINY DAY

You're in for a treat just queuing to see the **cathedral** (p185) by ogling its floors, walls and ceiling as you wait, regardless of the weather. Across Piazza del Duomo is the even more popular (and hence be prepared to queue) **Santa Maria della Scala** (p188), where you'll witness a rare sight in secular frescos and spend so much time underground that you'll forget what the day is like outside. Crossing Piazza del Duomo one last time, get your fill of Sienese art in the **Museo dell'Opera Metropolitana** (p186).

OUTDOOR SIENA

Half a day should be allotted for simply taking in the profusion of arresting streets in this massive, Gothic All-Star of a city. It's a daunting climb, but the views from the **Torre del Mangia** (p183) will make the mind swirl. After descending, take an extended break, have a drink or read a book from the reverse angle in **Piazza del Campo** (above), which is ostensibly compulsory for every resident and visitor to call on once per day.

CENTRAL TUSCANY

SIENA

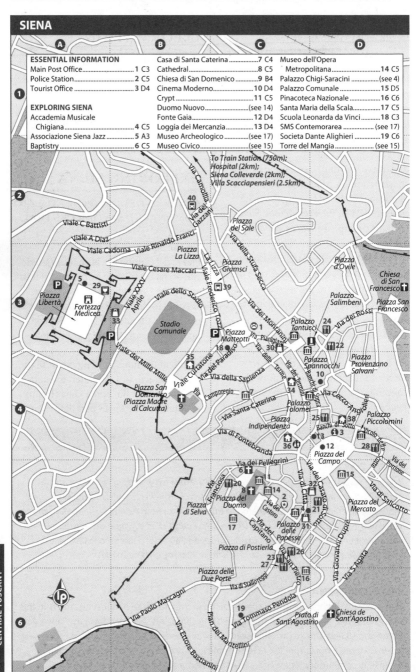

ESSENTIAL INFORMATION
Main Post Office.................................1 C3
Police Station.....................................2 C5
Tourist Office.....................................3 D4

EXPLORING SIENA
Accademia Musicale
  Chigiana..4 C5
Associazione Siena Jazz..................5 A3
Baptistry...6 C5

Casa di Santa Caterina..................7 C4
Cathedral...8 C5
Chiesa di San Domenico................9 B4
Cinema Moderno............................10 D4
Crypt...11 C5
Duomo Nuovo.........................(see 14)
Fonte Gaia.......................................12 D4
Loggia dei Mercanzia....................13 D4
Museo Archeologico.............(see 17)
Museo Civico..........................(see 15)

Museo dell'Opera
  Metropolitana.............................14 C5
Palazzo Chigi-Saracini..............(see 4)
Palazzo Comunale...........................15 D5
Pinacoteca Nazionale...................16 C6
Santa Maria della Scala.................17 C5
Scuola Leonarda da Vinci............18 C3
SMS Contemorarea.................(see 17)
Societa Dante Alighieri..................19 C6
Torre del Mangia......................(see 15)

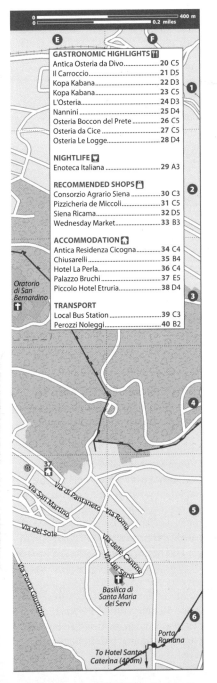

The fountain's panels are reproductions; the severely weathered originals, sculpted by Jacopo della Quercia in the early 15th century, are on display in the Complesso Museale di Santa Maria della Scala (p188). At the lowest point of the square stands the spare, elegant **Palazzo Comunale**, conceived by the Consiglio dei Nove as a nerve centre for the republican government, uniting the offices and courts in one building, thus greatly reducing the symbolic and actual power of the feudal nobles.

Dating from 1297 the palazzo is one of the most graceful Gothic buildings in Italy, with an ingeniously designed concave facade to mirror the opposing convex curve formed by the piazza. Also known as the Palazzo Pubblico, or town hall, it was purpose-built as the piazza's centrepiece, resulting in a wonderful amphitheatre effect.

The attached **Torre del Mangia** (1344), with a crown designed by painter Lippo Memmi, was a remarkable engineering feat and one of the tallest nonsectarian towers (102m) in Italy. Climb the 400 steps (admission €7; 10am-7pm mid-Mar–Oct, to 4pm Nov–mid-Mar) for splendid views across the city. Expect a wait in high season, as only 30 people are allowed up at any time.

Inside the Palazzo
Entry to the palazzo's ground-floor central courtyard is free. Adjacent is the entrance to the **Museo Civico** (0577 29 22 63; adult/student €7/4.50, museum & tower €12; 10am-7pm mid-Mar–Oct, 10am-5.30pm or 6.30pm Nov–mid-Mar), with a series of rooms containing frescos by artists of the distinctive Sienese school. These frescos are unusual in that they were commissioned by the governing body of the city, rather than the Church, and many depict secular

COMBINED TICKETS

Siena has a bewildering permutation of combined tickets:

★ Museo Civico and Torre del Mangia (€12)

★ Museo Civico, Santa Maria della Scala and SMS Contemporanea (€11, valid for two days)

★ Museo dell'Opera Metropolitana, Battistero di San Giovanni, crypt, Oratorio di San Bernardino, Museo Diocesano (€10, valid for three days)

★ Museo Civico, Santa Maria della Scala, SMS Contemporanea, Museo dell'Opera Metropolitana, Battistero di San Giovanni (€14, valid for seven days)

★ Museo Civico, Santa Maria della Scala, SMS Contemporanea, Museo dell'Opera Metropolitana, Battistero di San Giovanni, Museo Diocesano, Chiesa di Sant'Agostino and Oratorio di San Bernardino – the bumper bundle though not including Torre del Mangia (€17, valid for seven days)

★ 'Siena's Renaissance Trail': Museo Civico, Santa Maria della Scala, National Gallery, Duomo & Piccolomini Library, State Archive (€13.50)

subjects instead of the favoured religious themes of the time.

Upstairs, start in the **Sala del Risorgimento** with its impressive late-19th-century frescos serialising key events in the campaign to unite Italy. Next is the **Sala di Balia** (or Sala dei Priori). The 15 scenes depicted in frescos around the walls recount episodes in the life of Pope Alexander III (the Sienese Rolando Bandinelli), including his clashes with the Holy Roman Emperor Frederick Barbarossa. You then pass into the **Anticamera del Concistoro**, remarkable for the fresco (moved here in the 19th century) of *Santi Caterina d'Alessandria, Giovanni e Agostino* (Saints Catherine of Alexandria, John and Augustine), executed by Ambrogio Lorenzetti. The next hall, **Sala del Concistoro**, is dominated by the allegorical ceiling frescos of the Mannerist Domenico Beccafumi. Back in the Anticamera del Concistoro, you pass to your right into the **Vestibolo** (Vestibule), whose star attraction is a bronze wolf, the symbol of the city. Next

door in the **Anticappella** are frescos of scenes from Greco-Roman mythology and history, while the **Cappella** (Chapel) contains a fine *Sacra Famiglia e San Leonardo* (Holy Family and St Leonard) by Il Sodoma and intricately carved wooden choir stalls.

The best is saved for last. From the Cappella, you emerge into the **Sala del Mappamondo** where you can admire the masterpiece of the entire building, Simone Martini's powerful and striking *Maestà* (Virgin Mary in Majesty) fresco, his earliest known work and one of the most important works of the Sienese school.

The next room, the **Sala dei Nove** (or Sala della Pace), contains a three-panelled fresco series painted by Ambrogio Lorenzetti, depicting the *Allegories of Good and Bad Government*. The central allegory portrays scenes with personifications of Justice, Wisdom, Virtue and Peace, all unusually (at the time) depicted as women, rendered along with scenes of criminal punishment and rewards for righteousness. Set perpendicular from it are the frescos *Allegory of Good Government* and *Allegory of Bad Government,* which hold intensely contrasting scenes set in the recognisable environs of Siena. The good depicts a sunlit, idyllic, serene city, with joyous, dancing citizens and a countryside filled with crops; the bad city is filled with vices, crime and disease.

Finish by backtracking and climbing the stairs to the **loggia**, which looks southeast over Piazza del Mercato and the countryside.

☙ CATHEDRAL // ADMIRE THE MARBLE ORNAMENTATION

Siena's **cathedral** (Piazza del Duomo; admission €3; ☯ 10.30am-7.30pm Mon-Sat, 1.30-6.30pm Sun Mar-Oct, 10.30am-6.30pm Mon-Sat, 1.30-5.30pm Sun Nov-Feb) is one of Italy's great Gothic structures. Building began in 1196 and was largely completed by 1215, although work continued on features such as the apse and dome well into the 13th century. The magnificent **exterior** facade of white, green and red marble was begun by Giovanni Pisano – who completed

---

IL PALIO

This spectacular event, held twice yearly on 2 July and 16 August, in honour of the Virgin Mary, dates back to the Middle Ages and features colourful pageants, a wild horse race around Piazza del Campo, eating, drinking and celebrating in the streets.

This is one of very few major medieval spectacles of its type in Italy, which has survived through the sheer tenacity of Sienese traditionalism.

Ten of Siena's 17 town districts, or *contrade,* compete for the coveted *palio,* a silk banner. Each has its own traditions, symbol and colours, and its own church and *palio* museum. Along the streets you'll notice the various flags and plaques delineating these quarters, each with a name and symbol relating to an animal. On the downside, competition is so fierce that fist fights sometimes break out between *contrade,* and Il Palio jockeys often live in fear from rival *contrade.*

On festival days Piazza del Campo becomes a racetrack, with a ring of packed dirt around its perimeter. From about 5pm, representatives of each *contrada* with their banners parade in historical costume.

The race is run at 7.45pm in July and 7pm in August. For about one exhilarating minute, the 10 horses and their bareback riders tear three times around Piazza del Campo so fast and violently that it makes your hair stand on end. Even if a horse loses its rider, it still can win and, since many riders fall each year, it is the horses in the end who are the focus of the event. There is only one rule: riders mustn't interfere with the reins of other horses.

Book well in advance for a room and join the crowds in the centre of Piazza del Campo at least four hours before the start for a good view. Surrounding streets are closed off well before the race begins, except for Via Giovanni Dupré, which stays open right up until the flag drops. If you can't find a good vantage point, don't despair – the race is televised live and then repeated throughout the evening on TV.

A few days beforehand, jockeys and horses practise in Piazza del Campo – almost as good as the real thing. Between May and October, **Cinema Moderno** (☎ 0577 28 92 01; Piazza Tolomei; admission €5.50; ☯ 10am-5pm) runs a mini-epic 20-minute film of Siena and Il Palio that will take your breath away.

only the lower section before his death –
and was finished towards the end of the
14th century. The mosaics in the gables
were added in the 19th century. The
statues of philosophers and prophets
by Giovanni Pisano, above the lower
section, are copies; the originals are preserved in the adjacent Museo dell'Opera
Metropolitana. In 1339 the city's leaders
launched a plan to enlarge the cathedral
and create one of Italy's largest places of
worship. Known as the **Duomo Nuovo**
(New Cathedral), the remains of this
unrealised project are on Piazza Jacopo
della Quercia, at the eastern side of the
main cathedral. The daring plan, to build
an immense new nave with the present
cathedral becoming the transept, was
scotched by the plague of 1348.

The cathedral's **interior** is truly stunning. Walls and pillars continue the
black-and-white-stripe theme of the
exterior, while the vaults are painted
blue with gold stars. High along the
walls of the nave is a long series of papal
busts. After looking up, look down and
you'll see the cathedral's most precious
feature, the inlaid-marble floor, decorated with 56 glorious panels by about
40 artists and executed over the course
of 200 years (14th to 16th centuries),
depicting historical and biblical subjects.
The older, rectangular panels, including
Ruota della fortuna (Wheel of Fortune;
1372) and *Lupa senese e simboli delle
città alleate* (The She-Wolf of Siena with
the emblems of the confederate cities;
1373) are graffiti designs by unknown
artists, both restored in 1864. Domenico
di Niccoló dei Cori was the first known
artist to work on the cathedral, contrib-
uting several panels between 1413 and
1423, followed by renowned painter
Domenico di Bartolo, who contributed
Imperatore Sigismundo in trono (Em-

peror Sigismund Enthroned) in 1434.
In the 15th century, director Alberto
Aringhieri and celebrated Sienese artist Domenico Beccafumi created the
dramatic expansion of the floor scheme.
These later panels were done in more
advanced multicoloured marble, inlaid
with hexagon and rhombus frames. Unfortunately, about half are obscured by
unsightly, protective covering, and are
revealed only from August 21st through
October 27th each year (admission is €6
during this period). Seek out the exquisite 13th-century marble and porphyry
pulpit by Nicola Pisano, who was aided
by his equally talented son, Giovanni.
Intricately carved with vigorous, realistic
crowd scenes, it's one of the masterpieces of Gothic sculpture.

Off the north aisle, the **Libreria
Piccolomini** is another of the cathedral's
great treasures. Pope Pius III built this
compact hall to house the books of his
uncle, Enea Silvio Piccolomini, who became Pope Pius II; only a series of huge
choral tomes remains on display. The
walls have vividly coloured narrative
frescos by Bernardino Pinturicchio, depicting events in the life of Piccolomini.

♥ MUSEO DELL'OPERA METROPOLITANA // ARTISTIC RICHES AND PANORAMIC SIENA

This **museum** (☎ 0577 28 30 48; Piazza del
Duomo 8; admission €6; ◷ 9.30am-7pm Mar-May &
Sep-Nov, to 8pm Jun-Aug, 10am-5pm Dec-Feb), also
known as Museo dell'Opera del Duomo,
is in what would have been the southern
aisle of the nave of the Duomo Nuovo.
Among its great works of art, which formerly adorned the cathedral, are the 12
statues of prophets and philosophers by
Giovanni Pisano that decorated the facade. Their creator designed them to be
viewed from ground level, which is why

CENTRAL TUSCANY

they look so distorted as they crane uncomfortably forward. On the 1st floor is Duccio di Buoninsegna's striking early-14th-century *Maestà* (Madonna and Child Enthroned with 20 Angels and 19 Saints), painted on both sides as a screen for the cathedral's high altar. The front and back have now been separated and the panels depicting the Story of Christ's Passion hang opposite the *Maestà*. Duccio's narrative genius is impressive. Take the lower half of the bottom big middle panel, in which three scenes take place: Christ preaches to the Apostles in the Garden of Gethsemane; he then asks them to wait up for him; and is lastly portrayed while in prayer. In the half-panel above, he is kissed by Judas while Peter lops off a soldier's ear and the remaining Apostles flee.

Feature Artists

To the right of the *Maestà*, a door leads into a back room with statues by Jacopo della Quercia, while on the left is a room with 19th-century illustrations of the entire collection of marble floor panels in the cathedral. On the upper floors other artists represented include Ambrogio Lorenzetti, Simone Martini and Taddeo di Bartolo, and there's also a rich collection of tapestries and manuscripts. Haul yourself up the 131-step, very narrow, corkscrew stairway, to the **Panorama del Facciatone** (admission €6), at the top of the facade of the putative Nuovo Duomo. A combined admission ticket for the museum and panorama costs €10 and is valid for three days.

☙ CRYPT // EXAMINE 13TH-CENTURY PINTURA A SECCO

Located just north of the cathedral and down a flight of steps is the **crypt** (admission incl audio guide €6; ⏰ 9.30am-7pm Mar-May, 9.30am-8pm Jun-Aug, 9.30am-7pm Sep-Oct), a room

below the cathedral's pulpit discovered in 1999 during restoration work. After a period of clean-up and study – the room had been filled to the roof with debris in the 1300s and forgotten – it was opened to the public in 2003. The walls are completely covered with *pintura a secco* ('dry painting', better known as 'mural painting', as opposed to frescos which are painted on wet plaster, making them more durable) dating from the 1200s. There's some 180 sq metres, depicting several biblical stories, including the Passion of Jesus and the Crucifixion.

☙ BATTISTERO DI SAN GIOVANNI // BOUNTIFUL MARBLE AND FRESCOS

The **baptistry** (Baptistry of St John; Piazza San Giovanni; admission €3; ⏰ 9.30am-7pm Mar-May, to 8pm Jun-Aug, to 7pm Sep-Oct), its Gothic facade unfinished on the upper levels, is quite a remarkable extravagance in marble. Inside, the ceiling and vaults are lavishly decorated with frescos. The life of Jesus is portrayed in the apse of this oddly shaped rectangular baptistery. The one on the right showing Christ carrying the cross is of particular interest. If you look at the city from which it appears he and the crowd have come, it is hard to escape the feeling that among the imaginary buildings are Brunelleschi's dome and Giotto's Campanile in Florence. Could this be a nasty little anti-Florentine dig suggesting Siena's rival as the source of Christ's tribulations? The centrepiece, literally and figuratively, is a marble font by Jacopo della Quercia, decorated with bronze panels in relief depicting the life of St John the Baptist. The panels, executed by several top-notch artists, include Lorenzo Ghiberti's *Baptism of Christ* and *St John in Prison,* and Donatello's *Herod's Feast.*

❤ **COMPLESSO MUSEALE DI SANTA MARIA DELLA SCALA //** **TOUR RELIGIOUS ART, HISTORY AND RUINS**

Originally a hospice for pilgrims and until quite recently a working hospital with almost a millennium of history, the **Santa Maria della Scala** (☎ 0577 22 48 11; Piazza del Duomo 2; admission €6; 🕙 10.30am-6.30pm Apr-Oct, to 4.30pm Nov-Mar) has as its main attraction the vivid, secular frescos (a nice departure from the spiritual ones around town) by Domenico di Bartolo, lauding the good works of the hospital and its patrons. Before entering the hospital proper, pass by the **Chiesa della Santissima Annunziata**, a 13th-century church remodelled two centuries later. Turn right into the **Cappella del Manto**, decorated with frescos; the most striking is by Beccafumi (1514) and portrays the *Meeting of St Joaquim and St Anna,* the supposed parents of the Virgin Mary.

Pilgrim Hall

You'll pass into a long hall where, to the left, is the remarkable 14th-century **Sala del Pellegrinaio**, the pilgrim hall and subsequently the hospital's main ward. The bulk of its fresco series was done by di Bartolo in the 1440s. The first panel, by Il Vecchietta, depicts *gettatelli* (orphans) ascending to heaven. Taking in orphans was frequently one of the tasks of medieval hospitals throughout Tuscany. Later panels show *balie* (wet nurses) suckling orphans and other needy children. One jolly panel depicts a doctor nodding off as a patient describes his symptoms.

Downstairs you'll find the **Fienile**, once storage space for the hospital. The original panelling of the Fonte Gaia (and a few replicas) is now housed here. Through the Fienile is the **Oratorio di Santa Caterina della Notte** (Oratory of

St Catherine of the Night), a gloomy little chapel for sending up a prayer or two for the unwell upstairs.

Archaeological Museum

The **Museo Archeologico** (🕙 10.30am-6.30pm Apr-Oct, to 4.30pm Nov-Mar) is within Santa Maria della Scala. Most of the collection consists of pieces found near Siena, ranging from elaborate Etruscan alabaster funerary urns to gold Roman coins. In between you'll see some statuary, much of it Etruscan, a variety of household items, votive statuettes in bronze and even a pair of dice. The collection is well presented, and the surroundings – twisting, arched tunnels – perfectly complement it and are a cool blessing on stifling-hot summer days. Admission to the museum is included in the price for Santa Maria della Scala.

❤ **PINACOTECA NAZIONALE //** **A VAST COLLECTION OF SIENESE GOTHIC MASTERPIECES**

This **gallery** (☎ 0577 28 11 61; Via San Pietro 29; adult/child €4/free; 🕙 10am-6pm Tue-Sat, 9am-1pm Sun & Mon, 8.30am-1.30pm Mon), within the 14th-century Palazzo Buonsignori, displays an incredible concentration of Gothic masterpieces from the Sienese school. But the collection also demonstrates the subsequent gulf cleaved between artistic life in Siena and Florence in the 15th century. While the Renaissance flourished 70km to the north, Siena's masters and their patrons remained firmly rooted in the Byzantine and Gothic precepts that had stood them in such good stead from the early 13th century. Stock religious images and episodes predominate, typically pasted lavishly with gold and generally lacking any of the advances in painting, such as perspective, emotion or movement, that artists in Florence were exploring. Start your tour on the 2nd floor where, in the first two rooms, you can see some of the earliest surviving pre-Gothic works from the Sienese school, including pieces by Guido da Siena. Rooms 3 and 4 are given over to a few works by Duccio di Buoninsegna and his followers. The most striking exhibits in Room 3 are Simone Martini's *Madonna della misericordia* (Madonna of Mercy), in which the Virgin Mary seems to take the whole of society protectively under her wing, and his *Madonna col bambino* (Madonna and Child). The two brothers Pietro and Ambrogio Lorenzetti feature in Rooms 7 and 8, while the following three rooms contain works by several artists from the early 15th century. Rooms 12 and 13 are mostly devoted to Giovanni di Paolo; a couple of his paintings show refreshing signs of a break from strict tradition. His two versions of the *Presentazione nel tempio* (Presentation of Jesus in the Temple) have virtually no gold

and introduce new architectural themes, a hint of perspective and a discernible trace of human emotion in the characters depicted.

❦ CHIESA DI SAN DOMENICO // EXAMINE RELICS OF SAINT CATHERINE

This imposing 13th-century Gothic church (Piazza San Domenico; ⏲ 7.30am-6.30pm) has been altered time and time again over the centuries. The bare, barnlike interior is in keeping with the Dominican order's ascetic spirit. Near the entrance is the raised **Cappella delle Volte**, where Santa Caterina di Siena took her vows and, according to tradition, performed some of her miracles. In the chapel is a portrait of the saint painted during her lifetime. In the **Cappella di Santa Caterina**, off the south aisle, are frescos by Il Sodoma depicting events in Santa Caterina's life – and her head, in a

ACCOMMODATION

Central Tuscany's assortment of high-profile, desirable destinations sometimes means accommodation can be tight. Though the allure of staying in town is powerful, if you have a car, consider the constellation of *pensioni* (guest houses) and *agriturismi* (farm-stay accommodation) surrounding most cities. **Vacanze Senesi** (☎ 0577 4 59 00; www.vacanzesenesi.it) and **Siena Hotels Promotion** (☎ 0577 28 80 84; www.hotelsiena.com; Piazza San Domenico 5; ⏲ 9am-8pm Mon-Sat) are good resources. Full a full list of accommodation, see p391.

★ Occupying a 14th-centry mansion, **Hotel Leon Bianco** (p405) is a smoothly run, welcoming option facing San Gimignano's main square.

★ Just outside Cetona, **La Frateria di Padre Eligio** (p406) is a lovingly restored former convent dating from 1212 with seven unforgettable rooms and a gourmet restaurant.

★ Springless beds, soundproof windows, ornate frescos, wi-fi and antique furniture make **Antica Residenza Cicogna** (p402), a central option, justifiably popular.

★ Situated just south of Castiglione d'Orcia, **Le Case** (p402) is one of the best value *agriturismi* that we've seen, occupying a gorgeous, 18th-century stone farmhouse.

★ A historic collection of farmhouses called **Borgo Stomennano** (p404), dating from the 1600s, has been furnished and decorated with an amazing collection of heirlooms dating back hundreds of years.

15th-century tabernacle above the altar. She died in Rome, where most of her body is preserved, but, in keeping with the bizarre practice of collecting relics of dead saints, her head was returned to Siena. Another bit that managed to find its way here is her desiccated thumb, on grisly display in a small window box to the right of the chapel. Also on show is a nasty-looking chain whip with which she would apply a good flogging to herself every now and then for the well-being of the souls of the faithful.

♥ CASA DI SANTA CATERINA // EXPLORE SAINT CATHERINE'S HOME, NOW HOMAGE

If you want more of Santa Caterina – figuratively speaking – visit **Casa di Santa Caterina** (☎ 0577 22 15 62; Costa di Sant'Antonio 6; admission free; ☼ 9am-6.30pm Mar-Nov, 10am-6pm Dec-Feb), where the saint was born and lived with her parents plus, says legend, 23 siblings. The rooms, converted into small chapels in the 15th century, are decorated with frescos of her life and paintings by Sienese artists, including Il Sodoma. The lower-level bedroom, frescoed in 1893 by Alessandro Franchi, includes her untouched, nearly bare cell.

GASTRONOMIC HIGHLIGHTS

According to the Sienese, most Tuscan cuisine has its origins here, though Tuscans elsewhere may well dispute this. Traditional dishes include *ribollita* (a rich vegetable, bean-and-bread soup), *panzanella* (summer salad of soaked bread, basil, onion and tomatoes) and *pappardelle con sugo di lepre* (ribbon pasta moistened with hare ragù). Panforte (literally, 'strong bread') is a rich cake of almonds, honey and candied fruit, orig-

inally created as sustenance for Crusaders to the Holy Land. Keep an eye out for dishes featuring the region's signature *cinta senese* (indigenous Tuscan pig).

♥ ANTICA OSTERIA DA DIVO €€€

☎ 0577 28 43 81; www.osteriadadivo.it; Via Franciosa 29; meals €45-50

Here the background jazz is as smooth as the walls are rough-hewn. On the lower, cellar level you're dining amid Etruscan tombs. The inventive menu includes dishes such as cannelloni with ricotta, spinach, grilled sweet peppers, tomatoes and Tuscan pesto sauce. The buckwheat lasagne au gratin with pheasant and fennel seeds in a creamed garlic and squash sauce is, obviously, quite the sight.

♥ IL CARROCCIO €€

☎ 0577 4 11 65; Via del Casato di Sotto 32; meals €32; ☼ closed Tue dinner & Wed

This place serves exceptional pasta and it's exceptionally busy, so arrive early for lunch and call ahead for dinner. Try the *pici*, a thick spaghetti typical of Siena, followed by the *tegamate di maiale* (pork with fennel seeds), and select something a little special from the long and carefully nurtured wine list. The restaurant is a member of the Slow Food Movement (see p385) – always a good sign.

♥ KOPA KABANA €

Via dei Rossi 54

Flout the places with enviable locations and be rewarded with absurd mountains of Siena's freshest gelato, starting at €1.70. A second location is at Via San Pietro 20.

♥ L'OSTERIA €€

☎ 0577 28 75 92; Via dei Rossi 79/81; meals €25

We promised we wouldn't put this one in the book but it was just too good. Plus the place was half-filled with tourists when we visited, so it's not exactly a secret. L'Osteria serves no-nonsense, savoury dishes at prices locals will pay. Pop over to Kopa Kabana for something *dolce* afterward.

😺 NANNINI €
Banchi di Sopra 22

Always crowded, this is something of a Sienese institution, baking its finest cakes and serving good coffee with speed and panache. Its refrigerator is cooled by water carried from 16km away by the same 13th-century tunnels that fuel many of the city's fountains, including Fonte Gaia in Piazza del Campo.

😺 OSTERIA BOCCON DEL PRETE €€
☎ 0577 28 03 88; Via San Pietro 17; meals €28

A small, hectic, typical Sienese place, offering a daily changing menu. Dishes are largely composed of lighter fare – such as smoked swordfish and salmon salad – much appreciated when you're still carrying a food baby from a previous meal. There's downstairs seating, so don't back out if the place appears to be full.

😺 OSTERIA DA CICE €€
☎ 0577 28 80 26; Via San Pietro 32; meals €26; 😺 Tue-Sun

In the hands of a friendly team, reflecting its mainly youthful clientele, this extremely popular place is best for informal, relaxed meals. The menu has plenty of typical dishes such as *pappardelle al cinghiale* (pappardelle with wild boar sauce) and *bistecca alla fiorentina* (grilled T-bone steak), with a few vegetarian options among its *primi piatti* (first courses).

😺 OSTERIA LE LOGGE €€
☎ 0577 4 80 13; www.osterialelogge.it, in Italian; Via dei Porrione 33; meals €40-45; 😺 Mon-Sat

This place changes its menu of creative Tuscan cuisine almost daily. In the

downstairs dining room, which was once a pharmacy, bottles are arranged in cases, floor to ceiling, like books in a library; there are more than 18,000 more in the cellars, so you won't go thirsty. There's also a large street-side terrace.

NIGHTLIFE

😺 ENOTECA ITALIANA
☎ 0577 28 84 97; Fortezza Medicea; 😺 noon-1am Tue-Sat, to 8pm Sun

Within the fortress walls, the former munitions cellar has been artfully transformed into a classy *enoteca* that carries more than 1500 labels. The Italian wine display includes some dusty *reservas,* the oldest dating back to 1944.

RECOMMENDED SHOPS

😺 CONSORZIO AGRARIO SIENA
Via Pianagini 13

This farmer's co-op, operating since 1901, is a rich emporium of local food and wine, much of which has been locally produced.

😺 PIZZICHERIA DE MICCOLI
☎ 0577 28 91 64; Via di Città 93-5

Richly scented, this is a great place to stock up on picnic fodder. Its windows are festooned with sausages, piled-up cheeses and *porcini* mushrooms by the sackful.

😺 SIENA RICAMA
☎ 0577 28 83 39; Via di Città 61

A one-woman embroidery and needlepoint shop, where nearly every surface area is covered by crafts made onsite, largely inspired by local art and architecture.

😺 WEDNESDAY MARKET
😺 7.30am-1pm

Spreading all around Fortezza Medicea and seeping towards the Stadio

Comunale. One of Tuscany's largest, it's great for foodstuffs and cheap clothing, or just aimless browsing.

TRANSPORT

BUS // The hub for buses is Piazza Gramsci. Bus 'train' service TRAIN (☎ 0577 20 42 46; www.trainspa.it) runs two services daily between Pisa International Airport and Siena (one-way/return €14/26). It also operates city bus services (€0.90). Bus 8, 9 and 10 run between the train station and Piazza Gramsci. This operation and SITA (www.sitabus.it) have ticket offices underneath the piazza, where there's also a left-luggage office. Express buses race up to Florence (€6.80, 1¼ hours, up to 30 daily). Other regional TRAIN destinations include San Gimignano (€5.30, 1¼ hours, 10 daily either direct or changing in Poggibonsi), Montalcino (€3.30, 1½ hours, six daily), Poggibonsi (€3.80, one hour, up to 10 daily), Montepulciano (€4.50, 1¾ hours) and Colle di Val d'Elsa (€2.60, 30 minutes, hourly), with connections for Volterra. Other destinations in the area include San Quirico d'Orcia (€3.30), Pienza (€3.80) and Grosseto (€6.60). SENA buses run to/from Rome (€20, three hours, eight daily) and Milan (€29, 4¼ hours, three daily) and there are seven buses daily to Arezzo (€5.20, 1½ hours).

CAR // Cars are banned from the town centre, though visitors can drop off luggage at their hotel, then get out (don't forget to have reception report your licence number or risk receiving a 'souvenir' fine). To reach Florence, take the SS2, the *superstrada* (expressway), or the more attractive SS222, also known as the Chiantigiana, which meanders its way through the hills of Chianti.

PARKING // Park illegally inside the city and you'll be towed away in a flash. Try the large car parks at the Stadio Comunale and around the Fortezza Medicea, both just north of Piazza San Domenico.

TRAIN // Siena isn't on a major train line and buses are generally a better alternative. By train, change at Chiusi for Rome and at Empoli for Florence. Trains arrive at Piazza Fratelli Rosselli, north of the city centre.

BICYCLE & MOTORCYCLE // Perozzi Noleggi (☎ 0577 28 83 87; www.perozzi.it; Via dei Gazzani 16-18; ⏰ 8.30am-12.30pm & 3-7pm) rents mountain bikes (per day/week €10/50) and 125cc scoot-

ers (per day/week €45/260). If there's no one in the showroom, pop round the corner to Via del Romitorio 5.

TAXI // For a taxi, call ☎ 0577 4 92 22.

NORTH OF SIENA

· · · · · ·

Within easy reach of both Siena and Florence, San Gimignano is a tourist magnet. Come in winter or early spring to indulge your imagination a little; in summer you'll spend your time dodging fellow visitors in the middle of the day. But there's a time when the day-trippers leave, and this is when you'll discover a different, more peaceful town. Where San Gimignano has its towers, Volterra has its archaeological sites, extensive network of mysterious alleys to explore and steep, stone stairways to scale.

SAN GIMIGNANO

pop 7740

As you crest the hill coming from the east, the 14 towers of this walled town look like a medieval Manhattan – with modern Manhattan's population density. The towers, which once numbered 72, were symbols of the power and wealth of the city's medieval families. San Gimignano delle Belle Torri (meaning 'of the Fine Towers' – though they're actually almost devoid of design and rather dull unless sheer height impresses you) is surrounded by lush, productive land and the setting is altogether enchanting. The area around San Gimignano is famous for the cultivation of saffron. Originally an Etruscan village, the town was named after the bishop of

Modena, San Gimignano, who is said to have saved the city from Attila the Hun. It became a *comune* (self-governing city) in 1199, but fought frequently with neighbouring Volterra. Internal battles between Ardinghelli (Guelph) and Salvucci (Ghibelline) families over the next two centuries caused deep divisions. Most towers were built during this period – in the 13th century, one *podestà* (town chief) forbade the building of towers higher than his own 51m pile.

In 1348, plague wiped out much of the population and weakened the nobles' power, leading to the town's submission to Florence in 1353. Today, not even the plague would deter the summer swarms.

ESSENTIAL INFORMATION

TOURIST OFFICES // Tourist office (☎ 0577 94 00 08; www.sangimignano.com; Piazza del Duomo 1; ☺ 9am-1pm & 3-7pm Mar-Oct, 9am-1pm & 2-6pm Nov-Feb) Hires out audio guides of the town (€5) and organises Vernaccia di San Gimignano vineyard visits (two-hour tours, Tuesdays and Thursdays, from May to October; €20). Advance reservations are essential.

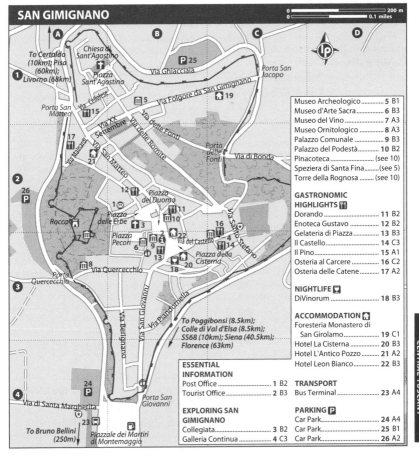

SAN GIMIGNANO

Museo Archeologico	5 B1
Museo d'Arte Sacra	6 B3
Museo del Vino	7 A3
Museo Ornitologico	8 A3
Palazzo Comunale	9 B3
Palazzo del Podestà	10 B2
Pinacoteca	(see 10)
Speziera di Santa Fina	(see 5)
Torre della Rognosa	(see 10)

GASTRONOMIC HIGHLIGHTS 🍴

Dorando	11 B2
Enoteca Gustavo	12 B2
Gelateria di Piazza	13 B3
Il Castello	14 C3
Il Pino	15 A1
Osteria al Carcere	16 C2
Osteria delle Catene	17 A2

NIGHTLIFE 🍷

DiVinorum	18 B3

ACCOMMODATION 🏠

Foresteria Monastero di San Girolamo	19 C1
Hotel La Cisterna	20 B3
Hotel L'Antico Pozzo	21 A2
Hotel Leon Bianco	22 B3

ESSENTIAL INFORMATION

Post Office	1 B2
Tourist Office	2 B3

EXPLORING SAN GIMIGNANO

Collegiata	3 B2
Galleria Continua	4 C3

TRANSPORT

Bus Terminal	23 A4

PARKING 🅿

Car Park	24 A4
Car Park	25 B1
Car Park	26 A2

CENTRAL TUSCANY

MONEY SAVER

If you're an assiduous sightseer, two combined tickets may be worth your while. One (adult/child €7.50/5.50) gives admission to the Palazzo Comunale and its Museo Civico, the archaeological museum, Torre Grossa and some secondary sights. The other (adult/child €5.50/2.50) gets you into the Collegiata and nearby Museo d'Arte Sacra.

EXPLORING SAN GIMIGNANO

Start in triangular Piazza della Cisterna, named after the 13th-century cistern at its centre. In the Piazza del Duomo, the Collegiata (basilica) looks across to the late-13th-century **Palazzo del Podestà** and its tower, the **Torre della Rognosa**. The Palazzo Comunale, to the right of the basilica, is the town hall.

♥ COLLEGIATA // ENJOY A MEDIEVAL COMIC STRIP

Access to the town's Romanesque **basilica** (adult/child €3.50/1.50; ☉ 9.30am-7.30pm Mon-Sat, 12.30-5pm Sun Apr-Oct, 9.30am-5pm Mon-Sat, 12.30-5pm Sun Nov–mid-Jan & Mar) is up a flight of stairs from Piazza del Duomo. Its bare facade belies the remarkable 14th-century frescos that stripe the interior walls like some vast medieval comic strip, stretching amid the black-and-white striped arches and columns that separate the three naves. A fresco by Taddeo di Bartolo covers the upper half of the rear wall and depicts the Last Judgment, while the lower half is dominated by Benozzo Gozzoli's rendering of the martyrdom of St Sebastian. Still facing the rear wall, on the upper-left side is a fresco depicting *Paradiso* (Heaven) and on the upper-

right *Inferno* (Hell). Both are by Taddeo di Bartolo, who seems to have taken particular delight in presenting the horrors of the underworld, considering the faithful in those times would have taken such images pretty much at face value.

Facing the altar, along the left (north) wall, are scenes from Genesis and the Old Testament by Bartolo di Fredi, dating from around 1367. The top row runs from the creation of the world through to the forbidden fruit scene. This in turn leads to the next level and fresco, the expulsion of Adam and Eve from the Garden of Eden, which has sustained some war damage. Further scenes include Cain killing Abel, and the stories of Noah's ark and Joseph's coat. The last level continues with the tale of Moses leading the Jews out of Egypt, and the story of Job.

On the right (south) wall are scenes from the New Testament by the school of Simone Martini, completed in 1336. Again, the frescos are spread over three levels, starting in the six lunettes at the top. Commencing with the Annunciation, the panels proceed through episodes such as the Epiphany, the presentation of Christ in the temple and the massacre of the innocents on Herod's orders. The subsequent panels on the lower levels summarise the life and death of Christ, the Resurrection and so on. Again, some have sustained damage, but most are in good condition.

The **Cappella di Santa Fina**, off to the right, has a pair of touching frescos by Domenico Ghirlandaio depicting events in the life of the saint, and a superb altar of alabaster and marble flecked with gold.

♥ MUSEO D'ARTE SACRA // BROWSE THE TOWN'S RELIGIOUS TREASURES

Across the square, the **Museo d'Arte Sacra** (☎ 0577 94 03 16; Piazza Pecori 1; adult/child

€3/1.50; ⊗ 9.30am-7.30pm Mon-Fri, to 5pm Sat, 12.30-5pm Sun Apr-Oct, 9.30am-5pm Mon-Sat, 12.30-5pm Sun Nov–mid-Jan & Mar) has some fine works of religious art, including a collection of medieval painted wooden statues, vestments, hangings, crosses and finely illuminated manuscripts culled, in the main, from the town's churches. Those who specialise in medieval religious objects will appreciate the items made from precious metals, including beautifully crafted chalices and thuribles (censers), as well as some exquisitely embroidered textiles.

♥ PALAZZO COMUNALE // VIEW ANCIENT ART AND SAN GIMIGNANO FROM ON HIGH

San Gimignano's other principal sight is this seat of secular power, which was founded in 1288, expanded in the 14th century and had a neo-Gothic facade tacked on in the late 19th century.

From the internal courtyard climb the stairs to the **Pinacoteca** (☎ 0577 99 03 12; Piazza del Duomo; museum & tower adult/child €5/4; ⊗ 9.30am-7pm Mar-Oct, 10am-5.30pm Nov-Feb). In the main room, the **Sala di Dante**, the great poet addressed the town's council, imploring it to join the Florentine-led Guelph League. You can't miss the *Maestà*, a masterful 1317 fresco by Lippo Memmi depicting the enthroned Virgin Mary and Christ child with angels and saints. Other frescos portray jousts, hunting scenes, castles and other medieval goings-on. Up two levels, the collection of medieval religious works includes a crucifix by Coppo di Marcovaldo, notable for its age (c 1261) and quality (some say it's superior to those of Giotto), and a pair of remarkable *tondi* (circular paintings) by Filippino Lippi. Also on this level, there's a small frescoed room. Opinion is divided on what these frescos, showing wedding scenes, are all about. It all looks like great fun, with the newlyweds taking a bath together and then hopping into the sack. Climb up the palazzo's **Torre Grossa** for a spectacular view of the town and surrounding countryside.

♥ MUSEO DEL VINO // TASTE CHOICE LOCAL WHITE WINES

In an unmarked gallery just outside the town's fortress is San Gimignano's **wine museum** (☎ 0577 94 12 67; Parco della Rocca; admission free; ⊗ 11.30am-6.30pm Thu-Mon, 3-6.30pm Wed Mar-Oct). A sommelier is on hand to lead a (paid) tasting. This is a one-man show – when the sommelier is sick or on holiday, the place unceremoniously shuts.

♥ MUSEO ARCHEOLOGICO & SPEZIERA DI SANTA FINA // EXAMINE CONTENTS FROM A 16TH-CENTURY PHARMACY

There are actually two **museums** (☎ 0577 94 03 48; Via Folgore da San Gimignano 11; both museums adult/child €3.50/2.50; ⊗ 11am-5.45pm mid-Mar–Dec) and a gallery in this complex. The Speziera section includes ceramic and glass storage vessels from the 16th-century Speziera di Santa Fina, a reconstructed 16th-century pharmacy and herb garden. Many are beautifully painted and still contain curative concoctions. Follow your nose to the side room in Gallery 7, called 'the kitchen', which is filled with herbs and spices used for elixirs. All descriptions are in Italian. Beyond here is a small archaeological museum divided into Etruscan/Roman and medieval sections with exhibits found locally. The museum also houses a good modern art gallery that in itself merits a visit. Permanent works include the distinctive swirly abstracts of Renato Guttuso and some excellent oils on canvas by Raffaele de Grada.

WINE: CHEAPER THAN WATER

It's true, a glass of house wine in an Italian restaurant will usually undercut the price of a bottle of water. You really have no choice but to imbibe. Since you're saving all that money, consider splashing out on the following top pours.

'It kisses, licks, bites, thrusts, and stings'. That's how Michelangelo, clearly drawing upon the purple end of his palate, described **San Gimignano's Vernaccia** white wine. Smooth and aromatic with a slightly bitter aftertaste and pale golden yellow in colour, it was Italy's first DOC wine and the second white to be awarded DOCG (see p375). But these are only recent accolades. It's been around, though scarcely unsung, for centuries. Dante in his *Divine Comedy* banished Pope Martin IV to purgatory because of it, Boccaccio fantasised about flowing streams of cool Vernaccia, Pope Paul III reputedly bathed in it and the ever-demure St Catherine of Siena used it as medicine.

Vino Nobile di Montepulciano dates back to 1350. Pope Paul III – presumably after towelling off from a good soak in Vernaccia – gushed about this red in his late-16th-century poem 'Bacchus in Tuscany'. It was granted the description of 'noble' in the second half of the 18th century, about the same time that Voltaire was name-checking it in his 1759 novel *Candide*. More recent admirers have included the American presidents Martin Van Buren and Thomas Jefferson. Some 250,000 cases of Vino Nobile di Montepulciano are produced each year, more than might be deemed 'noble', but still few enough to make a bottle a special occasion.

Brunello di Montalcino ranks among the world's top wines. Collectors pay hundreds of dollars for a respectable bottle at auction. The price tag skyrockets into the thousands for select bottles from the 1940s and a bottle of the Biondi-Santi 1955 Brunello, voted as one of the top dozen wines of the last century, could put a small nation's budget into deficit. 'Brunello' is the name used for a handful of mutations of the sangiovese grape found around Montalcino, the result of horticultural tinkering by Clemente Santi and his grandson, Ferruccio Biondi-Santi, in the mid-19th century. Brunello almost immediately developed an exalted reputation, its grapes coming from select boutique vineyards, creating a product known for its borderline outlandish exclusivity and price as much as for its extraordinary quality. It was the first wine appellation in Italy to be granted the coveted DOCG ranking in 1970. Total annual production, from grapes grown almost entirely within a 26-sq-km radius around Montalcino, is about 350,000 cases – not even what a medium-sized winery produces yearly.

🌿 **GALLERIA CONTINUA // CONTEMPORARY ART FROM AROUND THE WORLD**
Housed in the city's old theatre, **Galleria Continua** (☎ 0577 94 31 34; www.galleriacontinua .com; Via del Castello 11; admission free; ⏰ 2-7pm Tue-Sat) shows its collection of contemporary art by famous artists at nearly every major international art fair, with sister galleries in Le Moulin and Beijing. Exhibitions change about every two months.

GASTRONOMIC HIGHLIGHTS

Each Thursday morning there's a **produce market** (Piazza della Cisterna & Piazza del Duomo).

☺ DORANDO €€€

☎ 0577 94 18 62; www.ristorantedorando.it; Vicolo dell'Oro 2; mains €55-60; ☺ daily Easter-Oct, Tue-Sun Oct-Easter

Recognised by the Slow Food Movement, Dorando runs a classic five-course menu with dishes based on authentic Etruscan recipes. The à la carte menu is otherwise brief (four *primi* and four *secondi*). The atmosphere is swanky yet cool, with intimate corners and works of art.

☺ ENOTECA GUSTAVO €

☎ 0577 94 00 57; Via San Matteo 29; snacks & wine from €2.50; ☺ 9am-8pm

There isn't much elbow space inside, so go for one of the outside tables, which offer the bonus of enjoying longing looks from hungry passersby. Snacks include a large variety of bruschetta and plates of meats and cheeses with honey to go with your choice from the impressive selection of wines.

☺ GELATERIA DI PIAZZA €

☎ 0577 94 22 44; Piazza della Cisterna 4; ☺ Mar–mid-Nov

As the pictures around the wall attest, many celebrities have closed their lips around one of Gelateria di Piazza's rich ice creams ('all the family thought the ice cream was delicious' attested one Tony Blair). Master Sergio uses only the choicest ingredients: pistachios from Sicily and cocoa from Venezuela.

☺ IL CASTELLO €€

☎ 0577 94 08 78; enotecailcastello@iol.it; Via del Castello 20; meals €35; ☺ Mar–mid-Jan

Being both wine bar and restaurant, this place has a delightful patio with views and an all-brick, glass-domed courtyard. Most dishes are macho-meaty, like the frighteningly large *bistecca alla fiorentina* and *cinghiale alla sangimign-anese con polenta* (wild boar with polenta and tomato salad), though there's less macho fallbacks like the *pennette* with broccoli, wild mushrooms and saffron.

☺ IL PINO €€

☎ 0577 94 04 15; Via Cellolese 8-10; meals €37-42; ☺ Fri-Wed

The atmosphere here is spruce, vaulted and airy. Service is friendly and attentive and the seasonal menu, which includes massive pasta plates and several truffle-based specialities, is a winner. The 'chocolate mousse with chocolate' might sound funny, but the joke's over when you taste it – and realise it's factually correct.

☺ OSTERIA AL CARCERE €€

☎ 0577 94 19 05; Via del Castello 5; soups €8, meals €30-35; ☺ closed Thu lunch & Wed

A fine *osteria*, offering an atypical menu (the words '*primi*' and '*secondi*' are nowhere to be seen) loaded with distinctive plates. There are half a dozen soups, including *zuppa di farro e fagioli* (local-grain-and-white-bean soup) and creative flashes like *tacchina al pistacchi e arance* (turkey with pistachios and orange sauce).

☺ OSTERIA DELLE CATENE €€

☎ 0577 94 19 66; osteriadellecatene.oster@tin.it; Via Mainardi 18; menù degustazione €13-31, meals €33-38; ☺ closed Wed & mid-Dec–Feb

The brick-barrelled interior is softly lit while the menu is heavy on strong meats – hare, boar, duck and rabbit. Alongside many Tuscan stalwarts and saffron experimentation such as the *zuppa medievale*, there's the *spaghetti dell'Ostria* (spaghetti with zucchini, sausages and chilli pepper in puréed sauce) and a small but sublime carrot and leek soufflé.

NIGHTLIFE

♥ DIVINORUM

Piazza della Cisterna 30; ✆ 11am-8pm Mar-Oct, 11am-4pm Nov-Dec

Housed in cavernous former stables is this cool wine bar run by local lads. The light menu includes fruit and cheese plates, bruschetta and carpaccio. In summer, sip your drink on the tiny outdoor terrace from where you'll gain stunning valley views.

TRANSPORT

BUS // Buses arrive in Piazzale dei Martiri di Montemaggio, beside Porta San Giovanni. Services run to/from Florence (€6, 1¼ hours, more than 30 daily) and Siena (€5.30, one to 1½ hours, 10 daily). For Volterra (€4.30, 1½ hours, five daily except Sunday), you need to change in Colle di Val d'Elsa and maybe also in Poggibonsi. The tourist office carries timetables.

CAR & MOTORCYCLE // From Florence or Siena, take the SR2 to Poggibonsi, then the SS429 and finally the SP63. From Volterra, take the SS68 east and follow the turn-off signs north to San Gimignano. **Bruno Bellini** (✆ 0577 94 02 01; www.bellinibruno.com; Via Roma 41; ✆ 9am-1pm & 3-7.30pm Mon-Fri) rents mountain bikes (per day €15) and scooters (per day from €31).

PARKING // There are car parks (per hour €2 or per day €5 to €20) outside the city walls and beside and below Porta San Giovanni. There's free parking in the new parts of town, just northwest of the old centre, but this is quite a hike and competition is fierce.

TRAIN // Poggibonsi (by bus €1.80, about 30 minutes, frequent) is the closest train station.

VOLTERRA

pop 11,200

Volterra's well-preserved medieval ramparts give the windswept town a scrappy yet proud, forbidding air. This landscape was deemed ideal for the discriminating tastes of the planet's principal vampire

coven in the wildly popular book series *Twilight,* by Stephanie Meyer.

People looking for that perfect alabaster figurine for their garden, or simply wanting to see alabaster artists in action, will have plenty of shops to choose from, and the local collection of Etruscan artefacts is arguably unmatched in Tuscany.

The Etruscan settlement of Velathri was an important trading centre and senior partner of the Dodecapolis. It is believed that as many as 25,000 people lived here in its Etruscan heyday. Partly because of the surrounding inhospitable terrain, the city was among the last to succumb to Rome – it was absorbed into the Roman confederation around 260 BC and renamed Volaterrae. The bulk of the old city was raised in the 12th and 13th centuries under a fiercely independent free *comune.* The city first entered into Florence's orbit in 1361, but it was some time before Florence took full control. When this domination was first threatened, Lorenzo Il Magnifico made one of his few big mistakes and created lasting enemies in the people of Volterra; in 1472 he marched in and ruthlessly snuffed out every vestige of potential opposition to direct Florentine rule.

ESSENTIAL INFORMATION

TOURIST OFFICES // Volterra Tourist Office (✆ 0588 8 72 57; www.volterratur.it; Piazza dei Priori 19-20; ✆ 10am-1pm & 2-6pm) Offers a free hotel-booking service and rents out a good town audio guide (€5).

EXPLORING VOLTERRA

♥ PIAZZA DEI PRIORI & AROUND // VISIT THE CITY'S MOST STRIKING BUILDINGS

Piazza dei Priori is ringed by austere medieval mansions. The 13th-century **Palazzo dei Priori** (Piazza dei Priori; admission €1;

⊙ 10.30am-5.30pm mid-Mar–Oct, 10am-5pm Sat & Sun Nov–mid-Mar), the oldest seat of local government in Tuscany, is believed to have been a model for Florence's Palazzo Vecchio. Highlights are a fresco of the *Crucifixion* by Piero Francesco Fiorentino on the staircase, the magnificent cross-vaulted council hall and a small antechamber on the 1st floor giving a bird's-eye view of the piazza below. The **Palazzo Pretorio** is from the same era. From it thrusts the **Torre del Porcellino** (Piglet's Tower), so named because of the wild boar protruding from its upper section.

Cathedral & Surrounds

The **cathedral** (Piazza San Giovanni; ⊙ 8am-12.30pm & 3-6pm) was built in the 12th and 13th centuries. Highlights include a small fresco, the *Procession of the Magi* by Benozzo Gozzoli, behind a terracotta nativity group tucked away in the oratory at the beginning of the north aisle. An exquisite 15th-century alabaster tabernacle by Mino da Fiesole rises above the high altar.

Just west of the cathedral is the 13th-century **baptistry** with a small marble font by Andrea Sansovino. On the west side of Piazza San Giovanni, the porticoed

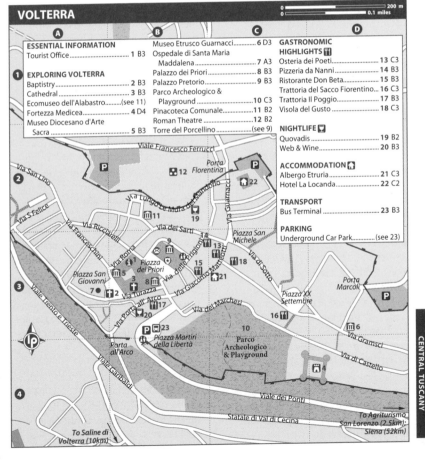

VOLTERRA

0 — 200 m
0 — 0.1 miles

ESSENTIAL INFORMATION
Tourist Office 1 B3

EXPLORING VOLTERRA
Baptistry 2 B3
Cathedral 3 B3
Ecomuseo dell'Alabastro .... (see 11)
Fortezza Medicea 4 D4
Museo Diocesano d'Arte
  Sacra 5 B3

Museo Etrusco Guarnacci 6 D3
Ospedale di Santa Maria
  Maddalena 7 A3
Palazzo dei Priori 8 B3
Palazzo Pretorio 9 B3
Parco Archeologico &
  Playground 10 C3
Pinacoteca Comunale 11 B2
Roman Theatre 12 B2
Torre del Porcellino .... (see 9)

GASTRONOMIC HIGHLIGHTS
Osteria dei Poeti 13 C3
Pizzeria da Nanni 14 B3
Ristorante Don Beta 15 B3
Trattoria del Sacco Fiorentino ... 16 C3
Trattoria Il Poggio 17 B3
Visola del Gusto 18 C3

NIGHTLIFE
Quovadis 19 B2
Web & Wine 20 B3

ACCOMMODATION
Albergo Etruria 21 C3
Hotel La Locanda 22 C2

TRANSPORT
Bus Terminal 23 B3

PARKING
Underground Car Park .... (see 23)

Viale Francesco Ferrucci
Porta Florentina
Via San Lino
Via Lungo Le Mura del Mandorlo
Via S-Felice
Via Ricciarelli
Via dei Sarti
Piazza San Michele
Via Guarnacci
Via Franceschini
Via Roma
Piazza dei Priori
Via delle Prigioni
Via di Sotto
Via Giacomo Matteotti
Piazza San Giovanni
Via Turazza
Via Porta all'Arco
Porta Marcoli
Via del Marchesi
Viale Trento e Trieste
Piazza XX Settembre
Piazza Martiri della Libertà
Parco Archeologico & Playground
Porta all'Arco
Viale Garibaldi
Via Gramsci
Via di Castello
Viale dei Ponti
Statale di Val di Cecina

To Agriturismo San Lorenzo (2.5km); Siena (52km)
To Saline di Volterra (10km)

CENTRAL TUSCANY

TICKETING

An €8 ticket covers visits to the Museo Etrusco Guarnacci, the Pinacoteca Comunale and the Museo Diocesano d'Arte Sacra. A €3 ticket allows entry to both the Roman theatre and the dilapidated Etruscan necropolis within the Parco Archeologico.

Ospedale di Santa Maria Maddalena was once a foundlings hospital. Nearby, the **Museo Diocesano d'Arte Sacra** (☎ 0588 8 62 90; Via Roma 1; 9am-1pm & 3-6pm mid-Mar–Oct, 9am-1pm Nov–mid-Mar) merits a peek for its collection of ecclesiastical vestments, gold reliquaries and works by Andrea della Robbia and Rosso Fiorentino.

Late Renaissance Art

The **Pinacoteca Comunale** (☎ 0588 8 75 80; Via dei Sarti 1; 9am-7pm mid-Mar–Oct, 8.30am-1.45pm Nov–mid-Mar), in the Palazzo Minucci Solaini, houses a modest collection of local, Sienese and Florentine art. A scholarly highlight is Rosso Fiorentino's *Deposition,* due to its emotional content and similarities with the works of Goya. It is considered Fiorentino's masterpiece, straddling late-Renaissance and Mannerism.

♥ ECOMUSEO DELL'ALABASTRO // ADMIRE CONTEMPORARY AND ETRUSCAN ALABASTER CREATIONS

As befits a town that has hewn the precious rock from nearby quarries since Etruscan times, Volterra has an **alabaster museum** (☎ 0588 8 75 80; Via dei Sarti 1; admission €3; 11am-5pm mid-Mar–Oct, 9am-1.30pm Sat & Sun Nov–mid-Mar), which shares the same building as the Pinacoteca. On the ground floor are contemporary creations, including a finely chiselled mandolin and a bizarre fried egg, while on the two upper floors are

choice examples from Etruscan times onwards and a re-created artisan's workshop.

♥ MUSEO ETRUSCO GUARNACCI // SEE ONE OF ITALY'S FINEST ETRUSCAN MUSEUMS

In terms of content, this **museum** (☎ 0588 8 63 47; Via Don Minzoni 15; adult/student €8/5; 9am-7pm mid-Mar–Oct, 8.30am-1.45pm Nov–mid-Mar) is one of Italy's finest Etruscan museums. Much of the collection is displayed in the old-style didactic manner – badly labelled, mostly in Italian, and stuffy – though some exhibits on the upper levels have been artfully displayed in modern, stylish cases with subdued lighting. The multilingual audio guide (€3) is worth the investment for much-needed descriptions and to boost the overall pep factor.

All exhibits were unearthed locally. They include a vast collection of some 600 funerary urns carved mainly from alabaster and tufa and displayed according to subject and period. The tiny casket-shaped urns typically have human figures lying in repose on the top with a scene captured on the front, often military in theme. Be selective; they all start to look the same after a while. The best examples (those dating from later periods) are on the 2nd and 3rd floors.

Original touches are the Ombra della Sera bronze *ex voto*, a strange, elongated nude figure that would fit harmoniously in any museum of modern art, and the urn of the Sposi, a terracotta rendering of an elderly couple, their wrinkled features depicted in portrait fashion rather than the usual stylised manner.

♥ ROMAN THEATRE // FEEL THE DRAMA OF ANCIENT THEATRE

On the city's northern edge is a **Roman theatre** (10.30am-5.30pm mid-Mar–Oct, to 4pm Sat & Sun Nov–mid-Mar), a well-preserved complex dating from the 1st century BC. Three arched niches, two stairways and 19 rows of seating are still easily identifiable. Behind the theatre is a Roman bathhouse dating from the 4th century AD. The site was completely buried in garbage during medieval times; excavations began in 1951.

GASTRONOMIC HIGHLIGHTS

☕ OSTERIA DEI POETI €€

☎ 0588 8 60 29; Via Giacomo Matteotti 55; meals €33, tourist menus €13-35; ⏰ Fri-Wed

Get here right at midday, before the business lunchers fill the last seat. It's equally hectic at dinner. Typical Tuscan fare is served with a backdrop of pleasing mellow brickwork and golden arches. The *antipasto del poeta* (€15), a rich assortment of canapés, cheeses and cold cuts, is a delight, and the veal is juicy good value.

☕ PIZZERIA DA NANNI €

☎ 0588 8 40 47; Via delle Pregioni 40; pizzas €6.20-8.50; ⏰ Mon-Sat

This is a hole-in-the-wall-plus – the plus being the excellent pizzas that Nanni spatulas from his oven, while sustaining a vivid line of backchat with his wife and drop-ins. Unscheduled closings are increasing as the couple eases into retirement.

☕ RISTORANTE DON BETA €€

☎ 0588 8 67 30; Via Giacomo Matteotti 39; meals €30-45, menus €12-21; ⏰ closed Mon Oct-Apr

With four truffle-based *primi piatti,* and five *secondi* enhanced by their fragrance, this is the place to sample the prized fungus, which abounds – in so far as it abounds anywhere – in the woods around Volterra. Do check on the prices first, though they are generally reasonable. Alternatively, choose the mouthwatering *tortellone di sfoglia di spinaci noci e radicchio* (spinach ravioli with walnut and radicchio sauce) or the *bistecca*

di cinghiale alla griglia (amazingly tender wild boar fillets grilled with rosemary).

☕ TRATTORIA DEL SACCO FIORENTINO €€

☎ 0588 8 85 37; Piazza XX Settembre 18; meals €28-32, menù degustazione €26-28; ⏰ Thu-Tue

A great little vaulted trattoria that serves up imaginative dishes with a happy selection of local wines. Try the *piccione al vin santo e radicchio rosso* (pigeon baked with red radicchio and holy wine) or the critical mass of flavour in the beef tartare with artichokes and fresh onions.

☕ TRATTORIA IL POGGIO €€

☎ 0588 8 52 57; Via Porta all'Arco 7; meals €28; ⏰ Wed-Mon

A popular restaurant where the cheery waitresses bustle around and find time to chat with the regulars between dashes to the electric dumbwaiter raising food from the subterranean kitchen. There's a good set menu, a long list of pizzas, two outdoor terraces, and rich dishes such as scampi and rocket, or ravioli with asparagus and ham in a parmesan cream sauce.

☕ VISOLA DEL GUSTO €

Via Antonio Gramsci 3

This hole-in-the-wall *gelateria* (ice-cream shop) serves the freshest gelato in town, starting at €1.50 for a 'small'. The signature flavour redefines the word 'creamy'.

NIGHTLIFE

☕ WEB & WINE

☎ 0588 8 15 31; Via Porta all'Arco 11-13; meals €32; ⏰ 9.30am-1am Fri-Wed

This is one of those splendid places that defy guidebook characterisation. It's at once internet point (web access per hour €3), a stylish *enoteca* (with a good selection of tipples), a snack stop, a hip designer cafe (it's not every day you step across a glass floor, revealing under-lit Etruscan remains and a 5m-deep Renaissance grain silo) and a full restaurant serving home-made pasta, sweets and bread.

TRANSPORT

BUS // The bus terminal is on Piazza Martiri della Libertà. CPT (☎ 800 57 05 30; www.cpt.pisa.it, in Italian) buses connect the town with Saline (€1.80, 20 minutes, frequent) and its train station. From Saline, 9km southwest, there are bus connections for Pisa (direct €5.50, two hours, or change at Pontedera €3.50) and Cecina (€3.50), to where there's also a train link. Buy tickets in *tabacchi* shops (buying on the bus is more expensive). For San Gimignano (€3.50, 1½ hours), Siena (€4.50, 1½ hours) and Florence (€7.40, two hours), change at Colle di Val d'Elsa (€2.50, 50 minutes), to where there are four runs daily from Volterra, except on Sunday. The rare, direct run to Florence from Volterra is €7.10. Other buses head south in the direction of Massa Marittima but only go as far as Pomarance (€2.40, 12 daily) and Castelnuovo di Valle di Cecina (€3.50, 10 daily). The tourist office carries timetables.

CAR & MOTORCYCLE // By car, take the SS68, which runs between Cecina and Colle di Val d'Elsa. A couple of back routes to San Gimignano are signposted north off the SS68. Driving and parking inside the walled town are more or less prohibited.

PARKING // Park in one of the designated parking areas around the circumference, most of which are free. There's a four-level paying underground car park beneath Piazza Martiri della Libertà.

TRAIN // From the small train station in Saline, you can catch a train to Cecina on the coast and change to the Rome-Pisa line.

SOUTH OF SIENA

· · · · · ·

Le Crete is an area of rolling clay hills scored by steep ravines offering a feast of classic Tuscan images – bare ridges topped by a solitary cypress tree and hills silhouetted one against another as they fade into the misty distance. For a while, similar countryside persists as you roam south amid the classic Tuscan landscape of rolling hills of hay topped with a huddle of cypress trees. Gradually the landscape gives way to more unruly territory. This part of the province offers everything: the haughty hilltop medieval wine centres of Montalcino and Montepulciano; hot sulphurous baths in spa towns such as Bagno Vignoni; the Romanesque splendour of the Abbazia di Sant'Antimo; and the Renaissance grace of Pienza, an early example of idealised town planning.

DRIVING TOUR: ABBAZIA DI SAN GALGANO TO PETROIO

Distance: 92km
Duration: six to eight hours
About 20km southwest of Siena on the SS73 is the 13th-century **Abbazia di San Galgano** (☎ 0577 75 67 00; admission free; ☸ 8am-7.30pm), one of the country's finest Gothic buildings in its day and now a ruin that still speaks strongly of its past. The monks of this former Cistercian abbey were among Tuscany's most powerful, forming the judiciary and acting as accountants for the *comuni* of Volterra and Siena. In 1786 the bell tower simply collapsed, as did the ceiling vaults a few years later. Today the great, roofless, stone-and-brick shell stands silent in the fields.

Next door to the church are what remain of the monastery buildings, as well as a brief stretch of cloister housing a small **tourist office** (☎ 0577 75 67 38; ☸ 10.30am-7pm Easter-Oct). On a hill overlooking the abbey is the tiny, round Romanesque **Cappella**

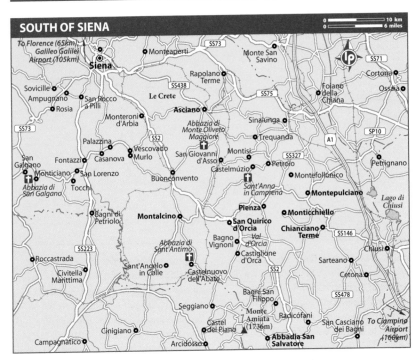

SOUTH OF SIENA

di Monte Siepi, which houses badly preserved frescos by Ambrogio Lorenzetti and a real life 'sword in the stone'.

The drive to **Buonconvento** is tricky – wiggle east past Monticiano, through San Lorenzo, Fontazzi and Murlo, then curl down the Strada Provinciale di Murlo 34. You could be forgiven mistaking Buonconvento for a large roadside rest stop. Lying perfectly flat in a rare stretch of plain, the low-slung fortified walls of this farming centre hide a quiet little town of medieval origins. The **Museo della Mezzadria Senese** (☎ 0577 80 90 75; Via Tinaia del Taja, Buonconvento; adult/child €4/2; ⏰ 10am-6pm Tue-Sun Apr-Oct, to 1.30pm Tue-Fri, to 1pm Sat & Sun Nov-Mar), with its life-sized figures and antique farm tools, offers a multimedia presentation of what life was like living off the land until quite recently. The **Museo d'Arte Sacra** (☎ 0577 80 71 90; www

.museoartesacra.it; Via Soccini 18, Buonconvento; adult/child €3.50/free; ⏰ 10am-1pm & 3-6pm Tue-Sun Apr-Oct, 10am-1pm & 3-5pm Sat & Sun Nov-Mar) contains religious art collected in the town and neighbouring hamlets.

A pretty 10km drive northeast from here is the 14th-century **Abbazia di Monte Oliveto Maggiore** (☎ 0577 70 76 11; admission free; ⏰ 9.15am-noon & 3.15-6pm Apr-Oct, to 5pm Nov-Mar). Still a retreat for around 40 monks, the congregation was founded in 1313 by John Tolomei, though construction didn't begin on the monastery until 1393. Visitors come here for the wonderful fresco series in the Great Cloister, painted by Luca Signorelli and Il Sodoma, illustrating events in the life of the ascetic St Benedict, founder of the Benedictine order. Signorelli, reputed to be a widely respected, kind man, had previously done minor work on the Sistine Chapel and

would later produce his masterpiece *Resurrection of the Flesh* in the Chapel of San Brizio, in Orvieto's Duomo. He started work in the monastery in 1497, producing nine frescos. The nine frescos by Signorelli line the east side and Il Sodoma picks up again on the northern wall. The decorations on the pillars between some of Il Sodoma's frescos are among the earliest examples of 'grotesque' art, copied from decorations found in the then-newly excavated Domus Aurea of Nero in Rome.

The road from Monte Oliveto Maggiore to **Asciano** is quite a thrill, both for drivers (a 1½ car-width, winding, heel-toe challenge) and for passengers (camera-ready countryside). This pretty little hamlet has a trio of small museums dedicated to Sienese art and Etruscan finds in the area. If you're hungry, there are several restaurants in town, including **La Brace** (☎ 0577 71 80 56; Via Mameli 9/11; meals €22; Wed-Sun), where the sweet staff serve simple lunches off handwritten menus.

Another twisting 20km brings you to **Montisi** (www.montisi.com), little more than a one-street, medieval blip capping a steep hill. Its allure speaks to a certain disposition, particularly the expat artist

community hunkered down here. A little asking around can win you entrance to a few of the town's small churches, stuffed with ageing paintings, town effects dating back to the 15th century and a tiny crypt. **Taverna Montisi** (☎ 0577 84 51 59; www.tavernamontisi.com; Via Umberto I 3; meals €25-28) has a seasonal menu fuelled by organic farmers in the immediate area.

Nearby, wedding cake–shaped **Petroio,** is a wanderable, quiet place and home to the **Museo della Terracotta** (☎ 0577 66 51 88; www.museoterracotta.it; Via Valgelata 10; adult/child €3/1.50; 4-7pm Thu & Fri, 10.30am-1pm & 4-7pm Sat & Sun), run by a prolific terracotta artist. If you can drive no further, **Palazzo Brandano** (p406) is a stylish place to spend the night.

MONTALCINO

pop 5190

Formerly known as 'the Republic of Siena in Montalcino', the last wily holdout against Florence even after Siena had fallen, Montalcino is these days a retiring hill town overlooking the Orcia valley. While this is a perfectly nice place to bulk up your calf muscles while wandering inhumanly steep 'streets', the real attraction is its internationally coveted wine, Brunello (see the boxed text, p196). You can also savour more modest but very palatable local reds such as Rosso di Montalcino.

Plenty of *enoteche* around town allow you to taste and buy Brunello (see p375; a bottle costs a minimum of €20, though some hunting in town shops can sometimes win you sale-priced bottles for as little as €15), and restaurant servers will impetuously assume you mean Brunello when you ask for a 'glass of red', because why else would you be in Montalcino? Glasses start at €5, while a bottle from an excellent year comes with a price tag of well over the €105 mark. There's no need to labour over prices however, as all Brunello is made to strict standards and any bottle will invariably be memorable.

ESSENTIAL INFORMATION

TOURIST OFFICES // Tourist office (☎ 0577 84 93 31; www.prolocomontalcino.it, in Italian; Costa del Municipio 1; ⏰ 10am-1pm & 2-5.40pm, closed Mon in winter) Has free maps and books hotels for walk-in customers. It also has a list of 183 local vineyards, showing which are open to the public and have English-speaking guides.

EXPLORING MONTALCINO

If you purchase a combined ticket (€6), it will give you entry to Montalcino's principal sights, the *fortezza* and the Museo Civico e Diocesano d'Arte Sacra.

♥ FORTEZZA // WALK THE RAMPARTS TOWARDS THE ENOTECA
The **fortezza** (☎ 0577 84 92 11; Piazzale Fortezza; courtyard free, ramparts adult/child €4/2; ⏰ 9am-8pm Apr-Oct, 10am-6pm Nov-Mar), an imposing 14th-century fortress that was later expanded under the Medici dukes, dominates the town from a high point at its southern

end. You can sample and buy local wines in the *enoteca* (p207) inside and also climb up to the fort's ramparts (though the view is almost as magnificent from the courtyard). Buy a ticket at the bar.

♥ MUSEO CIVICO E DIOCESANO D'ARTE SACRA // ADMIRE RELIGIOUS ART OF THE REGION
☎ 0577 84 60 14; Via Ricasoli 31; adult/child €4.50/3; ⏰ 10am-1pm & 2-5.40pm Tue-Sun
In the former convent of the neighbouring **Chiesa di Sant'Agostino**, this is an important collection of religious art from the town and surrounding region. Jewels include a triptych by Duccio di Buoninsegna and a *Madonna and Child* by Simone Martini. Other artists represented include the Lorenzetti brothers, Giovanni di Paolo and Sano di Pietro, and the museum has a fine collection of painted wooden sculptures by the Sienese school.

♥ POGGIO ANTICO // TOUR ONE OF THE TOP WINE PRODUCERS
☎ 0577 84 80 44; www.poggioantico.com; ⏰ 10am-7pm
Located about 4.5km down the road to Grosseto, at the end of a cypress-lined, dusty road, is this highly regarded winemaker, producing one Rosso, three Brunellos and one Super Tuscan. Tours (45 minutes; free) and a variety of tastings (€2 to €22) are available, as is an outstanding meal at the onsite restaurant (☎ 0577 84 92 00; tasting menu with/without wine €80/60).

GASTRONOMIC HIGHLIGHTS

There's a vigorous **Friday market** on and around Via della Libertà.

♥ AL BACCANALE €€
☎ 340 78 10 273; Via Matteoti 19; meals €27-32
A family operation favoured by locals, serving belt-challenging, pick-and-mix

INTERVIEW: JENA PATTERSON

How long have you been living in Italy and why Montalcino? I had been working in the restaurant business in New York and realised that it was the wine part of my job that really excited me. On a vacation with my sisters to Tuscany we were torn between the Vino Nobile of Montepulciano and the Brunello of Montalcino. In the end, having met a Montalcino producer at a wine tasting at the restaurant, I came to visit his estate and was offered a job.

Where did you come from and was the transition to Italy difficult? While I am American by passport, I was born and raised overseas due to my father's work. My love affair with this place has endured many things including cultural blunders and professional mishaps due to having been raised with a different set of standards and values. The inequality of the sexes both in the workplace and at home perseveres in this remote part of Tuscany. The first two years were particularly trying because of difficulties with the language, which at best was very good for a tourist but not for a working professional.

How much wine do you drink in an average week? Be honest. First, we must distinguish between tasting wine for work (spitting it out) and drinking wine for pleasure. In an average work day I taste/spit about a glass worth of various wines. In an average week of dining with friends, 90% of whom are in the wine business, I probably drink about two to three bottles of wine. One thing's for sure though, for me and many in this profession, after a long day of tastings and talking about wine, all you really want is a nice cold beer.

How do you respond to people who say 'Wow, you're living my dream!' Be careful about moving to your paradise. Once you do, it will no longer be your paradise. It can certainly be an improvement on your quality of life for the natural beauty, art, food, wine, the space and atmosphere for cultivating close relationships…the general rhythm of the Italian way of life. It's a wonderful place to live, it's home, but unless you have some place to go back to, Tuscany will no longer be your getaway.

Wine taster Jena Patterson settled in Montalcino in 2001. An impassioned Brunello educator/promoter, she has worked for producer Ciacci Piccolomini d'Aragona, wine shop Enoteca La Fortezza, and is currently with wine estate Poggio Antico.

pasta/sauce plates, including the popular, idiosyncratic *maltagliati*, or 'bad pasta', the random, leftover bits after other pasta has been cut.

♥ OSTERIA IL GIARDINO €€
☎ 0577 84 90 76; Piazza Cavour 1; meals €32-35;
🕙 closed Sun
All light wood and arches, this place has a good selection of traditional dishes, including *risotto al radicchio rosso, Brunello e pecorino* (risotto with red chicory,

Brunello wine, and *pecorino* cheese) and wild boar.

♥ OSTERIA PORTA AL CASSERO €€
☎ 0577 84 71 96; Via Ricasoli 32; meals €24;
🕙 Thu-Tue
A simple place selling hearty peasant-style fare such as bean-and-vegetable soup, Tuscan pork sausage with white beans, and a 'pan-roasted roasted rabbit'. Don't ask, as we did, how a rabbit can be roasted twice unless you want to ignite

a 30-minute, *osteria*-wide, impassioned debate on Tuscan cooking terminology.

☝ RE DI MACCHIA €€

☎ 0577 84 61 16; Via Soccorso Saloni 21; meals €32, fixed menu €23; ⏰ Fri-Wed

This is a very agreeable small restaurant run by an enterprising couple. Roberta selects the freshest of ingredients and the wine cellar is impressive; to sample a variety, try Antonio's personal selection of four wines (€16), each to accompany a course.

☝ TAVERNA IL GRAPPOLO BLU €€

☎ 0577 84 71 50; Scale di Via Moglio 1; meals €28

Does ingenious things with local ingredients – including the juicy *coniglio al Brunello* (rabbit cooked in Brunello wine) and wild boar with polenta. Non-Brunello-enriched options are scant – which may be local law.

NIGHTLIFE

☝ ALLE LOGGE DI PIAZZA

Piazza del Popolo 1; ⏰ closed Wed Sep-Mar & Jan

This is one of Montalcino's primary social hubs for the 25 to 40 crowd. The wine selection changes constantly, while the light menu doesn't. Staff shake cocktails something fierce and the choice is almost as long as the wine list. Happy hour runs from 7pm to 9pm.

☝ ENOTECA LA FORTEZZA DI MONTALCINO

☎ 0577 84 92 11; Piazzale Fortezza; wine by the glass from €4

Set within the fort itself, this *enoteca* is perfect for trying out or buying one of countless varieties of Brunello, or climbing up onto the ramparts, or both. It also puts on informal tastings, accompanied by delectable nibbles.

☝ FIASCHETTERIA

Piazza del Popolo 6

A fine tiled old cafe where crusty locals stand at the bar, putting the world to rights over a glass of wine, and visitors sit out on Montalcino's best piazza terrace.

TRANSPORT

BUS // The **bus terminal** is on Piazza Cavour. Regular TRAIN buses run to/from Siena (€3.20, 1½ hours, six daily).

SOUTH OF MONTALCINO

☝ ABBAZIA DI SANT'ANTIMO // ABSORB THE SIGHTS AND SOUNDS OF A RESTORED ABBEY

This beautiful isolated Romanesque church (☎ 0577 83 56 59; admission free; ⏰ 10.30am-12.30pm & 3-6.30pm Mon-Sat, 9am-10.30am & 3-6pm Sun) is best visited in the morning, when the sun, streaming through the east windows, creates an almost surreal atmosphere. At night too, it's impressive, lit up like a beacon. Set in a broad valley, just below the village of **Castelnuovo dell'Abate**, its architecture is clearly influenced by northern European versions of Romanesque architecture, especially that of the Cistercians. Tradition tells that Charlemagne founded the original monastery here in 781. In subsequent centuries, the Benedictine monks became among the most powerful feudal landlords in southern Tuscany, until they came into conflict with Siena in the 13th century. Until the mid-1990s, the church and abbey lay pretty much abandoned. Then a body of monks moved in and supervised restoration work. There are regular daily prayers and Mass in the church, which are open to the public. This is a worthwhile exercise as the monks sing Gregorian chants. If

CENTRAL TUSCANY

you can't make it, they can sell you the CD. The exterior, built in pale travertine stone, is simple but for the stone carvings, which include various fantastical animals, set in the bell tower and apsidal chapels. Inside, study the capitals of the columns lining the nave, especially the one representing Daniel in the lion's den (second on the right as you enter). Below it is a particularly intense polychrome 13th-century Madonna and Child and there's a haunting 12th-century Christ on the Cross above the main altar.

A twisting, narrow road leads directly to Castelnuovo dell'Abate from a roundabout just south of Montalcino's historic centre. Three buses a day run from Montalcino (€1.20) to Castelnuovo dell'Abate, from where it's a short walk to the church.

☝ RURAL TREATS // HEAD OFF THE TRACK FOR A MEAL WITH VIEWS

Less than 1km away from the Abbazia di Sant'Antimo, **Locanda Sant'Antimo** (☎ 0577 83 56 15; www.locandasantantimo.it; Via Bassomondo 8; meals €22-28), at Castelnuovo dell'Abate, serves solid traditional cooking. A three-course, fixed menu with wine and coffee is a mere €19. Should you wish to catch the early morning light over the abbey, there are four rooms (single/double €60/80).

You may want to consider an alternative lunch or dinner excursion west from Castelnuovo dell'Abate along a dirt road to **Sant'Angelo in Colle**. The views from the village are wonderful. A two-sister team serve highly recommended home-cooked food at **Trattoria Il Pozzo** (☎ 0577 84 40 15; meals €22-25), just off the square. **Trattoria Il Leccio** (☎ 0577 84 41 75; Costa Castellare 1; meals €32-38; ☺ Thu-Tue), on the square, is known for its ravioli and fried veggies. Some terrace tables have panoramic views. The proximity and volume of the church bell may cause a few wine spills.

☝ BAGNO VIGNONI // ADMIRE THE INGENUITY OF AN EARLY SPA TOWN

This tiny spa town dates back to Roman times and was later a popular overnight stop for pilgrims eager to soothe weary limbs. The hot sulphurous water bubbles up into a picturesque pool, built by the Medicis and surrounded by mellow stone buildings. Some 36 springs cook at up to 51°C and collect in the pool, although in winter the temperature of the water is considerably cooler.

You can't dunk yourself in the pool. To take to the waters, dive into nearby Hotel Posta Marcucci's open-air **Piscina Val di Sole** (day ticket adult/child €15/10).

You can dip your fingers into the hot-water streams trickling through **Il Parco dei Mulini di Bagno Vignoni**, just above the entrance to the hotel, and read at length about how the two vast cubes hewn into the rock were once holding tanks for water-driven windmills below.

A pleasantly lit, rustic building sporting a heavy-beamed ceiling, **Osteria del Leone** (☎ 0577 88 73 00; Piazza del Moretto 28; meals €35; ☺ Tue-Sun) is located a block back from the pool. You can eat solid Tuscan country fare, such as *coniglio con mele verde e vino bianco* (rabbit cooked with green apples and white wine).

☝ BAGNI SAN FILIPPO // SOAK IN A DO-IT-YOURSELF SPA

Those who prefer free hot-water frolics could press on about 15km south along the SR2 to Bagni San Filippo. Based just uphill from Hotel le Terme, the village's only hotel, follow a sign, 'Fosso Bianco', down a lane for about 150m to a bridge and a set of hot tumbling **cascades** where you can enjoy a relaxing soak. It's a pleasant if slightly whiffy spot for a picnic – and best in winter, when the hotel's closed and the water pressure is greater.

❦ RADICÓFANI // BE DRAWN BY THIS SINGULAR ROADSIDE ATTRACTION

On your travels in this part of Tuscany you'd have to be shortsighted not to notice the village of **Radicófani**, 17km southwest of Sarteano on the SS478 – or, more precisely, its **rocca** (fortezza; adult/child €4/3; ☺ 10am-7pm May-Oct, to 6pm Fri-Sun Nov-Apr). Built high on a blancmange-shaped hill, it's an impressive sight from any approach, and the views from its ramparts are stunning. It now houses a small **museum** devoted to medieval times.

❦ ABBAZIA DI SAN SALVATORE // AN INCREDIBLE ABBEY HIDDEN IN THE OLD TOWN

Eighteen kilometres further southwest is Abbadia San Salvatore, a largely ugly mining town that grew rapidly and tastelessly from the late 19th century. Its saving grace, the **Abbazia di San Salvatore** (☎ 0577 77 80 83; abbaziasansalvatore@ virgilio.it; Piazzale Michelangelo 8; ☺ 7am-5pm Mon-Sat, 10.30am-6pm Sun Apr-Oct, 7am-5pm Mon-Sat, 10.30am-5pm Sun Nov-Mar), lies in the centre of town. Founded in 743 by the Lombard Erfo, the abbey eventually passed into the hands of Cistercian monks, who still occupy it today. Little remains of the monastery, but the church more than compensates. Built in the 11th century and Romanesque in style, it was reconstructed in the late 16th century, when the whole area from the transept to the apse was raised and adorned with broad, frescoed arches that give the impression of walking into a tunnel. Best of all, however, is the 8th-century Lombard crypt, a remarkable stone forest of 36 columns. From Siena, two RAMA buses (€4.60, 1¾ hours) call by the abbey daily.

PIENZA

pop 2180

If the primary road to Montepulciano didn't pass right through town, little Pienza might not inspire people to take their foot off the accelerator. Fortunately it does, so pull over and take a few hours to absorb its few, but compelling attractions. Or stay longer and benefit from its great-value food and accommodation. Self-caterers will love (or loathe) that virtually all shops here are geared towards connoisseurs – cheese, meats and preserves are top choice and top price.

Urban-planning geeks will get a wicked buzz from Pienza's Renaissance town blueprint, instigated by Pope Pius II in an effort to jazz up his birthplace. He secured the services of architect Bernardo Rossellino, who applied the principles of his mentor, Leon Battista Alberti. The result was the superb Piazza Pio II and the surrounding buildings.

ESSENTIAL INFORMATION

TOURIST OFFICES // Tourist office (☎ 0578 74 99 05; Corso Il Rossellino; ☺ 10am-1pm & 3-7pm Wed-Mon) Located inside the Museo Diocesano.

EXPLORING PIENZA

❦ PIAZZA PIO II AND THE CATHEDRAL // EARLY RENAISSANCE URBAN PLANNING

Stand in Piazza Pio II and spin 360 degrees. You have just taken in Pienza's major monuments. Gems of the Renaissance and all constructed in a mere three years between 1459 and 1462, they're all grouped around Piazza Pio II. The square was designed by Bernardo Rossellino, who left nothing to chance. The space available to him was limited so, to increase the sense of perspective and dignity of the great edifices that would grace the square, he set the Palazzo Borgia and Palazzo Piccolomini off at angles to the cathedral.

Cathedral

The **cathedral** (⌚ 8.30am-1pm & 2.15-7pm) was built on the site of the Romanesque Chiesa di Santa Maria, of which little remains. The Renaissance facade, in travertine stone, is of clear Albertian inspiration. The interior of the building, a strange mix of Gothic and Renaissance, contains a collection of five altarpieces painted by Sienese artists of the period, as well as a superb marble tabernacle by Rossellino. The papal bull of 1462 forbade any changes to the church, so revel in the thought that views are virtually the same now as they were for visitors in the Middle Ages. Perhaps the most bizarre aspect of the building is the state of collapse of the transept and apse. Built on dodgy ground, the top end of the church seems to be breaking off. The huge cracks in the wall and floor are matched by the crazy downwards slant of this part of the church floor. Various attempts to prop it all up have failed to solve the problem.

Museum

To the left of the cathedral is the **Palazzo Borgia** (also known as Palazzo Vescovile), built by Cardinal Borgia, later Pope Alexander VI, and containing the **Museo Diocesano** (☎ 0578 74 99 05; Corso Il Rossellino 30; adult/child €4.10/2.60; ⌚ 10am-1pm & 2-7pm Wed-Mon mid-Mar–Oct, Sat & Sun only Nov–mid-Mar), which has an intriguing miscellany of artworks, illuminated manuscripts, tapestries and miniatures.

Palace

The **Palazzo Piccolomini** (☎ 0578 74 85 03; 30min guided tour adult/child €7/5; ⌚ 10am-12.30pm & 3-6pm Tue-Sun), to your right as you face the cathedral, was the pope's residence and is considered Rossellino's masterpiece. Built on the site of former Piccolomini family houses, the building demonstrates some indebtedness on Rossellino's part to Alberti, whose Palazzo Rucellai in Florence it appears in part to emulate. Inside is a fine courtyard, from which stairs lead you

---

～ WORTH A TRIP ～

If you're staying in the area of Monticchiello and Montefollonico, here are a few eating choices offering both out-of-the-way variety and small-town intimacy.

A few minor roads lead south of Pienza to **Monticchiello**. Don the best arch support at your disposal and take an hour to build up an appetite while wandering around this pretty medieval village. Positioned just inside the main gate, **Ristorante La Porta** (☎ 0578 75 51 63; www.osterialaporta.it; Via del Piano 3; meals €35) has a terrace with unspeakable views of Val d'Orcia and a reputation for food and service that behoves a reservation, even in low season.

Located north of Pienza is **Montefollonico**, even smaller and quieter. The only restaurant on its tiny square is **La Botte Piena** (☎ 0577 66 94 81; www.labottepiena.com; Via della Resistenza 153; meals €28-32), a family place with unusual pasta choices on the daily menu and great beef options.

up into the papal apartments, now filled with an assortment of period furnishings, minor art and the like. To the rear, a three-level loggia offers a spectacular panorama over the Val d'Orcia below.

Make time to visit the Romanesque **Pieve di Corsignano**, leaving Pienza by taking Via Fonti from Piazza Dante Alighieri. This church dates from the 10th century and boasts a strange circular bell tower. There are no fixed visiting times but it is usually open between Easter and November.

GASTRONOMIC HIGHLIGHTS

❦ IL ROSSELLINO €€€

☎ 0578 74 90 644; Piazza di Spagna 4; meals €42-48
One of Pienza's smarter restaurants, a mere six tables have been allotted for the opportunity to enjoy the options from the respected menu, featuring several preparations of Chianina beef, as well as regional nods to truffle and pesto dishes.

❦ TRATTORIA LATTE DI LUNA €€

☎ 0578 74 86 06; Via San Carlo 6; meals €25; ☽ Wed-Mon
On a kind of squarette where the street splits off from Corso Il Rossellino, this trattoria has a lovely terrace with plenty of shady umbrellas and a flirtatious, talking bird providing comic relief. Try the *anatra arrosto alle olive* (roast duck with olives) and the homemade hazelnut ice cream to top off the meal.

RECOMMENDED SHOPS

❦ BOTTEGA DEL NATURISTA

Corso Il Rossellino 16
Almost a monument in its own right, this pungent *bottega* has a truly mouthwatering choice of cheeses, from fresh to well-aged and smelly, from the classic *pecorino di Pienza* to ones lightly infused with peppers or truffles.

TRANSPORT

BUS // Up to four buses run on weekdays between Siena and Pienza (€3.80, 1¼ hours) and nine to/from Montepulciano (€1.80). The bus terminal is just off Piazza Dante Alighieri. Buy tickets at the nearby bar.

MONTEPULCIANO

pop 14,400
This reclaimed narrow ridge of volcanic rock will push your quadriceps to their failure point. When it happens, collapse against a centuries-old stone wall, drink in the views over the Valdichiana countryside, then fall into the nearest cantina and treat yourself to a generous pour of the highly reputed Vino Nobile.

A late-Etruscan fort was the first in a series of settlements here. During the Middle Ages, it was a constant bone of contention between Florence and Siena, until in 1404 Florence won the day. And so the Marzocco, or lion of Florence, came to replace the she-wolf of Siena as the city's symbol, atop a column just off Piazza Savonarola. The new administration introduced a fresh architectural style as Michelozzo, Sangallo il Vecchio and others were invited in to do some innovative spring cleaning, imparting a fresh wind of Renaissance vigour to this Gothic stronghold. That intriguing mix alone makes this town worth the sustained leg cramps.

ESSENTIAL INFORMATION

TOURIST OFFICE // Strada del Vino Nobile di Montepulciano Information Office (☎ 0578 71 74 84; www.stradavinonobile.it; Piazza Grande 7; ☽ 10am-1pm & 3-6pm Mon-Fri) Books accommodation and other activities such as cooking courses, Slow Food tours, wine tastings, bike rentals, and nonstrenuous country walks, culminating in lunch. Tourist office (☎ 0578 75 73 41; www.prolocomontepulciano

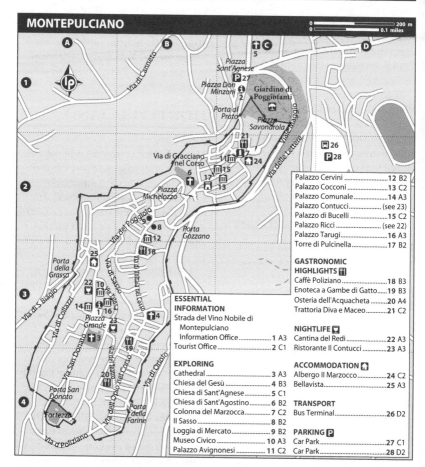

MONTEPULCIANO

Palazzo Cervini	....	**12** B2
Palazzo Cocconi	....	**13** C2
Palazzo Comunale	....	**14** A3
Palazzo Contucci	....	(see 23)
Palazzo di Bucelli	....	**15** C2
Palazzo Ricci	....	(see 22)
Palazzo Tarugi	....	**16** A3
Torre di Pulcinella	....	**17** B2

GASTRONOMIC HIGHLIGHTS

Caffè Poliziano	....	**18** B3
Enoteca a Gambe di Gatto	....	**19** B3
Osteria dell'Acquacheta	....	**20** A4
Trattoria Diva e Maceo	....	**21** B2

NIGHTLIFE

Cantina del Redi	....	**22** A3
Ristorante Il Contucci	....	**23** A3

ESSENTIAL INFORMATION

Strada del Vino Nobile di Montepulciano Information Office	....	**1** A3
Tourist Office	....	**2** C1

EXPLORING

Cathedral	....	**3** A3
Chiesa del Gesù	....	**4** B3
Chiesa di Sant'Agnese	....	**5** C1
Chiesa di Sant'Agostino	....	**6** B2
Colonna del Marzocca	....	**7** C2
Il Sasso	....	**8** B2
Loggia di Mercato	....	**9** B2
Museo Civico	....	**10** A3
Palazzo Avignonesi	....	**11** C2

ACCOMMODATION

Albergo Il Marzocco	....	**24** C2
Bellavista	....	**25** A3

TRANSPORT

Bus Terminal	....	**26** D2

PARKING

Car Park	....	**27** C1
Car Park	....	**28** D2

.it; Piazza Don Minzoni; 9.30am-12.30pm & 3-8pm Easter-Jul, Sep & Oct, 9.30am-8pm Aug, to 12.30pm Mon-Sat & 3-6pm Sun Nov-Easter) A friendly resource, which can reserve accommodation without charge. It sells local bus and train tickets, and rents bikes and scooters.

EXPLORING MONTEPULCIANO

♥ VIA DI GRACCIANO NEL CORSO // ADMIRE THE LANDMARKS ALONG THE CITY'S MAIN ARTERY

From the gate, walk southwards along Via di Gracciano nel Corso. At the upper end of Piazza Savonarola is the **Colonna del Marzocca**, erected in 1511 to confirm Montepulciano's allegiance to Florence. The splendid stone lion, squat as a pussy-cat atop this column is, in fact, a copy; the original is in the town's Museo Civico. The late-Renaissance **Palazzo Avignonesi** by Giacomo da Vignola is at No 91. Several mansions line Via di Gracciano nel Corso, including the **Palazzo di Bucelli** at No 73, the lower courses of whose facade are recycled Etruscan and Latin inscriptions and reliefs. Sangallo also designed **Palazzo Cocconi** at No 70. Continuing up Via di

CENTRAL TUSCANY

Gracciano nel Corso, you'll find Miche-lozzo's **Chiesa di Sant'Agostino** (Piazza Michelozzo; 9am-noon & 3-6pm) with its lunette above the entrance holding a terracotta Madonna and Child, John the Baptist and St Augustine. Opposite, **Torre di Pulcinella**, a medieval tower house, is topped by the town clock and the hunched figure of Pulcinella (Punch of Punch and Judy fame), which strikes the hours.

PIAZZA GRANDE AND AROUND // TOUR THE TOWN'S HISTORIC SQUARE

Overlooking Piazza Grande, the town's highest point, is the **Palazzo Comunale** (admission free; 10am-6pm Mon-Sat). Built in the 13th-century Gothic style and remodelled in the 15th century by Miche-lozzo, it still functions as the town hall. From the top of its **tower** (entry on 2nd fl; admission €1.60; Apr-Oct) on a clear day, you can see as far as the Monti Sibillini to the east and the Gran Sasso to the southeast.

Opposite is the **Palazzo Contucci**, and its extensive wine cellar, Enoteca Il Contucci, open for visiting and sampling (see p214).

Attributed to Giacomo da Vignola, **Palazzo Tarugi** is beside a well, sur-mounted by a particularly genial pair of lions. The beautiful 16th-century **cathedral** (Piazza Grande; 9am-noon & 4-6pm) has an unfinished facade. Above the high altar is a lovely triptych by Taddeo da Bartolo depicting the Assumption.

GASTRONOMIC HIGHLIGHTS

CAFFÈ POLIZIANO €€

0578 75 86 15; Via di Voltaia nel Corso 27; meals €24;

Established as a cafe in 1868, Poliziano has had a chequered past – at times cafe-cabaret, mini-cinema, grocery store and, once again since 1990, an elegant cafe,

lovingly restored to its original form by the current owners. Plan carefully to win a seat on one of the tiny, precipitous balc-ony tables with expansive views.

ENOTECA A GAMBE DI GATTO €€

0578 75 74 31; zelfdizekf@yahoo.it; Via dell Opio nel Corso 34; meals €21-30; closed Jan-Easter & Wed

Renowned throughout the region, this place is run by exacting husband-and-wife team of Emanuel and Laura, travel the country each winter to acquire the absolute best products from organic pro-ducers. The daily menu fluctuates in var-ied ways, depending on market offerings. The wine and oil served in the restaurant is available in the *enoteca*.

OSTERIA DELL'ACQUACHETA €

0578 75 84 43; www.acquacheta.eu; Via del Teatro 22; meals €18-24; Wed-Mon

This is a small eatery with the look and feel of a country trattoria and some of the most attentive staff in Tuscany. The food's excellent and mainly meaty, ranging from *misto di salami Toscani* (a variety of Tus-can sausages and salamis) to huge steaks. It fills fast at lunch. Arrive early or reserve.

TRATTORIA DIVA E MACEO €€

0578 71 69 51; Via di Gracciano nel Corso 90; meals €24-28; Wed-Mon

An uncomplicated place, Trattoria Diva e Maceo is popular with the locals and carries a good selection of local wines. You can feast on Tuscan cuisine like *ravioli in crema tartufata* (ravioli with truffle sauce) in simple surroundings.

NIGHTLIFE

There are plenty of places, including sev-eral long-established cantinas, where you can whet your palate on the local red, Vino Nobile.

THE TOMB OF THE INFERNAL CHARIOT

In 2003 archaeologists excavating an intact 4th-century-BC tomb in the necropolis of Pianacce, just outside Sarteano on the road to Cetona (signposted *'tombe etrusche delle Pianacce'*), discovered a unique fresco, its colours still as bright as the day they were applied. On the walls surrounding the alabaster sarcophagus, a demonic figure with wild flowing russet hair drives a chariot pulled by a pair of lions and two griffins. Fabulous monsters – a three-headed snake and a huge seahorse – rear up and two male figures, 'perhaps a father and son as their distinct age difference shows', have an affectionate moment.

The deceased had chosen his last resting place well, with its commanding views over the Val di Chiana, and it's worth the short diversion for the panorama alone. Tours cost €5 and are only possible on Saturdays. Reserve through the **Archaeological Civic Museum** (☎ 0578 26 92 61; Via Roma 24; adult/child €2.50/2) in Sarteano.

♥ CANTINA DEL REDI

Via Ricci 13; ⏰ 10.30am-1.30pm & 2.30-7.30pm
'No smoking, No microphones, Do not shout out, No dogs, No trash, Do not touch the casks' is the notice that welcomes you. This place doubles as a cool wine cellar that is free to tour.

♥ ENOTECA CONTUCCI

☎ 0578 75 70 06; www.contucci.it; Palazzo Contucci, Piazza Grande; ⏰ 10.30am-12.30pm & 2.30-6.30pm
Vintners since Renaissance times, this is another active cellar where you can sample a drop of the local wine. The owner is a great character and will give you a personal tour, tasting and photo session. The nearby restaurant (meals €30 to €35; open Tuesday to Sunday) is also cellar-fabulous.

TRANSPORT

BUS // TRAIN runs eight buses daily between Montepulciano and Siena (€4.70, 1¾ hours) via Pienza. Regular LFI buses connect with Chiusi (€2.30, 50 minutes, half-hourly) and continue to Chiusi-Chianciano Terme train station. There are three services daily to/from Florence (€9.40) and two to/from Arezzo (€3.70; change at Bettolle). Buses leave from the terminal shared with car park No 5, outside the Porta al Prato at the northern end of town.

CAR & MOTORCYCLE // By car, take the Chianciano Terme exit from the A1 and follow the SS146. Cars are banned from the town centre, but many hotels can issue on-the-spot parking permits, valid for their immediate vicinities, saving guests the death march up the hill with their bags.

PARKING // There are car parks near the Porta al Prato, from where minibuses weave their way to Piazza Grande.

TRAIN // Chiusi-Chianciano Terme, 18km southeast and on the main Rome–Florence line, is the most convenient train station (rather than Stazione di Montepulciano, which has very infrequent services).

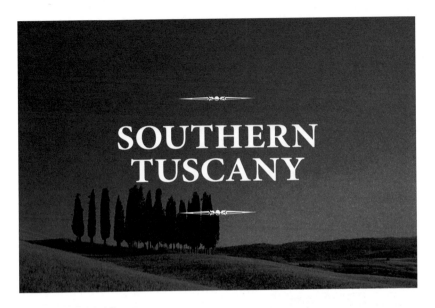

SOUTHERN TUSCANY

3 PERFECT DAYS

♥ DAY 1 // MEDIEVAL ELBOW ROOM

Although lacking in eye-popping sights, the atmospheric and compelling historic centres of Grosseto (p220) and Massa Marittima (p222) offer one of the rarest amenities in Tuscany: personal space. Well guarded from extraneous vehicle traffic, both are prime spots for the *passeggiata* (traditional evening stroll), and with tour buses roaring to higher-profile cities up north, your quiet sit-down and medieval reverie on the steps of the respective cathedrals will be nigh undisturbed. Respectable museums and select eating options make either city worthy of a sleepover.

♥ DAY 2 // A COASTAL CALL

The southern coast is relatively serene area, Monte Argentario in high season notwithstanding. All the nature and exercise you need can be found within Parco Regionale della Maremma (p225). The towns of Orbetello (p226), Porto Santo Stefano (p226) and Porto Ercole (p227) cumulatively contain seaside diversions, narrow lanes, outstanding eating and calf-blasting climbs to tenaciously located forts. The latter two bookend the sometimes dangerously overcrowded Via Panoramica, a circular route offering coastal views.

♥ DAY 3 // AN ETRUSCAN TOUR

A number of arresting Etruscan sites pepper Tuscany's southern extent. The extensive walls, foundations and roads at Roselle (p220) are well worth the detour, and Saturnia (p229) and the Ghiaccio Forte abitato Etrusco (p229) are powerful draws, but the strongest cluster of sites is in the area around Pitigliano, Sovana and Sorano (p230). There you can explore extensive tombs (p232), *vie cave* (sunken roads; p232) and even the Vitozza rock caves (p232), first inhabited in prehistoric times.

SOUTHERN TUSCANY

SOUTHERN TUSCANY

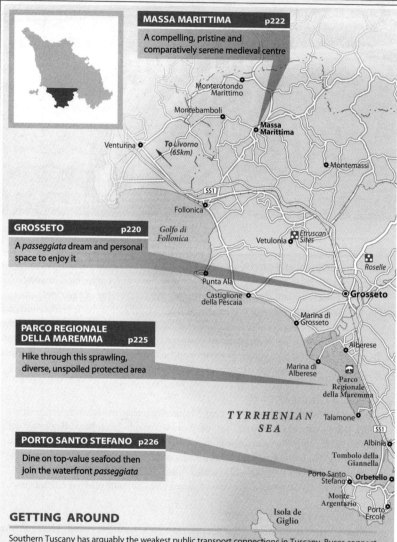

MASSA MARITTIMA p222

A compelling, pristine and comparatively serene medieval centre

GROSSETO p220

A *passeggiata* dream and personal space to enjoy it

PARCO REGIONALE DELLA MAREMMA p225

Hike through this sprawling, diverse, unspoiled protected area

PORTO SANTO STEFANO p226

Dine on top-value seafood then join the waterfront *passeggiata*

Monterotondo Marittimo

Montebamboli

Venturina

To Livorno (65km)

Massa Marittima

Montemassi

SS1

Follonica

Golfo di Follonica

Vetulonia

Etruscan Sites

Roselle

Punta Ala

Castiglione della Pescaia

Grosseto

Marina di Grosseto

Alberese

Marina di Alberese

Parco Regionale della Maremma

TYRRHENIAN SEA

Talamone

SS1

Albinia

Tombolo della Giannella

Porto Santo Stefano

Orbetello

Monte Argentario

Porto Ercole

Isola de Giglio

GETTING AROUND

Southern Tuscany has arguably the weakest public transport connections in Tuscany. Buses connect Grosseto with Massa Marittima, Magliano in Toscana, Castiglione della Pescaia, Pitigliano and Porto Santo Stefano. Grosseto is on the Rome–La Spezia train line, with some services stopping at Orbetello Scalo and Follonica, where shuttles go to Massa Marittima. The SS1 connects Grosseto with Rome and Livorno. Parking is tight anywhere on Monte Argentario. Both Massa Marittima and Grosseto have paid parking just outside the centre and free parking not much further beyond.

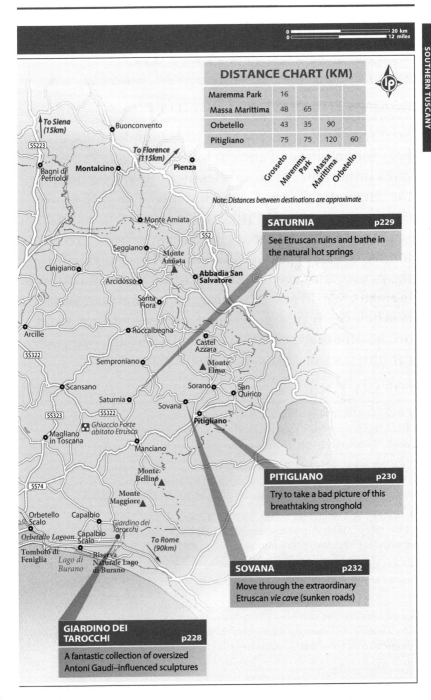

SOUTHERN TUSCANY

DISTANCE CHART (KM)

	Grosseto	Maremma Park	Massa Marittima	Orbetello
Maremma Park	16			
Massa Marittima	48	65		
Orbetello	43	35	90	
Pitigliano	75	75	120	60

Note: Distances between destinations are approximate

SATURNIA   p229

See Etruscan ruins and bathe in the natural hot springs

PITIGLIANO   p230

Try to take a bad picture of this breathtaking stronghold

SOVANA   p232

Move through the extraordinary Etruscan *vie cave* (sunken roads)

GIARDINO DEI TAROCCHI   p228

A fantastic collection of oversized Antoni Gaudí–influenced sculptures

To Siena (15km)

SS223

Buonconvento

To Florence (115km)

Bagni di Petriolo

Montalcino

Pienza

Monte Amiata

SS2

Seggiano

Monte Amiata

Cinigiano

Abbadia San Salvatore

Arcidosso

Santa Fiora

Arcille

Roccalbegna

SS322

Castel Azzara

Semproniano

Monte Elmo

Scansano

Sorano

San Quirico

Saturnia

Sovana

SS323

SS322

Pitigliano

Ghiaccio Forte abitato Etrusco

Magliano in Toscana

Manciano

Monte Bellino

SS74

Monte Maggiore

Orbetello Scalo

Capalbio

Giardino dei Tarocchi

Orbetello Lagoon

Capalbio Scalo

To Rome (90km)

Tombolo di Feniglia

Lago di Burano

Riserva Naturale Lago di Burano

SOUTHERN TUSCANY
GETTING STARTED

MAKING THE MOST OF YOUR TIME

Southern Tuscany is a land of lush rumpled hills, distant hazy mountains and ancient hilltop villages. Tuscany's most important Etruscan sites await inland, including the enigmatic *vie cave* (sunken roads). For pure drama, the medieval town of Pitigliano is inimitable, looming above a mountainous cliff face pitted with Etruscan tombs. Grosseto provides an atmospheric setting for the *passeggiata* (evening stroll), while Massa Marittima is equally placid and charming. Smart marinas, good beaches, shady pine groves and a craggy interior await on the Monte Argentario peninsula. Though compact, car hire is a must for comprehensive touring.

TOP DIY TOURS

♥ PARCO REGIONALE DELLA MAREMMA
Choose from 12 signed walking trails as well as horse and night tours on this protected stretch of coastline (p225).

♥ MONTE ARGENTARIO TO MANCIANO
A low-impact day trip with hilltop towns, Etruscan ruins, a sulphuric spring, unique shopping and opportunities for leg stretching and a self-catered picnic (p229).

♥ I CAN'T BELIEVE I ATE THE WHOLE PENINSULA!
As you cruise Monte Argentario, engineer a tour of the excellent eating options spread throughout Orbetello, Porto Santo Stefano and Porto Ercole (p226).

♥ WALK LIKE AN ETRUSCAN
Hire a car and hit the Etruscan sites scattered around southern Tuscany, which peak in the area around Pitigliano (p230).

♥ STRADA DEL VINO
Take a tour of the local wine routes; visit the regional office in Massa Marittima for comprehensive wine-tour information (p222).

GETTING AWAY FROM IT ALL

The beauty of southern Tuscany is that once you're here, you've already got away from almost everything you intended to get away from. That said, you can retreat even deeper into Tuscan obscurity at the following places.

★ **Vetulonia** This windswept, eccentric mountain village, within striking distance of several Etruscan sites, is an agreeable retreat (p221).

★ **Saturnia** If you don't mind a little guerrilla public bathing, the springs around Saturnia become more secluded and serene the further away from the road you forage (p229).

★ **Agriturismo Le Fontanelle** A pleasingly remote farmhouse stay with a veritable zoolike atmosphere of animals and nature (p407).

RESOURCES

★ **Alta Maremma Turismo** (www.alta maremmaturismo.it) Maremma tourism overview site with some booking services

★ **Maremma Tourism** (www.lamaremma .info) Thorough and interactive official site for the Maremma region

★ **Parco degli Etruschi** (www.parcodegli etruschi.it) Provides a comprehensive guide to the region's nature, culture and history

★ **Strada del Vino** (www.stradavino.it) Listing the region's wine-centric imperatives

FESTIVALS

Small but spirited festivals enliven the region each summer. Book a room (p407) far in advance if you plan to attend.

★ **Torciata di San Giuseppe** The Torch Festival of St Joseph, celebrating the coming of spring, is observed in Pitigliano in mid-March with a day of feasting from street stands followed by a torch parade ending in the main square with a bonfire.

★ **Balestro del Girifalco** This medieval festival held in Massa Marittima on the fourth Sunday in May and the second Sunday in August is punctuated by a crossbow competition.

★ **Toscana Foto Festival** (www.toscana fotofestival.com, in Italian) International professional photographers display works all over Massa Marittima from the first two weeks of July until mid-August.

TOP RESTAURANTS

❦ **RISTORANTE IL CANTO DEL GALLO**
Excellent food and eccentric use of the rooster theme; tops Grosseto's eating options (p220)

❦ **LA TANA DEL BRILLO PARLANTE**
The alleged 'smallest *osteria* in Italy', with a wild-boar fixation you'll want to humour (p224)

❦ **OSTERIA IL NOCCHINO**
Food like mamma used to make, with about the same seating capacity (p228)

❦ **GATTO E LA VOLPE**
The last stop on the Porto Ercole harbour, where the views are wonderful (p227)

GROSSETO & AROUND

· · · · · ·

Poor Grosseto (population 78,800), with an uninviting, Anglicised ring to its name and a lack of jaw-dropping sites, isn't exactly burdened with an overabundance of visitors. Yet it's these shortcomings that have contributed to the city's obscure charm. The old walls, raised in 1559, form a near-perfect hexagon. Within, where refreshingly few tourist buses penetrate, the historic Old Town has unpretentious enticements and genuinely friendly, good-value eating and sleeping options. It's also one of the rare places in Tuscany where the oft-proclaimed 'no car zone' means almost that. *Passeggiata* anyone?

Grosseto was one of the last Siena-dominated towns to fall into Medici hands in 1559. Once in control, Florence had the walls, bastions and fortress raised in order to protect what was then an important grain and salt depot for the grand duchy.

Worthwhile Etruscan artefacts and ruins at Roselle and Vetulonia are both within easy striking distance of Grosseto.

ESSENTIAL INFORMATION

TOURIST OFFICES // Permanent tourist office (☎ 0564 46 26 11; www.lamaremma.info; Via Monte Rosa 206, Grosseto; ⏰ 9.30am–noon & 4–6pm Mon-Sat) Offers town and regional information, including the Parco Regionale della Maremma. **Seasonal tourist office** (☎ 0564 42 78 58; Via Gramsci, Grosseto; ⏰ 9.30am–noon & 4–6pm Mon-Sat Apr-Oct) At the entrance to the Old Town.

EXPLORING GROSSETO & AROUND

♥ **OLD TOWN //** SAMPLE THE HISTORIC CENTRE'S ART AND ARCHITECTURE

Within the city walls, Grosseto's **cathedral** (⏰ 7.30am–noon & 3.30-7pm), started in the late 13th century, has a distinctive Sienese air. It has been added to over time and much of the facade was renewed along neo-Romanesque lines during the 19th century. Next door, on Piazza Dante, the **Palazzo della Provincia** seems to be Sienese Gothic, which is exactly what its early 20th-century architects hoped you might think.

Sharing common premises, the **Museo Archeologico e d'Arte della Maremma** and smaller **Museo d'Arte Della Diocesi di Grosseto** (☎ 0564 48 87 50; Piazza Baccarini 3; adult/child €5/2.50; ⏰ 9.30am-1pm & 4-7pm Tue-Sat, 10am-1pm & 4-7pm Sun) are well worth a visit. On the ground floor are Etruscan and Roman artefacts unearthed from Roselle (below); room 11 in particular has some imposing statues and fragments, ingeniously jigsawed together. The next floor displays items recovered from Vetulonia (opposite) and other Etruscan sites, while the top storey is mainly devoted to Grosseto's rich ecclesiastical heritage. Opening hours change frequently (and whimsically).

Ristorante il Canto del Gallo (☎ 0564 41 45 89; Via Mazzini 29; meals €32; ⏰ dinner Mon-Sat, lunch bookings only), aka ' The Cock Crow', offers further enticement for overnighting in Grosseto. It's a long, thin tunnel of a place, decorated with every possible variant upon the cockerel (rooster) theme, even down to the stoppers used on the grappa.

♥ **ROSELLE //** GET A TASTE OF ETRUSCAN URBAN PLANNING

Less than 7km northeast of Grosseto's historic centre, Roselle was a middle-ranking Etruscan town populated as early as the 7th century BC that came under Roman control in the 3rd century BC.

Although there are no great monuments left standing, the extensive **historic site** (☎ 0564 40 30 67; adult/child €4/2; ☺ 9am-sunset) retains its Roman defensive walls, an oddly elliptical amphitheatre, traces of houses, the forum and streets. You will also find remains of an abandoned medieval village. There are wonderful views down to the plains and out to the sea.

To get here, turn north on Via Senese (SS223) from Grosseto's massive Piazza Volterno.

❦ VETULONIA // A QUIETER POCKET OF TUSCANY WITH ETRUSCAN ACCENTS

This windswept mountain village 23km northwest of Grosseto seems to rise out of nothing from the surrounding plains. It retains elements of the ancient surrounding wall and has a small **Museo Archeologico** (☎ 0564 94 80 58; Piazza de Vetulonia; adult/child €4.50/2.50; ☺ 10am-2pm & 3-6pm Tue-Sat Oct-May, to 8pm Jun-Sep) that contains a rich display of artefacts revealed by excavations at the two nearby **Etruscan sites** (☎ 0564 94 95 87; admission free; ☺ 10am-7pm Apr-Sep). The more extensive area, known as **Scavi Città** (Town Excavations), is just below the village as you leave by the only road.

More interesting are four unearthed **Etruscan tombs** (Via dei Sepolcri; ☺ 10am-7pm) a couple of kilometres further downhill and along a turn-off to the right. Best is the last, about 1km down a rough dirt track.

A daily bus runs to/from both Grosseto and Castiglione della Pescaia.

TRANSPORT

BUS // **Rama** (☎ 199 848787; www.griforama.it, in Italian; Piazza Marconi) buses usually leave from the

ACCOMMODATION

Owing to its comparatively humble and understated attractions, southern Tuscany enjoys great-value accommodation options and a few luxurious standouts. The Accommodation chapter (p391) provides in-depth coverage, but here are some highlights of the region:

★ **Hotel Il Sole** (p407) Behind the rather impressive facade of this ideally located hotel in Massa Marittima reside 50 large and quiet rooms.

★ **Agriturismo Le Fontanelle** (p407) Claiming to be among the first *agriturismi* (farm-stay accommodation) in Tuscany, this is a wonderfully rustic, zoolike place south of Montemerano.

★ **Agriturismo Tenuta La Parrina** (p407) Attractive double rooms and apartments in an 18th-century building adorned with period furniture.

train station. Buses for Siena, where you can connect with either **TRAIN** (☎ 0577 20 41 11; www.trainspa.it) or **Vaibus** (www.vaibus.it) buses to Florence, run seven times per day (€10). Alternatively, there are three direct services of Rama buses (€18.10, 2½ hours). There is only one direct bus a day to Massa Marittima (€3.80, 1 hour). Other destinations include Piombino (€5.20, 1¼ hours, three daily), Magliano in Toscana (€2.30, one hour, two to five daily), Follonica (€3.80, one hour, three daily), Castiglione della Pescaia (€4.70, 50 minutes, 15 daily), Porto Santo Stefano (€3.80, one hour, three daily) and Pitigliano (€6, two hours, five daily).

TRAIN // Grosseto is on the main coastal train line between Rome (€10.45, two hours) and Livorno (€7.70, 1½ hours). For places such as Pisa (€8.60, two hours), Florence (€12.10, three hours) or Siena (€6.50, 1½ hours), the train is probably a smarter bet.

PARKING // There's plenty of parking, albeit paying, beneath the exterior of the city walls. Free parking spots start appearing, generally, about 100m from the walls.

MASSA MARITTIMA

• • • • • •

pop 8770

Massa Marittima is a compelling place with a pristine and comparatively serene medieval centre by Tuscan standards. Briefly under Pisan domination, it thrived on the local metal mining industry, even becoming an independent *comune* (self-governing city) in 1225, only to be swallowed up by Siena a century later. The plague in 1348, and the end of mining 50 years later, reduced the city to the brink of extinction. Not until the 18th century, with the draining of marshes and re-establishment of mining, did Massa Marittima finally come back to life.

ESSENTIAL INFORMATION

TOURIST OFFICES // Tourist office (☎ 0566 90 27 56; www.altamaremmaturismo.it; Via Todini 3/5; ☺ 9.30am-12.30pm & 3.30-7.30pm Mon-Sat, 10am-1pm & 4-7pm Sun Jun-Sep, 9.30am-12.30pm & 3.30-6.30pm Mon-Sat, 10am-1pm Sun Apr, May & Oct, 9.30am-12.30pm & 3-6pm Mon-Sat Nov-Mar) Down a side street, beneath the Museo Archeologico; takes bookings for tours and wine tastings, and has an exhaustive *Strada del Vino* map of the region.

EXPLORING MASSA MARITTIMA

♥ ST CERBONE'S CATHEDRAL // PROBE THE HEART OF MEDIEVAL MASSA

Piazza Garibaldi is watched over by the imposing bulk of the **cathedral** (☺ 8am-noon & 3-5pm). Cleverly set asymmetrical to the square to better show off its splendour, the cathedral is a snap-on conglomeration of enlargements and renovations supplementing its first, pre-Romanesque incarnation from the 12th century. The Pisan-Romanesque facade includes a central door flanked by two lion heads and topped by five panels depicting scenes from the life of St Cerbone. The roof was crowned with a polygonal dome in the 15th century. The lower half of the attached Gothic *campanile* (bell tower) dates from around 1400, while the upper part was redone at the beginning of the 20th century. The cathedral's interior is a standard basilica-plan layout with rib vaults in both the aisles (17th century) and nave (15th century), highlighted by the *Arca di San Cerbone* (St Cerbone's Ark; 1324) carved by Goro di Gregorio and adorned with bas-relief episodes of the saint's life. A wooden crucifix (early 14th century) by Giovanni Pisano sits on the huge marble altar by Flaminio del Turco (1626).

♥ MUSEO ARCHEOLOGICO // GO BC AND BEYOND

The 13th-century **Palazzo del Podestà** houses the **Museo Archeologico** (☎ 0566 90 22 89; www.coopcollinemetallifere.it/musei, in Italian; Piazza Garibaldi 1; adult/child €3/1.50; ☺ 10am-12.30pm & 3.30-7pm Tue-Sun Apr-Oct, 10am-12.30pm & 3-5pm Tue-Sun Nov-Mar). A monkey fossil from the Miocene era and a simple but compelling stela dating from the 3rd millennium BC are the hands-down highlights of the ground floor's archaeological collection. The upper levels have a modest collection of ancient Roman and Etruscan artefacts recovered from around town.

♥ MUSEO DELLA MINIERA // MIND THE MINE

The city's long mining history is told at the **Museo della Miniera** (☎ 0566 90 22 89; Via Corridoni; adult/child €5/3; ☺ guided visits 10am-

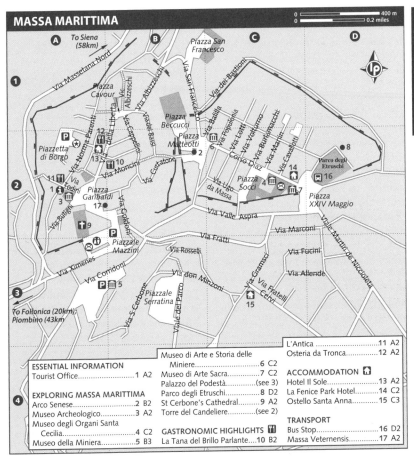

MASSA MARITTIMA

SOUTHERN TUSCANY

12.30pm & 3-5.30pm Apr-Sep, 10am-noon & 3-4.30pm Tue-Sun Oct-Mar), where the display includes a replica of a length of mine. Guided tours in Italian and optional English last around 45 minutes.

❤ CITTÀ NUOVA // APPRAISE A PARADE OF MUSEUMS

Passing under the vast sweep of the **Arco Senese** (Sienese Arch), you enter the Città Nuova (New Town). The arch links the defensive bastions in the wall to the **Torre del Candeliere** (Piazza Matteotti; adult/child €2.50/1.50; 10am-1pm & 3-6pm Tue-Sun Apr-

Oct, 11am-1pm & 2.30-4.30pm Tue-Sun Nov-Mar) – enter the tower and walk across the arch for stupendous views over the Città Vecchia (Old Town).

Corso Diaz, indeed the entire New Town, is notable for its several museums, starting with **Museo di Arte e Storia delle Miniere** (☎ 0566 90 22 89; Piazza Matteotti 4; adult/child €1.50/1; 3-5.30pm Tue-Sun Apr-Oct), a smaller counterpart to Museo della Miniera (opposite), with more mining material and a strong photographic collection.

Music lovers will enjoy the **Museo degli Organi Santa Cecilia** (☎ 0566 94 02 82;

www.museodegliorgani.it; Corso Diaz 28; adult/child €4/2; ⏰ 10am-1pm & 4-8pm Apr-Oct, 10.30am-12.30pm & 3-6pm Tue-Sun Nov-Mar) with its collection of antique organs, harpsichords and clavichords, which, if you strike it lucky, the curator will play for you.

At the far end of Corso Diaz is the **Museo di Arte Sacra** (☎ 0566 90 19 54; Corso Diaz 36; adult/child €5/3; ⏰ 10am-1pm & 3-6pm Apr-Sep, 11am-1pm & 3-5pm Oct-Mar), the new home for Ambrogio Lorenzetti's magnificent *Maestà* (Majesty) as well as a collection of alabaster bas-reliefs, sculptures, a wooden crucifix by Pisano, paintings by Sano di Pietro and Stefano di Giovanni, and other items collected from local churches.

Across Piazza XXIV Maggio and the park is the **Parco degli Etruschi** (☎ 0566 90 12 68; www.parcodeglietruschi.it; admission free; ⏰ 9.30am-12.30pm & 2.30-6.30pm Tue-Sun Apr-Sep, 9.30am-12.30pm & 3-6pm Fri-Sun Oct-Mar). Despite the name, this is not a park, nor is it a museum or archaeological site. Housed in the 13th-century Clarisse Church and Convent, it's a 'virtual park', detailing Etruscan sites and towns around the Maremma region. Interactive points, known as 'totems', and state-of-the-art, motion sensor–driven educational stations have pictures, short programs and games that will engross every age range.

GASTRONOMIC HIGHLIGHTS

☙ LA TANA DEL BRILLO PARLANTE €€
☎ 0566 90 12 74; Vicolo del Ciambellano 4; meals €30-35; ⏰ Thu-Tue
Satisfying the Slow Food checklist to the letter. The diminutive interior 'den' at the 'smallest *osteria* in Italy' seats a mere 12 people (in summer up to another six can squeeze into tiny alley tables). If you intend to dine here in summer or on the weekend, reserve two to seven days in advance. Pork is the fixation, particularly

the regional *cinghiale alla maremmana* (Maremma wild boar).

☙ L'ANTICA €€
☎ 0566 90 26 44; Via Norma Parenti 19; meals €25; ⏰ Mon-Sat
A great-value pizza place in the Neapolitan tradition. For those with the stomach capacity, the menu digresses to lip-smacking pasta. Vegetarian options include the cheese-filled ravioli with mushrooms.

☙ OSTERIA DA TRONCA €€
☎ 0566 90 19 91; Vicolo Porte 5; meals €23-28; ⏰ Tue-Sun
Squeezed into a side street, Da Tronca is an intimate stone-walled restaurant with a fine music playlist ranging from Dylan and Simon & Garfunkel to smooth salsa marathons. There are lots of antipasti (€3) to choose from and a singular *tortelli alla maremma* (pasta parcels filled with ricotta and a type of spinach, covered in homemade *ragù*). For mains, try anything with *cinghiale* (wild boar).

TRANSPORT

BUS // There are two daily buses to Siena (€4.40, 1½ hours) at 7.05am and 4.40pm, and around four to Volterra (changing at Monterotondo). All call at the stop on Piazza XXIV Maggio. **Massa Veternensis** (☎ 0566 90 20 62; Piazza Garibaldi 18) sells both bus and train tickets.
TRAIN // The nearest train station is Massa-Follonica in Follonica, 20km southwest of Massa Marittima, served by a regular shuttle bus (€2.30).

THE COAST
· · · · · ·

There are no great swaths of sand as you cruise the coast south from Piombino, where occasional stretches of pine-backed beach are pleasant without being breathtaking. What does deserve a detour along this southern stretch of mainland coast is the Parco Regionale della Maremma. Near the southern extent of the Tuscan coast is Monte Argentario, a popular, somewhat upscale weekend retreat for sea-seeking Romans, and the bird-dominated nature reserve at Lago di Burano.

PARCO REGIONALE DELLA MAREMMA

The Maremma is an area of long, sandy beaches and reclaimed marshland, criss-crossed by dykes and drainage ditches. A **nature park** (www.parco-maremma.it; admission €6-9), it protects its most spectacular parts and incorporates the **Monti dell'Uccellina**, which drop to a magnificent stretch of unspoiled coastline. Native wild boar, wild cats and porcupines share the area with cowboy-supervised herds of oxen and horses, all spread out over a string of adjacent but wildly diverse ecosystems.

The park's main **visitor centre** (☎ 0564 40 70 98; 8am-5pm mid-Mar–Sep, 8.30am-1.30pm Oct–mid-Mar) is in Alberese. It has shelves of information on the park and activities, including guided horse and night tours. There's a small **seasonal centre** (☎ 0564 88 71 73; 8am-noon & 5-8pm Jul & Aug, 8am-1pm Sep–Jun) at the park's southern extremity, 400m up a dirt lane about 1km before Talamone.

❦ EXPLORING THE PARK // TAKE IN MYRIAD LANDSCAPES AND WILDLIFE

Entry to the park is limited and cars must be left in designated areas. Walking is the best way to explore its riches – there are 12 signed walking trails, varying from 2.5km to 12km long. Trails lead through thick pine forests onto beaches, past caves, around bays, through marshes and bushland, skirting ponds and along coastline. Admission (by ticket bought at one of the visitor centres) varies according to whether a minibus transports you to your chosen route. Depending upon your trail, you stand a chance of spotting deer, wild boar, foxes and hawks.

The **Centro Turismo Il Rialto** (☎ 0564 40 71 02), 600m north of the main visitors centre, offers two-hour guided canoe outings (adult/child €16/8) and rents mountain bikes (€3/8 per hour/day). It doesn't have set opening hours, so call ahead or risk finding the place abandoned.

Between July and September, when the park gets very crowded, a couple of routes are closed and two others can only be undertaken in a guided group because of the high risk of forest fire. There are no shelters within the park, so make sure you wear sunblock and carry water.

❦ EATING SPOTS // REPLENISH YOUR POSTPARK ENERGY

A simple, good-value eating option is **Trattoria e Pizzeria Mancini e Caduro** (☎ 0564 40 71 37; Via del Fante 24; meals €19; Wed-Mon Apr-Sep), in Alberese. It has a short, affordable menu of homemade Tuscan standards – *tortelli ricotta espinace* (pasta with cheese and spinach), *aquacotta* (soup with bread, onion, tomatoes, celery and egg) – and pizzas, which are served on a small terrace.

Osteria la Nuova Dispensa (☎ 0564 40 73 21; Via Aurelia Vecchia 11; meals €28-32; Thu-Tue) occupies the old village store and also offers local specialities. If you like your food spicy, fire up on the *peposo* (a peppery stewed beef dish with vegetables), Tuscany's answer to a vindaloo. The restaurant's

4.5km south of Alberese, just before the junction with the SS1.

MONTE ARGENTARIO

Once an island, this rugged promontory came to be linked to the mainland by an accumulation of sand that is now the isthmus of Orbetello. Further sandy bulwarks form the Tombolo della Giannella and Tombolo di Feniglia to the north and south. They enclose a lagoon that is now a protected nature reserve.

Intense building, dated urban planning and stunning mobs of people have spoiled the northern side of the promontory (Porto Santo Stefano and around), but the south and centre have been left in peace (forest fires aside). The area is generally upmarket-leaning and a favourite weekend getaway for Romans in the summer, when it gets packed to the gunwales. Ambitious hotel prices make it poor value in high season, and parking, particularly in Porto Santo Stefano, is cutthroat. Late April to early May and late September to early October are optimum times to visit, when warm days, cool nights, reduced crowds and lower prices dramatically improve the atmosphere.

EXPLORING MONTE ARGENTARIO

❦ ORBETELLO // STROLL THE PEDESTRIAN-FRIENDLY GATEWAY TO MONTE ARGENTARIO

Set on a balance-beam isthmus running through the lagoon, Orbetello (population 15,000) is an easily digestible, less raucous regional destination. Its modest, main attraction is the **cathedral** (Piazza della Repubblica; ☽ 9am-noon & 3-6pm), which has retained its 14th-century Gothic facade despite being remodelled in the Spanish style during the 16th century.

Other reminders of the Spanish garrison that was stationed in the city for nearly 150 years include the viceroy's residence on Piazza Eroe dei Due Mondi, the fort and the city walls, parts of which are the original Etruscan fortification.

The **tourist office** (☎ 0564 86 04 47; ☽ 9.30am-12.30pm & 4-7pm Apr-Sep, to 8pm Jul & Aug, 9am-12.30pm & 4-7pm Oct-Mar) is opposite the cathedral and has maps of the town and region.

The best place for observing bird life on Orbetello Lagoon (where as many as 140 species have been identified) is out along the Tombolo di Feniglia, the southern strip of land linking Monte Argentario to the mainland. It is blocked to traffic, but you can park your car near the campsite and continue on foot or bicycle. The beach on the seaward side is one of the best on the peninsula.

❦ PORTO SANTO STEFANO // JOIN THE WATERSIDE BUSTLE

Porto Santo Stefano's linked, crescent waterfront layout divides the objectionable port from the fashionable harbour. Both sides are equally chaotic, though the Ferraris, yachts and scantily clad bodies on the harbour side are significantly more enthralling. From the waterline, the city shoots up the mountainside on ultrathin streets, devoid of parking and sidewalks. The harbour, however, is a *passeggiata* dream: spacious and lined with restaurants, cafes, *gelaterie* (ice-cream shops), and plenty of places to sit and observe this endearing social pageant.

The **tourist office** (☎ 0564 81 42 08; www .lamaremma.info; Piazzale Sant'Andrea; ☽ 9am-1pm & 4-8pm Mon-Sat, 9am-12.30pm Sun) is appallingly located at the eastern end of the port.

Several uneven streets and stairways lead from the harbour up to **Fortezza Spagnola** (☎ 0564 81 06 81; Piazza del Governatore;

adult/child €2/1; ⏰ 6pm-midnight Jun-Sep, 10.30am-12.30pm & 3-7pm Sat & Sun Oct-May), with a small collection of underwater archaeological finds and an exhibition of wooden boat-making. It affords breathtaking views of Porto Santo Stefano.

If you have wheels, follow signs for the narrow and sometimes dangerously overcrowded **Via Panoramica**, a circular route offering great coastal views over the water to the hazy whaleback of the Isola de Giglio.

There are several good **beaches**, mainly of the pebbly variety, just to the east and west of the city centre.

🍽 PORTO ERCOLE // FIND A LITTLE BREATHING SPACE

Situated in a picturesque position between two Spanish forts, Porto Ercole still manages to retain some of its fishing-village character. Far less hectic than the north side of the island, here you can wander the hillside historic centre, past the sandwiched Chiesa di Sant'Erasmo – final resting place of painter-hellion Caravaggio (1571–1610) – and sometimes wonder if you're the only person in town. The climb to the ho-hum fortress is a steep one. Down by the water, the beach is serviced, so it's clean but cluttered with deck chairs and umbrellas.

GASTRONOMIC HIGHLIGHTS

🍽 GATTO E LA VOLPE // PORTO ERCOLE €€

☎ 0564 83 52 05; Via dei Cannoni 3; meals €36-42; ⏰ Tue-Sun

This the last stop on the right as you sweep down the road to the far end of the harbour, where the views are wonderful. Try the speciality *linguine all'astice* (lobster linguine), leaving room for the homemade desserts. Nonlocal vehicles are banned from the port promenade after 6pm in summer. Dine at lunch or be prepared for a 500m walk.

🍽 IL MOLETTO // PORTO SANTO STEFANO €€

☎ 0564 81 36 36; www.moletto.it; Via del Molo 52; meals €28-33; ⏰ Thu-Tue

Among several enticing quayside seafood restaurants, this place wins for its location. At this wooden cabin, set apart from the rest at the end of a mole (pier), you can dine beside a picture window or on the jetty as the evening breeze cools your pasta. Seafood dishes largely depend on the catch of the day, though shrimp, calamari and Mamma Isabella's swordfish steak are fixtures.

🍽 IL VELIERO // PORTO SANTO STEFANO €€

☎ 0564 81 22 26; Via Panoramica 149-151; meals €37-42; ⏰ Tue-Sun Feb-Oct, Fri-Sun Nov-Jan

It's a steep climb from the harbour (head up the steps, guarded by a terracotta lion, just above Pensione Weekend), but the prize is some of the freshest fare of the sea, supplied by the owner's father who runs a fish shop in town. An excellent restaurant with a fondness for presentation – the *pici* (thick, hand-rolled pasta, like a fat spaghetti) with crab sauce is frame-worthy. The *tagliolini di pasta fresca dello chef* (ribbon-thin pasta with a light tomato-lobster sauce) is also a highlight.

🍽 OSTERIA DEL LUPACANTE // ORBETELLO €€

☎ 0564 86 76 18; Corso Italia 103; tasting/tourist menus €23-45, meals €33-38; ⏰ Thu-Tue

You really must begin with one of the splendid soups, which is almost a meal in itself, at this *osteria* run by a local family. The *spaghetti alla messinese* (Messina style, with swordfish, tomato, peppers, sunflower seeds and spices) and *scottiglia di cappone* (local fish and mussels, with a slightly spicy red sauce) are only two of the imaginative creations.

🐦 OSTERIA IL NOCCHINO // ORBETELLO €€

☎ 0564 86 03 29; Via Furio Lenzi 64; meals €25-33; ⏰ Wed-Mon Mar-Oct, Fri-Sun Nov-Feb

Another exceptional choice, serving moderately priced food like mamma used to make, with about the same seating capacity as mamma's (supplemented in summer by outdoor seating). The *gnocchetti pinoli e gamberi* (small gnocchi with pine nuts and prawns) and the *risotto alla pescatora* (fisherman's risotto) are excellent representations of regional pasta dishes.

🐦 PIZZERIA DA GIGETTO // PORTO SANTO STEFANO €

☎ 0564 81 44 95; Via del Molo 9; pizza €4-6

For great views without paying panoramic prices, munch on one of over a dozen pizzas on this popular waterfront terrace. Finish off with an ice cream from Bar Gelateria Chioda, right next door.

TRANSPORT

BUS // Frequent **Rama** (☎ 199 848787; www .griforama.it, in Italian) buses connect most towns on Monte Argentario with downtown Orbetello (€1.50, 20 minutes) and continue to the train station. They also run to Grosseto (€3.40, one hour, up to four daily).

CAR & MOTORCYCLE // By car, follow signs for Monte Argentario from the SS1, which connects Grosseto with Rome.

LAGO DI BURANO & AROUND

🐦 RISERVA NATURALE LAGO DI BURANO // MINGLE WITH MIGRATORY BIRDS

Little more than 10km further east along the coast from Monte Argentario, this saltwater flat is a **nature reserve** (☎ 0564 89 88 29; Capalbio Scalo; admission €8; ⏰ guided visits 10am & 2.30pm Sun Sep-Apr) run by the World Wide Fund for Nature (WWF). Covering 410 hectares and stopping about 5km short of the regional frontier with Lazio, it is typical of the Maremma in its flora but interesting above all for its migratory bird life. Tens of thousands of birds of many species winter here, including several kinds of duck and even falcons. Among the animals, the most precious is the beaver. A path with seven observation points winds its way through the park. To get here, take the Capalbio Scalo exit from the SS1.

🐦 GIARDINO DEI TAROCCHI // CONTEMPLATE THE FUSION OF TAROT, ART AND NATURE

About 8km east of the lake turn-off, you can see the terraces of the **Giardino dei Tarocchi** (☎ 0564 89 51 22; www .nikidesaintphalle.com; Località Garavicchio-Capalbio; adult/child €10.50/6; ⏰ 2.30-7.30pm May–mid-Oct), a fantastic collection of oversized Antoni Gaudí–influenced sculptures tumbling down a hillside. On a theme-park scale, the profusion of dreamy, mosaic-covered sculptures skilfully merges with surrounding nature. The colossal effort, by Franco-American artist Niki de Saint Phalle (1930–2002), depicts the main players from the tarot card pack, such as the Moon, the Fool, the High Priest of Feminine Intuitive Power – and the Empress, within whose innards the artist lived for months during construction. Your interest in divination notwithstanding, these pleasing exhibits transcend age and aesthetic leanings and are the kind of roadside fun that many tourists drive miles out of their way to see. To get here, take the Pescia Fiorentina exit from the SS1.

INLAND & ETRUSCAN SITES

· · · · · ·

The deep south of Tuscany is home to thermal springs, medieval hill towns and Etruscan archaeological finds.

DRIVING TOUR: MONTE ARGENTARIO TO MANCIANO

Map p230
Distance: 106km
Duration: six to seven hours

Departing from Monte Argentario, head for **Albinia** along the SS1, at the northern tip of the Orbetello Lagoon. At Albinia, take the SS74 (signed for Manciano) and quite soon there'll be a right turn for **La Parrina** and the lovely Agriturismo Tenuta La Parrina (p407). The real draw at the *agriturismo* (farm-stay accommodation) is its mesmerising, impulse-buy shop where you can outfit one of the greatest picnics in modern history. An eye-popping assortment of sauces, wine, oil, pasta, honey, cheese, meat and even bath products are tantalisingly displayed. Sadly, there's no bread. The fill-your-own-jug table-wine station starts at €1 per litre.

Head back toward the SS74, cross it, and continue north on the SS323 toward **Magliano in Toscana**, impressive above all for its largely intact city walls. Some date from the 14th century, while most were raised by Siena in the 16th century. The town is a little scrappy on the inside. If you've chosen to forgo the picnic, lunch in the pretty sheltered garden at **Antica Trattoria Aurora** (☎ 0564 59 20 30; Via Chiasso Lavagnini 12/14; meals €40-48; ⊙ Thu-Tue)

is a good idea. The cutting-edge menu includes *cinghiale al finocchio selvatico* (wild boar tortellini with wild fennel).

Next, continue up to **Scansano**. Although there are no monuments of great importance, the old centre, all narrow lanes and archways, is a pleasure to wander around and offers some great views over the surrounding countryside.

Continue through Scansano and exit on the SS322 to Manciano. After about 6.5km, turn right on a road marked 'Aquilaia' (blue sign) and '**Ghiaccio Forte abitato Etrusco**' (brown sign), which is your objective. After about 3km, when the asphalt road curves right, continue straight (no sign) on the dirt road. One more right turn (signed) and you're there. The Etruscan ruins are meagre and information boards severely weathered, but the top-of-the-world panoramic views are unbeatable. Serviceable picnic tables are where you should unfurl the feast you prepared at La Parrina.

Backtrack to the SS322, turn right and you'll soon hit the small, walled medieval town of **Montemerano**. Pick up a bottle of the excellent local Morellino di Scansano wine at **La Vecchia Dispensa** (Via Italia 31; ⊙ 9am-1pm & 5-7pm), a richly scented delicatessen that presses its own olive oil, then drop into **Chiesa di San Giorgio**, decorated with 15th-century frescos of the Sienese school. Finally, stroll up to harmonious, oh-so-photogenic **Piazza del Castello**.

From Montemerano it's 6km to **Saturnia**, with its Etruscan remains, including part of the town wall. A tomb at **Sede di Carlo**, just northeast of the town, is one of the area's best preserved.

The sulphurous spring and thermal baths at **Terme di Saturnia** (☎ 0564 60 01 11; www.termedisaturnia.it; day admission €22, after 3pm €17; ⊙ 9.30am-7.30pm Apr-Sep, to 5.30pm Oct-Mar;

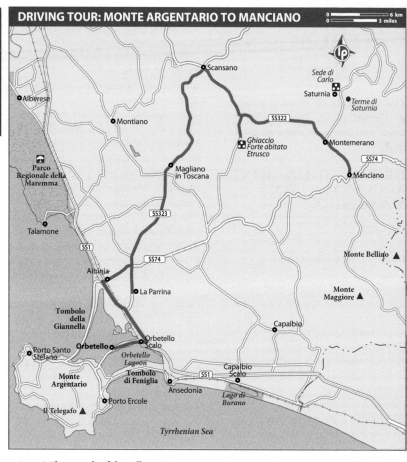

DRIVING TOUR: MONTE ARGENTARIO TO MANCIANO

(P) are 2.5km south of the village. You can happily spend a whole day dunking yourself in the hot pools and signing on for some of the ancillary activities such as the alluring 'four-hand massage shower'. Econo-bathers can avail themselves of the waters running parallel to the road for several hundred metres, starting just south of the Terme di Saturnia turn-off. Look for the telltale sign of other bathers' cars parked on the road, then forage down the dirt path until you find a suitable spot of gratis cascading water, with temperatures at a constant 37.5°C.

Last stop is **Manciano**, another former Sienese stronghold. Apart from the much-interfered-with *rocca* (fortress), there is not much else to keep you here.

PITIGLIANO & AROUND

Check your mirrors before screeching to a halt outside Pitigliano (population 4010). This hilltop stronghold, organically sprouting from a volcanic rocky outcrop towering over the surrounding country, is photo-op fodder that will make your blog visitors swoon. Return at night to see it lit up. The gorges that surround the town on three sides constitute a natural bastion, completed to the east by the manmade fort. Within the town, twisting stairways disappear around corners, cobbled alleys bend tantalisingly out of sight beneath arches, and the stone houses seem to have been piled up higgledy-piggledy by some giant child playing with building blocks.

Originally built by the Etruscans, Pitigliano remained beyond the orbit of the great Tuscan city-states, such as Florence and Siena, until it was finally absorbed into the grand duchy under Cosimo I de' Medici.

In the course of the 15th century, a Jewish community settled here, increasing notably when Pope Pius IV banned Jews from Rome in 1569. They moved into a tiny ghetto, where they remained until 1772. From then until well into the following century, the local community of 400 flourished and Pitigliano was dubbed 'Little Jerusalem'. By the time the Fascists introduced the race laws in 1938, most Jews had moved away; only 80 or so were left and precious few survived the war.

Both an easy drive from Pitigliano, Sovana and Sorano jointly hold Tuscany's most riveting Etruscan ruins.

ESSENTIAL INFORMATION

TOURIST OFFICES // Tourist office (☎ 0564 61 71 11; Piazza Garibaldi, Pitigliano; ☉ 10.20am-1pm & 3-7pm Tue-Sun Apr-Oct, 10.20am-1pm & 2-6pm Tue-Sun Nov-Mar)

EXPLORING PITIGLIANO & AROUND

If you plan to visit most of the archaeological sites around Pitigliano, invest in a €7 combined ticket. It gives entry to the Tomba della Sirena and Tomba di Ildebranda at the Necropoli di Sovana (p232), the Fortezza Orsini in Sorano, the Necropoli di San Rocco just out of Sorano, and the Vitozza rock caves (p232) outside San Quirico. Buy a ticket at any of the sites.

♥ PIAZZAS GARIBALDI & PETRUCCIOLI // COLLIDE WITH THE OLD AND OLDER

An imposing 16th-century viaduct keeps watch over the interlinked Piazza Garibaldi and Piazza Petruccioli. Opposite is the 13th-century Palazzo Orsini (☎ 0564 61 44 19; adult/child €3/1.50; ☉ 10am-1pm & 3-7pm Tue-Sun Apr-Sep, 10am-1pm & 3-5pm Tue-Sun Oct-Mar). Twenty-one of its rooms are open to the public and decked out with a generous collection of ecclesiastical objects, assembled, it occasionally seems, as much to fill the vast empty space as for any aesthetic merit. Opposite is the altogether more organised Museo Archeologico (☎ 0564 61 40 67; Piazza della Fortezza; adult/child €2.50/1.50; ☉ 10am-1pm & 3-7pm Tue-Sun Apr-Sep, 10am-1pm & 3-6pm Tue-Sun Oct-Mar), which has a rich display of finds from local Etruscan sites. They're well displayed, but descriptive panels are in Italian only.

♥ LA PICCOLA GERUSALEMME // PLUNGE INTO A REVIVED GHETTO

The town's medieval lanes and steep alleys are a delight to wander, particularly around the small Ghetto quarter. Head down Via Zuccarelli and turn left at a sign indicating La Piccola Gerusalemme (Little Jerusalem; ☎ 0564 61 60 06; Vicolo Manin 30; adult/child €3/2; ☉ 10am-12.30pm & 4-7pm Sun-Fri May-Oct, 10am-12.30pm & 3-6pm Sun-Fri Nov-Apr). The area fell into disrepair with the demise of Pitigliano's Jewish community at the end of WWII, and was practically rebuilt from scratch in 1995.

VIE CAVE

There are at least 15 rock-sculpted passages spreading out in every direction from the valleys below Pitigliano. These *vie cave* (sunken roads) are enormous – up to 20m deep and 3m wide – and are believed to be sacred routes linking the necropolises and other sites associated with the Etruscan religious cult. A less popular, more mundane explanation is that these strange megalithic corridors were used to move livestock or as some kind of defence, allowing people to move from village to village unseen. Whatever the reason, every spring on the night of the equinox (19 March) there is a torchlit procession down the Via Cava di San Giuseppe, which culminates in a huge bonfire in Pitigliano's Piazza Garibaldi. It serves as a symbol of purification and renewal marking the end of winter.

The countryside around Pitigliano, Sovana and Sorano is also riddled with *vie cave*. Two particularly good examples, 500m west of Pitigliano on the road to Sovana, are Via Cava di Fratenuti, with its high vertical walls and Etruscan graffiti, and Via Cava di San Giuseppe, which passes the Fontana dell'Olmo, carved out of solid rock. From this fountain stares the sculpted head of Bacchus, the mythological god of fruitfulness, as the water flows from his mouth. Via Cava San Rocco, near Sorano, is another fine example. It winds its way through the hills for 2km between the town and the Necropoli di San Rocco, another Etruscan burial site.

There's a fine **walk** from Pitigliano to Sovana (8km, three hours) that incorporates parts of the *vie cave*. Enquire at the tourist office in Pitigliano (p231) for routes and the all-important return transport.

The open-air **Museo Archeologico all'Aperto** (☎ 338 469 92 79; adult/child €4/2; ☿ 10am-3pm Mon-Fri, to 6pm Sat & Sun), south of town on the road to Grosseto/Saturnia, contains sections of *vie cave*, and several necropolises.

A visit includes the tiny, richly adorned synagogue and a small museum of Jewish culture, including the old bakery, kosher butcher and dyeing workshops.

❦ NECROPOLI DI SOVANA // EXPLORE TUSCANY'S MOST SIGNIFICANT ETRUSCAN TOMBS

Within the **Necropoli di Sovana** (admission €5; ☿ 9am-7pm Mar-Nov, 10am-5pm Fri-Sun Dec-Feb), 1.5km south of the nearby village of Sovana, are Tuscany's most significant Etruscan tombs. Look for the yellow sign on the left for the **Tomba della Sirena**, where you follow a trail running alongside a rank of tomb facades cut from the rock face, as well as walk along a *via cava*.

The **Tomba di Ildebranda**, by far the grandest of Etruscan mausoleums and the only surviving temple-style tomb, still preserves traces of its columns and stairs. **Tomba del Tifone** is about 300m down a trail running alongside a rank of tomb facades cut from the rock face. A few arresting lengths of *via cava* exist here as well.

Due east of the village, just outside the tiny hamlet of San Quirico and signposted from the main square, are the **Vitozza rock caves** (☎ 0564 61 40 74; admission €2; ☿ 10am-6pm Tue-Sun Mar-Oct, by appointment Nov-Feb), more than 200 of them, peppering a high rock ridge. One of the largest troglodyte dwellings in Italy, the complex was first inhabited in prehistoric times.

GASTRONOMIC HIGHLIGHTS

In Pitigliano, pick up a stick or two of *sfratto,* a gorgeously sticky local confection of honey and walnuts, from **Il Forno** (Via Roma 16). Counterbalance the sweetness with a glass of the town's lively dryish Bianco di Pitigliano wine from **Il Ghetto** (Via Zuccarelli 47), a smart flagstone-and-brick wine bar with cheese and salami snacks.

❦ OSTERIA IL TUFO ALLEGRO // PITIGLIANO €€

☎ 0564 61 61 92; Vico della Costituzione 2; meals €29; ☺ Wed-Mon

The aromas emanating from the kitchen door facing Via Zuccarelli should be enough to draw you down to the cavernous chamber, carved out of tufa foundations. The excruciatingly small-portioned lamb is admittedly succulent. Truffle and vegetarian options dominate the *primi* section.

TRANSPORT

BUS // Rama (☎ 199 848787; www.griforama.it, in Italian) buses leave from the train station at Grosseto for Pitigliano (€6, two hours, four daily). They also connect Pitigliano with Sorano (€1.20, 15 minutes, seven daily) and Sovana (€1.20, 20 minutes, one daily). For Saturnia, change at Manciano.

EASTERN TUSCANY

3 PERFECT DAYS

☙ DAY 1 // NAME THAT FILM SCENE

In recent years, film location scouts have twice deemed this tiny corner of Tuscany as being the region's scenic superlative. Roberto Benigni filmed scenes of his Oscar-winning film *La vita è bella* (Life Is Beautiful) in Arezzo and Cortona, while Audrey Wells chose Cortona as a backdrop for some scenes from *Under the Tuscan Sun* (not wholly surprising, as the novel is set there). Even if you haven't committed these films to memory, both cities have backdrops powerful enough to inspire a film of your own.

☙ DAY 2 // PIERO DELLA FRANCESCA TRAIL

The Museo Civico in Sansepolcro (p245), where the great artist's life both began and ended, is only the beginning of a thorough tour of his surviving works in the area. Evidence of his previously unequalled skill in applied geometry and mathematical foreshortening to achieve perspective and backgrounds can be found in his *Madonna del Parto* in Monterchi (p247) and the renowned *Legend of the True Cross* in Arezzo's Chiesa di San Francesco (opposite).

☙ DAY 3 // EXPLORE CASENTINO

The undeservedly obscure hill country of the Casentino is a lush forested landscape, making for a low-key drive with copious photo ops. There's an assortment of minor castles and noteworthy monasteries, including the truly vast Sanctuario di San Francesco in Verna (p248). Wandering the Parco Nazionale delle Foreste Casentinesi will fill a day on its own (p247).

AREZZO

. . . . . .

pop 97,500

Bombed back to the Renaissance during WWII, the surviving parts of Arezzo's historic centre and ancillary attractions are still worthy competition for any destination in the region. Day trips here from Florence or Perugia are easy enough, but with both accommodation and eating value being superior in Arezzo, shifting your bags for a night or two will be well rewarded. Furthermore, the city serves as an ideal staging area for day trips to Sansepolcro or the Casentino region.

The lopsided, architectural jumble of Piazza Grande is riveting, particularly from the many restaurants and *enoteche* (wine bars) on the perimeter offering choice people-watching. The renowned five-star fresco cycle by Piero della Francesca in the Chiesa di San Francesco will beguile, whether you adore art or just endure it, as will the Romanesque epitome of Pieve di Santa Maria.

Long a vital Etruscan trading post, Arezzo later prospered while part of the Roman Empire. The staunch Ghibelline city was a free republic by the 10th century, lending its support to the emperor during bloody clashes with the papacy. The city went into a centuries-long period of decline after being swallowed by Guelph-bent Florence in 1384. It would not experience significant prosperity again until after the unification of Italy and the arrival of the railroad in 1866.

It's the birthplace of the Renaissance poet Petrarch, who popularised the sonnet, penning his verses in both Latin and Italian, and Giorgio Vasari, the prolific painter and architect whose contributions to Renaissance Florence included the Uffi-zi Gallery, the Palazzo dei Cavalieri and the tomb of Michelangelo in San Croce.

Another illustrious son, born in a nearby village, is comic actor and director Roberto Benigni, who created and starred in the Oscar-winning film *La vita è bella* (Life Is Beautiful).

ESSENTIAL INFORMATION

EMERGENCIES // Nuovo Ospedale San Donato (☎ 0575 25 50 01; Via A de Gasperi) Arezzo's hospital, located outside the city walls. Police station (☎ 0575 31 81; Via Fra Guittone 3)

TOURIST OFFICES // Centro di Accoglienza Turistico (☎ 0575 40 35 74; Via Ricasoli; 9.30am-6.30pm Jun-Oct, 10am-5pm Nov-May) An alternative tourist office, it hires out audio guides to Arezzo (adult/child per day €2.50/2) with an accompanying map. Its 'Room 180' shows a 30-minute film about Arezzo (adult/child €2.50/2) in six languages on a 180-degree screen. The tourist office (☎ 0575 2 08 39; www.apt.arezzo.it; Piazza della Repubblica 28; 9am-1pm & 3-7pm Apr-Sep, 10am-1pm & 3-6pm Mon-Sat, 10am-1pm Sun Oct-Mar) has a representative from Colori Toscani on-site who can arrange accommodation and tours free of charge.

EXPLORING AREZZO

❤ CHIESA DI SAN FRANCESCO // FOLLOW PIERO DELLA FRANCESCA'S MEDIEVAL CARTOON TALE

Gracing the apse of this 14th-century church (Piazza San Francesco; 9am-7pm

TICKETING

You can buy a combined ticket (€10) giving entry to the Piero della Francesca frescos in the Chiesa di San Francesco, plus the Museo Archeologico, Museo Statale d'Arte Medievale e Moderna and the Casa di Vasari, at any of the four venues.

(Continued on page 240

EASTERN TUSCANY

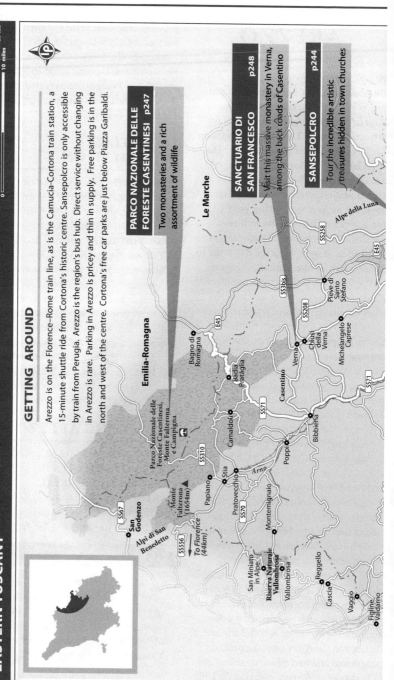

GETTING AROUND

Arezzo is on the Florence–Rome train line, as is the Camucia-Cortona train station, a 15-minute shuttle ride from Cortona's historic centre. Sansepolcro is only accessible by train from Perugia. Arezzo is the region's bus hub. Direct service without changing in Arezzo is rare. Parking in Arezzo is pricey and thin in supply. Free parking is in the north and west of the centre. Cortona's free car parks are just below Piazza Garibaldi.

PARCO NAZIONALE DELLE FORESTE CASENTINESI   p247
Two monasteries and a rich assortment of wildlife

SANCTUARIO DI SAN FRANCESCO   p248
Visit this massive monastery in Verna, among the back roads of Casentino

SANSEPOLCRO   p244
Tour the incredible artistic treasures hidden in town churches

Le Marche

Emilia-Romagna

Alpe della Luna

SS258

E45

SS5bis

Pieve di Santo Stefano

SS208

Bagno di Romagna

Badia Prataglia

Verna

Chiusi della Verna

Michelangelo Caprese

Casentino

SS71

Camaldoli

SS71

Bibbiena

SS571

Parco Nazionale delle Foreste Casentinesi, Monte Falterona e Campigna

SS310

Poppi

Stia

Arno

Papiano

Pratovecchio

SS70

Montemignaio

SS567

Monte Falterona (1654m)

San Godenzo

Alpi di San Benedetto

SS556

To Florence (44km)

San Miniato in Alpe

Riserva Naturale Vallombrosa

Vallombrosa

Reggello

Cascia

Vaggio

Figline Valdarno

0   10 miles
0   20 km

EASTERN TUSCANY

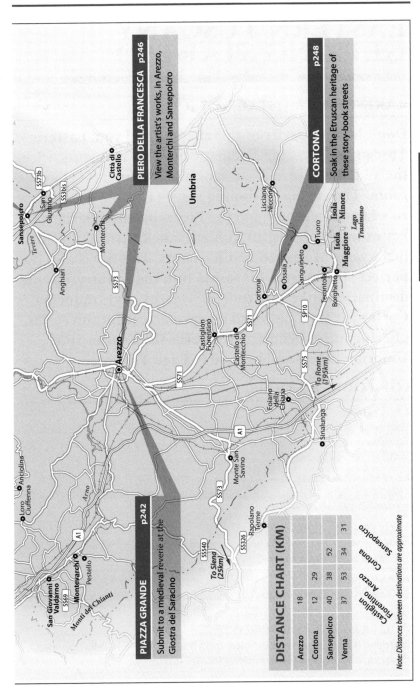

PIERO DELLA FRANCESCA p246

View the artist's works, in Arezzo, Monterchi and Sansepolcro

CORTONA p248

Soak in the Etruscan heritage of these story-book streets

PIAZZA GRANDE p242

Submit to a medieval reverie at the Giostra del Saracino

Umbria

Città di Castello

Sansepolcro
San Giustino
SS73b
SS3bis
Monterchi
Tevere
Anghiari
SS73

Lisciano Niccone
Tuoro
Isola Minore
Isola Maggiore
Lago Trasimeno
Ossaia
Sanguineto
Cortona
Terontola
Borghetto
SP10

Castiglion Fiorentino
Castello di Montecchio
SS71
Arezzo
SS71
SS75
To Rome (195km)

Foiano della Chiana
A1
Sinalunga

Loro Ciuffenna
Anjiolina
Arno
Monte San Savino
SS73

Monti del Chianti
Pestello
San Giovanni Valdarno
Montevarchi
A1
SS69

SS540
To Siena (25km)
SS326
Rapolano Terme

DISTANCE CHART (KM)

	Arezzo	Castiglion Fiorentino	Cortona	Sansepolcro
Arezzo				
Cortona	29	18		
Sansepolcro	38	40	52	
Verna	53	37	34	31

Note: Distances between destinations are approximate

EASTERN TUSCANY GETTING STARTED

MAKING THE MOST OF YOUR TIME

Don't let the brevity of this chapter fool you. Eastern Tuscany holds some cinematic oh-wow moments, with the added pleasure of comparatively abundant elbow-room. The curiously sloping Piazza Grande in Arezzo's Etruscan centre and the Pieve di Santa Maria, a key example of Tuscan Romanesque construction, are just a taste of Arezzo's enticements. The city is also the perfect staging area for forays into the countryside and destinations like Sansepolcro. Nearby, sigh-inducing Cortona is the final word on spectacular hilltop eyries, offering mind-bending views over the Tuscan and Umbrian plains and beyond to Lago Trasimeno.

TOP TOURS & COURSES

☙ POLYMNIA
Also known as Koine, this Cortona-based operation offers Italian language courses and cultural activities such as day trips to the Chianti area and cooking classes. (☎ 0575 61 25 82; www.polymnia.net)

☙ ALESSANDRO MADIAI
A passionate cyclist, Alessandro runs five-hour bicycle tours around Arezzo. (Cortona; ☎ 338 6491481; torrequebrada@virgilio.it)

☙ CORTONA WELLNESS
Provides a comprehensive list of nearby excursions, bicycle hire and walks. (☎ 0575 60 31 36; www.cortonawellness.com, in Italian)

☙ CASA OMBUTO
Hosts week-long, all-inclusive cooking courses (p247) in Poppi. (www.italiancookerycourse .com)

☙ THE PIERO DELLA FRANCESCO TRAIL
The region is home to several renowned works by the artist Pierro della Francesco, which can be viewed in a full-day driving tour (p246).

GETTING AWAY FROM IT ALL

Cortona can get pretty crowded during tour-bus season, and Arezzo is always hectic with local busyness. Nevertheless, you'll find that blissful quiet you crave is only a quick drive away.

* **Sansepolcro** (p244) The narrow streets of Sansepolcro may be busy, but weak public transport connections mean comparatively light tourism and value for money.

* **Parco Nazionale delle Foreste Casentinesi** (p247) This national park is a cool summer refuge, ideal for walking and observing a rich assortment of wildlife in incredibly scenic surrounds.

TOP EATING EXPERIENCES

♥ LANCIA D'ORO
One of Arezzo's more sophisticated places, with fresh flowers on the tables and excellent snacks arriving unannounced (p243)

♥ RISTORANTE FIORENTINO
A Sansepolcro institution, where the pasta's homemade and the imaginative menu changes with the seasons (p245)

♥ TRATTORIA DARDANO
Cortona's leading, no-nonsense, yet still unexpectedly wonderful, trattoria, destined to be someone's travel-memoir fodder (p251)

♥ TORRE DI GNICCHE
This traditional restaurant located just off the Piazza Grande in Arezzo offers a vast selection of antipasti and local *pecorino* cheeses (p243)

FESTIVALS

* **Giostra dell'Archidado** A week of trumpeting, parading and a crossbow competition first held in the Middle Ages take place in Cortona, in either May or June, coinciding with Ascension day.

* **Giostra del Saracino** A horse-jousting competition involving neighbourhood rivalries in Arezzo (p241).

* **Arezzo Wave** (www.arezzowave.com, in Italian) An annual music festival featuring artists and bands from Italy and abroad, held over six days in mid-July.

* **Sagra del Fungo Porcino** Honouring this delectable mushroom, the Porcini Festival takes place in Cortona, mid-August.

* **Palio della Balestra** A crossbow contest pitting costumed archers from Gubbio against Sansepolcro's best, in Sansepolcro on the second Sunday in September.

* **Sagra della Bistecca** Giardino del Parterre becomes one vast open-air grill at Cortona's Steak Festival (14/15 August).

RESOURCES

* **Arezzo Tourist Agency** (www.apt.arezzo.it) Website of the city's official tourist body

* **Piero della Francesca** (www.pierodellafrancesca.it) Describes the artist and his principal works

* **Comune di Sansepolcro** (www.comune.sansepolcro.ar.it, in Italian) The city's official website

* **Parco Nazionale Foreste Casentinesi** (www.parcoforestecasentinesi.it) Online guide to the park and around

(Continued from page 235)

Apr-Oct, to 6pm Nov-Mar) is one of the greatest works of Italian art, Piero della Francesca's fresco cycle of the *Legend of the True Cross*. Painted between 1452 and 1466, it relates in 10 episodes the story of the cross on which Christ was crucified.

The illustration of this medieval legend, as entertaining as it is inconceivable, begins in the top right-hand corner and follows the story of the tree that Seth plants on the grave of his father, Adam, and

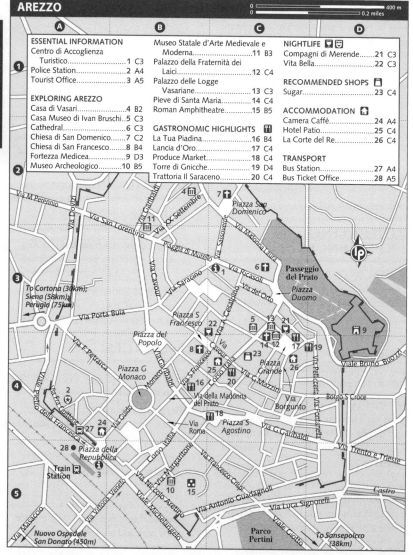

AREZZO

0   400 m
0   0.2 miles

ESSENTIAL INFORMATION	
Centro di Accoglienza Turistico	1 C3
Police Station	2 A4
Tourist Office	3 A5

EXPLORING AREZZO	
Casa di Vasari	4 B2
Casa Museo di Ivan Bruschi	5 C3
Cathedral	6 C3
Chiesa di San Domenico	7 C2
Chiesa di San Francesco	8 B4
Fortezza Medicea	9 D3
Museo Archeologico	10 B5

Museo Statale d'Arte Medievale e Moderna	11 B3
Palazzo della Fraternità dei Laici	12 C4
Palazzo delle Logge Vasariane	13 C3
Pieve di Santa Maria	14 C4
Roman Amphitheatre	15 B5

GASTRONOMIC HIGHLIGHTS 🍴	
La Tua Piadina	16 B4
Lancia d'Oro	17 C4
Produce Market	18 C4
Torre di Gnicche	19 D4
Trattoria Il Saraceno	20 C4

NIGHTLIFE 🍷 🍸	
Compagni di Merende	21 C3
Vita Bella	22 C3

RECOMMENDED SHOPS 🛍	
Sugar	23 C4

ACCOMMODATION 🏠	
Camera Caffé	24 A4
Hotel Patio	25 C4
La Corte del Re	26 C4

TRANSPORT	
Bus Station	27 A4
Bus Ticket Office	28 A5

EASTERN TUSCANY

from which, eventually, the True Cross is made. A scene on the opposite wall shows the long-lost cross being rediscovered by Helena, mother of the emperor Constantine; behind her, the city of Jerusalem is represented by a medieval view of Arezzo. Even Khosrow, the Persian emperor accused of making off with the cross, features ignominiously. Rarely will you get a better sense of medieval frescos as strip cartoon, telling a tale with such vigour and sheer beauty. Likewise, art buffs will be struck by Piero's innovations with perspective and geometric perfection and the stillness he created by his lack of naturalism.

As is often the case, the mere survival of these frescos has been part extraordinary luck, part back-breaking restoration. Damage endured/eluded from fires, earthquakes and allied bombs notwithstanding, time and the elements also conspired to sully the work. When Piero's *Dream of Constantine* was cleaned up during major restoration, the piece that was formerly thought to be 'the first realistic nocturnal scene in Italian art' turned out to be set at dawn. It was just dirty.

You can get some sense of the frescos from beyond the cordon in front of the altar, but to really appreciate them up close you need to plan ahead for a **visit with audio guide** (☎ 0575 35 27 27; www .pierodellafrancesca.it; admission €6; ⏱ 9am-7pm Apr-Oct, to 6pm Nov-Mar). As only 25 people are allowed in every half-hour, it's essential to prebook, either by phone or at any of the sights that participate in the combined ticket scheme. The ticket office is at Piazza San Francesco 4, to the right of the church's main entrance.

❤ PIEVE DI SANTA MARIA & AROUND // APPRAISE INTRIGUING ART AND ARCHITECTURE

This 12th-century **church** (Corso Italia 7; ⏱ 8am-1pm & 3-7pm May-Sep, 8am-noon & 3-6pm Oct-Apr) has a magnificent Romanesque arcaded facade adorned with dozens of carved columns, each uniquely decorated. Its 14th-century bell tower, with 40 apertures, is something of an emblem for the city. Above the central doorway are carved reliefs representing the months of the year. The monochrome of the interior's warm stone is relieved by Pietro Lorenzetti's fine polyptych *Madonna and Saints,* beneath the semidome of the apse. Below the altar is a 14th-century silver bust reliquary of the city's patron saint, San Donato. Other treasures on display include a 13th-century crucifix by

GIOSTRA DEL SARACINO

Originating in the time of the Crusades, the 'Joust of the Saracen' is one of those grand, noisy affairs involving extravagant fancy dress and neighbourhood rivalry that Italians delight in. Like many such Tuscan folk spectacles, the tournament was revived in its present form in 1931 after long neglect. The day begins with a herald reading a proclamation, followed by a procession of precisely 311 people in 14th-century dress and 31 horses. It's the highlight of the year for the city's four *quartieri* (quarters), each of which puts forward a team of 'knights' armed with lances. In the Piazza Grande, the knights try their hand jousting at a wooden effigy, known as the *buratto*. In one hand the *buratto* holds a shield, etched with various point-scores, which the knights aim for while trying to avoid being belted with the *mazza-frustro* – three heavy leather balls on ropes – which dangle from the *buratto*'s other hand. The winning team takes home the coveted Golden Lance, bringing glory to its *quartiere*.

Margherito di Arezzo and a carved marble bas-relief of the *Adoration of the Magi*.

For slightly less ecclesiastical art and antiques, pop over the road to the **Casa Museo di Ivan Bruschi** (☎ 0575 35 41 26; Corso Italia 14; admission €5; ◷ 10am-6pm Tue-Sun Apr-Sep, 10am-1pm & 2-6pm Tue-Sun Oct-Mar). Cast an eye over the large and varied collection, amassed by the man who founded the Arezzo antiques fair (see below).

☙ PIAZZA GRANDE & AROUND // EXPLORE THIS COBBLED BEAUTY

Curiously lopsided, architecturally disarrayed and newly recobbled by the same team that did Piazza del Campo in Siena, mesmeric Piazza Grande is overlooked at its upper end by the porticos of the **Palazzo delle Logge Vasariane**, completed in 1573. The **Palazzo della Fraternità dei Laici** with its churchlike facade, in the northwest corner, was started in 1375 in the Gothic style and finished after the onset of the Renaissance. In addition to being the venue for the Giostra del Saracino (see the boxed text, p241), a frenzied **antiques fair** that attracts more than 500 exhibitors to the piazza and the surrounding streets is held here on the first Saturday and Sunday of every month.

☙ CATHEDRAL & AROUND // CONTINUE THE DELLA FRANCESCA EDUCATION

Arezzo's **cathedral** (Piazza Duomo; ◷ 7am-12.30pm & 3-6.30pm), at the top of the hill, was started in the 13th century, yet was not completed until well into the 15th century. In the northeast corner, to the left of the bulky, intricately carved main altar, there's an exquisite fresco of *Mary Magdalene* by Piero della Francesca, itself dwarfed in size but not beauty by the multitiered, rich marble reliefs of the adjoining tomb of Bishop Guido Tarlati,

featuring a frieze of priests and an acolyte chanting while holding a censer, a prayer book and candles.

Off the north aisle, the Capella della Madonna del Conforto has a pair of fine glazed terracotta images from the della Robbia workshop. On the right as you enter is the tomb of Pope Gregory X, who died in Arezzo in 1276.

Up high to the southeast of the cathedral, across the peaceful gardens of the **Passeggio del Prato**, rears the **Fortezza Medicea** (admission free; ◷ 7am-8pm Apr-Oct, 7.30am-6pm Nov-Mar), completed in 1560 and offering grand views of the town and surrounding countryside.

☙ ART CRAWL // MEDIEVAL GREATS FROM CIMABUE TO SIGNORELLI

The short detour to the **Chiesa di San Domenico** (Piazza San Domenico 7; ◷ 8.30am-6pm), with its unusual, asymmetrical facade, is a must. Above the main altar rears a haunting *Crucifixion,* one of Cimabue's earliest works, painted around 1265. Note too the pair of well-preserved frescos by Spinello Aretino (1350–1410) at the western end, and, in the south aisle, a statue by the della Robbia school of San Pietro Martire with a sword cleaving his skull.

To the west, **Casa di Vasari** (☎ 0575 40 90 40; Via XX Settembre 55; adult/child €2/1; ◷ 8.30am-7.30pm Mon & Wed-Sat, to 1pm Sun) was built and sumptuously decorated (overwhelmingly so in the case of the Sala del Camino, the Fireplace Room) by the architect himself. Ring the bell if the door's closed.

Further west again, the **Museo Statale d'Arte Medievale e Moderna** (☎ 0575 40 90 50; Via San Lorentino 8; adult/student €10/7; ◷ 9am-6pm Tue-Sun) primarily houses works by local artists. The two small rooms on the ground floor mostly contain sculptures from local churches, while on the next floor is a display of medieval paintings, including works by Bartolomeo della Gatta and Domenico Pecori, a collection of glazed terracotta pieces by the della Robbia family, and colourful majolica plates. Upstairs, in addition to works by Luca Signorelli and several canvases on the grand scale by Vasari, the chronology continues into the 19th century.

♥ MUSEO ARCHEOLOGICO & ROMAN AMPHITHEATRE // VIEW SOME VIVID ART AND ARTEFACTS

The Museo Archeologico (☎ 0575 2 08 82; Via Margaritone 10; adult/child €4/2; ☼ 8.30am-7pm) is in a former convent overlooking the remains of the Roman amphitheatre (admission free; ☼ 8.30am-7pm Apr-Oct, to 6pm Nov-Mar), which once seated up to 10,000 spectators. Inside, there's a sizeable collection of Etruscan and Roman artefacts, including locally produced ceramics and bronzes. Among the highlights is the Cratere di Euphronios, a large 6th-century-BC Etruscan vase, decorated with vivid scenes showing Hercules in battle, and, upstairs, an exquisite tiny portrait of a bearded man executed on glass in the 3rd century AD.

GASTRONOMIC HIGHLIGHTS

A veritable melee erupts in Piazza Sant'Agostino each Tuesday, Thursday and Saturday at the local produce market.

♥ LA TUA PIADINA €

☎ 0575 2 32 40; Via de' Cenci 18; snacks €3.50
A justifiably popular takeaway place hidden away down a side street, where you can get a range of hot, tasty *piadine*, Emilia-Romagna's version of the wrap. A busy mix of neighbourhood folk, students and visitors jockeys for the limited seating out on the street.

EASTERN TUSCANY

ACCOMMODATION

Even in the busier parts of the region, good accommodation value can be found with very little effort.

★ **Locanda Giglio** (p409) Four rooms with oak floors, underfloor lighting and period furniture recovered from the family loft.

★ **Hotel San Michele** (p409) Cortona's finest hotel, with elements dating from the 12th century, offering frequent room discounts.

★ **La Corte Del Re** (p409) Six apartments, centimetres from Piazza Grande, harmoniously blending contemporary design into elements of the historic building.

For a full list of accommodation options in Eastern Tuscany, see p391.

♥ LANCIA D'ORO €€

☎ 0575 2 10 33; Piazza Grande 18-19; meals €45; ☼ closed Sun evening & Mon
A sophisticated place with fresh flowers on the tables where your order is supplemented by excellent snacks and titbits that arrive unannounced. There's a jolly, waggish waiter, while the interior, painted with swags and green-and-white stripes, is like dining in a marquee. Good 'light' lunch menus (€15, two courses, plus glass of wine) are served on the terrace under the loggia that looks down over Piazza Grande. Service charge 10%.

♥ TORRE DI GNICCHE €

☎ 0575 35 20 35; Piaggia San Martino 8; meals €21-26; ☼ Thu-Tue
Just off the Piazza Grande, this is a fine old traditional restaurant (lunch service starts at 12.30pm and not one second

before) that offers a rich variety of anti-pasti. The ample range of local *pecorino* cheeses is enriched by an extensive red wine list.

♥ TRATTORIA IL SARACENO €€

☎ 0575 2 76 44; www.ilsaraceno.com; Via G Mazzini 6; meals €24-28; ⊙ Thu-Tue

With 60 years in business, this trattoria serves quality, varied Tuscan fare attracting a lunch crowd that keeps the swarm of servers dashing. The impressive wine collection is hard to miss, as it conspicuously lines the walls along with classic pictures of Arezzo. Pizzas start at €5.

NIGHTLIFE

♥ COMPAGNI DI MERENDE

☎ 0575 182 23 68; Logge Vasari 16

Occupying one of the most enviable positions in the city, what you'd expect to be an overpriced tourist trap is in fact a friendly, unassuming little wine bar, tucked under the loggia overlooking Piazza Grande. Enjoy a plate of cheese or cold cuts, or simply sit with a restorative glass of wine.

♥ VITA BELLA

Piazza San Francesco 22

Opposite the Chiesa di San Francesco, Vita Bella is an agreeable place with wrought-iron chairs on a large terrace. You can sip a negroni and nibble on a crostini while watching the world go by.

RECOMMENDED SHOPS

♥ SUGAR

☎ 0575 35 48 46; Corso Italia 43

One of a growing number of superchic boutique shops appearing in small Tuscan towns, Sugar offers a fusion of top fashion names and modern art exhibitions rotating in the windows.

TRANSPORT

BUS // Services from the bus station at Piazza della Repubblica include Cortona (€2.80, one hour, more than 10 weekdays, three Saturdays), Sansepolcro (€3.30, one hour, seven daily) and Siena (€5.20, 1½ hours, seven daily). For Florence, you're better off hopping on the train. Buy tickets in the bus ticket office just outside the train station.

TRAIN // Arezzo is on the Florence–Rome train line, with frequent services to Rome (€11.70, 2½ hours) and Florence (€5.60, 1½ hours). Trains call by Cortona (€2.40, 20 minutes, hourly).

CAR & MOTORCYCLE // Arezzo is a few kilometres east of the A1, and the SS73 heads east to Sansepolcro.

NORTHEAST OF AREZZO

· · · · · ·

In addition to being low-key, agreeable walled cities, Monterchi and Sansepolcro are irresistible enticements for Piero della Francesca enthusiasts.

SANSEPOLCRO

pop 16,200

An unusually flat, but captivating Tuscan walled town dating from AD 1000, Sansepolcro is best known as the probable birthplace of Piero della Francesca (p246).

Reaching its current size in the 15th century and walled in the 16th century, the historic centre is tightly packed with stone structures abutting somewhat less historic structures in a pleasant jumble.

Sansepolcro's light tourist scene is largely due to poor transport connections; it's only accessible by bus from Arezzo or the agonisingly slow train from Perugia.

Via Matteotti connects Piazza Torre di Berta and Piazza Fra Luca Pacioli, with the Duomo, Museo Civico and the Palazzo delle Laudi.

ESSENTIAL INFORMATION

TOURIST OFFICES // The recently enlarged **tourist office** (☎ 0575 74 05 36; infosansepolcro@apt.arezzo.it; Via Matteotti 8; 🕙 9.30am-1pm & 3-6pm Apr-Sep, 9.30am-12.30pm & 3.30-5.30pm Mon-Sat, 9.30am-12.30pm Sun Oct-Mar) is packed with multilingual information.

EXPLORING SANSEPOLCRO

🏛 MUSEO CIVICO // MEET PIERO AND HIS PROTÉGÉS

The **Museo Civico** (☎ 0575 73 22 18; www .comune.sansepolcro.ar.it, in Italian; Via Aggiunti 65; adult/child €6/4.50; 🕙 9.30am-1.30pm & 2.30-7pm Jun-Sep, 9.30am-1pm & 2.30-6pm Oct-May) features a couple of Piero della Francesca's masterpieces. In the *Resurrezione* (Resurrection), the newly risen Christ stares out at the viewer, banner in hand like a triumphant warrior, while his guards slumber. In the splendid *Madonna della Misericordia* polyptych, the Virgin spreads her protective cloak over the painting's benefactors.

There are also works by distinguished Piero protégés Pontormo, Raffaellino dal Colle and Santi di Tito, whose *Riposo Durante la Fuga in Egitto* (Rest during the Flight into Egypt) portrays the Holy Family in a tender and humanistic light.

Upstairs there's a display of 14th- and 15th-century frescos, including a haunting portrait of St Sebastian, while the basement holds a small gathering of archaeological finds and ecclesiastical knick-knackery. There are also two notable works by Matteo Di Giovanni: *Crocifissione* and *Pala dei Santi Pietro e Paolo*.

🏛 CHURCH ART // DISCOVER SANSEPOLCRO'S HIDDEN RELIGIOUS ART

Step into any church with open doors, as they're all lovely, but make a point of calling at the following.

Just south of the tourist office, the newly renovated **cathedral** contains the recently cleaned *Volto Santo* (Sacred Face), a striking wooden crucifix with a wide-eyed Christ, dating back to AD 950 and one of only three in the world. Also gawk-worthy is a fresco by Bartolomeo della Gatta.

If you're looking for work by Luca Signorelli, head to the **San Antonio church** (cnr Via San Antonio & Via del Campaccio), which has a magnificent processional banner with paintings on two sides by the Cortona-born artist.

In the **Chiesa di San Lorenzo** (1556; cnr Via di San Croce & Via Lucca Pacioli) you'll find the Rosso Fiorentino manneristic masterpiece *Deposition of Christ* (1528), 'crowned' with a lunette painted by Raffaellino del Colle, depicting 'God the Father Giving His Blessing', while the **Chiesa Santa Maria dei Servi** (Piazza Dotti) contains a *Madonna del Parto* that predates Piero della Francesca's *Parto* in Monterchi and is now thought to have inspired the work, taking away, some say, from della Francesca's credit. When a della Francesca fanatic at Santa Maria decided to destroy this evidence, Sansepolcro's pregnant women protested, so a column was judiciously placed making it all-but-impossible to see the original *Parto*. It's on the left as you enter church, in an alcove behind the column. Bring a flashlight or a very bright mobile phone.

Ristorante Fiorentino (Via L Pacioli 60; meals €28-32) is the city's stand-out restaurant and a fine accommodation option (p409).

TRANSPORT

BUS // SITA buses link Sansepolcro with Arezzo (€3.50, one hour, 20 daily).
TRAIN // Several trains leave daily to Perugia (€4.15, 1¾ hours) where you can change for Rome (2¾ hours).

EASTERN TUSCANY

EASTERN TUSCANY

DRIVING TOUR: SANSEPOLCRO TO AREZZO ON THE PIERO DELLA FRANCESCA TRAIL

Distance: 46km
Duration: seven hours

Though many details about his life are hazy, it is believed that Piero della Francesca was born around 1420 in Sansepolcro to a privileged family, his father being a successful tanner and shoe-maker, allowing him to receive a good education and indulge in the study of painting with Siena-trained artists in the area. He spent the bulk of his productive life in Arezzo, though he also worked in Rimini, Ferrara, Rome and Florence, where he worked with Domenico Veneziano on frescos for the Ospedale di Santa Maria

Nuova. He returned to Sansepolcro in his twilight years to write several treatises, most notably *De Prospectiva Pingendi* (On Perspective in Painting). Though it has never been confirmed, it is believed that della Francesca lost his sight near the end of his life. He died on 12 October 1492, the same day that Columbus arrived in the New World.

Piero's distinction revolved around his use of perspective and his skill with backgrounds, creating an overall, salient 'serene humanism'. He cultivated his methods of applied geometry and mathematical foreshortening for all objects on the canvas at a level previously unknown to, never mind unachievable by, most painters.

A profusion of Piero della Francesca's works survive in Eastern Tuscany, easily filling a full-day tour. Starting in **Sansepolcro**, seek out his masterpieces the *Resur-*

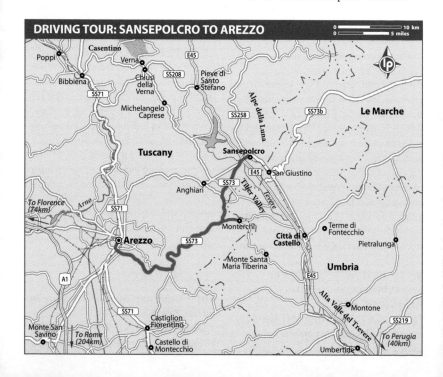

rezione (Resurrection) and the *Madonna della Misericordia* polyptych (p245).

From there it's a 17km drive to **Monterchi**, one of the more atmospheric, atoll-like protuberances in the High Tiber Valley, where you'll find della Francesca's renowned fresco **Madonna del Parto** (☎ 0575 7 07 13; Via della Reglia 1; adult/child €3.50/ free; 9am-1pm & 2-7pm Tue-Fri, to 7pm Sat & Sun Apr-Sep, to 5pm Oct-Mar). Painted in just seven days, the Pregnant Madonna is considered one of the key works of 15th-century Italian art and the only known representation from the period. The fresco depicts two angels pulling back tabernacle flaps, presenting the Pregnant Madonna to a group of believers, thus associating her (a mortal) with God, a sacred no-no in the 15th-century. As such, the church routinely destroyed such images, this being one of the few to survive. A nice touch: pregnant women get free admission.

The 29km leg to **Arezzo** probably won't take as long as finding reasonable parking there and walking to Chiesa di San Francesco (p235), but it's wholly worth the effort to see the renowned *Legend of the True Cross,* painted between 1452 and 1466, relating in 10 episodes the story of the cross on which Christ was crucified.

THE CASENTINO REGION

· · · · · ·

♠ PARCO NAZIONALE DELLE FORESTE CASENTINESI, MONTE FALTERONA E CAMPIGNA // TRAVERSE A PROTECTED PARK AND FOREST

This **national park** (www.parcoforestecasentinesi .it) goes over both sides of the Tuscany–Emilia-Romagna border, taking in some of the most scenic stretches of the Apennines. The Tuscan part is gentler than the Emilian side.

One of the highest peaks, **Monte Falterona** (1654m), marks the source of the Arno. Apart from the human population, including the inhabitants of two monasteries, the park is also home to a rich assortment of wildlife, including foxes, wolves, deer and wild boar, plus nearly 100 bird species. The dense forests are a cool summer refuge. The Grande Escursione Appenninica (GEA) trekking trail passes through here, and myriad walking paths criss-cross the park.

From Arezzo take the SS71 northwards through Bibbiena and on up to **Badia Prataglia**, a pleasant little mountain village in the Alpe di Serra, near the border with Emilia-Romagna. Its **visitors centre** (☎ 0575 55 94 77; www.badiaprataglia.com, in Italian; 9am-12.30pm & 3.30-6pm Tue-Sun Jun-Sep, 9am-12.30pm Tue-Sat, 9am-12.30pm & 3.30-6pm Sun Oct-May) carries a wealth of information about the park, including two useful titles in English.

♠ POPPI & BIBBIENA // ENJOY A MULTIATTRACTION CASTLE

The most striking town of the Casentino region is Poppi, perched on a hill in the Arno plain. It's topped by the gaunt, commanding presence of the **Castello dei Conti Guidi** (☎ 0575 52 05 16; www.buon conte.com, in Italian; Piazza Repubblica 1; adult/child incl audio guide €6/5; 10am-6.30pm Jul-Oct), built by the same counts who raised the Castello di Romena.

Interior attractions include a small 'ancient prison', a fairy-tale courtyard, the Sala delle Feste with its restored medieval frescos and the internationally acclaimed library, containing hundreds of medieval texts and manuscripts. The main attraction, however, is the chapel on the 2nd floor, with frescos by Taddeo Gaddi. The scene of *Herod's Feast* shows Salome apparently clicking her fingers as she dances, accompanied by a lute player, while John the Baptist's headless corpse lies slumped in the corner.

Poppi is home to **Casa Ombuto** (www.italiancookerycourse.com), which hosts week-long, highly reputed (and highly priced), all-inclusive cooking courses.

Bibbiena has reasonable transport links to the national park. Buses depart from the train station to Verna (€2.30, four daily), each taking around 45 minutes.

♥ SANTUARIO DI SAN FRANCESCO (VERNA) // AN INCREDIBLE MONASTERY ONCE HOME TO ST FRANCIS

This Franciscan monastic complex is 23km east of Bibbiena in Verna. It's where St Francis of Assisi is said to have received the stigmata.

By car, follow signs just outside Verna for the **sanctuary** (☎ 0575 53 41; www.santu ariolaverna.org; ☽ 6.30am-8.30pm) or take the mildly taxing but agreeable 30-minute uphill hike from the visitor centre in the city. The Chiesa Maggiore (also known as the Basilica) has some remarkable glazed ceramics by Andrea della Robbia. Here, you will also discover reliquaries containing items associated with the saint, including his clothing, stained with blood from stigmatic wounds and the whip he used to impose a little self-discipline.

Beside the Basilica entrance is the **Cappella della Pietà**. From it, the **Corridoio delle Stimmate**, painted with frescos recounting the saint's life, leads to a cluster of chapels, with a short detour to the cave and the unforgiving slab of rock that St Francis called a bed. At the core of the sanctuary is the **Cappella delle Stimmate**, beautifully decorated with terracotta works by Luca and Andrea della Robbia.

SOUTH OF AREZZO

· · · · · ·

CORTONA

pop 22,900

With a layout indicative of someone spilling a bucket of 'Etruscan town' down a hillside, Cortona started as a small Etruscan settlement in the 8th century BC, later becoming a Roman town. In the late 14th century Fra' Angelico lived and worked here, and fellow artists Luca Signorelli (1450–1523) and Pietro da Cortona (1596–1669) were both born within its walls.

The town, with its steep captivating streets, twisting off at mirthfully impossible angles, can be easily seen in a few hours, though overnighters will be treated to sensational dusk and dawn views over Val de Chiana, as far as Lago di Trasimeno.

ESSENTIAL INFORMATION

TOURIST OFFICES // The friendly **tourist office** (☎ 0575 63 03 52; Via Nazionale 42; ☽ 9am-1pm & 3-7pm Mon-Sat, 9am-1pm Sun May-Sep, 9am-1pm & 3-6pm Mon-Fri, 9am-1pm Sat Oct-Apr) has excellent maps, brochures, and timetables, sells bus and train tickets, and can book rooms.

EXPLORING CORTONA

♥ MUSEO DELL'ACCADEMIA ETRUSCA // TAKE A PHOTO 700 YEARS IN THE MAKING

To the north of Piazza della Repubblica and its brooding **Palazzo Comunale**

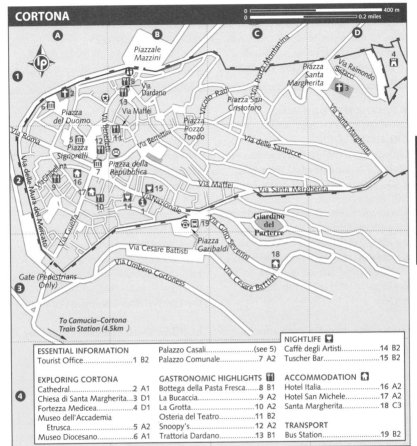

CORTONA

EASTERN TUSCANY

ESSENTIAL INFORMATION		Palazzo Casali.....................(see 5)	NIGHTLIFE
Tourist Office.....................1 B2		Palazzo Comunale.................7 A2	Caffè degli Artisti..............14 B2
			Tuscher Bar........................15 B2
EXPLORING CORTONA		GASTRONOMIC HIGHLIGHTS	
Cathedral............................2 A1		Bottega della Pasta Fresca......8 B1	ACCOMMODATION
Chiesa di Santa Margherita....3 D1		La Bucaccia...........................9 A2	Hotel Italia...........................16 A2
Fortezza Medicea................4 D1		La Grotta.............................10 A2	Hotel San Michele..............17 A2
Museo dell'Accademia		Osteria del Teatro................11 B2	Santa Margherita................18 C3
Etrusca............................5 A2		Snoopy's.............................12 A2	TRANSPORT
Museo Diocesano................6 A1		Trattoria Dardano................13 B1	Bus Station..........................19 B2

(built in the 13th century, renovated in the 16th and again in the 19th), you'll find Piazza Signorelli and the 13th-century **Palazzo Casali**. The Casali's 17th-century facade may be plain, but inside lives the fascinating **Museo dell'Accademia Etrusca** (☎ 0575 63 04 15; Piazza Signorelli 9; adult/child €7/4; ☼ 10am-7pm Apr-Oct, to 5pm Tue-Sun Nov-Mar), with an eclectic array of art and antiquities, including Etruscan bronzes, medieval paintings, and 18th-century furniture. One of the most intriguing pieces is an elaborate 2nd-century-BC bronze Etruscan oil lamp, decorated with satyrs, sirens and a gorgon's head, weighing in at a hefty 55kg. The Medici Room contains a pair of early-18th-century globes of heaven and earth, where the cartographer takes artistic licence portraying the 'Isola di California' floating free from the western coast of America. Upstairs you can see material recently excavated from local Etruscan tombs. The basement contains well-executed displays of Etruscan and Roman ruins, archaeological models, jewellery, bronze accoutrements, pottery and mosaics. Book in advance for a guided tour of the museum in English (€5, minimum six people) and three Etruscan tombs (adult/child with guide €10.50/7.75) in the surrounding countryside. Combined tours of both cost €15/9.50.

♥ PIAZZA DEL DUOMO //
SEEK OUT BOTH ART AND
ARCHITECTURE

Little is left of the original Romanesque character of the **cathedral** (Piazza del Duomo), situated northwest of Piazza Signorelli. It was completely rebuilt late in the Renaissance and again, indifferently, in the 18th century. Its true wealth lies in the riches contained within the **Museo Diocesano** (☎ 0575 6 28 30; Piazza del Duomo 1; adult/child €5/3; ⏰ 10am-7pm Tue-Sun Apr-Oct, to 5pm Tue-Sun Nov-Mar) in the former church of Gesù.

Room 1 features a remarkable Roman sarcophagus decorated with a frenzied battle scene between Dionysus and the Amazons. Here and continuing into the adjoining Room 4 are paintings by Luca Signorelli, including his *Compianto sul Cristo Morto* (Grief over the Dead Christ; 1502), a masterpiece of colour, composition and pathos. In Room 3 there's a moving *Crucifixion* by Pietro Lorenzetti and the star work of the collection: Fra' Angelico's *Annunciazione* (Annunciation; 1436), one of the most recognisable images of Renaissance art that by its sheer luminosity leaves all the surrounding works in the shade. This is one of a number of versions of this painting, the most famous of which resides in the Museo di San Marco in Florence (p67). Also by Fra' Angelico and almost as moving is his exquisite *Madonna*. Downstairs the Oratorio is decorated with biblical frescos by Vasari's workshop.

♥ CHIESA DI SANTA MARGHERITA
& FORTEZZA MEDICEA // ASCEND
TO GREAT HEIGHTS

The 800m journey from Piazza della Repubblica to the largely 19th-century **Chiesa di Santa Margherita** (Piazza Santa Margherita; ⏰ 7.30am-noon & 3-7pm Apr-Oct, 8.30am-noon & 3-6pm Oct-Apr) is one of the steepest, and cruellest, cobblestone climbs in Italy (it's approximately a 110m vertical gain, for the record). It's drivable from an access road to the north, but then you'd miss the achingly quaint, rewarding labyrinth of quiet lanes. The remains of Saint Margaret, the patron saint of Cortona, are on display here in an ornate, 14th-century, glass-sided tomb above the main altar.

A sinner-to-saint story if there ever was one, St Margaret's early life as a mistress and mother to an illegitimate son was transformed after arriving in Cortona. After a few regrettable false-starts with local dreamboats, Margaret formed her own congregation, opened a hospital, received ecstasy-charged messages from heaven, prophesised the date of her death and surrounded herself with the poor, ill, reformed, pious and penitent. She was canonised in 1728 by Pope Benedict XIII.

It's a stiff climb, but it's worth pushing even further uphill to the forbidding **Fortezza Medicea** (☎ 0575 63 04 15; adult/child €3/1.50; ⏰ 10am-1.30pm & 2.30-6pm Apr, May, Jun & Sep, to 7pm Jul & Aug). This is Cortona's highest point, with stupendous views over the surrounding countryside.

GASTRONOMIC HIGHLIGHTS

Snoopy's on Piazza Signorelli serves the freshest gelato in town with generous portions, starting at €1.50 for a 'small'.

♥ LA BUCACCIA €€
☎ 0575 606 039; www.labucaccia.it; Via Ghibellina 17; meals €40-45

Decidedly tourist-targeted, with Etruscan cellar ambience: wine racks, grape press, tiny wine barrels, cheese wheels and an Etruscan cistern displayed under a glassed floor. The service is indisputably warm, and the food notable in both taste and presentation, but lofty wine prices push the final total quite high.

❦ LA GROTTA €€
☎ 0575 63 02 71; Piazzetta Baldly 3; meals €20-28; ۞ Wed-Mon

At the end of a blind alley just off Piazza della Repubblica, this is a rock-reliable choice. Twin-roomed and intimate, it has all the virtues of a traditional trattoria. If you go for strong flavours, begin with the beef carpaccio (thin slices of meat), followed by the cheese ravioli with truffle sauce.

❦ OSTERIA DEL TEATRO €€
☎ 0575 63 05 56; www.osteria-del-teatro.it; Via Maffei 2; meals €32-40; ۞ Thu-Tue

Friendly service, fresh flowers on every table and a liberal meting out of truffle shavings awaits diners here. Featured in nearly every Italian gastronomic guide, its walls are clad with photos of actors who have dined here. In summer try the *ravioli ai fiori di zucca* (pumpkin-flower ravioli). Watch your head when the unwieldy phallus of a pepper grinder is heaved out for random seasoning.

❦ TRATTORIA DARDANO €
☎ 0575 60 19 44; Via Dardano 24; meals €19-24; ۞ Thu-Tue

Dardano is one of those no-nonsense yet still unexpectedly wonderful trattorias that feature prominently in every Tuscany travel memoir, doing amazing things with ostensibly simple dishes. You'll be elbow-to-elbow with locals and giddy, idealistic visitors, seriously considering

buying and fixing up a nearby farmhouse on the strength of their lunch.

NIGHTLIFE

❦ CAFFÈ DEGLI ARTISTI
☎ 0575 60 12 37; Via Nazionale 18

One of the precious few places in Cortona allowing patrons to linger past midnight, Caffè degli Artisti offers lazy rounds of wine and coffee augmented by antipasti, pastas, pizzas and a lengthy bruschetta menu. The pedestrian scenery from the miniscule terrace is better than TV.

❦ TUSCHER BAR
☎ 0575 6 20 53; Via Nazionale 43; ۞ closed Mon

Hypoglycaemics and the severely jet-lagged will appreciate that food service never stops at this stylish place, starting with breakfasts, done in both Continental and English style. Though coffee is available as ever, the swank-leaning decor lends itself more to a wine-y lunch or after-dinner cocktails.

TRANSPORT

BUS // From the bus station at Piazza Garibaldi, LFI buses connect the town with Arezzo (€2.80, one hour, more than 10 daily), via Castiglion Fiorentino. Shuttle buses (€1, 15 minutes) run almost hourly to Camucia-Cortona train station, on the main Rome–Florence line.

TRAIN // Destinations include Arezzo (€2.40, 20 minutes, hourly), Florence (€7.10, 1½ hours, hourly), Rome (€9.40, 2¼ hours, every two hours) and Perugia (€3.15, 40 minutes, over 12 daily).

CAR & MOTORCYCLE // By car, the city is on the north–south SS71 that runs to Arezzo. It's also close to the SS75 that connects Perugia to the A1.

NORTHERN UMBRIA

3 PERFECT DAYS

❦ DAY 1 // HISTORY MEETS NATURE IN THE NORTH
Start your day in the Gothic wonderland of Gubbio. Take the **Funivia Colle Eletto** (p284) up the mountain before admiring the architecture and history in the **Piazza Grande** (p283). Drop your bags off at **Le Tortorelle** (p412) and wander the Umbrian countryside for a few hours before heading to Città di Castello to view the artwork at the **Pinacoteca Comunale** (p287) and dining in style at **Il Postale** (p289).

❦ DAY 2 // TOUR UMBRIA'S ROLLING HILLS
Grab a good map or GPS and drive through the countryside in between Brufa and Deruta in the north and Montefalco and Spello in the south – a kind of Golden Parallelogram of stone farmhouses and wildflower-covered rolling hills. Part of the joy in this day is discovery, but wine tasters will want to sip in **Montefalco** (p280) and **Bevagna** (p279). Stop in **Deruta** (p268) to throw ceramics on the wheel at **Maioliche Nulli** (p269) and dine in elegance at **I Quattro Sensi** (p268), making sure to arrive in Assisi for an early night's sleep.

❦ DAY 3 // LET YOUR SPIRIT SOAR IN UMBRIA'S SPIRITUAL HOME
Set your alarm for 6am to make it to the **Basilica di San Francesco** (p270) by sunrise, when it will just be you and the nuns. Contemplate the life of St Francis in the crypt before venturing into Foligno to dine at the shrine of all that is holy about Umbrian cuisine: **Il Bacco Felice** (p279). Make it to Lago Trasimeno by dinnertime to sample any one of the excellent restaurants, or hop on the ferry by 7pm to sleep in the peaceful isolation at **Fattoria il Poggio** (p413).

PERUGIA

· · · · · ·

pop 163,300

One of Italy's best-preserved hill towns, replete with museums and churches, Perugia is also a hip student town with a never-ending stream of cultural events and concerts. Within the city walls, little has changed architecturally for several hundred years and a few hotels and restaurants are in triple-digit ages. Culturally, however, Perugia is on the edge. Two major universities, a steady stream of foreigners and a thriving art scene ensure that Perugia melds the modern with the past.

Although the Umbri tribe once inhabited the surrounding area and controlled land stretching from present-day Tuscany into Le Marche, it was the Etruscans who founded the city, leading to its zenith in the 6th century BC. It fell to the Romans in 310 BC and was given the name Perusia.

During the Middle Ages the city was racked by the internal feuding of the Baglioni and Oddi families. In 1538 the city was incorporated into the Papal States under Pope Paul III, remaining under papal control for almost three centuries.

Perugia has a strong artistic tradition. In the 15th century it was home to fresco painters Bernardino Pinturicchio and his master Pietro Vannucci (known as Perugino), who would later teach the famous painter Raphael. Its cultural tradition continues to this day with both the University of Perugia and several universities, including the famous Università per Stranieri (University for Foreigners), which teaches Italian, art and culture to thousands of students from around the world.

Old Perugia's main strip, Corso Vannucci (named for Perugino), runs north from the top of Rocca Paolina, through Piazza Italia and into the heart of the city, Piazza IV Novembre, where you'll find the Fontana Maggiore and the cathedral. Almost every listing in this chapter is within a kilometre of here. *Urbano* (city) buses originate from Piazza Italia, while *extraurbano* (intercity) buses drop you off at Piazza Partigiani. From here, take a few sets of *scale mobili* (elevators) through the Rocca Paolina to reach Piazza Italia. If you have heavy luggage, watch out: *scale mobili* interchange with staircases up the steep hillside. From the train station it's an enormous hike, especially with that luggage, or a quick €1 bus ride, 1.5km up the hill to Piazza Italia.

ESSENTIAL INFORMATION

EMERGENCIES // After-hours doctor (☎ 075 36 584) **Hospital** (Ospedale Silvestrini; ☎ 075 57 81; S Andrea delle Frate) **Police Station** (☎ 075 572 32 32; Palazzo dei Priori)

TOURIST OFFICES // Info Umbria (☎ 075 57 57; www.infoumbria.com; Piazza Partigiani Intercity bus station, Largo Cacciatori delle Alpi 3; ☉ 9am-1pm & 2.30-6.30pm Mon-Fri, 9am-1pm Sat) A private tourist office offering information on *agriturismi* (farm-stay accommodation), festivals, sights and general information. **Tourist Office** (☎ 075 573 64 58; www.comune .perugia.it; Piazza Matteotti 18; ☉ 8.30am-6.30pm) The government tourist office; not particularly helpful but with hundreds of brochures and maps for the entire region.

EXPLORING PERUGIA

❦ PIAZZA IV NOVEMBRE // PERUGIA'S MEETING PLACE FOR 2000 YEARS

The centre of Perugia (and therefore the centre of Umbria) is **Piazza IV Novembre**. More than 2000 years ago, it was the meeting point for the ancient Etruscans and

(Continued on page 259)

LONELYPLANET.COM

NORTHERN UMBRIA

NORTHERN UMBRIA

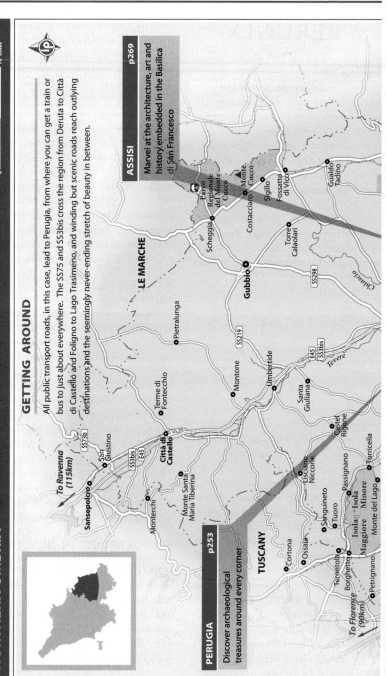

GETTING AROUND

All public transport roads, in this case, lead to Perugia, from where you can get a train or bus to just about everywhere. The SS75 and SS3bis cross the region from Deruta to Città di Castello ad Foligno to Lago Trasimeno, and winding but scenic roads reach outlying destinations and the seemingly never-ending stretch of beauty in between.

ASSISI   p269

Marvel at the architecture, art and history embedded in the Basilica di San Francesco

PERUGIA   p253

Discover archaeological treasures around every corner

LE MARCHE

TUSCANY

Parco Regionale del Monte Cucco

Monte Cucco

Gualdo Tadino

Fossato di Vico

Sigillo

Costacciaro

Torre Calaolari

Scheggia

Gubbio

SS298

Chiascio

Pietralunga

SS219

Montone

Umbertide

E45
SS3bis

Tevere

Terme di Fontecchio

Santa Giuliana

San Giustino

SS73b

Città di Castello

SS3bis
E45

Monte Santa Maria Tiberina

To Ravenna (115km)

Sansepolcro

Monterchi

Castel Rigone

Lisciano Niccone

Torricella

Passignano

Isola Maggiore
Isola Minore

Monte del Lago

Sanguineto

Tuoro

Cortona

Ossaia

Teontola

Borghetto

Petrignano

To Florence (90km)

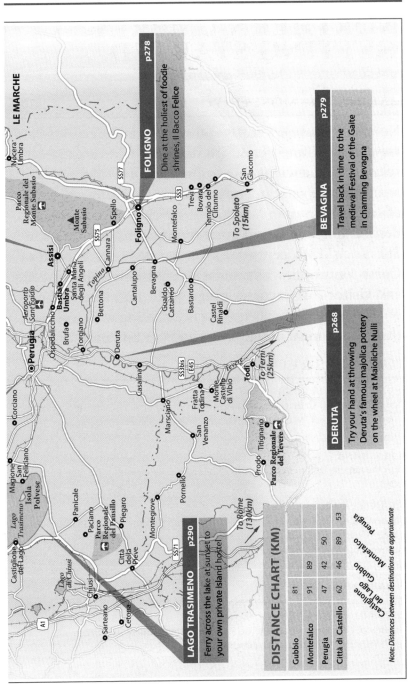

FOLIGNO p278
Dine at the holiest of foodie shrines, Il Bacco Felice

BEVAGNA p279
Travel back in time to the medieval Festival of the Gaite in charming Bevagna

DERUTA p268
Try your hand at throwing Deruta's famous majolica pottery on the wheel at Maioliche Nulli

LAGO TRASIMENO p290
Ferry across the lake at sunset to your own private island hostel

DISTANCE CHART (KM)

	Castiglione del Lago	Gubbio	Montefalco	Perugia
Gubbio	81			
Montefalco	91	89		
Perugia	47	42	50	
Città di Castello	62	46	89	53

Note: Distances between destinations are approximate

NORTHERN UMBRIA GETTING STARTED

MAKING THE MOST OF YOUR TIME

Northern Umbria's softly rolling hills and never-ending views of wildflowers and gnarled olive trees are interspersed with ancient stone villages, world-class museums, a lake retreat, vineyards and a healthy smattering of serenity. Even in Northern Umbria's most popular destination, you'll find quiet reminiscent of native son St Francis' 13th-century Assisi. Perugia centres around Corso Vannucci, which pulsates with university students and visitors on warm evenings, while nightlife in the rest of Northern Umbria consists of drinking wine over a three-hour meal of truffles, wild boar and pasta.

TOP TOURS & COURSES

☙ UNIVERSITÀ PER STRANIERI

Sign up for courses in literature, art history, music and opera at Italy's most famous school for foreigners. Alternatively, join one of the excellent language courses and immerse yourself in all things Italian (p262).

☙ PERUGINA CHOCOLATE FACTORY

Tour the famous facilities and pick up some chocolate kisses for great take-home gifts (p262).

☙ CANTINA APERTE

The best time to undertake a wine tour in Umbria is to come for Cantina Aperte (Open Wineries), held annually on the last Sunday in May. Almost every winery in the area is open for tours, tastings, food and concerts. The most famous is the Mangialonga from Arnaldo Caprai (p281).

☙ MARCO BELLANCA

Marco Bellanca is an art and history specialist who gives guided tours (from €100 to €150 for three hours to €200 to €300 for six hours) and will meet guests in any town in Umbria, but his favourite is Perugia. Umbrian-born, fluent in German and English. (☎ 075 573 68 53, 347 600 22 09; bellsista@yahoo.it)

GETTING AWAY FROM IT ALL

Although more populous than Southern Umbria, the northern half of Umbria has pockets where it's still possible you'll hear church bells rather than foreign languages.

* **Strike a yogic pose at Torre Colombaia** This *agriturismo* (farm-stay accommodation) is set in its own oasis of country activity (p410).

* **Scour the back roads** Search for wild boar and flowers on a scenic drive to Città di Castello (p287) or through any one of the Strade di Vini wine routes.

* **Sleep in peace** Rest your head on your own private island hostel in the middle of Lago Trasimeno (p413).

* **Get lost** Drive through the hills around Bevagna and Montefalco in search of secret wineries.

RESOURCES

* **Lago Trasimeno** (www.lagotrasimeno .net) A full slate of restaurants, sights and activity information

* **Perugia Online** (www.perugiaonline.com) Comprehensive guide to Perugia's sights and events

* **Strada dei Vini del Cantico** (www .stradadeivinidelcantico.it) The wine route covering Perugia, Assisi, Spello and Tor-giano, on down to Todi

* **Strada del Sagrantino** (www.stradadel sagrantino.it) Covering the region around Bevagna and Montefalco, replete with tourist information

ADVANCE PLANNING

* **Perugina Chocolate Factory** (☎ 075 527 67 96; Van San Sisto, Perugia; admission free; ☷ 9am-1pm & 2-5.30pm Mon-Fri year-round, 9am-1pm Sat Oct-Jan & Mar-May) While you can usually latch on to an Italian-language tour, call ahead to guarantee an English version.

* **Bicycle Tours** (www.lifeitalianstyle.com) Book a day trip with American-Italian restaura-teur Jennifer McIlvaine (p281), who leads bicycle tours and cooking classes from Cannara, in the heart of the wine region.

* **Cantina Aperte** Time your stay for the last Sunday in May; wineries throughout Italy open to visitors, with entertainment, food and, of course, plenty of wine.

TOP EATING EXPERIENCES

❦ **IL BACCO FELICE**
A visit to Salvatore's neighbourhood joint in Foligno is a must (p279)

❦ **IL POSTALE**
Nouvelle cuisine in Città di Castello (p289)

❦ **RISTORANTE LA FORNACE DI MASTRO GIORGIO**
Masterful culinary traditions blend tradi-tional and modern (p286)

❦ **RISTORANTE SIRO**
Packed with locals who've been coming here for at least a generation (p267)

❦ **LA LOCANDA DI GULLIVER**
Well worth the 10km drive away from Lago Trasimeno for the food (and view) (p296)

NORTHERN UMBRIA

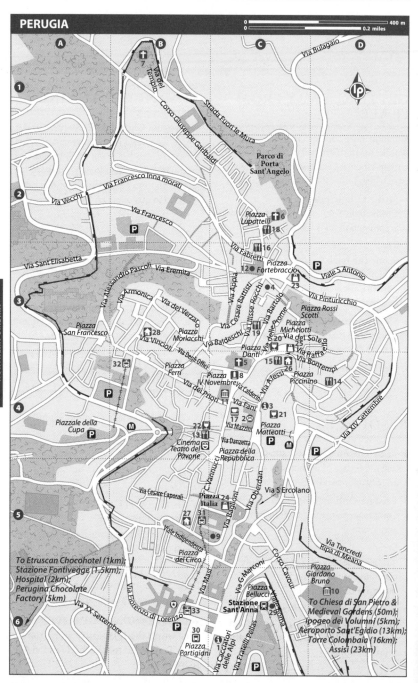

PERUGIA

0   400 m
0   0.2 miles

Via Bulagaio

Via del Tempio

Corso Giuseppe Garibaldi

Strada Fuori le Mura

Parco di Porta Sant'Angelo

Via Francesco Inna morati

Via Vecchi

Via Francesco

Piazza Lupattelli

Via Sant'Elisabetta

Via Fabretti

Piazza Fortebraccio

Viale S Antonio

Via Pinturicchio

Via Alessandro Pascoli   Via Eremita

Via Armonica

Via del Verzaro

Via Appia

Via Cesare Battisti

Via Ulisse Rocchi

Via Bartolo

Via delle Prome

Piazza Rossi Scotti

Piazza San Francesco

Via Vincioli

Piazza Morlacchi

Via Baldeschi

Piazza Michelotti

Via del Sole

Piazza Danti

Via Raffa

Via delle Offici

Via Bontempi

Piazza Ferri

Piazza IV Novembre

Via Calderini

Piazza Piccinino

Via dei Priori

Via Fani

Via Aless...

Piazzale della Cupa

Via Mazzini

Piazza Matteotti

Via XIV Settembre

Cinema Teatro del Pavone

Via Danzetta

Piazza della Repubblica

Via Cesare Caporali

Clanucci

Via Oberdan

Via S Ercolano

Piazza Italia

Via Baglioni

Viale Indipendenza

Piazza del Circo

Via Masi

Via G. Marconi

Corso Cavour

Piazza Giordano Bruno

To Etruscan Chocohotel (1km);
Stazione Fontivegge (1.5km);
Hospital (2km);
Perugina Chocolate
Factory (5km)

Via Fiorenzo di Lorenzo

Via XX Settembre

Piazza Bellucci

Stazione Sant'Anna

Via Tancredi Ripa di Meana

To Chiesa di San Pietro &
Medieval Gardens (50m);
Ipogeo dei Volumni (5km);
Aeroporto Sant'Egidio (13km);
Torre Colombaia (16km);
Assisi (23km)

Via Caccatori delle Alpi

Piazza Partigiani

Via Fratelli Pellas

NORTHERN UMBRIA

(Continued From Page 253)

Romans. In the medieval period, it was the political centre of Perugia. Now students and tourists gather here to eat gelato and do the *passeggiata*. Much of Perugia's nightlife parades outside the cathedral and around Fontana Maggiore. Hundreds of local and foreign students congregate here practically every night, playing guitars and drums and chatting with friends. Tourists mix in easily, slurping gelati and enjoying this fascinating version of outdoor theatre.

In the centre of the piazza stands the **Fontana Maggiore** (Great Fountain). It was designed by Fra Bevignate, and built by father-son team Nicola and Giovanni Pisano between 1275 and 1278. Along the edge are bas-relief statues representing scenes from the Old Testament, the founding of Rome, the 'liberal arts', and a griffin and lion. Look for the griffin all over Perugia – it's the city's symbol. The lion is the symbol for the Guelphs, the Middle Ages faction that favoured rule by the papacy over rule by the Holy Roman Empire.

🌿 CATTEDRALE DI SAN LORENZO // MARVEL AT 400 YEARS OF ART AND ARCHITECTURE

Anchoring the north end of the piazza is the **Cattedrale di San Lorenzo** (☎ 075

572 38 32; Piazza IV Novembre; ☷ 10am-1pm & 2.30-5.30pm Tue-Sun). Although most of the excitement these days happens on its front steps, the land has hosted a church since the 10th century. The current version was begun in 1345 from designs created by Fra Bevignate in 1300, but it's the facade – incomplete for over 400 years, with pieces of an old Roman wall – that gets the most attention. Inside, check out Signorelli's altarpiece and a crucifix, a relic of the 1540 salt war that changed the direction of Umbrian history.

🌿 PALAZZO DEI PRIORI // VIEW THE FINEST ART COLLECTION IN UMBRIA

The Palazzo dei Priori houses some of the best museums in Perugia. The foremost art gallery in Umbria is the stunning **Galleria Nazionale dell'Umbria** (www .gallerianazionaleumbria.it/; ☎ fax 800 69 76 16; Palazzo dei Priori, Corso Vannucci 19; adult/concession €6.50/3.25; ☷ 8.30am-7.30pm), entered from Corso Vannucci. It's an art historian's dream, with 30 rooms of artwork dating back to Byzantine-like art from the 13th century, as well as rooms dedicated to works from hometown heroes Pinturicchio and Perugino.

Also in the same building is what some consider the most beautiful bank

NORTHERN UMBRIA

in the world, the **Nobile Collegio del Cambio** (Exchange Hall; ☎ 075 572 85 99; Corso Vannucci 25; adult/concession €4.50/2.60; ◷ 9am-12.30pm & 3-7pm Mon-Sat summer, 2.30-5.30pm winter), which has three rooms: the Sala dei Legisti (Legist Chamber), with wooden stalls carved by Giampiero Zuccari in the 17th century; the Sala dell'Udienza (Audience Chamber), with frescos by Perugino; and the Chapel of San Giovanni Battista, painted by a student of Perugino's, Giannicola di Paolo. The **Nobile Collegio della Mercanzia** (Merchant's Hall; ☎ 075 573 03 66; Corso Vannucci 15; admission €3.10; ◷ 9am-12.30pm & 2.30-5.50pm Tue-Sun summer, often closed afternoons winter) highlights an older audience chamber from the 13th century, which is covered in wood panelling by northern craftsmen.

The **Sala dei Notari** (Notaries' Hall; ☎ 075 577 23 39; Palazzo dei Priori, Piazza IV Novembre; admission free; ◷ 9am-1pm & 3-7pm Tue-Sun) was built between 1293 and 1297 and is where the nobility met. The arches supporting the vaults are Romanesque, covered with frescos depicting biblical scenes and Aesop's fables. To reach the hall, walk up the steps from Piazza IV Novembre.

♥ **ROCCA PAOLINA // TAKE AN ESCALATOR THROUGH HISTORY**
At the southern end of Corso Vannucci is the tiny **Giardini Carducci**, which has lovely views of the countryside and hosts the antiques market. The gardens stand atop a once-massive 16th-century fortress, now known as the **Rocca Paolina** (main entrance Piazza Italia, entrances on Via Marzia, Via Masi & Viale Indipendenza; admission free; ◷ 8am-7pm). Pope Paolo III Farnese built the monstrosity in the 1540s, wiping out entire sections of what had been a wealthy neighbourhood. Now used as the throughway for the *scale mobili*, you

---

48 HOURS IN PERUGIA

PERUGIA ON THE CHEAP
Recently deemed the world's sexiest small city, Perugia oozes romance, charm and youth. On your first full day, get your espresso fix at **Sandri** (p264) before heading into the **Cattedrale di San Lorenzo** (p259) and the **Sala dei Notari** (p259) – both of which have free admission. Lunch at the student favourite **Dal Mi'Cocco** (p264) before heading through the **Arco Etrusco** (opposite) for local Perugian chocolate and gelato at **Augusta Perusia** (p265). Stroll down to the **Chiesa di Sant' Angelo** (opposite) for a 1500-year-old look at Christian history and end with dinner at **Pizzeria Mediterranea** (p264).

ROMANTIC PERUGIA
Gather picnic supplies before heading towards the **Chiesa di San Pietro** (opposite). Behind the church, you'll find the otherworldly **Medieval Gardens** (opposite), perfect for a romantic lunch. For dessert, pick up some chocolates on the **Perugina chocolate factory** (p262) tour. During the evening's *passeggiata* (traditional evening stroll), wander arm-in-arm with your sweetie along Corso Vannucci. Whisk through the cobblestone streets to a quiet table at **Il Gufo** (p263) for an inventive dinner. End the night at **Hotel Brufani Palace** (p410), where you can wake up the next day with a sunrise view over the valley and stone churches below.

HISTORY TOUR

For a thorough self-guided archaeological tour from Etruscan to Renaissance Perugia, pick up the *Archaeological Itineraries* booklet at the Perugia tourist office. Plan on it taking about three or four hours, and wear comfortable shoes.

can still see former homes of Perugia's powerful medieval families, capped with the bricked-over roof of the Papal fortress. Its nooks and crannies are now used for art exhibits throughout the year, and the last weekend of every month sees the antiques market.

❧ CORSO GIUSEPPE GARIBALDI // WALK ALONG 3000 YEARS OF ARCHAEOLOGICAL KNOW-HOW

At the end of Via Ulisse Rocchi facing Piazza Fortebraccio and the Università per Stranieri are the ancient city gates, the **Arco Etrusco** (Etruscan Arch), dating from the 3rd century BC. The imposing structure is the most significant Etruscan monument still standing in Umbria and a good example of this Etruscan invention. The upper part is Roman and bears the inscription 'Augusta Perusia', after Marc Antony and Octavian battled over control of Perugia. As a visually stark contrast, the delicate Renaissance loggia perched atop the monstrous arch is a mini-study in striated Italian history.

North along Corso Giuseppe Garibaldi is the **Chiesa di Sant'Agostino** (Piazza Lupatelli; ☺ 8am-noon & 4pm-sunset), a church that boasts a beautiful 16th-century choir by sculptor and architect Baccio d'Agnolo. Small signs forlornly mark the places where artworks once hung before they were carried off to France by Napoleon and his men. Further north

along the same thoroughfare, Via del Tempio branches off to the Romanesque **Chiesa di Sant'Angelo** (☎ 075 57 22 64; Via Sant'Angelo; ☺ 10am-noon & 4-6pm). You won't find many churches older than this one in all of Italy. Dating back to the 5th and 6th centuries, it incorporates touches from several epochs, including Roman columns and Templar symbols.

❧ MUSEO ARCHEOLOGICO NAZIONALE DELL'UMBRIA // TOUR THE ETRUSCAN AGE IN AN HOUR

The **Museo Archeologico Nazionale dell'Umbria** (☎ 075 572 71 41; Piazza Giordano Bruno 10; adult/concession €4/2; ☺ 8.30am-7.30pm Tue-Sun, 10am-7.30pm Mon) will boggle the mind with its collection of Etruscan and prehistoric artefacts – carved funerary urns, coins, Bronze Age statuary – dating back to the 16th century BC. The Cippo Perugino (Perugian Memorial Stone) has the longest Etruscan-language engraving ever found, offering a new window into the language.

❧ CHIESA DI SAN PIETRO & MEDIEVAL GARDENS // WHILE AWAY AN AFTERNOON WITH A PICNIC

Just past the Porta di San Pietro is the 10th-century **Chiesa di San Pietro** (☎ 075 3 47 70; Borgo XX Giugno; ☺ 8am-noon & 4pm-sunset), the entrance through a frescoed doorway in the first courtyard. The interior is an incredible mix of gilt and marble and contains a *pietà* (a sculpture, drawing or painting of the dead Christ supported by the Madonna) by Perugino. Many of the paintings in this church feature depictions of biblical women.

Take a stroll or picnic at the **Medieval Gardens** (☎ 075 585 64 32; Borgo XX Giugno 74; admission free; ☺ 8am-6.30pm Mon-Fri), entered behind the Chiesa di San Pietro. During the medieval period, monasteries often created gardens reminiscent of the Garden of Eden and biblical stories, with plants that symbolised myths and sacred stories. Be sure to check out the groovy alchemist's studio.

☙ IPOGEO DEI VOLUMNI // EXPLORE THE STREETS OF THE ETRUSCAN DEAD

About 5km southeast of the city is the **Ipogeo dei Volumni** (☎ 075 39 33 29; Via Assisana 53; adult/concession €3/1.50; ☑ 9am-1pm & 3.30-6.30pm Sep-Jun, 9am-12.30pm & 4.30-7pm Jul & Aug), a 2nd-century-BC Etruscan burial site. An underground chamber contains a series of recesses holding the funerary urns of the Volumnio family. The surrounding grounds are a massive expanse of partially unearthed burial chambers with several buildings housing artefacts that haven't been stolen over the years. To get here, take a train or APM bus 3 from Piazza Italia to Ponte San Giovanni and walk west from there. By car, take the Bonanzano exit heading south on the E45.

☙ PERUGINA CHOCOLATE FACTORY // CHANNEL YOUR INNER OOMPA LOOMPA

The trick for independent travellers visiting the **Perugina chocolate factory** (☎ 075 527 67 96; Van San Sisto; admission free; ☑ 9am-1pm & 2-5.30pm Mon-Fri year-round, 9am-1pm Sat Oct-Jan & Mar-May) is to either call ahead to arrange a guided tour, or simply latch on to a tour group (conducted in either Italian or English). After visiting the simple museum, you'll wend your way through an enclosed sky bridge, watching as the white-outfitted Oomp-, er, factory workers demonstrate their god-given talent for creating chocolate. Drive through the gates of the humor-

NORTHERN UMBRIA

TOP TIP

If you're planning on staying a while, pick up a copy of Perugia's must-have *The Little Blue What-to-Do*, available at **Cinema teatro del Pavone** (Corso Vannucci 67). The free biannual compendium of activities, housing information, transport, restaurant reviews and the popular 'Perugia Personalities' section is a handy guide to Perugia's eclectic populace, like the communist declaimer and tracksuit-sporting prophet.

---

ously nondescript factory entrance marked Nestlé, or take the bus to San Sisto.

☙ UMBRIA JAZZ // CATCH INTERNATIONAL ACTS IN UNUSUAL VENUES

Umbria Jazz (☎ 800 46 23 11, 075 500 11 07; www.umbriajazz.com, in Italian) is known the world over as a top-notch 10-day festival, attracting an astounding number of international performers in mid-July every year. From Pat Metheny to the Buena Vista Social Club and Chick Corea, all of jazz shows up for this. Single tickets cost €10 to €100, and week-long or weekend passes are also available.

☙ LANGUAGE SCHOOLS // LEARN THE LINGO

Perugia is a thriving university town and one of the best places in Italy to take a language course. The **Università per Stranieri** (☎ 075 5 74 61; www.unistrapg.it; Palazzo Gallenga, Piazza Fortebraccio 4) is Italy's foremost academic institution for foreigners, offering courses in language, literature, history, art, music, opera and architecture, to name a few. A series of degree courses is available, as well as one-, two- and three-month intensive language courses starting at €300 a month and semester-long accredited programs for students. Catering to a more serious crowd is the **Comitato Linguistico** (☎ 075 572 14 71; www.comitatolinguistico.com; 3rd fl, Largo Cacciatori delle Alpi 5), with lessons that are slightly more rigorous than at Università per Stranieri. Two- and four-week courses start throughout the year, starting at €150 per week. The school can arrange private or family accommodation. Check with the tourist office for lists of all current classes in and around Perugia.

FESTIVALS & EVENTS

Sagra Musicale Umbra (Holy Music Festival; ☎ 075 572 22 71; www.perugiamusicaclassica.com, in Italian; ticket office Via Danzetti 7; tickets €7-50) One of the oldest music festivals in Europe. Begun in 1937, it's held in Perugia from mid- to late September and features world-renowned conductors and musicians.

Eurochocolate (☎ 075 502 58 80; www.euro chocolate.com) Most Perugians keep their distance from this festival, which often sees up to one million visitors heading into town. Held around the third week of October, Eurochocolate involves hundreds of booths selling every known concoction of cacao, cocoa and chocolate. We think it's overhyped, but if you're thinking of attending, plan your hotel stay months in advance and don't even think of driving.

GASTRONOMIC HIGHLIGHTS

Because of the great volume of students and tourists, the number of places to dine in Perugia is staggering. The first days of spring when the mercury rises above 15°C or so (usually in March) see dozens of open-air locales spring up along Corso Vannucci.

♥ AL MANGIAR BENE €€
☎ 075 573 1047; Via della Luna 21; pizza €5-8, meals €25
Ahead of its time, this underground pizza and pasta restaurant is Umbria's first almost entirely organic restaurant. Pizzas and calzones, baked in a hearth-like brick oven, are all made with organic ingredients, including organic beer and local wine, and flour from Torre Colombaia *agriturismo* (p410).

♥ IL GUFO €€
☎ 075 573 41 26; Via della Viola 18; meals €29; ⏱ 8pm-1am Tue-Sat
The owner-chef of Il Gufo gathers ingredients from local markets and cooks up whatever is fresh and in season. Try dishes such as *cinghiale* (wild boar) with fennel (€12.50) or *riso nero* (black rice)

ACCOMMODATION

Outside of Perugia, the northern half of the green region is chock full of brilliant accommodation options, from rural *agriturismi* to historic residences. There's a full listing in the Accommodation chapter (p391) and here are our three favourite great-value places:

★ **Al Grappolo d'Oro** (p410) With an outdoor pool, inclusive breakfast, in-room DSL connection and breathtaking vista, you'll feel like you should be paying double.

★ **La Casa sul Lago** (p413) With every amenity known to hostelkind – including laundry, free internet access, free bicycles, a bar, comforting home-cooked meals etc – Mum will trust you're in good hands.

★ **Residenza di Via Piccardi** (p412) Start your day off with breakfast in the quiet garden in this sweet and romantic home away from home.

with grilled vegetables and brie (€12.50). Note: credit cards are not accepted.

🏮 PIZZERIA MEDITERRANEA €
☎ 075 572 13 22; Piazza Piccinino 11/12; meals €11; 🕑 Wed-Mon

Perugini know to come here for the best pizza in town. A spaceship-sized wood-fired brick oven heats up pizzas, from the simplest *margherita* to the 12-topping 'his and hers'. Add delectable *mozzarella di bufala* (fresh buffalo-milk mozzarella) to any pizza for an additional €1.60. It gets busy enough to queue, especially Thursday and Saturday nights.

🏮 RISTORANTE DAL MI'COCCO €
☎ 075 573 25 11; Corso Garibaldi 12; set meals €14; 🕑 Tue-Sun

Don't ask for a menu because there isn't one at this most traditional Perugian restaurant. Diners receive a set menu of a starter, main course, side dish and dessert. You may enjoy wild asparagus risotto in May, or tagliatelle (long, ribbon-shaped pasta) with peas and ham in November. Extremely popular with students, it's best to call ahead.

🏮 SANDRI €
☎ 075 572 41 12; Corso Vannucci 32; 🕑 10am-8pm Tue-Sun

When you enter into your third century of business, something must be right. Known for delectable chocolate cakes, candied fruit, espresso and pastries, the staff wrap all take-home purchases (picked up at the counter but paid for at the till), no matter how small, in beautiful red paper with a ribbon bow.

🏮 TUTTOTESTO €
☎ 075 573 66 66; Corso Garibaldi 15; meals €9; 🕑 Tue-Sun

Beyond Perugia's pasta and meat focus is this casual university spot where professors and students debate Nietzsche over sweet and savoury crêpes, salads and *torta al testo* (Umbrian flatbread sandwiches).

🏮 WINE BARTOLO HOSTERIA €€
☎ 075 571 60 27; Via Bartolo 30; meals €32; 🕑 Thu-Tue

Descend a staircase into a low-ceilinged hobbit-like burrow lined with walls of wine bottles set around a handful of cosy tables. The chef does beautiful things with Chianina beef – stewed with Sangiovese or as a carpaccio with lemon over radicchio.

NIGHTLIFE

🏮 BOTTEGA DEL VINO
☎ 075 571 61 81; Via del Sole 1; 🕑 7pm-1am Mon-Sat

A fire or candles burn atmospherically on the terrace. Inside, live jazz and hundreds of bottles of wine lining the walls add to the romance of the setting. You can taste dozens of Umbrian wines, which you can purchase with the help of sommelier-like experts.

🏮 LA TERRAZZA
Piazza Matteotti 18a; 🕑 summer

Should you sit in the park and enjoy the view of the sun setting over the Umbrian hillside, or head into a darkened pub for a drink? Well, you can come here for both. On the back terrace of the building that houses the Coop and covered markets is this open-air bar, perfect for an evening *aperitivo*.

🏮 LUNABAR
☎ 075 572 29 66; Via Scura 1/6 at Corso Vannucci; 🕑 8am-2am Tue-Sun

Atmospherically equidistant between New York and Umbria, the city-centre lounge spins together frescoed, Venetian plaster walls with a grey and onyx bar and space-age restrooms. Smokers enjoy their own room and the hungry will appreciate the *apertivo* selection.

RECOMMENDED SHOPS

☙ AUGUSTA PERUSIA CIOCCOLATO E GELATERIA

☎ 075 573 45 77; www.cioccolatoaugustaperusia .it, in Italian; Via Pinturicchio 2; ☺ 10.30am-11pm Mon-Sat, 10.30am-1pm & 4-8pm Sun

Giordano worked for Perugino for 25 years. In 2000 he opened his own shop, creating delectables from the old tradition, including *baci* (hazelnut 'kisses' covered in chocolate) from the original Perugian recipe. Handmade chocolate bars come in boxes with old paintings of Perugia – great for gifts – or pick up some of the city's best gelato for yourself.

☙ MERCATO MENSILE ANTIQUARIATO

Antiques Market; Giardini Carducci; ☺ 9am-6pm or 7pm

If you are lucky enough to be in Perugia on the fourth weekend of the month, spend a few hours wandering through this market around Piazza Italia and in the Giardini Carducci. It's a great place to pick up old prints, frames, furniture, jewellery, postcards and stamps.

☙ UMBRIA TERRAVIVA

Organic Market; ☎ 075 835 50 62; Piazza Piccinino

On the first Sunday of the month, check out this market located along the side of the Duomo heading towards Via Bonanzi. You'll find all sorts of organic fruits and vegetables, and there are fabulous canned or packaged items to take home as gifts.

TRANSPORT

Current train and bus routes, company details and timetables are listed in the monthly booklet *Viva Perugia* (€1), available at the tourist office, hotels and some newsstands.

TO/FROM THE AIRPORT

AIRPORT // Sant'Egidio Airport (PEG; ☎ 075 59 21 41; www.airport.umbria.it), 13km east of the city, has daily Alitalia flights to Milan and Ryanair flights to London Stansted.

TAXI // To the airport from the city centre costs approximately €30, or there's a shuttle (€3.50) that coincides with arrivals and departures.

SHUTTLE BUS // Leaves Piazza Italia about two hours before each flight, stopping at the train station. From the airport, buses leave when all passengers are on board.

NORTHERN UMBRIA

ARRIVING FROM ROME

It's quite easy to take a direct bus from Rome's Leonardo da Vinci (FCO; commonly known as Fiumicino) airport to Perugia. Pick up a blue **Sulga** (☎ 800 09 96 61; www.sulga.it) bus across the street from international terminal C. From Monday to Saturday, there are four daily buses to Perugia (€21, 3½ to four hours) departing at 9am, 12.30pm, 2.30pm and 5pm, and two buses on Sundays and holidays at 12.30pm and 4.30pm. Heading back to Fiumicino, buses leave Piazza Partigiani at 6am, 8am and 9am Monday to Saturday, and 7.30am and 8.30am on Sundays and holidays. Several buses stop in Assisi. Check the website for details.

GETTING AROUND

TRAIN // Stazione Fontivegge is the main train station; the sign at the station says 'Perugia'. There are self-service ticket machines and a ticket office. Regular trains run to Rome (€10.50 to €29.50, two hours) and Arezzo (€4.50 to €6.85, 70 minutes, every two hours). Within Umbria, it's easy to reach Assisi (€2.05, 25 minutes, hourly), Gubbio (€4.75, 1½ hours, seven daily), Spello (€2.65, 30 minutes, hourly), Orvieto (€6.15 to €9.60, 1¼ hours, at least every other hour) and Narni (€5.35 to €8.35, 1¾ hours, eight daily). It's a 1.5km uphill climb from Perugia's train station. Ferrovie Centrale Umbra (FCU; ☎ 075 57 54 01; www.fcu.it, in Italian; Stazione Sant'Anna, Piazzale Bellucci) trains head to Rome (switch in Terni). Validate tickets on board. Take the FCU south to Fratta Todina for Monte Castello di Vibio, Todi or Terni. The Sansepolcro line heads north to Umbertide and Città di Castello.

BUS // Intercity buses leave from Piazza Partigiani. Buses run to Florence (€10.50, 2½ hours, 7.30am Monday and Friday), Assisi (€3.10, 50 minutes, nine daily), Todi (€5.40, 70 minutes, seven daily), Gubbio (€4.50, 70 minutes, 10 daily) and Castiglione del Lago (€4.90, one hour, six to 10 daily). Frequent APM (www.apmperugia.it) local buses run to Deruta and Torgiano. The city bus costs €1 and takes you as far as Piazza Italia. Validate your ticket upon boarding. Tickets on board cost €1.50. A 10-ticket pass costs €9.20.

PARKING // Perugia has seven fee-charging car parks: Piazza Partigiani and the Mercato Coperto are the most central. The free car park is located at Piazza Cupa. *Scale mobili* or *ascensori* (lifts) lead from each car park towards the city centre but don't operate 24 hours a day. Parking fees cost €0.80 to €1.20 per hour in the city centre lots. You can buy a tourist *abbonamento* (unlimited parking ticket pass) from the ticket office at the car park.

MINIMETRÒ // These single-car people-movers traverse between the train station and Pincetto (just below Piazza Garibaldi) every minute. The same €1 tickets work for the bus and minimetrò. From the train station facing the tracks, head right up a long platform.

CAR & MOTORCYCLE // From Rome, leave the A1 at Orte and follow signs for Terni. Once there, take the SS3bis/E45 for Perugia. You can rent cars at the train station with Avis, Maggiore or Hertz. Perugia is famously difficult to navigate and most of the city centre is only open to residential or commercial traffic (although tourists may drive to their hotels to drop off luggage).

TAXI // Taxi services are available from 6am to 2am (24 hours a day in July and August) – call ☎ 075 500 48 88 to arrange pick-up. A ride from the city centre to the main train station costs about €15. Add €1 per suitcase.

SOUTH OF PERUGIA

Just south of Perugia are three charming villages, each known for something particularly special. Deruta has ceramics, Torgiano is known as the wine country of the famed Lungarotti family and tiny Brufa boasts an outdoor modern sculpture route. However, the surrounding area also calls for a visit. The landscape is seemingly laid out solely for a leisurely drive through wheat fields and vineyards, cresting each hill only to discover the next castle, trattoria or winery.

TORGIANO

pop 6230

Fans of wine and olive oil will appreciate this town, a monument to these two most important Umbrian, and indeed Italian, products. Torgiano, just a 25-minute bus ride from Perugia's Piazza Partigiani, is famous throughout the world for its fine wines, and the Lungarotti family, the closest thing Umbria has to a ruling noble clan these days, owns many of the local vineyards, the excellent wine museum and the second of Umbria's two five-star hotels.

You can pick up information on wine tasting, the Strada dei Vini del Cantico or the Brufa sculpture garden from the **tourist office** (☎ 075 988 60 37; Piazza Baglioni; 9am-noon & 2.30-5pm Tue-Sun).

❦ MUSEO DEL VINO // LEARN THE SECRETS OF ITALIAN WINE PRODUCTION

The most important wine museum in Europe, Torgiano's **Museo del Vino** (☎ 075 988 02 00; Corso Vittorio Emanuele 31; adult/concession €4.50/2.50, incl Museo dell'Olivo e dell'Olio €7, audio guide €2; 9am-1pm & 3-7pm summer, to 6pm winter) was started in 1974 by the Lungarotti matriarch, Maria Grazie. The 20-room former palace traces the history of the production of wine in the region back to Etruscan times. Displays of utensils, graphic art, wine containers and production techniques sit alongside a personal collection of photos from the 1950s.

❦ MUSEO DELL'OLIVO E DELL'OLIO // GET TO GRIPS WITH THE OLIVE OIL ECONOMY

With support from research institutes in Italy and abroad, the Lungarotti family helped organise the **Museo dell'Olivo e dell'Olio** (☎ 075 988 03 00; Via Garibaldi 10; adult/concession €4.50/2.50; 10am-1pm & 3-7pm summer, to 6pm winter), which opened in 2000. Contained in a series of medieval houses, the museum traces the production cycle of the olive, displays olive-oil accoutrements and documents the culture and use of olives and how they relate to the economy, the landscape, religion, medicine, diet, sport, crafts and traditions.

❦ LE MELOGRANE // SAVOUR THE VERY BEST UMBRIAN CUISINE

One of Umbria's most exclusive restaurants can be found in the luxury hotel **Le Tre Vaselle** (☎ 075 988 04 47; www.3vaselle.it; Via Garibaldi 48; s €170, d €205-230, ste €270; P 🛏 🖵) owned by the Lungarotti family – are you starting to see a theme here? The restaurant serves deluxe Umbrian cuisine (meals €90) amid sumptuous furnishings and beautiful brick floors. Dishes include veal carpaccio topped with black truffles, and risotto cooked with Rubesco red wine produced by, of course, the Lungarottis.

❦ RISTORANTE SIRO // SAMPLE AUTHENTIC FARE IN AN OLD-SCHOOL EATERY

One of those spots where waiters and customers all know each other by name, **Ristorante Siro** (☎ 075 98 20 10; Via Giordano Bruno 16; meals €24.50; lunch & dinner) has an *antipastone al tagliere* (a huge board of antipasti; €15 for two) starter that could feed a hungry family easily. The *gnochetti al rubesco e radicchio* (little gnocchi with Rubesco wine and radicchio) takes full advantage of the local tipple, and the homemade tiramisu is to die for.

BRUFA

Art fans looking for something a bit more modern shouldn't miss the hamlet of Brufa. This former *frazione* (defence town) of Torgiano, Brufa is just minutes away from Perugia's Ponte San Giovanni neighbourhood and is home to a top resort and spa, and several excellent restaurants. Since 1987 the Strada del Vino e dell'Arte (Street of Wine and Art) that leads into the countryside town has been decorated with sculptures from many of Italy's best sculptors. There are more than two dozen pieces of art, ranging in size from above 6m tall to a mere fraction of that. Torgiano's tourist map *In Viaggi*, available at the tourist office (opposite), carries an inset map detailing Brufa's sculptures.

NORTHERN UMBRIA

TOP FIVE

VIEWS IN NORTHERN UMBRIA

If you do nothing else, admiring the views in Northern Umbria will be worth the price of your ticket. Here are five of our favourites.

* **Funivia Colle Eletto** (p284) The view from this 'birdcage' funicular is as hair-raising as it is beautiful.

* **The garden at Il Torrione** (p413) Grab a couple of chairs and a bottle of wine and watch the sun set over Lago Trasimeno from in front of the 15th-century tower at this inn's perfect garden.

* **The patio at Hotel Brufani Palace** (p410) Overlooks fields of flowers, hill towns and churches.

* **Bar Giardino Bonci** (p277) The view from the back patio of the nondescript bar is a worthwhile surprise.

* **Strada del Vino e dell'Arte** (p267) The road that circles the tiny hamlet of Brufa has been enhanced with more than a dozen modern sculptures.

♥ I QUATTRO SENSI // DINE IN OPULENT SURROUNDINGS

For a truly magnificent experience, dine in sumptuous luxury at the newly refurbished **Relais Borgo Brufa** (☎ 075 98 52 67; www.borgobrufa.it; Via del Colle 38; meals €40). Formerly a quiet, out-of-the-way country estate, the relais is now an homage to opulence, destined for greatness. In addition to elegant surroundings, food from the hotel restaurant is tastefully and ingeniously presented: *porcini* mushroom tempura, pumpkin soup with caviar, and shrimp softer than butter. Its **Wellness Centre** (☎ 075 988 78 50; treatments €30-75; ☼ 10am-1pm & 2.30-8pm) is something of a secret, but it is open to the public. The six treatment rooms have warm lighting, a mosaic Turkish bath with twinkling lights and a hydromassage pool.

♥ I BIRBI OSTERIA // SIT HEARTHSIDE AND ENJOY DINNER IN FAMIGLIA

For a lighter dinner, stop in at **I Birbi Osteria** (☎ 075 988 90 41; Località Le Casacce, Miralduoro di Torgiano; meals €30; ☼ dinner Tue-Sun, lunch Sat & Sun, closed 2 weeks Nov, 3 weeks Jan) on a beautiful hill just east of Brufa. A Tuscan/Umbrian couple hosts their extended family and friends in front of a great hearth. Sure, there's technically a menu, but go with the menu of the day, much of it local meats grilled over the wood-fired hearth.

DERUTA

pop 9130

While it's not quite steel or forestry, Deruta is an ancient 'company' town known for one thing: majolica ceramic technique. The Etruscans and Romans worked the clay around Deruta, but it was not until the bright blue and yellow metallic-oxide majolica glazing technique was imported from Majorca in the 15th century that the ceramics industry took off.

Prices for ceramics in Deruta can be lower or higher than towns such as Gubbio or Assisi, but realise what you're getting (ie either pricier quality handmade items at boutique outlets or cheaper, mass-produced factory knockoffs at the larger operations). For the best quality, head to a smaller shop that follows the centuries-old Deruta traditions.

Contact the **tourist office** (Pro Loco; ☎ 075 971 15 59; Piazza dei Consoli; ☺ 9am-noon & 2.30-6.30pm, closed Mon afternoon) for general information or details about additional accommodation (be aware it's staffed by volunteers and often closes on slow off-season days). APM buses connect the town with Perugia.

♥ CERAMIC SHOPPING // SOURCE QUALITY, HANDCRAFTED CERAMICS FOR SOUVENIRS

At **Maioliche Nulli** (☎ /fax 075 97 23 84; Via Tiberina 142; ☺ 9am-1pm & 4-7pm), Rolando Nulli creates each item by hand, while his brother Goffredo, wife Tiziana or son Luca finishes them with intricate paintings, specialising in classic medieval designs. If they're not busy and you ask nicely in Italian, they might even bring you downstairs and teach you to throw a bowl on the wheel. They'll even package and ship your purchases anywhere in the world. Parking's available. Bring your camera!

Otherwise, browse the shelves of **Maioliche CAMA Deruta** (☎ 075 971 11 82; www.camaderuta.com; Via Tiberina 112). It is one of the biggest operations in town, but is also one of the most respected in Deruta. It sells wine and food as well, and offers almost everything online, which it also packs and ships.

♥ MUSEO REGIONALE DELLA CERAMICA // LEARN THE BACK STORY TO DERUTA'S CERAMICS FAME

You can get a taste for the genuine article at the **Museo Regionale della Ceramica** (☎ 075 971 10 00; Largo San Francesco 1; adult/child/concession €7/2/5 Sat & Sun incl pinacoteca, €5/1/4 Mon-Fri; ☺ 10.30-1pm & 3-6pm, closed Tue afternoon Oct-Mar), in the former Franciscan convent. The history of the production of pottery in Deruta from the 14th century until the beginning of the 20th century is presented here, along with an explanation of the development of the special glaze, including some splendid examples.

♥ COUNTRY DINING // ENJOY EATING JUST LIKE THE LOCALS

Just south of Deruta in the village of Casalina is **Ristorante Country House L'Antico Forziere** (☎ 075 972 43 14; www .anticoforziere.com; Via della Rocca 2, Località Casalina di Deruta; r €65-150; P ⋈ ⊠), a charming country house with several well-decorated rooms in an enviable position to reach most of northern Umbria (although a tad close to the highway). However, the **restaurant** (meals €32) is what brings travellers (and food critics) in the know out here. Three brothers perform magic with dishes such as turnip pasta with leek and poppy seeds and saffron risotto with cinnamon pork. Don't even think of leaving before trying (and photographing) the dessert sampler.

For a great and cheap meal, try **Hotel Ristorante Asso di Coppe** (☎ 075 971 02 05; SS3bis/E45, Km 73,400; meals €22), a place populated by locals and serving basic but delicious Umbrian cuisine.

ASSISI

· · · · · ·

pop 27,300

The spiritual capital of Umbria is Assisi, a town that is more tied to its most famous son than anywhere else. To visit Assisi now is to see it almost as St Francis himself saw it. Except, of

course, for the millions of other pilgrims and tourists who are all attempting to share in the same tranquillity as you.

Assisian history dates back to 1000 BC, when Umbrians built small settlements in the hospitable countryside. It has bounced around between almost a dozen ruling factions since, including Roman rule as far back as 295 BC and Ostrogoth invaders in the 6th century. In the 13th century when Assisi was a free *comune* (self-governing city), the Ghibelline (pro-Empire) residents often fought against its Guelph (pro-Papacy) neighbour, Perugia. One such soldier was the future St Francis of Assisi, who was born here in 1182. He preached his message throughout Umbria until his death in 1224.

Piazza del Comune is the centre of Assisi. At the northwestern edge of this square, Via San Paolo and Via Portica both eventually lead to the Basilica di San Francesco. Via Portica also leads to the Porta San Pietro and the Piazzale dell'Unità d'Italia, where most intercity buses stop, although APM buses from smaller towns in the area terminate at Piazza Matteotti. Train riders arrive at Piazza Matteotti by shuttle bus (€1) from Santa Maria degli Angeli.

ESSENTIAL INFORMATION

EMERGENCIES // Hospital (Ospedale di Assisi; ☎ 075 81 39 1; Via Fuori Porta Nuova) Police Station (☎ 075 81 28 20; Piazza del Comune)
TOURIST OFFICES // Branch office Outside Porta Nuova from Easter through October 8. Tourist Office (☎ 075 813 86 80; www.assisi.regioneumbria .eu; Piazza del Comune 22; ☺ 8am-2pm & 3-6pm Mon-Sat, 10am-1pm & 2-5pm Sun summer, 9am-1pm Sun winter)

EXPLORING ASSISI

☙ BASILICA DI SAN FRANCESCO // ADMIRE INCREDIBLE FRESCOS IN ST FRANCIS' CHURCH

The fabulous Basilica di San Francesco (☎ 075 81 90 01; Piazza di San Francesco) was built on a hill known as Colle d'Inferno (Hell Hill). People were executed at the gallows here until the 13th century. St Francis asked his followers to bury him here in keeping with Jesus, who had died on the cross among criminals and outcasts. The area is now known as Paradise Hill. The basilica has a separate information office (☎ 075 819 00 84; www.sanfrancescoassisi .org; ☺ 9am-noon & 2-5pm Mon-Sat) opposite the entrance to the lower church.

Upper Church

The upper church (☺ 8.30am-6.45pm Easter-Oct, to 6pm Oct-Easter) was built just after the lower church, between 1230 and 1253, and the change in style and grandiosity is readily apparent. One of the most famous pieces of art in the world is the 28-part fresco circling the walls. The fresco has been attributed to Giotto, but there have been a few who have debated its attribution within the art-history community. The fresco starts just to the right of the altar and continues clockwise around the church. Above each image is a corresponding biblical fresco with 28 corresponding images from the Old and New Testament. The frescos in the basilica literally revolutionised art in the Western world. All the gold leaf and flat iconic images of the Byzantine and Romanesque periods were eschewed for natural backgrounds, people of all classes and a human, suffering Jesus. This was in keeping with Francis' idea that the human body was 'brother' and the earth around him 'mother' and 'sister'.

ASSISI

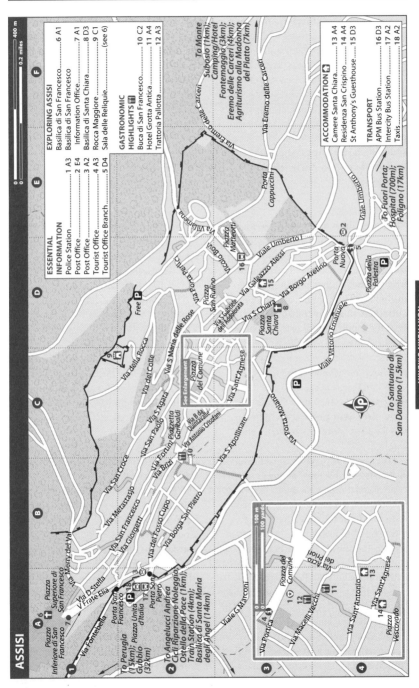

NORTHERN UMBRIA

These fresco painters were the storytellers of their day, turning biblical passages into Bibliae Pauperum: open public Bibles for the poor, who were mostly illiterate. The scenes in St Francis' life were tied to the scenes as a way to translate the Bible through images. For instance, the fifth fresco shows St Francis renouncing his father, while the corresponding biblical fresco shows the disobedient Adam and Eve in the Garden of Eden.

Lower Church

The **lower church** (⏰ 6am-6.45pm summer, to 6pm winter) was built between 1228 and 1230. The stained-glass windows are the work of master craftsmen brought in from Germany, England and Flanders during the 13th century, and were quite an architectural feat at that time.

In the centre of the lower church, above the main altar, are four frescos attributed to Maestro delle Vele, a pupil of Giotto, which represent what St Francis called 'the four greatest allegories'. The first was the victory of Francis over evil, and the other three were the precepts his order was based on: poverty, obedience and chastity.

Lorenzetti's triptych in the left transept ends with his most famous and controversial *Madonna Who Celebrates Francis*. Mary is seen holding the baby Jesus and indicating with her thumb towards St Francis. On the other side of Mary is the apostle John, whom we're assuming is being unfavourably compared with Francis. In 1234 Pope Gregory IX decided that the image was not heretical because John had written the gospel, but Francis had lived it.

Cimabue was the most historically important painter who worked in this church because he was the only artist to get a first-hand account from St Francis' two nephews, who had personally known the saint. In the *Madonna in Majesty,* in the right transept, much has been tampered with, but Cimabue's intact depiction of St Francis is considered the most accurate. Francis appears peaceful and calm in this painting. The first biographer of St Francis, Thomas of Celano, wrote in the middle of the 13th century that Francis was an eloquent man, of cheerful countenance and of a kindly aspect.

One of the most moving locations in the basilica complex is downstairs from the lower church: the crypt of St Francis, where the saint's body has been laid to rest. Bench seating around the tomb allows for quiet reflection.

The basilica's **Sala delle Reliquie** (Relics Hall; ☎ 075 81 90 01; admission free; ⏰ 9am-6pm, 1-4.30pm holidays) contains items from St Francis' life, including his simple tunic and sandals and fragments of his celebrated *Canticle of the Creatures*. The most important relic here is the Franciscan Rule parchment, the *Book of Life* composed by Francis.

❦ BASILICA DI SANTA CHIARA // DISCOVER ST FRANCIS' FEMALE COUNTERPART

The **Basilica di Santa Chiara** (☎ 075 81 22 82; Piazza Santa Chiara; ⏰ 6.30am-noon & 2-7pm summer, to 6pm winter) is a 13th-century Romanesque church, with steep ramparts and a striking facade. The white-and-pink stone that makes up the exterior here (the same stone that makes many buildings in Assisi look like they glow in the sunlight) came from nearby Subasio. The daughter of an Assisian nobleman, St Clare (Santa Chiara) was a spiritual contemporary of St Francis and founded the Sorelle Povere di Santa Chiara (Order of the Poor Sisters), now known as the Poor Clares. She is buried in the church's crypt. The Byzantine cross that is said to have spoken to St Francis is also housed here.

❧ SANTUARIO DI SAN DAMIANO // BE INSPIRED BY ST FRANCIS AND ST CLARE

Get in touch with the spirit of St Francis and St Clare at the quiet and reflective **Santuario di San Damiano** (☎ 075 81 22 73; admission free; ⏱ 10am-noon & 2-6pm summer, 10am-noon & 2-4.30pm winter, vespers 7pm summer & 5pm winter), where St Francis first heard the voice of God telling him to rebuild his church and where he wrote his *Canticle of the Creatures*. The serene locale is more popular with pilgrims than tourists, as you can practically feel the spirit of St Francis and St Clare (who died here in 1253) at this simple church. Many walk the 1.5km path (a fairly easy stroll past olive fields).

❧ EREMO DELLE CARCERI // FIND PEACE AT ST FRANCIS' ISOLATED HERMITAGE

Find out why St Francis chose the caves of **Eremo delle Carceri** (☎ 075 81 23 01; www.eremocarceri.it; admission free; ⏱ 6.30am-7pm summer, to 6pm winter) as his hermitage after hearing the word of God. The *carceri* (isolated places, or 'prisons') along the slopes of Monte Subasio are as peaceful today as they were 800 years ago when St Francis and his followers retreated into the caves for prayer. These days, many use the locale as a jumping-off point for contemplative walks through Monte Subasio or to picnic under the oaks. It's about a 4km drive (or walk) east of Assisi, and hiking trails heading out of the hermitage are extremely well signposted.

❧ BASILICA DI SANTA MARIA DEGLI ANGELI // VISIT THE CHURCH WITHIN THE CHURCH

A quick walk from the train station is the imposing **Basilica di Santa Maria degli Angeli** (☎ 075 8 05 11; www.porziuncola .org; Santa Maria degli Angeli; ⏱ 6.15am-12.50pm & 2.30-7.30pm), built between 1565 and 1685 around the first Franciscan monastery and tiny Porziuncola Chapel. Perugino fans will appreciate his intact *Crucifixion*, painted on the rear wall. St Francis died at the site of the Cappella del Transito on 3 October 1226.

❧ ROCCA MAGGIORE // GAZE OVER ALL OF NORTHERN UMBRIA

Dominating the city, with an equally dominant view of the valley, is the massive 14th-century **Rocca Maggiore** (☎ 075 81 52 92; Via della Rocca; adult/concession €5/3.50; ⏱ 10am-sunset), an oft-expanded, pillaged and rebuilt hill fortress offering 360-degree views of seemingly all of Northern Umbria. Walk up winding staircases and claustrophobic passageways to reach the archer slots that served Assisians as they went medieval on Perugia.

❧ OUTDOOR ASSISI // HIKE THE PILGRIMAGE TRAILS AROUND ASSISI

St Francis buffs and nature lovers will appreciate the plethora of strolls, day hikes and overnight pilgrimage walks leading into and out of Assisi. Many make the trek to Eremo delle Carceri or Sanctuario di San Damiano on foot. The tourist office has maps for those on such a peregrination, including a route that follows in St Francis' footsteps to Gubbio (18km).

A popular spot for hikers is nearby Monte Subasio. Local bookshops sell all sorts of walking and mountain-biking guides and maps for the area, and the tourist office can help with brochures and maps as well.

Bicycle rentals are available at **Angelucci Andrea Cicli Riparazione Noleggio** (☎ 075 804 25 50; www.angeluccicicli.it; Via Risorgimento 54a) in Santa Maria degli Angeli and at Ostello della Pace (p411).

FESTIVALS & EVENTS

Settimana Santa Celebrated with processions and performances. Easter week.
Festa di Calendimaggio Colourful festival which celebrates spring in medieval fashion. It starts the first Thursday after 1 May.
Festa di San Francesco The main religious event in the city takes place on 3 and 4 October.
Marcia della Pace This is Europe's largest peace march. It began in 1961 and attracts more than 150,000 pilgrims who walk the 24km route between Perugia and Assisi. First week in October.

GASTRONOMIC HIGHLIGHTS

While we sometimes recommend staying away from hotel restaurants, most of Assisi's better restaurants (even the more inexpensive ones) are part of hotels.

☙ BUCA DI SAN FRANCESCO €€
☎ 075 81 22 04; Via Brizi 1; meals €31; ☺ Tue-Sun
Sample traditional Umbrian dishes and specialities of the house in an elegant medieval setting. Choose from bruschetta, local sausage, *spaghetti alla buca* (house-speciality spaghetti made with roasted mushrooms), gnocchi and homemade desserts, and from the extensive wine list with the help of one of Assisi's only sommeliers.

☙ HOTEL GROTTA ANTICA €
☎ 075 81 34 67; Vicolo Buscatti 6; meals €16
Although there are only a handful of menu items, the Ligurian owners and

chefs ensure that you needn't look past the pesto dishes for a cheap and filling main course. Wine prices can't be beaten anywhere in Assisi.

☙ TRATTORIA PALLOTTA €€
☎ 075 81 26 49; Vicolo della Volta Pinta; meals €25; ☺ Wed-Mon
Head through the Volta Pinta (Painted Vault) off Piazza del Comune, careful not to bump into someone as you gaze at the 16th-century frescos above you, into this gorgeous setting of vaulted brick walls and wood-beamed ceilings. All the Umbrian classics are cooked here: rabbit, homemade *strangozzi* (round stringlike spaghetti), even pigeon. Readers have assured us its selection for vegetarians is excellent.

TRANSPORT

TRAIN // Assisi is on the Foligno–Terontola line with regular services to Perugia (€2.05, 25 minutes, hourly) and Spoleto (€3.25 to €5, one hour, 12 daily). You may have to change at Terontola for Florence (€10.55 to €16.50, 1¾ to 2¾ hours, 10 daily) and at Foligno for Rome (€9.40 to €25.50, two to three hours, hourly). Assisi's train station is 4km west in Santa Maria degli Angeli; shuttle bus C (€1) runs between the train station and the APM bus station on Piazza Matteotti every half-hour. Buy tickets from the station's *tabacchi* and in town.
BUS // Take **APM Perugia** (☎ 800 51 21 41; apmperugia.it) to Perugia (€3.10, 50 minutes, nine daily) and Gubbio (€5.20, 70 minutes, 11 daily) from Piazza Matteotti. **Sulga** (☎ 800 09 96 61; www.sulga.it) buses leave from Porta San Pietro for Florence (€12, 2 ½ hours, departs 7am daily) and Rome's Stazione Tiburtina (€17.50, 3¼ hours, two daily).
PARKING // There are many car parks scattered outside the city centre; driving within the city walls is nearly impossible. Six car parks dot the city walls (connected to the centre by orange shuttle buses), or head for Via della Rocca where, for the price of a short but fairly steep walk, you should be able to find free parking. Covered parking is at the Maiano car park.

TAXI // For a 24-hour taxi, dial ☎ 075 81 31 00 or head to Piazza Unità d'Italia's taxi stand.

SPELLO

· · · · · ·

pop 8600

Sometimes it seems like it's just not possible for the next Umbrian town to be any prettier than the last. And then you reach Spello. It's often overlooked, as tourists head to nearby Assisi or Perugia, but the proliferation of arched stone walkways and hanging flowerpots make it well worth a visit, especially in spring when the whole bloomin' town smells of flowers.

ESSENTIAL INFORMATION

EMERGENCIES // Doctor (☎ 0742 30 20 16) Police Station (☎ 0742 65 11 15; Piazza della Repubblica)

TOURIST OFFICES // Pro Loco (☎ 0742 30 10 09; prospello@libero.it; Piazza Matteotti 3; ⏱ 9.30am-12.30pm & 3.30-5.30pm) Can provide you with a list of

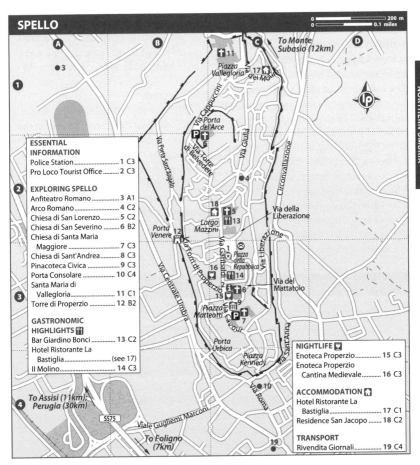

SPELLO

ESSENTIAL INFORMATION		
Police Station	1	C3
Pro Loco Tourist Office	2	C3
EXPLORING SPELLO		
Anfiteatro Romano	3	A1
Arco Romano	4	C2
Chiesa di San Lorenzo	5	C2
Chiesa di San Severino	6	B2
Chiesa di Santa Maria Maggiore	7	C3
Chiesa di Sant'Andrea	8	C3
Pinacoteca Civica	9	C3
Porta Consolare	10	C4
Santa Maria di Vallegloria	11	C1
Torre di Properzio	12	B2

GASTRONOMIC HIGHLIGHTS		
Bar Giardino Bonci	13	C2
Hotel Ristorante La Bastiglia	(see 17)	
Il Molino	14	C3

NIGHTLIFE		
Enoteca Properzio	15	C3
Enoteca Properzio Cantina Medievale	16	C3
ACCOMMODATION		
Hotel Ristorante La Bastiglia	17	C1
Residence San Jacopo	18	C2
TRANSPORT		
Rivendita Giornali	19	C4

To Monte Subasio (12km)

Piazza Vallegloria

Via Cappuccini

Via Porta del Arce

Via Torre di Belvedere

Via Porta Sant'Angelo

Via Giulia

Circonvallazione

Via della Liberazione

Arco Romano

Largo Mazzini

Porta Venere

Via Torri di Properzio

Via Centrale Umbra

Via Garibaldi

Piazza della Repubblica

Via Liberazione

Via del Mattatoio

Piazza Matteotti

Via Cavour

Via Sant'Anna

Porta Urbica

Piazza Kennedy

Via Roma

To Assisi (11km); Perugia (30km)

SS75

Viale Guglielmi Marconi

To Foligno (7km)

accommodation and has maps of walks in the surrounding area, including an 8km walk across the hills to Assisi. Purchase a city map here for €0.50.

EXPLORING SPELLO

Spello isn't known for any one site, so a leisurely walking tour is the best way to see the town.

♥ A TOUR OF TOWN // ADMIRE ANCIENT ARCHITECTURE AND RELIGIOUS ART

As you enter Spello, you'll come across Piazza Kennedy, the main entrance to the town, with a partially Roman gate, **Porta Consolare.** Further into town, Piazza Matteotti features the stunning 12th-century **Chiesa di Santa Maria Maggiore** (8.30am-noon & 2-7pm Mar-Oct, to 6pm Nov-Mar). You'll also find the town's real treat, Pinturicchio's beautiful frescos in the Cappella Baglioni. The fresco is in the right-hand corner as you enter, behind glass, but be aware that you need to pay to illuminate the fresco. This is done not just to make money; constant light damages the paint. Also of note is the Cappella's exquisite floor (dating from 1566) made of tiles from Deruta. Next stop is the **Pinacoteca Civica** (☎ 0742 30 14 97; Palazzo dei Cannonica, Piazza Matteotti; adult/concession €4/3; 10.30am-1pm & 3-6.30pm Tue-Sun Apr-Sep, 10.30am-12.30pm & 3-5pm Tue-Sun Oct-Mar), which shows off Spello's artistic, religious and architectural past. Stop in briefly at the austere **Chiesa di Sant'Andrea** (Piazza Matteotti; varies), where you can admire *Madonna with Child and Saints* by Bernardino Pinturicchio.

Continue through to **Piazza della Repubblica** and the **Chiesa di San Lorenzo** (8.30am-12.30pm & 3-7pm summer, to 6pm winter), with a collection of sacred works. At the far north of town is yet another imposing church, **Santa Maria di Vallegloria,** built in the 1320s in Gothic style with frescos by Spacca. The **Torre di Properzio** (Porta Venere) stands guard over the western Roman walls. Named after the Roman poet Propertius, the gate and its towers are a hodgepodge of Roman, medieval and 20th-century reconstructionist architecture.

Perhaps the best sight in all of Spello is to head past the **Arco Romano** to the **Chiesa di San Severino** (closed to the public), an active Capuchin monastery with a Romanesque facade. From here you can get the best view of the **Anfiteatro Romano** (closed to the public) – the amphitheatre used for spectacles thousands of years ago in Roman 'Hispellum' (the Roman name for modern-day Spello) – and the surrounding countryside.

THE PASSEGGIATA

One of the very best things to take advantage of during your stay in Umbria is the *passeggiata* (traditional evening stroll). No matter how big or small a town, locals and visitors of all ages take to the streets with friends or family, by themselves or, these days, accompanied by a mobile phone. Most towns in Umbria are built concentrically around a main square that might have started out as a Roman forum or medieval gathering place. Best of all, *'un passeggio'* is free, doesn't require any preplanning and practically forces you to eat a double gelato. Think of it as improvised urban street theatre. In Perugia, watch as the students preen and flirt, jostling their way towards adulthood. In Orvieto, sit around the cathedral with older locals, who come to deliver Italian lessons to unsuspecting visitors. In Castelluccio, your *passeggiata* will most likely be shared with the town's herd of goats.

FESTIVALS & EVENTS

During **L'Infiorata del Corpus Domini**, teams of friends, families and neighbours create flower carpets decorating the streets. It's usually held in June on Corpus Domini, the Sunday 60 days after Easter.

GASTRONOMIC HIGHLIGHTS

❦ BAR GIARDINO BONCI €

Via Garibaldi 10; mains €6; ⏱ 7am-10pm Fri-Wed, to midnight summer

This simple bar has decent light meals and gelati, but the best thing is the back veranda, where you can while away hours admiring the view. The sheltered outdoor space offers plenty of plastic tables and chairs overlooking the rolling hills and valley below.

❦ HOTEL RISTORANTE LA BASTIGLIA €€€

☎ 0742 65 12 77; Via dei Molini 17; meals €55; ⏱ Fri-Tue & dinner Thu

Connoisseurs come from all over the world to dine here. The food is beyond outstanding and a rare example of Umbrian nouvelle cuisine. Who would have thought blood and gnocchi would go together, or pigeon and puff pastry? But they do, artfully served with impeccable manners in elegant surroundings.

❦ IL MOLINO €€

☎ 0742 65 13 05; Piazza Matteotti 6/7; meals €31; ⏱ Wed-Mon

Housed in an ancient olive-oil mill, the restaurant for the Hotel Palazzo Bocci harks back to the 14th-century building in which it resides. A wood-burning grill centrepiece and arched brick ceilings set the scene for wild game, foraged herbs and earthy truffles, creating a modern medieval atmosphere worthy of a special occasion dinner or a casual lunch.

NIGHTLIFE

❦ ENOTECHE PROPERZIO & PROPERZIO CANTINA MEDIEVALE

Umbrian vineyards aren't usually open to the public, so one of the only chances visitors have to taste several wines at once without breaking the bank (or getting sloshed) is to stop at an *enoteca* in town. And there's no better place in Umbria to do so than **Enoteca Properzio** (☎ 0742 30 15 21; www.enoteche.it; Palazzo dei Canonici, Piazza Matteotti 8/10; ⏱ 9am-11pm Apr-Oct, to 8pm Nov-Mar), where for €30 you can try half a dozen Umbrian wines while snacking on cheese, prosciutto and bruschetta. For €144, you can have a dozen bottles shipped abroad. **Enoteca Properzio Cantina Medievale** (☎ 0742 30 16 88; Via Torri di Properzio 8a) is a more intimate bar around the corner. It's set in a medieval vault and sells many edibles.

TRANSPORT

TRAIN // Spello is on the line between Perugia and Foligno, so trains run at least hourly to Perugia (€2.65, 30 minutes) and Assisi (€2.05, 10 minutes). It's a quick walk into town from the station (often unstaffed). Buy tickets at either the self-service ticket machine or at the **Rivendita Giornali** (Piazza della Pace 1) newsstand.

LA STRADA DEL SAGRANTINO

· · · · · ·

Wine connoisseurs are not the only ones who will enjoy the tourist-friendly 'route of Sagrantino wine'. It is one of four Umbrian driving (or, for the brave, bicycling) wine routes

NORTHERN UMBRIA

NORTHERN UMBRIA

that follow signposted roads through stunningly beautiful landscape filled with vineyards, castles, sunflower fields and five charming villages. The two main towns in the area are the postcard-perfect burgs of Montefalco and Bevagna, but meandering countryside roads through Gualdo Cattaneo, Giano dell'Umbria and Castel Ritaldi are equally lovely.

All tourist offices near the region carry Strada del Sagrantino brochures with detailed driving maps, vineyards and *enoteche* (wine bars), or find information on accommodation (including *agriturismi* and B&Bs), restaurants, public transport and history at the region's tourism website www.stradadelsagrantino.com. For more information on the Le Strada del Vino in Umbria, see p379.

TRANSPORT

BUS // SSIT (☎ 0742 67 07 47; www.spoletina .com) buses travel from Foligno to Montefalco (€3.20, 30 minutes, eight daily) and Bevagna (€2.60, 20 minutes, six daily). From Foligno you can continue north to Perugia or south towards Spoleto. Buses go between Bevagna and Montefalco (€2.20 to €3.40, 20 to 40 minutes, five daily), some direct and others through Foligno.

TRAIN // To get to Trevi it is best to take the train from Foligno.

FOLIGNO

pop 56,400

If you've come to Foligno, you've landed in the centre of the universe, at least that's what its proud residents will assure you. Although Foligno is now a commercial city and has lost some of its charm to industry and earthquakes, its city centre is still filled with historic buildings and narrow pathways. The city is Umbria's main transport hub, it has good shopping and boasts Umbria's most famous neighbourhood restaurant. If you want to see the 'real' Umbria, Foligno is for you.

Many public transport users will go through Foligno at some point. If you arrive by train and are switching to a bus, head out of the train station down Viale Mezzetti. The main bus terminal is about 50m to your left. To get to Trevi, head about 40m further to the grandiose Porta Romana.

ESSENTIAL INFORMATION

TOURIST OFFICE // Tourist office (☎ 0742 35 44 59; www.comune.foligno.pg.it/cultura/servizio turistico, in Italian; Corso Cavour 126; ☼ 9am-1pm & 3.30-7pm Mon-Sat, 9am-1pm Sun) has information behind the desk (no one speaks English) for Foligno, Bevagna, Gualdo Cattaneo, Montefalco, Spello and Trevi. It's located near the Porta Romana.

EXPLORING FOLIGNO

♣ **PIAZZA DELLA REPUBBLICA //** **EXPLORE THE TRINCI FAMILY'S ARTISTIC TREASURE TROVE**
The cathedral is in Piazza della Repubblica, in which St Feliciano is buried. The building dates from the 12th century and is a hodgepodge of many architectural styles, from Roman-Gothic to 16th-century Renaissance additions. There are some stunning 16th-century frescos by Baroque painter Vespasiano Strada. In the same square is the worthwhile Palazzo Trinci (☎ 0742 35 07 34; admission free; ☼ 10am-7pm Tue-Sun), which has some paintings and frescos from the 15th century. The Trinci family was part of the *seigniories* (feudal lordships) that ruled over much of papal-controlled Umbria in the later medieval period. (You'll notice buildings all over Umbria named after these families: the Baglionis in Perugia or the Vitellis in Città di Castello.)

The Trincis paid Ottaviano Nelli to decorate their palace – although they didn't score like the Vitellis in Città di Castello, with Raphael and Giorgio Vasari. There's a small museum (descriptions in Italian only) in the palazzo, which features some of the historic costumes you'd find at the Quintana festival.

♣ LA GIOSTRA DELLA QUINTANA // GET IN THE MEDIEVAL MOOD WITH AN ANNUAL JOUST

If you're in the area during the beginning of June or in September, the main festival you'll come across is **La Giostra della Quintana** (☎ 0742 35 40 00; www.quintana.it), a medieval equestrian tournament reinvented from the 1400s. Ten neighbourhoods vie against each other in a friendly jousting competition complete with elaborate velvet-and-lace traditional costumes, and dishes from the 15th century.

♣ IL BACCO FELICE // DINE AT SALVATORE'S AND MEET A LOCAL LEGEND

The walls at **Il Bacco Felice** (☎ 0742 34 10 19; Via Garibaldi 73; meals €60; ☯ Tue-Sun) are held up by graffiti, books and bottles, but this neighbourhood joint has reached a mythic level – fitting for a town that calls itself 'the centre of the universe'. The godhead figure, then, is Salvatore Denaro, the chef and owner who will turn away anyone on a mobile phone or to whom he takes a dislike. Tourists Salvatore dislikes often subsidise the meals of those he does, so check your bill at the end to find out how you measure up. Don't worry about the lack of a menu; diners might find fava beans from his garden and organic locally grown pork one day and Chianina beef the next.

TRANSPORT

TRAIN // You can buy train tickets at the Blu Bar, next to the petrol station at the bus terminal. There are hourly trains to Perugia (€3.05, 40 minutes) and Assisi (€2.05, 15 minutes).

BEVAGNA

pop 5020
If a visitor had only one day to spend in Umbria, Bevagna wouldn't be a bad choice. The town was once named the most beautiful village in Italy, and the townsfolk do seem a little happier here. Ancient city walls ring the main drag, Corso Matteotti, and everything listed is within about a 10-minute walk of the square, Piazza Silvestri. Bevagna began first as an Umbrian settlement, then became Etruscan and eventually a Roman *municipium* on the Via Flaminia. For visitors, Romanesque churches, *enoteche* and a dearth of tourists add to the charm.

ESSENTIAL INFORMATION

TOURIST OFFICES // Pro Loco tourist office (☎ 0742 36 16 67; pbevagna@bcsnet.it; Piazza Silvestri 1; ☯ 9.30am-1pm & 2.30-7pm) can help with accommodation and wine tasting.

EXPLORING BEVAGNA

♣ PINACOTECA COMUNALE // BROWSE ROMAN MOSAICS AND LOCAL ARCHAEOLOGICAL FINDS

The **Pinacoteca Comunale** (☎ 0742 36 00 31; Corso Matteotti 70; adult/concession €5/2; ☯ 10.30am-1pm & 3-7pm summer, 10.30am-1pm & 3-5.30pm or 6pm Tue-Sun winter) features a rudimentary exhibit on local archaeology and ceramics.

The ticket for the *pinacoteca* also includes admission to the **Roman Mosaic Museum of Antiquities** (☎ 075 572 71 41; Via di Porta Guelfa; ☯ 10.30am-1pm & 3-4.30pm Tue-Sun), whic features a well-preserved tile floor from ancient Roman baths. There are also the remains of an old Roman theatre, and a Roman and medieval wall, plus a monastic winery.

♥ PAOLO BEA // NIBBLE CROSTINI AS YOU SAMPLE FOUR SPECIAL WINES

On the road out of Bevagna heading towards Spoleto, stop by **Paolo Bea** (☎ 0742 37 81 28; www.paolobea.com; Località Cerrete 8; ☽ Sun in summer, varies) for a true tasting experience. The family creates four special wines, which you can taste for €18 along with homemade bruschetta and *crostini*. They also sell their own olive oil and Parmesan. During the summer, a harp player entertains visitors on Sunday. In a very Umbrian fashion, the vineyard is also open when the owners are home and not busy.

♥ LOCAL FESTIVALS // JOIN THE LOCALS CANDLE-MAKING AND SNAIL SAMPLING

At the end of June, Bevagna goes medieval with the **Festival of the Gaite**. For two days, the town goes back in time a few hundred years. Artisans give demonstrations on the crafts of the day – glassblowing, candle-making, ironworks – dressed in period attire.

If you happen upon the area during the last third of August and are in the mood for eating a mollusc or three, the little town of Cantalupo di Bevagna celebrates its **Sagra della Lumaca** (Festival of the Snail), with snail dishes cooked in every way imaginable (snail pasta, bruschetta with snail sauce, roasted snails, snail antipasti etc), as well as exhibits, dancing and general slug-related merriment. Accordingly, you'll find *lumache* (snails) on the menu at many restaurants

(including Coccorone in Bevagna; see below).

GASTRONOMIC HIGHLIGHTS

♥ COCCORONE €€

☎ 0742 37 95 35; Largo Tempestivi; €29; ☽ Thu-Tue
Hidden along a quiet side street, Coccorone has tables outside where you can enjoy the stone walkway. Bring out your adventurous side for the menu, heavy on game and unusual meats, such as rabbit *alla cacciatore* (Italian tomato sauce with green peppers), pigeon and snails.

♥ ENOTECA AND LOCANDA PIAZZA ONOFRI €

☎ 0742 36 19 20, 335 718 89 03; www.enoteca onofri.it; Piazza Onofri 2; mini-apt €80-130; ☽ enoteca Thu-Tue
For one-stop shopping, the always cheerful Assú runs this delicious restaurant and good-value hotel in addition to her wine shop, La Bottega di Piazza Onofri. You only have to stumble upstairs after dinner to relax under arched stone windows, or feel free to cook up a light meal in your own kitchenette.

♥ LA BOTTEGA DI PIAZZA ONOFRI €

☎ 339 374 57 05; 102 Corso Matteotti 102; meals €4-8; ☽ 10.30-3.30pm & 6-9pm Thu-Tue Mar–mid-Jan
Head to this central location to enjoy a selection of homemade small meals served up by Assú of Enoteca and Locanda Piazza Onofri fame. She pours about half a dozen tasting wines each day (purchased by the glass).

MONTEFALCO

pop 5720

The ancient town of Montefalco looks as if it grew organically, along with the local vines, out of the ground. Known as the *ringhiera dell'Umbria* (the banister, or balcony, of Umbria), the perfectly perched village sits atop a hill with a view so lyrically beautiful, it practically begs for an ode. As if that wasn't enough, Montefalco is the headquarters for the distinctly Umbrian red, Sagrantino di Montefalco. Imbibe in the main square, Piazza del Comune, in no less than four *enoteche* (Enoteca L'Alchimista has the best reputation).

❤ MUSEO CIVICO SAN FRANCESCO // ADMIRE PAINTED PEOPLE IN PERSPECTIVE

The most important building in Montefalco is the **Museo Civico San Francesco** (☎ 0742 37 95 98; Via Ringhiera Umbra 6; adult/concession €5/2; ☷ 10.30am-1pm & 2.30-5pm Nov-Feb, 10.30am-1pm & 2-6pm Mar-May & Sep-Oct, 10.30am-1pm & 3-7pm Jun & Jul, 10.30am-1pm & 3-7.30pm Aug, closed Mon Nov-Feb). The museum is housed next to the deconsecrated St Francis Church, with a 'narrated' fresco cycle by the painter Benozzo Gozzoli, who was the first Umbrian painter of the 1400s to use perspective to paint human form. There's also a decent *pinacoteca*, plus tools from a medieval monastic vineyard. Ask for the well-written guides in Italian, English and French.

❤ WINE TASTING // TASTE THE LOCAL GRAPE

Next to Torgiano's Lungarotti (see p266), the second most famous vineyard in Umbria is **Arnaldo Caprai** (☎ 742 37 88 02; www.arnaldocaprai.it; Località Torre di Montefalco; ☷ 9am-1pm & 3-7pm Mon-Fri, 9am-1pm Sat), the winemakers who single-handedly

NORTHERN UMBRIA

INTERVIEW: JENNIFER MCILVAINE

What's the history of wine in Umbria? The Etruscans made wine in Umbria starting in the 6th century BC, soon to be followed by the Romans. It wasn't until the Middle Ages, around 1200, that the popes of the time discovered the sweet wines of Orvieto, and they turned Lake Corbara into their official summer retreat. A little bit later, the sweet wine Sagrantino, from Montefalco, began to be used as the 'sacred' wine in Catholic ceremonies.

What are the main Umbrian varietals visitors should try? The main varietals of Umbria are Grechetto, Trebbiano, Sangiovese and Sagrantino. All are cultivated vigorously, producing the excellent wines we drink today.

What's the best time for oenophiles to visit Umbria? The best way to wine tour in Umbria is to come for Cantina Aperte (Open Wineries), held annually on the last Sunday in May. Almost every winery in the area is open for tours, tastings, food and concerts. The most famous is the Mangialonga from Arnaldo Caprai (above), a frolic through the vineyards with stops at picnic stations, all accompanied by live music, and lots of wine!

What's your favourite local find? Definitely Vernaccia di Cannara. Vernaccia is a local sweet wine from Cannara (my home town). It's made from the Cornetta grape and is traditionally drunk on Easter morning for breakfast. It is almost impossible to find in stores, except for one winery, di Filippo. The best way to find it, other than knocking on farmers' doors (which does work, by the way) is to check out the Vernaccia festival the Sunday before Easter, or the famous Onion Festival in September, both in Cannara.

Jennifer McIlvaine is a chef and restaurant owner who leads cooking classes and bicycle tours from her home in Cannara, Umbria. See her website at www.lifeitalianstyle.com.

brought the now-famous Denominazione d'Origine Controllata e Garantita
(DOCG) Sagrantino back from obscurity. The Caprai vineyard has just built a
beautiful new tasting room and is one
of the few vintners in Umbria open to
the public on a regular basis. Plus, if you
love the wine (we suggest the white fruity
Grecchetto and the earthy Sagrantino),
you're in luck; Caprai is one of the largest
Umbrian wine exporters and distributes
its goods in about two-dozen countries,
from Australia to Brazil and Korea to the
US. To reach the winery, follow the signs
on the road towards Bevagna to Località
Torre or Torre di Montefalco.

Another impressive Umbrian winery
is **Antonelli** (☎ 0742 37 91 58; www.antonelli
sanmarco.it; SS316 km15, Località San Marco 60, Montefalco; ☒ 8.30am-12.30pm & 2.30-6.30pm Mon-Sat),
which produces not only delicious local
varietals like Grecchetto, Sagrantino,
Passito and Trebbiano, but olive oil and
grappa as well. The grounds alone are
worth a visit. Try to call ahead, as they
often close to visitors in the low season.

❤ RISTORANTE RINGHIERA UMBRA // DINE ON TRUFFLES AND LOCAL WINES

The basic **Hotel Ristorante Ringhiera
Umbra** (☎ 0742 37 91 66; www.ringhieraumbra
.com; verziere@tiscali.it; Via Mameli 20; d €75, q €150,
all incl breakfast) has a fantastic, inexpensive
restaurant located in a cosy stone-and-
brick cave, and serves excellent *strangozzi*
with truffles and Sagrantino sauce.

TREVI

pop 8240

A tiny picturesque hillside town just south
of Foligno, Trevi has miraculously avoided any sort of bowing to Umbria's burgeoning tourist industry, and would feel

downright foreign to anyone just coming
from San Gimignano or Siena. Nowadays,
you can actually hear the z-z-z-zip as it
rolls itself up for siesta, and nary a local
soul ventures out between 1pm and 4pm.
The town calls itself a low City (p385),
and residents pride themselves on its utter mellowness. Greenish-grey olive trees
swathe every inch of hill-side around
Trevi, and the olive oil here is reputedly
some of the best in Italy.

The **Pro Loco** (☎ /fax 0742 78 11 50; www
.protrevi.com; Piazza Mazzini 5; ☒ 9am-1pm & 3.30-
7pm) is run entirely by volunteers, so be
warned you might find it closed sporadi-
cally. The easiest way to access Trevi is
by car or train. The town is on the main
Perugia–Assisi–Spoleto line.

❤ CENTRO STORICO // IDLE AWAY A FEW HOURS IN TREVI'S HISTORIC CENTRE

Trevi was a theatre town back in Roman
times. The **Teatro Clitunno** (☎ 0742 38 17
68; Piazza del Teatro) remains the town's most
important gathering point. Remnants of
concentric rings of a Mura Romana (Roman Wall) and a Mura Medievali (Medieval Wall) still encircle the historic centre
of the town. The **Museo della Civiltá dell'
Ulivo** (Olive Museum; ☎ 0742 33 22 22; ☒ 10.30am-
1pm & 3-6pm Tue-Sun summer, Fri-Mon winter) is a
must-see while in the area, as it details the
history of olive-oil production in Umbria
for millennia. For something a little more
contemporary, the **Flash Art Museum**
(☎ 0742 38 19 78; Palazzo Luncarini; free admission;
☒ 4-7pm Tue-Fri) has a funky collection of
multimedia modern art.

❤ LOCAL DINING // BE CHARMED BY THE LOCAL RESTAURANTS

Named after its location as the old post
office, **La Vecchia Posta** (☎ 0742 38 54 01,
rooms ☒ 333 392 47 37; www.lavecchiaposta.net;

Piazza Mazzini 14; s €35-50, d €50-70, ste €70-90) is a charming restaurant (meals €27, open Friday to Wednesday) with a few rooms to let. The *strangozzi* and truffles or chicken in *porcini* cream should satisfy just about any taste. The candied pear dessert with mint and chocolate sauce is legendary.

Maggiolini (☎ 0742 38 15 34; Via San Francesco 20; meals €26), a beautiful restaurant, is best in summer when you can dine alfresco on several reasonably priced truffle dishes and homemade pasta.

☙ TRAMPETTI OLIVE OIL // SAVOUR THE FAMOUS LOCAL OLIVE OIL

Does Trevi really have the best olive oil in Italy? Try some for yourself. Stop by **Trampetti** (☎ 0742 67 02 62; www.trampetti.it; Via delle Industri 25, San Eraclio di Foligno) for a full service tasting. The award-winning olive oil (available in gourmet stores in the United States) isn't the only thing on tap here: bruschetta, light meals and drinks in front of a toasty fire complete the scene. Just off the highway in the industrial zone between Foligno and Trevi, the shop is well worth the detour.

GUBBIO

· · · · · ·

pop 32,800

While most of Umbria feels soft and rounded, Gubbio is angular, sober and imposing. Perched along the steep slopes of Monte Ingino, the Gothic buildings wend their way up the hill towards Umbria's closest thing to an amusement park ride, its open-air funicular. During Christmastime, the side of the mountain becomes the world's largest Christmas tree.

Gubbio is famous for its Eugubine Tablets, which date from 300 to 100 BC and constitute the best existing example of ancient Umbrian script. An important ally of the Roman Empire and a key stop on the Via Flaminia, the town declined during the Saracen invasions. In the 14th century it fell into the hands of the Montefeltro family of Urbino and was later incorporated into the Papal States.

The city is small and easy to explore. The immense traffic circle known as the Piazza Quaranta Martiri, at the base of the hill, is where buses to the city terminate, and it also has a large car park. The square was named in honour of 40 local people who were killed by the Nazis in 1944 in reprisal for partisan activities.

ESSENTIAL INFORMATION

EMERGENCIES // Hospital (Ospedale Civile; ☎ 075 927 08 01; Località Branca) About 2km from the city centre. Police station (☎ 075 927 37 70; Via Mazzatinti)

TOURIST OFFICES // Tourist office (☎ 075 922 06 93; info@iat.gubbio.pg.it; www.gubbio-altochiascio.umbria2000.it; Via della Repubblica 2; 🕙 8am-2pm & 3-6pm Mon-Fri, 9am-1pm & 3-6pm Sat, 9.30am-12.30pm & 3-6pm Sun & holidays)

EXPLORING GUBBIO

Gubbio's most impressive buildings look out over Piazza Grande, where the heart of the Corsa dei Ceri (p286) takes place.

☙ PIAZZA GRANDE // SURROUND YOURSELF WITH GOTHIC BEAUTY

The piazza is dominated above all by the 14th-century **Palazzo dei Consoli**, attributed to Gattapone. The crenellated facade and tower can be seen from all

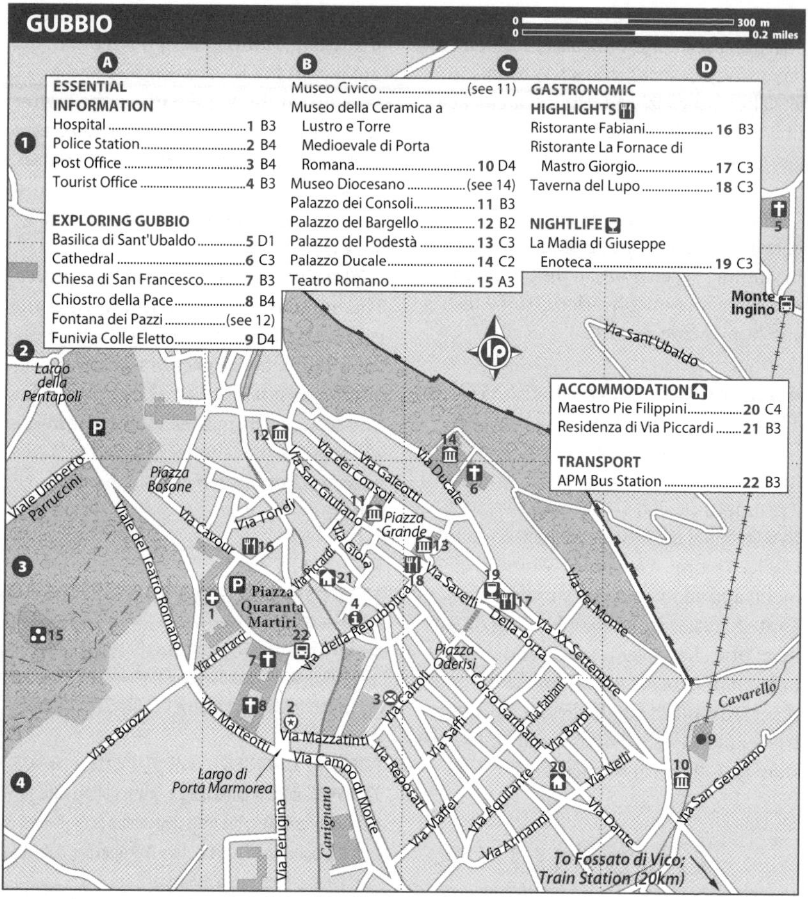
GUBBIO
0 300 m
0 0.2 miles
A
B
C
D
1
2
3
4
ESSENTIAL INFORMATION
Hospital 1 B3
Police Station 2 B4
Post Office 3 B4
Tourist Office 4 B3
EXPLORING GUBBIO
Basilica di Sant'Ubaldo 5 D1
Cathedral 6 C3
Chiesa di San Francesco 7 B3
Chiostro della Pace 8 B4
Fontana dei Pazzi (see 12)
Funivia Colle Eletto 9 D4
Museo Civico (see 11)
Museo della Ceramica a Lustro e Torre Medioevale di Porta Romana 10 D4
Museo Diocesano (see 14)
Palazzo dei Consoli 11 B3
Palazzo del Bargello 12 B2
Palazzo del Podestà 13 C3
Palazzo Ducale 14 C2
Teatro Romano 15 A3
GASTRONOMIC HIGHLIGHTS
Ristorante Fabiani 16 B3
Ristorante La Fornace di Mastro Giorgio 17 C3
Taverna del Lupo 18 C3
NIGHTLIFE
La Madia di Giuseppe Enoteca 19 C3
ACCOMMODATION
Maestro Pie Filippini 20 C4
Residenza di Via Piccardi 21 B3
TRANSPORT
APM Bus Station 22 B3
Monte Ingino
Via Sant'Ubaldo
Largo della Pentapoli
Piazza Bosone
Viale Umberto Parruccini
Viale del Teatro Romano
Via Cavour
Via Tondi
Via San Giuliano
Via dei Consoli
Via Galeotti
Via Ducale
Piazza Grande
Via Gioia
Via Piccardi
Via della Repubblica
Via Savelli
Della Porta
Via XX Settembre
Via del Monte
Piazza Quaranta Martiri
Via d'Ortacci
Piazza Oderisi
Via Cairoli
Corso Garibaldi
Via Fabiani
Via Barbi
Via Nelli
Via B Buozzi
Via Matteotti
Via Mazzatinti
Via Campo di Marte
Via Reposati
Via Saffi
Via Maffei
Via Aquilante
Via Armanni
Via Dante
Largo di Porta Marmorea
Via Perugina
Camignano
Cavarello
Via San Gerolamo
To Fossato di Vico; Train Station (20km)

over the town. The building houses the **Museo Civico** (☎ 075 927 42 98; Piazza Grande; adult/concession incl gallery €4/2.50; ⏲ 10am-1pm & 3-6pm Apr-Oct, 10am-1pm & 2-5pm Nov-Mar), which displays the Eugubian Tablets, discovered in 1444. The seven bronze tablets are the main source for research into the ancient Umbrian language. Upstairs is a picture gallery featuring works from the Gubbian school. Across the square is the **Palazzo del Podestà**, also known as the Palazzo Pretorio, built along similar lines to its grander counterpart. Now the city's active town hall, if you ask nicely, you might win a peek at the impressive vaulted ceilings.

FUNIVIA COLLE ELETTO // TAKE AN UNEXPECTED BIRDCAGE RIDE ABOVE GUBBIO

Although the **Basilica di Sant'Ubaldo** – where you'll find the body of St Ubaldo, the 12th-century bishop of Gubbio – is a perfectly lovely church, the adventure is in the getting there. Take the **Funivia Colle Eletto** (☎ 075 922 11 99; adult/child return €5/4; ⏲ 9am-8pm Jul & Aug, 9.30am or 10am-1.15pm & 2.30-5.30pm or 7pm Mar-Jun, Sep & Oct, 10am-

1.15pm & 2.30-5pm Thu-Tue Nov-Feb), where your first rule is to believe the man when he tells you to stand on the dot. He will then throw you into a moving metal contraption that looks frighteningly like an open-topped human birdcage. You're whisked instantly away on a cable car that looks more like a precarious ski lift, dangling dozens of metres above a rocky hill (bring a camera, but hold tight). The ride up can be as frightening as it is utterly beautiful. There's a restaurant on top of the hill and the aforementioned church, but the nicest way to spend the day is to bring a picnic and have a wander.

♥ CERAMIC MUSEUM & MEDIEVAL TOWER // IMAGINE A WORLD WITH CHASTITY BELTS AND CROSSBOWS

Just below the Funivia Colle Eletto is the **Museo della Ceramica a Lustro e Torre Medioevale di Porta Romana** (☎ 075 922 11 99; Via Dante 24; admission €2.50; ⏰ 10.30am-1pm & 3.30-7pm). The *a lustro* ceramic style has its origins in 11th-century Muslim Spain. On the museum's 2nd floor, ceramics from prehistoric times share space with medieval and Renaissance pieces. There's also a collection of crossbows from the 18th century, some of which have a target range as far as 50m. Check out the really un-fun-looking chastity belt on the 4th floor and appreciate the fact that you are alive today instead of 300 years ago.

♥ VIA FEDERICO DA MONTEFELTRO // EXPLORE GUBBIO'S ARCHITECTURAL HISTORY

Walk up Via Federico da Montefeltro (also called Via Ducale or Via della Cattedrale) to a trio of sights detailing Gubbio's past, from late medieval to early Renaissance. The 13th-century pink **cathedral** (Via Federico da Montefeltro; donations welcome) has a fine 12th-century stained-glass window and a fresco attributed to Bernardino Pinturicchio. Opposite, the 15th-century **Palazzo Ducale** (☎ 075 927 58 72; Via Federico da Montefeltro; adult/concession €2/1; ⏰ 9am-7.30pm Tue-Fri & Sun, to 10.30pm Sat) was built by the Duke of Montefeltro family as a scaled-down version of their grand palazzo in Urbino; its walls hide an impressive Renaissance courtyard. Next door is the **Museo Diocesano** (☎ 075 922 09 04; Via Federico da Montefeltro; adult/concession €5/2.50; ⏰ 10am-7pm Mon-Sat summer, to 6pm Mon-Sat winter, to 6pm Sun & holidays year-round), a winding homage to Gubbio's medieval history.

♥ CHIESA DI SAN FRANCESCO // CONTEMPLATE FRESCOS THROUGH ROSE-COLOURED WINDOWS

Perugia's Fra Bevignate is said to have designed the **Chiesa di San Francesco** (Piazza Quaranta Martiri; ⏰ 7.15am-noon & 3.30-7.30pm). It features impressive frescos by local artist Ottaviano Nelli. Built in a simple Gothic style in the 13th century, it has an impressive rose window. Wander into the **Chiostro della Pace** (Cloister of Peace) in the adjoining convent to view some ancient mosaics and stroll around the peaceful garden.

♥ PALAZZO DEL BARGELLO // WALK AROUND THE FOUNTAIN OF LUNATICS

In the western end of the medieval section is the 13th-century **Palazzo del Bargello**, the city's medieval police station and prison. In front of it is the **Fontana dei Pazzi** (Fountain of Lunatics), so-named because of a belief that if you walk around it three times, you will go mad. On summer weekends the number of tourists actually carrying out this bizarre ritual is indeed cause for concern about their collective sanity.

♥ TEATRO ROMANO // LISTEN TO TUNES, ROMAN STYLE
Southwest of Piazza Quaranta Martiri, off Viale del Teatro Romano, are the overgrown remains of a 1st-century-AD **Roman Theatre** (☎ 075 922 09 22; admission free; 🕑 8.30am-7.30pm Apr-Sep, 8am-1.30pm Oct-Mar). In the summer, check with the tourist office about outdoor concerts held here.

FESTIVALS & EVENTS

Gubbio is host to some colourful festivals:

Corsa dei Ceri (Candles Race) A centuries-old event held annually on 15 May to commemorate the city's patron saint, Sant'Ubaldo. It starts at 5.30am and involves three teams, each carrying a *cero* (these 'candles' are massive wooden pillars weighing about 400kg, each bearing a statue of a 'rival' saint) and racing through Gubbio's streets. This is one of Italy's liveliest festivals and has put Gubbio on the map.

Palio della Balestra Held on the last Sunday in May, this annual archery competition involves medieval crossbows, in which Gubbio competes with its neighbour Sansepolcro. The festival continues all through the year in tourist shops, which are alive with crossbow paraphernalia.

GASTRONOMIC HIGHLIGHTS

♥ RISTORANTE FABIANI €€
☎ 075 927 46 39; Piazza Quaranta Martiri 26; meals €28; 🕑 Wed-Mon
A fabulous spot to sit on the back patio and enjoy the garden for a few hours. The selection here is vast, and it offers a rotating €15 tourist menu or a €20 *menù gastronomico* of whatever is in season. Stop in on Thursday or Friday for its fish specials.

♥ RISTORANTE LA FORNACE DI MASTRO GIORGIO €€€
☎ 075 922 18 36; Via Mastro Giorgio 2; meals €46; 🕑 Wed-Mon
Named after Gubbio's most famous medieval ceramicist (whose oven still graces one of the restaurant's ancient walls), Mastro Giorgio is our favourite place for a special occasion (and not just for the 500-item wine list). The seasonal menu includes modern takes on traditional dishes: venison carpaccio wrapped with salt, olive oil and asparagus, and its signature dish, a *stinco* (veal shank) stewed to falling-off-the-bone perfection.

♥ TAVERNA DEL LUPO €€€
☎ 075 927 43 68; Via Ansidei 21; meals €42; 🕑 Tue-Sun
Il Lupo was the wolf that St Francis domesticated; a wolf that supposedly came back to this restaurant to dine. He made an excellent choice. The atmosphere is sophisticated, if a bit stiff, and diners will feel more comfortable if smartly dressed. Most ingredients are locally produced in the surrounding Apennines, including its cheese, truffles and olive oil. Set aside at least two hours for a meal.

NIGHTLIFE

♥ LA MADIA DI GIUSEPPE ENOTECA
☎ 075 922 18 36; Via Mastro Giorgio 2; 🕑 10am-midnight Thu-Mon, Wed dinner
Fairly new on the scene in Gubbio is this stone-walled *enoteca*, one of the rare locations in Umbria where guests can sample several different glasses of wine. But it is not just for drinking – beautiful plates of nibbles (€5 to €14) such as prosciutto and cheeses, bruschetta and sweets grace the cafe tables. What's

more: it sells a selection of local goods for you to take away and enjoy.

TRANSPORT

BUS // APM Perugia (☎ 800 51 21 41; apm perugia.it) has buses to Perugia (€4.40, 70 minutes, 10 daily). Buses depart from Piazza Quaranta Martiri.

CAR & MOTORCYCLE // Take the SS298 from Perugia or the SS76 from Ancona and follow the signs.

PARKING // Parking in the large car park in Piazza Quaranta Martiri costs €0.80 per hour.

CITTÀ DI CASTELLO

· · · · · ·

pop 40,100

Most travellers to Umbria don't make it too far north of Perugia, but those who do will be rewarded with the area nicknamed 'Museum Valley', thanks to its extraordinary collection of art and history. The area surrounds the Tiber river, so is known as the Alta Valle del Tevere, and the history is laid on thick, especially in the largest and most central town of Città di Castello.

The town is surrounded by some pretty awful suburbs, but if you can look past this, it has a beautiful historic centre, many grand buildings and the second-most important art museum in Umbria, after the Galleria Nazionale dell'Umbria (p259) in Perugia.

Note: don't come to Città di Castello on a Monday. Most museums are closed, as are many restaurants.

Known as Tifernum Tiberium in the Roman era, Castrum Felicitatis (Town of Happiness) in the medieval period and Città di Castello today, it actually has neither a castle nor is it a city. The town was

economically depressed until the 1960s, but is now known for its thriving paper, book, ironworks and furniture industries. The town's favourite son is artist Alberto Burri, and two galleries proudly display much of his lifetime's work. The town's current favourite daughter is well-known actress Monica Bellucci.

The entire town, including its historic centre, is within a valley, so it's almost all on flat ground and easily walkable (a rarity in Umbrian towns).

ESSENTIAL INFORMATION

EMERGENCY // Hospital (☎ 075 8 50 91; Via Angelini) Police station (☎ 075 852 92 22; Piazza Garibaldi)

TOURIST OFFICES // Tourist Office (☎ 075 855 49 22; info@iat.citta-di -castello.pg.it; Logge Bufalini, Piazza Matteotti; ☾ 9am-1.30pm & 3.30-6.30pm Mon-Sat, 9.30am-12.30pm Sun)

ORIENTATION

From the train station, walk straight ahead for 200m. Turn right under Porta Santa Maria Maggiore and take Corso Vittorio Emanuele to Piazza Matteotti. Driving is mostly forbidden in the walled city, but there's plenty of free parking just outside the walls, mostly around Porta San Giacomo and Piazza Garibaldi.

EXPLORING CITTÀ DI CASTELLO

❧ PINACOTECA COMUNALE // GET ACQUAINTED WITH UMBRIA'S SECOND-BEST ART COLLECTION
The collection at the **Pinacoteca Comunale** (☎ 075 855 42 02; Via della Cannoniera 22; adult/child €6/4; ☾ 10am-1pm & 2.30-6.30pm daily Apr-Oct, 10am-1pm & 3-6pm Tue-Sun Nov-Mar), in the imposing 15th-century **Palazzo**

Vitelli alla Cannoniera, is filled with paintings from the masters who lived here when Città di Castello was the second-most important artistic centre in Umbria, behind Perugia. Luca Signorelli painted his *Martyrdom of Saint Sebastian* here in 1498. Raphael also painted

in Città; two of his works still stand in the *pinacoteca*. Ask for the information booklet in English, which will guide you through the paintings, giving explanations and context to the more prominent works. A cool astrological fresco cycle graces the staircase, with depictions

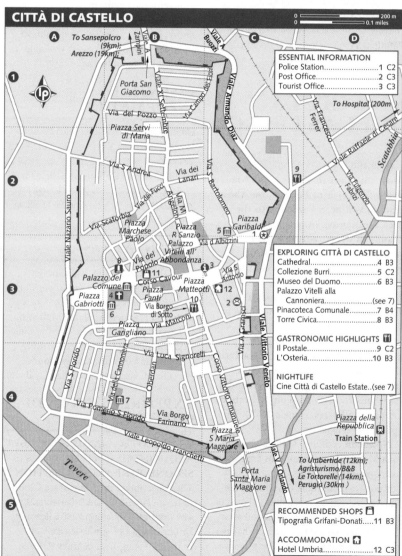

CITTÀ DI CASTELLO

To Sansepolcro (9km); Arezzo (19km)

Porta San Giacomo

Via del Pozzo

Piazza Servi di Maria

Via S Andrea

Via dei Lanari

Via Scatorbia

Piazza Marchese Paolo

Piazza R Sanzio

Palazzo Vitelli all' Abbondanza

Via d'Albizzini

Piazza Garibaldi

Palazzo del Comune

Corso Cavour

Piazza Fanti

Piazza Matteotti

Via S Antonio

Piazza Gabriotti

Via Borgo di Sotto

Via Marconi

Piazza Gangliano

Via Luca Signorelli

Via Oberdan

Via Pomerio S Florido

Via Borgo Farinano

Piazza S Maria Maggiore

Viale Leopoldo Franchetti

Tevere

Porta Santa Maria Maggiore

To Hospital (200m)

To Umbertide (12km); Agriturismo/B&B Le Tortorelle (14km); Perugia (30km)

Piazza della Repubblica

Train Station

ESSENTIAL INFORMATION
Police Station........................1   C2
Post Office............................2   C3
Tourist Office.........................3   C3

EXPLORING CITTÀ DI CASTELLO
Cathedral.............................4   B3
Collezione Burri....................5   C2
Museo del Duomo................6   B3
Palazzo Vitelli alla
  Cannoniera.....................(see 7)
Pinacoteca Comunale...........7   B4
Torre Civica...........................8   B3

GASTRONOMIC HIGHLIGHTS
Il Postale...............................9   C2
L'Osteria..............................10   B3

NIGHTLIFE
Cine Città di Castello Estate..(see 7)

RECOMMENDED SHOPS
Tipografia Grifani-Donati.....11   B3

ACCOMMODATION
Hotel Umbria......................12   C3

NORTHERN UMBRIA

of Apollo and the muses, erudites and emperors, sea horses and winged cherubs. The halls include wall frescos from Cristoforo Gherardi, depicting historical subjects, such as Hannibal, Caesar and Alexander the Great.

❧ COLLEZIONE BURRI // SEE ONE OF ITALY'S MOST POPULAR MODERN ARTISTS

The artist Alberto Burri began his art career in 1946 after a stint as a prisoner of war in Texas. His contemporary work with paint and physical materials has been immensely popular throughout the world. His early work influenced the New Dada and Pop Art movements, and artists such as Rauschenberg, Christo and Jasper Johns credit him as an inspiration. The **main collection** (☎ 075 855 46 49; Palazzo Albizzini, Via Albizzini 1, secondary exhibit at Ex Seccatoi del Tabacco, Via Pierucci; adult/child €6/4; ☺ 9am-12.30pm & 2.30-6pm Tue-Sat, 10.30am-12.30pm & 3-6pm Sun & holidays) is definitely worth seeing. A secondary exhibit of mostly larger pieces is housed in an old tobacco-drying warehouse – a site in itself – and is closed from November to March, except by special requests made three days in advance.

❧ CATHEDRAL // VIEW LIFE IN PALEO-CHRISTIAN DAYS

Not much remains of the original Romanesque **cathedral**, but the building houses some treasures. **Museo del Duomo** (☎ 075 855 47 05; Piazza Gabriotti 3/a; adult/child €6/4; ☺ 10am-1pm & 3-6.30pm Tue-Sun) holds an impressive collection of sacred artefacts dating back to Paleo-Christian times (the 6th century AD). Attached, take a look at the statuesque **Torre Civica** (Piazza Gabriotti), the city's bell tower that dates back to medieval times, which is temporarily closed for renovation.

❧ MOSTRA MERCATO TARTUFO E PRODOTTI DEL BOSCO // ATTEND ONE OF UMBRIA'S LARGEST TRUFFLE TRADE SHOWS

During the first week in November, the town plays host to this festival dedicated to the area's ubiquitous white truffle. Farmers and growers bring every type of truffle product that is imaginable to this epicurean trade show, as well as honey, mushrooms and many other local delicacies available for sampling.

GASTRONOMIC HIGHLIGHTS

❧ IL POSTALE €€€

☎ 075 852 13 56; Via Raffaele di Cesare 8; 3-course menu €65; ☺ lunch & dinner Tue-Fri & Sun, dinner Sat
If there's such a thing as nouvelle Umbrian cuisine, this is the place to try it. Over several courses, the husband and wife team at Il Postale serves dishes such as duck with fennel compote, or carp with hazelnuts. House specialities include its lentil dishes and, of course, truffles.

❧ L'OSTERIA €

☎ 075 855 69 95; Via Borgo di Sotto; meals €21
Nothing fancy, but good typical Umbrian food. Locals know to come here on Friday, when fish specialities dominate the daily chalkboard menu. Try the asparagus when it's in season (late spring to early summer).

NIGHTLIFE

❧ CINE CITTÀ DI CASTELLO ESTATE

☎ 075 852 92 49; adult/child €5/4
During the summer, the *pinacoteca*'s lawn is the perfect place to take in some open-air cinema. All genres of movies are shown – from *Harry Potter* to art-

DRIVING UMBRIA

With a few basic hints, getting around Umbria can be a stress-free experience.

★ **Driving** Driving in Umbria is relatively easy for an Italian region. Major highways run north to south on either side of the region, but traversing east to west might take quite a bit longer. However, it's these secondary roads where Umbria shines. Sure, it might take you two hours to drive 50km, but you're guaranteed untold fields of wildflowers, stone farmhouses and maybe even a castle or two. Here are a few clues: if you see the words Torre (tower), Castel (castle) or Fiore (flower) in a town name, take off and check it out. (However, this rule doesn't work in reverse: Bastardo, Pornello and Schitto are all perfectly lovely towns.)

★ **Parking** Most towns in Umbria – especially walled or hill towns – have exterior car parks, as city centre parking is often mostly reserved for residents. Paid spots for visitors are always marked in blue (free parking spots have no lines and white is usually for residents). An automatic pay machine nearby will dispense tickets (be sure to keep a stack of euros in your car), which you can slot in the affixed plastic sleeve on the dashboard reserved for this purpose.

house Italian films. Movies are usually screened on Fridays and Saturdays at 9.15pm from July through to the end of August.

RECOMMENDED SHOPS

❦ RETRO ANTIQUES & OLD THINGS MARKET

Piazza Matteoti; 3rd weekend every month

The town hosts this market in central Piazza Matteotti. It's not as big as the one in Perugia, but it's still a great place to get a hands-on history lesson (and to purchase unique gifts not found anywhere else).

❦ TIPOGRAFIA GRIFANI-DONATI

☎ 075 855 43 49; Corso Cavour 4; 8.30am-12.30pm & 3-7pm Mon-Sat

Città di Castello has been known for its paper-making prowess since the 1400s, and this shop (and museum) has been open since 1799. Hundreds of years of printmaking supplies are on display, and you can also buy modern handmade paper or books.

TRANSPORT

TRAIN // The Ferrovia Centrale Umbra railway connects Città di Castello with Perugia (€3.05, 70 minutes, 16 daily) and onto Todi.

CAR & MOTORCYCLE // Città di Castello is just east of the E45.

LAGO TRASIMENO

· · · · · ·

It would have been easy for drop-dead gorgeous Lago Trasimeno to become a holiday haven for busloads of Northern European sunseekers, à la the coast of Le Marche. Granted, you'll find plenty of such folks during the summer months, but the bulk of the area – outside Passignano and a strip leaving San Feliciano – has thankfully eschewed the Stalinist high-rise mono-architecture of such Adriatic holiday villages. *Agriturismi* cover the hills like sunflowers, historic

Castiglione del Lago folds travellers in gently to allow room for all and everyone respects the delicate ecology of the precious lake.

Outside of overcrowded August, relaxed visitors enjoy the water sports, local cuisine, never-ending walking trails and Umbria's best hostel, located on its own (almost) private island.

The region known as Lago Trasimeno is made up of eight different *comuni* (municipalities): Castiglione del Lago, Città della Pieve, Magione, Paciano, Panicale, Passignano, Piegaro and Tuoro. Castiglione del Lago and Panicale are the most pleasant places in which to spend a day or two, while Città della Pieve is a further drive but chock-full of artwork for the connoisseur.

Popular activities at the lake include hiking, wine tasting, camping, water sports and *dolce far niente* (the sweet enjoyment of doing nothing). Many also go for the culinary delights. The locals are very proud of their excellent produce, most notably their high-quality DOC (Denominazione di Origine Controllata) wines and DOP (Denominazione d'Origine Protetta, or Protected Denomination of Origin) olive oils. See the boxed texts Lakeside Activities (below) and Markets & Food Tours (p292) for details.

ESSENTIAL INFORMATION

TOURIST OFFICES // Castiglione del Lago Tourist office (☎ 075 965 24 84; www.castiglionedellago.it; Piazza Mazzini 10, Castiglione del Lago; ☼ 8.30am-1pm & 3.30-7pm Mon-Sat & 9am-1pm Sun) The most comprehensive tourist office in the region, it will help make hotel and *agriturismi* reservations, and offers a host of maps and advice on walking and biking trails and water sports. Panicale (☎ 075 837 80 17; www.lagodarte.com; Piazza Umberto I; ☼ 10am-12.30pm & 3.30-7.30pm Easter-Oct, closed Sun winter)

NORTHERN UMBRIA

LAKESIDE ACTIVITIES

Tourist offices can provide you with fold-out maps, such as *Le Mappe di Airone per il Trekking* or *Le Mappe di Airone per il Cicloturismo*. The walking guide has 13 maps and the *cicloturismo* (cycle tourism) guide has six maps. The *Kompas Lago Trasimeno* map (€6.95) is extremely thorough for both sightseers and walkers.

Do as the locals do and head out for a day of **fishing** (☎ 075 847 60 05; www.albaTrasimeno.it, in Italian; Via Alicata 19, San Feliciano; fishing per person €55) – for eel, trout, perch, tench and carp – on the lake. Two people at a time can join locals for a four-hour angling or early-morning fishing trip. After reeling in your catches at dawn, the fisherman can guide you to restaurants that will cook up your fish using traditional recipes. Book at least one day in advance. Nature trips (for up to 10 people, €90) are also available.

Ask at one of the tourist offices for a booklet of walking and horse-riding tracks. Horse-riding centres include the **Maneggio Oasi** (☎ 0337 65 37 95; Località Orto, Castiglione del Lago) and **Poggio del Belveduto** (☎ 075 82 90 76; www.poggiodelbelveduto.it; Via San Donato 65, Località Campori di Sopra, Passignano), which also offers archery courses if you're feeling particularly medieval.

Canoe, windsurfing and sailboat rentals can be found in Castiglione del Lago at **La Merangola** (☎ 075 965 24 45; Località Lido Arezzo) or in Tuoro at **Belneazione Tuoro** (☎ 328 454 97 66; Località Punta Navaccia). La Merangola also has a small beach and restaurant, and turns into a *discoteca* at night.

Offers tours of the town's major sites at 10.10am, 11.30am, 3.40pm, 5pm and 6.10pm in summer. **Passignano** (☎ 075 829 62 11; Piazza Trento e Trieste 6, Passignano; ⏰ 10.30am-12.30pm & 4-7pm Mon-Sat, 10.30am-12.30pm Sun)

EXPLORING LAGO TRASIMENO

♥ PANICALE // BROWSE DAINTY LACE OR MARVEL AT PERUGINO'S ARTWORK

Perched on a hill with an expansive view of the lake, the entire town of Panicale is one giant fortress. In the **Chiesa di San Sebastiano** is Perugino's *Martyrdom of St Sebastian*, painted by the master in 1505. In the background of the painting is a landscape of the lake as it looked in Perugino's day. If you look closely, especially at the bottom of the painting, you'll see what's known as the *tratteggio* restoration technique, where artists create tiny vertical brushstrokes to fill in damaged artwork. The result is seamless from far away but art historians can tell what is original and what has been restored. In 2005 art historians discovered another fresco in the church, *Madonna in Trono con Angeli Musicanti,* which they have attributed to Raphael.

Craft fans will appreciate the **Museo del Tulle** (Lace Museum; ☎ 075 83 78 07; Chiesa Sant'Agostino; ⏰ 10am-12.30pm & 4.30-7pm Jun-Sep, Fri-Sun winter & by appt), with examples of traditional lace and tulle from the area, housed in a deconsecrated frescoed church.

The **Museo della Chiesa della Sbarra** (admission €2; ⏰ 9am-12.30pm & 3-5.30pm), in the church of the same name, offers an up-close view of church vestments, statues and altar regalia from the past five centuries. Of particularly creepy note are the relic boxes filled with the bones of saints. Entry here is payable at the lace museum.

The **Teatro Cesare Caporali** is an 18th-century theatre, beautifully designed, which has concerts all year long. During the summer, the Musica Insieme Panicale runs a series of concerts from July until September, in addition to the Mosaico Sonoro free concert every Thursday in the main square at 9pm.

♥ CASTIGLIONE DEL LAGO // STROLL TRASIMENO'S QUINTESSENTIAL VILLAGE

Castiglione del Lago's history dates back to an Etruscan settlement and is now a popular (but not overwhelmingly so)

MARKETS & FOOD TOURS

For a fun cultural and gastronomic experience, don't miss the **weekly markets**, which have all sorts of fresh local produce and basic goods. They take place from 8.30am to 1pm at the following locations: Castiglione del Lago (Wednesday), Magione (Thursday), Tuoro (Friday) and Passignano (Saturday). Ask at each town's tourist office for more information.

If you are interested in following the Strada del Vino of the Colli del Trasimeno (Trasimeno Hill district), the **Associazione Strada del Vino Colli del Trasimeno** (☎ 075 58 29 41; www.montitrasimeno.umbria.it, in Italian) produces a brochure with suggested itineraries. It lists open cellars, which means you can stop by and try wine, but you almost always need to call ahead. You can also pick up this brochure at the tourist office in Castiglione del Lago. Look out, too, for the guide to local restaurants, *Trasimeno a Tavola,* which includes sample menus and price guides in English, also available from the tourist office.

tourist destination. In the 7th century, the town became an important defensive promontory for Byzantine Perugia. It was fought over and traded between the papacy, the emperor and various territories for about 1000 years.

An ancient ducal palace, **Palazzo della Corgna** (☎ 075 965 82 10; Piazza Gramsci; admission incl Rocca del Leone adult/concession €3/2; ⏰ 10am-1pm & 4-7.30pm Mar-Oct, 9.30am-4.30pm Sat & Sun Nov-Feb) houses an important series of 16th-century frescos by Giovanni Antonio Pandolfi and Salvio Savini. It was built in the 16th century by Jacopo Barozzi, who incorporated parts of ancient houses once owned by the feudal Baglioni family from Perugia.

A covered passageway connects the palace with the 13th-century **Rocca del Leone** (Fortress of the Lion), a pentagon-shaped fortress built in 1247 and an excellent example of medieval military architecture. Seen from the lake, rearing up on a rocky promontory, it cuts a striking pose.

♥ ISOLA POLVESE // TRADE CROWDS FOR SOLITUDE ON YOUR PRIVATE ECO-ISLAND

There's not much to do in Isola Polvese, which, to those who seek out its tranquillity, is its charm. The main attraction is that the entire island is a scientific and educational park. Many school groups come here to use the environmental labs that are devoted to teaching preservation of biodiversity and sustainable technologies. Make sure you visit the **Garden of Aquatic Plants** to see biodiversity at work. Also of interest are the **Monastery of San Secondo** and the **Church of St Julian**. There are also remains of a 14th-century castle. The only inhabited building is the **Fattoria Il Poggio** (see p413).

♥ CITTÀ DELLA PIEVE // VISIT PERUGINO'S BIRTHPLACE FOR IN SITU ART

Città della Pieve is culturally and geographically considered part of Lago Trasimeno, but it's about 20km to the south. Although he became known as 'Il Perugino' (the Perugian), the famous Renaissance painter Pietro Vannucci was born here in 1445 and his paintings are all over the town. Buy a 'museum circuit' ticket at the tourist office or one of the museums listed below for €4.

The **Cattedrale di San Gervasio e Protasio** houses Perugino works and was developed from the ancient baptismal church (known as a *pieve*). Perhaps Perugino's most famous work in his hometown is *Adoration of the Magi,* on view at the **Oratory of Santa Maria dei Bianchi** (admission €2; ⏰ 9.30am-12.30pm & 4-7.30pm Mar-Oct, 10am-12.30pm & 3.30-6pm Nov-Feb).

The head of the della Corgna family was appointed as governor of the town by his uncle, Pope Julius III, and subsequently commissioned artists to paint works for the town, known then as Castel della Pieve (it was elevated to a city in 1600). The frescos located in the statuesque **Palazzo della Corgna** (☎ 0578 29 81 85; Piazza Antonio Gramsci 1; admission €2) include ones by Il Pomarancio and Salvio Savini. It is now a library that is open to the public, so feel free to step inside and have a wander around.

♥ ISOLA MAGGIORE // RIDE THE FERRY TO A FESTIVE ISLAND

The lake's main inhabited island, Isola Maggiore, near Passignano, was reputedly a favourite with St Francis. The hill-top **Chiesa di San Michele Arcangelo** contains a Crucifixion by master painter Bartolomeo Caporali. The island is famed for its lace and embroidery production and you can see examples in the **Museo del Merlotto** (Lace Museum; ☎ 075 825 42 33; Via Gugliemi, Isola Maggiore; admission €3; ☺ 10am-1pm & 2.30-6pm), near the port.

♥ SAN FELICIANO // DROP IN ON YOUR WAY TO ISOLA POLVESE

This working town still sees fishermen leave to trawl for fish in the morning. It now hosts many a Northern European on holiday, and its…ahem, 'quaint' **Fishing Museum** (☎ 075 847 92 61; museodellapesca @tiscali.it; Via Lungolago della Pace e del Lavoro 20; adult/child/concession €3/1/2; ☺ 10.30am-1pm & 4-9pm daily Jul & Aug, 10am-12.30pm & 3-6pm Tue-Sun Apr-Jun & Sep, 10.30am-12.30pm & 2.30-5.30pm Thu-Sun Feb, Mar & Oct, 10.30am-1pm & 2.30-5pm Sat & Sun Nov-Jan), worth a quick look if killing time waiting for the ferry to Isola Polvese.

♥ PASSIGNANO // PICK UP SOUVENIRS IN TRASIMENO'S HOLIDAY HEADQUARTERS

Passignano is the most holiday-ish of the Trasimeno towns, with many restaurants, hotels, gelato joints and souvenir shops. The medieval castle on the top of the hill is closed to visitors, but the view from in front of it is as good as it gets. Check out the 16th-century **Chiesa della Madonna dell'Uliveto** (☎ 075 82 71 24; ☺ 5-7pm Wed & Thu, 4-8pm Fri & Sat, 10am-noon & 5-7pm Sun) on the road to Tuoro. Inside, the sanctuary features a *Madonna* by Bartolomeo Caporali and a decorated holy-water trough. A must-see for anyone stopping here on the last Sunday of July is the **Palio delle Barche** (Boat Race), when groups of neighbourhood men carry a heavy boat to the castle on the top of the hill.

♥ TUORO // FOLLOW IN THE FOOTSTEPS OF HANNIBAL

The only reason to visit Tuoro, otherwise a rather sleepy residential area with a handful of decent hidden *agriturismi* in the surrounding hills, is to take a drive through the grounds of the Battle of Trasimeno (see below). Stop off at the **Tuoro tourist office** (City Library ☎ 075 82 52 20; ☺ 9am-noon & 4-7pm Mon-Fri, 9am to noon Sat 12 Jun-12 Sep) to check out the permanent exhibition before heading out around town. There is an archaeological connect-the-dots walking or driving tour of the battle-field, signposted by 12 numbered stops, describing the events that took place 2300 years ago.

Also visit **Field of the Sun** (Campo del Sole), a group of 27 contemporary sand sculptures made by celebrated artists and looking like a modern-day Stonehenge.

HANNIBAL V ROMANS

During the second Punic War between Rome and Carthage, Lago Trasimeno was the site of one of the deadliest battles in all of Roman history. Roman troops led by Consul Caius Flaminius were set up around the area that is now Tuoro. Quite the wartime strategist, Carthaginian general Hannibal made it look as though he was just passing by on his way to Rome, as nonchalantly as one can with 50,000 troops, 9000 horses and 37 elephants. Hannibal's men even lit a series of torches far from the lake, leading Flaminius' forces to believe the Carthaginians were too far away to be a threat. Under the cover of the lake's typical misty morning, Hannibal staged such a rapid ambush that the Romans hardly had time to suit up, with over three-fifths of Flaminius' 25,000-strong army killed. A local stream ran with the blood of Flaminius and his soldiers for three straight days, earning the new name Sanguineto (the bloody).

You will find it near Località Navaccia Lido, close to the lake's edge.

♥ MAGIONE // STOP ON YOUR WAY IN OR OUT OF TOWN

You may end up here if you suddenly realise that you need a heap of groceries or a mosaic table. It's the commercial centre of the lake and, as such, not terribly interesting. However, the train stops here and it does have a fascinating castle. Originally constructed between 1160 and 1170, the Templars used Magione's fortified abbey as a hospital for crusaders going back and forth to fight in the crusades in Jerusalem. The Knights of Malta took the abbey from the Templars and still own it to this day. You can drive up to the **Castle of the Knights of Malta** (☎ 075 84 38 59; admission free), which is open in summer only.

FESTIVALS & EVENTS

Lago Trasimeno hosts countless events throughout the year.

Art & Culture festival In Città della Pieve over the first weekend in June.

Palio delle Barche Passignano's annual boat race of a different sort; see opposite. Held on the last Sunday in July.

Palio dei Terzieri This showcases the town's Renaissance past with some serious revelry, including acrobatics, fire-eating and archery. Held in mid-August.

GASTRONOMIC HIGHLIGHTS

The main specialities of the Trasimeno area are *fagiolina* (little white beans), olive oil and wine. In addition, you'll find many fish dishes, such as carp *in porchetta* (cooked in a wood oven with garlic, fennel and herbs) and *tegamaccio*, a kind of soupy stew of the best varieties of local fish, cooked in olive oil, white wine and herbs.

♥ DA SETTIMIO SAN FELICIANO €€

☎ 075 847 60 00; Via Lungolago Alicata, San Feliciano; meals €28; ⏰ Fri-Wed Jan-Oct

If you stay on Isola Polvese, you'll most likely pass by this restaurant near the ferry terminal in San Feliciano. It doesn't look like much, but locals know it as the best fish restaurant in the area, handed down from father to son for four generations. Try the *risotto alla pescatora* (fisherman's risotto) or the appetiser of 'fried little fishies'.

♥ IL LIDO SOLITARIO CASTIGLIONE DEL LAGO €€

☎ 075 95 18 91; Via Lungolago 16, Castiglione del Lago; meals €28

It isn't often we recommend a heavily trafficked waterfront restaurant with the bright plastic signs, but it isn't often you get to try a delicate fish cake topped with sweet Castelluccian lentils or a tender Chianina beef infused with Sagrantino wine. Grab a front veranda table overlooking the nearby lake for a true summer experience.

♥ LA CANTINA CASTIGLIONE DEL LAGO €

☎ 075 965 24 32; Via Emanuele 93, Castiglione del Lago; meals €22; ⏰ Tue-Sun

Not only is this well-priced restaurant fabulous – a stately interior with a lovely outdoor terrace for summer dining – but there's also an adjacent *magazzino* (shop) where you can sample and buy the area's best wine, olive oil and treats. Try the delicious trout with local *fagiolina* (€9).

♥ L'ACQUARIO CASTIGLIONE DEL LAGO €€

☎ 075 965 24 32; Via Vittoria Emanuele 69, Castiglione del Lago; meals €29; ⏰ Thu-Tue

This rather refined restaurant is a great place to try out the local carp *in porchetta* fresh from the lake or have an

NORTHERN UMBRIA

appetiser of eel *in tegamaccio*. The fish
dishes are, of course, remarkable, but
truffles, fresh herbs and homemade wine
also feature strongly.

❤ LA LOCANDA DI GULLIVER PETRIGNANO €€

☎ 075 952 82 28; Vocabulo I Cucchi, Petrignano;
meals €27

Even if the food wasn't absolutely fantastic (which it is), the drive out here would
be reason enough to stop in. Housed in
an old brick farmhouse near sunflower-
draped fields of yellow, the inventive
menu features gems like *cinghiale* (wild
boar) bruschetta with local olive oil, eel
and yellow pumpkin risotto, and tagliatelle with local smoked lake fish. Did we
mention the homemade pizzas, hot out
of the brick oven?

NIGHTLIFE

❤ TRATTORIA/HOTEL IL FALIERO (DA MARIA)

☎ 075 847 63 41; www.hotelfaliero.it; Località Monte-
buono di Magione; meals €12; ⏱ to midnight in season

Dine, dance and sleep it off at Lago
Trasimeno's most famous institution.
For Umbrians, a trip to the lake simply
isn't complete without a visit to this
temple of folk dancing, camaraderie and
the famous Umbrian sandwich, *torta
al testo*. Known as 'Da Maria' after the
owner, Il Faliero is hopping on most
summer weekends with dancers, but the
casual, counter-service restaurant has
garnered just as much fame. In a pinch,
13 business-casual hotel rooms (around
€65) are far enough from the noise for a
good night's sleep.

TRANSPORT

CAR // Two major highways skirt the lake: the SS71
heads from Chiusi to Arezzo on the west side (in Tuscany)
and the SS75bis crosses the north end of the lake, heading from the A1 in Tuscany to Perugia.

BICYCLE // Hire bikes from **Cicli Valentini**
(☎/fax 075 95 16 63; Via Firenze 68b, Castiglione del
Lago) and **Marinelli Ferrettini Fabio** (☎/fax
075 95 31 26; Via B Buozzi 26, Castiglione del Lago);
most camping grounds have bikes.

BUS // APM (☎ 800 51 21 41; www.apmperugia.it)
buses connect Perugia with Passignano (€3, 70 minutes,
nine daily) and Castiglione del Lago (€4.60, 1¼ hours,
nine daily).

FERRY // APM (ampperugia.it) operates ferry
services. Offices (with timetables) are on the waterfront
at each town. From approximately Easter until the end
of September, hourly ferries head from San Feliciano to
Isola Polvese (€3.30, 20 minutes), Tuoro to Isola Maggiore (€3.30, 20 minutes) and Passignano or Castiglione
del Lago to Isola Maggiore (€3.90, 30 minutes). Ferries
stop running at 7pm.

TRAIN // The main hub near the lake is Terontola in
Tuscany; trains originating in Umbria often stop there
first. Trains run about every hour from Perugia to Magione (€2.05, 20 minutes), Tuoro (€2.95, 40 minutes),
Passignano (€2.65, 35 minutes), Castiglione del Lago
(€3.45, change at Terontola) and Torricella (€2.05 to
€3.55, change at Tuoro).

SOUTHERN UMBRIA

3 PERFECT DAYS

❦ DAY 1 // TRUFFLES & WILDFLOWERS

Start in Norcia (p320), the regional seat of all things deliciously Umbrian. Wander through shops filled with ubiquitous stuffed boar heads to buy provisions for the next day's drive – *cinghiale* (wild boar) salami, *pecorino* cheese, Sagrantino wine. Take a three-hour lunch detour at Ristorante Vespasia (p321) before heading to the Piano Grande (p322) with a good pair of hiking boots. In May and June, no less than 17 gazillion wildflowers surround ancient Castelluccio (it's beautiful year-round, backed by snowcapped mountains). End the day at San Pietro in Valle's abbey-cum-hotel and restaurant (p325).

❦ DAY 2 // ETHEREAL UMBRIA

The morning starts with a contemplative breakfast in the garden of San Pietro in Valle. Give yourself sufficient time to digest before visiting the murderously creepy Museo delle Mummie (p323) before winding up at Cascata delle Marmore around 3pm, when the Roman waterfalls 'open'. Spend the evening dining and strolling in the rarely visited hamlet of Narni (p325), the historic town of Spoleto (p314) or the art mecca of Todi (p310).

❦ DAY 3 // HISTORY, ART & GOD

Spend the morning visiting La Rocca Albornoz in Narni (p328), the archaeological museum in Spoleto (p315), or the shops of Todi (p313) before making the scenic trek to Umbria Grill (p309) for wine tasting, a cooking course or a meal. Just be sure to make it to Orvieto (p302) to witness the cathedral's golden facade during sunset.

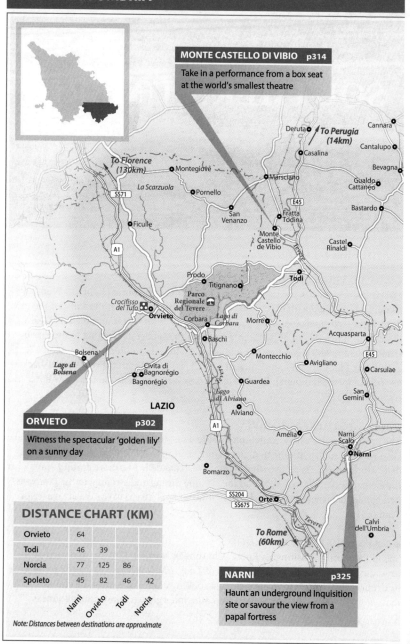

SOUTHERN UMBRIA

MONTE CASTELLO DI VIBIO   p314

Take in a performance from a box seat at the world's smallest theatre

To Perugia (14km)

To Florence (130km)

ORVIETO   p302

Witness the spectacular 'golden lily' on a sunny day

LAZIO

To Rome (60km)

NARNI   p325

Haunt an underground Inquisition site or savour the view from a papal fortress

DISTANCE CHART (KM)

	Narni	Orvieto	Todi	Norcia
Orvieto	64			
Todi	46	39		
Norcia	77	125	86	
Spoleto	45	82	46	42

Note: Distances between destinations are approximate

SOUTHERN UMBRIA

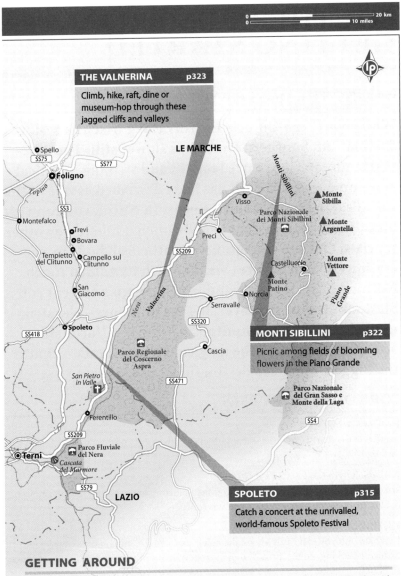

THE VALNERINA   p323

Climb, hike, raft, dine or museum-hop through these jagged cliffs and valleys

MONTI SIBILLINI   p322

Picnic among fields of blooming flowers in the Piano Grande

SPOLETO   p315

Catch a concert at the unrivalled, world-famous Spoleto Festival

0   20 km
0   10 miles

LE MARCHE

Spello
SS75
SS77
Foligno
Topino
SS3
Montefalco
Trevi
Bovara
Tempietto del Clitunno
Campello sul Clitunno
San Giacomo
SS418
Spoleto
San Pietro in Valle
Ferentillo
SS209
Terni
Cascata del Marmore
SS79
LAZIO

Visso
Parco Nazionale dei Monti Sibillini
Preci
SS209
Serravalle
SS320
Cascia
SS471
Parco Regionale del Coscerno Aspra
Parco Fluviale del Nera
Castelluccio
Monti Sibillini
Monte Sibilla
Monte Argentella
Monte Vettore
Piano Grande
Monte Patino
Norcia
Monte
Parco Nazionale del Gran Sasso e Monte della Laga
SS4

Neri
Valnerina

SOUTHERN UMBRIA

GETTING AROUND

Travelling north–south is quite easy throughout Umbria. Take the A1 on the western border with Tuscany, which connects Rome and Florence through Orvieto. Further to the east, it's either the E45 for Todi or Terni or the SS75/SS3 for Spoleto, or to head into the Valnerina or Monti Sibillini. Conveniently, trains shadow these major highways. Driving the same distances east–west can take three or four times as long, but the views of mountains and rolling hills make the lengthy drives well worth it.

SOUTHERN UMBRIA
GETTING STARTED

MAKING THE MOST OF YOUR TIME

While Northern Umbria is easily categorised as a 'slow' destination, Southern Umbria is slower still. The ethereal landscape is at once languid and striking, mystical and unmanicured. Todi has been described as one of the world's most perfect small towns. In Narni, you can visit lions, saints and castles, usually unencumbered by other tourists. Orvieto's magnificent cathedral, built by generations of artists, lures visitors with its golden touch. Nothing beats simply wandering Spoleto's ancient cobblestone streets. However, it's the outdoors – the striking Valnerina, the ubiquitous *agriturismi* (farm-stay accommodation) or the magical Piano Grande – that is the biggest must-see destination.

TOP TOURS & COURSES

❦ LA LINGUA LA VITA
Spend one week or six months learning Italian in the most cosmopolitan hill town in Umbria (p312).

❦ BIANCONI HOSPITALITY GROUP
Norcia is the food capital of Umbria, and the Bianconi family knows how to show you all of it, from truffle hunts to wine tastings (p320).

❦ UMBRIA GRILL
It's a haul, but you can easily spend the better part of a day and night taking a wine-tasting or cooking course, then dining in front of live performances in the amphitheatre (p309).

❦ EUROLINKS
Italian classes, wellness retreats, cooking courses and local tours (p331).

GETTING AWAY FROM IT ALL

Outside of Orvieto, there is no better place to escape the crowds of central Italy than in Southern Umbria. Even in May or June (or September or October), you might have some towns practically to yourself.

★ **See all of Southern Umbria** Head to the top of La Rocca Albornoz in Narni (p328).

★ **Explore the Piano Grande** Bring your best hiking shoes to the plains around Castelluccio, including a hike to the lake where Pontius Pilate was supposedly buried (p322).

★ **Visit the undead** Get away from civilisation – and the living – at the rousingly creepy Museo delle Mummie in Ferentillo (p325).

★ **Casale Santa Brigida** Focus on finishing a piece of art or planning a performance, or hang out with those who are, at an Art Monastery/Agriturismo near Calvi dell'Umbria p309.

RESOURCES

★ **Umbrian Tourist Board** (www.regioneumbria.eu) Official Umbrian tourist board site

★ **Bella Umbria** (www.bellaumbria.net) Unofficial tourism information, including hotel bookings

★ **Umbria Online** (www.umbriaonline.com) Private tourist information site

★ **Valnerina** (www.valnerina.it) Information on each town in the Valnerina

★ **Sistema Museo** (www.sistemamuseo.it) Comprehensive information about Umbrian museums

FESTIVALS

Festivals and *sagre* (fairs) in Southern Umbria can mean medieval costumes and music, delicious food and wine or races and revelry. Almost every decent-sized town has its own festival; check with your hotel, *agriturismo* or at the local tourist office.

★ **Corsa all'Anello** Narni's medieval festival is one of Umbria's oldest (p329).

★ **Festival dei Due Mondi** World famous, the Spoleto Festival features dancers, musicians and even mock jury trials (p318).

★ **Umbria Jazz Winter** The sister festival to Perugia's Umbria Jazz; takes place in late Dec and early Jan (p306).

TOP EATING EXPERIENCES

❦ **RISTORANTE PIERMARINI**
Far from the crowds yet maintains gastronomic perfection (p325)

❦ **RISTORANTE I SETTE CONSOLI**
Typical Umbrian fare meets haute cuisine (p306)

❦ **IL GATTEMELATA**
Narni's best restaurant, mixing inventive fare with classic Umbrian cuisine (p329)

❦ **IL CANTICO**
San Pietro in Valle's subterranean restaurant (p325)

❦ **UMBRIA GRILL**
Experiential cooking courses and dining (p309)

❦ **VISSANI**
One of Europe's highest-rated restaurants (p310)

SOUTHERN UMBRIA

ORVIETO

· · · · · ·

pop 21,000

The entire town of Orvieto is placed precariously on a cliff made of the area's tufaceous stone, a craggy porous limestone that seems imminently ready to crumble under the weight of Orvieto's magnificent Gothic cathedral (or at least under all the tourists who are drawn to it). Just off a main autostrada, Orvieto can get a bit crowded with summer bus tours, but rest assured – they've all come for good reason.

Orvieto held a lofty position as one of Umbria's most influential towns for almost 3000 years. The Etruscan settlement was founded as far back as the 8th or 9th century BC, and thrived as a centre for bronze and ceramics. The ancient evidence is still on display at several of Orvieto's museums, including the Museo Claudio Faina e Civico and the Museo Archeologico Nazionale. The second zenith in Orvieto's history was the late Middle Ages, when it reigned as a leader of the papal states, a position that led to the construction of the stunning cathedral and the stately civic and religious buildings that now create a leisurely way to stroll back in time.

ESSENTIAL INFORMATION

EMERGENCIES // After-hours doctor (☎ 0763 30 18 84) Farmacia del Moro (☎ 0763 34 41 00; Corso Cavour 89; ☺ 9am-1pm & 4pm-7.30pm) Posts 24-hour pharmacy information. Hospital (☎ 0763 30 71) In the Ciconia area, east of the railway station. Police (☎ 0763 3 92 11; Piazza Cahen)
TOURIST OFFICES // Campo della Fiera tourist information In the car park, near the entrance to the funicular. Tourist Office (☎ 0763 34 17 72; info@iat.orvieto.tr.it; Piazza Duomo 24; ☺ 8.15am-1.50pm & 4-7pm Mon-Fri, 10am-1pm & 3-6pm Sat, Sun & holidays)

EXPLORING ORVIETO

♥ CATHEDRAL // A SPECTACULAR VISUAL FEAST OF GOLD-PLATED CHRISTIANITY

Little can prepare you for the visual feast that is the cathedral (☎ 0763 34 11 67; Piazza Duomo; ☺ 7.30am-12.45pm & 2.30pm-7.15pm Apr-Sep, shorter evening hours off-season), often called the 'golden lily' of cathedrals. Originating in 1290, this remarkable edifice was originally planned in the Romanesque style but, as work proceeded and architects changed, Gothic features were incorporated into the structure. The facade harmoniously blends mosaic with sculpture and plain stone with dazzling colour, and has been likened to a giant outdoor altar screen.

The building took 30 years to plan and three centuries to complete. It was

MONEY SAVER

For one-stop visitor shopping, pick up an **Orvieto Unico Card** (adult/concession valid 1yr €18/15). It entitles its owner to entrance to the nine main attractions (including the Cappella di San Brizio in the cathedral, Museo Claudio Faina e Civico, Orvieto Underground, Torre del Moro, Museo dell'Opera del Duomo and the Crocifisso del Tufo Etruscan Necropolis) and either five hours' free car parking at the Campo della Fiera car park next to the funicular or a round-trip on the funicular and city buses. It can be purchased at the Campo della Fiera car park, the attractions listed earlier, the tourist office or the funicular car park.

ORVIETO

ESSENTIAL INFORMATION

Campo della Fiera Tourist	
Information.......................1 F1	
Farmacia del Moro................2 C3	
Police Station......................3 E2	
Post Office..........................4 D3	
Tourist Office......................5 D3	

EXPLORING ORVIETO

Cathedral.............................6 D3	
Museo Archeologico	
Nazionale...........................7 D3	
Museo Claudio Faina e	
Civico...............................8 C3	
Museo dell'Opera del	
Duomo..............................9 D3	
Museo di Emilio Greco......(see 9)	
Orvieto Underground........10 C4	
Torre del Moro..................11 C3	

GASTRONOMIC HIGHLIGHTS

Cantina Foresi...................12 D3	
Le Grotte del Funaro........13 B3	
Osteria dell'Angelo...........14 D2	
Ristorante I Sette Consoli...15 D3	
Ristorante Zeppelin..........16 B3	
Vinosus............................17 D3	

NIGHTLIFE

Il Palazzo del Gusto..........18 B3	
Teatro Mancinelli..............19 C3	

ACCOMMODATION

Villa Mercede....................20 D3	

TRANSPORT

Bus Station........................21 E1	
Funicular Station...............22 E2	

SOUTHERN UMBRIA

probably started by Fra Bevignate and later additions were made by Lorenzo Maitani (responsible for Florence's cathedral), Andrea Pisano and his son Nino Pisano, Andrea Orcagna and Michele Sanicheli. The great bronze doors, the work of Emilio Greco, were added in the 1960s.

In the **Cappella di San Brizio** (admission €3) is Orvieto's most famous piece of art, *The Last Judgment* fresco cycle, mostly by Luca Signorelli. The rather shocking frescos include scenes about the end of the world, demons receiving the damned in hell and the preaching of the Anti-Christ. Tickets for the Cappella di San Brizio are available from the tourist office.

The **Cappella del Corporale** houses the blood-stained altar linen of the miracle of the Eucharist, preserved in a silver reliquary decorated by artists of the Sienese school. The walls feature frescos depicting the miracle, painted by Ugolino di Prete Ilario. Mass is celebrated here daily at 9am (in Italian); both *capelle* (chapels) are closed to the public during Mass.

❦ MUSEO CLAUDIO FAINA E CIVICO // WITNESS 3000 YEARS OF ARCHAEOLOGICAL HISTORY

An absolutely fantastic museum for ancient history is the **Museo Claudio Faina e Civico** (☎ 0763 34 15 11; www .museofaina.it; Piazza Duomo 29; adult/concession €4.50/3; ☺ 9.30am-6pm Apr-Sep, 10am-5pm Oct-Mar, closed Mon Nov-Feb), opposite the cathedral. Much of the display here comes from the Etruscan Necropolis found on the outskirts of town. There are examples of gorgons, an incredibly thorough collection of numismatics (coins, many with the likeness of famous Roman emperors) and bronze figures from the 2nd and 3rd centuries BC. Kids will enjoy following

the questions (in Italian and English) for developing little historians to ponder along the way.

❦ AROUND THE CATHEDRAL // WANDER DOWN MUSEUM ROW FOR ART AND HISTORY

Next to the cathedral is the **Museo dell'Opera del Duomo** (☎ 0763 34 24 77; Palazzo Soliano, Piazza Duomo; adult/concession €5/4; ☺ 10am-1pm & 3-7pm Jul & Aug, 10-6pm Apr-Jun & Sep-Oct, 10am-5pm Nov-Mar, closed Tue in winter), which houses a clutter of religious relics from the cathedral, as well as Etruscan antiquities and works by artists such as Simone Martini and the three Pisanos: Andrea, Nino and Giovanni.

Around the corner in the Palazzo Papale you can view Etruscan antiquities in the **Museo Archeologico Nazionale** (☎ 0763 34 10 39; Palazzo Papale, Piazza Duomo; adult/concession €3/1.50; ☺ 8.30am-7.30pm). It doesn't have information in English, so visit the Museo Claudio Faina e Civico first to get your bearings on the background of these ancient artefacts.

Museo di Emilio Greco (☎ 0763 34 46 05; Palazzo Soliano, Piazza Duomo; combined ticket with Cappella San Brizio adult/concession €6.50/5; ☺ 10.30am-1pm & 2.30-6pm Apr-Sep, 10.30am-1pm & 2-5.30pm Tue-Sun Oct-Mar) displays a collection of modern pieces donated by the creator of the cathedral's bronze doors.

❦ TORRE DEL MORO // CLIMB 250 STEPS TO SEE ORVIETO FROM ABOVE

Near the end of the main drag is the **Torre del Moro** (Moor's Tower; ☎ 0763 34 45 67; Corso Cavour 87; adult/concession €2.80/2; ☺ 10am-8pm May-Aug, 10am-7pm Mar, Apr, Sep & Oct, 10.30am-1pm & 2.30-5pm Nov-Feb). Climb all 250 steps (or take an elevator part of the way) for a sweeping pigeon's-eye view of the entire city.

❧ ORVIETO UNDERGROUND // EXPLORE THE UNDERSIDE OF ORVIETO

The coolest place in Orvieto – literally – is the **Orvieto Underground** (☎ 0763 34 06 88, 339 733 27 64; Parco delle Grotte; adult/concession €5.50/3.30; ☼ tours 11am, 12.15pm, 4pm & 5.15pm daily Mar-Jan, Sat & Sun Feb), a series of 440 caves used by locals for millennia for various purposes. The caves were initially used as wells by the Etruscans, who needed water but couldn't risk leaving the hill when the Romans were about. During the Middle Ages, locals experiencing a high volume of sieges used the caves for protected sustenance, this time trapping pigeons in dovecotes for food (pigeon is still found on Umbrian menus to this day – look for *palomba* or *piccione*). During WWII, the caves were converted into bomb shelters, but luckily they never had to be used, as the tufaceous volcanic rock that makes up the hill crumbles easily. Tours depart from in front of the tourist office.

Hint: during summer, take the 12.15pm tour, as you'll enjoy the year-round temperature of around 15°C while most sights and shops are closed.

❧ CROCIFISSO DEL TUFO ETRUSCAN NECROPOLIS // TOUR A CITY OF THE DEAD

Besides the Hypogea di Volumni outside of Perugia, the **Crocifisso del Tufo Etruscan Necropolis** (☎ 0763 34 36 11; Località Le Conce, SS71, Km 1.6; adult/concession €3/1.50; ☼ 8am-7pm) is one of only two Etruscan necropolises that travellers can visit in Umbria (and is much more complete than the Hypogeo di Volumni). It dates back to the mid-6th century BC. Several series of burial chambers feature the etched names of their deceased residents. The manner in which the graves are laid out shows the precision of good ancient urban planning, albeit one whose residents couldn't quite appreciate it. Many of the furnishings from the Necropolis can be found at the Louvre, British Museum and various other museums, though some of the collection hasn't left: the Museo Claudio Faina e Civico still holds a good chunk.

ACCOMMODATION

Almost every location in this chapter is within an hour or two's drive of another (besides Castelluccio), meaning it's possible and even desirable to pick one location to spend a few days, or better yet, an entire week. We can't stress it enough; having your own wheels means you can choose whatever *agriturismo* (farm-stay accommodation), villa or village inn you'd like, and day-trip from there. If you're worried about navigating, our box about driving and parking in Umbria (p290) will give you a few rules to follow. For a full list of accommodation in the regiona, see p391.

* **Todi Castle and Villa Pianegiani** (p414) is its own self-contained holiday retreat, with an interactive restaurant, ancient ruins and cooking classes
* **Casale Santa Brigida, Calvi dell'Umbria** (p309) will leave guests feeling like they've just spent a few days at creativity summer camp for adults
* **Residenza d'Epoca Abbazia, San Pietro in Valle** (p416), in the heart of the Valnerina, invites guests to relax in ancient rooms and a contemplative garden

♥ **ORVIETO FESTIVALS // PARTIES, TRADITIONAL RITES AND ALL THAT JAZZ**

If you're in Orvieto on Pentecost Sunday, make time for the world-famous **Palombella**, which includes parades and craft fairs, and a sacred rite that disturbs animal-rights activists. Palombella has been celebrating the Holy Spirit and good luck since 1404: take one bewildered dove, cage it, surround the cage with a wheel of exploding fireworks, and hurtle the cage 300m down a wire towards the cathedral steps. If the dove lives (which it usually does), the couple most recently married in the cathedral become its caretakers (and, presumably, the ones who pay for posttraumatic dove-stress disorder counselling).

From the end of December to early January there's **Umbria Jazz Winter** (www.umbriajazz.com), with a great feast and party on New Year's Eve. Ask at the tourist office for a program of events. See p263 for details of the summer jazz festival.

GASTRONOMIC HIGHLIGHTS

Orvieto has a staggering number of cafes, restaurants and gourmet food shops, many of them with outdoor seating, a plus in the hot, Orvieto summer sun.

♥ **CANTINA FORESI €**
☎ /fax 0763 34 16 11; Piazza Duomo 2; snacks from €4.50; ☺ daily 10am-10pm, to at least 11pm Fri and Sat
A family-run *enoteca* (wine bar) and cafe serving up panini and sausages, washed down with dozens of local wines from the ancient cellar. Directly in front of the cathedral and with low prices, it's the perfect spot to grab a snack and rest your feet.

♥ **LA BADIA RISTORANTE €€€**
☎ 0763 30 19 59; Località La Badia 8; meals €45; ☺ Thu-Tue
The restaurant at La Badia is as refined as its hotel (p413). The chef's speciality is suckling pig and *tagliolini* pasta with truffles. If you enjoy the Orvieto Classico here, tell the owner, Count Fiumi, as it comes from his vineyards. Even if you don't stay or eat here, you can still see it; when you're in the Orvieto Underground, look for the 8th-century abbey in the fields below.

♥ **LE GROTTE DEL FUNARO €€**
☎ 0763 34 32 76; Via Ripa Serancia 41; meals €27; ☺ Tue-Sun
The hollowed-out cavern is worth a visit just for the piano bar, display of antique agricultural objects and the to-die-for view. The restaurant is embedded in the ancient Orvieto cliffside, a former rope maker's grotto. If you're sick of truffles (which is technically possible, although we can't imagine), try the regional classic Chianina beef, especially topped with *cipolline* (baby onions) and rosemary in an *agrodolce* (sweet-sour) sauce.

♥ **OSTERIA DELL'ANGELO €**
☎ 0763 34 18 05; Piazza XXIX Marzo 8a; mains €22; ☺ Tue-Sun
Judged by local food writers to be one of the best restaurants in Umbria, this is certainly an elegant place. Your meal is being cooked by the winner of the 2000 'Chef to Watch' competition. The banana soufflé with a rum-and-cream sauce is recommended and the wine list is extensive.

♥ **RISTORANTE I SETTE CONSOLI €€€**
☎ /fax 0763 34 39 11; www.isetteconsoli.it; Piazza Sant'Angelo 1a; meals €45; ☺ Thu-Tue

Foodies have been known to flock here from Rome or Milan just for lunch, as it is quickly gaining fame as one of Umbria's top restaurants. With dishes like pan-fried pigeon with caramelised grapes or *tagliolini* pasta with zucchini blossoms and baby squid, it's no wonder it's considered a leader in nouvelle cuisine. In summer, dine under the gauzy tent out in the private garden. Reservations highly recommended for dinner.

❤ RISTORANTE ZEPPELIN €€

☎ 0763 34 14 47; Via Garibaldi 28; meals €32; ☺ Mon-Sat, lunch Sun

This natty place has a cool 1920s atmosphere, jazz on the stereo and a long wooden bar where Ingrid Bergman would have felt right at home. It serves creative Umbrian food, including well-priced tasting menus for vegetarians (€25), children (€20), truffle lovers (€40) and traditionalists (€25). Ask about its daylong cooking courses.

❤ VINOSUS €

☎ 0763 34 19 07; Piazza Duomo 15; tapas €6-10; ☺ Tue-Sun

Within photo-op range of the cathedral's northwest wall is a wine bar and eatery that features not only the best wines of the region but also delectables such as a local cheese and honey plate or cured Umbrian meats. The elegant establishment is especially desirable in summer, when outdoor tables beckon and wine

TOP FIVE

UMBRIAN DELICACIES TO SAMPLE

While considered a backwater region for years, much of the world is now striving to catch up with Umbria's instinctive culinary commitment to Slow Food. For hundreds of years, three-hour dinners, organic ingredients and locally grown peasant cuisine has remained Umbria's culinary claim to fame. Here are a few of our favourite ingredients you might want to try when here.

★ **Cinghiale** Wild boar is ubiquitous on most Umbrian menus, and rightfully so. Richly gamy but tender, the flavourful meat often comes served over pasta or stewed in sauce.

★ **Tartufi** Umbrian black truffles (the stronger *nero* preferably over *estivo*) in particular are a menu mainstay, often featured in the autumn harvest months. The earthy fungus is especially delicious sliced over long, thick pasta such as Umbrian *strangozzi*.

★ **Lenticchie** The small, green lentils from Castelluccio (or Colfiorito) are partially responsible for the Piano Grande's floral explosion each spring and summer, and are at their best in a thick soup topped with bruschetta and a fabulous virgin olive oil.

★ **Piccione** English uses the euphemistic 'squab', but Umbrians readily order pigeon, often from the highest-end restaurants. The delicate poultry was a mainstay for townsfolk under siege in the Middle Ages, when hunting and farming were too dangerous.

★ **Farro** Spelt was the daily staple in ancient times, and still graces many Umbrian menus. Classic *zuppa di farro* is a rich, nutty and distinctly Umbrian experience, perfect for a warm lunch on a cold, misty day in the hills.

SOUTHERN UMBRIA

tasting into the wee hours is a pastime for visitors and locals alike.

NIGHTLIFE

Like the rest of Umbria, nightlife in Orvieto consists mostly of eating good food, drinking wine and the *passeggiata* (traditional evening stroll). Dinner, especially on weekends, rarely lasts less than two hours, and the Corso Cavour is *the* place to stroll every night between about 7pm and midnight.

♥ IL PALAZZO DEL GUSTO

☎ 0763 39 35 29; www.orvietowine.info; Via Ripa Serancia I 16; wine tastings €5-11; ⏰ 11am-1pm & 3-5pm Mon-Fri winter, 11am-1pm & 5-7pm Mon-Fri summer

This Etruscan subterranean wine cellar is as infused with atmosphere as it is with yeast. Several tunnels have been redecorated for wine tastings and parties. Peek behind the glass doors for a look at ancient Etruscan tunnels. Check with the tourist office if one of its many weekend events is open to the public.

♥ TEATRO MANCINELLI

☎ 0763 39 31 27; Corso Cavour 122; tour adult/concession €2/1, tickets €10-60; ⏰ 10am-1pm & 4-7pm Mon-Sat, 4-8pm Sun

The stunning 19th-century theatre plays host to Umbria Jazz Winter but offers everything from ballet and opera to folk-music concerts and Pink Floyd tributes all year. If you're not able to catch a performance, it's worth a visit during the day to see the allegorical frescos and tufa walls.

TRANSPORT

TRAIN // Main connections from Orvieto Scalo train station include Rome (€7.10 to €15, 1¼ hours, hourly), Florence (€10.80 to €16.90, 1½ to 2½ hours, hourly) and Perugia (€6.10 to €14.20, 1¼ hours, at least every other hour).

BUS // Intercity buses depart from the bus station on Piazza Cahen, stopping at the train station. **Bargagli** (☎ 057 778 62 23) runs a daily bus service to Rome's Tiburtina Station (€8, 80 minutes, 8.10am, also 7.10pm Sun). Local bus 1 runs up to the Old Town from the train station (€0.95).

FUNICULAR // A century-old cable car connects the train station to Piazza Cahen, west of the town centre. Carriages leave every 10 minutes from 7.20am to 8.30am Monday to Friday, and every 15 minutes from 8am to 8pm Saturday and Sunday (€1.80 round-trip, including the bus from Piazza Cahen to Piazza Duomo, the city centre stop).

CAR & MOTORCYCLE // The city is on the A1 between Rome and Florence, and the SS71 heads north to Lago Trasimeno. Note: The A1 is a toll road, so be sure to have small bills or change. Heading anywhere else in Umbria can be taxing, as there are few east–west routes out of Orvieto, so even crossing the SS448 to Todi can take an hour.

PARKING // At the bottom of the funicular entrance, just next to the train station, is an enormous car park, the Campo della Fiera (at the roundabout in front of the station, head in the direction of 'Arezzo' and turn left). There is plenty of metered parking in Piazza Cahen and around town.

TAXI // For a taxi, dial ☎ 0763 30 19 03 at the train station or ☎ 0763 34 26 13 at Piazza Repubblica.

AROUND ORVIETO

· · · · · ·

While Orvieto sometimes feels like a tufaceous stone monolith standing out in the softly green rolling hills of Umbria, the area just to the east embodies the classic Umbrian countryside. From the winding roads along Lago di Corbara (the southern route, still a long drive, is perhaps a third as time-consuming as the northern) to once reputed 'most liveable town in the world' of Todi, the landscape gently welcomes visitors looking for a bit more tranquillity.

LAGO DI CORBARA

In between Orvieto and Todi lies a lake retreat once popular with popes on holiday. While the lake itself is not as picturesque as Lago Trasimeno, the rural area surrounding it has some of the best restaurants in Umbria, and two of its *agriturismi* (p414) are housed in castles.

❦ TRIPPINI // LEARN TO COOK LIKE A MASTER

Although Vissani and Trippini (see p310) went to school together, Trippini opened a simple **restaurant** (☎ 0744 95 03 16; www.trippini.net; Civitella del Lago; meals €50; ❧ Tue-Sun) while Vissani opened an empire. Adolfo Trippini's restaurant is in the centre of Civitella del Lago, where one could describe it as elegant but not cloyingly so, creative without the over-kill. He does beautiful things to shrimp and seafood, and even teaches cookery

courses (call the number listed for information).

❦ UMBRIA GRILL // ENJOY DINNER AND A PERFORMANCE AT A UNIQUE RESTAURANT

Already garnering international press, **Umbria Grill** (☎ 340 757 39 41; www.todi castle.com/site/Umbria_Grill; Vocabolo Pianesante, Morre; meals €40; ❧ wine tastings Mon, cooking classes Thu, dinner Sat & Sun, reservations required) is the region's most unique dining experience, recently opened for travellers willing to make the trek. The outdoor hillside restaurant looks like a natural Roman amphitheatre, and in keeping with the theme, performers often take the stage during dinner. The full experience includes weekly cookery and tasting courses (English spoken), a children's medieval playground and footpath to medieval ruins, tasting menus (meat, fish and vegetarian) and an authentic brick wood-fired pizza oven. If this all sounds exhausting, look no further; Todi Castle (p414) rents rooms next door.

∽ WORTH A TRIP ∽

Fancy a Nick Drake number performed on lute with your dinner? How about late-night improv games after a round of *limoncello* (lemon liqueur) you helped make? For a retreat like no other, recharge for a few days at the B&B arm of the **Art Monastery Project** (www .artmonastery.org). **Casale Santa Brigida** (☎ 069 835 72 94, www.casalesantabrigida.org; Via del Acqua-vigna 3, Calvi dell'Umbria; per person incl breakfast €35; P ❧) is a guest house/former *agriturismo* that houses resident artists and performers associated with the Art Monastery, but is open to guests year-round. You'll get the requisite pink sunsets over the terrace, swimming pool with view over the idyllic countryside below and odd wild boar jogging past, but you'll also experience working side-by-side in the permaculture garden, learning to bake bread or starting a morning with yoga on the terrace. Just over an hour north of Rome in the far southern tip of Umbria near undiscovered Calvi dell'Umbria (the Art Monastery itself is in the middle of this picture-perfect town), the Casale folks will gather you at Leonardo da Vinci (Fiumicino) airport for €60, or at the nearby Orte or Civita Castellana train stations.

♥ VISSANI // JUDGE ITALY'S BEST RESTAURANT FOR YOURSELF

The hype surrounding Gianfranco Vissani's eponymous **restaurant** (☎ 0744 95 02 06; www.vissani.net; meals €145; ☺ closed lunch Mon, lunch & dinner Wed, lunch Thu, dinner Sun, closed late Jul, late Aug & Christmas) has hit astronomical levels of name recognition, even for Italian standards. While the rest of Italy and the world flock to Umbria just to eat at the famed restaurateur's lakeside abode (located down a locked private drive), and Gambero Rosso (the source of all food knowledge in Italy) has rated Vissani as Italy's top restaurant – Umbrians are not yet convinced. Watch Vissani through – yes – gilt-framed windows as the master chef or his protégé cook. Dishes change seasonally, but the tuxedoed service remains the same. After dinner, guests are invited to move to the dessert room, where an after-dinner drink apothecary serves espresso and tea while diners sup gorgeously designed sweets.

TODI

pop 17,200

Todi embodies all that is good about a central Italian hill town. Ancient structures line even more ancient roads, and the pace of life inches along, keeping time with the fields of wildflowers that languidly grow and shift with the seasons. Foreign artists share Todi's cobblestone streets with local families who have lived amid Todi's enclosed Roman and Etruscan walls for generations.

Like rings around a tree, Todi's history can be read in layers: the interior walls show Todi's Etruscan and even Umbrian influence, the middle walls are an enduring example of Roman know-how, and the 'new' medieval walls boast of Todi's economic stability and prominence during the Middle Ages.

Todi has been thriving for millennia. Three thousand years ago, the Umbri tribe developed the area, sharing it for a spell with the Etruscans. Rome conquered Todi around the 2nd century BC. In Roman days, Todi was known as Tuder and was the home to temples of Jupiter and Minerva and Roman baths. The Dark Ages weren't terribly kind to Todi, but in 1213 the city cemented its reputation as an area powerhouse.

ESSENTIAL INFORMATION

EMERGENCIES // **Hospital** (☎ 075 8 85 81; Via Giacomo Matteotti) **Police station** (☎ 075 895 62 43; Piazza Jacopone)

TOURIST OFFICES // **Tourist office** (☎ 075 894 54 18; Piazza del Popolo 37; ☺ 9.30am-1pm & 3.30-6.30pm Mon-Sat, 10am-1.30pm Sun & holidays Mar-Oct, 9.30am-1pm & 3-6pm Mon-Sat, 10am-1pm Sun & holidays Nov-Mar)

EXPLORING TODI

♥ PIAZZA DEL POPOLO // WRITE YOUR POSTCARD FROM AN ALMOST-PERFECT PIAZZA

Just try to walk through the **Piazza del Popolo** without feeling compelled to sit on medieval building steps and write a postcard home. This town centre is one of the most renowned squares in all of

TICKETING

If you'll be spending a day or two in Todi, it's a good idea to buy a **Biglietto Cumulativo** (adult/concession/child €6/5/4), which will allow you to gain entry into the Museo Pinacoteca, Cisterno Romano and the Tempio di San Fortunato. The ticket can be purchased at any of the museums or at the tourist office.

SOUTHERN UMBRIA

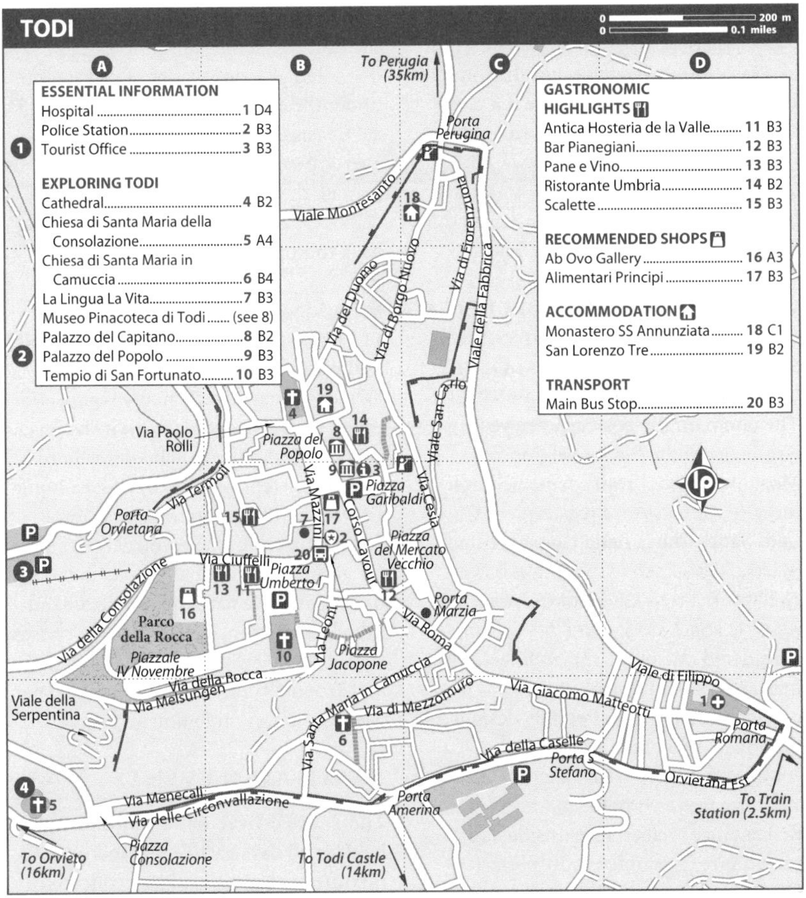
TODI
0 200 m
0 0.1 miles
A
B
C
D
1
2
3
4
ESSENTIAL INFORMATION
Hospital 1 D4
Police Station 2 B3
Tourist Office 3 B3
EXPLORING TODI
Cathedral 4 B2
Chiesa di Santa Maria della Consolazione 5 A4
Chiesa di Santa Maria in Camuccia 6 B4
La Lingua La Vita 7 B3
Museo Pinacoteca di Todi (see 8)
Palazzo del Capitano 8 B2
Palazzo del Popolo 9 B3
Tempio di San Fortunato 10 B3
GASTRONOMIC HIGHLIGHTS
Antica Hosteria de la Valle 11 B3
Bar Pianegiani 12 B3
Pane e Vino 13 B3
Ristorante Umbria 14 B2
Scalette 15 B3
RECOMMENDED SHOPS
Ab Ovo Gallery 16 A3
Alimentari Principi 17 B3
ACCOMMODATION
Monastero SS Annunziata 18 C1
San Lorenzo Tre 19 B2
TRANSPORT
Main Bus Stop 20 B3
To Perugia (35km)
Porta Perugina
Viale Montesanto
Via del Duomo
Via di Borgo Nuovo
Via di Fiorenzuola
Viale della Fabbrica
Viale San Carlo
Via Paolo Rolli
Piazza del Popolo
Via Termoli
Porta Orvietana
Via Mazzini
Corso Cavour
Piazza Garibaldi
Via Cesia
Piazza del Mercato Vecchio
Via Ciuffelli
Piazza Umberto I
Via della Consolazione
Parco della Rocca
Piazzale IV Novembre
Via della Rocca
Via Melsungen
Viale della Serpentina
Via Leoni
Piazza Jacopone
Porta Marzia
Via Roma
Via Santa Maria in Camuccia
Via di Mezzomuro
Via Giacomo Matteotti
Viale di Filippo
Porta Romana
Via della Caselle
Porta S Stefano
Orvietana Est
Via Menecali
Via delle Circonvallazione
Porta Amerina
Piazza Consolazione
To Orvieto (16km)
To Todi Castle (14km)
To Train Station (2.5km)

Italy. Its lugubrious medieval cathedral and buildings cradle the interior piazza, enclosed with four gates during the medieval years but now filled with bustling shops, cappuccino-sipping residents and travellers gazing in wonder at living history. The Lombard-style 13th-century **Palazzo del Capitano** links to the **Palazzo del Popolo** to create what is now the **Museo Pinacoteca di Todi** (☎ 075 895 62 16; Piazza del Popolo; admission €3.10; 🕑 10am-1.30pm & 3-6pm Tue-Sun Mar-Oct, 10.30am-1pm & 2.30-5pm Tue-Sun Nov-Feb), which features an elegant triple window and houses the city's recently restored *pinacoteca* (picture gallery) and an expansive archaeological museum housing exhibits on archaeology, numismatics (coins), weaving and ceramics.

The **cathedral** (☎ 075 894 30 41; Piazza del Popolo; 🕑 8.30am-12.30pm & 2.30-6.30pm), at the northwest end of the square, has a magnificent rose window and intricately decorated doorway.

However, there are two much more impressive churches that no visit to Todi should go without. The lofty **Tempio di San Fortunato** (Piazza Umberto 1; admission free;

9am-1pm & 3-7pm Wed-Mon Mar-Oct, 10am-1pm & 2.30-5pm Wed-Mon Nov-Mar) contains frescos by Masolino da Panicale and the tomb of Beato Jacopone. Inside, make it a point to climb the **Campanile di San Fortunato** (adult/concession €1.50/1; 10am-1pm & 3-6.30pm Mar-Oct, 10.30am-1pm & 2.30-5pm Nov-Mar, closed Mon), where you can gaze across the hills and castles surrounding Todi.

🍷 CHIESA DI SANTA MARIA DELLA CONSOLAZIONE // WITNESS THE SOARING BLUE-DOMED MAJESTY OF A RENAISSANCE MASTERPIECE

The photo on the postcard you've just written from the Piazza del Popolo? Most likely it's of Todi's famed church, the early-Renaissance masterpiece **Chiesa di Santa Maria della Consolazione** (Via della Consolazione & Via della Circonvallazione; 9.30am-12.30pm & 2.30-6.30pm Wed-Mon Mar-Oct, 9.30am-12.30pm & 2.30-5pm Wed-Mon Nov-Mar), considered one of the top architectural masterpieces of the 16th century, is just outside the city walls. Possibly designed by Donato Bramante in 1508 but not completed until 99 years later, its construction was a veritable modern feat in Renaissance architecture. Inside, fans can admire its geometrically perfect Greek cross design. Outside, its soaring cupola-topped dome is visible from 10km away.

🍷 CHIESA DI SANTA MARIA IN CAMUCCIA // TOUR A MEDIEVAL AND ROMAN UNDERGROUND

While you might walk past this fairly nondescript church, we are here to let you in on the little secret that lies below the **Chiesa di Santa Maria in Camuccia** (347 3162381; Via Santa Maria in Camuccia; vary, tours by appt). A Dominican monastery founded in 1394, it's certainly worth a look-see for the stunning examples of

wooden Madonna sculptures. However, the lead archaeologist, Carlo Zoccoli, has offered to give our readers a private tour under the church, where an archaeological treasure trove awaits. Sift through an ever-growing collection of pottery shards or walk through ancient roads, burial chambers and houses, much of it dating back to Roman times.

🍷 LA LINGUA LA VITA // LEARN ITALIAN IN SOPHISTICATION AND SOLACE

While Perugia attracts many young and rowdy university students in its language courses, Todi offers a school for those a tad more…refined. Sign up at **La Lingua La Vita** (075 894 83 64; www.lalingualavita .com, Via Mazzini 18), where you can sign up for group or individual lessons, but both options involve participation in a handful of activities including cooking classes, Italian film viewings and field trips in and around Todi. Costs start at €400 per week for accommodation and classes.

FESTIVALS & EVENTS

The **Todi Festival** (www.todiartefestival.it), held for 10 days each September, is a mixture of classical and jazz concerts, theatre, ballet and cinema.

GASTRONOMIC HIGHLIGHTS

🍷 ANTICA HOSTERIA DE LA VALLE €€

075 894 48 48; Via Ciuffelli 17/19/21; meals €27; Tue-Sun

Art vies with food for top billing at this most creative of restaurants. Every three to four months, new artists not only display their work on the walls, but their illustrations adorn the new seasonal menus. Although the *zuppa di farro* (€7, best in winter) is a mainstay, the chef suggests the spinach ravioli in walnut cream sauce or tagliatelle with truffles.

❦ BAR PIANEGIANI €

☎ 075 894 23 76; Corso Cavour 40; ☺ 6am-midnight Tue-Sun

Just like Clark Kent, this nondescript neighbourhood bar puts on an innocent front to conceal the magic that lies beneath, but 50 years of tradition has created the world's most perfect gelato. Try the *spagnola* (black cherry) or *nocciola* (hazelnut) or, in winter, the hot chocolate with fresh whipped cream. In 2010, it's opening a beautiful back patio.

❦ PANE E VINO €€

☎ 075 894 54 48; Via Ciuffelli 33; meals €28; ☺ Tue-Thu

Now you're definitely in Italy. Dine on dishes such as risotto with yellow pumpkin (€8) or just nibble on the antipasto plate (€11) while tasting from the extensive wine list that includes wines from all over Italy. Relax on the outdoor patio or at candlelit tables under the curved brick ceiling in this narrow, atmospheric *enoteca*.

❦ RISTORANTE UMBRIA €€

☎ 075 894 27 37; Via Santa Bonaventura 13; meals €29; ☺ Thu-Tue

What's more enjoyable: the food or the outdoor patio with a view back in time? Look in the display case to salivate over which goodies you'd like for your meal, perhaps some prosciutto or *salumi* (cured meats)? Try the *palombaccio* (a type of pigeon; €13), a risotto dish or its speciality (truffles, of course).

❦ SCALETTE €

☎ 075 894 44 22; Via delle Scalette 1; meals €24; ☺ Tue-Sun

Wander off the main road down this ancient stairway for a reasonably priced feast in a hobbit-like abode. This ancient farmhouse feels like it's practically in Middle Earth and, with its stone walls, roasted meat dishes and decadent desserts, is a precious spot for a mini-medieval banquet.

RECOMMENDED SHOPS

Todi has become quite the artist community. Folk from across the world have set up shop in town and visitors from all over come to buy new and antique artwork.

❦ AB OVO GALLERY

☎ 075 894 55 26; www.abovogallery.com; Via del Forno 4; ☺ 10.30am-1.30pm & 3.30-7.30pm

One of the more unusual art galleries in Todi, Ab Ovo looks forward rather than back in time. Museum-quality applied art – from jewellery to blown glass – adorns the modern space. Guest artists rotate about every two months, so check in for art openings and special events (open to the public).

❦ ALIMENTARI PRINCIPI

☎ 075 894 27 37; Via Santa Bonaventura 13; meals €29; ☺ 8.45am-1pm & 4-8pm, closed Thu afternoon & end Jul-beg Aug

Foodie gifts, picnic supplies, hundreds of bottles of wine – it's all here. Alimentari Principi will package and ship anything in the store, from jars of truffles to wild-boar sausage and fresh pasta, perfect for sending home a few culinary souvenirs. (Check on import laws in your country first, as some items such as meats and cheeses aren't allowed.)

❦ SATURDAY MARKET

Piazza Garibaldi; ☺ 7am-noon Sat

One of the area's better weekly markets, with clothing, household items, groceries, knick-knacks and munchies. It's a great place to pick up local fruits and vegetables. Plus, unique souvenirs are just a bottle of local honey away.

TRANSPORT

TRAIN // Todi is on the FCU (☎ 075 57 54 01; www.fcu.it, in Italian) train line, which runs through Deruta to Perugia (€2.55, 50 minutes, 18 daily). Although the train station is 3km away, city bus C (€0.90, eight minutes) coincides with arriving trains, every other hour on Sundays.

BUS // APM (☎ 800 51 21 41; www.apmperugia.it, in Italian) heads to Perugia (€5.40, 1 ½ hours, five daily; most originate in Piazza Consolazione but a few depart from Piazza Jacapone) and Spoleto (€5.40, 1½ hours, 6.50am).

CAR & MOTORCYCLE // Todi is easily reached on the SS3B-E45, which runs between Perugia and Terni, or take the Orvieto turnoff from A1 (the Milan–Rome–Naples route).

MONTE CASTELLO DI VIBIO

pop 1670

The real draw in this tiny speck of a town about 20km from Todi is its even tinier speck of a theatre. Throw in gorgeous views and a working *agriturismo* (see p414) and you're set for one or two days.

Monte Castello di Vibio feels like it's in the middle of nowhere, but it's just a few kilometres from the SS3B-E45 that links Perugia and Terni (just north of Todi).

Take the SS3-E45 from Todi to Perugia. Exit at the Monte Castello di Vibio sign and continue for about 4km. At the roundabout that doesn't tell you where to turn, veer left. It's on the S397 between Todi and Marsciano.

Tourist information is at the Associazione Culturale (Via Roma 1), just behind the theatre. The post office next door sells stamps with the image of the theatre.

♥ **TEATRO DELLA CONCORDIA // BE ENTERTAINED IN THE WORLD'S SMALLEST THEATRE**
In keeping with the proportions of the tiny town, **Teatro della Concordia** (Teatro Piccolo; ☎ 075 878 07 37, 328 9188892; www .teatropiccolo.it; admission free but donations accepted; ☺ 10am-12.30pm & 3-6pm Sat, Sun & holidays Sep-Mar, 10am-12.30pm & 4-7pm Sat, Sun & holidays Apr-Aug, daily 1 Jul-10 Sep & 25 Dec-6 Jan) is billed as the smallest theatre in the world. It seats 99 people, 32 on the main floor and 67 in frescoed stalls. In 1808, nine highly motivated local families decided their town needed a theatre and construction began. Frescos and red velvet seats came 50 years later, and the theatre's sophisticated interior rivals larger, grander spaces even today. In 1951 the theatre was almost shut down due to its lack of revenue, but the community voted to pay extra taxes to keep the theatre going. Saturday night is the best time to catch a performance, but the theatre is also open weekend days.

SPOLETO & AROUND

· · · · · ·

Just a few kilometres from the Valnerina, Spoleto feels like an urban destination with a striking rustic backdrop. Almost the 'big city' when compared to the rest of Umbria's hill towns, Spoleto nevertheless manages to exude a relaxed feel, despite having the grandest live arts festival in Central Italy and dozens of in situ Roman relics, which have made it somewhat of a hot spot. Nearby Campello sul Clitunno is more relaxed still, and a visit to a Romanesque church and swan-flecked lake

will make visitors feel like they're on a Roman holiday, albeit one from two millennia ago.

SPOLETO

pop 38,900

This was one of those sleepy Umbrian hill towns until, in 1957, Italian-American composer Gian Carlo Menotti changed everything. For a while, Spoleto saw its tourist season peak for only 10 days from the end of June to the beginning of July during its immensely popular Spoleto Festival (p318). During the festival this quiet town takes centre stage for an international parade of drama, music, opera and dance.

Now so many people have discovered the town via the festival that it's become a popular destination for most of the year (although as in the rest of Umbria, you'll have the town mostly to yourself in winter). Even outside the festival season, Spoleto has enough museums, Roman ruins, wander-worthy streets and vistas to keep you busy for a day or two.

Umbria was first divided in half between the Etruscans and Umbrians. After Rome fell, it was divided again: Byzantines on the east of the Tiber River, Lombards to the west. Spoleto, which was just to the west of the Tiber, became the capital of the Lombardy duchy and in AD 890, the title of Holy Roman Emperor went to a duke from Spoleto. Although much of its pre-Lombard artwork has been lost, you'll see many of the signature religious buildings and hermitages in the area.

ESSENTIAL INFORMATION

EMERGENCIES // Ospedale San Mateo
(☎ 0743 21 01; Via Madonna di Loreto) **Police**
(Polizia Municipale; ☎ 0743 2 32 41; 191 Via la Marconi)

TOURIST INFORMATION // Tourist
Office (☎ 0743 23 89 20/1; www.visitspoleto.it;
Piazza della Libertà 7; ☑ 8.30am-1.30pm & 4-7pm
Mon-Fri, 9.30am-12.30pm Sat & Sun Apr-Oct, 8.30am-
1.30pm & 3.30-6.30pm Mon-Sat, 9.30am-12.30pm Sun
Nov-Mar) **Con Spoleto** (☎ 0743 22 07 73; www.
conspoleto.com; Piazza della Libertà 7) A privately
owned service that can book accommodation.

EXPLORING SPOLETO

❦ MUSEO ARCHEOLOGICO // CHECK OUT ROMAN ARCHAEOLOGY AND CATCH A PERFORMANCE

Make your first stop the **Museo Archeologico** (☎ 0743 22 32 77; Via S Agata; adult/child/concession €4/free/2; ☑ 8.30am-7.30pm), located on the western edge of Piazza della Libertà. Since 1985 this former Benedictine monastery and prison has been used as a museum. It holds a well-displayed collection of Roman and Etruscan bits and bobs from the area, including two marble statues of Augustus and possibly Caesar. Step outside to view the mostly intact 1st-century **Teatro Romano** (Roman Theatre), which often hosts live performances during the summer (check with the museum or the tourist office) and is an understandably popular venue during the Spoleto Festival.

❦ CASA ROMANA // DESPERATE HOUSEWIVES – ANCIENT STYLE

The excavated **Casa Romana** (☎ 0743 23 42 50; Via di Visiale; adult/child €2.50/2; ☑ 10am-6pm) isn't Pompeii, but it gives visitors a peek into what a typical Roman house of the area would have looked like in the 1st century BC, and still has vestiges of mosaics and paintings. East of Piazza della Libertà, around the Piazza Fontana, are more Roman remains, including the *Arco di Druso e Germanico* (Arch of Drusus and Germanicus; sons of the Emperor Tiberius), which marked the

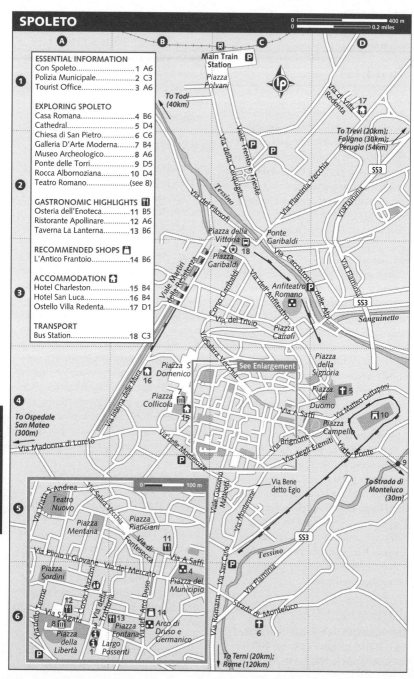

SPOLETO

0 — 400 m
0 — 0.2 miles

ESSENTIAL INFORMATION
Con Spoleto...........................1 A6
Polizia Municipale.................2 C3
Tourist Office.......................3 A6

EXPLORING SPOLETO
Casa Romana.......................4 B6
Cathedral..............................5 D4
Chiesa di San Pietro.............6 C6
Galleria D'Arte Moderna......7 B4
Museo Archeologico.............8 A6
Ponte delle Torri..................9 D5
Rocca Albornoziana............10 D4
Teatro Romano..................(see 8)

GASTRONOMIC HIGHLIGHTS
Osteria dell'Enoteca...........11 B5
Ristorante Apollinare..........12 A6
Taverna La Lanterna...........13 B6

RECOMMENDED SHOPS
L'Antico Frantoio.................14 B6

ACCOMMODATION
Hotel Charleston.................15 B4
Hotel San Luca....................16 B4
Ostello Villa Redenta...........17 D1

TRANSPORT
Bus Station.........................18 C3

Main Train Station
Piazza Polvani
To Todi (40km)
Via di Villa Redenta
17
To Trevi (20km); Foligno (30km); Perugia (54km)
SS3
Via della Cerquiglia
Viale Trento e Trieste
Tessino
Via del Filosofi
Via Flaminia Vecchia
Via Flaminia
Piazza della Vittoria
Ponte Garibaldi
Via Caccatori delle Alpi
2
18
Piazza Garibaldi
Anfiteatro Romano
SS3
Via dell'Anfiteatro
Sanguinetto
Viale Martiri della Resistenza
Corso Garibaldi
Via del Trivio
Piazza Cairoli
Piazza S. Domenico
16
Via Sabra Vecchia
Piazza S. Vecchia
See Enlargement
Piazza della Signoria
Piazza del Duomo
5
Via Matteo Gattaponi
10
Via Interna delle Mura
Piazza Collicola
7
15
Via A. Saffi
Piazza Campello
To Ospedale San Mateo (300m)
Via Madonna di Loreto
Via delle Monterozze
Via Brignone
Via degli Eremiti
Viale Ponte
9
To Strada di Monteluco (30m)
Via Giacomo Matteotti
Via Bene detto Egio
Via Montrone
SS3
Tessino
Via San Carlo
Via Romana
Via Flaminia
Strada di Monteluco

0 — 100 m
Via S. Andrea
Via Salara Vecchia
Teatro Nuovo
Piazza Pianciani
Piazza Mentana
Via di Fontesecca
11
Via A. Saffi
Via Plinio il Giovane
Via del Mercato
4
Piazza Sordini
Corso Mazzini
Via della Trattoria
Piazza del Municipio
12
13
Via dell'Arco Druso
14
Via S. Agata
8
3
Piazza Fontana
Arco di Druso e Germanico
Via del Duomo Terme
Piazza della Libertà
1
Largo Possenti
To Terni (20km); Rome (120km)

grandiose entrance to the Roman forum. The city boasts an Anfiteatro Romano (Roman Amphitheatre), one of the country's largest. Unfortunately it is within military barracks and closed to the public. Wander along Via dell'Anfiteatro, off Piazza Garibaldi, in search of a glimpse.

❧ ROMAN AQUEDUCT // STROLL ACROSS AN ANCIENT AQUEDUCT TO A MEDIEVAL CHURCH

An hourlong stroll or an all-day hike is a lovely way to while away an afternoon along the Via del Ponte to the **Ponte delle Torri**, erected in the 14th century on the foundations of a Roman aqueduct. The bridge is 80m high and 230m across, built in an imposing set of 10 arches. Cross the bridge and follow the lower path, Strada di Monteluco, to reach the **Chiesa di San Pietro** (☎ 0743 4 48 82; Località San Pietro; admission free; 9.30am-11am & 3.30-6.30pm). The 13th-century facade, the main attraction of the church, is liberally bedecked with sculpted animals.

❧ ROCCA ALBORNOZIANA // VISIT A PAPAL FORTRESS ABOVE SPOLETO

The **Rocca Albornoziana** (☎ 0743 22 30 55; Piazza Campello; admission €6, combined ticket to Rocca & museum €7.50; 10am-8pm summer & weekends, 10am-1pm & 3-6pm late Mar-Jun, Sep & Oct, 10-11.45am & 2-4.15pm Mon-Fri, 10am-4pm Sat & Sun Nov-Feb), an example of a Cardinal Albornoz–built fortress from the mid-14th century. Cardinal Albornoz led Pope Innocent VI's forces in the fight to take back control of Umbria. He fostered the building of many of the *rocche* (fortresses) in the area, including the one still standing in Narni (p325) and one in Perugia (p260) that was destroyed in an uprising against the Pope just three

years after it was built. The monstrosity dominates the city. For hundreds of years, until as recently as 1982, Spoleto's *Rocca* was used as a high-security prison housing such notables as Pope John Paul II's attempted assassin, Ali Agca. It now hosts open-air concerts (most notably during the Spoleto Festival) and a museum displaying local history. Now it's home to the **National Museum of the Dukedom of Spoleto** (☎ /fax 0743 22 30 55; Piazza Campello; admission €6, combined ticket to Rocca & museum €7.50; 10am-7pm Thu-Sun) which houses historical information as well as artwork from Spoleto's *pinacoteca*, which will remain closed for several years.

❧ CATHEDRAL // LOOK THROUGH A STRIATED HISTORY OF RELIGION AND ART

The stunning **cathedral** (Santa Maria Assunta; ☎ 0743 4 43 07; Piazza del Duomo; 7.30am-12.30pm & 3-6pm summer, 7.30am-12.30pm & 3-5pm winter) in Spoleto was consecrated in 1198 and remodelled in the 17th century. The Romanesque facade is fronted by a striking Renaissance porch. In the 11th century, huge blocks of stone salvaged from Roman buildings were put to good use in the construction of the rather sombre bell tower. The mosaic floors are from a 12th-century reconstruction effort. Inside, the first chapel to the right of the nave (Chapel of Bishop Constantino Eroli) was decorated by Bernardino Pinturicchio. Check out the apse's fresco *Life of the Virgin Mary*, done by Fra' Filippo Lippi and his assistants, Fra Diamante and Piero Matteo d'Amelia (who painted a starry sky on the Sistine Chapel ceiling 20 years before Michelangelo covered it up). Lippi died during the commission. Lorenzo de' Medici travelled to Spoleto from Florence and ordered Lippi's son, Filippino, to build a mausoleum for the artist. This now stands in the cathedral's right transept.

The spectacular closing concert of the Spoleto Festival is held on the piazza, in front of the cathedral.

❤ GALLERIA D'ARTE MODERNA // EXPLORE THE WORK OF ITALIAN SCULPTOR LEONCILLO

To check out some modern artwork, head towards the **Galleria D'Arte Moderna** (☎ 0743 4 64 34; Palazzo Collicola; adult/child €4/3; ⏲ 10.30am-1pm & 3-5.30pm Wed-Mon 16 Oct-14 Mar, 10.30-1pm & 3.30-7pm Wed-Mon 15 Mar-15 Oct) a homage to Spoleto's commitment to its ongoing artistic support. The Italian sculptor Leoncillo has a dedicated room here.

❤ SPOLETO FESTIVAL // ENJOY A MONTH-LONG CULTURE FEST

The world-famous **Spoleto Festival** (☎ 800 56 56 00; www.spoletofestival.it) was conceived by Italian-American composer Gian Carlo Menotti as the Festival dei Due Mondi (Festival of Two Worlds) in 1958, and has since become a cultural phenomenon. Spanning late June to mid-July, it holds opera, theatre, ballet and art performances all around town. One inventive new tradition is re-enacting famous historical court proceedings. Tickets cost €5 to €200, but most are in the €20 to €30 range. The most famous performances sell out as early as March or April, but you can still buy tickets that week for many shows. There are usually several free concerts in various churches.

GASTRONOMIC HIGHLIGHTS

Spoleto is one of Umbria's main centres for the *tartufo nero* (black truffle), which you'll often find shaved over pasta.

❤ OSTERIA DELL'ENOTECA €
☎ 0743 22 04 84; Via A Saffi 7; tourist menu €15; ⏲ Wed-Mon

Extremely fit waiters carry dishes up and down a curving iron staircase into this 12th-century tavern. Diners sit on dark-wood benches under a high stone ceiling surrounded by rows and rows of local wines from which to choose. Dishes are typical of the area – *strangozzi alla spoletina* ('shoelace' pasta in a tomato, garlic and chilli sauce, €6.20), truffle omelette (€6.20) – and priced to allow at least one or two meals while in town.

❤ RISTORANTE APOLLINAIRE €€
☎ 0743 22 32 56; Via S Agata 14; tasting menus incl veg €30-40; ⏲ Wed-Sun

A delight for the senses, Apollinare is an extraordinary culinary experience set amid ancient 12th-century walls and low oak-beam ceilings lit by flickering candlelight. The menu changes seasonally, but you can choose to go with one of its tasting menus – vegetarian, truffle or traditional – or choose from its 'nouvelle' menu. Somehow this restaurant manages to figure out that squid-ink pasta does go with pesto and crayfish, and rabbit feels quite at home in a black-olive sauce. No matter what, make sure you have dessert.

❤ TAVERNA LA LANTERNA €
☎ 0743 4 98 15; Via della Trattoria 6; tasting menus around €15; ⏲ Thu-Tue

Reasonable prices draw folks in, but it's the Italian hosts and locally grown ingredients that will convince you you've made the right choice. Well-priced tasting menus include vegetarian, Umbrian or special *porcini* mushroom or *tartufo* (truffle), and all come with several filling courses. Try the local *strangozzi alla spoletina,* typical Umbrian pasta in a mildly spicy tomato sauce.

SOUTHERN UMBRIA

RECOMMENDED SHOPS

❤ L'ANTICO FRANTOIO

☎ 0743 4 98 93; Via dell'Arco Druso 8

Sells plenty of pasta, *lenticchie* (small, green lentils), wine, oil and cheese for a great gift or picnic. Each town in Umbria has several of these gourmet-goods stores, but here the fiery owner, Sandra, makes many of her own sauces. Try anything with *tartufi* (truffles), olive or *carciofi* (artichokes). She will carefully package and FedEx any purchases you make to anywhere in the world.

TRANSPORT

TRAIN // Main connections include Rome (€7.45 to €14.30, 1½ hours, hourly), Florence (€12.10 to €20, 1½ to 2½ hours, every two hours or so), Perugia (€4.15, one hour, nine daily) and Assisi (€3.25, 40 minutes, hourly).

CAR & MOTORCYCLE // The city is on E45 and an easy connection to the SS209 to the Valnerina.

BUS // Intercity buses depart from the train station. Since the train is so convenient, you'll need a bus only for nearby towns not served by the train. SSIT (☎ 0743 21 22 09; www.spoletina.com) runs buses to Norcia (€4.90, one hour, six daily) from the bus station. Every 20 minutes, an orange shuttle bus (€0.90) marked A, B or C heads to Piazza della Libertà from the train station.

CAMPELLO SUL CLITUNNO

pop 2490

If you're heading between Foligno and Spoleto, a pleasant place for a stroll is the Campello sul Clitunno.

❤ FONTI DEL CLITUNNO // ENJOY AN ATMOSPHERE WHERE ZEN AND ROME MEET

The Fonti del Clitunno (☎ 0743 52 11 41; Località Pissignano; admission €2; ⏱ 10am-12.30pm & 2.30-5.30pm winter, 9am-8pm summer) marks the source of the Clitunno river. This Zen-like garden proffers crystal clear springs, a tranquil lake and exquisitely lush foliage. In ancient times, it was a popular site for religious pilgrimages. Caligula was known to come here to consult the god of the Clitunno river and it was also used for theatre performances, feasts and gladiator matches. While you can't witness gladiator matches, you can stroll the lovely grounds.

❤ TEMPIETTO DEL CLITUNNO // VISIT A SECRET MEDIEVAL TEMPLE

Keep your eye out for the **Tempietto del Clitunno** (☎ 0743 27 50 85; Via Flaminia, Km 139; ⏱ 9am-8pm Apr-Oct, 8am-6pm Nov-Mar), as the tiny outdoor church has the smallest, most nondescript signpost in all of tourism-dom (on the left 1.1km north of the Fonti). This Paleo-Christian building has been attributed to just about every period, from the Roman 4th century to the Romanesque 13th century. However, 8th-century frescos and the proclivity of locals in the Middle Ages to procure building supplies from Roman ruins might give away the date. It has many of the classic Roman features, such as Corinthian columns and neo-Augustan inscriptions (in big block lettering).

THE VALNERINA & MONTI SIBILLINI

· · · · · ·

Norcia is the natural jumping-off place to travel through the Umbrian wilderness of the Valnerina and Monti Sibillini. After filling up on cured meats and cheese, head into the magical hills of the Monti Sibillini, where

SOUTHERN UMBRIA

you can hike, hang-glide and look for fairies (or so say the locals). The Valnerina is full of unique restaurants and the spectacular Cascata delle Marmore, one of the biggest waterfalls this side of the Atlantic.

NORCIA

pop 4980

As the jumping-off point to the Valnerina and Monti Sibillini, venerable Norcia more than delivers its share of impressive churches and museums (and it's the birthplace of St Benedict, patron saint of Europe). But that's not the reason most people come here. No, visitors come for the pigs, in all their delicious forms – *prosciutto crudo* and *cotto,* salami, *porchetta* (suckling pig). And the wild boar. And the lentils, cheese, chocolate, *farro,* mushrooms and, of course, black truffles.

ESSENTIAL INFORMATION

TOURIST INFORMATION // Bianconi Hospitality (www.bianconi.com) Serving Norcia-bound tourists for 160 years now, this hospitality group's website includes info on its hotels and restaurants as well as truffle hunts and activities in the Valnerina and Monti Sibillini. **Casa del Parco** (☎ 0743 81 70 90; Via Solferino 22; ⏰ 9.30am-12.30pm & 3-6pm Mon-Fri, 9.30am-12.30pm & 3.30-6.30pm Sat & Sun) Offers tourist info and plenty of Monti Sibillini information, including guided trips, public transport to the area, detailed walking maps and local products. During the summer, ask about low-priced English-language excursions throughout Monti Sibillini.

EXPLORING NORCIA

♥ **BASILICA DI SAN BENEDETTO // VISIT THE BASILICA OF EUROPE'S PATRON SAINT**

The **Basilica di San Benedetto** (Piazza San Benedetto) is an impressive show of architec-

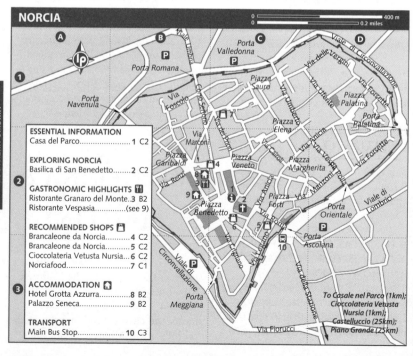

NORCIA

0   400 m
0   0.2 miles

To Casale nel Parco (1km);
Cioccolateria Vetusta
Nursia (1km);
Castelluccio (25km);
Piano Grande (25km)

SOUTHERN UMBRIA

tural know-how. Named after St Benedict, patron saint of Europe, who was born in Norcia, it was built in the shape of a Latin cross with a polygonal apse. The bell tower dates back to 1389 and its portico is Gothic. Frescos inside the church date to the 16th century, including *Resurrezione di Lazzaro* (Resurrection of Lazarus) by Michelangelo Carducci (not *the* Michelangelo, but one from Norcia) and *San Benedetto e Totila* (St Benedict and Totila) by Filippo Napoletano, completed in 1621. If you're in town on a Sunday, be sure to stop in at 5.30pm or 7.45pm, when Benedictine monks from the attached monastery chant in the crypt.

✹ MOSTRA MERCATO DEL TARTUFO // JOIN THE FOODIES IN THE ANNUAL TRUFFLE HUNT

Truffle lovers, foodies and moochers should head to Norcia on the last weekend in February and the first weekend in March for the **Mostra Mercato del Tartufo Nero** (www.neronorcia.it). Thousands of visitors from all over the world sift through dozens of booths, tasting, of course, all things truffle from Norcia, but also sweets from Sicily, cheese from Tuscany and other goodies. The entrance (and most tastings) are free and any gifts will be well loved.

GASTRONOMIC HIGHLIGHTS

The town is full of *norcinerias* – butchers serving Norcia-produced dried meats. In fact, the word *norcineria* is now used to mean a butcher throughout all of Italy. The techniques used in Norcia date back to Roman times when the harsh terrain led area inhabitants to focus on animal husbandry as the main food source. Famous food items from the area also include *cinghiale*, lentils and *pecorino* cheese.

✹ RISTORANTE GRANARO DEL MONTE €€

☎ 0743 81 65 13; Via Alfieri 12; meals €28

One of the most famous restaurants in Umbria for visitors, it has been open daily for 150 years running. It is a tad touristy, but the food is still excellent and comes in great piles of *porcini* mushrooms, sausages and prosciutto, truffles and *cinghiale*. In the winter, sit inside next to the grand fireplace in the enormous banquet-sized interior, and in summer, relax on the pleasant outdoor dining area. Its signature dish is *filetto tartufato del cavatore,* a veal dish sautéed in butter, black truffles and red wine – as rich as it is delicious.

✹ RISTORANTE VESPASIA €€€

☎ 0743 81 65 13; Via Cesare Battisti 10; ☽ lunch & dinner; restaurant meals €55, lounge meals €32

Set in a 16th century *palazzo,* the restaurant's elegantly simple furnishings complement the understated gourmet cuisine. A simple organically grown egg is topped with a generous helping of Norcia black truffles, or locally grown saffron accompanies risotto and local pork. Herbs come from, of course, their own garden. In warmer months, dine in the garden to jazz or blues.

RECOMMENDED SHOPS

Norcia is lined with shops selling local products, cheeses and every conceivable piece of pig in every conceivable form of pork product. Be careful, though: you can't ship meat to most countries.

✹ BRANCALEONE DA NORCIA

☎ 0743 82 83 11, 0743 81 75 15; www.gustus italiano.com; Corso Sertorio 17

A savvy shop specialising in locally produced products of every sort, size and type – cheese, lentils, jam, and every conceivable cut of pork known to humankind. Once you're home, order anything you want from their website. There's another branch at Via Roma 24.

♥ CIOCCOLATERIA VETUSTA NURSIA

☎ 0743 81 73 70, shop 0743 82 80 70; Viale della Stazione 41/43

A kilometre outside Norcia on the road to Castelluccio you'll pass what looks like a boring warehouse. Step inside and you'll find the best prices on a huge selection of chocolate, wine, lentils and local (non-meat) products. Best of all, there is always something available to taste. There's also a smaller and more expensive shop in town at Via Mazzini 6.

♥ NORCIAFOOD

☎ 0743 82 83 62; www.norciafood.com; Via dei Priori 38

This is one of the largest and most complete *norcinerie* and local-produce shops. It ships to anywhere in the world and you can order many of its products on the website. Peruse dozens of types of truffles, from sliced to whole, black to white, or try local pasta, jam or cured meats.

TRANSPORT

BUS // Buses leave from near Porta Ascolana. **SSIT** (☎ 0743 21 22 11; www.spoletina.it) runs trips to Spoleto (€4.40, one hour, five daily) and Perugia (€6.80, two hours, daily at 2.10pm).
CAR & MOTORCYLCE // From Spoleto, take the SS209 to the SS396.
TRAIN // The closest train station is in Spoleto.

MONTI SIBILLINI

Monti Sibillini is one of those places it would be great to discover by accident, but there's no way you're going to haul yourself up from Norcia (if you make

it to Norcia at all) unless you hear how beautiful this area is.

This area is really, really, really beautiful. Really. Go. Even during summer, its jagged peaks keep a healthy dusting of snow. Mt Vettore – the highest peak in Monti Sibillini – stands at 2476m. In May and June, infinite expanses of wildflowers blanket the Piano Grande, the great plain surrounding Castelluccio. Wolves run free, icy streams flow and fairies dance. Well, so the story goes. During the Middle Ages, the Sibillini mountains were known throughout Europe as a place that harboured demons, necromancers and fairies. A woman named Sybil was said to live in a cave and tell fortunes. These days, the area is home to peregrine falcons, royal eagles and porcupines (brought over in the last few decades). Eighteen hundred botanical species have been counted just in this one area.

Before going off into the Monti Sibillini, you can pick up a host of maps at the Casa del Parco (p320) in Norcia, depending on how strenuous or leisurely you want to be. Any level of activity is possible here, spanning from day paths to weeklong survival treks circling the mountain chain. The office has a lot of useful information available on different kinds of inexpensive guided trips in English, as well.

For information, try the official **Parco Nazionale dei Monti Sibillini** (www.sibillini .net).

CASTELLUCCIO

Castelluccio looks impossible. The crumbling village sits atop a lonely hilltop like an outpost in the middle of the vast expanse of the Piano Grande. It's difficult enough these days to traverse the dozen kilometres (at least) over treacherous mountain passes to reach the nearest village in any direction, especially during winter when temperatures can reach -30°C, but Castelluccio was even more isolated in the past and as such, has stayed relatively poor.

The hamlet now boasts a smattering of small eateries and a few places to stay, but what has put it on the map is the Castelluccio *lenticchie:* small, thin-skinned legumes that keep many of the hundred or so permanent residents in business and many Umbrian bellies warm and full during the winter. The town is also famous for its *pecorino* and ricotta cheeses.

During the day, head out in any one direction to hike, ski, hang-glide or go horse riding. Or wander the perimeter of the main square (the area around the car park) to chow down in small shops selling all sorts of Castelluccian goodies. Since the nightlife consists mostly of chasing goats around dilapidated stone buildings, a good night's sleep is practically guaranteed.

The Casa del Parco (p320) in Norcia has information about the town of Castelluccio. The only bus runs once a week, so you'll need your own car. Those without wheels might want to sign up for a day excursion with Bianconi Hospitality (p320).

❦ HANG-GLIDING // ENJOY THE BEST VIEWS IN UMBRIA WITH THE EXPERTS

One of the most well-respected hang-gliding institutions in Europe is **Pro Delta** (☎ 0743 82 11 56, 339 563 54 56; www .prodelta.it; Via della Fate 3, Castelluccio), which has a solid reputation for safety. A basic five-day hang-gliding or paragliding course costs €400 and refresher courses start at €120. Those with a sense of adventure but neither time nor money can take a

two-person paragliding and hang-gliding ride for €25 to €70. Check the requirements page of its website before arriving for a course.

Another school is **Fly Castelluccio** (☎ 0736 34 42 04; www.flycastelluccio.com; Via Copernica 12, Ascoli Piceno), in the neighbouring region of Le Marche. It offers weekend, five- or 10-day elementary courses in paragliding and hang-gliding, as well as paramotoring.

❦ ASSOCIAZIONE SPORTIVA PIANGRANDE // EXPLORE MONTI SIBILLINI ON HORSE OR BIKE

For horse riding, contact **Associazione Sportiva Piangrande** (☎ 0743 81 72 79; Castelluccio), which is open from Easter to October, and on weekends in winter. The organisation offers half- and full-day treks throughout Monti Sibillini, plus bicycle tours of the region. Mountain-bike riders should pick up the *Pedalling in the Park* brochure at any Casa del Parco office.

❦ TAVERNA DI CASTELLUCCIO // FILL UP ON LENTIL SOUP AMID GOOD COMPANY

A ramshackle edifice on the outside, Taverna di Castelluccio (☎ 0743 82 11 58; Via Dietro la Torre 6; meals €22.50; ⏰ Thu-Tue Easter-Oct, daily in August) has the sort of hearty, filling meals that bring the hang-gliders and paragliders out by the wingful. The dish to try, of course, is the lentil soup, and truffle frittatas and *farro* soup round out the territory's offerings.

DRIVING TOUR: THE VALNERINA

Map p324
Distance: 80km
Duration: one to two days
Forget all those softly rolling hillsides and delicate vineyards gracing much of

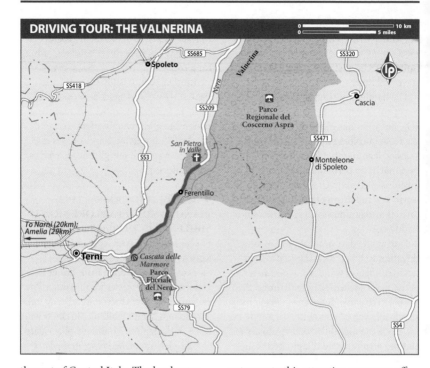

the rest of Central Italy. The landscape
in the Valnerina is a geographically feral
contrast to the nearby time-worn topog-
raphy, but is as beautiful as it is mystical.
Named for the valley of the Nera River,
the ancient flow created steep valleys
and jagged mountains, and millennia
of isolated history has placed hidden
monasteries and castles throughout.
The entire area has been nominated as
a Unesco World Heritage Site, although
it remains one of the most overlooked
spots in Umbria.

The Valnerina is easily accessed as a
day trip from Spoleto, Narni, Norcia or
Amelia, and is little over an hour from
Foligno or Todi. Coming from points
west through industrial Terni is the first
stop, **Cascata delle Marmore** (☎ 0744 6 75
61; www.cascatadellemarmore.it; SR209; adult/conces-
sion €5/2.50; ☟ vary). Don't let the tourist-trap

entrance to this attraction scare you off
(except on weekends in August – then
you should run screaming). These waterfalls are the highest in Europe, plus it's
not often one gets to witness waterfalls
turn 'on' or 'off'. The Romans created
this sight-to-behold in 290 BC, when
they diverted the Velino River into the
Nera River. These days, the waterfalls
provide hydroelectric power to the region. They're surrounded by kilometres
of forested grounds and hiking trails.
One ticket buys you entrance into a lower
and upper parking area, and it's worth it
to see the falls from both. The bizarrely
complex operating hours change monthly
(check with any local tourist office or on
the website), but in the warmer months,
the area is generally open from 9am to
10pm. However, it's when the falls turn
on and off (really) that is the must-see.

Plan on arriving by 10am or 11am most mornings.

As you head from the waterfalls north up the SS209 you'll see a set of medieval walls placed precariously over a hill that mark the entrance to **Ferentillo**, a quiet town set in the midst of the fluvial Valnerina. If you're visiting on a Sunday (call ahead to see if it's open on other days), stop in for lunch at **Ristorante Piermarini** (☎ 0744 78 07 14; www.saporipiermarini.it; Via Ancaiano 23; meals €46; ❤ Tue-Sat, Sun lunch, bookings required for lunch Tue-Fri), where expert service and elegant presentation meet astonishingly good cookery. Many of the ingredients are grown or raised within the Valnerina – grains, fish and, of course, boatloads (well, gravy boat-loads) of truffles. Signore Piermarini himself hunts the truffles with his two trusty hounds (dogs are much better than pigs, he says, because they're not as quick to gobble down the fungi treats). After the first sign announcing Ferentillo, head left into town on Via della Vittoria.

After lunch is well, well digested, head across the SS209, where fans of the macabre will have a deathly good time at the goosebump-inducing **Museo delle Mummie** (Museum of the Mummies; ☎ 0743 543 95; Via delle Torre; adult/concession €3/2; ❤ 9am-12.30pm & 2.30-7.30pm Apr-Sep, 10am-12.30pm & 2.30-6pm Oct & Mar, 10am-12.30pm & 2.30-5pm Nov-Feb), reached through an eerie subterranean 4th-century crypt. You'll find a collection of ancient Ferentillian mummies – glorified desiccated corpses, really – in various stages of decay, mummified naturally with a process of salt, ammonia and mushrooms. Dozens of mummies – one, a visiting 19th-century Chinese doctor – sit, stand or lie down, some still clothed, others with a full set of teeth or hair, a mother and child, and the ever-popular display of disembodied heads.

Six kilometres further north is the ancient abbey of **San Pietro in Valle**. Evidence suggests it was a pagan temple before two wandering Syrian hermits happened upon it in the 5th century. The interior of the abbey has pre-Giotto frescos from the Roman and Lombard epochs.

Much of the abbey has been turned into a hotel, and it would do you wonders to extend your day trip into night at the **Residenza d'Epoca Abbazia San Pietro in Valle** (p416). Or just stop for dinner at its restaurant, **Il Cantico** (☎ 0744 78 00 05; meals €31; ❤ mid-Mar–Oct), tucked under the abbey in a centuries-old subterranean stone vault. Seasonal dishes include crayfish ravioli with Trasimeno bean soup, pumpkin flan with *pecorino* sauce and truffles, and pigeon breast in Sagrantino wine sauce, all made with fresh, local ingredients. A great bet is to order one of the four enormous tasting menus: vegetarian (€35), rivers and lakes (€40), Valnerina specialities (€38) or meat (€40).

Look up information on accommodation, activities, events and dining in English or Italian at www.valnerinaonline.it.

NARNI

· · · · · ·

pop 20,400

While Umbria is called the 'Green Heart of Italy', the town of Narni could be called the true heart of Italy. It's the closest town to the geographic centre of the Italian peninsula, a symbolic position not lost on its inhabitants. Umbria is one of the more rural provinces in Italy, and Narni exudes the friendly, laid-back charm that pervades the southern part of Umbria.

You're not just imagining it: people here are friendlier.

Narni became a Roman stronghold in the 2nd century BC, as the Via Flaminia ran from Rome to Rimini through Narni. Its importance grew partly because of the Nera river, which flowed at the bottom of Narni's great hill. The town developed into a *comune* (city-state) as early as the 11th century but was partially destroyed in the 14th century by northern mercenaries on their way home from sacking Rome. After rebuilding, Narni regained its status as a centre for art and goldsmithing, and held artistic prominence in the Renaissance.

Narni has two historic centres: the quieter Piazza dei Priori, housing the tourist office and Palazzo del Podestà; and Piazza Cavour, home to the cathedral. Just outside the main town gate (the Arco Romano) is Piazza Garibaldi, along the back of the cathedral, where you'll find restaurants, cafes and the bus stop. Everything's a short walk from these two, except the Rocca, which is a drive or a pretty decent hike up the hill. At the bottom of the hill is the Nera and the Roman Ponte d'Augusto.

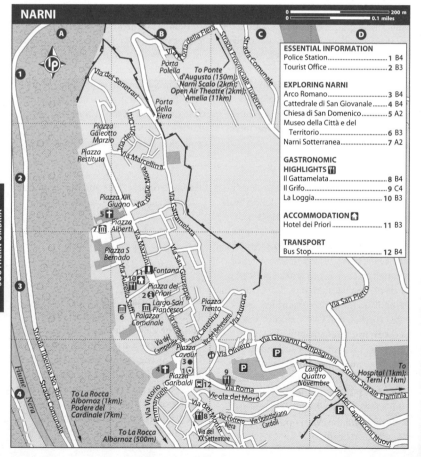

NARNI

ESSENTIAL INFORMATION	
Police Station	1 B4
Tourist Office	2 B3
EXPLORING NARNI	
Arco Romano	3 B4
Cattedrale di San Giovanale	4 B4
Chiesa di San Domenico	5 A2
Museo della Città e del Territorio	6 B3
Narni Sotterranea	7 A2
GASTRONOMIC HIGHLIGHTS	
Il Gattamelata	8 B4
Il Grifo	9 C4
La Loggia	10 B3
ACCOMMODATION	
Hotel dei Priori	11 B3
TRANSPORT	
Bus Stop	12 B4

SOUTHERN UMBRIA

NARNI/NARNIA

One might notice the mythical setting of Narnia from CS Lewis' *The Chronicles of Narnia* bears a striking etymological similarity to the town of Narni, and even more remarkably like its old Roman name, Narnia.

While researching Roman history at Oxford, CS Lewis was inspired by several descriptions of the ancient town of Narnia. He most likely remembers the name from reading books by Livy or Pliny the Elder, which described a stunning Roman village with beautiful villas and baths. In fact, Lewis showed his biographer, Walter Hooper, the ancient atlas in which he'd underlined the town name. Hooper eventually made a literary pilgrimage to Narni in the 1990s.

Although CS Lewis never visited, *narnese* (residents of Narni) like to point out the similarities between mythical and historical Narnia. Narni's symbol is the flying griffin, and fans of the movie will undoubtedly remember seeing them there. In the fourth nave on the right side of the **Cattedrale di San Giovenale** (p328) lies the rather creepy remains of Beata Lucia, Blessed Lucy. At the **Palazzo Comunale** on the town square, look for the stone lion statue, Narni's own Aslan. And if you head down the Via Flaminia towards the **Ponte d'Augusto** (p328), stop off at the halfway point to hunt for the pre-Roman stone altar, similar to the one where Aslan was sacrificed.

ESSENTIAL INFORMATION

EMERGENCIES // Hospital (☎ 0744 74 01; Via Cappuccini Nuova) **Police station** (☎ 0744 71 52 34; Via Portecchia)

TOURIST OFFICES // Tourist office (☎ 0744 71 53 62, 0744 74 72 47; www.comune.narni.tr.it; Piazza dei Priori 3; ☷ 9.30am-12.30pm daily, 4.30-7pm Mon & Tue, 3.30-7pm Wed-Sun)

EXPLORING NARNI

♥ NARNI SOTTERRANEA // WALK IN THE FOOTSTEPS OF THE INQUISITION

Plan your visit to Narni around the concise opening hours of the tortuously fascinating **Narni Sotterranea** (Subterranean Narni; ☎ 0744 72 22 92; www.narnisotterranea.it; Via San Bernardo 12; admission €5; ☷ tours 10.15am, 11.15am, 12.30pm, 3pm, 4.15pm, 5.30pm Sun & public holidays, 3pm-6pm Sat Apr-Oct, 11am, 12.15pm, 3pm, 4.15pm Sun Nov-Mar). The 1½-hour tour (in Italian, English or both) guides you

through millennia of history, starting with a look into Roman plumbing and an underground Romanesque frescoed church, and moving on to an Inquisition prisoner's cell from 1759 and the torture devices with which he might have been familiar. Skulls and bones abound throughout the tour. The subterranean was rediscovered in 1979 on the advice of an older town resident whose grandfather had heard the stories passed down for centuries. The current archaeological director rents a tranquil apartment outside of town, **Podere del Cardinale** (p416), and guests or visitors might be able to lend a hand during the week for the ongoing archaeological excavations. In addition to the above hours the subterranean is also open weekdays during the Corso all'Anello and Ferragosto, or by appointment during the week.

Above the subterranean is the **Chiesa di San Domenico**, where the Dominican inquisitors preached love and kindness when they weren't conducting their inquisition and torturing. The Sotterranea's archaeologist is spending several years excavating the floors under the church. There was a pathway recently discovered that led the monks from the church into the subterranean. Search for the hidden symbols – a Templar 'rosy' cross (a cross hidden in a four-sided rose) and the sun and the moon, the Lombard symbols for the beginning and the end.

♥ LA ROCCA ALBORNOZ // LEARN ABOUT GUELPHS AND GHIBELLINES

Above town is the fortress **La Rocca Albornoz** (admission €3; ☑ 11am-1.30pm & 3.30-6.30pm weekends & holidays; ℗), built by Cardinal Albornoz, who was the heavy charged with switching Narni from a free *comune* to a papal-controlled state in the 13th century. The pope needed an imposing bastion to guard against the pro-Emperor Ghibellines and to scare the people into submission. Some original frescos still exist, but its use as a prison for hundreds of years took its toll on the building. The climb up the tower stairs can be treacherous but it is well worth it for the 360-degree perfect Umbrian views when you get to the top. La Rocca now opens its doors to choirs and orchestras and has a collection of photos from its medieval festival. Also housed is a fascinating motorcycle collection, including a 1906 foldable motorcycle, a rare surviving joint venture from Aermacchi (a popular Italian manufacturer) and Harley Davidson. Imagine the bomber helmet you might have worn sitting in the 1938 BMW sidecar. Contact the tourist office for information.

♥ PONTE D'AUGUSTO // PASS BY HISTORY JUST LIKE A LOCAL

The Romans built the **Ponte d'Augusto**, a bridge on the ancient route of the Via Flaminia, in 27 BC. The bridge now has only one remaining arch, but it's not every day you see a giant Roman arch (unless, of course, you live here).

♥ CATTEDRALE DI SAN GIOVENALE // SEARCH FOR TRACES OF NARNIA

The 12th-century **Cattedrale di San Giovenale** (Piazza Cavour; ☑ 7.30am-12.30pm & 3.30-7pm) is dedicated to Narni's patron saint, San Giovenale, who became the first bishop of Narni in AD 386. You'll see the remains of Beata Lucia, who received the stigmata, and now reminds visitors to Narni of Lucy Pevensie, one of the four children in *The Chronicles of Narnia*. In the courtyard is the Roman statue of a lion, Narni's own version of Aslan from *The Chronicles*.

♥ MUSEO DELLA CITTÀ E DEL TERRITORIO// EXPERIENCE NARNESE HISTORY

It isn't often Umbria gets a new museum, which makes the **Museo della Città e del Territorio** (☎ 0744 71 71 17; www.museoeroli.it; Via Aurelio Saffi 1; ☑ 10.30am-1pm & 3.30-6pm Tues-Sun Apr-Jun & Sep, 10.30am-1pm & 4.30-7pm Tues-Sun Jul-Aug, 10.30am-1pm & 3-5.30pm Sat, Sun & holidays Oct-Mar) an especially rare treat for a small town. Diverse pieces include a Ghirlandaio painting, headstones from residents of Roman Narnia and an Egyptian mummy, but don't forget to stop by the lion (Narni's Aslan?) just past the entrance.

♥ OPEN AIR THEATRE // ENJOY A CONCERT UNDER THE STARS

Built specifically for the Narni Opera Open Air concert series is the 1840-seat, brand-new **Open Air Theatre** (☎ 0744 75 11 97; www.narniopera.it; Parco dei Pini, Piazza Rossellini, Narni Scalo; tickets €12-170, average performances €30-60, reduced prices for under 26yr & over 65yr; ☑ performances May-Sep) puts on world-class

SOUTHERN UMBRIA

performances in a stunning outdoor setting, reminiscent of a Roman theatre. While opera is the main draw, the theatre also hosts a fine array of jazz, classical and world-music performances.

FESTIVALS & EVENTS

Corsa all'Anello (The Race for the Ring) The town's major festival of the year is held three weekends from the end of April to the beginning of May. The town goes all out for this festival, with medieval costumes, sombre processions, cultural events and neighbourhood feasts. The race itself is held on the second Sunday of May.

International Folklore Festival This festival sees folklorist groups from all over the world perform nightly at the Piazza dei Priori. Held from mid-July to mid-August.

GASTRONOMIC HIGHLIGHTS

❦ IL GATTAMELATA €€
☎ 0744 71 72 45; Via Pozzo della Comunità 4; meals €27; ☽ Tue-Sun

Named after the *capitano di ventura* (mercenary captain) Il Gattamelata, this simply decorated restaurant serves wonderful meals that are a little more imaginative than the typical Umbrian cuisine. You can try dishes such as ravioli with smoked cheese in herb-infused butter (€8). The dish you can't leave without trying, however, is the chocolate mousse pyramid dessert, flambéed with essence of vermouth. You can order from two tasting menus that feature foods served during medieval times.

❦ IL GRIFO €
☎ 0744 72 66 25; Via Roma 3; meals €21.50, ☽ Thu-Tue

Specialising in Umbrian and international cuisine, this large restaurant's food is as enticing as its view. Set along the outer walls of the city, the large plate glass-windows overlook the green valley below. Try the sinfully rich gnocchi with black truffles and *taleggio* cream sauce (€10)

OUTDOOR ACTIVITIES

Umbria is a haven for outdoor enthusiasts.

★ **Centro Canoe e Rafting Le Marmore** (☎ 330 753420; www.raftingmarmore.com; Via Carlo Neri) The skittish and the completely insane are both welcome here. One can try 'hydrospeeding' – the white-water equivalent of bobsledding – or take what is called a 'soft rafting' excursion down the Nera River, more appropriate for all ages and skill levels.

★ **Rafting Umbria** (☎ 0742 2 31 46, 348 351 17 98; www.raftingumbria.it; Via Santi Brinati 2, Foligno) Canoeing, kayaking, horseback riding, free climbing, mountain biking, white-water rafting, orienteering and survival skills.

★ **Associazione Gaia** (☎ 338 7678308; www.asgaia.it; Via Cristoforo Colombo 1a, Foligno) In addition to rafting trips, it offers environmental education, mountain biking, horse riding and free climbing.

If you want to take an independent hike, try the tourist brochure *Hiking Trails in the Valnerina and Spoleto Valley*, available at any large office near Spoleto. The English-language guide has maps, directions and durations of 14 hikes (including one that takes you hiking past six monasteries).

SOUTHERN UMBRIA

or the pizzas (€4.50 to €5). A very simple tourist menu costs €12.90.

❧ LA LOGGIA €

☎ 0744 72 27 44; Vicolo del Comune 4; meals €23
Owned by the Hotel dei Priori, this restaurant serves excellent dishes at even better prices. Bright yellow walls and small tables set in front of an open fireplace make for an intimate dinner. The menu blends typical Umbrian dishes with intricate flavours, such as lamb with artichokes (€11) or pork with juniper berries (€8).

TRANSPORT

BUS // Intercity **ATC Terni** (☎ 0744 71 52 07; www.atcterni.it, in Italian) buses leave from Piazza Garibaldi to Amelia (€1.80, 30 minutes, every 45 minutes or so) and Orvieto (€5.20, 80 minutes, five daily).

CAR & MOTORCYCLE // To get to Narni from the A1 autostrada, take the Magliano Sabina exit from the south, and Orte exit from the north.

TRAIN // The station is in Narni Scalo (4km below Narni's city centre) and called Narni/Amelia. Trains connect to Rome (€5.35, 1 to 1 ½ hours, hourly), Orvieto (€3.85 to €9.75, almost hourly). Buses (€1.25, 15 minutes, hourly) trek up the hill into the city centre, usually in connection with arriving trains.

AMELIA

· · · · · ·

pop 11,900

Few words describe this town as aptly as 'sweet'. Perhaps 'quaint', 'delightful' or 'adorable' come close. It's a tiny village, unassuming and unspoiled, with one of the oldest histories in Umbria. The legend goes that Amelia was founded by a mythological king named Ameroe in the 12th century BC. Latin texts mention the existence of Amelia as a settlement as early as the 11th century BC (four centuries before Rome was founded). A good chunk of the original walls (believed to have been constructed sometime around the 6th century BC) can still be seen by the theatre, but much of the wall is of newer construction…you know, the 4th century BC.

Signs in front of monuments are in Italian and English, so it's easy to get around.

ESSENTIAL INFORMATION

TOURIST INFORMATION // Pro Loco Città di Amelia (☎ 0744 98 25 59; web.tiscali.it/proloco

SOUTHERN UMBRIA

～ WORTH A TRIP ～

The most complete example of a Roman city in Umbria, **Carsulae** (☎ 0744 33 41 33; adult/ concession €4.40/3.30; ☺ 8.30am-7.30pm Apr-Sep, to 5.30pm Oct- Mar) isn't quite the size of Pompeii or Rome, but it does offer some spectacular Roman history in a beautiful setting. During the reign of Augustus in the 3rd century BC, Romans built the strategically important Via Flaminia. Carsulae was one of the many outposts systematically built along this Roman version of a highway. It was on the part of the road that joined Narnia to Vicus Martis Tudertium (Narni to the Todi region), so when reconstruction started on a more easterly route, Carsulae fell into decline. Then barbarians from the north began using this part of the road to head towards Rome, and Carsulae had no chance.

To arrive here, take the road to Perugia from Terni. Look for the sign indicating SS75/San Gemini and you'll then see signs for Carsulae. The closest place to spend the night around Carsulae is in San Gemini.

.amelia; Piazza Augusto Vera 8; ⏰ 9.30am-12pm & 3.30-5pm Mon-Sat) **Amelia** (www.amelia.it)

EXPLORING AMELIA

Amelia is almost entirely surrounded by pre-Roman polygonal walls, possibly dating back to the 6th century BC. The huge stones have held together without mortar for over 2500 years. Piazza Matteotti was the site of an ancient Roman forum.

If you're with your darling be sure to walk down from Piazza Matteotti past the Palazzo Municipale to Vicolo Baciafemmine (Girl-Kissing Alley), so named because its narrowness has been known to cause passers-by to get close enough to let their passions run amok.

❤ MUSEO ARCHEOLOGICO DI AMELIA // FIND RELICS OF THE TROJAN WAR

Don't miss the fascinating **Museo Archeologico di Amelia** (☎ 0744 97 81 20; www .sistemamuseo.it, in Italian; Piazza Augusto Vera 10; adult/concession €5/4; ⏰ 10.30am-1pm & 3.30-6pm Fri-Sun Oct-Mar, 10.30am-1pm & 4-7pm Tue-Sat Apr-Jun & Sep, 10.30am-1pm & 4.30-7.30pm Tue-Sun Jul-Aug), with its famous bronze statue of Germanico, Roman captain and adopted son of Tiberius. Over 2m high, this almost fully restored statue is covered in armour featuring Achilles' ambush of Troilus in the Trojan War. You'll also find a painting by one of Amelia's most famous residents, Piermatteo d'Amelia. Piermatteo was instrumental in securing Christopher Columbus the three ships he used to discover America and was also the painter of the original Sistine Chapel ceiling.

❤ EUROLINKS // LEARN TO COOK OR SPEAK THE LINGO

If you're looking for somewhere easygoing to learn Italian, try **Eurolinks** (☎ 0744 98 18 60; www.eurolinkschool.com; Viale Rimembranze 48), which runs live-in classes at all levels from €660 per week for accommodation and instruction. It also arranges wellness retreats, cooking courses and tours of local wineries.

GASTRONOMIC HIGHLIGHTS

Be sure to try the local sweet *fichi girotti* at any shop in town. It's kind of like eating the hardened insides of a fig biscuit mixed with chocolate and nuts.

❤ OSTERIA DEI CANSACCHI €

☎ 0744 97 85 57; Piazza Cansacchi 4; meals €22; ⏰ Thu-Tue

Set in a medieval atmosphere, this restaurant combines two excellent local delicacies by serving *bistecche di cinghiale e porcini* (wild boar with *porcini* mushrooms). Pizza is a good and inexpensive bet here, but the fish comes most highly recommended. For an excellent pasta dish, try the *tagliata tartufo*, homemade local pasta with black truffles.

TRANSPORT

BUS // Intercity **ATC Terni** (☎ 0744 49 27 11, www.atcterni.it, in Italian) buses leave from in front of the main gate to Narni (€1.85, 30 minutes, every 45 minutes or so) and Orvieto (€4.45, 70 minutes, seven daily).
TRAIN // The station is in Narni Scalo (4km below Narni's city centre) and called Narni/Amelia. Buses run about 15 times daily between Amelia and the station (€1.25, 20 minutes).

BACKGROUND

♥ HISTORY
Plague, plotting and patronage – Tuscany and Umbria's wild and wonderful history makes for great reading (opposite).

♥ LIVING THE IDYLL
Life is sweet in this privileged pocket of Italy, but dress well and order the right coffee if you want to fit in (p347).

♥ ART & ARCHITECTURE
This is where the Renaissance kicked off and saw its greatest triumphs – thousands of them (p351); check out our who's-who of artists and their masterworks (p362).

♥ RENAISSANCE FRESCOS
They may look like bible stories now, but in their heyday, Renaissance frescos provided running social commentary as well as religious inspiration (p364).

♥ VENTURE OUTDOORS
Useful information for those who are keen to walk, cycle, swim, ski or fish in these splendid natural landscapes (p369).

♥ ON THE WINE TRAIL
Comparing the relative merits and demerits of DOCGs, DOCs and Super Tuscans is sometimes difficult – but boy, it's fun (p375).

♥ THE TUSCAN & UMBRIAN TABLE
Food in Tuscany and Umbria is seasonally driven, flavour-charged and best savoured slowly (p381).

♥ FOOD GLOSSARY
Words and phrases to help you order everything from a sweet snack to a Florentine feast (p389).

HISTORY

· · · · · · ·

No one knows exactly why the ancient Etruscans headed to Tuscany and Umbria from parts east (probably Anatolia) in the 9th century BC, but Etruscan artefacts give some idea why they stayed: dinner. The wild boar that roam the Tuscan and Umbrian hills was a favourite item on the Etruscan menu, and boar hunts are a recurring theme on Etruscan ceramics, tomb paintings and even bronze hand mirrors. In case the odd boar bristle tickled the throat or a truffle shaving headed down the windpipe while eating, Etruscans washed down their meals with plenty of wine, thereby introducing viticulture to Italy.

Tomb paintings show Etruscan women keeping pace with men in banquets so decadent they scandalised even the orgy-happy Romans. Many middle-class and aristocratic women had the means to do what they wished, which apparently included music, romance, politics and overseeing a vast underclass of servants. Roman military histories boast of conquests of Etruscan women along with Etruscan territory starting in the 3rd century BC, but these accounts are probably exaggerated. According to recent genetic tests, Etruscans did not mingle much with their captors – their genetic material is distinct from modern Italians, who are the descendants of ancient Romans.

Etruscans didn't take kindly to Roman authority, nor were they keen on being enslaved to establish Roman plantations. They secretly allied with Hannibal to bring about the ignominious defeat of the Romans at Lago Trasimeno, where some 16,000 Roman soldiers were lost in approximately three hours (see the boxed text, p294). After that Rome began to take a more hands-off approach with the Etruscans, granting them citizenship in 88 BC to manage their own affairs in the new provinces of Umbria and Tuscia (Tuscany), and in return securing safe passage along the major inland Roman trade route is the Via Flaminia. Little did the Romans suspect when they paved the road that they were also paving the way for their own replacements in the 5th to 8th centuries AD: first came German emperor Theodoric, then Byzantine emperor Justinian, then the Lombards and finally Charlemagne in 800.

MAROZIA & MATILDA: HOW TO MAKE (& BREAK) POPES

In medieval times political power constantly changed hands. Nevertheless, two notorious women managed to wield power effectively against a shifting backdrop of kings and popes. The daughter of a Roman senator and a notorious prostitute-turned-

» 9TH CENTURY BC	» 265 BC	» 88 BC
Etruscans bring wine, women and song to the hills of Tuscany and Umbria, but fail to invite the Romans; war ensues.	Etruria falls to Rome, but remains unruly and conspires with Hannibal against Rome during the Punic Wars.	Roman headaches are solved by granting the Etruscans citizenship to manage their own affairs.

BACKGROUND

senatrix, Marozia already had one illegitimate son by her lover Pope Sergius III and was pregnant again when she married the Lombard duke of Spoleto, Alberic I, in 909 AD. He was hardly scrupulous himself: he'd achieved his position by murdering the previous duke, and he soon had Sergius III deposed. When Alberic was in turn killed, Marozia married Guy of Tuscany and conspired with him to smother Pope John X and install (in lethally rapid succession) Pope Leo VI and Stephen VIII.

After Guy's death, she wooed his half-brother Hugh of Arles, the new king of Italy. No matter that he already had a wife: his previous marriage was soon annulled. But at the wedding ceremony, Marozia's son, Alberic II, who had been named Pope John XI, had the happy couple arrested – he was reportedly scandalised that his mother had turned the papacy into a 'pornocracy'. Marozia spent the rest of her life in prison, but her legacy lived on: no fewer than five popes were her direct descendants.

Countess Matilda of Tuscany (1046–1115) was another powerful woman. Rumour has it that she was more than just an ally to Pope Gregory VII, and there's no doubt that she was a formidable strategist both on and off the battlefield. To consolidate her family's Tuscan holdings, she married her own stepbrother, Godfrey the Hunchback. She soon arranged for him to be sent off to Germany, annulling the marriage soon after and finding herself a powerful prince 26 years her junior to marry.

When Matilda's ally Pope Gregory VII excommunicated Holy Roman Emperor Henry IV in 1077 for threatening to replace him with an antipope, the emperor showed up outside her castle barefoot and kneeling in the snow to beg the pope's forgiveness. Gregory, who was Matilda's guest, kept him waiting for three days before rescinding the excommunication. Henry retaliated for what he saw as Matilda's complicity in his humiliation by conspiring with Matilda's neighbours to seize her property, and even turned her trophy husband against her – but Matilda soon dislodged Henry's power base in the north with the support of his own son, Conrad. Disgraced by his own family and humbled on the battlefield by a woman, Henry died in 1106. Matilda outlived him by nine years, and at her death left behind substantial holdings to the Church, a lineage that would claim among its descendants one Michelangelo Buonarroti, and her mortal remains to be interred at St Peter's Basilica in Rome.

AGONY & ECSTASY

Lashings, starvation, solitary confinement: in the Middle Ages it wasn't always easy to distinguish religious practices from criminal punishments. Among the privileged classes it became a mark of distinction to renounce worldly ties for a life of piety – not

» 59 BC	» AD 476	» 570–774
After emerging victorious from a corrupt election campaign for the position of Roman consul, Julius Caesar establishes a soldier-retiree resort called Florentia.	German king Odovacar snatches Rome out from under Romulus Augustulus, and becomes the first of many foreign kings of Italy.	The Lombards rule Italy as far south as Florence, and manage to turn the tiny duchy of Spoleto into a booming trade empire.

to mention it was a handy way to winnow the number of eligible heirs to a title. A nobleman from Norcia named Benedict set the example and started a monastery-building spree in AD 500, when he ditched his studies to seek a higher purpose among hermits in the hills. His rule of peace, prayer and work was taken up by Benedictine religious orders, which limited food intake and downtime but didn't require the vows of silence, fasting or hard labour practised by more hermetic believers. Some Benedictine orders had help tilling their fields from tenant farmers and hired workers, freeing up monks for reading and creative tasks such as manuscript illumination and winemaking.

But not all medieval monks and nuns whiled away the hours with a good book and a nice glass of wine. 'Hair shirts' woven of scratchy sackcloth, horsehair or chain mail became all the rage among the aristocracy after Holy Roman Emperor Charlemagne (c AD 742–814) was buried in his. The first known case of religious self-flagellation dates from the mid-13th century in Perugia, when a strange, spontaneous parade of believers began whipping themselves while singing. By 1260 roving bands of Flagellants appeared in major cities across Tuscany and Umbria, stripped to the waist, hooded and ecstatically whipping themselves while sing-

> *'in the Middle Ages it wasn't always easy to distinguish religious practices from criminal punishments'*

ing *laudi,* songs about the passion of Christ. They made quite an impression in Florence, Siena and Gubbio, where adherents formed *scuole di battuti* (schools of beatings) to build *case di Dio* (houses of God) that served as charity centres and hospices and also hosted mass flagellation sessions using specialised equipment.

The sudden popularity of mortification of the flesh may be tied to the popular outpouring of grief at the death of St Francis of Assisi in 1226; legend has it that even his trusty donkey wept to see him go. Although he did practise strict poverty and periodic fasting and wore chafing friar's robes, the gentle Francis was apparently too preoccupied with caring for the sick, needy and animals to make a conspicuous display of his own personal suffering, even when going blind.

The Church remained neutral on the issue until the fledgling Flagellants claimed that like scratching an itch, their activities could grant temporary relief from sin. This posed direct competition for the Church's practice of confession, not to mention its steady business in indulgences, pardons and tithes. The Flagellant movement was banned in 1262, only to regain momentum a century later during the plague and recur periodically until the 15th century, when the Inquisition subjected Flagellants to

» 773–74	» 800	» 1082
Charlemagne crosses the Alps into Italy, fighting the Lombards and having his ownership of Tuscany, Emilia, Venice and Corsica confirmed by Pope Hadrian I.	Pope Leo III crowns Charlemagne Holy Roman Emperor on Christmas Day.	Florence picks a fight with Siena over ownership of the Chianti region, starting a bitter rivalry that will last the next 400 years.

the ultimate mortification of the flesh: burning at the stake. Self-flagellation processions continued to be held in Tuscany under the Church's guidance into the late 19th century, and self-flagellation continues to be practised privately by zealous penitents today.

DEMOCRACY AMONG DEVIANTS

Not all agony came with a side order of religious ecstasy in medieval Tuscany and Umbria. Legal records indicate that no one was exempt from violence: leaders of powerful families were stabbed by rivals while attending Mass; peasants were ambushed by brigands roaming the deceptively bucolic landscape; and bystanders were maimed in neighbourhood disputes that all too easily escalated to kill-or-be-killed brawls.

But if crime seemed vicious, medieval criminal justice was often worse. Even petty crimes such as theft were subject to some combination of steep fines, corporal punishment and public humiliation, such as public flogging or mutilation. Nobles could demand satisfaction for the rather capriciously defined crime of *laesa maiestas* (insulting nobility), but an alarming number skipped such legal niceties and kidnapped or suffocated the children of their rivals instead. Jails were rare, since suspects received only cursory trials and incarceration was deemed insufficient to extract true penitence. The earliest known jail in the region (and among the first in Europe) was Le Stinche prison, founded in Florence in 1297. Niccolò Machiavelli (1469–1527) endured six rounds of interrogation on Le Stinche's notorious rack for an alleged plot to overthrow the government, and amazingly survived to describe the place.

By the 13th century, many Tuscan and Umbrian communities were well and truly ready for change. Farmers who had painstakingly reclaimed their fields wanted to get their produce to market alive; merchants needed peaceful piazzas in which to conduct their business; and the populace at large began to entertain hopes of living past the age of 40. *Comuni* (town councils) were established in cities and towns such as Gubbio, Siena and Perugia, with representatives drawn from influential families, guilds and the merchant classes in a new power-sharing arrangement. Across Tuscany and Umbria, ambitious building projects were undertaken to give citizens a new sense of shared purpose and civic identity. Hospitals and public charities helped serve the city's needy, and new public squares, marketplaces and town halls became crucial meeting places and testing grounds for civic society. Law and order was kept (relatively speaking) by a *podesta,* an independent judiciary often brought in from outside the city for limited terms of office to prevent corruption.

» 1080	» 1136	» 1167
Henry IV deposes Pope Gregory VII for the second time, installing Clement III in his place and marching against Gregory's supporter Matilda of Tuscany.	Scrappy, seafaring Pisa adds Amalfi to its list of conquests, which included Jerusalem, Valencia, Tripoli and Mallorca, and colonies in Constantinople and Cairo, among others.	The Siena *comune* establishes a written constitution declaring elected terms should be short and money should be pretty; it's later amended to guarantee public boxing matches.

Each *comune* developed its own style of government, and the most imaginative of these was Siena's. To curb bloody turf battles among its *contrade* (neighbourhoods), Siena channelled that fighting spirit into organised boxing matches, bullfights and Il Palio, the annual horse race that is still run today (see the boxed text, p185). Anyone who broke the peace was subject to heavy fines, and the city's coffers soon swelled with monies collected in the city's *osterie* (wine bars serving some food) for cursing. After Florence won yet another battle against Siena by cutting off the town's water supply, Siena's *comune* was faced with a funding choice: either build an underground aqueduct to fend off Florence, or build a cathedral that would establish Siena as a creative capital of the medieval world. The council voted unanimously for the cathedral. Work began almost immediately in 1215 and continued for more than three centuries, through bouts of famine, banking disasters and plague that nearly wiped out the city. From these dark days emerged a magnificent Duomo (p185) and an expressive, eerily glowing style of painting known as the Sienese School, which is recognised as a precocious precursor to the Renaissance.

DISASTERS & SAVING GRACES

'Midway on our life's journey, I found myself in dark woods, the right road lost…' So begins the ominous year 1300 in Dante Alighieri's *Inferno*, where our hero Dante escapes from one circle of hell only to tumble into the next. Gloomy? Certainly – but also uncannily accurate. In the 14th century, Dante and his fellow Tuscans would face a harrowing sequence of events, including famine, economic collapses, plague, war and tyranny. Umbrians had all this to contend with plus a series of earthquakes, not to mention lowlands that tended to revert to marsh when not diligently drained. It's no small miracle that anyone in the region survived the 14th century – but it's an even greater wonder that the early Renaissance emerged from this hellish scenario.

When medieval mystics predicted that the year 1300 would bring certain doom for all but a few, they were off by barely 50 years. Approximately two-thirds of the population were decimated in cities across Tuscany and Umbria in the bubonic plague outbreak of 1348, and since the carriers of the plague (fleas and rats) weren't correctly identified or eradicated, the Black Death repeatedly ravaged the area for decades afterwards. Blame for the disease was placed on the usual suspects – lepers, immigrants, Romany people, heretics, Jewish communities, women of loose morals – but no amount of scapegoating could cure the afflicted. Entire hospital and monastery populations were wiped out, leaving treatment to opportunists promising miracle

» 1223	» 1314–21	» 1348–50
Franciscan order founded in Assisi, with strict vows of poverty and lifelong manual labour requirements; monasteries are soon overflowing with new recruits.	Dante writes his *Divina Commedia*, told in the first person, using Tuscan dialect instead of formal Latin, and peppered with political satire, pathos, adventure and light humour.	Black Death ravages Tuscany and Umbria, wiping out around two-thirds of the population in dense urban areas; 40 more outbreaks are recorded in Umbria before 1500.

cures. Flagellation, liquor, sugar and spices were prescribed, as was abstinence from bathing, fruit and olive oil – all to no avail. Florentine author and 1348 plague eyewitness Giovanni Boccaccio writes of entire families left to starve under quarantine, sick children abandoned by parents and family members hastily dumped still breathing in mass graves.

But amid the ample evidence of human failings there were also more reassuring signs of humanity. Meals were shared, and orphans cared for by strangers. Doctors and devout clergy who cared for the sick were the most obvious heroes of the day; though they lacked the medical knowledge to save plague victims, they knowingly risked their own lives just to provide a dignified death for their patients. At age 19, St Catherine of Siena overruled her family's understandable objections and dedicated her life to serving the plague ridden. She also wrote long, eloquent letters to the pope and heads of powerful families in the region, imploring them to reconsider their warring ways and allow the troubled region a moment's peace.

Painful though those days must have been to record, writers such as Dante (1265–1321), Boccaccio (1313-75) and Marchione di Coppo Stefani (c 1336–85) wrote frank assessments of their time, believing that their critiques might one day serve the greater good. More than any painterly tricks of perspective or shading, it's this rounded view of humanity that brought truth to Renaissance art.

This legacy was almost lost centuries later in another disaster, the 1966 Great Flood of Florence, which deluged the city with more than 4m of water, left thousands of people homeless, and buried three million rare manuscripts and thousands of works of art under some 500,000 tonnes of mud, stone and sewage. People arrived in force from across Italy and around the world to rescue the city and its treasures from the mud, and today these heroes are honoured as *gli angeli del fango* (angels of mud).

BETWEEN BELLIGERENCE & BEAUTY

The Renaissance was a time of great art and great tyrants, between which there was an uneasy relationship. The careful balance of power of the *comuni* became a casualty of the plague in the 14th century; political control was mostly left to those who managed to survive and were either strong enough or unscrupulous enough to claim it. In 1353 Spanish-born cardinal Gil Álvarez Carrillo de Albornoz (1310–67), known in Italian as Egidio Albornoz, was sent to Italy by Pope Innocent VI to seize the moment. With the help of a small army of mercenaries he extended the Church's control across central Italy, building fortifications for new religious authorities in formerly independent

» 1353–57	» 1375–1406	» 1378
Cardinal Gil de Albornoz exerts Church control across central Italy. Wherever appeals to faith fail to convince locals, he barges in with troops and sets up a fortified castle atop the town.	Philosopher-politician Coluccio Salutati serves as chancellor of Florence, promoting a secular civic identity to trump old feudal tendencies – a bold, new model that occasionally even works.	The Florentine city council ignores a petition from the city's wool carders, who want guild representation: cue the Revolt of Ciompi, an ultimately unsuccessful democratic uprising.

secular municipalities such as Perugia. In *comuni* such as Florence and Siena, powerful families assumed control of the *signoria,* the city council ostensibly run by guild representatives and merchants.

Most unelected Renaissance rulers weren't great tyrants but rather petty ones, obsessed with accumulating personal power and wealth, and their lasting contributions to civic life were costly wars of conquest and internal strife. Cities, commercial entities and individual families took sides with either the Rome-backed Guelphs or the imperial Ghibellines, loyalists of the Holy Roman Empire. Since each of these factions was eager to put itself on the map, this competition might have meant a bonanza for artists and architects – but shifting fortunes in the battlefield meant funds for pet art projects could disappear just as quickly as they appeared.

Tuscany began to resemble a chess game, with feudal castles appearing only to be overtaken, powerful bishops aligning with nobles before being toppled, and minor players backed by key commercial interests occasionally rising to power. Nowhere was the chess game harder to follow than in the Ghibelline *comune* of Pistoia: first it was conquered by the Florentine Guelphs, then it split into White and Black Guelph splinter groups, then it was captured by Lucca (which was at that time Ghibelline backed) before being reclaimed by the Florentines.

> '*The Renaissance was a time of great art and great tyrants*'

The Medici family were by no means exempt from the usual failings of Renaissance tyrants, but early on in his rise to power Cosimo the Elder (Cosimo il Vecchio; 1389–1464) revealed a surprisingly enlightened self-interest and an exceptional eye for art. Although he held no elected office, he served as ambassador for the Church, and through his behind-the-scenes diplomatic skills managed to finagle a rare 25-year stretch of relative peace for Florence. When a conspiracy led by competing banking interests exiled him from the city in 1433, some of Cosimo's favourite artists split town with him, including Donatello and Fra' Angelico. But they weren't gone long: Cosimo's banking interests were too important to Florence, and he returned triumphant after just a year to crush his rivals, exert even greater behind-the-scenes control and sponsor masterpieces such as Brunelleschi's legendary dome for Florence's Duomo (p44).

But sponsorship from even the most enlightened and powerful patrons had its downside: their whims could make or break artists and they attracted powerful enemies. Lorenzo de' Medici (Lorenzo the Magnificent; 1449–92) was a legendary supporter of the arts and humanities, providing crucial early recognition and support for

» 1469–92	» 1478–80	» 1494
Lorenzo de' Medici unofficially rules Florence, despite the 1478 Pazzi Conspiracy, an attemped overthrow that left his brother Giuliano torn to shreds in the Duomo.	A confusing set of wars breaks out among the papacy, Siena, Florence, Venice, Milan and Naples. Individual families broker secret pacts; the Tuscan population pays the price.	The Medici are expelled; Savonarola declares a theocratic republic with his Consiglia di Cinquecento – a kind of religious Red Guard that denounces neighbours for owning books.

Leonardo da Vinci, Sandro Botticelli and Michelangelo Buonarroti, among others. But after Lorenzo narrowly escaped an assassination attempt by a conspiracy among the rival Florentine Pazzi family, the king of Naples and the pope, the artists he supported had to look elsewhere for sponsorship until Lorenzo could regain his position. Religious reformer Savonarola took an even darker view of Lorenzo and the classically influenced art he promoted, viewing it as a sinful indulgence in a time of great need and suffering. When Savonarola ousted the Medici in 1494, he decided their decadent art had to go, too, and works by Botticelli, Michelangelo and others went up in flames in a massive Bonfire of the Vanities on Florence's Piazza della Signoria (p50).

THE SUN & OTHER TOUCHY SUBJECTS

Savonarola's theocratic rule over Florence lasted just four years, until his denunciation of decadence got him excommunicated and executed by Pope Alexander VI (1431–1503), who didn't appreciate Savonarola critiquing his extravagant spending, illegitimate children and pursuit of personal vendettas. But Savonarola's short reign would have an impact on Tuscany and Umbria for centuries to come. The church now saw the need to exert more direct control over the independent-minded region, and to guard against humanist philosophies that might contradict the Church's divine authority. The Inquisition made heretical ideas punishable by death, which had an understandably chilling effect on intellectual inquiry. The celebrated universities in Pisa, Perugia and Siena were subject to close scrutiny, and the University of Pisa was effectively closed for about 50 years until Cosimo I de' Medici (1519–74) reinaugurated it in 1543.

One of the most notable faculty members at the revitalised University of Pisa was a professor of mathematics named Galileo Galilei (1564–1642). To put it in mathematical terms, Galileo was a logical paradox: a Catholic who fathered three illegitimate children; a man of science with a poetic streak, who lectured on the dimensions of hell according to Dante's *Inferno;* and an inventor of telescopes whose head was quite literally in the clouds, yet who kept in close contact with many friends who were the leading intellectuals of their day.

Galileo's meticulous observations of the physical universe attracted the attention of the Church, which by the 16th century had a difficult relationship to the stars. Pope Paul III kept several astrologers on hand, and no major papal initiative or construction project could be undertaken without first searching the sky with an astrolabe for auspicious signs. Yet theologian (and sometime astrologer) Tommaso Campanella was

» 1498	» 1527–30	» 1571
To test Savonarola's beliefs, rival Franciscans invite him to a trial by fire. He sends a representative to be burned instead, but is eventually tortured, hung and burned as a heretic.	Florentines run the Medici out of town. The Republic of Florence holds out for three years, until the emperor's and pope's combined cannon power reinstalls the Medici.	Painters are no longer obliged to belong to guilds, so individual artistic expression means you don't have to pay your dues first.

BACKGROUND

MACHIAVELLI'S MANOEUVRES

Born in 1469 into a poor offshoot of one of Florence's leading families, Niccolò Machiavelli got off to a bad start. His father, an impoverished, small-time lawyer, was continually in debt, but was at least rich in books, which his son devoured.

Somehow the young Machiavelli managed to swing a post in the city's second chancery at the age of 29 and so embarked on a colourful career as a Florentine public servant. Our man must have shown early promise, as by 1500 he was in France on his first diplomatic mission in the service of the Republic.

Impressed by the martial success of Cesare Borgia and the centralised state of France, Machiavelli came to the conclusion that Florence needed a standing army.

The city, like many others on the Italian peninsula, had formerly employed mercenaries to fight its wars. The problem was that mercenaries had few reasons to fight and die for anyone. They took their pay and often did their best to avoid mortal combat. Machiavelli convinced the Republic of the advantages of a conscripted militia, which he formed in 1506. Three years later it was blooded in battle against the rebellious city of Pisa, whose fall was mainly attributed to the troops led by the wily statesman.

The return to power of the Medici family in 1512 was a blow for Machiavelli, who was promptly removed from office. Suspected of plotting against the Medici, he was even thrown into the dungeon in 1513 and tortured. He maintained his innocence and, once freed, retired a poor man to his little property outside Florence.

It was in these years, far from political power, that he did his greatest writing. *Il Principe* (The Prince) is his classic treatise on the nature of power and its administration, a work reflecting the confusing and corrupt times in which he lived and his desire for strong and just rule in Florence and beyond.

Machiavelli never got back into the mainstream of public life. He was commissioned to write an official history of Florence, the *Istorie Fiorentine,* and towards the end of his life he was appointed to a defence commission to improve the city walls and join a papal army in its ultimately futile fight against imperial forces. By the time the latter had sacked Rome in 1527, Florence had again rid itself of Medici rule. Machiavelli hoped that he would be restored to a position of dignity, but by now he was suspected almost as much by the Medici opponents as he had been years before by the Medici. He died in 1527 frustrated and, as in his youth, on the brink of poverty.

» 1633

Galileo Galilei is condemned for heresy in Rome. True to his observations of a pendulum in motion, the Inquisition's extreme measures yield an opposite reaction: Enlightenment.

» 1656

Oh no, not again: the plague kills at least 300,000 people across central and southern Italy.

» 1737

Maria Theresa ends the Medici's dynastic rule by installing her husband as grand duke of Tuscany. She remains the brains of the operation, reforming Tuscany from behind the scenes.

BACKGROUND

found guilty of heresy for dissenting views that emphasised observation. Research into the universe's guiding physical principles was entrusted by Paul III to his consulting theologians, who determined from close examination of the scriptures that the sun must revolve around the earth.

Equipped with telescopes that he'd adjusted and improved, Galileo came to a different conclusion. His observations supported Nicolaus Copernicus' theory that the planets revolved around the sun, and a cautious body of Vatican Inquisitors initially allowed him to publish his findings as long as he also presented a case for the alternate view. But when Galileo's research turned out to be dangerously convincing, the Vatican reversed its position and tried him for heresy. By then Galileo was quite ill, and his weakened state and widespread support may have spared him the usual heresy sentence of execution. Under official threat of torture, Galileo stated in writing that he may have overstated the case for the Copernican view of the universe, and was allowed to carry out his prison sentence under house arrest. Pope Urban VIII alternately indulged his further studies and denied him access to doctors, but Galileo kept on pursuing scientific research even after he began losing his sight. Meanwhile, Tommaso Campanella was taken out of prison and brought to Rome, where he became Urban VIII's personal astrologer in 1629.

GOING FOR BAROQUE

With his astrologers on hand, the pope might have seen Italy's foreign domination coming. Far from cementing the Church's authority, the Inquisition created a power vacuum on the ground while papal authorities were otherwise occupied with lofty theological matters. While local Italian nobles and successful capitalists vied among themselves for influence as usual, the Austrian Holy Roman Empress Maria Theresa took charge of the situation in 1737, and set up her husband Francis as the grand duke of Tuscany.

The mother of 16 children (including the now-notorious Marie Antoinette) and self-taught military strategist soon put local potentates in check, and pushed through reforms that curbed witch burning, outlawed torture, established mandatory education and allowed Italian peasants to keep a modest share of their crops. She also brought the Habsburgs' signature flashy style to Tuscany and Umbria, and kicked off a frenzy of redecoration that included flamboyant frescos packed with cherubs, ornate architectural details that were surely a nightmare to dust, and gilding whenever and wherever possible. Perhaps fearing that her family's priceless art collection might

BACKGROUND

» 1765–90	» 1796–1801	» 1805–14
Moved by Cesare Beccaria's case for criminal justice reform, Enlightenment leader Leopold I makes Tuscany the first sovereign state to outlaw the death penalty.	Italy becomes a battleground between Napoleon, the Habsburgs and their Russian allies; Tuscan and Umbrian cultural patrimony is divvied up as spoils of war.	Napoleon establishes himself as king of Italy, with the military assistance of Italian soldiers he'd conscripted; when his conscripts desert, Napoleon loses Tuscany to Ferdinando III.

factor into Maria Theresa's redecorating plans, Medici heiress Anna Maria Luisa de' Medici willed everything to the city of Florence upon her death in 1743, on the condition that it all must remain in the city.

Naturally the glint of gold captured the attention of Napoleon Bonaparte, who took over swaths of Tuscany and Umbria in 1799. So appreciative was Napoleon of the area's cultural heritage, in fact, that he decided to take as much as possible home with him. What he couldn't take he gave as gifts to various relatives – never mind that all those Tuscan villas and church altarpieces were not technically his to give. When Habsburg Ferdinando III took over the title of grand duke of Tuscany in 1814, Napoleon's sister Elisa Bonaparte and various other relations refused to budge from the luxe Lucchesi villas they had usurped, and concessions had to be made to accommodate them all.

Still more upmarket expats arrived in Tuscany and Umbria with the inauguration of Italy's cross-country train lines in 1840. Soon no finishing-school education would be complete without a Grand Tour of Italy, and the landmarks and museums of Tuscany and Umbria were required reading. Trainloads of debutantes, dour chaperones and career bachelors arrived, setting the stage for EM Forster novels, Tuscan timeshare investors and George Clooney wannabes.

RED & BLACK: A CHEQUERED PAST

While an upper-crust expat community was exporting Romantic notions about Italy, the country was facing some harsh realities. Commercial agriculture provided tidy sums to absentee royal Austrian landlords while reducing peasants to poverty and creating stiff competition for small family farms. In rural areas, three-quarters of the family income was spent on a meagre diet of mostly grains. The promise of work in the burgeoning industrial sector lured many to cities, where long working hours and dangerous working conditions simply led to another dead end, and 70% of family income was still spent on food. Upward mobility was rare, since university admissions were strictly limited, and the Habsburgs were cautious about allowing locals into their imperial army or bureaucratic positions. Increasingly, the most reliable means for Tuscans and Umbrians to support their families was emigration to the Americas.

Austrian rule provided a common enemy that, for once, united Italians across provinces and classes. The Risorgimento (reunification period) was not so much a reorganisation of some previously unified Italian state (which hadn't existed since Roman times) as a revival of city-state ideals of an independent citizenry. The secret

» 1861	» 1871	» 1915
Two decades of insurrections culminate in a new Italian government, with parliament and king. Florence becomes Italy's capital in 1865, despite extensive poverty and bread riots.	After French troops are withdrawn from Rome, the forces of the Kingdom of Italy defeat those of the Papal States to take power in Rome; the capital moves there from Florence.	Italy enters WWI fighting a familiar foe: the Austro-Hungarian Empire. War casualties, stranded POWs, heating-oil shortages and food rationing make for a hard-won victory by 1918.

societies that had flourished right under the noses of the French as a local check on colonial control soon formed a network of support for nationalist sentiment. During 1848 and 1849 revolution broke out, and a radical government was temporarily installed in Florence. Nervous that the Austrians would invade, conservative Florentine leaders invited Habsburg Leopold II to return as archduke of Tuscany. But when rural unrest in Tuscany made Austria's return to power difficult, Austrian retaliation and brutal repression galvanised nationalist sentiment in the region. Although the country was united under one flag in 1861, this early split between radicals and conservatives would define the region's political landscape in the years ahead.

Unification didn't end unemployment or unrest; only 2% of Italy's population gained the right to vote in 1861 – the same 2% that controlled most of the country's wealth. Strikes were held across the country to protest working conditions, and their brutal suppression gave rise to a new Socialist Party in 1881. The new Italian government's money-making scheme to establish itself as a colonial power in Ethiopia and Eritrea proved a costly failure – 17,000 Italian soldiers were lost near Adowa in 1896, in what was the worst defeat of any European colonial power in Africa. When grain prices were raised in 1898, many impoverished Italians could no longer afford to buy food, and riots broke out. Rural workers unionised, and when a strike was called in 1902, 200,000 rural labourers came out en masse.

Finally Italian politicians began to take the hint and initiated some reforms. Child labour was banned, working hours were set and the right to vote was extended to all men over the age of 30 by 1912 (women would have to wait for their turn at the polls until 1945). But as soon as the government promised the Socialists to fund an old-age pension scheme, it reneged, and opted to invade Tunisia instead. Italy then got more war than it had budgeted for in 1914, when WWI broke out. A young but prominent Socialist firebrand named Benito Mussolini (1883–1945) led the call for Italy to intervene in support of the Allies, though most Socialists were opposed to such an action. As a result, Mussolini was expelled from the Socialist Party and went on to join the Italian army and serve in the war. After being injured and discharged from the army, he formed the Italian Combat Squad in 1919, the forerunner of the National Fascist Party.

Though Italy had been on the winning side in WWI, few Italians were in the mood to celebrate. In addition to war casualties, 600,000 Italians served time as POWs (prisoners of war), and another 100,000 died primarily due to the Italian government's failure to send food, clothing and medical supplies to its own soldiers. Wartime decrees that extended working hours and outlawed strikes had made factory conditions so deplorable that women led mass strikes even under threat of prison. Bread shortages

» 1921	» 1940–43	» 1943–45
Mussolini forms the Fascist Party. The 1924 elections are 'overseen' by Fascist *squadristi* (paramilitary groups, aka Blackshirts) and the Fascists win a parliamentary majority.	The Fascist Italian Empire joins Germany in declaring war on Great Britain and France. Italy surrenders in 1943 but Mussolini refuses to comply and war continues.	The Italian Resistance joins the Allies against Mussolini and the Nazis; Tuscany is liberated. When civil warfare ends in 1945, a coalition government is formed.

THE BIKER, THE FRIAR & THE ACCOUNTANT

Unbelievable though it may sound, this trio became heroes of the Italian Resistance. Giorgio Nissim was a Jewish accountant in Pisa who belonged to a secret Tuscan Resistance group that helped Jewish Italians escape from fascist Italy. The network was discovered by the Fascists, and everyone involved was sent to concentration camps, except for Giorgio, who remained undetected.

It seemed nowhere was safe for Jewish refugees – until Franciscan friar Rufino Niccacci helped organise the Assisi Underground, which hid hundreds of Jewish refugees from all over Italy in convents and monasteries across Umbria in 1943 and 1944. In Assisi, nuns who'd never met Jewish people before learned to cook kosher meals for their guests, and locals risked their lives to provide shelter to total strangers.

The next problem was getting forged travel documents to the refugees, and quick. Enter Gino Bartali, world-famous Tuscan cyclist, Tour de France winner and three-time champion of the Giro d'Italia. After his death in 2003, documents revealed that during his 'training rides' during the war years, Bartali had carried Resistance intelligence and falsified documents that were used to transport Jewish refugees to safe locations. Suspected of involvement, Bartali was once interrogated at the dreaded Villa Triste in Florence, where political prisoners were held and tortured – but he revealed nothing. Until his death he refused to discuss his efforts to save Jewish refugees, even with his children, saying, 'One does these things, and then that's that.'

spread nationwide, along with bread riots. Mussolini had found support for his call to order in the Tuscan countryside, and by 1922 his black-shirted squads could be seen parading through Florence, echoing his call for the ousting of the national government and the purging of Socialists and Communists from all local positions of power. In 1922 the Fascists marched on Rome and staged a coup d'etat, installing Mussolini as prime minister.

But no amount of purging prevented the country from plunging into recession in the 1930s after Mussolini demanded (and obtained) a revaluation of the Italian *lira*. While the free fall of wages won Mussolini allies among industrialists, it created further desperation among his power base. New military conquests in Libya and Ethiopia initially provided a feeble boost to the failing economy, but when the enormous bill came due in the late 1930s, Mussolini hastily agreed to an economic and military alliance with Germany. Contrary to the bold claims of Mussolini's propaganda machine, Italy was ill prepared for the war it entered in 1940.

» 1946	» 1959–63	» 1969
Umberto II is exiled after a referendum to make Italy a republic is successful; 71.6% of Tuscans and 71.9% of Umbrians vote for a republic.	Italy's economy revives via industrialisation, entrepreneurship and US Marshall Plan investments. Florence revives its textile industry and becomes Italy's first fashion capital.	Mass strikes and ongoing student uprisings demand social change and promote sweeping reforms in working conditions, housing, social services, pensions and civil rights.

BACKGROUND

A powerful Resistance movement soon emerged in Mussolini's former stomping grounds in the Tuscan countryside – tragically, not soon enough to prevent hundreds of thousands of Italian casualties, plus a still-unknown number of Italians shipped off to 23 Italian concentration camps (including one near Arezzo) and death camps in Germany. A new Italian government surrendered to the Allies in 1943, but Mussolini refused to concede defeat, and dragged Italy through two more years of civil war, Allied campaigns and German occupation. Tuscany and Umbria emerged from these black years redder than ever, and Tuscany in particular became a staunch Socialist power base.

Today the region's true colours are neither red nor black, but more of a trendy neutral. Agriculture and travel are once again the defining features of the region, just as they were three millennia ago – and just like then, you never know who'll take the stage next.

BACKGROUND

» 1970s–80s

The Anni di Piombo (Years of Lead) terrorise the country with extremist violence and reprisals; police kill anarchist Franco Serantini in Pisa, and Red Brigades kill Florence's mayor.

» 1993

A string of Mafia-motivated bombings that kill five people and cause US$10 million damage to art in the Uffizi galvanises the country and spurs Mani Pulite (Clean Hands) reformers.

» 2008

Silvio Berlusconi and his right-wing allies triumph in the national elections. Tuscany's traditional support of leftist candidates and parties is diluted.

LIVING THE IDYLL

· · · · · · ·

Deeply attached to their patch of land, people in this predominantly rural neck of the woods are not simply Italian or Tuscan or Umbrian. Harking back to centuries of coexistence as rival political entities with their own style of architecture, school of painting and so on, it is the *paese* (home town) or, in the case of Siena, the *contrada* (neighbourhood) in which one is born that reigns supreme.

Passionate, proud, reserved, hard-working, family-oriented, fond of food and wine, pernickety about their appearance and thrifty are characteristics attributed to Tuscans across the board. With their gargantuan artistic heritage and tradition of master craftsmanship, Florentines are known for their attention to detail, quest for perfection, appreciation of beauty, pride in their dialect (they believe it is 'pure' Italian) and deep respect for the past.

Landlocked Umbria has always had to lean on its own land for sustenance and remains devout to its past as a port-less place unaccustomed to foreign influences. Umbrians are self-reliant, honest and unabashedly direct; they have little time for vanity or conceit – what you see is what you get. That said, Umbrians are Italian, too (albeit salt-of-the-earth Italians) and, even in the pokiest of towns, they still don big sunglasses when it's cloudy.

The quintessential Umbrian never travels, their family has lived in the same place for 400 years and they have little worldliness to share. They're aloof, distant and unlikely to offer a warm welcome to strangers.

LA DOLCE VITA

Life is *dolce* (sweet) for this privileged pocket of Italy – two of the country's wealthiest enclaves – where the family reigns supreme, and tradition and quality reign over quantity. From the great names in viticulture to the flower-producing industry of Pescia and the small-scale farms of Umbria, it is family-run businesses handed between generations that form the backbone of this proud, strong region.

In Florence – the only city with a whiff of cosmopolitan air wafting through it – daily life is the fastest paced. City-slick Florentines rise early, drop the kids at school by 8am, then flit from an espresso (taken standing up at their favourite cafe) to the office by 9am. Lunch is a lengthy affair for these food- and wine-mad people, as is the early-evening *aperitivo*, enjoyed in a bar with friends to whet the appetite for dinner (usually enjoyed between 7pm and 9pm). The *aperitivo* system is simple – for the price of a drink you get the opportunity to graze on a buffet of snacks or are given your own small plate of the same. Sometimes the buffets are so lavish that they can replace dinner. Smokers – fast dwindling – puff on pavements outside due to recent EU-initiated laws banning smoking in hotels, bars and restaurants.

Theatre, concerts, art exhibitions and *il calcio* (football) entertain after hours. Indeed, the region's two top professional football clubs, ACF Fiorentina and less lucky Perugia Calcio, enjoy fanatical fan bases. Weekends see many flee their city apartments for less urban climes, where the din of *motorini* (scooters) whizzing through the night lessens

BACKGROUND

and there's more space and light: green countryside is a mere 15-minute getaway from lucky old Florence, unlike many urban centres where industrial sprawl really sprawls.

Like Umbrians, Tuscans by their very nature travel little (many spend a lifetime living in the town of their birth) and place great importance on their family home – the local rate of 75% home ownership is among Europe's highest. At one time the domain of Tuscany's substantial well-off British population (there's good reason why playwright John Mortimer dubbed Chianti 'Chiantishire' in his 1989 TV adaptation *Summer Lease*), the region's bounty of stylish stone villas and farmhouses with terracotta floors, wood-burning fireplaces and terraces with views are now increasingly passing back into the hands of Tuscans eagerly rediscovering their countryside.

Rural lifestyle, particularly in Umbria, is slavishly driven by close-knit, ancient communities in small towns and villages where local matters and gossip are more important than national or world affairs. Everyone knows everyone to the point of being clannish, making assimilation for outsiders hard – if not impossible. Farming is the self-sufficient way of life, albeit one that is becoming increasingly difficult – hence the mushrooming of *agriturismi* (farm-stay accommodation) as farmers stoically utilise every resource they have to make ends meet.

Urban or rural, children typically remain at home until they reach their 30s, often only fleeing the nest to wed. In line with national trends, Tuscan and Umbrian

COFFEE LEXICON

Like all Italians, locals here take their coffee seriously. They only occasionally sit down in cafes to enjoy a caffeine fix – instead preferring to down their cup of choice while standing at the bar, where the coffee is between two and four times cheaper than its table-served equivalent. There is one cardinal rule: cappuccino, caffè latte or latte macchiato are only ever drunk at breakfast or in the early morning – never, *ever* after a meal. Here's a guide of what to order:

Caffè corretto Espresso with a dash of grappa or other spirit.

Caffè doppio Double espresso shot.

Caffè freddo Long glass of cold, black, sweetened coffee.

Caffè freddo amaro Former minus the sugar.

Caffè granita Sweet and strong, traditionally served with a dollop of whipped cream.

Caffè latte Milkier version of a cappuccino with less froth.

Caffè lungo Literally 'long coffee', also called *caffè americano;* espresso with extra water run through the grinds to make it mug-length (and occasionally bitter).

Cappuccino Espresso topped with hot, frothy milk.

Cappuccino freddo Bit like an iced coffee, popular in summer.

Cappuccino senza schiuma Cappuccino minus the froth.

Espresso Short, sharp shot of strong, black coffee; acceptable any time of day but the *only* coffee to end a meal with.

Latte macchiato Warmed milk 'stained' with a spot of coffee.

Macchiato 'Stained' coffee'; an espresso with a dash of cold milk.

Macchiato caldo/freddo Espresso with a dash of hot, foamed/cold milk.

Un caffè Literally 'a coffee', meaning an espresso and nothing else.

families are small – one or two kids, with around 20% of families childless and 26% of households being single. Despite increasing numbers of women working, chauvinistic attitudes remain well entrenched in more rural areas.

E' QUI LA FESTA?

E' Qui la Festa literally translates as 'It's here the party?' Delve into the mindset of a Tuscan or Umbrian and a holy trinity of popular folklore, agricultural tradition and religious rite of passage dances before your eyes. No cultural agenda is more jam-packed with ancient festivity than theirs: patron saints alone provide weeks of celebration given that every village, town, profession, trade and social group has a saint they call their own and venerate religiously.

Festivities climax (twice!) with Siena's soul-stirring Il Palio (p185), a hot-blooded horse race conceived in the 12th century to honour the Virgin Mary and revamped six centuries on to celebrate the miracles of the Madonna of Provenzano (2 July) and Assumption (16 August). Deeply embroiled in its religious roots is a fierce *contrada* rivalry, not to mention a fervent penchant for dressing up and a widespread respect of tradition that sees horses blessed before the race, jockeys riding saddleless, the silk banner for the winner of August's race ritually designed by local Sienese artists and July's by non-Sienese, and so on. Legend says that a Sienese bride marrying in far-off lands took earth from her *contrada* with her to put beneath the legs of her marital bed to ensure her offspring would be conceived on home soil. Other folkloric festivals such as Arezzo's Giostra del Saracino (p241) reflect the same historic division of cities and all-consuming *campanilismo* (literally, loyalty to one's bell tower).

Although it's by no means the social force it once was, Catholicism (the religion of 85% of the region) and its rituals nevertheless play a key role in daily lives: first Communions, church weddings and religious feast days are an integral part of Tuscan and Umbrian society.

LA BELLA FIGURA

A sense of style is vital to Tuscans, who take great pride in their dress and appearance – not surprising given this is where the Italian fashion industry was born. Guccio Gucci and Salvatore Ferragamo got the haute-couture ball rolling in the 1920s with boutiques in Florence. But it was in 1951 when a well-heeled Florentine nobleman called Giovanni Battista Giorgini held a fashion soirée in his Florence home that Italy's first prêt-à-porter fashion shows were spawned. The catwalk quickly shifted to Florence's Palazzo Pitti, where Europe's most prestigious fashion shows dazzled until 1971, when the women's shows moved to Milan. The menswear shows stayed put, though, and

---

DON'T MISS...

LOCAL EXPERIENCES

* ★ **Aperitivo** // Enjoy a predinner drink or two.

* ★ **Coffee culture** // Bolt an espresso at the bar with the locals.

* ★ **Florentine fashion houses** // Pop into Gucci or Ferragamo for a souvenir you'll cherish.

* ★ **Il Palio** // Witness the most famous of the region's many festivals.

BACKGROUND

top designers still leg it to Florence twice a year to unveil their menswear collections at the Pitti Immagine Uomo fashion shows and their creations for *bambini* (kids) at Pitti Bimbo; both events waltz around the Fortezza da Basso. Local designers to look for include Roberto Cavalli, Michele Negri, Enrico Coveri, Patrizia Pepe, Emilio Pucci and Ermanno Daelli.

DESIGN ICONS

The local sense of style isn't limited to fashion. Italian design icons such as the Vespa scooter (p14) hail from this part of the country, as does Richard Ginori porcelain and handmade marbled paper with the colourful Fiorentina pattern. Alessi product designers Cisotti Biagio (the Daibolix bottle opener), Marta Sansoni (the Cactus! collection), Massimo Morozzi (the famous Pasta Set) and Elena Danti and Enrica Zanzi (the Turn Me On candlestick) are local, as is high-profile international architect, designer and critic Andrea Branzi (although these days he lives in Milan). And last but by no means least in the style stakes is Salvatore Ferragamo's chain of glamorous hotels and restaurants (www.lungarnohotels.com), most designed by Florentine architect Michele Bonan.

ART & ARCHITECTURE

Tuscany and Umbria's treasury of architectural styles and artistic expression was the work of a colourful cast of characters, whose stubborn independent-mindedness and ingenuity bordering on insanity left a legacy like no other.

Improbably enough, the region's art and architecture survived plague, war, Fascism, earthquakes and a rather nasty rash of postwar housing projects. Examples can be found everywhere from cities to small towns and cathedrals to municipal museums across the region, making travel to Tuscany and Umbria supremely satisfying for the artistically or architecturally inclined. For more information on frescos in particular, see p364.

ELEGANT DEATH: THE ETRUSCANS

Roughly 2800 years before you started dreaming of a hill-top getaway in Tuscany or Umbria, the Etruscans had a similar idea. Dotting the countryside are towns that were founded to keep a watchful eye on the crops below – as well as on the neighbours across the valley. Perugia's Etruscan character is still in evidence today with its Arco Etrusco (p261) in the ancient city walls and an Etruscan well in the town centre, built presumably in case the neighbours got nasty and cut off the water supply downhill.

From the 8th to the 3rd century BC, Etruscan towns held their own against friends, Romans and countrymen, worshipped their own gods and goddesses, and farmed lowlands using sophisticated drainage systems of their own invention. How well the Etruscans lived between sieges and war is unclear, but they sure knew how to throw a funeral: a wealth of jewellery, ceramics and other creature comforts for the afterlife have been found in the Etruscan stone tombs of Ipogeo dei Volumni near Perugia (p262) and Crocifisso del Tufo outside Orvieto (p305).

Despite the tantalising clues they left behind, no one seems to know who the Etruscans were or where they came from. Recent studies of their genetic material suggest they have more in common with Anatolia than with modern Italians, and early Roman historians suggested a connection with Asia Minor. Come up with your own theories at the Museo Claudio Faina e Civico in Orvieto (p304) and the Museo Archeologico Nazionale dell'Umbria in Perugia (p261), where you'll notice that Etruscan ceramic urns and iron horses seem distinctly Greek, while their scarab-beetle jewellery and tomb paintings look quite Egyptian.

The Romans knew a good thing when they plundered it. After conquering swaths of Etruscan territory in Umbria and Tuscany in the 3rd century BC, they incorporated the Etruscans' highly refined, geometric style seen in artefacts at Spoleto's Museo Archeologico e Teatro Romano (p315) into their own art and architecture. But even after another 800 years of trying, Rome never entirely succeeded in establishing its authority throughout Etruscan territory. This would become a recurring theme, with local municipal authorities battling with papal emissaries from Rome for control over the region right through the 15th century AD.

WELCOME, PILGRIMS: RELIGIOUS ATTRACTIONS

Roman centurions may have failed to make much of an impression on Etruscan territory, but Christianity began to take hold when a lovelorn young man from Norcia named Benedict abandoned his studies and a promising career in Rome to join the growing community of hermits in the hills of Umbria c AD 500. Fledgling monasteries nearby sought his spiritual leadership, but his appointment as abbot didn't go so well – the monks tried to poison him twice.

Miraculously he survived, and monasteries sprang up in the valley beyond his cave as word of his piety spread. One of these, San Pietro in Valle (p323), founded by Longobard duke of Spoleto Faroaldo II after St Peter commanded him in a dream to build a church, features five Roman sarcophagi as well as 8th-century Romanesque frescos on the upper part of the nave showing scenes from the Old Testament and crusaders galloping through arches on a couple of pin-headed horses and a camel.

This building and others in the area helped establish the blend of Lombard and Roman styles known as Romanesque as the decor scheme of choice for local ecclesiastical structures. The basic template was simple: a stark nave stripped of extra columns ending in a domed apse, surrounded by chapels usually donated by wealthy patrons. Gone were the colonnaded Roman facades seen on earlier buildings, such as the 4th-century Tempietto del Clitunno near Spoleto (p319); the new look was more spare and austere, befitting a place where hermits might feel at home and nobles may feel inspired to surrender worldly possessions.

While Umbria kept the architecture relatively simple in local *tufo* volcanic stone, Tuscany couldn't resist showing off just a bit. In the 11th century, the grand colonnade and loggia in Lucca's Cattedrale di San Martino (p131) and two-tone striped marble nave of Pisa's Duomo (p115) gave Romanesque a Tuscan makeover, and this new look was then applied to the Chiesa di San Miniato al Monte in Florence (p81). Nicola Pisano's marble pulpit for the baptistry in Pisa (p115) was another spectacle in marble: a hexagonal structure covered with deep reliefs of Old and New Testament characters who are almost twisting free of the structure.

Siena was not about to be outdone by its neighbours and rivals, Florence and Pisa, and so in 1215 its city council approved a no-expenses-spared program to rebuild and redecorate its greenish-black-and-white striped marble cathedral (p185). They got what they paid for in the 13th century, endowing the project with a Tuscan Gothic facade by Giovanni Pisano, a pulpit by Nicola Pisano, a rose window designed by Duccio di Buoninsegna and the *Annunciation* painted by his star pupil Simone Martini (now in the Uffizi; see p53). If that's not enough, the cathedral also features inlaid marble floors, which are at the receiving end of many a dropped jaw and, the crowning glory by Sienese artist Pinturicchio, the Libreria Piccolomini frescos, which tell the life story of Sienese pope Pius II in jewel-like colours. Siena's desire to outshine Florence succeeded for about 150 years, until the Florentines picked up a few cues from Sienese painters, and started a little something called the Renaissance.

But while Tuscany's churches were becoming quite spectacular, nothing prepared pilgrims for what they would find inside the upper and lower churches of the Basilica di San Francesco in Assisi (p270). Not long after St Francis' death in 1226, an all-star team of artists was hired to decorate the churches in his honour. Cimabue, Giotto, Pietro Lorenzetti and Simone Martini captured the life and gentle spirit of St Francis while his memory was still fresh in the minds of the faithful. For medieval pilgrims unaccustomed to multiplexes and special effects, entering a space that had been covered from floor to ceiling with stories told in living colour must have been a dazzling, overwhelming experience. Painter, art historian and Renaissance man Giorgio Vasari praised Cimabue for setting the standard for realistic modelling and perspective with his lower church frescos, which you can still make out despite the extensive damage caused over the years by earthquakes – not to mention art thieves who plundered fresco fragments after the devastating 1997 quake.

But the most startling achievement in the Basilica di San Francesco is Giotto's fresco cycle, which shows Francis not just rolling up but tearing off his sleeves to provide aid to lepers and the needy, as onlookers and family members gasp and look away in shock. These images had an emotional, immediate impact on viewers, creating a much more theatrical setting for church services. Chants and solos added to the liturgy provided a surround-sound component to the fresco cycles, and the drama reached fever pitch with passion plays and other theatrical elements. The basilica drew hundreds of thousands of pilgrims each year when its decoration was in progress and even more when it was completed; today, annual attendance figures top four million.

ENLIGHTENED DARK AGES: THE RISE OF THE COMUNE

While communities sprang up around hermits and holy men in the hinterlands, cities began taking on a life of their own in the 13th and 14th centuries. Some public facilities were hold-overs from Roman times: the theatre in Spoleto (up and running each year during the Spoleto Festival; see p315) being a good example. Ancient road networks also served as handy trade routes starting in the 11th century, and farming estates and villas began to spring up outside major trading centres as a new middle class of merchants, farmers and skilled craftspeople emerged. Taxes and donations sponsored the building of hospitals such as Filippo Brunelleschi's Spedale degli Innocenti (p68), which is considered the earliest Florentine Renaissance building (1419–36). Streets were paved, town walls erected and sewage systems built to accommodate an increasingly sophisticated urban population not keen on sprawl or squalor.

Once townsfolk came into a bit of money they weren't necessarily keen to part with it, and didn't always agree how their tax dollars should be spent. Town councils were formed to represent the various interests of merchants, guilds and competing noble families, and the first order of business on the agenda in major medieval cities such as Perugia, Todi, Siena, Florence and Gubbio was the construction of an impressive town hall to reflect the importance and authority of the *comune*. Surprisingly, these democratic monuments don't look as though they were designed by committee, and Siena's Palazzo Comunale (p181) has become a global icon of civic pride with its pointed Sienese arches, a splendid marble loggia contributed by Sienese Black Death survivors, and the tall Torre del Mangia clock tower that serves as the compass needle orienting the entire city.

But in addition to being savvy political lobbyists and fans of grand architectural projects that kept their constituents gainfully employed, medieval *comune* were masters of propaganda. Nicola and Giovanni Pisano's carved-relief Fontana Maggiore (p253) in Perugia's central piazza and the frescoed town-council hall (now called the Sala dei Notari) in the Palazzo dei Priori (p259) were part of a brilliant chamber-of-commerce-style PR campaign. Such a campaign positioned Perugia as the embodiment of ancient virtues and Christian belief, using imagery that blended ancient mythology, biblical themes and Perugia's contemporary history.

> 'Like the best campaign speeches, this cautionary tale was brilliantly rendered, but not always heeded'

Ambrogio Lorenzetti's *Allegories of Good and Bad Government* in Siena's Palazzo Comunale is better and bigger than any political billboard could ever be. In the *Allegory of Good Government* (see p365), townsfolk make their way through town in an orderly fashion, pausing to do business, greet one another, join hands and dance a merry jig. In the *Allegory of Bad Government,* a horned, fanged Tyrannia rules over a scene of chaos surrounded by winged vices, while Justice lies unconscious, her scales shattered. Like the best campaign speeches, this cautionary tale was brilliantly rendered, but not always heeded.

TRADING UP: IMPORTS & COSMOPOLITAN INFLUENCES

When they weren't busy politicking, late medieval farmers, craftspeople and merchants did quite well for themselves. Enterprising Umbrians drained marshlands to grow additional crops to sell. Elegant, locally made ceramics, tiles and marbles were showcased in churches, villas and workshops across Tuscany and Umbria and became all the rage throughout Europe and the Mediterranean. Artisans were kept busy applying their skills to civic works projects and churches, which had to be expanded and updated to keep up with the growing numbers and rising expectations of pilgrims in the area.

With outside interest came outside influence, of course, and local styles adapted to international markets. Florence, Deruta and Orvieto became famous for lustrous, tin-glazed *maiolica* (majolica ware) tiles and plates painted with vibrant metallic pigments that were inspired by the Islamic ceramics of Majorca (Spain). The prolific Florentine della Robbia family created ceramic reliefs that are now enshrined at the Museo Nazionale del Bargello (p71). Modest Romanesque cathedrals were given an International Gothic makeover befitting their appeal to pilgrims of all nations, but the Italian take on the French style was both more colourful and more subdued than the grey-stone spires and flying buttresses of Paris. The local version of International Gothic in Tuscany and Umbria often featured a simple layout and striped stone naves fronted by multilayer birthday-cake facades, which might be frosted with pink paint, glittering mosaics and rows of arches capped with sculptures. Particularly fabulous examples of this confectionary approach are the cathedrals in Siena, Orvieto and Florence. The last

BACKGROUND

two were the creations of Arnolfo di Cambio, also known for his work in Florence's Palazzo Vecchio (p51).

The evolution from solid Romanesque to airy Gothic to a yin and yang balance of the two can be witnessed in several standout buildings in the region. The Gothic trend started while the upper church of the Basilica di San Francesco in Assisi was under construction, and the resulting blend of a relatively austere Romanesque exterior with high Gothic drama indoors set a new ecclesiastical architecture standard, which was exported by Franciscan monks all over Europe. The pointed arches on the lower half of the facade of the Basilica di Santa Maria Novella (p57) reveal a Gothic underbelly below the lofty classical proportions of the Corinthian columns and pediment, with ingenious side scrolls to pull the look together. But while humanist and religious idioms and cross-cultural influences were seamlessly blended in lofty Renaissance architecture, the reality on the ground looked quite different.

UNFRIENDLY COMPETITION: RIVALRIES TO THE DEATH

By the 14th century, the smiling Sienese townsfolk of Ambrogio Lorenzetti's *Allegory of Good Government* and the placid Umbrian countryside backdrop of the Basilica di San Francesco frescos must have seemed like figments of fertile imaginations. The Black Death swept through cities in Umbria and left communal government hobbled, giving Church authorities and warlords an excuse to impose new and decidedly less democratic authority. But while municipalities fended off tyranny, fields returned to swampland, roads became toll-collecting opportunities for thugs, and merchants abandoned the region for greener, safer pastures. The Assisi fresco painters who miraculously survived the plague would not live to see their work finished due to some rather unkindly acts of God: major earthquakes erupted in Umbria every 20 years for some 250 years.

Meanwhile in Tuscany, the great medieval arts capital of Siena was suffering. After a major famine in 1329 and a bank collapse, the municipality went into debt to maintain roads, continue work on the cathedral, help the needy and jump-start the local economy. But just when Siena seemed set for a comeback, the plague devastated the city in 1348. Three-quarters of Siena's population was soon dead, and virtually all economic and artistic activity ground to a halt. The *comune* rallied with tough fines on lawbreakers, new business taxes and rules against wearing black mourning attire (too depressing), and within five years Siena was going strong. But when another plague hit in 1374 and killed 80,000 Sienese, and was followed by a famine, the city never entirely recovered.

Florence was also hit by the plague in 1348, and despite fervent public prayer rituals, 96,000 Florentines died in just seven months. Those who survived experienced a crisis of faith, making Florence fertile territory for humanist ideals – not to mention macabre superstition, attempts to raise the dead, and a fascination with corpses that the likes of Leonardo da Vinci would call science and others morbid curiosity. Power struggles also ensued among Florence's great families, many of whom had well-placed relatives at the Vatican to make their case for power. Florence's booming postplague

BACKGROUND

textile trade helped fund military campaigns against its comparatively weaker neighbours Arezzo, Pisa and Cortona, and even brought commercial power players Lucca and Siena into the Florentine sphere of influence.

A building boom ensued as Church and secular authorities competed to become the defining fixtures of the local landscape. In Florence, Cosimo the Elder commissioned his favourite architect, Michelozzo di Bartolomeo Michelozzi, to build Palazzo Medici-Riccardi (p65), an imposing three-storey building on a base of rough-hewn, 'rusticated' stone. This kicked off a competitive *palazzo*-building frenzy in Florence, involving many of the city's powerful families, including Medici arch-enemies the Strozzi.

THE RENAISSANCE: PICTURING AN IMPERFECT WORLD, PERFECTLY

So who came out ahead in all this jockeying for position? Oddly enough, the architects. To put an end to the competing claims of the Tuscan Ghibelline faction that was allied with the Holy Roman Empire, the Rome-backed Guelph faction marked its territory with impressive new landmarks. Guelph Florence hired Giotto to design the city's iconic 85m-tall square *campanile* (bell tower; p45), one-upping the 57m-tall tower (p113) under construction in Ghibelline Pisa that was already looking a bit off kilter. Pisa battled with Florence throughout the 14th and 15th centuries, and was otherwise too preoccupied with shoring up its sagging political position to keep up with its construction-happy Guelph neighbours.

'Mess with Florence, and you take on Rome' was the not-so-subtle hint delivered by Florentine architecture, which made frequent reference to the glories of the ancient power and its classical architecture. Filippo Brunelleschi and Michelangelo Buonarotti recycled the coffered ceiling of the Parthenon in Rome for the Basilica di San Lorenzo (p63), with Andrea del Verrocchio providing the classically styled Medici family sarcophagus. This new Florentine style became known as Renaissance or 'rebirth' – but there was also much to Renaissance architecture that was truly novel. Today's red-carpet appearances simply can't compare with entrances made on the grand staircase at the Biblioteca Laurenziana Medicea (p63) in Florence's San Lorenzo, which Michelangelo framed for dramatic effect with two curving stairways.

> *'This new Florentine style became known as Renaissance or "rebirth"'*

Meanwhile, Florentine artists enjoyed a bonanza of commissions to paint heroic battle scenes, fresco private chapels and carve busts of the latest power players – works that sometimes outlived their patrons' clout. The Peruzzi family rose to prominence in 14th-century Florence as bankers with interests reaching from London to the Middle East, and set the trend for art patronage by commissioning Giotto to fresco the family's memorial chapel in Santa Croce, completed in 1320. When Peruzzi client King Edward III of England defaulted on loans and war with Lucca interfered with business, the Peruzzi went bankrupt – but as patrons of Giotto's precocious experiments in perspective and Renaissance illusionism, their legacy set the tone for the artistic flowering of Florence.

BACKGROUND

One Florentine family to follow the Peruzzi's lead were the prominent Brancacci, who commissioned a chapel in the Basilica di Santa Maria del Carmine in Florence (p76), to be painted by Masolino and his precocious assistant Masaccio. After Masaccio's premature death aged only 27, the frescos were completed by Filippino Lippi. In these dramatic frescos, framed in astonishingly convincing architectural sets, select scenes from the life of St Peter allude to pressing Florentine concerns of the day: the new income tax, unfair imprisonment and hoarded wealth. Masaccio's image of the expulsion of Adam and Eve from the Garden of Eden proved especially prophetic: the Brancacci were allied with the Strozzi family, and were similarly exiled by the Medici before they could see the work completed.

But the patrons with the greatest impact on the course of art history were the Medici. Patriarch Cosimo the Elder

> ## DON'T MISS...
>
> ### BUILDINGS
>
> * ★ **Spedale degli Innocenti, Florence** // Brunelleschi's classically inspired foundling hospital portico (p68)
> * ★ **Cappella de' Pazzi, Florence** // Another Brunelleschi Renaissance masterpiece (p71)
> * ★ **Chiesa di Santa Maria della Spina, Pisa** // A diminutive Gothic gem (p117)
> * ★ **Chiesa di San Miniato al Monte, Florence** // A Tuscan Romanesque triumph (p81)
> * ★ **Biblioteca Laurenziana Medicea, Florence** // Michelangelo's sinuous library staircase (p63)
> * ★ **Piazza Pio II, Pienza** // A magnificent Renaissance-era public space (p209)

was exiled in 1433 by a consortium of Florentine families who considered him a triple threat: powerful banker, ambassador of the Church, and consummate politician with the savvy to sway emperors and popes. But the flight of capital from Florence after his departure created such a fiscal panic that the exile was hastily rescinded and within a year the Medici were back in Florence. To announce his return in grand style, Cosimo funded the 1437 rebuilding of the Convento di San Marco (now Museo di San Marco, p67) by Michelozzo, and commissioned Fra' Angelico to fresco the monks' quarters with scenes from the life of Christ. Another artist pleased with Cosimo's return was Donatello, who had completed his lithe bronze statue of *David* with Cosimo's patronage (now in the Museo Nazionale del Bargello, p71).

Through such commissions, early Renaissance innovations in perspective, closely observed realism, and chiaroscuro (the play of light and dark) began to catch on throughout Tuscany and Umbria. Cosimo's grandson Lorenzo de' Medici (aka 'the Magnificent') gave an early and important nod of approval to Cortona-born painter Luca Signorelli, who took foreshortening to expressive extremes in his *Last Judgment* in Orvieto, offering up-the-nostril angles on angels and creepy between-the-toes peeks at demons (p302). A painter from Sansepolcro named Piero della Francesca earned a reputation for figures who were glowing with otherworldly light, and who were caught in personal predicaments that people could relate to: Roman soldiers snoozing on the job, crowds left goggle-eyed by miracles, bystanders distressed to witness cruel persecution (p246).

BACKGROUND

THE GREAT DEBATE: SCANDAL, SCIENCE & CENSORSHIP

The High Renaissance is often seen as a kind of university faculty meeting, with genteel, silver-haired sages engaged in a collegial exchange of ideas. A bar brawl might be closer to the metaphorical truth, with artists, scientists, politicians and clergy mixing it up and everyone emerging bruised. The debate was never as simple as Church versus state, science versus art or seeing versus believing; in those days, politicians could be clergy, scientists could be artists, and artists could be clergy. Nor was debate strictly academic: any statement, however artistic, could mark a person as a menace, a has-been, a heretic or a dead man.

Giorgio Vasari's gossipy *Lives of the Artists* (1st edition 1550) documents shocking behaviour from his Renaissance contemporaries that may not have happened quite as he describes but is entirely possible given what we know of those tumultuous times. Legal records show that after being exiled from Florence for stabbing a man with a wooden stake, Pietro Vanucci attracted more positive notice for frescoing the better part of the city of Perugia c 1500 under the pseudonym Perugino. He also gained fame as the tutor of a promising young painter named Raphael, who promptly stole papal commissions right out from under him. But you'd never guess this back story by looking at Perugino's serene figures of Justice, Prudence, Temperance and Fortitude in Perugia's Collegio del Cambio (p259). They're painted under the same starry sky as biblical figures, suggesting that the universe might be able to accommodate both secular and sacred ideals – an idea ahead of its time in 1503. A dispute over salt taxes led to a clash between Perugia's ruling Baglioni family and Pope Paul III, and the ensuing Salt War ended Perugia's relative independence from papal authority in 1540. Papal forces levelled the homes of the Baglioni and with them untold art treasures, though the Collegio del Cambio mercifully was left intact.

War wasn't the only danger to Renaissance art. Inspired by Masaccio, tutored by Fra' Filippo Lippi and backed by Lorenzo de' Medici, Sandro Botticelli was a rising art star who'd worked alongside Perugino and was sent to Rome to paint a fresco celebrating papal authority in the Sistine Chapel. The golden boy who'd painted the Venus with the golden hair for Lorenzo de' Medici's private villa in 1485 (now in Florence's Uffizi in the Botticelli Room; see p53) could do no wrong, until he was accused of sodomy in 1501. The charges didn't stick but the rumours did, and Botticelli's work was critiqued as too decadently sensual for religious subjects. When religious reformer Savonarola ousted the Medici and began to purge Florence of decadent excess in the face of surely imminent Armageddon, Botticelli paintings went up in flames in the massive Bonfire of the Vanities. Botticelli repudiated mythology and turned his attention to Madonnas, some of whom bear a marked family resemblance to his Venus.

Michelangelo's classically inspired work was also alternately admired and rejected. Lorenzo de' Medici personally took charge of the young sculptor's schooling from age 13, and Michelangelo remained the darling of Florence until the Medici were ousted by Savonarola in 1494. By some accounts, Savonarola tossed rare early paintings by Michelangelo onto his bonfires (ouch). Without his Medici protectors, Michelangelo seemed unsure of his next move: he briefly hid in the basement of San Lorenzo and then roamed around Italy. In Rome he carved a Bacchus for Cardinal Raffaele Riaro that the patron deemed unsuitable – which only seemed to spur Michelangelo to make a bigger and still more sensuous statue of *David* in 1501 (p66).

Although he was the one artist whom Vasari positively gushed about, by all other accounts Michelangelo was fiercely competitive, denigrating the work of Perugino, openly gloating when his rival Leonardo da Vinci failed to complete a commission, and accusing Raphael and Bramante of setting him an impossible task with his Sistine Chapel commission in Rome.

The constraints imposed by papal emissaries and petty tyrants caused a creative backlash in the 16th century, as mannerist artists explored darker visions and eerie special effects in the manner of the High Renaissance. In the 1520s, scenes depicting the Deposition (when Jesus' body is taken down from the cross) provided the ideal opportunity to explore extreme perspective and twisting, restless bodies in works at the Cattedrale di Volterra in Arezzo by Il Rosso Fiorentino (aka the Redhead from Florence) and at Santa Felicità in Florence by Jacopo Pontormo. In both works, the figures seem lit as if by a camera flash and their bodies appear boneless under layers of drapery – movie magic ahead of its time. The Sienese painter known as 'Il Sodomo' (for reasons unknown but rather maliciously insinuated by Vasari) combined Leonardo's High Renaissance illusionism with moody Sienese drama in his 1542 *Saint Sebastian with Madonna and Angels* (now at Pisa's Museo Nazionale di San Matteo; p116). The same year, the Inquisition arrived in Italy, marking a definitive end to the Renaissance exploration of humanity, in all its glorious imperfections.

OUR SUMMER PLACE: COLONIAL POWER & INFLUENCE

In the centuries that followed the sack of Rome by Charles V in 1527, artistic production in Tuscany and Umbria came to be defined by passing trends, imperial excess and periodic pillaging. Umbria began to reclaim its farms from marshlands and make a comeback in the late 15th century, but regular looting by passing armies made it slow going. Deruta and Gubbio struggled to regain their reputations as ceramics centres, but a steady stream of pilgrims and tourists en route to Rome helped keep Umbrian artistic traditions limping along. Unfortunately, anything that wasn't nailed down was lifted by Napoleonic forces in the 18th century, making artistic progress from this period hard to track.

'anything that wasn't nailed down was lifted by Napoleonic forces in the 18th century'

Tuscany had the rather more dubious luck of being the holiday destination of choice for despots, generals and imperial relations. Imported Roman baroque touches started to make an appearance on the Florentine cityscape in the 17th century: Gherardo Silvani's bodaciously curvy, sculpture-bedizened interior of the Chiesa di San Gaetano (p60), and Pietro da Cortona's ornately obsequious frescos at the Palazzo Pitti (p76) that celebrate the four ages of man – and the power of the Medici. But Cortona's prediction did not hold, and the Medici power waned despite Maria de' Medici's convenient and turbulent marriage to King Henry IV of France in 1600.

Lucca in particular began to look distinctly French, with wide boulevards, neoclassical buildings and more than 300 baroque villas. As a consolation prize for separating from her husband, Elisa Bonaparte was dubbed Duchess of Tuscany by her brother Napoleon Bonaparte, and soon established the trend for Italian vacation villas with her Villa Reale near Lucca (p136). When Napoleon lost Tuscany in 1814, former grand duke of Tuscany Ferdinando III was briefly reinstated, only to lose Lucca in a treaty to Elisa in 1815. But the Bourbon queen Maria Luisa of Etruria (western Tuscany) had an eye on a villa herself, and through treaty negotiations took control of Lucca in 1817.

A 'Grand Tour' of Italy became an obligatory display of culture and class status by the 18th century, and Tuscany and Umbria were key stops on the itinerary. German and English artists enraptured with Michelangelo, Perugino and other early High Renaissance painters took the inspiration home. This resulted in the high-octane romanticism of Henry Fuseli (1741–1825), the Swiss-German naturalised British painter best known for his unruly horses, and the moody, craft-conscious Pre-Raphaelite movement of Dante Gabriel Rossetti (1828–82), William Morris and friends. Conversely, Italian artists picked up on artistic trends making a splash in northern Europe without having to leave home. Impressionism, plein-air painting and romanticism became trendy among Italian artists, as witnessed in the collection at Florence's Galleria d'Arte Moderna (p78). But the most fascinating case of artistic import-export is Italian art nouveau, often referred to as Liberty after the London store that put William Morris' Italian-inspired visual ideals into commercial action.

SHOCKS TO THE SYSTEM: WAR, FUTURISM & FASCISM

After centuries under the thumbs of popes and sundry imperial powers, Tuscany and Umbria had acquired a certain forced cosmopolitanism, and local artists could identify with Rome or Paris in addition to their own *campanile*. The wave of nationalism that came with Italian unification didn't have a clear, immediate artistic effect within Tuscany or Umbria, whose biggest star in the early 20th century was Livorno-born painter and sculptor Amedeo Modigliani (1884–1920), who lived most of his adult life in Paris. A precocious and precarious talent, Modigliani made pilgrimages to the Uffizi, read Nietzsche, seduced maids and smoked hashish – all of which have been suggested as possible inspirations for his iconic long-faced, blank-eyed female figures.

Forward momentum for the local scene was provided by futurism and Gerardo Dottori's 1914 *Ciclista,* which echoed experiments by Umberto Boccioni in picturing movement and seems to have been the working prototype for Fortunato Depero's famous 1924 futurist poster for Bianchi Bicycles. But what started out as a radical experiment in *aeropittura,* the sensation of flight, became codified into a staunch nationalist aesthetic under the Fascists, and Dottori became better known for his 1933 portrait of Il Duce, aka Benito Mussolini. The Fascists also took quite a shine to the striking medieval buildings of Umbria, and decreed that all Umbrian buildings should be stripped of postmedieval ornament – a decision thankfully not put into practice, since soon thereafter the Fascists became otherwise occupied with losing the war. Still, Mussolini got his wish with austere, rationalist tower blocks that sprang up in the suburbs of Terni, Spoleto and Foligno, which have since been disparaged as only marginally liveable.

Cracks in the futurist fabric were memorably rendered by Alberto Burri (1915–95), who was born in Città di Castello, went to Africa as a doctor, got captured by the Americans and started to paint while in a prisoners of war (POW) camp in Texas. His abstract works combine oil paint and lowly materials such as burlap and salvaged wood – an instinct shared by radical 1970s Arte Povera (Poor Art) artists, who used only materials they could get for free or on the cheap. Burri's earthy, exposed-seam works proved the ideal foil to Victor Vasarely's giddy, airtight op art at the 1965 Sao Paolo Biennial, where the artists jointly landed the top prize. To judge for yourself, head to Città di Castello to visit the Collezione Burri (p289).

CONTEMPORARY ART: WHAT'S PAST IS PROLOGUE

Tuscany and Umbria can still draw crowds with its past glories; there are 120 museums in Umbria and 1.5 million visitors annually head to the Uffizi alone in Tuscany. But though 2800 years of rich artistic tradition means job security for legions of art conservation specialists and art historians, it can have a stultifying effect on artists attempting to create something wholly new. Look beyond the usual etchings of key landmarks and the inevitable sunflowers, though, and you'll find contemporary art in progress.

Most notable is Massimo Bartolini (b 1962), who radically alters the local landscape with just a few deceptively simple (and quintessentially Tuscan) adjustments of light and perspective that fundamentally change our experience: a bedroom where all the furniture appears to be sinking into the floor, Venice style, or a gallery where the viewer wears special shoes that subtly change the lighting in the gallery with each step. Bartolini has also changed the local flora of the tiny Tuscan town of Cecina, near Livorno, where he lives and works, attracting colourful flocks of contemporary art collectors and curators. These days you might be more likely to find his work at the Shanghai or Venice Biennale, but his installations can occasionally be found interrupting the countryside at the biennial Tuscia Electa arts festival (www.tusciaelecta.it).

Florentine Gianfranco Masi (b 1979) also works with local material; his digital videos show the ever-changing configurations of clouds and tourists that define the Tuscan landscape. Check out his work online at www.etraarte.com, and find out about other upcoming contemporary art events.

The region has some wonderful contemporary sculpture gardens, which showcase site-specific works in gorgeous surrounds. These include the Fattoria di Celle (see the boxed text, p100) outside Pistoia, Il Giardino dei Tarocchi (p228) in Southern Tuscany and the Parco Sculture del Chianti (p106) near Siena.

GREAT TUSCAN & UMBRIAN ARTISTS

❦ ANDREA DELLA ROBBIA // (1435–1525)

KNOWN FOR taking ceramics way beyond teacups with eye-catching, sometimes garish high-contrast reliefs; this is where Wedgwood found its blue-and-white inspiration. **LOOK FOR** his *Madonna of the Apple* in the Museo Nazionale del Bargello, Florence (p71) and medallions on the Spedale degli Innocenti in Florence (p68).

❦ DOMENICO GHIRLANDAIO // (1449–94)

KNOWN FOR his crisp, revealing portraits that capture every last detail with a lively line, blending the earthiness of his peer Fra' Filippo Lippi and the elegance of Sandro Botticelli. **LOOK FOR** his frescos in the Cappella di Filippo Strozzi of the Basilica di Santa Maria Novella, Florence (p57).

❦ DONATELLO // (1386–1466)

KNOWN FOR his taut, lithe, twisting sculptures in bronze, marble and wood that evoke the Humanist ideal in bodily form. **LOOK FOR** his *David* and *St George* in Florence's Museo Nazionale del Bargello (p71) and his *Prophet Habakkuk* and *Mary Magdelene* in the Museo dell'Opera del Duomo (p48).

❦ DUCCIO DI BUONINSEGNA // (C 1255–1318)

KNOWN FOR spearheading the Sienese school: ethereal, riveting figures with level gazes and pale-green skin against glowing gold backgrounds, like elegant aliens. **LOOK FOR** his *Maestà* (Madonna and Child Enthroned with 20 Angels and 19 Saints) at Siena's Museo dell'Opera Metropolitana (p186).

❦ FRA' ANGELICO (AKA BEATO ANGELICO) // (C 1400–1455)

KNOWN FOR his frescos of relatable religious figures with wry expressions and casual poses, conveying a sense of light coming from within. **LOOK FOR** the frescos in the Museo di San Marco (p67), particularly the *Annunciation*. A painter so revered that he was made a saint.

❦ FRA' FILIPPO LIPPI // (1406–69)

KNOWN FOR pure charm and uncanny empathy: moon-faced Madonna, squirming baby Jesus, and crowd scenes where you can read the minds of each character. **LOOK FOR** the *Coronation of the Virgin* and *Madonna and Child with Two Angels* in the Uffizi (p53).

BACKGROUND

♥ GIOTTO // (1267–1337)
KNOWN FOR kick-starting the Renaissance with action-packed frescos that you'll swear are in motion; each character pinpoints emotions with facial expressions and poses that need no translation. **LOOK FOR** his *Life of St Francis* fresco cycle at the Basilica di San Francesco in Assisi (p270) and his frescos in Santa Croce, Florence (p69).

♥ LEONARDO DA VINCI // (1452–1519)
KNOWN FOR being a genius of such flabbergasting proportions, the term polymath (aka Renaissance Man) had to be coined to explain him, and new painting terms defined to describe his style (eg sfumato, chiaroscuro). **LOOK FOR** his *Annunciation* in the Leonardo Room at the Uffizi, Florence (p53).

♥ LUCA SIGNORELLI // (C 1450–1523)
KNOWN FOR bringing irresistible beauty to the grotesque, with sunny scenes of eternal damnation and eerie shading in contrasting colours. **LOOK FOR** his *Last Judgment* in the Capella di San Brizio in Orvieto Cathedral (p302).

♥ MICHELANGELO BUONAROTTI // (1475–1564)
KNOWN FOR turning raw marble into imposing figures with impeccable balance, muscular movements and subtle emotion; he wasn't kidding when he claimed he saw the angel in the marble and set it free. **LOOK FOR** his *David* in the Galleria dell'Accademia, Florence (p66) and the *Tondo Pitti* in the Museo Nazionale del Bargello (p71).

♥ PIERO DELLA FRANCESCA // (1412–92)
KNOWN FOR luminous figures with lovely, limpid eyes and penetrating gazes that seem to follow you across the room and into your next life. **LOOK FOR** his *Legend of the True Cross* frescos in the Chiesa di San Francesco in Arezzo (p235) and *Madonna del parto* at Monterchi (p247).

♥ SANDRO BOTTICELLI // (C 1444–1510)
KNOWN FOR his Renaissance beauties: translucent, floating figures that glide across the canvas and glow from within. **LOOK FOR** *Primavera, Birth of Venus* and *Adoration of the Magi* at the Uffizi, Florence (p53).

BACKGROUND

RENAISSANCE FRESCOS

· · · · · · ·

War protests, healthcare crises, prison conditions: today's newspaper coverage sounds like a Renaissance fresco. They may look like ordinary bible stories now, but in their heyday, Renaissance frescos provided running social commentary as well as religious inspiration. Masaccio's *Tribute Money* spoke for Florentines whose taxes funded wars; Giotto's frescos of St Francis among lepers touched those left orphaned and ostracised by plague; and eternal torment in Taddeo di Bartolo's frescos looked suspiciously like the late-medieval justice system.

Human adversity never looked so divine, and vice versa. Early masters mostly used the demanding *buon fresco* technique, painting pigment on wet plaster walls. Today we can appreciate the brilliance of this technique, since many brightly coloured frescos remain bonded to walls across Tuscany and Umbria despite centuries of exposure, earthquakes and grime. But *buon fresco* offers very little margin for error. Mistakes must be chipped out of the wall and painstakingly patched to match the rest of the image. To touch up goofs or add shimmering colour, artists would sometimes mix ground-up semiprecious stones with a binder and apply it to the dry wall. This *a secco* technique has its downsides, too: it often flakes off and fades.

> 'what keeps many Renaissance frescos fresh even when they're crumbling is their remarkable empathy'

But what keeps many Renaissance frescos fresh even when they're crumbling is their remarkable empathy. They brought those haughty Byzantine saints, hovering overhead on medieval mosaic domes, down to eye level, where fresco details revealed awestruck eyes, quivering lips and clenched fists. Renaissance fresco artists made even dire predicaments pretty, proving that no human experience is entirely beyond understanding – or even redemption.

❦ **CIMABUE:** *MAESTÀ CON SAN FRANCESCO* **(MADONNA ENTHRONED WITH THE CHILD, ST FRANCIS & FOUR ANGELS; 1278–80) // LOWER CHURCH, BASILICA DI SAN FRANCESCO, ASSISI (P270)**
Of all the miracles Cimabue's Madonna is said to have performed over the centuries – restoring eyesight, delivering prescription-free fertility treatments and other feats widely advertised in spam email – perhaps the most amazing is its comeback after the 1987 earthquake that reduced much of Assisi's Basilica di San Francesco to rubble. While the dust was still clearing, thieves made off with precious fresco fragments, making the thousands of remaining pieces even harder to puzzle back together. The sleek contours that Cimabue outlined seemingly effortlessly in sludgelike drying plaster had to be laboriously pieced back together with a special computer-modelling program. Years of restoration work later, St Francis again stands shyly by while the four angels fawn over a baby Jesus, who is too busy tugging his mother's robes to notice either angelic hosts or earthquakes.

BACKGROUND

♥ **GIOTTO:** *NOLI ME TANGERE* **(JESUS & MARY MAGDALENE; 1307–08) //**
LOWER CHURCH, BASILICA DI SAN FRANCESCO, ASSISI (P270)
It's hard not to feel for Mary Magdalene in this image, as she reaches out to the man
who cast out her demons only to be told 'Don't touch me.' But Jesus had his reasons:
at this point he'd already died, and had places to go and God to see. When two angelic
ushers beckon on a flying red carpet, it's clearly time to leave, and Giotto's gentle Jesus
entrusts reformed sinner Mary Magdalene to pass the word. This is markedly different
from the scenes of near-certain damnation that loomed large in many Romanesque
churches, capped by stern saints who look like school principals. Even more than
the perspective he applies to the rocky background landscape, it's Giotto's appeal to
humanity that makes this fresco a sign of the Renaissance ahead.

♥ **AMBROGIO LORENZETTI:** *THE ALLEGORY OF GOOD GOVERNMENT*
(1338–40) // PALAZZO COMUNALE, SIENA (P181)
Some people move to the suburbs to find a place with less crime and welcoming
neighbours – but not Ambrogio Lorenzetti. In his *Good Government* frescos for
Siena's city hall, he imagined that these civic ideals might be achieved in inner-city
Siena, despite the city's chequered history of elected government and gang warfare, organised charity and public stonings, booming trade and dire famines. In *The Allegory
of Good Government,* his grey-bearded figure of Legitimate Authority is flanked by an
entourage who'd put White House interns to shame. They've got beauty, brains and
ethics, too, representing key governmental virtues, from left to right: Peace unwinding
with her olive branch; armed and ever-vigilant Fortitude; finger-wagging Prudence;
learned Magnanimity, with book in hand; Temperance pointing at an hourglass, cau-
tioning against hasty action; and a somewhat rough Justice bearing a head on a pike.
Above them flit Faith, Hope and Charity, and to the left Concord sits confidently on
her throne while the reins of justice are held taut overhead.

Next to this fresco is another depicting the effects of good government: farmers
bringing donkey loads of food to a spotlessly clean Siena marketplace, where all classes
of citizens mingle, haggle and gleefully crash a wedding. Sadly, Lorenzetti's extraordinary vision had yet to be fully realised by 1348 when he died of the plague – and like
many a glorious campaign promise, remains to be seen.

♥ **TADDEO DI BARTOLO:** *FINAL JUDGMENT* **(1396) // COLLEGIATA, SAN
GIMIGNANO (P194)**
As Renaissance painters knew, sweetness and light needs some brooding darkness to
put it into perspective – and Taddeo di Bartolo more than obliged in his *Final Judgment*. Snickering demons tormenting wayward souls are everywhere: here a disem-
bowelment, there a tongue being pierced with a mallet. Tuscan waiters may have
their surly moments, but that can't compare to the treatment at the devil's table,
where defrocked monks are force-fed Communion wafers. Fifty years before Hiero-
nymus Bosch was born, di Bartolo defined grotesque with a cross-eyed, chicken-
footed Lucifer, inhaling people whole and expelling them out the other end – all the
while gripping a human in each hand and banging their heads together like cymbals.

This may not seem like such a stretch from early Romanesque gargoyles or B-movie horror scenes, but there's a perversely gleeful gallows humour here that makes sense in its late-medieval context. Three-quarters of the city's population was wiped out in the plague by 1350, followed by bouts of war, more plague outbreaks and economic depression as the once-thriving trade centre was reduced to a Florentine vassal state. Those who did not willingly submit to Florentine authority might be convinced using the extreme methods and spiked implements today displayed in San Gimignano's Museo della Tortura e di Criminologia Medievale (Museum of Torture and Medieval Criminology). By 1396 it would've taken a lot more than hellfire to shock locals who had seen worse, and the notion of brutal justice for their subjugators may have held a certain appeal, too. That this fresco still appeals today speaks volumes about Taddeo di Bartolo's skills and, perhaps, our society.

☙ PINTURICCHIO: LIBRERIA PICCOLOMINI FRESCOS (1502–07) // CATHEDRAL, SIENA (P185)

After more than 150 years of war, famine and plague followed by plague, famine and more war with Florence, Siena seemed to be running alarmingly low on people and resources, let alone inspiration. To rally the city, church elders hired Umbrian painter Bernardino Pinturicchio to reassert the glory of Siena in 10 fresco panels celebrating Enea Silvio Piccolomini, aka the humanist Pope Pius II of Siena, with a cameo appearance by St Catherine of Siena.

Siena briefly outlawed black attire to lift the city's spirits after the plague and Pinturicchio seems to have had a similar impulse in these frescos. The sombre shadows and murky green tones of early Sienese painting are long gone. Pinturicchio's characters make their appearance in full party dress, in rosy hues, lush greens and an astonishing blue that appears jewel-like because it is – ultramarine was made of ground semiprecious lapis lazuli, then worth its weight in gold. To keep this lavish display of civic pride from seeming too heavy-handed, Pinturicchio covered the ceiling in frolicking grotesques: weight-lifting cherubs, griffins sticking out their tongues, banner-waving satyrs in red capes, and bouncing, bat-winged babies. In the crowd scene below Pope Pius II canonising St Catherine, the artist included a self-portrait alongside his early collaborator on the Libreria Piccolomini: a young painter named Raphael.

☙ FRA' ANGELICO: *ANNUNCIATION* (C 1440) // MUSEO DI SAN MARCO, FLORENCE (P67)

All those high-and-mighty religious figures on medieval cathedrals began to seem outmoded in the Renaissance with the rise of elected leadership. So instead of painting religious figures as domineering authorities, Renaissance artists painted them caught in all-too-human moments of uncertainty. Take, for example, Fra' Angelico's *Annunciation*, which shows an angel appearing before Mary to inform her she's been chosen to be the mother of God. Mary's blushing, bent-forward 'Come again?' posture and 'Who, me, a baby?' hand gesture make her instantly relatable. Anyone coming to terms with a religious calling could especially identify with Mary's predicament here, making this image ideally suited for a monastery. Fra' Angelico returned to this scene

BACKGROUND

several times, but the directness and poignant simplicity of the Museo di San Marco *Annunciation* makes it a masterpiece.

☙ TOMMASO MASACCIO: *EXPULSION OF ADAM & EVE FROM PARADISE* (C 1427) // CAPPELLA BRANCACCI, SANTA MARIA DEL CARMINE, FLORENCE (P76)

Take a close look at Masaccio's *Expulsion from Paradise* and the adjacent *Tribute Money* in the Cappella Brancacci and you'll appreciate not only his astounding architectural perspective but also his sly political satire. Florence had suffered five years of war at taxpayer expense by 1427, when the powerful Medici clan proposed a new tax to fund another military campaign. Florentines rejected it with near unanimity, but Giovanni de' Medici pushed through the measure. Before they even had a chance to see Masaccio's finished work on their chapel, the Brancacci were exiled from Florence for allying against the Medici. Masaccio died unexpectedly not long after this work was completed – insert conspiracy theory here – but his work stands as a brilliant rebuke to unchecked powers who wage war at taxpayer expense, and oust all opposition.

Later authorities objected not to Masaccio's message but its anatomical correctness, and had Adam and Eve's bits painted over with a fig leaf in about 1680. The leaf was removed in recent restorations, so now you can see the duo as nature and Masaccio intended.

☙ PIERO DELLA FRANCESCA: *LEGEND OF THE TRUE CROSS (C 1452–66)* // CHIESA DI SAN FRANCESCO, AREZZO (P235)

If the story of an inanimate object doesn't sound gripping, wait until you see what Piero della Francesca does with it. In 10 episodes he traces the story of the cross used to crucify Jesus, from when it was uprooted from the Garden of Eden and replanted as Adam's headstone *(The Death of Adam)* to its role as a holy relic fought over by kings *(The Victory of Constantine over Massentius)*. But thanks to a recent 15-year restoration effort, we can also read the cycle of frescos as an encyclopaedia of Renaissance painting tricks. Piero's realistic, directional lighting takes on nocturnal drama in *Constantine's Dream,* where light is shed from above by an angel hovering overhead like a holy street light. An accomplished mathematician, Piero experimented with a building shown in steep perspective in *The Discovery of the True Cross,* and a vanishing point that carefully positions Jerusalem on a distant Tuscan hill top.

☙ LUCA SIGNORELLI: *LAST JUDGMENT* (1499–1504) // DUOMO, ORVIETO (P302)

Have you heard the end is near? So it must have seemed in 1499, when Signorelli picked up where Fra' Angelico left off on the Orvieto cathedral and began his startling *Apocalypse* and *Last Judgment*. Green, orange and red devils ruthlessly stomp on the wayward and the weak, and winged demons raise up lost souls just to watch them fall. The chaos of this image has some basis in reality: religious crusader Savonarola had just been burned alive in Florence, the all-powerful Medici had been booted and France had invaded Italy. The Umbrian countryside had been bedevilled by a century of earthquakes and plague, and Signorelli lost a son and his assistant to the disease.

BACKGROUND

The handsome devils Signorelli painted break free of all Renaissance architectural constraints and seem ready to twist right off the wall – you'd never guess the man had worked under calm, rational Piero della Francesca. These writhing, muscular souls in torment may remind you of Michelangelo's *Last Judgment* in the Sistine Chapel, but they were done 35 years earlier. Signorelli's imagery also served as a visual reference for Sigmund Freud, the devil-child film *The Omen* and contemporary video artist Bill Viola. But when it comes to Signorelli's masterwork, the sincerest form of flattery isn't imitation, but sheer terror: as recently as 2000, doomsday predictors studied this work for signs that the end was nigh.

♀ PERUGINO: *THE ALMIGHTY WITH PROPHETS & SYBILS* (1503) // COLLEGIO DEL CAMBIO, PALAZZO DEI PRIORI, PERUGIA (P259)

Renaissance humanism flowered early in Perugia, the home of a university of secular law and theology as early as 1308, and never entirely faded, thanks in part to Perugino's still-vibrant frescos in the Collegio di Cambio. Old Testament prophets, classical sybils and a grey-bearded God are united here against an idyllic Umbrian landscape, under starry skies mapped with the latest Renaissance technology. For his insistence on ideals at a time when Perugia was sliding towards dictatorship and brooding mannerist imagery, Perugino's style was dismissed as outmoded and he was skipped for Vatican commissions in favour of his star pupil, Raphael. Although the Collegio was later occupied by the Church and various powerful Perugian interests, this fresco has never been dismantled or defaced. Perugino's delicate balance of faith, intellectual rigor, new technology and time-tested values remains intact, waiting for its time to come.

VENTURE OUTDOORS

· · · · · · ·

The gorgeous landscapes of Tuscany and Umbria beg to be explored and enjoyed, slowly. Those who tear through the countryside on the highways miss out on a rich variety of outdoor activities that underscore the area's splendour.

Because Tuscany and Umbria are year-round destinations, there's something to do in every season, from adrenalin-inducing winter skiing to leisurely countryside strolls. Families will be delighted to discover how accessible these activities are, while those in search of more demanding pursuits won't be disappointed either. There will still be plenty of time left to lounge around the villa and sip Chianti – which tastes all the better after a day in the region's fresh air.

WALKING

Tuscany and Umbria are eminently suited to walking. Indeed, large hiking groups, mostly from the UK, are a common sight throughout the region and frequently distinguishable at 200m by the floppy white sunhats they so often seem to sport.

The patchwork countryside of the centre, the wilder valleys and mountains in the south and northwest and, even more dramatically, the Apuane Alps and Apennine ranges all offer colourful variety.

'Because Tuscany and Umbria are year-round destinations, there's something to do in every season'

A truly ambitious hiker could undertake the 24-stage Grande Escursione Appenninica (GEA), an arc that takes you from the Due Santi pass above La Spezia southeast all the way to Sansepolcro. Alternatively Umbria's Monti Sibillini is superb for walkers using Castelluccio as a base, with a choice of demanding backpack hikes to the summit or casual day hikes.

People have been criss-crossing Tuscany for millennia, creating paths and trails as they went. One of the most important pilgrim routes in Europe during the Dark Ages was the Via Francigena (or Via Romea), in its time a veritable highway across Tuscany. Starting in the Magra river valley and winding through the wild Lunigiana territory of the northwest, the trail hugged the coast for a while before cutting inland to Siena via San Gimignano and then turning south to Rome, the capital of Christianity. Parts of the route can still be walked today and there's a movement afoot to restore even more of it as a resource for hikers. For more information, see p148.

PRIME SPOTS

Chianti is a favourite among walkers of all levels. One of the classic walks takes you rambling over several days (perhaps as many as five or six) from Florence to Siena. A good map resource is *Chianti Classico: Val di Pesa–Val d'Elsa* (1:25,000) published by Edizioni Multigraphic (see www.edizionimultigraphic.it, in Italian, for its full map catalogue), which covers most of the area and has hiking trails superimposed.

BACKGROUND

Another area within easy reach of Florence for a day's walking is Il Mugello, northeast of the city and extending to the border with Emilia-Romagna. Sorgenti Firenze Trekking (SOFT; Florence Springs Trekking) is a network of signed day or half-day trails criss-crossing the area. *Mugello, Alto Mugello, Val di Sieve,* produced by SELCA, is a decent map for hikers at 1:70,000.

For a day of history and hiking, you could walk from San Gimignano to Volterra or vice versa. Both your point of departure and your goal are fascinating medieval towns, each of which has reasonable transport links and plenty of accommodation.

DON'T MISS...

THERMAL BATHS

After a day on the hoof or in the saddle, nothing rivals a good long soak to ease the stiffness. Here's our choice of the best thermal baths in the region, many of which have been functioning since Roman times.

★ **Bagni di Lucca** (p138)

★ **Bagno Vignoni** (p208)

★ **Montecatini Terme** (p137)

★ **Terme di Saturnia** (p229)

History buffs may want to walk in the tracks of the Etruscans, basing themselves in Suvereto, Campiglia Marittima or Pitigliano. In Pitigliano, you can follow the Via Cave (p232), a three-hour walk that traverses sunken sacred routes linking Etruscan necropoli.

Back on the spine of the Apennines, the Garfagnana, up in the northwest, and Lunigiana, spilling into Liguria, both offer exciting medium-mountain walking. Castelnuovo di Garfagnana makes a good base and its **Centro Visite Parco Alpi Apuane** (garfagnana@tin.it) is well stocked with information and maps.

You can enjoy these two areas in their own right or do a couple of limbering-up hikes, then attack the Apuane Alps. The serious hikes are stunning and challenging, but there are also possibilities for less arduous itineraries.

The island of Elba is especially well geared for short walks and you will generally be able to plan your own routes quite easily. For more information, contact **Il Genio del Bosco – Centro Trekking Isola d'Elba** (☎ 0565 93 08 37; www.geniodelbosco.it, in Italian).

In Umbria, hiking in the scenic Monti Sibillini is wonderful, although there are relatively few marked trails. For information, contact the **Ente Parco Nazionale Monti Sibillini** (☎ 0737 97 27 11; www.sibillini.net). A good base for shorter day hikes is Castelluccio, where there is a choice of trails threading from the village. One of the most popular leads to Lago di Pilato under Monte Vettore; here, legend tells, Pontius Pilate is buried. The Club Alpino Italiano (CAI) map *Parco Nazionale dei Monti Sibillini* covers the park at 1:25,000, as does the Edizioni Multigraphic alternative of the same name. *Italy's Sibillini National Park: Walking and Trekking Guide* by Gillian Price is a useful resource.

INFORMATION

Edizioni Multigraphic publishes a couple of series of maps that are designed for walkers and mountain-bike riders (*mulattiere,* or mule trails, are especially good for mountain bikes). The *Carte dei Sentieri* series is at 1:25,000, while the *Carte Turistica e dei Sentieri* maps are at a scale of either 1:25,000 or 1:50,000. Edizioni Multigraphic's catalogue is online at www.edizionimultigraphic.it (in Italian).

In addition to Edizioni Multigraphic and the CAI, the German cartographers Kompass produce 1:25,000 scale, walker-friendly maps of various parts of Italy, including Tuscany and Umbria.

Walking in Tuscany, by Gillian Price, is an excellent guide that describes more than 50 walks and hikes of a none-too-strenuous nature (the text spills over into neighbouring Umbria and Lazio). Its ample selection takes you from Chianti country to the island of Elba, and to plenty of less-explored parts of the Tuscan region as well; however, it doesn't cover the more arduous hiking possibilities in the Apuane Alps in Tuscany's northwest.

The series of *Guide dei Monti d'Italia,* grey hardbacks published by the Touring Club Italiano (TCI) and CAI, are exhaustive walking guides containing maps. *Walking & Eating in Tuscany and Umbria* by James Lasdun and Pia Davis embraces two of the region's most delightful activities, offering 40 varied itineraries across these two central regions of Italy and plenty of tips for restaurants and overnight stays.

CYCLING

Italy is generally a cycle-friendly country and Tuscany and Umbria are no exception. Whether you're out for a day's gentle pedalling around town with the children in tow, a sybaritic weekend winery tour in Chianti with a bunch of friends, or a serious workout on that muscle tone with a week or more of pedal power, these regions provide plenty of cycling scope.

Matching the varied landscape, there is also a wide choice of roads and routes. Paved roads are particularly suited to high-tech racing bikes (watch out for the Sunday swarm of identically clad riders from the local club as the peloton sweeps by) or travelling long distances on touring bikes. Country roads, known as *strade bianche,* have dirt surfaces covered with gravel for stability.

Back roads and trails are another option if you are fairly fit and have a multigear mountain bike, as this is mainly hilly terrain. There are also plenty of other challenges for the more ambitious cyclist: Monte Amiata is the perfect goal for aspiring hill climbers, while hilly itineraries with short but challenging climbs beckon from Umbria through to Chianti and Le Crete. Don't despair; there are also plenty of itineraries with gentler slopes for amateur cyclists and even for families with children.

The best time of year for serious pedalling is spring, not only because of the obvious advantage of a cooler temperature, but also because the scenery is at its most breathtaking at this time of year, with valleys drenched in poppies and wildflowers. Easter and the days either side of 25 April and 1 May, both national holidays, are best avoided because of the crowds that infiltrate the region.

Autumn is also a good season, although there's a greater chance of rain, which can lead to slippery roads and poor visibility.

The most versatile bicycle for most of the roads of Umbria and Tuscany is a comfortable all-terrain bike capable of travelling over both paved and country roads and, even more importantly, able to climb hills without forcing you to exert yourself excessively. Ideally, it should give you a relaxed riding posture, have front suspension and be equipped with a wide range of gears, similar to a mountain bike.

BACKGROUND

If you are bringing your own bike from home, check in advance with your airline if there's a fee and how much, if any, disassembling and packing it requires. Bikes can be transported by train in Italy, either with you or to arrive within a couple of days.

PRIME SPOTS

The picturesque SS222, also known as the Strada Chiantigiana, runs between Florence and Siena, cleaving right through Chianti country. Although it's far from traffic free, you'll find it's a scenic and justifiably popular cycling route. More importantly, there are more than 400km of traffic-free roads.

The hills around San Gimignano and Colle di Val d'Elsa are another favourite venue for cyclists. One challenging route starts from Casole d'Elsa, following the road as it climbs to Monteguidi, then descending to cross the Cecina river before reaching the village of Montecastelli in the province of Pisa. An easier ride starts with a panoramic circuit around the town walls of Monteriggioni, carrying on to Colle di Val d'Elsa, and continuing towards San Gimignano and Volterra.

The rolling landscape of Le Crete and Val d'Orcia is similar to Chianti's, except that instead of pedalling through woodlands, you pass between vast swaths of wheat fields. Among the most stunning routes are the Monte Sante Marie road from Asciano to Torre a Castello and the Pieve a Salti road from Buonconvento to San Giovanni d'Asso. Both are unpaved and require all-terrain or mountain bikes. An alternative for cyclists with touring bikes is the legendary Lauretana road from Siena to Asciano and onwards towards Chiusure, Monte Oliveto Maggiore and Buonconvento.

Only die-hard peddlers should attempt to climb the steep flanks of Monte Amiata, a 1738m-long extinct volcano. The good news is that, at a mere 1370m, you'll come across a restaurant (Prato Le Macinaie) to revive you, roughly a 4km ride from the peak. You can also spend the night here, should your exertions exhaust you. You can attack the mountain by several routes: the easiest are those leading up from Arcidossa and Abbadia San Salvatore; the latter is a 14km uphill ride with a steady but reasonably slight gradient. The most difficult approach is via Castel del Piano, 15km of unremitting uphill work with a steady, steep 7% gradient for the first 10km. But, oh, the exhilarating joy of whooshing down without a single turn of the pedals…

The broad valleys of the Umbria region around Orvieto, Spello and Lago di Trasimeno are not too physically demanding. They're well suited for cyclists who want to experience the beauty of the unique and varied landscape at a leisurely pace.

INFORMATION

Bicycle Touring in Tuscany by David Cleveland describes eight multiday tours, each with a detailed route map. In defiance of its title, it also embraces cycle trips in Umbria and Le Marche. Tourist offices in Tuscany stock free information including *Cycling on the Tuscan Coast and the Islands of the Archipelago,* a handy kit comprising a booklet and 48 glossy itinerary cards; the *Discovering Tuscany by Bike* booklet; and *Trekking Bike* magazine. Edizioni Multigraphic's *Chianti e le Colline Senesi* is a useful map with mountain-bike trails superimposed.

BACKGROUND

Siena-based **Amici Della Bicicletta** (☎ 0577 45159; www.adbsiena.it, in Italian) is an active, ecologically minded group that promotes cycling as a daily form of urban transport and organises day-long and sometimes more extensive bike trips. It also dedicates considerable effort to developing and promoting cycling paths and itineraries for visiting cyclists.

From Florence, a handful of operators offer one-day cycling excursions into Chianti, complete with cycle rental, often with lunch and sometimes with a visit to a winery thrown in. For more details, see p101. **Parco Ciclistico del Chianti** (☎ 0577 74 94 11; www .parcociclisticodelchianti.it), based in Gaiole in Chianti, is an ecologically committed local cycling organisation that offers both tailor-made and 'ready-to-ride' tours. From Arezzo, **Alessandro Madiai** (☎ 338 649 14 81; torrequebrada@virgilio.it), himself a passionate cyclist, runs day and overnight tours around the enchanting southern Tuscan countryside.

SKIING

The region's skiing scene centres upon **Abetone** (www.abetone.com), on the border with the region of Emilia-Romagna. While the Apennines are smaller and less majestic than the Alps, they have a charm of their own. Abetone and the neighbouring, much smaller resort of Cutigliano have between them some 50km of downhill pistes. Abetone has a couple of cross-country trails, while Cutigliano offers a more demanding, more attractive 15km circuit.

The ski season generally runs from December to late March. Abetone gets pretty busy during weekends as skiers head up here from Florence and other nearby cities, such as Lucca and Pisa, by the bus and car load.

If you are here in late March, you may catch Pinocchio Sugli Sci, a keenly contested ski competition for children.

PRIME SPOTS

A couple of shops on the main square in Abetone hire boots and skis – you'll have to supply your own woolly hat. From here it is a couple of minutes' walk to the chairlift that takes you to the top of Monte Selletta (1711m). There's a good choice of blue runs and a couple of red, although the latter should pose little problem even to relatively novice skiers. The red runs are exhilarating with dips that allow you to pick up speed, followed by slower, flat sections where you can regain control.

Once you've warmed up with a couple of easy runs, ski across the face of the ridge to lift 17, then take lift 15 and whoosh down the trail to lift 18. This is the heart of the ski area with trails leading into all the valleys on the Tuscan side. It's also the access point for the Val di Luce (Valley of Light), a beautiful, appropriately named valley that has most of the area's more rewarding intermediate trails. If you head to the Alpe Tre Potenze (1940m), you will be rewarded with gorgeous panoramic views stretching all the way to the Tuscan coast.

INFORMATION

For ski-lift passes and more information contact the **Ufficio Centrale Biglietti** (☎ 0573 6 05 56; Piazza Piramidi, Abetone; 1-day weekday/weekend €28/33, 3-day weekday/weekend €72/84,

BACKGROUND

7 days €135). You can sign up for lessons with four ski schools: **Scuola Zeno Colò** (☎ 0573 6 00 32), **Scuola Sci Montegomito** (☎ 0573 6 03 92; www.scuolascimontegomito.it), **Scuola Sci Colò** (☎ 0573 60 70 77; www.scuolascicolo.it), all in Abetone, and **Italian Ski School Scuola Amerigo Colò** (☎ 0573 62 93 91; www.freesnowclub.it) in Cutigliano.

WATER SPORTS

Enjoying the water needn't involve any special effort, equipment or outlay but if you are keen on more than an idle paddle or swim, there are plenty of activities on offer. Diving facilities are generally of a high standard, and scuba-diving courses are not that expensive, with good rental gear widely available. Snorkelling, the low-tech alternative, still allows you to get dramatically close to fascinating aquatic life. Although there are several areas, such as Monte Argentario (Porto Ercole), that are excellent for diving, the island of Elba is where most divers of all levels head. The main tourist office in Portoferraio carries a list of schools and courses that are available.

If you're into wrecks, you can dive at Pomonte where the *Elvisco* cargo boat is submerged at a depth of 12m. Alternatively, a Junker 52, a German plane from WWII, lies on the seabed near Portoferraio at a more challenging depth of 38m.

The coves of the Tuscan archipelagos and around Monte Argentario are superb for sailing, as well as windsurfing, kite surfing and sea kayaking. You can rent equipment and receive instruction at the major resorts.

In Monte Argentario and Elba it's possible to enjoy most water sports, including diving, throughout autumn and winter as the water temperature remains relatively temperate year-round. For diving, however, you'll shiver without a semidry wetsuit between November and May. You can switch to a regular wetsuit for summer.

Windsurfing is also very popular on the Costa Fiorita near Livorno. Further up the coast, Viareggio holds several annual sailing regattas, including the Coppa di Primavera in March and the Vela Mare Cup in May. For more information, check out the website www.circolovelamare.it (in Italian).

Fishing in the sea is unlikely to lead to a very plentiful catch because of commercial overfishing that, in turn, has led to occasional fishing bans. For a more certain catch, you are better off heading for the trout farms, lakes and streams of the interior. Lago Trasimeno is one popular choice. Before you cast your line in fresh water, you will need a permit, available from the **Federazione Italiano della Pesca Sportiva e Attività Subacquee** (www.fipsas.it, in Italian), which has offices in every province.

ON THE WINE TRAIL
· · · · · · ·

The viticultural powerhouses of Tuscany and Umbria provide plenty of excitement for visiting oenophiles. Wine tasting here is an endless pleasure, with myriad *enoteche* (wine bars) and *cantine* (wine cellars) to ensure that your tastebuds stay titillated. Trattorias are the province of inexpensive and robust *vino di tavola* (table wine), but most restaurants have wine lists covering every price range and regional origin.

TUSCANY

Tuscany is largely about reds, Brunello di Montalcino being up there at the top with Italy's most prized: count on €8 for a glass, €30 to €100 for an average bottle and €5000 for a 1940s collectible. The product of Sangiovese grapes grown south of Siena, it must spend at least two years ageing in oak. It is intense and complex with an ethereal fragrance, and is best paired with game, wild boar and roasts. Brunello grape rejects go into Rossi di Montalcino, Brunello's substantially cheaper but wholly drinkable kid sister.

Prugnolo Gentile grapes (a clone of Sangiovese) form the backbone of the distinguished Vino Nobile di Montepulciano (2006 was an exceptional year). Its intense but delicate nose and dry, vaguely tannic taste make it the perfect companion to red meat and mature cheese.

Then there's Chianti, a cheery full and dry fellow known the world over, easy to drink, suited to any dish and wholly affordable. More famous than it was good in the 1970s, contemporary Chianti gets the thumbs up from wine critics today. Produced in seven subzones from Sangiovese and a mix of other grape varieties, Chianti Classico – the traditional heart of this longstanding wine-growing area – is the best known, with a DOCG (Denominazione d'Origine Controllata e Garantita; Protected Designation of Origin and Quality) guarantee of quality and a Gallo Nero (Black Cockerel) emblem that once symbolised the medieval Chianti League. Young, fun Chianti Colli Senesi

APPELLATIONS

You will encounter three official classifications used to signify derivation and quality in the local wines:

Denominazione d'Origine Controllata (DOC) Protected Designation of Origin; must be produced within a specified region using defined methods and meeting a defined quality standard.

Denominazione d'Origine Controllata e Garantita (DOCG) Protected Designation of Origin and Quality; subterritories of DOC areas producing wines of particularly high quality.

Indicazione Geografica Tipica (IGT) Protected Geographical Indication; high-quality wines that don't meet DOC or DOCG definitions but are high quality nevertheless. Super Tuscans fall into this category.

Superiore marked on the label denotes DOC wines above the general standard (perhaps with greater alcohol content or longer ageing) and *riserva* is applied only to DOC or DOCG wines aged for a specified amount of time.

BACKGROUND

from the Siena hills is the largest subzone; Chianti Colli Pisane is light and soft in style; and Chianti Rùfina (p105) comes from the hills east of Florence.

> *'Then there's Chianti, a cheery full and dry fellow known the world over'*

One result of Chianti's 'cheap wine for the masses' reputation in the 1970s was the realisation by some Tuscans – including the Antinoris, Tuscany's most famous wine-producing family – that wines with a rich, complex, internationally acceptable taste following the New World tradition of blending mixes could be sold for a lot more than local wines. Thus, innovative, exciting wines were developed and cleverly marketed to appeal to buyers both in New York and in Florence. And when an English-speaking scribe dubbed the end product Super Tuscans the name stuck. Sassacaia, Tignanello, Solaia and Luce are superhot Super Tuscans.

Tuscan whites amount to one label loved by popes and artists alike during the Renaissance: Vernaccia di San Gimignano (p196).

UMBRIA

Umbria was first recognised for its whites, most notably the dry Orvieto Classico, which is as gorgeous as the southern Umbrian town that it takes its name from. Orvieto is where Etruscans first cultivated vines. Ironically, some of the most prestigious wines from this area, such as the fruity, well-structured Cervaro della Sala (literally 'stag of the hall', made from Grechetto and Chardonnay grapes) and the sweet, golden dessert wine Muffato della Sala (a blend of four grapes), are made by Tuscany's Antinori family. The Antinoris bought Castello della Sala, a centuries-old estate complete with 52 hectares of vines and olive groves, 29 farms and a dilapidated 14th-century castle located in Ficulle, 18km from Orvieto, in 1940 and slowly made it into the highly respected label it is today. The man behind the transformation: Umbrian-born Renzo Cotarella.

Queen of Umbrian wine is Chiari Lungarotti, whose family transformed Torgiano, south of Perugia, into the royal wine-making area it is today; Torgiano was the first wine-producing area of Umbria to gain both the DOC (Denominazione d'Origine Controllata, Protected Designation of Origin; 1968) and DOCG (1990) quality recogni-

HOT DATES

Dedicated oenophiles should consider timing their visit around the last weekend in May, when dozens of wine-producing estates in Tuscany and Umbria open their cellars to wine tasters during **Cantine Aperte**, an annual festival organised by Italy's dynamic **Movimento Turismo del Vino** (www.movimentoturismovino.com).

Other hot dates to consider include **Benvenuta Vendemmia**, a grape harvest festival on a Sunday in September when wine estates open their cellar doors; **San Martino in Cantina**, an opportunity to taste the *vino novello* (new wine) in the second week of November; and the festive **Calci di Stelle** on 10 August, when town squares host wine tastings, classical- and jazz-music performances, fireworks and historical parades. For more info on all of these, check out www.movimentoturismovino.com.

BACKGROUND

tions. Lungarotti wine production is vast and covers the whole gamut of wine today – white, red, rosé and sparkling. The Lungarotti Estate's Museo del Vino (p267) and neighbouring *cantina* provide a prime opportunity to discover Umbrian viticulture and taste its wine, as does the extraordinary wine list in the estate's top-notch restaurant and hotel (p267). Torgiano Rosso Riserva DOCG is its most renowned appellation.

Bevagna and Montefalco, east of Perugia, make up the other wealthy wine area thanks to the Sagrantino di Montefalco, which comes as a *passito* (sweet) or *secco* (dry) white – best drunk with sweet biscuits and venison or roasts respectively – or as a red. Taste all three versions along the well-marketed Strada del Sagrantino (see p379).

THE WINE ROADS

There is nothing quite so idyllic as following *le strade del vino*, well-marked wine trails that take motorists and cyclists along scenic Tuscan and Umbrian back roads, past a plethora of vineyards and vintner's wine cellars (look for the sign '*cantine aperte*') where you can taste or buy wine. Some of the *strade* incorporate olive-oil producers, and others *sapori* (good food) producers and provedores.

Each *strada* has its own distinct emblem; look for a sign that has something resembling a bunch of grapes and you're probably on the right track. All have their own map, with listings of wineries and sometimes *agriturismi* (farm-stay accommdation), restaurants, wine-tasting *enoteche*, olive mills and other producers.

To date, 10 Tuscan and four Umbrian *strade del vino* have been marked, crisscrossing famous wine-production areas. Tourist offices have maps and information, as does www.terreditoscana.it and www.umbriadoc.com (both in Italian). In Tuscany, try to source a copy of *Guida alle Strade del Vino, dell'Olio e dei Sapori di Toscana*, a book of 22 enogastronomic itineraries covering the entire region of Tuscany.

LE STRADE DEL VINO: TUSCANY

🍇 STRADA DEI VINI CHIANTI RÙFINA E POMINO // WWW.CHIANTIRUFINA.COM

Tours the area around Pontassieve, Rùfina, Pelago, Londa and Dicomano east of Florence where Pomino DOC and Chianti Rùfina wines are produced. Known for its locally grown saffron, berries and late-ripening Londa peaches. See the boxed text, p105, for more.

🍇 STRADA DEL VINO COSTA DEGLI ETRUSCHI // WWW.LASTRADADELVINO.COM

Follows the Tuscan coastline and includes Elba; taste the famous Sassicaia Super Tuscan, the Elba Aleatico Passito DOCG and the Terratico di Bibbona, Bolgheri, Val di Cornia and Montescudaio DOCs along the way.

🍇 STRADA DEL VINO DEI COLLI DI CANDIA E DI LUNIGIANA // WWW.STRADADELVINOMS.IT

Traverses the dramatic scenery between Pontremoli and Montignoso in northwestern Tuscany; famous for fruits of the forest, including chestnuts and honey, and its Candia and Colli di Luni DOCs.

❦ STRADA DEL VINO DELLE COLLINE PISANE
Through the Pisan hills, home to Chianti delle Colline Pisane DOCG and Bianco Pisano di San Torpè DOC. This area incorporates San Miniato, known for its white truffles and *mallegato* (blood sausage).

❦ STRADA DEL VINO MONTESPERTOLI //
WWW.CHIANTI-MONTESPERTOLI.IT
Tours the area just outside Florence, in the northern part of Chianti, which is home to Chianti Montespertoli and Chianti Colli Fiorentini DOCGs, Vin Santo del Chianti DOC and Tuscan IGT (Indicazione Geographica Tipica; Protected Geographical Indication) wines. It's known for its locally baked bread (sold throughout Florence) and white truffles.

❦ STRADA DEL VINO NOBILE DI MONTEPULCIANO //
WWW.STRADAVINONOBILE.IT
Around Montepulciano between Valdichiana and Val d'Orcia. Home to big guns including the Vino Nobile di Montepulciano and Chianti Colli Senesi DOCGs; Rosso di Montepulciano, Vin Santo di Montepulciano and Valdichiana DOCs. Also known for its Terre di Siena DOP (Denominazione d'Origine Protetta; Protected Designation of Origin) extra-virgin olive oil and for *cinta senese* (indigenous Tuscan pig), which is roasted, grilled and made into salami.

❦ STRADA DEL VINO ORCIA // WWW.STRADAVINORCIA.IT
Tours south of Siena in the Val d'Orcia, incorporating the famous wine region of Montalcino, home to the Brunello di Montalcino DOCG. You'll also find the Orcia DOP and Terre di Siena DOP extra-virgin olive oil. Local delicacies include *pecorino* cheese, truffles, *porcini* mushrooms and *cinta senese*.

❦ STRADA DEL VINO TERRE DI AREZZO //
WWW.STRADADELVINO.AREZZO.IT
Incorporates Arezzo and the Casentino. Best known for its Chianti Colli Arentini DOCG and Cortona, Valdichiana and Pietraviva DOCs. Local foods include honey and *pecorino*.

❦ STRADA DEL VINO VERNACCIA DI SAN GIMIGNANO
Attracts devotees of the famously crisp and dry Vernaccia di San Gimignano DOCG but is also home to the Chianti Colli Senesi DOCG and San Gimignano DOC. Local products include extra-virgin olive oil and saffron.

❦ STRADA MEDICEA DEI VINI DI CARMIGNANO //
WWW.CARMIGNANODIVINO.PRATO.IT/STRADA
This route to the northwest of Florence tours Medici villas and vineyards producing the Carmignano DOCG and Barco Reale, Rosato di Carmignano and Vin Santo di Carmignano DOCs, the last of which is delicious served with the local speciality of Carmignano dried figs.

LE STRADE DEL VINO: UMBRIA

❦ LA STRADA DEI VINI DEL CANTICO // WWW.STRADADEIVINIDELCANTICO.IT

The most sprawling route, it criss-crosses a triangle between Perugia, Todi and Spello, stopping in Torgiano, Assisi and Marsciano. Local tipples include the Torgiano Rosso Riserva DOCG and the Assisi, Colli Martani, Colli Perugini and Torgiano DOCs.

❦ LA STRADA DEI VINI ETRUSCO ROMANA // WWW.STRADADEIVINIETRUSCOROMANA.IT

Connects Orvieto with Amelia and many points in between. Local DOCs include Orvieto, Rosso Orvietano, Lago di Corbara and Colli Amerini and there are also a number of IGT wines that are typical of the geographical region. The local extra-virgin olive oil, truffles and vegetables are also of note.

❦ LA STRADA DEL SAGRANTINO // WWW.STRADADELSAGRANTINO.IT

The area surrounding Bevagna and Montefalco is the fastest-growing wine area in the region. Home to the Montefalco Sagrantino/Sagrantino di Montefalco DOCG and the Montefalco Rosso and Colli Martani Grechetto DOCs. Local delicacies include *lardo* (thin slices of local pork fat marinated in a mix of herbs and oils), emmer wheat, black truffles, honey and extra-virgin olive oil.

❦ LA STRADA DEL VINO COLLI DEL TRASIMENO // WWW.STRADADELVINOTRASIMENO.IT

Starts at Corciano near Perugia and circles through the *colli* (hills) around the lake. The local DOCs are Colli del Trasimeno, Colli Altotiberini and Colli Perugini. The proximity to the lake means that freshly caught fish are a local treat.

LE STRADE DEL VINO & DELL'OLIO

There are also six routes in Tuscany that give equal emphasis to wine, olive oil and local produce.

❦ STRADA DELL'OLIO E DEL VINO MONTALBANO

Hit the hills between Capraia and Serravalle Pistoiese, passing Leonardo da Vinci's home town of Vinci en route. Local wines to investigate are the Chianti Montalbano, Barco Reale di Carmignano and Vin Santo di Carmignano DOCs. Produce includes salamis and prosciutto, local chocolate and an excellent olive oil.

❦ STRADA DEL VINO E DEI SAPORI COLLI DI MAREMMA // WWW.STRADAVINIMAREMMA.IT

This route southeast of Grosseto highlights Morellino di Scansano DOC and DOCG; Ansonica Costa dell'Argentario, Bianco di Pitigliano, Capalbio, Parrina and Sovana DOCs; extra-virgin olive oil Toscano IGP (Indicazione Geografica Protetta; Protected Geographical Indication); and the Maremma breed of cattle.

BACKGROUND

❧ STRADA DEL VINO E DEI SAPORI MONTEREGIO DI MASSA MARITTIMA // WWW.STRADAVINO.IT

This route travels trough the hills of the Upper Maremma around Grosseto. This is where the Monteregio di Massa Marittima DOC is produced, and where the locals like to claim that *ricciarelli* and *cavallucci* biscuits originated (a claim that Siena disputes).

❧ STRADA DEL VINO E DELL'OLIO CHIANTI CLASSICO

Tours the Chianti Classico district between Florence and Siena, following the Via Chiantigiana running from Greve in Chianti, through Panzano and to Siena, tasting the Chianti Classico DOCG, extra-virgin olive oil DOP, and Chianti Classico and Vin Santo del Chianti Classico DOCs along the way. Features a wealth of *agriturismo* choices and wonderful regional produce.

❧ STRADA DEL VINO E DELL'OLIO LUCCA MONTECARLO E VERSILIA // WWW.STRADAVINOEOLIOLUCCA.IT

Travels between Seravezza in the Apuane Alps to Lucca and then east to Montecarlo and Pescia, passing dramatic scenery and ornate villas on the way. Features Lucca's famous DOP olive oil and the Colline Lucchesi and Montecarlo di Lucca DOCs.

❧ STRADA DEL VINO MONTECUCCIO E DEI SAPORI D'AMIATA // WWW.STRADADELVINOMONTECUCCO.IT

Take to the roads south of Montalcino, which are home to Montecuccio DOC and Seggiano DOP extra-virgin olive oil.

THE TUSCAN & UMBRIAN TABLE

· · · · · · ·

Be it by sinking your teeth into a bloody *bistecca alla fiorentina* (T-bone steak), sampling wild boar salami in Norcia, savouring a flavoursome fish stew in Livorno or sniffing out truffles in the dank woods outside San Miniato (see p130), you'll discover this region cooks up a feast of gastronomic experiences.

The cuisine in this part of Italy has stayed faithful to its humble rural roots, relying on fresh local produce and eschewing fussy execution. During the 13th and 14th centuries, when Florence prospered and the wealthy started using silver cutlery instead of their fingers, simplicity remained the hallmark of dishes cooked up at the lavish banquets held by feuding families as a show of wealth. And while the Medici passion for flaunting the finer things in life gave Tuscan cuisine a fanciful kick during the Renaissance, with spectacular sculptures of sugar starring alongside spit-roasted suckling pig on the

> *'cuisine in this part of Italy has stayed faithful to its humble rural roots'*

banquet table, ordinary Tuscans continued to rely on the age-old *cucina povera* (poor dishes) that kept hunger at bay. Contemporary Tuscan and Umbrian cuisine continues this tradition.

THE COUNTRY KITCHEN

It was over an open wood fire in *la cucina contadina* (the farmer's kitchen) that Tuscan and Umbrian cuisine was cooked up. Its basic premise: don't waste a crumb.

MEAT & GAME

The icon of Tuscan cuisine is Florence's *bistecca alla fiorentina,* a char-grilled T-bone steak rubbed with olive oil, seared on the char grill, garnished with salt and pepper and served *al sangue* (bloody).

Tuscan markets conjure up an orgy of animal parts most of us wouldn't even dream of digesting. In the past, prime beef cuts were the domain of the wealthy. Offal was the staple fare of peasants, who cooked tripe in the pot for hours with onions, carrots and herbs to make *lampredotto* or with tomatoes and herbs to make *trippa alla fiorentina* – two Florentine classics still going strong.

Fortunately *pasto,* a particularly gruesome mix of *picchiante* (cows lungs) and chopped potatoes, is not even a gastronomic curiosity these days – unlike *cibrèo* (chicken's kidney, liver, heart and cockscomb stew) and *colle ripieno* (stuffed chicken's neck), two dishes not for the faint-hearted that can still be sampled at Trattoria Cibrèo in Florence (p88). Another fabulous golden oldie (cooked by the Etruscans, no less, as many a fresco illustrates) still going strong is *pollo al mattone* – boned chicken splattered beneath a brick, rubbed with herbs and baked beneath the brick. The end result is handsomely crispy.

BACKGROUND

Cinghiale (wild boar), hunted in autumn, is turned into *salsicce di cinghiale* (wild-boar sausages) or simmered with tomatoes, pepper and herbs for hours to make a rich stew.

Pork reigns supreme in Umbria, where historically every last morsel of the family pig was eaten. Butchers from Norcia were so well known for their craft in medieval times that, to this day, a pork butcher anywhere in Italy is known as a *norcino* and works in a *norcineria*. *Porchetta* (suckling pig) is roasted whole on a spit, or slaughtered, butchered and conserved (to eat in the long, hard winter traditionally) as *prosciutto di norcia*, a coarse, salty cured ham. Other porky Umbrian specialities include *capocollo* (seasoned cured pork sausage), *barbozzo* (pig-cheek bacon) and *mazzafegati* (pork liver, orange peel and sultana sausages).

In Tuscany the family pig invariably ended up on the plate as a salty slice of *soprassata* (head, skin and tongue boiled, chopped and spiced with garlic, rosemary and other herbs and spices), *finocchiona* (fennel-spiced sausage), prosciutto (the best is from Casentino), nearly black *mallegato*, spiked with nutmeg, cinnamon, raisins and pine kernels from San Miniato, or *mortadella* (a smooth-textured pork sausage speckled with cubes of white fat). Butcher legend Dario Cecchini (p104) in Chianti will happily sell you these and explain their provenance. *Lardo di colonnata* (thin slices of local pork fat marinated in a mix of herbs and oils for at least six months; p146) is among the Tuscan food products highlighted by Slow Food's Ark of Taste (p19).

FISH

Livorno leads the region in seafood, fishy *cacciucco* (one 'c' for each type of fish thrown into it) being its signature dish. Deriving its name from the Turkish *kukut*, meaning 'small fry', *cacciucco* is a stew of five fish simmered with tomatoes and red peppers, and served atop stale bread. *Triglie alla livornese* is red or white mullet cooked in tomatoes, and *baccalà alla livornese*, also with tomatoes, features cod traditionally salted aboard the ships en route to the old Medici port. *Baccalà* (salted cod), not to be confused with *stoccofisso* (unsalted air-dried stockfish) is a Tuscan trattoria mainstay, served on Fridays as tradition – and old-style Catholicism –demands.

The area around Lago Trasimeno in Umbria is another *pesce* (fish) hot spot, where you can fish and eat your own catch (p291), or dine out on *carpa regina in porchetta* (carp cooked in a wood oven with loads of fennel and garlic) and *tegamaccio* (a kind of soupy stew of the best varieties of local lake fish – eel, whiting, perch, trout, and so on – simmered in olive oil, white wine and herbs).

PULSES, GRAINS & VEGETABLES

Poor man's meat was precisely what pulses (beans, peas and lentils) were to Tuscans and Umbrians centuries ago. Jam-packed with protein, cheap and available year-round (eaten fresh in summer, dried in winter), pulses – of which an incredible variety exist – make some of the region's most traditional dishes, *minestra di fagioli* (bean soup) and *pasta e ceci* (chickpea pasta) included. Throw the other dirt-cheap staple, bread, into the pot and you get *minestra di pane* (bread and bean soup) and *ribollita* (a 'reboiled' bean, vegetable and bread soup with black cabbage, left to sit for a day before being served).

BACKGROUND

White *cannellini* beans drizzled in olive oil are an inevitable accompaniment to meat. Amid the dozens of different bean varieties, *cannellini* and dappled *borlotti* are the most common; the round, yellow *zolfino* from Pratomagno and silky smooth *sorano* bean from Pescia are the most prized. The greenish *verdino di cave* and yellowish *giallo di cave,* cultivated in Cave, a hamlet near Foligno in northern Umbria, is harvested and the entire crop sold at the village's Sagra del Fagiolo di Cave in October. Another Umbrian variety, the small white *fagiolo del purgatorio* (purgatorial bean), alludes to the centuries-old Lenten tradition of eating beans on Ash Wednesday to purge sins.

Lenticchie (small, green lentils) from Castelluccio, near Norcia in Umbria, are another source of local pride, as are the 18 local varieties of *farro dicocco* (emmer wheat), an ancient grain cultivated in the Valnerina area and around Spoleto, southern Umbria. Of a similar age to emmer but with a tougher husk is *farro della garfagnana* (spelt), a grain grown in Central Europe as early as 2500 BC and one that has never died out in the Garfagnana, northwestern Tuscany.

The Tuscan vegetable garden is lush, strictly seasonal, and one that sees medieval vegetables cultivated alongside tomatoes, zucchini, mushrooms and others common to most European tables. Wild fennel, black celery (braised as a side dish), sweet red onions (delicious oven-baked), artichokes and zucchini flowers (both stuffed and oven-baked), black cabbage, broad beans, chicory, chard, thistle-like cardoons and green tomatoes are among the more unusual to look out for.

Practically an antique and prized the world over as one of the most expensive spices, saffron is fast becoming all the rage again, particularly around San Gimignano where it was enthusiastically traded in medieval times. Fiery red and as fine as dust by the time it reaches the kitchen, saffron in its rawest state is, in fact, the dried flower stigma of the saffron crocus. Should you want to learn how it is grown, stay at Podere Castellare (p396).

PASTA

Florentine chef Fabio Picchi (p72) says it is a fallacy to suggest that pasta is not part of Tuscan cuisine: he has a good guffaw every time the press yet again cites the absence of pasta in his Florence restaurant as a reflection of true Tuscan gastronomy. Indeed, no Tuscan banquet would be quite right without a *primo* of homemade *maccheroni* (wide, flat ribbon pasta), pappardelle (wider flat ribbon pasta) or Sienese *pici* (a thick, hand-rolled version of spaghetti) served with a duck, hare, rabbit or boar sauce.

Umbria has its own pasta: round stringlike *umbricelli* (also spelled *ombricelli*), fatter than spaghetti, and *strangozzi (strozzapreti* in some towns), which is like *umbricelli* but with a rougher surface to better absorb the accompanying meat, tomato, *porcini* mushroom (bliss!) or truffle (double bliss!) sauce.

BREAD

One bite and the difference is striking – *pane* (bread) here is unsalted, creating a disconcertingly bland taste many a bread lover might never learn to love.

Yet it is this centuries-old staple, deliberately unsalted to ensure it lasted for a good week and to complement the region's salty cured meats, that forms the backbone of Tuscany's most famous dishes: *pappa al pomodoro* (a thick bread and tomato soup,

BACKGROUND

eaten hot or cold), *panzanella* (a tomato and basil salad mixed with a mush of bread soaked in cold water) and *ribollita*. None sound or look particularly appetising, but their depth of flavour is extraordinary.

Thick-crusted *pane toscana* (also known as *pane casalingo*) is the basis of two antipasti delights, traditionally served on festive occasions but today appearing on most menus – *crostini* (lightly toasted slices of bread topped with liver pâté) and *fettunta* (also called *crogiantina* or bruschetta; toast fingers doused in garlic, salt and olive oil).

CHEESE

So important was cheesemaking in the past, it was deemed a dowry skill. Still highly respected, the sheep's-milk *pecorino* crafted in Pienza, a Tuscan town near the Umbrian border, ranks among Italy's greatest *pecorini*: taste it young and mild in the company of fava beans; or try it more mature and tangier, spiked with *toscanello* (black pepper corns) or as *pecorino di tartufo* (infused with black-truffle shavings). *Pecorino* massaged with olive oil during the ageing process turns red and is called *rossellino*.

Pecorino is commonly served regionwide as a first course with either fresh pear or chestnuts and honey. Mild-tasting *caciotta* is made from cow's milk and laced with truffle shavings by Umbrians to become *caciotta al tartufo*. Shepherds in the Umbrian hills traditionally salted ricotta (*ricotta salata*) to preserve it.

OLIVE OIL

Olive oil heads the culinary trinity (bread and wine are the other two) and epitomises the earthy simplicity of Tuscan and Umbrian cuisine: dipping chunks of bread into pools of this liquid gold or biting into a slice of oil-doused *fettunta* are sweet pleasures in life here.

The Etruscans were the first to cultivate olive trees and press the fruit to make oil, a process later refined by the Romans. As with wine, strict rules govern when and how olives are harvested (October through to 31 December), the varieties used and so on. Extra virgin oil originating from the terraced hillsides in Umbria is covered by one state-regulated DOP while the best Tuscan oils bear a Chianti Classico DOP or Terre di Siena DOP label and an IGP certificate of quality issued by the region's Consortium of Tuscan Olive Oil.

SWEETS, CHOCOLATE & ICE

Be it the simple honey, almond and sugar-cane sweets traditionally served at the start of 14th-century banquets in Florence, or the sugar sculptures made to impress at the flamboyant 16th- and 17th-century feasts of the power-greedy Medici, *dolci* (sweets) have always been reserved for festive occasions. In more humble circles street vendors sold *bomboloni* (doughnuts) and *pandiramerino* (rosemary-bread buns), while Carnivale in Florence was marked by *stiacchiata* (Florentine flat bread made from eggs, flour, sugar and lard, then dusted with icing sugar).

As early as the 13th century, servants at the Abbazia di Montecelso near Siena paid tax to the nuns in the form of *panpepato* (a pepper and honey flat bread), although legend tells a different tale: following a siege in Siena, the good-hearted Sister Berta

BACKGROUND

baked a revitalising flat cake of honey, dried fruit, almonds and pepper to pep up the city's weakened inhabitants. Subsequently sweetened with spices, sprinkled with icing sugar and feasted on once a year at Christmas, Siena's *panforte* (literally 'strong bread') – a flat, hard cake with nuts and candied fruit – is eaten year-round today. An old wives tale says it stops couples quarrelling.

SLOW FOOD, SLOW CITIES

In 1986 McDonald's was about to open a restaurant at the famed Spanish Steps in Rome. Carlo Petrini, a wine writer, was so appalled at this prospect that he started a movement that has since grown to include more than 100,000 members in 132 countries. Called Slow Food (www.slowfood.com), about half of its members are based in Italy, but branches are opening around the world at a rapid pace as people follow the Italian lead, seeking to preserve local food traditions and encouraging interest in the food they eat, where it comes from, how it tastes and how our food choices affect the rest of the world.

There are a number of regional Slow Food specialities that you should try to sample when travelling through these regions. In Tuscany, look for Garfagnana potato bread and *biroldo* (the local equivalent of haggis), *cinta senese* (indigenous Tuscan pig), Chianina oxen, Certaldo onions, Orbatello *bottarga* (salted fish roe), Prato *mortadella* (a smooth-textured pork sausage speckled with cubes of white fat), sea *palamita* (fish), Valdarno chicken and *tarese* (pancetta), Zeri lamb, *zolfino* beans, *farro* (spelt), Pistoian mountain *pecorino*, *fiori di zucca* (zucchini flowers), *bazzone* prosciutto, *bollo* cakes and biscuits (spiced with anise), Calvana beef, Carmignano dried figs, Casentino prosciutto, Casola chestnut bread, Cetica red potatoes, *lardo di colonnata* (thin slices of local pork fat marinated in a mix of herbs and oils), Florentine *bardiccio* (salami made with bloodied meat, entrails and fennel seeds), Garfagnana beef and sheep, Londa peaches, *mallegato* (blood sausage), Maremma ox, Pecciolo Colombana grapes, *sfratto* cakes and biscuits (confection of honey and walnuts), sheep *raviggiolo* (cheese), Siena *buristo* (sausage) and Sorana beans. In Umbria, there are only three Slow Food–flagged products: Lago Trasimeno beans, *roveja* (a pulse) and Trevi black celery. For more information check out www.fondazioneslowfood.com.

From the Slow Food Movement grew the Slow City Movement (www.cittaslow .blogspot.com). Its members are concerned that globalisation is wiping out differences in traditions and culture and replacing them with a watered-down homogeneity.

To become a Slow City (or Città Lenta as they're known in Italy), towns have to pass a rigid set of standards, including having a visible and distinct culture. The towns must follow principles such as relying heavily on autochthonous (from within) resources instead of mass-produced food and culture; cutting down on air and noise pollution; and increasingly relying on sustainable development, such as organic farming and public transport. Tuscany boasts the Slow Cities of Anghiari, Barga (p139), Greve in Chianti (p102), Massa Marittima (p222), Pratovecchio, San Miniato (p129), San Vincenzo and Suvereto (p161). The Umbrian portfolio includes Amelia (p330), Castiglione del Lago (p292), Montefalco (p280), Trevi (p282), Todi (p310), Torgiano (p266), San Gemini and Orvieto (p302).

As you travel through these towns, you will never hear a car alarm; you can be assured you'll find plenty of public space; and there will never, ever, be a McDonald's.

BACKGROUND

Unsurprisingly it was at the Florentine court of Catherine de' Medici that Italy's most famous product, gelato (ice cream), first appeared thanks to court maestro Bernardo Buontalenti (1536–1608), who engineered a way of freezing sweetened milk and egg yolks together; the ice house he designed still stands in the Giardino di Boboli in Florence (p80). For centuries, ice cream and sherbets – a mix of shaved ice and fruit juice served between courses at Renaissance banquets to aid digestion – only appeared on wealthy tables.

Tuscan *biscotti* (biscuits) – once served with candied fruits and sugared almonds at the start of and between courses at Renaissance banquets – are dry, crisp and often double-baked. *Cantucci* are hard, sweet biscuits traditionally studded with almonds but these days come spiked with anything from chocolate to apricots. *Brighidini di lamporecchio* are small, round aniseed-flavoured wafers; *ricciarelli* are almond biscuits, sometimes with candied orange; and *lardpinocchiati* are studded with pine kernels. All these biscuits are best sampled when dipped in a glass of Vin Santo dessert wine. In Lucca, locals are proud of their *buccellato* (a ring-shaped loaf made with flour, sultanas, aniseed seeds and sugar), a treat that is both given by godparents to their godchild on their first Holy Communion and eaten with alacrity at all other times.

Umbrian chocolate is legendary – the world-famous *baci* (hazelnut 'kisses' covered with chocolate) are made at the now Nestlé-owned Perugina chocolate factory (p262), which can be visited in Perugia.

TUTTI A TAVOLA

Walk into a trattoria or restaurant half an hour before opening time and the chatter of its entire staff merrily dining around a communal table will strike you instantly.

Tutti a tavola (the shared table) is an integral part of culinary culture. Traditionally gathering for a hearty *pranzo* (lunch) around noon, families now tend to share the main family meal in the evening – during the working week at least. Sunday lunch does, however, remain sacred. *Colazione* (breakfast), a quick dash into a bar or cafe on the way to work for a cappuccino and *cornetto* (croissant), scarcely counts as a meal.

An everyday *cena* (dinner) comprises a *primo* (first course) and *secondo* (second course), usually accompanied by a *contorno* (vegetable side dish) and a piece of fruit as dessert. The traditional Italian belt-busting five-course whammy of *antipasto* (appetiser), *primo*, *secondo* with *contorno*, *insalata* (salad) and *dolci* (dessert) generally only happens on Sundays and feast days. In true

DON'T MISS...

REGIONAL DELIGHTS

* ★ **Truffles** // White or black, in anything
* ★ **Porcini mushrooms** // Especially in autumn and on pasta
* ★ **Chianina beef** // Char-grilled and sliced in a *tagliata*
* ★ **Bistecca alla fiorentina** // T-bone steak; remember – it must be bloody
* ★ **Beans** // Any of the local varieties, preferably drizzled with new-season olive oil
* ★ **Castagnaccio** // The local chestnut cake is guaranteed to delight

Italian style, the only thing that is served at the end of a meal is coffee – as in a short, sharp espresso shot and *nothing* else – alongside, on special occasions, a digestive of grappa or other fiery liqueur. Bread is plentiful but don't expect a side plate; put it on the table and know you'll pay for it – restaurants charge a fixed €1.50 to €3 per head *coperto* (cover) whether you eat the bread or not. Sauce-mopping is not allowed.

Italians don't go to restaurants to eat pasta – every Italian thinks they can cook pasta better at home. Should your pasta involve fish, don't ask for parmesan, and if it happens to be long and thin, twirling it around your fork as if you were born twirling is the only way. Should you be confronted with a long dangling piece, bite rather than suck.

Dress decently when dining and strike a pose by resting your forearms or wrists (never elbows) on the table. Finally, if you want to avoid dishes tampered to suit tourist tastebuds, avoid the fixed-price *menù turistico*. Good value as it might appear, it is a pale reflection of authentic fare consumed by locals.

BUONE FESTE

Be it the start of a harvest, a wedding, a birth or a religious holiday, traditional celebrations are intrinsically woven into Tuscan culinary culture. These are by no means as raucous as festivals of the past when an animal was sacrificed, but most remain meaty affairs. As integral to the festive calendar as these madcap days of overindulgence are the days of eating *magro* (lean) – fasting days, usually preceding every feast day and in place for 40 days during Lent.

Tuscans have baked simple breads and cakes such as ring-shaped *berlingozzo* (Tuscan sweet bread) and *schiacciata alla fiorentina* (a flattish spongey bread-cum-cake best made with old-fashioned lard) for centuries during Carnevale, the period of merrymaking leading up to Ash Wednesday. Fritters are another sweet Carnevale treat: *cenci* are plain twists (literally 'rags') of fried, sweet dough sprinkled with icing sugar; *castagnole* look like puffed-up cushions; and *fritelle di mele* are slices of apple battered, deep fried and eaten warm with plenty of sugar.

'traditional celebrations are intrinsically woven into Tuscan culinary culture'

Pasqua (Easter) is big. On Easter Sunday, families take baskets of hard-boiled white eggs covered in a white-cloth napkin to church to be blessed, and return home to a luncheon feast of roast lamb gently spiced with garlic and rosemary, preempted by the blessed eggs. In Umbria, *ciaramicola* is the traditional Easter cake. Shaped in a ring with five humps representing Perugia's five historical quarters, it comes iced in white and sprinkled with multicoloured hundreds-and-thousands.

September's grape harvest sees grapes stuck on top of *schiacciata* to make *schiacciata con l'uva* (grape cake), and autumn's chestnut harvest brings a flurry of chestnut festivals and *castagnaccio* (chestnut cake baked with chestnut flower, studded with raisins, topped with a rosemary sprig and delicious served with a slice of ricotta) to the Tuscan table. Come Natale (Christmas), a *bollito misto* (boiled meat) with all the trimmings

BACKGROUND

is the traditional festive dish in many families: various meaty animal parts, trotters et al, are thrown into the cooking pot and simmered for hours with a vegetable and herb stock. The meat is later served with mustard, salsa verde and other sauces. A whole pig, notably the recently revived ancient white-and-black *cinta senese* indigenous breed, roasted on a spit is the other option.

Food festivals – a great excuse to dine well, drink and sometimes dance 'til dawn – stud the region's rich cultural calendar (see p16).

FOOD GLOSSARY

· · · · · · ·

For pronunciation guidelines, see p441.

THE BASICS

coltello kol·*te*·lo knife
cucchiaio koo·*kya*·yo spoon
forchetta for·*ke*·ta fork

STAPLES

aceto a·*che*·to vinegar
aglio *a*·lyo garlic
burro *boo*·ro butter
formaggio for·*ma*·jo cheese
miele *mye*·le honey
olio *o*·lyo oil
pane *pa*·ne bread
panna *pa*·na cream
pepe *pe*·pe pepper
riso *ree*·zo rice
sale *sa*·le salt
soya *so*·ya soy
tartufo tar·*too*·fo truffle
uovo/uova *wo*·vo/*wo*·va egg/eggs
zucchero *tsoo*·ke·ro sugar

DRINKS

acqua *a*·kwa water
birra *bee*·ra beer
caffè ka·*fe* coffee
tè te tea
vino (rosso/bianco) *vee*·no (*ro*·so/*byan*·ko) wine
(red/white)

MEAT & SEAFOOD

agnello a·*nye*·lo lamb
aragosta a·ra·*go*·sta lobster
baccalà ba·ka·*la* dried salted cod
carpaccio kar·*pa*·cho very fine slices of raw meat

coniglio ko·*nee*·lyo rabbit
cozze *ko*·tse mussels
frutti di mare *froo*·tee dee *ma*·re seafood
gamberoni gam·be·*ro*·nee prawns
granchio *gran*·kyo crab
pollo *po*·lo chicken
polpi *pol*·po octopus
prosciutto pro·*shoo*·to cured ham
salsiccia sal·*see*·cha sausage
tonno *to*·no tuna
trippa *tree*·pa tripe
vitello vee·*te*·lo veal

VEGETABLES

asparagi as·*pa*·ra·jee asparagus
carciofi kar·*cho*·fee artichokes
carota ka·*ro*·ta carrot
cavolo *ka*·vo·lo cabbage
cavolo nero *ka*·vo·lo *ne*·ro black cabbage
fagiolini fa·jo·*lee*·nee green beans
finocchio fee·*no*·kyo fennel
funghi *foon*·gee mushrooms
insalata in·sa·*la*·ta salad
melanzane me·lan·*dza*·ne eggplants/aubergines
oliva o·*lee*·va olive
patate pa·*ta*·te potatoes
peperoni pe·pe·*ro*·nee capsicums/peppers
piselli pee·*ze*·lee peas
pomodori po·mo·*do*·ree tomatoes
rucola *roo*·ko·la rocket
spinaci spee·*na*·chee spinach

GELATO FLAVOURS & FRUIT

amarena a·ma·*re*·na wild cherry
arancia a·*ran*·cha orange
bacio *ba*·cho chocolate and hazelnuts
ciliegia chee·*lye*·ja cherry
cioccolata cho·ko·*la*·ta chocolate

cono *ko*·no cone
coppa *ko*·pa cup
crema *kre*·ma cream
fragola *fra*·go·la strawberry
frutta di bosco *froo*·ta dee *bos*·ko fruit of the forest
(wild berries)
limone lee·*mo*·ne lemon
mela *me*·la apple
melone me·*lo*·ne melon
nocciola no·*cho*·la hazelnut
pere *pe*·ra pear
pesca *pe*·ska peach
uva *oo*·va grapes
vaniglia va·*nee*·lya vanilla
zuppa inglese *tsoo*·pa een·*gle*·ze 'English soup', trifle

ACCOMMODATION

FINDING ACCOMMODATION

Travellers are spoiled for choice when it comes to finding places to stay in this part of Italy. The most alluring options come in the form of *agriturismi* (working farms and country houses that offer rooms to visitors on holiday), villa rentals and boutique hotels, but there are also business hotels, hostels, *locande* (country inns), *pensioni* (small, family-run guesthouses offering B&B) and *affittacamere* (rooms in private houses) galore.

Accommodation can also be found in convents and monasteries throughout the region. A useful guide is *Guida ai Monasteri d'Italia* by Gian Maria Grasselli and Pietro Tarallo (2004, €14.50); otherwise tourist offices have lists. Another interesting option to investigate is the **WWOOF** (World Wide Opportunities on Organic Farms; www.wwoof.it) program, where you can trade your labour for accommodation on an organic farm.

Those planning to hike in the mountain areas can bunk down in a *rifugio* – a mountain hut kitted out with rooms

sleeping anything from two to a dozen or more people. Check **Club Alpino Italiano** (CAI; www.cai.it) for details.

Useful starting points for online research are www.tourism-in-tuscany.com and www.bellaumbria.net. There are also many online resources to help you plan an *agriturismi* stay (see p395) or arrange villa and farmhouse rentals (see p397).

PRICES & BOOKING

In our reviews we have cited the price range from low to high season. Low-season rates usually apply from November to March (with the exception

---

BOOK YOUR STAY ONLINE

For more accommodation reviews and recommendations by Lonely Planet authors, check out the online booking service at www.lonelyplanet.com/hotels. You'll find the true, insider low-down on the best places to stay. Reviews are thorough and independent. Best of all, you can book online.

of the Christmas and Easter periods); in cities and towns they may also apply in July and August. In the high season, it is wise to book well ahead for all accommodation.

Many hotels do not have *camera singola* (single rooms); instead, you'll pay a slightly lower price for the use of a double room with *camera doppia* (twin beds) or *camera matrimoniale* (double bed).

In reviews, the Parking icon indicates that the hotel has on-site parking or can organise a nearby car space. These usually cost between €10 and €20 per night.

FLORENCE

DUOMO & PIAZZA DELLA SIGNORIA

❦ CONTINENTALE €€€
Map pp46-7; ☎ 055 2 72 62; www.lungarno hotels.com; Vicolo dell'Oro 6r; d €300-390, ste €1250-1550, incl breakfast; P ⌧ ⌨ ⌂

Owned by the Ferragamo fashion house and designed by fashionable Florentine architect Michel Bonan, this glamorous hotel references 1950s Italy in its vibrant decor and is about as hip as Florence gets. Classic rooms are smallish; superior and deluxe rooms are larger, lighter and have views of the Arno.

❦ HOTEL CESTELLI €€
Map pp46-7; ☎ 055 21 42 13; www.hotelcestelli .com; Borgo SS Apostoli 25; s with shared bathroom

PRICE GUIDE

The following is a guide to the pricing system used in this chapter. Unless otherwise stated, prices quoted are for a double room with private bathroom.

€	up to €80
€€	€80 to €180
€€€	€180-plus

€40-60, d with shared bathroom €50-80, d with private bathroom €70-100; ☙ closed 2 weeks Jan, 3 weeks Aug

The scent of joss sticks and flicker of night lights add a soothing Zen air to this eight-room hotel on the floor of a 12th-century *palazzo*. The location off Via de' Tornabuoni is wonderful, and though the rooms are dark, they are attractively furnished, quiet and cool.

❦ RELAIS DEL DUOMO €€
Map pp46-7; ☎ 055 21 01 47; www.relaisdel duomo.it; Piazza dell'Olio 2; s €50-70, d €80-100, incl breakfast; ⌧ ⌨

Location is the prime selling point of this upscale B&B, perfectly placed in a 17th-century *palazzo* on a quiet, traffic-free street around the corner from the cathedral. The four elegant, pastel-coloured rooms are simple but comfortable, and staff are extremely helpful.

SANTA MARIA NOVELLA

❦ HOTEL PARIS €€
Map pp58-9; ☎ 055 28 02 81; www.parishotel.it; Via dei Banchi 2; s €80-125, d €90-180, incl breakfast; P ⌧ ⌨ ⌂

This pair of 15th-century palaces is linked on the 2nd floor by a glass walkway. Three-star rooms sport high ceilings, and window pelmets and bedheads are adorned with rich, embroidered drapes. The painted ceiling in the breakfast room is breathtaking.

❦ HOTEL SANTA MARIA NOVELLA €€
Map pp58-9; ☎ 055 27 18 40; www.hotelsanta marianovella.it; Piazza di Santa Maria Novella 1; incl breakfast d €135-200, ste €180-235; P ⌧ ⌨ ⌂

The bland exterior of this excellent four-star choice gives no hint of the spacious and elegant rooms within. All are beautifully appointed, featuring marble bathrooms, comfortable beds and toiletries from the nearby Officina Profumo-Farmaceutica di Santa Maria Novella (p59). The breakfast spread is lavish and the online booking rates (cited here) are generous.

♥ HOTEL SCOTI €€

Map pp58-9; ☎ 055 29 21 28; www.hotelscoti .com; Via de' Tornabuoni 7; s €40-75, d €65-125

Wedged between Dior, Prada and Mc-Queen, this *pensione* is a splendid mix of old-fashioned charm and great value for money. Run with smiling aplomb by Australian Doreen and Italian Carmello, the hotel is enthroned in a 16th-century *palazzo* on Florence's smartest shopping strip. The 11 rooms are clean and comfortable, but the star of the show is the floor-to-ceiling frescoed living room (1780). Breakfast costs an extra €5.

SAN LORENZO

♥ JOHANNA & JOHLEA €€

Map p64; ☎ 055 463 32 92, 055 48 18 96; www .johanna.it; s €70-120, d €80-170, incl breakfast; ⚡ ⚙

One of the most established B&Bs in town, J&J has more than a dozen tasteful, impeccable, individually decorated rooms split between five historic residences, some with wi-fi connections. Those desiring total luxury can ask about the suite apartments.

SAN MARCO

♥ HOTEL MORANDI ALLA CROCETTA €€

Map p67; ☎ 055 234 47 47; www.hotelmorandi .it; Via Laura 50; s €70-90, d €90-170, incl breakfast; ⓟ ⚡ ⚙

This medieval convent-turned-hotel away from the madding crowd is a stunner. Rooms are refined, tasteful

and full of authentic period furnishings and paintings. A couple of rooms have handkerchief-sized gardens to laze in, but the pièce de résistance is frescoed No 29, the former chapel.

♥ PALAZZO ALFANI €€

Map p67; ☎ 055 29 15 74, 346 0339931; www .palazzoalfani.com; Via Ricasoli 49; apt for 4 people €120-300, for 8 people €240-500; ⚡ 💻

Close to the Galleria dell'Accademia, this convent-turned-palace has five beautiful apartments decorated with original prints and richly upholstered furniture; some overlook a pretty, internal garden. Amenities include satellite TV, jacuzzi, shower and kitchen complete with breakfast equipment.

♥ RESIDENCE HILDA €€€

Map p67; ☎ 055 28 80 29; www.residencehilda.it; Via dei Servi; apt for 2 people €200-400, for 4 people €300-400; ⚡ ⚙

The superstylish lounge foyer gives a strong clue as to what can be found in the 12 upstairs suites at this recently opened residence. Apartments are serviced daily and have equipped kitchenettes, excellent bathrooms, decent work benches and wonderfully comfy beds. The family suites are perfect if you have little ones in tow. Check the website for specials.

SANTA CROCE

♥ BORGHESE PALACE ART HOTEL €€

Map p70; ☎ 055 28 43 63; www.borghesepalace .it; Via Ghibellina 174r; s €120-140, d €140-190, ste €230-240; ⓟ ⚡ ⚙

A key address for art lovers, this stylish ode to design with glass-topped courtyard and sculptures looming large in reception showcases original works of art from the 18th century to the present day. The location couldn't be more central, breakfast is served on a terrace with magnificent views and there's an in-house spa.

💗 HOTEL ORCHIDEA €

Map p70; ☎ 055 248 03 46; www.hotelorchidea florence.it; Borgo degli Albizi 11; s €30-60, d €50-80

This old-fashioned *pensione* in the mansion where the Donati family roosted in the 13th-century (Dante's wife, Gemma, was allegedly born in the tower) is charm itself. Its seven rooms with sink and shared bathroom are simple; rooms 5, 6 and 7 have huge windows overlooking a gorgeous garden while room 4 spills out onto a terrace. No credit cards.

OLTRARNO

💗 ALTHEA €

Map pp74-5; ☎ 055 233 53 41; www.florence althea.it; Via delle Caldaie 25; s €40-65, d €65-90, incl breakfast; 🕸 🖳

The decor might be 1970s flower power with plenty of chintz, but the good value for money that's provided by Althea's seven rooms is outstanding. Each is spotlessly clean and has its own bathroom, fridge and computer terminal.

💗 PALAZZO MAGNANI FERONI €€€

Map pp74-5; ☎ 055 239 95 44; www.florence palace.com; Borgo San Frediano 5; ste incl breakfast €300-720; 🅿 🕸 🖳 🛜

This extraordinary old palace is the stuff of dreams. The 12 suites, which occupy four floors with the family's private residence wedged in between, are vast and ooze elegance, featuring authentic period furnishings, rich fabrics and Bulgari toiletries. The 360-degree city view from the rooftop is unforgettable.

💗 RESIDENZA SANTO SPIRITO €€

Map pp74-5; ☎ 055 265 83 76; www.residenza sspirito.com; Piazza Santo Spirito 9; d €90-120; 🕸

Brilliantly placed on Florence's most buzzing summertime square, the romantic trio of rooms with sky-high ceilings in Palazzo Guadagni (1505) are a popular choice. The frescoed Gold Room is the first to be booked out and the Green Room with two connecting double rooms is the family favourite. Breakfast is pricey, so it's best to hit the local cafes instead.

BOBOLI & SAN MINIATO AL MONTE

💗 ALLE RAMPE €€

Map pp78-9; ☎ 055 680 01 31; www.villaalle rampe.com; Piazza F Ferrucci 6-7; d incl breakfast €60-140; 🅿 🕸 🛜

This five-room B&B is a lovely spot in which to escape the mayhem on the streets. Rooms are modern and comfortable, pots of flowers add a warm welcome, and there's space for five cars to park in the driveway.

AROUND FLORENCE

FIESOLE

💗 VILLA AURORA €€€

☎ 055 5 93 63; www.villaaurora.net; Piazza Mino da Fiesole 39; s €135-185, d €120-245, incl breakfast; 🅿 🕸 🖳

Built right on the main square in 1860, Villa Aurora offers relatively bland standard rooms and far more impressive deluxe rooms featuring original frescos – one has a spectacular panoramic view of Florence from its private balcony. The same view is enjoyed from the pagoda-covered terrace, where guests dine in style during the summer months.

AGRITURISMI

We've listed a number of *agriturismi* (working farms and country houses that offer rooms to visitors on holiday) in this chapter, but there are hundreds to choose from in this region. They're not easy to find, so it takes a bit of preplanning to arrange a stay. To start your research, browse *Osterie & Locande d'Italia: A Guide to Traditional Places to Eat & Stay in Italy* (Slow Food Editore), *Go Slow Italy* (Alistair Sawday Publishing) or *Special Places to Stay: Italy* (Alistair Sawday Publishing). After that, check out the following websites:

★ **Agriitalia** (www.holidayfarm.net)

★ **Agritour** (www.agritour.net)

★ **Agriturismo.it** (www.agriturismo.it)

★ **Agriturist** (www.agriturist.it)

★ **Farmhouse Italy** (www.agriguida.com)

★ **Italy Farm Holidays** (www.italyfarmholidays.com)

★ **Knowital.com** (www.knowital.com)

★ **Responsibletravel.com** (www.responsibletravel.com)

★ **Slow Travel** (www.slowtrav.com)

★ **Turismo.intoscana.it** (www.agriturismo.regione.toscana.it)

★ **Via Travel Design** (www.viatraveldesign.com)

PISTOIA

❦ TENUTA DI PIEVE A CELLE €€
Off Map p99; ☎ 0573 91 30 87; www.tenutadi
pieveacelle.it; Via di Pieve a Celle 158; r €110-130;
Ⓟ ✖ ⓡ
You'll find this peaceful 1850s country house in the hills 3km outside Pistoia. Set in expansive gardens, it offers five pretty bedrooms and elegant common areas. There's a lovely swimming pool and host Fiorenza will cook meals on request using produce from the estate's organic vegetable gardens.

CHIANTI

❦ AGRIFUTURISMO // BARBERINO VAL D'ELSA €
☎ 339 5019849; www.agrifuturismo.com; Strada San Silvestro 11; 2-/4-/6-bed apt €70/100/120; ⓢ

Woods filled with oak, juniper, cypress and pine trees sit next to ancient terraces of olive trees on this farm estate near Madonna di Pietracupa. All cultivation is pesticide-, herbicide- and fertiliser-free, and sustainable features such as solar panels, rain collection and recycling are utilised. The apartments are charming, with a strong and attractive design ethos. All have kitchens. No credit cards.

❦ CASTELLO DI MELETO // GAIOLE IN CHIANTI €€
☎ 0577 74 91 29; www.castellomeleto.it; Meleto; castle d €138-148, farmhouse d €95-125, incl breakfast; Ⓟ ⓡ
This place is part 15th-century castle, part historic villa. Castle rooms ooze romance (think canopied beds, high ceilings, exposed beams), while those in the

Casa Canonica (Priest's House), where farm workers once lived, are marginally more functional. Self-catering apartments are also available.

♥ FATTORIA DI RIGNANA // BADIA DI PASSIGNANO €€

☎ 055 85 20 65; www.rignana.it; Val di Rignana 15, Rignana; villa d €130-140, farmhouse d €95-105, incl breakfast; ⊗ Apr-Nov; Ⓟ 🖳 🖳

This old farmstead and noble villa 3.8km from Badia di Passignano offers a textbook Chianti experience – namely great views, wine and food in a tranquil and comfortable vineyard environment. Two accommodation options are on offer: utterly gorgeous frescoed rooms in the 17th-century villa and more rustic rooms in the adjoining *fattoria* (farmhouse). There's an excellent restaurant, La Cantinetta di Rignana (p103), in the former oil mill on the estate and an idyllic infinity swimming pool with sweeping Tuscan views.

♥ LOCANDA LA CAPANNUCCIA // CASTELLINA IN CHIANTI €€

☎ 0577 74 11 83; www.lacapannuccia.it; Borgo di Pietrafitta; d incl breakfast €95-125; ⊗ Mar–mid-Nov; Ⓟ 🖳

Tucked down a valley at the end of a 1.5km dirt road, this is a true Tuscan getaway. A pretty country inn, it offers five rooms furnished with antiques. Reserve in the morning for one of Daniela's very special dinners (€24 to €28). To get here, head north along the SS222 from Castellina and turn left to Pietrafitta.

♥ OSTELLO DEL CHIANTI // TAVARNELLE VAL DI PESA €

☎ 055 805 02 65; www.ostellodelchianti.it; Via Roma 137; dm €14.50, d with shared/private bathroom €35/45; ⊗ mid-Mar–Oct, reception 8.30-11am & 4pm-midnight; Ⓟ 🖳

One of Italy's oldest hostels (it's been going strong since the 1950s), Ostello del Chianti oozes dynamism. The recently renovated dorms max out at six beds (those in the original wing even have two bathrooms), bike hire can be arranged and it has a great garden for *aperitivi*. Breakfast costs €1.70.

♥ PODERE CASTELLARE // DIACETTO €€

☎ 055 832 60 82; www.poderecastellare.it; Via Case Sparse; d incl breakfast €80-200; Ⓟ 🖳 🖳

An essential stop for design buffs, this stylish *agriturismo* in the heart of the Rùfina Chianti wine region 20 minutes from Florence was renovated with the help of well-known Florence architect studio MBLR, and features furniture and fittings by Kartell, Luceplan and other Italian design houses. During the day, lazing around the jacuzzi and pool with view is a big temptation; come dusk, guests mingle over complimentary aperitifs in the Corbusier-styled salon, followed by dinner (€25) around a shared table. Arriving by car, drive past the eastern end of Diacetto village, then turn left.

♥ VILLA VIGNAMAGGIO // GREVE IN CHIANTI €€

☎ 055 85 46 61; www.vignamaggio.it; Via Petriolo 5; d €135-450; Ⓟ 🎿 🖳 🖳

Used as a location in Kenneth Branagh's film *Much Ado About Nothing*, this exquisite 15th-century manor house is a vast complex 5km south of Greve. It makes wine and grappa; has self-catering apartments and cottages to rent; and sports an Italian garden, two swimming pools and a tennis court. From Greve, follow the S222 south for 2km, then turn left towards Lamole.

VILLA & FARMHOUSE RENTAL

Be it hanging in a hammock strung between poplars, dropping off beneath medieval frescos or rising with the sun amid rolling hills, there is no better way to revel in the extraordinary peace and tranquillity of rural Tuscany and Umbria than by renting a villa, farmhouse or medieval hilltop village house. The following agencies are worth considering:

- ★ **Cottages to Castles** (www.cottagestocastles.com)
- ★ **Cuendet** (www.cuendet.com)
- ★ **Merry-Go-Round** (www.merrygoround.org)
- ★ **Summer's Leases** (www.sumlea.com)
- ★ **Traditional Tuscany** (www.traditionaltuscany.co.uk)
- ★ **Tuscan Way** (www.tuscanway.com)
- ★ **Veronica Tomasso Cotgrove** (www.vtcitaly.com)
- ★ **Villa Escapes** (www.villaescapes.com)
- ★ **Windows on Tuscany** (www.windowsontuscany.com)

NORTHWESTERN TUSCANY

PISA

♥ HOTEL BOLOGNA €€

Map p114; ☎ 050 50 21 20; www.hotelbologna.pisa.it; Via Mazzini 57; s €60-100, d €120-180, incl breakfast; P ⊠ ▯ ☎

This four-star choice on the south side of the Arno offers quiet, well-equipped rooms, efficient service and a generous breakfast buffet. It's only a 1km walk to Piazza dei Miracoli. The fact that it offers on-site parking is a big plus.

♥ HOTEL FRANCESCO €€

Map p114; ☎ 050 55 41 09; www.hotelfrancesco.com; Via Santa Maria 129; r €70-100; ⊠ ▯ ☎

On a busy street leading to the Leaning Tower, the San Francesco offers 13 clean but characterless rooms. Though quiet and relatively well equipped, the standard choices are slightly overpriced; go for one of the 1st-floor rooms (Nos 201 and 202), which share a terrace.

♥ HOTEL IL GIARDINO €€

Map p114; ☎ 050 56 21 01; www.hotelilgiardino.pisa.it; Piazza Manin 1; s/d incl breakfast €80/100; P ⊠ ☎

A gaggle of souvenir traders might hit you the second you walk out the door, but the Garden Hotel – an old Medici staging post the other side of the cathedral square wall – does have the advantage of a peaceful garden terrace to breakfast on while enjoying the view of the baptistery dome. Decor is contemporary, with original artworks in all rooms.

♥ ROYAL VICTORIA HOTEL €€

Map p114; ☎ 050 94 01 11; www.royalvictoria.it; Lungarno Pacinotti 12; r with shared bathroom €80, r with private bathroom €100-150, incl breakfast; P ⊠

This doyen of Pisan hotels, run with love and tender care by the Piegaja family for five generations, offers old-world luxury accompanied by warm, attentive service. The central location overlooking the Arno couldn't be better. Garage parking costs €20.

SAN MINIATO

♥ BARBIALLA NUOVA FATTORIA €€

☎ 0571 67 70 04; www.barbiallanuova.it; Via Casastada 49, Montaione; d/q €85/125, 2-/4-/6-person apt €420/680/850; P ♿

Creamy Chianina cows graze and wild boars ferret for truffles between tree roots on this heavily wooded 500-hectare working farm located roughly 20km south of San Miniato village and 20km north of San Gimignano. Apartments in farmhouses dotted throughout the property offer basic but comfortable accommodation, and there are plenty of opportunities to feed pigs, admire the livestock, stock up on fresh organic produce or hunt for truffles (guests get a 50% discount on the farm's famous truffle hunts; see p130).

♥ FATTORIA DI STIBBIO €€€

☎ 0571 29 02 47; www.fattoriadistibbio.com; Via San Bartolomeo 72, Stibbio; d €250-340; P ♿ ♞ ♿

Built by the Medicis in the 15th century and renovated with style and sophistication in 2008, this grand farmhouse is set in an extensive garden surrounded by olive groves and vineyards. Base yourself here for day trips to Pisa, Florence, Chianti and San Gimignano, relaxing on the gorgeous terrace or in the library/TV room (a former granary) at night.

LUCCA & AROUND

♥ AFFITTACAMERE STELLA // LUCCA €

Off Map p132; ☎ 0583 31 10 22; www.affittacamerestella.com; Via Pisana Traversa 2; s €45-55, d €60-70; P ♞ ♿

Just outside the Porta Sant'Anna, this well-regarded guesthouse in an early

20th-century apartment building offers small but comfortable and attractive rooms with cheerful decor. There's a kitchen for guests' use, free tea and coffee and private parking.

♥ FATTORIA DI PIETRABUONA // PESCIA €€

☎ 0572 40 81 15; Via di Medicina 2; www.pietrabuona.com; apt per week €400-1200; P ♿

The hills outside Pescia stay green all year round. This fact, joined with the area's proximity to both Lucca and Florence, makes it an excellent base for a Tuscan sojourn. On a huge family estate that produces chestnuts, olives, pigs and honey, the 14 apartments in seven renovated stone farmhouses have a rustic aesthetic, great views and mod cons such as satellite TV.

♥ LA BOHÈME // LUCCA €€

Map p132; ☎ 0583 46 24 04; www.boheme.it; Via del Moro 2; d incl breakfast €90-140; ♞

A hefty dark-wood door located on a peaceful backstreet heralds the entrance to this five-room bed and breakfast, which is run with charm and style by former architect Ranieri. Rooms are furnished in antique Tuscan style; some have breathtaking high ceilings and all have decent-sized bathrooms. Breakfast is generous.

♥ LA CORTE DEGLI ANGELI // LUCCA €€

Map p132; ☎ 0583 46 92 04; www.allacortedegliangeli.com; Via degli Angeli 23; d incl breakfast €140-180; P ♞ ♿ ♞

Occupying three floors of a 15th-century townhouse, this four-star boutique hotel oozes charm. Frescoed rooms are named after flowers: lovers in the hugely romantic Rosa room can lie beneath a pergola and swallow-filled sky.

❤ OSTELLO SAN FREDIANO // LUCCA €

Map p132; ☎ 0583 46 99 57; www.ostellolucca
.it; Via della Cavallerizza 12; dm with shared/private
bathroom €20/18, d/tr/q with private bathroom
€55/75/100; P 🖳

Flags flutter outside as if you're entering a five-star hotel at this staggeringly
historic, atmospheric and magnificent…
hostel. Top notch in comfort and service,
this Hostelling International–affiliated
hostel with 141 beds in voluminous
rooms is serviced with a bar and grandiose dining room (breakfast €3, lunch or
dinner €11). Non–HI members can buy
a €3 one-night stamp. Internet is €5 per
hour.

❤ VILLA MICHAELA // LUCCA €€€

Off Map p132; ☎ 0583 97 13 71; www.villamichaela
.com; Via di Valle 8, Vorno; d €250, villa per week
€35,000, incl breakfast; P 🞮 🖳 🛜 🖾

Even superlatives seem inadequate when
describing this 19th-century villa 10
minutes' drive from Lucca. The English
owners have furnished it in exquisite
taste, with antiques and amenities galore. There's a huge pool, floodlit tennis
court and manicured garden, as well as
formal dining room and private chapel.
Rentals are usually for the full villa only
between Easter and October, but it's
worth enquiring just in case rooms are
available.

❤ VILLA PRINCIPESSA // LUCCA €€

Off Map p132; ☎ 0583 37 00 37; www.hotelprinci
pessa.com; Via Nuova per Pisa 1616; d €100-130, ste
€320-450, incl breakfast; P 🞮 🖳 🖾

You will indeed feel like a *principessa*
(princess) at this aristocratic country mansion, residence of Lucca duke
Castruccio Castracani in the late-13th
and early-14th century. Smothered with
an abundance of foliage outside and full

of fine chandeliers, period furnishings
and rich wallpapers inside, it really is a
stunner. Find it 3km south of Lucca.

THE GARFAGNANA

❤ CASA CORDATI // BARGA €

☎ 0583 72 34 50; www.casacordati.it; Via di Mezzo
17; d €40, 2-person apt €60; 🕐 Mar-Oct; 🖳

Run by genial Giordano Martinelli,
who operates a small art gallery on the
ground floor and often hosts musical
evenings in his magnificent upstairs
apartment, this atmospheric accommodation in Barga Vecchia offers excellent
value. Rooms have lovely views, simple
decor and good-sized bathrooms (some
shared); the apartment is dark but well
sized.

❤ IL BENEFIZIO // BARGA €€

☎ 0583 72 22 01; www.albenefizio.it; Località
Ronchi 4; apt €65-110; P 🖳 🛜 🖾

Squeeze your car along the narrow
road to this welcoming *agriturismo*
2km from Barga. There are two well-
equipped apartments (one sleeping two
and the other four), both of which enjoy
spectacular views. Owner Francesca is
a walking guide who can give you lots
of advice about local trails, and her
husband Francesco is a sound engineer,
which explains the welcome presence
of a state-of-the-art home theatre. No
credit cards.

❤ PRADACCIO DI SOPRA // CASTELNUOVO DI GARFAGNANA €

☎ 0583 66 69 66; www.agriturismopradaccio.it;
Pieve Fosciana; d incl breakfast €50-70; P 🞮 🖾

With chestnut woods in the background,
this working family farm (wheat, *farro*,
pigs and corn) is an excellent-value *agriturismo* option. The friendly owners
offer four spick-and-span rooms in the
old farmhouse and are proud of their

dinners (€22), which feature home-grown products and are often cooked in the outdoor oven. It's a five-minute drive from Castelnuovo di Garfagnana.

APUANE ALPS

❤ ALBERGO PIETRASANTA // PIETRASANTA €€€

☎ 0585 79 37 26; www.albergopietrasanta.com; Via Garibaldi 35; d €295-375, ste €375-420; P X ❑
This art-filled *palazzo* in the historic centre of Pietrasanta makes a wonderful base for exploring the Apuane Alps or when attending the Puccini Festival in Torre del Lago. After a day spent sight-seeing, relax in the gorgeous courtyard, the conservatory or your beautifully appointed, classically elegant room.

THE LUNIGIANA

❤ COSTA D'ORSOLA // PONTREMOLI €€

☎ 0187 83 33 32; www.costadorsola.it; Orsola; per person B&B €47-57, half-board €63-75; P ❑ ❑
For a true taste of this beautiful, un-tamed region, spend a few nights in the restored stone buildings of this 16th-century village hamlet. You can wander through olive groves filled with grazing sheep, lounge by the swimming pool and admire the fabulous views, or take easy day trips through the Lunigiana or into the Apuane Alps. The apartments and rooms on offer are simple but comfort-able. It's 3.3km from the centre of Pon-tremoli and 1.6km from the motorway exit, at the end of a country lane.

THE CAMPY SIDE OF ITALY

Boy, do Italians like their outdoors. Camping grounds are descended upon almost as soon as the earmuffs are packed away. Properties range from pitiable dirt lots overlooking the motorway to three-star seaside facilities with bungalows, restaurants, bars and water-sports centres. No tent? No problem. Many sites have permanent tents with camp cots – or modern cabins for those who only like their nature until shower time. The choices on Elba are dizzying. Check www.elbalink.it or www.aptelba.it for exhaustive options. Here are a couple of sites that appealed to us:

★ **Acquaviva** (☎ 0565 91 91 03; www.campingacquaviva.it; high-season camping per person/tent/car €13.70/15/3.50; ⌖ mid-Mar–mid-Oct) Portoferraio's nearest camping ground, situated about 4km west of town, is a more traditional campground experience compared to many island schemes. Dirt paths encased in foliage connect pitches and modular Lego-like 'chalets' with common areas, including a tent restaurant. Modest apartments and 'mobile homes' are available as well. The beach, a humble but private 70m affair, is steps away, while other beaches are within reasonable walking distance.

★ **Camping Village Rosselba le Palme** (☎ 0565 93 31 01; www.rosselbalepalme.it; high-season camping per person/tent €16/21, r €23-90) Set around a genuine botanical garden, and said to be one of the best camping grounds in Europe, this 'village' covers all the bases from tents to apartments enshrouded by palm trees that have been imported from around the world. Activities include tennis, archery and diving classes taught by Jean-Jacques Mayol, son of legendary free diver Jacques Mayol. A minimarket, bar and pizzeria are located on site, although Portoferraio is only about a 10-minute drive away by car.

CENTRAL COAST & ELBA

LIVORNO

☙ CAMPING MIRAMARE €

Map p157; ☎ 0586 58 04 02; www.campingmira mare.it; Via del Littorale 220; camping per person €9-10, pitch €20-40; 🖳

This is a shady place with its own restaurant and pizzeria, right beside the beach in Antignano, about 8km south of town. There are three categories of campsite, including some with sea views, sun chairs and umbrellas.

☙ HOTEL AL TEATRO €€

Map p157; ☎ 0586 89 87 05; www.hotelalteatro .it; Via Enrico Mayer 42; s €95-110, d €130-150, incl breakfast; P ⛛ 🖳

Opened in 2004, this popular eight-room boutique hotel has smallish colour-themed rooms with understated, classic furniture and tapestry bedspreads. A few have views of the garden with a 200-year-old tree. Rooms have safes and minibar; some have shower massage. Parking is available for €20, though nearby street parking is free.

☙ HOTEL CITTÀ €€

Map p157; ☎ 0586 88 34 95; www.hotelcitta.it; Via di Franco 32; s €75-85, d €95-120, incl breakfast; P ⛛ 🖳 📶

You pay for location at this friendly, family-owned, three-star option in the heart of town. It looks unattractive from the outside, but rooms, though smallish, are just fine and come equipped with fridge, safe and new bathrooms. Parking will set you back €15.

☙ PENSIONE DANTE €

Map p157; ☎ 349 6260076; mihaela.b@hotmail .it; Scali d'Azeglio 28, 1st fl; s/d/tr incl breakfast €30/40/50

New management brought in new floors, new beds and vastly improved bathrooms and kitchen. Rooms are large and bare, some with a view of the canal, but everything is squeaky clean. The new breakfast room opens to the canal as well, and has a TV and coffee machine.

THE ETRUSCAN COAST

☙ AGRITURISMO LA CERRETA // SASSETTA €€

☎ 0565 79 43 52; www.lacerreta.it; Località Pian delle Vigne; per person half-board €55-65

Over 20 years in the engineering of a 'self-sufficient, biodynamic, harmonic project', this farmhouse is more about providing a simple, gastronomically authentic Tuscan lifestyle than serving up typical tourist services – though it can do that too. The owners raise *cinta senese* (indigenous Tuscan pigs), Maremma cows, and the rare Livornese chicken, among others. Cooking instruction, guided hiking and biking, farm activities and even photography are arranged on site. Horse tours are available nearby and a brand-new, three-pool thermal spa was near completion when we visited.

☙ AGRITURISMO LE FORNACINE // BIBBONA €€

☎ 328 4770769; www.agriturismolefornacine.com; d €65-90; 🖳

Recommended to us by an ecstatic traveller, this is a small, modern and welcoming place just outside Bibbona with a guest kitchen and barbecue. Nearby activities include thermal pools, walks, beaches (7km) and mountain biking, and the affable hostess has meticulously researched a book of tailor-made day trips to Pisa, Florence and Volterra among others. Wine tastings can be arranged in

ACCOMMODATION

nearby vineyards or the on-site wine cellar. Minimum one-week stay in August.

☙ PENSIONE BARTOLI // CASTIGLIONCELLO €

☎ 0586 75 20 51; www.albergobartoli.com; Via Martelli 9; s €43-50, d €60-72; ☺ Easter-Oct; ℗

Located in the unpretentious seaside town of Castiglioncello, this villa is rich in character and offers unbeatable value. It's an old-fashioned 'let's stay with grandma' kind of place with 18 well-dusted, large rooms, lace curtains and venerable family furniture. Room 19, the largest, and room 21 have the best sea views.

ELBA

In the height of summer many hotels operate a compulsory half-board policy.

☙ ALBERGO APE ELBANA // PORTOFERRAIO €€

☎ 0565 91 42 45; www.ape-elbana.it; Salita de' Medici 2; s €45-80, d €60-110, incl breakfast; ℗ ✖

In the Old Town, overlooking Piazza della Repubblica (where guests can park for free), this butter-coloured building is the island's oldest hotel, where guests of Napoleon are reputed to have stayed. The position is its best feature as rooms, while large, are a little soulless. Ask for one of the larger ones looking onto the piazza.

☙ HERMITAGE // LA BIODOLA €€€

☎ 0565 97 40; www.hotelhermitage.it; half-board per person €158-295; ℗ ✖ ▯ ⧉ ▣

If James Bond were to parachute onto Elba in a tuxedo, he'd land in the tennis courts of the Hermitage. One of the island's truly luxurious hotels, it's a gorgeous retreat complete with infinity pool overlooking the sea and a golf course

just over the fence. Amenities include a beauty centre and a massive jacuzzi.

☙ MONTECRISTO // MARINA DI CAMPO €€

☎ 0565 97 68 61; www.hotelmontecristo.it; Viale Nomelini; per person €40-140; ℗ ▣

The low-end rooms are a little spare, otherwise this is a pleasantly posh beachside hotel, with flower-framed balconies and a bar and pool overlooking the sea. The large sunny rooms have Scandinavian-style light furnishings and king-size beds. Amenities include fitness centre, sauna and free bicycle use.

☙ VILLA OMBROSA // PORTOFERRAIO €€

☎ 0565 91 43 63; www.villaombrosa.it; Via De Gasperi 3; s €60-130, d €80-225, incl buffet breakfast; ℗ ⧉

One of the very few hotels on the island open year-round. With a great location overlooking the sea and Spiaggia delle Ghiaie, it also has its own small private beach. Half-board that is considerably more creative than many other hotels' bland buffet fare is obligatory in summer. Wi-fi costs €5 for three hours.

CENTRAL TUSCANY

SIENA

☙ ANTICA RESIDENZA CICOGNA €€

Map pp182-3; ☎ 0577 28 56 13; www.antica residenzacicogna.it; Via dei Termini 67; s/d/ste €70/90/130, incl breakfast; ☺ reception 8am-1pm; ℗ ✖ ⧉

Springless beds, soundproof windows, ornate frescos, wi-fi and antique furniture make this central option justifiably popular. With a mere five rooms and two suites, class exudes from prominent elements such as the four-poster beds,

ACCOMMODATION

elaborate, thick-framed mirrors and the breakfast space (enormous buffet style). Reception has limited hours, so arrange your arrival in advance. Parking costs €18.

❦ CHIUSARELLI €€

Map pp182-3; ☎ 0577 28 05 62; www.chiusarelli .com; Viale Curtatone 15; s €65-90, d €90-135, incl breakfast; P ✕ 🛜

Functioning continuously since its construction in 1870, this hotel has a pleasant, spacious breakfast room and attractive, though somewhat dark, bedrooms. The rear ones are for lovers of quiet and lucky football fans – they overlook the stadium where Siena plays home matches on alternate Sundays in season. The hotel has a popular restaurant (meals €20) where you'll be dodging elbows to find a seat among the locals. Wi-fi costs €5 for three hours.

❦ HOTEL LA PERLA €

Map pp182-3; ☎ 0577 22 62 80; www.hotella perlasiena.com; Piazza Indipendenza 25; s €40-60, d €70-85; 🖳 🛜

A very friendly and well-run budget option. Bathrooms are small and a few rooms are musty, but that's a small price to pay for this otherwise excellent-value hotel, seconds from Piazza del Campo. Room 28 has an amazing view of Chiesa di San Domenico and Room 26 overlooks the cathedral. Wi-fi costs €5 for 24 hours; use of the PC is €5 per hour. No breakfast.

❦ HOTEL SANTA CATERINA €€

Off Map pp182-3; ☎ 0577 22 11 05; www.hscsiena .it; Via Piccolomini 7; s €95-125, d €125-185, incl breakfast; P ✕ 🛜

This elegant, renovated 18th-century villa, just outside the city walls, is a stone's throw beyond the Porta Romana. It's a tranquil haven: its 22 rooms are

tastefully furnished, the breakfast room is light and airy, and there's a lovely garden with open views to the surrounding hills. Parking costs €15; wi-fi costs €3 per hour.

❦ PALAZZO BRUCHI €€

Map pp182-3; ☎ 0577 28 73 42; www.palazzo bruchi.it; Via di Pantaneto 105; s €80-90, d €90-100, d 'superior' €120-150, incl breakfast; 🖳 🛜

The six rooms in the 'ancient and noble' Landi-Bruchi family home may be the only place in Siena where one wakes up to church bells and chirping birds, rather than street noise. The hospitality of Maria Cristina and her daughter Camilla is warmly consistent. There's a shared kitchen and a peaceful inner courtyard. Wi-fi and PC use are free.

❦ PICCOLO HOTEL ETRURIA €€

Map pp182-3; ☎ 0577 28 80 88; www.hotel etruria.com; Via delle Donzelle 3; s €45-55, d €80-110; ✕

Another equally welcoming family hotel, just off Piazza del Campo. The rooms are rather plain, with zero soundproofing, but there's a central light, airy sitting area and the location is outstanding. There's a 1am curfew. Breakfast is €6.

❦ SIENA COLLEVERDE €

Off Map pp182-3; ☎ 0577 28 00 44; www.camping colleverde.com; Via Scacciapensieri 47; camping per person/site €9.50/5.70, twin-bed mobile home €45; 🕑 mid-Apr–mid-Oct; 🛆

This recently renovated camping ground, 2km north of the historical centre, rents mobile homes that sleep two to five people (some have full kitchens) and has standard camp sites. There's an on-site restaurant and minimarket. To get there take bus 3 from Piazza Gramsci, heading for Siena Due Ponti (last bus 11.45pm).

♥ VILLA SCACCIAPENSIERI €€

Off Map pp182-3; ☎ 0577 4 14 41; www.villascac ciapensieri.it; Via Scacciapensieri 10; s €75-140, d €110-265, incl breakfast; ⓟ ⌘ ⌂ ⌂

Around 2.5km north of Siena, this four-star 19th-century villa has carved wooden ceilings, oil paintings, antiques, formal gardens and an old family chapel. Use of the tennis courts and bicycles is complimentary. Public buses to central Siena pass by every 15 to 30 minutes.

NORTH OF SIENA

♥ AGRITURISMO SAN LORENZO // VOLTERRA €€

Off Map p199; ☎ 0588 3 90 80; www.agriturismo sanlorenzo.it; d B&B €90, apt €95-110; ⌂ ⌂

Just 3km outside Volterra on the road to Siena, this is a giddying fusion of sustainable tourism, countryside vistas, mod cons and wonderful food (dinner per person €28). The biological swimming pool, fed by mountain springs and complete with frogs and salamanders, fronts the converted farmhouse. Rooms are 'farmhouse chic', individually decorated and colourful with modern kitchens and bathrooms. Walking, biking, horse riding and hands-on, seasonal olive-oil production (October to November) are available, as are cooking classes (per person €90) with meals served in the 12th-century Franciscan chapel. Curse or blessing, some mobile-phone services don't work out here.

♥ ALBERGO ETRURIA // VOLTERRA €€

Map p199; ☎ 0588 8 73 77; www.albergoetruria.it; Via Giacomo Matteotti 32; s €60-70, d €80-90, incl breakfast; ⌕ Feb-Dec; ⌂ ⌂

This is a good-value, cosy hotel, realised by two friendly English-speaking ladies. There's a self-catering kitchen and, of all things, an ice machine. Look for the remains of an Etruscan wall upstairs and savour the fine views from the roof garden – a genuine garden with lawns and bushes. Free PC and wi-fi internet.

♥ BORGO STOMENNANO // MONTERIGGIONI €€

☎ 0577 30 40 33; www.stomennano.it; apt for 4 people per week €800-1100; ⌂ ⌂

On an unforgettable, sprawling property 2km outside Monteriggioni, this historic collection of farmhouses dating from the 1600s has been converted into apartments furnished and decorated with an amazing collection of heirlooms dating back hundreds of years – children under 14 are not permitted due to the delicate nature of these items. Though geared for large groups (six to 32 people) and events, couples are welcome during select periods. Self-cater or request full board. Special touches include an infinity pool, welcome bottles of wine with personalised labels and a private trail from the property through undulating fields to Monteriggioni.

♥ FORESTERIA MONASTERO DI SAN GIROLAMO // SAN GIMIGNANO €

Map p193; ☎ 0577 94 05 73; www.monasterosan girolamo.it; Via Folgore da San Gimignano 26-32; per person €27; ⓟ

Run by friendly Benedictine nuns, this is an excellent, quiet budget choice. Rooms sleeping two to five people are basic, but spacious and comfortable with attached bathrooms. Breakfast is €3. Ring ahead as it is perpetually booked. If you don't have a reservation, arrive between 9am and 12.30pm or between 3pm and 5.45pm and ring the monastery bell (not the Foresteria one, which is never answered). Kitchen use costs €3 per day.

ACCOMMODATION

☙ HOTEL LA CISTERNA // SAN GIMIGNANO €€

Map p193; ☎ 0577 94 03 28; www.hotel cisterna
.it; Piazza della Cisterna 24; s €60-80, d €90-145, incl
breakfast; ✗ 🖳 �{}
Nearly 100 years in business, this hotel
offers 21st-century comfort in quiet, spacious rooms in a splendid 14th-century
building with vaulted ceilings and modest
chandeliers. Be sure to request a room
with a view of the square or the valley or
risk getting one facing a dull courtyard.

☙ HOTEL LA LOCANDA // VOLTERRA €€

Map p199; ☎ 0588 8 15 47; www.hotel-lalocanda
.com; Via Guarnacci 24-28; s €70-95, d €90-120;
✗ 🖳 �{}
In a former nunnery, there is nothing
austere about the classy rooms here,
most with a choice of massage shower or
hot tub. A suite with sauna will cost you
a cool €250 and a handicapped-equipped
double is €80 to €105. Free wi-fi.

☙ HOTEL L'ANTICO POZZO // SAN GIMIGNANO €€

Map p193; ☎ 0577 94 20 14; www.anticopozzo.com;
Via San Matteo 87; s €85-100, d €110-140, incl breakfast; ✗ closed Jan & first 2 weeks Nov; ✗ �{}
Named after the old, softly illuminated
pozzo (well) just off the lobby. Each room
has its own personality, with thick stone
walls, high ceilings, wrought-iron beds,
frescos, antique prints and peach-col-
oured walls. Room 20 has a magnificent
domed ceiling. Wi-fi costs €3 per hour.

☙ HOTEL LEON BIANCO // SAN GIMIGNANO €€

Map p193; ☎ 0577 94 12 94; www.leonbianco.com;
Piazza della Cisterna 13; s €65-80, d €80-135, incl
breakfast; ✗ 🖳 �{}
This hotel faces Hotel La Cisterna across
the square and also occupies a 14th-

century mansion. Smoothly run, it's
equally welcoming and friendly with a
ground-floor abundance of plants, pretty
inner courtyard, breakfast patio, billiard
table and fitness room. Wi-fi is free and
available in common spaces; PC internet
costs per hour €2.50.

SOUTH OF SIENA

☙ ALBERGO IL MARZOCCO // MONTEPULCIANO €€

Map p212; ☎ 0578 75 72 62; www.albergoilmar
zocco.it; Piazza Savonarola 18; s €60-75, d €90-95,
incl breakfast; 🅿 🖳
This fabulous 16th-century building has
been run as a hotel by the same family for
over a century. The rooms are large, comfortable and well furnished, and those with
a balcony and views come at no extra cost.

☙ BELLAVISTA // MONTEPULCIANO €

Map p212; ☎ 347 8232314; bellavista@bccmp.com;
Via Ricci 25; d €65-70; 🅿
An excellent budget choice, where nearly
all of the 10 high-ceiling, double rooms
have fantastic views – room 6 has a private terrace. Some rooms have refrigera-
tors and all have great beds. No-one lives
here so phone ahead in order to be met
and given a key (if you've omitted this
stage, there's a phone in the entrance
lobby from where you can call).

☙ HOTEL IL GIGLIO // MONTALCINO €€

☎ 0577 84 81 67; www.gigliohotel.com; Via Soccorso Saloni 5; s/d incl breakfast €82/122-135, annexe
s/d incl breakfast €60/92, apt €90-120; 🅿 �{}
Montalcino's oldest hotel, recently and
substantially renovated, is another family concern. Rooms have comfortable
wrought-iron beds – each gilded with
a painted giglio (lily) – and all doubles
have panoramic views. Il Giglio also has

a small annexe just up the street and a couple of apartments sleeping two to four people. Free wi-fi.

❧ HOTELITO LUPAIA // PIENZA €€€

☎ 0577 66 80 28; www.lupaia.com; d €240; 🖳
Just north of Pienza, this farm dates from 1237. Each room has been uniquely and meticulously designed by the family matriarch, a 30-year veteran of fashion and interior design. The main house, containing the sitting/dining rooms and open kitchen, is similarly bedecked with restored and agreeably weathered furniture. Stays here are largely occupied by sigh-inducing countryside views, doing as little as possible and admiring the dazzling creative use of medieval space.

❧ IL GIARDINO // MONTALCINO €

☎ /fax 0577 84 82 57; albergoilgiardino@virgilio.it; Piazza Cavour 4; s €40-45, d €55-60
An excellent-value, friendly, family-run two-star hotel. Occupying a venerable building overlooking Piazza Cavour, its decor has a distinct 1970s feel. The adjacent Osteria Il Giardino (p206) is one of the town's best eateries.

❧ LA FRATERIA DI PADRE ELIGIO // CETONA €€€

☎ 0578 23 82 61; www.lafrateria.it; Via di San Francesco; s €140-160, d €220-240, incl breakfast
For those who are seeking a special retreat, this is it. Situated up a signed lane ('Mondox la Frateria Conv S Francesco') 1km from Cetona on the road to Sarteano, this former convent dating from 1212 has been lovingly restored and converted into an unforgettable, seven-room hotel and gourmet restaurant (meals cost €110 without wine, open Monday to Wednesday, closed January

to mid-February), where you can expect a lavish eight-course dining experience, 90% of which is made from local products.

❧ LE CASE // CASTIGLIONE D'ORICA €

☎ 0577 88 89 83; www.agriturismolecase.com; Strada Provinciale 323; s/d incl breakfast €45/70; 🗓 mid-Mar–Dec; 🖳 🛜
Located just 1km south of Castiglione d'Orcia, this 18th-century stone farmhouse is one of the best-value *agriturismi* we have found. Somewhat remote and fittingly peaceful, it's run by a warm Italian couple and all five rooms are tastefully decorated and charming in their simplicity. Two elderly farmers can be regularly spotted around the property, resolutely undertaking their daily chores. Nearby diversions include horse riding, hiking, wine tasting and the bathing in the spas. Discounts are available for long stays. Free PC and wi-fi internet.

❧ OLIVIERA CAMERE // PIENZA €

☎ 0578 74 82 74, 338 9520459; www.nautilus -mp.com/oliviera; Via Condotti 4b; s/d incl breakfast €35/50, apt €65
Squeezed into a side street and as close to dead-centre Pienza as the un-sainted can hope to get, this former olive-oil mill represents excellent value. Its four rooms are simple but fresh and attractive. There are also three larger studio apartments.

❧ PALAZZO BRANDANO // PETROIO €€€

☎ 0577 66 51 69; www.palazzobrandano.com; Via di Valgelata 18; s/d incl breakfast €150/225; 🖾 🖳 🛜
Within the 12th-century walls of peaceful Petroio, the four-star Brandano is practically an attraction on its own.

Rooms are sumptuous, wood-beamed affairs with frescos, classic furniture, plush beds, sensational views and jacuzzis. There's an impressive on-site restaurant, with a chef who's available for cooking classes.

SOUTHERN TUSCANY

❤ AGRITURISMO LE FONTANELLE // MONTEMERANO €€
☎ 0564 60 27 62; www.lefontanelle.net; s/d incl breakfast €47/85; 🖳

Claiming to be among the first farmhouse stays in Tuscany, this wonderfully rustic place is 1.2km down a turnoff 2.5km south of Montemerano. A large variety of cabin and chalet accommodation allows you to choose your optimum level of exposed wood and/or modern bathrooms. The massive, zoolike property has a duck pond, plenty of shady trees, geese, mallards, herons, goats and deer. Daughter Daniella is a sparkling hostess for dinner (€24), which includes wine, grappa and coffee, taken alfresco with other guests around a large communal table.

❤ AGRITURISMO TENUTA LA PARRINA // LA PARRINA €€
☎ 0564 86 26 26; www.parrina.it; r €120-200; 🖳 🍽

This legendary purveyor of high-quality farm products (see p229) also maintains several attractive double rooms and apartments in an 18th-century building complete with period furniture. The decor is elegant, with exposed wooden beams, but not overdone. The rooms have garden views, but for lounging retire to the immense sitting room, adorned with couches, books, games and a massive terrace. Weekly rates and half-board are available. From the SS1 at Albinia,

take the turn for Manciano; there's a signed right turn soon after exiting the town.

❤ BASTIANI GRAND HOTEL // GROSSETO €€
☎ 0564 2 00 47; www.hotelbastiani.com; Piazza Gioberti 64; s €90-110, d €130-180, incl breakfast; 🅿 ✻ 🛜

A smart hotel within a grand old building, complete with a *Gone with the Wind*–type, dance-down-me staircase. Rooms are woody and elegant, with bathrooms (most with a bathtub) that are tiled, gold-fixtured and gleaming. The buffet breakfast is vast. The parking garage, a 10-minute walk away, costs €21. Wi-fi is €4 per hour.

❤ DUCA DEL MARE // MASSA MARITTIMA €€
Map p223; ☎ 0566 90 22 84; www.ducadelmare.it; Piazza Dante Alighieri 1/2; s €50-60, d €85-100, incl buffet breakfast; 🅿 ✻ 🛜 🛌

Duca del Mare is a steep 10-minute walk from the historic centre. This modern, sunny hotel has a Scandinavian air with lots of shiny light wood and Ikea-style furnishings. All ground-floor rooms have terraces, some party-sized, with tree-obscured views of the countryside. Wi-fi costs €1 per hour.

❤ HOTEL IL SOLE // MASSA MARITTIMA €€
Map p223; ☎ 0566 90 19 71; www.ilsolehotel.it; Via della Liberta 43; s €55-65, d €85-95, incl breakfast; 🅿 ✻

The ideal location and the free, lift-accessed underground parking are the two primary perks of this cavernous hotel. Behind the rather impressive facade reside 50 large, spare, but quiet rooms. Some of the tiny windows reveal fine views.

ACCOMMODATION

❦ IL CORNACCHINO // SORANO €€

☎ 0564 95 15 82; www.cornacchino.it; full board per person €70-80; ⚇ Apr-Nov; ▢

About 10km north of Sorano, 3km off the SS2, is this 100-hectare *agriturismo-cum-village*, offering a great selection of hiking trips and horse-riding courses. Choose from a three-day, on-site class (all ages) or one of the week-long themed horse-riding treks, like 'Mountain-Sea', 'Etruscan' and 'Maremma Park'. It has about 55 horses, including 12 Haflingers, six Appaloosas, two Paints, six Maremmans, six part-Arabs and four Arab-Haflingers. While horse enthusiasts gallop around, nonequestrian companions can engage in standard *agriturismo* diversions, like hiking and mountain biking the countryside.

❦ PENSIONE WEEKEND // PORTO SANTO STEFANO €

☎ 0564 81 25 80; www.pensioneweekend.it; Via Martiri d'Ungheria 3; d €50-80; ℗

This *pensione* is a true gem and the only pseudo-budget option in town. Rooms are small and scrubbed, some with eccentric components like the intercom surviving from an upgrade done in the 1960s. New bathrooms have been recently shoehorned into every room. The friendly, polyglot owner can give you a parking permit for the tiny lot across the road.

❦ TAVERNA ETRUSCA // VETULONIA €

☎ 0564 94 98 02; www.tavernaetrusca.it; Piazza Stefani 12; s €55-65, d €60-75; ⚇ Easter-Oct; ▨ ⚏

At the apex of the village, these 10 large rooms, some with terraces, have panoramic views fantastic enough to successfully distract from the spartan furnishings. There is an on-site restaurant that serves satisfying meals (€24) and the village itself is a quaint, little *passeggiata* superlative.

EASTERN TUSCANY

❦ CAMERA CAFFÉ // AREZZO €

Map p240; ☎ 347 0324405; www.cameracaffe.net; Via Guido Monaco 92; s with shared/private bathroom €35/40, d with private bathroom €55, incl breakfast; ▨

The dorm-room decor at Camera Caffé is supplemented by cushy beds and fat duvets, and some of the rooms also have air-con. The huge, self-service kitchen has a gorgeous dining terrace with city views. Across the street from the train station.

❦ HOTEL ITALIA // CORTONA €€

Map p249; ☎ 0575 63 02 54; www.hotelitalia cortona.com; Via Ghibellina 5/7; s €85-90, d €110-115, incl breakfast; ▨ 🛜

Hotel Italia is a casual but atmospheric 17th-century *palazzo* just off Piazza della Repubblica. Standard rooms have traditional cross-beamed ceilings and are decorated in warm orange tones, while each of the unique superior rooms features giant bathtubs. Views are breathtaking from the roof-level breakfast room. Oriental massages and mountain-bike hire are also available. Wi-fi costs €10.

❦ HOTEL PATIO // AREZZO €€

Map p240; ☎ 0575 40 19 62; www.hotelpatio.it; Via Cavour 23; s €115-130, d €155-176, ste €190-230, incl breakfast; ℗ ▨ ▢ 🛜

Arezzo's most characterful hotel, with 10 themed rooms, each dedicated to one of Bruce Chatwin's travel books. Each has original furnishings from the various countries represented, including Australia, Morocco and China. Valet parking is €18.

ACCOMMODATION

❤ HOTEL SAN MICHELE // CORTONA €€

Map p249; ☎ 0575 60 43 48; www.hotelsanmichele .net; Via Guelfa 15; d incl breakfast €80-220; ⊙ mid-Mar–Dec; P ✕ ☎

Cortona's finest hotel. Primarily Renaissance, but with elements dating from the 12th century and modifications over subsequent centuries, it's like a little history of Cortona in stone. Rooms are airy, spacious and exquisitely furnished. Prices vary wildly due to frequent special offers and festivals. Parking costs €20. Wi-fi is €3 per hour.

❤ LA CORTE DEL RE // AREZZO €€

Map p240; ☎ 0575 29 67 20; www.lacortedelre.com; Via Borgunto 5; s €60-75, d €70-90; ✕ ⬛

A collection of six apartments, centimetres from Piazza Grande, harmoniously blending contemporary design into elements of the historic building. The Pietro Aretino Suite has an ultramodern bathroom that bleeds right into an Etruscan wall. Some apartments have kitchenettes and views of the square. Three-night minimum stay.

❤ LOCANDA GIGLIO // SANSEPOLCRO €€

☎ 0575 74 20 33; www.ristorantefiorentino.it; Via Luca Pacioli 60; s/d incl buffet breakfast €55/80; P ✕ ☎

This exceptionally friendly place has been in the same family for four generations. The four hotel rooms, with their oak floors, under-floor lighting and period furniture recovered from the family loft, have been imaginatively renovated by daughter Alessia, an architect-sommelier. Request 'La Torre', with a lovely low bed and the best view. Dad, Alessio, still runs the Ristorante Fiorentino (meals €28 to €32) with panache. The pasta's homemade and the imaginative menu changes with the seasons (Alessio tells you with pride that there'll never be a freezer in *his* kitchen).

❤ SANTA MARGHERITA // CORTONA €

Map p249; ☎ 0575 63 03 36; comunitacortona@smr .it; Via Cesare Battisti 15; s/d/tr/q €40/54/70/80

Run by sweet, obliging nuns from the religious institute, this is a popular place with Italian groups, so call ahead (with Italian phrasebook at the ready). A total renovation in 2009 included new beds, fresh paint and sparkling bathrooms. Breakfast costs €5.

NORTHERN UMBRIA

PERUGIA

❤ CENTRO INTERNAZIONALE PER LA GIOVENTÙ €

Map p258; ☎ 075 572 28 80; www.ostello.perugia .it; Via Bontempi 13; dm €15, sheets €2; ⊙ mid-Jan–mid-Dec; ⬛

If the 10am to 4pm lockout doesn't scare you off, then you'll appreciate the sweeping countryside view and wafting sounds of church bells from the hostel's terrace, where guests often gather after making dinner. Enjoy the 16th-century frescoed ceilings and tidy four- to six-person rooms.

❤ ETRUSCAN CHOCOHOTEL €€

Off Map p258; ☎ 075 583 73 14; www.chocohotel .it; Via Campo di Marte 134; s €55-75, d €90-140; P ✕ ⬛ ☎ ⬛

The first hotel in the world dedicated to chocolate. Try items from the restaurant's 'chocomenu', shop at the 'chocostore', or swim in the rooftop pool (sadly, filled with water). Free on-site parking, lobby wi-fi and triple-paned windows make up for the location on a busy street near the main train station.

❤ HOTEL BRUFANI PALACE €€€

Map p258; ☎ 075 573 25 41; www.sinahotels
.com; Piazza Italia 12; s €215, d €320, ste €440-850;
P ✖ ☐ ☎ ☒

One of Umbria's two five-star hotels
(the second is Le Tre Vaselle in Torgiano) and a truly spectacular experience. Special touches include frescoed
main rooms, impeccably decorated
bedrooms and suites, a garden terrace
on which to dine during summer, and
helpful trilingual staff. Swim over Etruscan ruins in the subterranean fitness
centre. For last-minute discounts of
more than 50%, check hotel and travel
websites.

❤ PRIMAVERA MINI HOTEL €

Map p258; ☎ 075 572 16 57; www.primaveramini
hotel.it; Via Vincioli 8; s €40-50, d €60-70; ✖ ☐ ☎

This central and quiet hotel run by a
dedicated English- and French-speak-
ing mother-daughter team is a fabulous
find, quietly tucked away in a corner.
The magnificent views complement the
bright and airy rooms and common
areas.

TORRE COLOMBAIA €€

Off Map p258; ☎ 075 878 73 41; www.torre
colombaia.it; San Biagio delle Valle; per person
incl breakfast €40, apt €85-135; dinner Fri-Sun
€25; P

The iron staircase curling around the
tree-draped fairy-tale cottage will make
any urban dweller's heart instantly melt.
Just 15 minutes southwest from downtown Perugia, this former Benedictine
monastery was confiscated during the
Napoleonic era and has been in the family since 1860. It was the first organic
farm in Umbria, and Alfredo (the owner's great-great-grandson) grows lentils,
spelt and other grains in a setting both
rustic and idyllic. Better yet, you can

try their ingredients in a home-cooked
dinner, available Friday, Saturday and
Sunday for €25.

SOUTH OF PERUGIA

❤ AL GRAPPOLO D'ORO // TORGIANO €€

☎ 075 98 22 53; www.algrappolodoro.net; Via
Principe Umberto 22/24; s €50, d €90-105, incl breakfast; P ✖ ☎ ☒

One of the best hotel deals in Umbria
and worth a stay just for the vineyard
view from the pool. Smartly furnished
19th-century rooms have been upgraded
with DSL, satellite TV, DVD, hairdryers
and towel warmers.

ASSISI

❤ AGRITURISMO ALLA MADONNA DEL PIATTO €€

Off Map p271; ☎ 075 819 90 50; www.incampagna
.com; Pieve San Nicolo 18; d incl breakfast €85-120;
☼ Mar–mid-Nov; P

As beautiful as it is seemingly isolated,
this *agriturismo* is less than 15 minutes from the basilica. Each of the six
Moroccan- or Indian-designed guest
chambers is truly a room with a view.
But the real reason to stay here is the
intimate cooking classes Letizia runs (in
Italian or English). Start the day in local markets and finish it off with a feast
of your own creation. Minimum stay is
two nights.

❤ CAMERE SANTA CHIARA €

Map p271; ☎ 075 81 34 67; camere.santachiara@
yahoo.it; Via Sant'Antonio 1; s/d incl breakfast
€35/55

Depending on which of the eight rooms
you choose, you might sleep on top of a
glass-covered Roman ruin, watch a TV
propped up on a medieval wall or enjoy
breakfast on your private patio. Curl

ACCOMMODATION

up with a book, headphones or DVD in the video library or have a drink at the piano bar.

CAMPING/HOTEL FONTEMAGGIO €
Off Map p271; ☎ 075 81 23 17; www.fontemaggio.it; Via Eremo delle Carceri 8; per person/tent/car €6/5/3, dm/s/d €20/35/52, bungalows €32-110

The sort of place St Francis himself probably would have stayed at. On the way to Eremo delle Carceri, 3km northeast of town, it offers a full complement of campsites, hotel rooms and bungalows (sleeping four to six people and equipped with kitchens) with a bed for just about any taste. It's a beautiful walk into town, but the restaurant might just keep you for the evening.

OSTELLO DELLA PACE €
Off Map p271; ☎ 075 81 67 67; www.assisihostel .com; Via Valecchie 177; dm incl breakfast €15-18; 1 Mar–8 Nov & 27 Dec–6 Jan; P

Student groups, couples appreciating the handful of private rooms, backpackers and pilgrims all can find their bliss at Assisi's HI hostel. Beautiful and quiet, it's just off the road coming in from Santa Maria degli Angeli. Thrifty travellers will appreciate the dinners (€10) and hikers will appreciate the boxed lunches (€6.50).

RESIDENZA SAN CRISPINO €€€
Map p271; ☎ 075 815 51 24; www.sancrispino residence.com; Via Sant'Agnese 11; ste incl breakfast €170-340;

Rooms are medieval old but have been upgraded with armoire kitchenettes to become blissful apartment suites named after St Francis' Canticle of the Creatures – Brother Sun, Sister Water etc. If the short stroll to the Basilica di Santa Chiara or monastic-quiet garden hasn't

calmed you down quite enough, jump on the shuttle to its sister property, the Resort & Spa San Crispino (www.assisi benessere.it), a luxurious wellness centre.

ST ANTHONY'S GUESTHOUSE €
Map p271; ☎ 075 81 25 42; atoneassisi@tiscali.it; Via Galeazzo Alessi 10; s/d/tr incl breakfast €40/60/80; P

Look for the iron statue of St Francis feeding the birds and you've found your Assisian oasis. Rooms are austere but welcoming and six have balconies with breathtaking views. Gardens, ample parking, an 800-year-old breakfast salon and an ancient Door of Death make this a heavenly choice. Like most religious accommodation, it requires a two-night minimum stay and has an 11pm curfew.

SPELLO

HOTEL RISTORANTE LA BASTIGLIA €€
Map p275; ☎ 0742 65 12 77; www.labastiglia.com; Via dei Molini 7; s €70-105, d €80-155, ste €210-300; P

Welcoming well-heeled pilgrims, bicyclists and tour participants for decades. Three classes of rooms open the hotel's stunning grounds to a large segment of the travelling public, all of whom enjoy seasonal breakfast (Italian style) on the terrace. The restaurant is one of Umbria's best.

RESIDENCE SAN JACOPO €
Map p275; ☎ 0742 30 12 60, 333 2232899; www .residencesanjacopo.it, in Italian; Via Borgo di Via Giulia 1; apt for 2/3 people €62/93

This vacation house saw its first incarnation in 1296 as the hospice of San Jacopo, a way station for pilgrims heading to Compostella in Galicia. Seven mini-apartments feature kitchenettes, bathrooms and TVs, and are furnished with rustic antiques. Vanya, the owner, also runs a nearby *enoteca* and knows everything about local wine and delicacies.

LA STRADA DEL SAGRANTINO

❤ ALBERGO RISTORANTE IL TERZIERE // TREVI €€

☎ 0742 7 83 59; www.ilterziere.com; Via Coste 1; d incl breakfast €80-100; Ⓟ ⚒ ⚑

Everything you'd want in a family-owned hotel. An impressive upgrade makes four of the 12 rooms feel modern rather than austere, with DSL and Sky TV in each room. Try to snag one of the two rooms with balconies to enjoy the stunning view below.

❤ VILLA PAMBUFFETTI // MONTEFALCO €€

☎ 0742 37 94 17; www.villapambuffetti.com; Viale della Vittoria 20; r incl breakfast €120-245; Ⓥ Feb-Dec; Ⓟ ⚒ ⚑

Hippie nobility reigns over this country house. She, a chef; he, a sommelier – together, they run the 'shabby chic' noble villa. Each of the 15 rooms is decorated with antiques used by the family before they turned the estate into a hotel in 1992. Alessandra's cooking courses are reason enough to stay, as all recipes are from her own cookbook.

❤ VILLA ZUCCARI // MONTEFALCO €€

☎ 0742 39 94 02; www.villazuccari.com; San Luca di Montefalco; s €95-170, d €110-240; Ⓟ ⚒ ⚑ ⚑

The most recent Zuccari family lineage turned this ancestral home (inhabited since the end of the 15th century) into a hotel, as it felt a tad large. Now, guests in 34 unique rooms and suites can know what it's like to sip champagne

on one's own private balcony or bathe in an in-suite jacuzzi under a frescoed ceiling.

GUBBIO

❤ MAESTRO PIE FILIPPINI €

Map p284; ☎ 075 927 37 68; Corso Garibaldi 100; per person €20

Six basic rooms serve up to 16 guests in this religious accommodation. A few have bathtubs, and there's an open salon for reading. There's a minimum two-night stay and 10.30pm curfew, and advance reservations are required.

❤ RESIDENZA DI VIA PICCARDI €

Map p284; ☎ 075 927 61 08; www.agriturismo colledelsole.it; Via Piccardi 12; s/d/mini-apt incl breakfast €30/55/60; Ⓥ Mar-Dec

Step through the arched gate into the romantic garden of this period residence. Share an amorous breakfast for two in the garden or cook up a simple dinner in the mini-apartment's kitchenette. Family owned, the characteristically medieval stone building has cosy rooms decorated in cheery florals with all the basic comforts. Great value.

CITTÀ DI CASTELLO

❤ AGRITURISMO/B&B LE TORTORELLE €

Off Map p288; ☎ 075 941 09 49, in English 347 9754467; www.letortorelle.it, in Italian; Località Molino Vitelli 180, Umbertide; per person incl breakfast €35-40, full board €55; Ⓟ ⚑ ⚑

Potential farmhands and travelling softies alike can find their bliss at 'turtle doves' organic farm. Aldo and Teresa left Milan to raise their family in the hills of northern Umbria, growing organic wheat, aloe and herbs, and eating only natural, organic fare. Either volunteer as part of the WWOOF (www.wwoof.org)

program or chill out as a guest, learning to make organic pasta or, if you're lucky during summer, cooking homemade pizza in the 200-year-old outdoor brick oven. Two-night minimum stay.

♥ HOTEL UMBRIA €

Map p288; ☎ 075 855 49 25; www.hotelumbria.net, in Italian; Via S Antonio 6; s/d incl breakfast €35/55
As the least expensive hotel within the city walls, the Hotel Umbria is a simple but good-value minimalist hotel. The location can't be beaten, and comfortable beds and typical Italian breakfasts (good coffee!) are enough to get you up and moving in the morning.

LAGO TRASIMENO

♥ FATTORIA IL POGGIO // ISOLA POLVESE €

☎ 075 965 95 50; www.fattoriaisolapolvese.com; dm/f incl breakfast €15/17; ✆ Mar-Oct, reception closed 3-7pm; 💻
You would hardly ever know you're staying in a HI youth hostel. Impeccably run, this former barn has dorms, doubles and family rooms all with views of the surrounding lake. Kayaks, private beaches, games, TV with DVDs, and laundry room are all on offer. Homemade dinners might include wild cherries or fava beans grown on the island, or the hostel's own production of olive oil.

♥ IL TORRIONE // CASTIGLIONE DEL LAGO €

☎ 075 95 32 36; www.iltorrionetrasimeno.com; Via delle Mura 4; r incl breakfast €65-70; ✆ Mar–mid-Nov
Romance abounds at this artistically minded tranquil retreat. Each room is decorated with artwork painted by the owner and a private flower-filled garden overlooks the lake, complete with chaise

longues from which to watch the sunset and a 16th-century tower. Rent the 'tower' mini-apartment, complete with kitchenette, for an amorous hideaway.

♥ LA CASA SUL LAGO // TORRICELLA €

☎ 075 840 00 42; www.lacasasullago.com; Via del Lavoro; dm €16, r per person €22-44, incl breakfast; 💻 📶
The private rooms could be in a three-star hotel, and all rooms have access to every amenity known to hostelkind: laundry, bicycles and wi-fi (both free), internet access, home-cooked meals, bar, football pitch, foosball table, pedal boat and private garden…all within 50m of the lake. A short walk from the Torricella train station, but use the bicycles to get around the lake.

SOUTHERN UMBRIA

ORVIETO

♥ HOTEL LA BADIA €€€

Off Map p303; ☎ 0763 30 19 59; www.labadiahotel.it; Località La Badia 8; d €180-250, ste €280-420; 🅿 🍴 📶 🏊
Occupied 1200 years ago by Benedictine monks, this hotel is one of the oldest in Italy and has been a holiday retreat since the 15th century. For the past century it's been under the ownership of a noble family who turned it into the hotel it is today. Twenty-one rooms and seven suites consist of modern comforts along with attractive antiques and furnishings. There's also a swimming pool and tennis court.

♥ VILLA MERCEDE €

Map p303; ☎ 0763 34 17 66; www.argoweb.it/casareligiosa_villamercede; Via Soliana 2; s/d incl breakfast 50/70; 🅿
Heavenly close to the cathedral, with 23 rooms there's space for a gaggle of

ACCOMMODATION

pilgrims. The building dates back to the 1500s, so the requisite frescos adorn several rooms. High ceilings, a quiet garden and free parking seal the deal. Vacate rooms each morning by 9.30am or you'll earn the housekeepers' wrath.

AROUND ORVIETO

❦ AGRITURISMO CASTELLO TITIGNANO // LAGO DI CORBARA €€

☎ 0763 30 80 00; www.titignano.it; Località Titignano di Orvieto; s/d €60/90; P 🏊

Even for Umbrian standards, the castle at Titignano is astonishingly old: AD 937, with its 'new' court (where you'll be staying) built in the 16th and 17th centuries. As expected, rooms are dripping with historic charm. The castle's dining room is now a restaurant (meals €29) serving Titignano's famous wines and olive oils; guests can request a tour of the mill or wine cellar.

❦ FATTORIA DI VIBIO // MONTE CASTELLO DI VIBIO €€€

☎ 075 874 96 07; www.fattoriadivibio.com; Località Buchella 9, Doglio; half-board per person €90-160, cottages per week €980-2100; P 🍴 🏊

The view from the spa pool – out a plate-glass window, overlooking an enormous expanse of perfectly rolling, villa-capped hills – is reason enough to make the haul here. In the middle of nowhere but with absolutely every amenity a world-class *agriturismo* might need, the *fattoria* offers enough activities to keep guests busy for a week of dining, massage, wine tasting, horse riding…or, just relaxing and staring at the view.

❦ MONASTERO SS ANNUNZIATA // TODI €

Map p311; ☎ 075 894 22 68; www.monasterosmr .net; Via San Biagio 2; s/d incl breakfast €32/60

Take off for a getaway to this tranquil retreat within the city walls. Set around a lovely garden, all rooms come with private bathroom and bed linen, and some with furnishings from the 1400s. Try to catch a meal with your host nuns – from the Mary's Servant of Repair order.

❦ SAN LORENZO TRE // TODI €€

Map p311; ☎ 075 894 45 55; www.sanlorenzo3.it; Via San Lorenzo 3; s with shared/private bathroom €55/75, d with shared/private bathroom €75/110, incl breakfast; ❧ Mar-Dec

Five generations of the same family have lived at this bed and breakfast, set in a historic private residence that is impressive enough to have been used as a filming location recently. Filling, home-cooked breakfasts, a library dating back a century and a stunning rooftop view of the surrounding valley add to the romance.

❦ TODI CASTLE // LAGO DI CORBARA €€€

☎ 0744 95 20 04; www.todicastle.com; Vocabolo Capecchio, Morre; villa €120-200, castle €160-350; P 🛜 🏊

Here's your chance to live in an honest-to-goodness castle, or one of three equally perfect (and more affordable) private villas. With on-site private pools, the famed Umbria Grill (p309) restaurant, medieval ruins, a deer park and the most attentive staff in Umbria, you'll hardly want to leave. Weekly rates available.

SPOLETO

❦ HOTEL CHARLESTON €€

Map p316; ☎ 0743 22 00 52; www.hotelcharleston .it; Piazza Collicola 10; s €40-75, d €52-135, incl breakfast; P 🍴 🖥 🛜

With a sauna (€15), fireplace and outdoor terrace, the Charleston is an enticing option in both winter and summer, and provides wine tastings or *aperitivi* every evening. The 17th-century building, covered in distinguished modern art, has been thoroughly renovated with double-paned windows and some rooms come with bathtubs.

❤ HOTEL SAN LUCA €€

Map p316; ☎ 0743 22 33 99; www.hotelsanluca .com; Via Interna delle Mura 21; s €95-170, d €110-240, ste €210-300, incl breakfast; Ⓟ ⌗
Practically perfect hospitality is one of the main draws of the Zuccari family's (p412) second hotel. With enough services to rival any of the five-stars in Umbria (soundproofed rooms, babysitting, laundry service), San Luca has an atmosphere that is rather relaxed, enough to cater to bicyclists and walking tours. Hand-painted pastel walls and antique furnishings inside complement the 17th-century manicured outdoor garden. Extra touches include €4 for room-service breakfast, hydromassage showers and homemade pastries.

❤ OSTELLO VILLA REDENTA €

Map p316; ☎ 0743 22 49 36; www.villaredenta .com; Via di Villa Redenta 1; dm €18-23, s €25-35, d €52-60, incl breakfast; ☽reception 8am-1pm & 3.30-8pm; Ⓟ
Pope Leone XII slept here. Literally. The 17th-century home is set within a quiet park just outside the historic centre and comes complete with a bar, and private bathroom in most rooms. The architecturally stunning hostel is sophisticated enough for travellers of any age and, with its car park and proximity to the Valnerina and surrounds, is the perfect spot from which to day-trip.

THE VALNERINA & MONTI SIBILLINI

❤ CASALE NEL PARCO // NORCIA €€

Off Map p320; ☎/fax 0743 81 64 81; www .casalenelparco.com; Località Fontevena 8; s €55-65, d €90-110, incl breakfast; Ⓟ ⌗
Only 1km from Norcia towards Castelluccio, this working organic *agriturismo* grows its own lentils, spelt and vegetables. Swim in the terracotta-tiled pool under the eye of snowcapped Monte Patino, ride the horses through the foothills of Monti Sibillini or dine on the home-grown ingredients in the organic restaurant.

❤ HOTEL GROTTA AZZURA // NORCIA €€

Map p320; ☎ 0743 81 65 13; www.bianconi.com; Via Alfieri 12; s €40-90, d €50-135; ⌗
A suit of armour greets guests in the reception of this 18th-century *palazzo*. The family-run hotel can be a fabulous deal during the week and low season, and is steeped in the area's history. Cross-vaulted rooms are stately if a bit dark, complete with carved ceilings and recently upgraded bathrooms.

❤ PALAZZO SENECA // NORCIA €€€

Map p320; ☎ 0743 81 74 34; www.palazzoseneca .com; Via Cesare Battisti 12; r €120-300, ste €270-800; ⌗
Perhaps it's as you play chess in an overstuffed leather chair in front of the fireplace or maybe it's while you're enjoying your Thai massage in the subterranean spa that you truly feel like you live in a palace, even just for a night or two. Four-poster beds and marble bathrooms meld seamlessly with ancient stone walls, and the accompanying, practically perfect Ristorante Vespasia (p321) means you never have to leave.

ACCOMMODATION

❤ RESIDENZA D'EPOCA ABBAZIA SAN PIETRO IN VALLE // VALNERINA €€

☎ 0744 780 129; www.sanpietroinvalle.com; SS209 Valnerina, Km 20; s €100-110, d €130-140; ⊙ Easter-Oct; Ⓟ

Rooms have been upgraded quite a bit since their days as medieval nunnery cells, but the stone fireplaces and breathtaking view over the cloisters are the same. Ask for myriad hiking maps and activity suggestions, or start a leisurely morning with freshly baked bread and homemade preserves on the abbey's outdoor patio.

NARNI

❤ HOTEL DEI PRIORI €

Map p326; ☎ 0744 72 68 43; www.loggiadeipriori .it; Vicolo del Comune 4; s €48-55, d €60-75, incl breakfast; ⌗

This fabulous three-star hotel has contemporary amenities (hairdryer, TV, minibar) and 15th-century charm aplenty, but it's the fabulous restaurant, La Loggia (p330), that attracts many visitors. Some of the 17 rooms have incredible views or balconies, but the penthouse *camere di torre* (tower room) is the pièce de résistance.

❤ PODERE DEL CARDINALE €

Off Map p326; ☎ 0744 71 70 31; www.podere delcardinale.com; Strada di Massa Bassa 7, Taizzano; per person €20-35

This country house with its own adobe oven is what country chic strives for – gnarled farmhouse tables, huge wooden beds, solar-powered shower, full kitchen, horse stables nearby. You'll dig it. Literally. The owner is the lead archaeologist for the Narni Sotteranea, and keen guests are invited to join Roberto for a spot of Inquisition archaeology.

DIRECTORY

BUSINESS HOURS

Shops generally open from 9am to 1pm and reopen in the afternoon from 3.30pm or 4pm to 7.30pm or 8pm Monday to Friday. In cities and tourist towns it's increasingly popular for shops to remain open all day. In small towns, shops often close one afternoon a week, generally on a Wednesday or Thursday. Bank hours are generally from 8.30am to 1.30pm and 3pm to 5pm on weekdays, but times can vary. Post offices open from 8.30am to 1.30pm Monday to Friday and for several hours in the afternoon. In large towns, they might open on Saturday mornings. Pharmacies open from 9am to 12.30pm and 3.30pm to 7pm Monday to Friday, and are open on Saturday and Sunday mornings. It is the law that one pharmacy in every town must stay open each night and weekend; the location of this pharmacy is posted on all pharmacy doors.

Restaurants usually serve from 12.30pm to 2.30pm and 7.30pm to 10pm. Bars usually open from 8am until the early hours. The law requires restaurants to close one day a week, but some ignore this rule and others close two days a week. Nightclubs open their doors at about 10pm but don't fill up until midnight.

CHILDREN

Most places happily accommodate children, with *agriturismi* (farm-stay accommodation) and hotels usually supplying baby cots for free and/or a child's bed for a small fee. Few offer babysitting services, though. Kids under aged 12 often get discounts on public transport, museum and gallery admissions etc, and those aged under three are almost always free.

Kids are welcomed with open arms in restaurants, and many go out of their way to cater to younger children's needs – serving a half-portion of pasta, serving it at the same time as the adults' antipasti, supplying smaller hands with teaspoons, and so on. Just don't count on high chairs.

DIRECTORY

PRACTICALITIES

* Italy uses the metric system for weights and measures.

* Plugs have two or three round prongs (standard to Europe); the electric current is 220V, 50Hz.

* Pick up Italian news with national dailies *Corriere della Sera* (www.corriere.it, in Italian), which has a section in English, and the Florence edition of *La Repubblica* (www .firenze.repubblica.it, in Italian); or regional broadsheets *La Nazione* and *Corriere dell' Umbria* (www.corrieredellumbria.it, in Italian).

* Get news, views, and classifieds in English-language biweekly newspaper the *Florentine* (www.theflorentine.net), freely distributed at select hotels, restaurants, bookshops and bars in Florence.

* Tune in to state broadcaster RAI-1 (1332AM or 89.7FM), RAI-2 (846AM or 91.7FM) and RAI-3 (93.7FM) for classical and light music with news, and Radio 105 (www.105.net, in Italian) for contemporary and rock.

* Italy's commercial TV stations are Canale 5, Italia 1, Rete 4 and La 7, alongside state-run RAI Uno, RAI Due and RAI Tre.

Car seats can be hired with rental cars (for a sometimes extortionate fee), but if you plan to do a lot of travelling you might be better off taking your own (which will almost certainly be more comfortable than the nonadjustable, sparsely cushioned seats usually provided).

Farmacie (pharmacies) sell baby formula in powder or liquid form as well as sterilising solutions. Disposable nappies are widely available at supermarkets and pharmacies.

For more information, see Lonely Planet's *Travel with Children*.

DANGERS & ANNOYANCES

THEFT

Although Tuscany and Umbria are relatively safe regions, pickpockets and bag snatchers are never more than a crowded bus or slashed strap away. Keep an eye out in much of Florence, as well as in larger towns such as Perugia, and around

train stations and popular tourist draws. Buses between the train station and city centres are notoriously filled with pickpockets, and be mindful of groups of dishevelled-looking women and children. Often working in groups, thieves sometimes employ children as young as six or seven to cause a commotion. While you are paying attention to the coffee spilled on your suitcase or the baby being handed to you, you probably won't even notice your bag has been cut from the bottom or your camera has been removed straight from your pocket. As soon as you get that sinking feeling something isn't right, pay extra attention. Better to hold on too tight than lose a camera.

Parked cars, particularly those with foreign number plates or rental-company stickers, are also prime targets for thieves. Never leave anything visible in your car, and make sure you are adequately insured. See p433 for more details. In case of theft or loss, always report the incident to the police within 24 hours and ask for a statement, otherwise your travel insurance company may not pay out.

TRAFFIC

Italian driving varies dramatically between city and country, but expect to have to stay alert at all times. The city is fast, chaotic and not overly friendly to pedestrians. Crossing the street can be a life-threatening event, as Italians would rather swerve around a pedestrian than (heaven forbid) stop and wait. Scooter drivers often act more like cyclists and it's not uncommon to see them driving on a footpath or going the wrong way down a one-way street. Always look both ways before crossing a street.

DISCOUNT CARDS

Seniors over 60 or 65 can get many discounts, including museum entrance fees, simply by presenting their passport or ID card as proof of age.

Student and youth cards can provide you with worthwhile discounts on travel, and reduced prices at some museums, sights and entertainment spots. The International Student Identity Card (ISIC), for full-time students, and the International Teacher Identity Card (ITIC), for full-time teachers and professors, are accepted in the majority of Italian museums. In Australia, the USA or the UK, try **STA Travel** (www.statravel.com) to obtain either of these cards.

Anyone under 26 can get a Euro26 card. This gives similar discounts to the ISIC. See www.euro26.org for details.

Centro Turistico Studentesco e Giovanile (CTS; www.cts.it) youth and student travel organisation branches in Italy can issue ISIC, ITIC and Euro26 cards. Note that many places in Italy give discounts according to age rather than student status. An ISIC may not always be accepted without proof of age (eg passport).

FOOD & DRINK

This section covers the nuts and bolts of dining and drinking. For a more in-depth portrait of culinary culture, history, wine and cuisine, see p375 and p381.

Tap water is perfectly drinkable, but Italians generally drink bottled *acqua minerale* (mineral water) – *frizzante* (sparkling) or *naturale* (still) – which rarely costs more than €2 in a restaurant for a 1L bottle.

Italian beers tend to be crisp, light Pilsener-style lagers, which younger Italians guzzle down with a pizza. Moretti, Peroni and Nastro Azzurro are all very drinkable and cheaper than imported varieties. If you want a local beer, ask for a *birra nazionale* in a bottle or *alla spina* (on tap).

Wine is cheap – often cheaper than bottled water – and generally very good. Most restaurants' *vino da tavola* (table wine) or *vino della casa* (house wine) is fine and costs in the range of €4 to €6 for a litre.

Serious etiquette surrounds coffee, easily Europe's best. To avoid any wrath, never order a cappuccino after 11am, and certainly not after a meal. At most, order a *caffè macchiato* ('stained' coffee) – an espresso with a dollop of foam. Worth a try in the summer is the *caffè shakerato* – a chilled, shaken espresso with cream, served elegantly in a martini glass. For the complete low-down, see the boxed text, p348.

WHERE TO EAT & DRINK

Meal prices quoted within Gastronomic Highlights listings of this guide are the average price you can expect to pay for

PRICE GUIDE

The following is a guide to the pricing system used for Gastronomic Highlights in this book. Prices include three courses and cover charge per person.

€	up to €25
€€	€25 to €45
€€€	€45-plus

a *primo* (first course, usually pasta), *secondo* (main meat or fish course), *dolce* (dessert) and a *coperto* (cover charge, usually €1 to €3, which covers bread and water and means additional tipping usually isn't expected). Naturally, meals in each respective place can cost a lot more or a lot less, depending on what you order. These days in Italy, you certainly don't have to order a three-course meal, so you can walk out of a restaurant we list as costing €35 with an €11 plate of pasta, €1.50 *coperto* and a €2 glass of wine.

Restaurants generally display their menu outside, and many have an additional board featuring the day's specials. Some of the smaller, most endearing and authentic trattorias simply have the day's market-dictated menu chalked up on a blackboard or rely on the waiter to tell you what's cooking. Generally, the quality of food goes down as the number of language translations on the menu goes up. A fixed *menù turistico* is offered at places geared first and foremost to the region's less-discerning tourist trade. For typical opening hours, see p417.

Fast food usually takes the form of a panino while standing up at a bar, pizza *al taglio* (by the slice), tripe from a street cart in Florence (p84), or a cake or pastry from one of the region's many delectable *pasticcerie* (cake shops).

For dining with children, see p417.

VEGETARIANS & VEGANS

Cibo biologico (organic food) is becoming increasingly popular in Italy, and often tends to be vegetarian. Nevertheless most Italians, especially those outside of major cities, are mystified by special diets or restrictions, such is their (understandable) dedication to traditional Italian cuisine. You may find yourself being asked, *Ma, che cosa mangi?* (What do you eat?).

Check out NaturaSi (www.naturasi.it, in Italian), an Italian organic supermarket with outposts in Siena, Lucca, Florence and Perugia. In restaurants, *primi piatti* (first courses) usually include many rice or pasta dishes suitable for vegetarians; however, vegan diets can be nearly impossible to accommodate as pasta is often made with egg. Watch out for bits of meat in sauces such as *amatriciana* (spicy pasta sauce made with tomatoes, pancetta or bacon, and basil) or carbonara. A *secondi* such as *scamorza* (smoked grilled cheese) is a great option for vegetarians, and Tuscan white-bean soup and Umbrian *zuppa di farro* (spelt soup) are also excellent typical alternatives found on most menus.

GAY & LESBIAN TRAVELLERS

The age of consent for homosexuals in Italy is 16 and homosexuality is mostly well tolerated in larger cities, including Florence, Pisa and Perugia. On the Tuscan coast, Torre del Lago has a lively gay scene, best expressed by **Friendly Versilia** (www.friendlyversilia.it), a summer campaign that encourages gays and lesbians to revel in Torre del Lago's fun-in-the-sun frolics from late April to September.

Online, www.gayfriendlyitaly.com (connected to the Italian-language site www.gay.it) helps with information on tour groups and gay-friendly hotels, and runs a homophobia rating system of Italian cities. Gay-friendly bars and clubs can be tracked down on the website or through local gay organisations such as **ArciGay** (☎ 051 649 30 55; www.arcigay.it) or Florence-based **Azione Gay e Lesbica** (☎ 055 67 12 98; www.azionegayelesbica.it, in Italian; Via Pisana 32r).

HEALTH

Italy is a relatively safe country, health-wise. Throughout central Italy, tap water is safe to drink and the risk of infectious or food-borne disease is low. Italy is currently ranked second on the WHO (World Health Organization) list of top countries for health care, although this isn't always apparent in hospitals (many of which, for instance, still turn a blind eye to smoking).

HOLIDAYS

SCHOOL HOLIDAYS

Avoid Tuscany and Umbria in mid-August when most Italians take their holidays, school kids in tow. Beaches are overly crowded and many restaurants and shops are closed, especially during the week of Ferragosto (15 August). Settimana Santa (Easter) is another busy holiday period when many schools take pupils on cultural excursions. Museums and places of interest may be more crowded than usual. Allow for long queues and be sure to make hotel reservations in advance, especially on weekends.

PUBLIC HOLIDAYS

In addition to the following national public holidays, almost every town in Italy celebrates its patron saint day with a festival or event of some kind; see regional chapters for details or contact the local tourist office.

New Year's Day (Anno Nuovo) 1 January
Epiphany (Befana) 6 January
Easter Sunday (Pasqua) March/April
Easter Monday (Pasquetta) March/April
Liberation Day (Festa della Liberazione) 25 April
Labour Day (Festa dei Lavoratori) 1 May
Foundation of the Italian Republic (Festa della Repubblica) 2 June
Assumption of the Virgin (Ferragosto) 15 August
All Saints' Day (Ognissanti) 1 November
Day of the Immaculate Conception (L'Immaculata Concezione) 8 December
Christmas Day (Natale) 25 December
St Stephen's Day/Boxing Day (Festa di Santo Stefano) 26 December

INSURANCE

For information on car insurance, see p433.

MEDICAL INSURANCE

If you're an EU citizen, arm yourself with the European Health Insurance Card, a handy piece of plastic that entitles you to emergency treatment throughout the EU. The card is not meant to take the place of travellers' insurance or provide any ongoing care in the host country.

Citizens from other countries should find out if there is a reciprocal arrangement for free medical care between their country and Italy. If you need health insurance, get a policy that covers you for the worst possible scenario, such as an accident requiring an emergency flight home. Find out in advance if your insurance plan will make payments directly to providers or reimburse you later for overseas health expenditures.

TRAVEL INSURANCE

A travel-insurance policy to cover theft, loss and medical problems is a good idea. Some policies specifically exclude dangerous activities, which can include scuba diving, motorcycling and even hiking.

You may prefer a policy that pays doctors or hospitals directly rather than you having to pay on the spot and claim later. If you have to claim later, ensure you keep all documentation. Check that the policy covers ambulances or an emergency flight home. Paying for your airline ticket with a credit card often provides limited travel-accident insurance. Ask your credit-card company what it's prepared to cover.

INTERNET ACCESS

With each passing week, wi-fi availability in Italy seems to be on the rise, but the starting point was rather dire (travellers are often surprised to find that many Italians don't have home internet connections, or have connections that rarely work). Wi-fi spots are popping up in cities and even smaller towns – at cafes, hotels and even public libraries.

Internet cafes are fairly abundant in towns and cities, and those in Florence and Perugia alone each number into the dozens. Expect to pay €1 to €5 per hour and don't forget your passport – an anti-terrorism law requires internet cafes take a photocopy of your *documento* (any ID will do) before they allow you online access.

If you're using your laptop, check it is compatible with the 220V electrical current in Italy; if not, you will need a converter.

For useful website resources on the region, see p9.

LEGAL MATTERS

Some Italians are likely to react with surprise, if not annoyance, if you point out that they might be breaking a law. Few people pay attention to speed limits and many motorcyclists and drivers don't stop at red lights – and certainly not at pedestrian crossings. No one bats an eyelid about littering or dogs pooping in the middle of the footpath, even though many municipal governments have introduced laws against these things. But these are minor transgressions when measured up against the country's organised crime, the extraordinary levels of tax evasion, and corruption in government and business.

There are several different types of 'police' in Italy. The *polizia* (police) are a civil force and take their orders from the Ministry of the Interior, while the *carabinieri* (military police) fall under the Ministry of Defence. *Polizia* headquarters are called the *questura,* which is where tourists wanting resident permits or reporting thefts will need to visit (see p427).

Other varieties of police in Italy include the *vigili urbani,* basically traffic police, who you will have to deal with if you get a parking ticket or if your car is towed away; and the *guardia di finanza,* who are responsible for fighting tax evasion and drug smuggling.

In an emergency, you can always go to the nearest people in uniform. Even if they're not the right uniforms, they'll know whom to contact. Or call ☎113 for the police or ☎112, the EU general emergency number.

Italy's drug laws are lenient on users and heavy on pushers. If you're caught with drugs that the police determine are for your own personal use, you'll be let off with a warning (and, of course, the drugs will be confiscated). If, instead, it is determined that you intend to sell the drugs, you could find yourself in prison. It's up to the police to determine whether or not you're a pusher, since the law is not specific about quantities. The sensible option is to avoid illicit drugs altogether.

When driving, the legal limit for blood-alcohol level is 0.05%. Random breath tests are carried out by the authorities, and penalties can range from an on-the-spot fine to the confiscation of your licence.

The average tourist will probably have a brush with the law only if they are unfortunate enough to be robbed by a bag snatcher or pickpocket.

MAPS

CITY MAPS

The city maps in this book, combined with tourist-office maps, are generally adequate for getting you around. Most tourist offices stock free maps of their city that are perfectly adequate for most travellers, and commercial maps of larger cities are available from newsstands and bookshops. For suggestions on maps for other cities covered in this book, refer to each destination: many bookshops with good selections of maps and guidebooks are listed in each section.

Tourist offices in Florence dole out free maps, and bookshops sell Touring Club Italiano's *Florence* (1:12,500), with a city-centre cutaway (1:6500).

DRIVING MAPS

Those motoring around Tuscany and Umbria will find the Istituto Geographico de Agostini's spiral-bound, 100-page *Atlante Turistico Toscana* (1:200,000), with 32 pages of city maps, 30 pages of regional maps and 14 pages of itineraries, indispensable; local bookshops in the region sell it. In the UK and USA, the road atlases for Italy published by the AA are likewise invaluable, if less detailed, for the region.

The AA also publishes regional maps for Tuscany and Umbria, as does Michelin, whose excellent orange-jacketed *Tuscana, Umbria, San Marino, Marche, Lazio and Abruzzo* (1:400,000) includes two Florence city maps.

Our favourite map for Umbria is the free Touring Club Italiano's *Carta Regionale 1:200,000,* available at almost all tourist offices and many hotels in Umbria. It marks many features that make it extremely helpful: tertiary/dirt roads and sites of interest including sanctuaries, Etruscan tombs, grottos, ruins and monasteries. On the reverse side are maps of tourist towns such as Perugia, Castiglione del Lago and Todi. Most maps of Umbria are combined with either Le Marche or Tuscany, except Mappe Iter's *Umbria 1:200,000 Carta Turistica e Automobilistica* (€6).

A note about the terrain: 94% of Umbria is hilly. Industrial complexes have taken advantage of the remaining flat 6%, so if you want attractive landscapes, stay away from anywhere on your map that is white (read: flat) and near a city.

GPS

GPS (Global Positioning System) devices can be a godsend in the confusing jumble that is the Tuscan and Umbrian road system. Almost all rental-car companies offer GPS; the price is usually around €70 to €100 per week and all have an English-language option. However, you can also bring your own device. Companies like

Garmin (www.garmin.com), Magellan (www.magellangps.com) and TomTom (www.tomtom.com) carry pricier versions that come with Western European maps, or you can purchase a less expensive device and add on an Italy (or an Italy and Greece) map for around €70.

WALKING & CYCLING MAPS

Tuscany and Umbria are great destinations for those who love the outdoors. Edizione Multigraphic publishes a couple of series designed for walkers and mountain-bike riders, scaled at 1:50,000 and 1:250,000. Ask for the *Carta dei Sentieri e Rifugi* or *Carta Turistica e dei Sentieri.* Another publisher is Kompass, which produces 1:50,000 scale maps of Tuscany and surrounding areas. Occasionally you will also come across useful maps put out by the Club Alpino Italiano (CAI).

For cycling enthusiasts, Verlag Esterbauer produces a *Cycling Tuscany: Cycle Guide and Map,* a spiral-bound 1:100,000 guide detailing the best cycling spots in the region. Regione Umbria produces the excellent *Umbria by Bike,* available free at most tourist offices in the area. The 130-page booklet describes in great detail (in English or Italian) 30 bicycling routes, including elevation, directions and sights along the way.

MONEY

The euro (€) has been the official currency of Italy since 2002. One euro is divided into 100 cents or centimes, with one-, two-, five-, 10-, 20- and 50-centime coins. Notes come in denominations of five, 10, 20, 50, 100, 200 and 500 euros. Euro notes and coins issued in Italy are valid throughout the other 15 countries in the euro zone: Austria, Belgium, Cyprus, Finland, France, Germany, Greece, Ireland, Luxembourg, Malta, the Netherlands, Portugal, Slovakia, Slovenia and Spain.

Travellers cheques – which are very sparingly used these days in Italy – can be cashed at most banks and exchange offices (bring your passport as proof of identity). Amex, Thomas Cook and Visa are the most widely accepted brands in this region.

Exchange rates are given on the inside front cover of this book and a guide to budget ranges used in this book can be found on p8.

Exceedingly often, Italian shopkeepers will not have change. Try to keep a collection of coins and small bills handy.

ATMS

Automated teller machines (ATMs) – known as *bancomat* in Italian – are the cheapest and most convenient way to get money. ATMs are situated in virtually every town or halfway populated village in Tuscany and Umbria, and usually offer an exchange rate far superior to travellers cheques. Cash advances on credit cards are also possible at ATMs, but incur charges.

It's not uncommon for Italian ATMs to reject foreign cards for no reason whatsoever. If this happens, try a few branches or another day. For this reason, always arrive with a few euros, just in case.

CREDIT & DEBIT CARDS

Credit and debit cards are convenient, relatively secure and will usually offer a better exchange rate than travellers cheques or cash exchanges. Visa and MasterCard (Access or Eurocard) are widely accepted; American Express

(Amex) cards are useful at more upmarket establishments and allow you to get cash at Amex offices and certain ATMs. In general, all three cards can be used in shops, supermarkets, for train travel, car rentals, motorway tolls and cash advances. Bear in mind that a few establishments – including shops, restaurants and a few budget hotels – only accept cash.

Getting a cash advance against a credit card is usually an expensive way to go as fees (and interest) are charged. Debit card fees are usually much less.

For lost cards, these toll-free Italy-wide numbers operate 24 hours:

Amex (☎ 800 91 49 12)
MasterCard, Eurocard & Access (☎ 800 87 08 66)
Visa (☎ 800 87 72 32)

POST

Italy's **postal service** (www.poste.it) is notoriously slow, unreliable and expensive. If you're sending a package, you might want to send your things home using DHL or FedEx. Shops such as Mail Boxes Etc can be found in most major towns.

Francobolli (stamps) are available at post offices and authorised *tabacchi* (tobacconists; look for the official sign: a big 'T', often white on black). Main post offices in the bigger cities are generally open from around 8am to at least 5pm; many open on Saturday morning too.

Postcards and letters up to 20g sent by airmail cost €1 to Australia and New Zealand (zone 3), €0.85 to the USA, Asia and Africa (zone 2), and €0.65 within Europe (zone 1); mail weighing between 20g and 50g costs €1.80, €1.50 and €1.45 respectively. Within Italy, a letter up to 20/50g costs €0.60/1.40. You can also send express letters *(posta prioritaria)* and registered letters *(rac-comandata)* at additional cost; charges vary depending on the type of post and weight of the letter. While the Italian postal system has improved greatly, normal airmail letters can take up to two weeks to reach the USA, while a letter to Australia will take between two and three weeks. The service within Italy is not much better: local letters take at least three days and up to a week to arrive in another city.

TELEPHONE

Privatised **Telecom Italia** (www.telecomitalia.com) is Italy's telephone company, but its once ubiquitous orange pay phones have been for the most part removed because of mobile (cell) phone use. Most only accept *carte/schede telefoniche* (phone cards), sold at post offices, *tabacchi*, newspaper stands and Telecom offices for €5 and €10 (snap off the perforated corner before use), although you might stumble upon the odd relic that still accepts coins. Most phones have clear instructions in English.

Landline telephone numbers comprise a two- to five-digit area code (always starting with zero) followed by a number of four to eight digits. Area codes are an integral part of all telephone numbers and must always be dialled.

Telephone numbers change often in Italy, so check the local directory for up-to-date information. *Numeri verdi* (free phone numbers) usually begin with ☎ 800 (some start with ☎ 199 and ☎ 848).

Italy's mobile system is GSM 900/1800, which is compatible with the rest of Europe and Australia, but travellers from other countries (including the USA and Japan) will need to verify that their mobile is GSM compatible.

DIRECTORY

If you have a GSM phone, check with your service provider about using it in Italy and beware of calls being routed internationally (which is very expensive for a 'local' call). Better still, once you arrive in Italy, sign up at any mobile-phone shop for a pay-as-you-go plan. If you don't have your own phone, buying a cheap new one starts at about €29 (still cheaper than, say, 10 international roaming calls). To buy an Italian SIM card, you'll need to register with a mobile-phone shop; bring your passport and have your Italian address with you. Your new number will be ready in about 12 to 24 hours. After that, buy *ricarica* (pre-paid minutes) from your selected mobile company at shops and *tabacchi* everywhere, usually about €0.20 within Italy and €0.60 to North America. Italy's main providers are **TIM** (www.tim.it), **Vodafone** (www.vodafone.it), **Wind** (www.wind.it) and **Tre** (www.tre.it). If staying in affordable touch internationally is a priority, Tre offers an International No Limit plan – €15 gets you 50 hours of airtime with any landline or mobile phone in North America, as well as European landlines.

Mobile-phone numbers always start with a three-digit prefix, such as ☎ 330, ☎ 339, ☎ 347 etc – never a zero.

Italy's country code is ☎ 39 and the international access code is ☎ 00.

National and international phone numbers can be requested at ☎ 1254 (in Italian) or online at http://1254.virgilio.it. Another handy number, where operators will respond in several languages, is ☎ 89 24 12.

TIME

Italy operates on a 24-hour clock. It is one hour ahead of GMT/UTC. Daylight-saving time starts on the last Sunday in March, when clocks are put forward one hour. Clocks are put back an hour on the last Sunday in October. This is especially valuable to know in Italy, as 'summer' and 'winter' hours are usually based on DST.

TIPPING

For the most part, Italians don't expect tips. In fact, in a refreshing about-face, a tip in Italy is what it was meant to be – appreciation for truly excellent service. The base pay for service-industry folk is quite good and a *coperto* (cover charge) of €1 to €3 per person is already factored into the bill. Tipping is customary in only a few places, including upscale hotels and restaurants.

If you'd like to reward particularly helpful or friendly service, we suggest 5% to 10% in restaurants (or simply round up the bill), €1 to €2 per bag for porters and €5 per night for the concierge.

TOURIST INFORMATION

Practically every village and town has a tourist office of sorts (listed under the relevant towns and cities throughout this book), operating under a variety of names but most commonly known as Pro Loco or, in larger towns, the Azienda di Promozione Turistica (APT; these offices usually provide information on the surrounding area).

English and French are widely spoken in Tuscany. Umbrian tourist boards, however, are legendary for staff who speak only Italian, and for sometimes closing on slow days when the volunteer staff don't show up.

Regional tourist offices offer a wealth of information, touristic itineraries and brochures on everything from wine routes to bicycle paths through their websites. For Tuscany go to www.tur ismo.toscana.it; for Umbria, www.regio neumbria.eu.

TRAVELLERS WITH DISABILITIES

Tuscany and Umbria are far from easy for travellers with physical disabilities. Cobblestone streets, stairs and tricky or no disabled access at train stations mean some towns are extremely difficult to navigate with wheelchairs or limited mobility. Happily though, this is changing in many towns.

Our favourite towns for wheelchairs (and strollers) are Florence in Tuscany and Assisi and Città di Castello in Umbria. Assisi outpaces the lot: go to **Assisi Accessibile** (www.assisiaccessibile.it) to read a paraplegic Assisian's assessment of the wheelchair accessibility of the city's hotels, restaurants and monuments. Another excellent resource is **Accessible Italy** (www.accessibleitaly.com), which publishes an online catalogue of accommodation suitable for travellers with disabilities, and organises both small group tours and independent travel for customers with physical or visual disabilities. It can coordinate an entire holiday, including airport pick-up and hotel reservations, and it also provides a listing of accessible monuments. **Accessible Italian Holiday** (www.accessibleitalianholiday.com) offers airport transfers and advice on rental cars and accessible hotels and monuments.

VISAS & PERMITS

The following information on visas was correct at the time of writing, but restrictions and regulations can change. Use the following as a guide only, and contact your embassy for the latest details. You may want to visit lonelyplanet.com for useful links and up-to-date information, or the **Italian Ministry of Foreign Affairs** (www.esteri.it) for updated visa information, including links to every Italian consulate in the world and a list of nationalities needing a visa.

Be sure to understand the difference between a visa and a *permesso di soggiorno* (see below). A visa gets you into the country and a *permesso di soggiorno* (permit to stay) allows you to stay. To apply for a visa, visit an Italian consulate in your home country. To apply for a *permesso di soggiorno,* apply at a *questura* (police station) within eight days of your arrival. Check www.portaleimmigrazi one.it for more information.

PERMITS

EU citizens do not need permits to live, work or start a business in Italy. They are, however, advised to register with a *questura* if they take up residence – in accordance with an anti-Mafia law that aims to keep an eye on everyone's whereabouts. EU citizens do not require a *permesso di soggiorno*. All other *stranieri* (foreigners) staying in Italy for more than eight days are supposed to report to the police station to receive a *permesso di soggiorno*. Tourists staying in hotels are not required to do this.

A *permesso di soggiorno* only becomes a necessity if you plan to study, work or live in Italy. Obtaining one is never a pleasant experience; it involves long queues and the frustration of arriving at the counter only to find you don't have the necessary documents.

The exact requirements change: depending on what type of *permesso di soggiorno* you're applying for, you might need to bring with you anything from eight extra passport-sized photos to a vial of the blood of a six-toed cat born on a Tuesday. In general you need at least a valid passport (if possible containing a visa stamp indicating your date of entry into Italy); a special visa issued in your own country if you are planning to study; four passport-sized photographs; and proof of your ability to support yourself financially. Recently they have changed the system: you apply with a form through the *Sportello Unico*, located at some but not all post offices, and then sometimes are given an additional appointment at the local *questura*. (Do not expect that you will be seen on time.)

Non-EU citizens wishing to work in Italy will need to obtain a *permesso di lavoro* (work permit). If you intend to work for an Italian company and will be paid in euros, the company must organise the *permesso di lavoro* and forward it to the Italian consulate in your country – only then will you be issued an appropriate visa.

If non-EU citizens intend to work for a non-Italian company or will be paid in foreign currency, or wish to go freelance, they must organise the visa and *permesso di lavoro* in their country of residence through an Italian consulate. This process can take many months, so look into it early.

VISAS

At the time of writing, Italy is one of 25 countries to have signed the Schengen Convention, an agreement where countries within the EU have agreed to abolish checks at common borders. Legal residents of one Schengen Area country do not require a visa for another Schengen country. In addition, nationals of a number of other countries – the USA, Canada, Australia, Ireland, Japan, New Zealand and Mexico – can stay for up to 90 days without a visa (plus the UK and Ireland, which are not part of the Schengen Agreement's open border). There are several dozen countries whose citizens require tourist visas, including Bosnia and Hercegovina, Peru, India and South Africa. Check with your nearest Italian consulate.

The Bossi-Fini law has recently tightened restrictions on immigration and penalties for *clandestini* (illegal immigrants). All non-EU nationals (except those from Iceland, Norway and Switzerland) entering Italy for any reason other than tourism (such as study or work) should contact an Italian consulate, as they may need a specific visa. They should also insist on having their passport stamped on entry as, without a stamp, they could encounter problems when trying to obtain a *permesso di soggiorno*.

STUDY VISAS

Non-EU citizens who want to study at a university or language school in Italy must have a study visa. These visas can be obtained from your nearest Italian embassy or consulate. You will normally need confirmation of your enrolment and payment of fees, as well as proof of adequate funds to be able to support yourself. The visa will then cover only the period of the enrolment. This type of visa is renewable within Italy but, again, only with confirmation of ongoing enrolment and proof that you are able to support yourself (bank statements are preferred).

TOURIST VISAS

The standard tourist visa is the Schengen visa, whic is valid for up to 90 days. A Schengen visa issued by one Schengen country is generally valid for travel in all other Schengen countries. However, individual Schengen countries may impose additional restrictions on certain nationalities. It is therefore worth checking the visa regulations with the consulate of each Schengen country you plan to visit.

It's mandatory to apply for a visa in your country of residence. You can apply for no more than two Schengen visas in any 12-month period, and they are not renewable inside Italy. For more information see www.eurovisa.info/Schengen Countries.htm.

WOMEN TRAVELLERS

Tuscany and Umbria in general are not dangerous regions for women, who mostly contend with overly long gazes or catcalls. However, women travelling alone will want to keep an eye open for more sinister attention from local and foreign men, especially in nightclubs or discos.

It is not uncommon for Italian men of all ages to try to strike up conversations with foreign women. Do as Italian women do, and don't be afraid to gently but firmly rebuff any advances or ignore them. If that doesn't work, politely tell them that you are waiting for your *marito* (husband) or *fidanzato* (boyfriend) and, if necessary, walk away. Most men are exceedingly polite in Umbria and most of Tuscany, but women in Florentine bars and coastal resorts – and college students in Perugian nightclubs – might want to keep up an additional guard.

TRANSPORT

ARRIVAL & DEPARTURE

AIR

High season for air travel to Italy is June to September. Shoulder season will often run from mid-September to the end of October and again in April. Low season is generally November to March, but tickets around Christmas and Easter often increase in price or sell out well in advance.

Full-time students and those under 26 have access to discounted fares: show a document proving your date of birth or a valid International Student Identity Card (ISIC) when buying your ticket. Other cheap deals are the discounted tickets released to travel agents and specialist discount agencies. Most major newspapers carry a Sunday travel section with ads for these agencies, often known as brokers in Europe and consolidators in the USA.

Check the websites of budget carriers, such as Ryanair, Jet2 and Easyjet, directly. But be on the alert; many aren't as low cost as their come-on publicity alleges, once you factor in taxes and fuel charges.

Some even charge for hold luggage (Ryanair, for example, slaps on €10 for the first piece and €20 per piece thereafter).

AIRLINES

Airlines flying into the region:

Air Berlin (AB; ☎ 848 39 00 54; www.airberlin.com)

Air France (AF; ☎ 848 88 44 66; www.airfrance.com)

Air One (AP; ☎ 199 20 70 80; www.flyairone.it)

Alitalia (AZ; ☎ 06 22 22; www.alitalia.it)

Austrian (OS; ☎ 02 89 63 4296; www.aua.com)

THINGS CHANGE...

The information in this chapter is particularly vulnerable to change. Check directly with the airline or a travel agent to make sure you understand how a fare (and ticket you may buy) works and be aware of the security requirements for international travel. Shop carefully. The details given in this chapter should be regarded as pointers and are not a substitute for your own careful, up-to-date research.

ONLINE TICKETS

Cheap Flights (www.cheapflights.com)
Ebookers.com (www.ebookers.com)
Expedia (www.expedia.com)
Kayak (www.kayak.com)
Last Minute (www.lastminute.com)
Orbitz (www.orbitz.com)
Priceline (www.priceline.com)
Travelocity (www.travelocity.com)

British Airways (BA; ☎ 199 712 266; www
.ba.com)
Brussels Airlines (SN; ☎ 899 800 903; www
.brusselsairlines.com)
Delta (DL; ☎ 848 78 03 76; www.delta.com)
EasyJet (U2; ☎ 899 67 89 90; www.easyjet.com)
Finnair (AY; ☎ 199 4000 99; www.finnair.com)
Iberia (IB; ☎ 199 101 191; www.iberia.com)
Jet2 (LS; ☎ 199 309 240; www.jet2.com)
Lufthansa (LH; ☎ 199 400 044; www.lufthansa
.com)
Meridiana (IG; ☎ 199 111 333; www.meridiana.it)
Norwegian (DY; ☎ 47 21 49 00 15; www.norweg
ian.com)
Ryanair (FR; ☎ 899 67 89 10; www.ryanair.com)
Swiss (LX; ☎ 848 868 120; www.swiss.com)
Thomsonfly (TOM; ☎ 02 36 00 3582; www
.thomsonfly.com)

AIRPORTS

The increasingly important **Galileo Galilei airport** (Pisa International Airport; PSA; ☎ 050 84 93 00; www.pisa-airport.com) is the most convenient destination for Tuscany and Umbria. From here, more than 20 airlines serve nearly 50 national and international destinations.

From the small **Amerigo Vespucci airport** (FLR; ☎ 055 306 13 00; www.aeroporto .firenze.it), just outside Florence, Meridiana flies to/from Amsterdam and London (Gatwick), while Lufthansa serves Frankfurt and Air France serves Paris (Charles de Gaulle).

From Umbria's even tinier **Sant'Egidio airport** (PEG; ☎ 075 59 21 41; www.airport.umbria .it), on the outskirts of Perugia, there are flights to/from Milan (Malpensa) and London (Stansted; Ryanair).

Most long-haul flights use Rome's **Leonardo da Vinci airport** (FCO; ☎ 06 659 51; www.adr.it), also known as Fiumicino, or Milan's **Malpensa** (☎ 02 748 522 00; www .sea-aeroportimilano.it) airports.

Trenitalia's new Alta Velocità service, opened in late 2009, promises to connect Bologna to Florence in a blistering 35 minutes, making **Aeroporto G Marconi di Bologna** (BLQ; ☎ 051 647 96 15; www.bologna -airport.it) into a legitimate Tuscany access point.

BUS

Eurolines (www.eurolines.com) is a consortium of European coach companies that operates across Europe with offices in all major European cities. Italy-bound buses head to Milan, Rome, Florence, Siena or Venice. Its multilingual website gives comprehensive details of prices, passes and travel agencies throughout Europe where you can book tickets. There are discounts for seniors and travellers under 26 years.

Another option is the backpacker-friendly **Busabout** (☎ 44 (0)8450 267 514; www.busabout.com), which covers at least 60 European cities and towns with a hop-on, hop-off pass – the shortest is a six-stop ticket. Its season runs from May to October and buses usually leave between large cities every other day. In Tuscany, its buses call by Florence and Siena.

CAR & MOTORCYCLE

Coming from the UK, you can take your car across to France by ferry, or via the Channel Tunnel on **Eurotunnel** (☎ 08705 35 35 35; www.eurotunnel.com). The latter runs

CLIMATE CHANGE & TRAVEL

Climate change is a serious threat to the ecosystems that humans rely upon, and air travel is the fastest-growing contributor to the problem. Lonely Planet regards travel, overall, as a global benefit, but believes we all have a responsibility to limit our personal impact on global warming.

FLYING & CLIMATE CHANGE

Pretty much every form of motor travel generates CO_2 (the main cause of human-induced climate change) but planes are far and away the worst offenders, not just because of the sheer distances they allow us to travel, but because they release greenhouse gases high into the atmosphere. The statistics are frightening: two people taking a return flight between Europe and the US will contribute as much to climate change as an average household's gas and electricity consumption over a whole year.

CARBON OFFSET SCHEMES

Climatecare.org and other websites use 'carbon calculators' that allow jetsetters to offset the greenhouse gases they are responsible for with contributions to energy-saving projects and other climate-friendly initiatives in the developing world – including projects in India, Honduras, Kazakhstan and Uganda.

Lonely Planet, together with Rough Guides and other concerned partners in the travel industry, supports the carbon offset scheme run by climatecare.org. Lonely Planet offsets all of its staff and author travel.

For more information check out our website: lonelyplanet.com.

at least 10 crossings (35 minutes) daily between Folkestone and Calais year-round. You pay for the vehicle only and fares vary according to time of day, season and advance purchase, starting at £55 one way.

For breakdown assistance both the British **RAC** (☎ 0800 55 00 55; www.rac.co.uk) and **Automobile Association** (AA; ☎ 0800 085 72 53; www.theaa.com) offer comprehensive cover in Europe. In the USA, contact **AAA** (www.aaa.com), which has an affiliation with ACI in Rome, or contact the automobile association in your own country for more information.

BORDER CROSSINGS

Entering Italy is relatively simple. If you are arriving from a neighbouring EU country, you do not require a passport check. The main points of entry to Italy

are the Mont Blanc Tunnel from France at Chamonix, which connects with the A5 for Turin and Milan; the Grand St Bernard Tunnel from Switzerland, which also connects with the A5; and the Gotthard Tunnel from Switzerland. The brand new, 34km-long Swiss Lötschberg Base Tunnel, the world's longest beneath land, connects with the century-old Simplon Tunnel into Italy. To the east, the Brenner Pass from Austria leads to the A22 to Bologna. All are open year-round. Mountain passes are often closed in winter and sometimes even in autumn and spring, making the tunnels a more reliable option. Make sure you have snow chains if driving in winter.

Every vehicle travelling across an international border should display a valid national licence plate and an accompanying registration card.

DRIVING LICENCES & DOCUMENTATION

All EU member states' driving licences are fully recognised throughout Europe. Drivers with a non-EU licence are supposed to obtain an International Driving Permit (IDP) to accompany their national licence, though copious anecdotal testimonies indicate that this rule is rarely enforced. An IDP, issued by your national automobile association, costs around €12 and is valid for a year. People who have held residency in Italy for one year or more must apply for an Italian driving licence.

INSURANCE

Third-party motor insurance is a minimum requirement in Italy. If your vehicle is registered outside Italy, you need an International Insurance Certificate, also known as a Carta Verde (Green Card); your car-insurance company will issue this. Also ask for a European Accident Statement form, which can simplify matters in the event of an accident. Never sign statements you don't understand – insist on a translation.

SEA

Ferries connect Italy with its islands and countries all over the Mediterranean. However, the only options for reaching Tuscany directly by sea are the ferry crossings to Livorno from Sardinia, Corsica and Sicily. See p160 for more details.

For a comprehensive guide to all ferry services into and out of Italy, check out **Traghettionline** (www.traghettionline.com, in Italian). The website lists every route and includes links to ferry companies, where you can buy tickets or search for deals.

TRAIN

Florence is an important hub, so it's easy to get to Tuscany and Umbria from many points in Europe. The *Thomas Cook European Timetable* has a complete listing of train schedules. It's updated monthly and available from Thomas Cook offices worldwide for about €15 or online at www.thomascookpublishing.com for €14.39. It is always advisable, and sometimes compulsory, to book seats on international trains to and from Italy. Some of the main international services include transport for private cars – an option worth examining to save wear and tear on your vehicle before it arrives in Italy. Consider taking long journeys overnight, as a sleeper fee can cost substantially less than a night in a hotel.

Train timetables at stations generally display *arrivi* (arrivals) on a white background and *partenze* (departures) on a yellow one. Imminent arrivals and departures are also signalled on electronic boards.

Regular trains connect Italy with the main cities in Austria, Germany, France and Eastern Europe. Those crossing the frontier at the Brenner Pass go to Innsbruck, Stuttgart and Munich. Those crossing at Tarvisio in the east proceed to Vienna, Salzburg and Prague. Trains from Milan head for Switzerland, then on into France and the Netherlands. The main international train line to Slovenia crosses near Trieste.

For information on getting around Italy by train, see p438.

GETTING AROUND

Most towns and cities in the region have reasonable bus services, but you'll probably find that amenities and places of interest are usually within walking distance. Buses and trains connect Pisa International Airport with Pisa and

TRANSPORT

Florence, as well as two buses per day to Siena. Buses link Amerigo Vespucci airport, just outside Florence, with central Florence. Buses from Perugia's Piazza Italia coincide with flights at Perugia's Sant'Egidio airport.

BICYCLE

Cycling is a national pastime in Italy. Bikes can be taken on any train that carries the bicycle logo. The cheapest way to do this is to buy a separate bicycle ticket (€3.50, or €5 to €12 on Intercity, Eurostar and Euronight trains), which are available even at the self-service kiosks. You can use this ticket for 24 hours, making a day trip quite economical. Bicycles that are dismantled and stored in a bag can be taken for free, even on night trains, and all ferries allow free bicycle passage.

If you shop around, bargain prices for basic bikes are about €120 for a standard machine to €210 for a mountain bike with 16 gears. Check university bulletin boards for used bicycles.

There are bikes available for rent in most Italian towns and many rental places offer both city and mountain bikes. Rental costs for a city bike start at around €10/40 per day/week.

Check out p371 for more information about cycling around the region. You cannot use bikes on the autostrada (highway).

BOAT

Regular ferries connect Piombino with Elba. On Elba, summertime trips depart from Portoferraio for the island of Capraia, and from both Porto Azzurro and Marina di Campo for the tiny island of Pianosa. From Livorno, ferries run to Capraia via the prison island of Gorgona. See the relevant chapters for more details.

BUS

Although trains are the most convenient and economical way to travel between major towns, a bus is often the best link between small towns and villages. For a few intercity routes, such as the one between Florence and Siena, the bus is your best bet.

Dozens of different companies offer a multiplicity of itineraries. Most reduce or even drop services on holidays and weekends, especially Sundays. Local tourist offices normally carry bus timetables or will call the companies for you.

The Lazzi and CLAP bus companies have merged to make **Vai Bus** (www.vaibus .it, in Italian), which runs services from Florence to parts of Tuscany, mostly in the northwest, including Pisa, Lucca and Pistoia. Note, buses are still sometimes marked as 'Lazzi' and 'CLAP'. **CAP** (www .capautolinee.it, in Italian) serves mainly northwest towns, though it runs one service to Siena. Pisa's **CPT** (Compagnia Pisana Trasporti; ☎ 800 012 773; www.cpt.pisa.it, in Italian) services destinations to that city's west and south. **SITA** (www.sitabus.it, in Italian) and **TRAIN** (☎ 0577 20 41 11; www.trainspa.it) serve Florence, Siena, Chianti, Val d'Elsa, Arezzo and others. In Umbria, look out for the companies ATC and SSIT, which serve southern Umbria, and APM, which covers Perugia, Assisi and the north. **Anglo Info Tuscany** (http://tuscany.angloinfo.com) breaks down bus company routes in English.

You can purchase tickets at most *tabacchi* and newsstands, or from ticket booths and dispensing machines at bus stations; they must be validated in the machine on board. Tickets are also usually available on board for a slightly higher cost. In larger cities, ticket companies often have offices at the bus terminal and some larger cities offer good-value daily tourist tickets.

Turn up on time; in defiance of deep-seated Italian tradition, buses are almost always punctual.

CAR & MOTORCYCLE

The north–south autostrada, signed by a white 'A' followed by a number on a green background, slices through the region. This apart, you'll mostly be driving on the wider web of *strade statali* (main roads). They're represented by 'S', 'SS' or 'SR' and vary from four-lane, toll-free highways to two-lane roads. Even thinner are the *strade provinciali* (main provincial roads), which connect smaller communities, and the string-thin *strade locali* (local roads), which might not even be paved. Seek the latter out; they can often lead to the most enticing, least-frequented places.

When on highways (autostradas), it is mandatory to drive with headlights on.

When driving in Italy always carry proof of vehicle ownership or your rental-car papers. See p446 for a list of common Italian road signs.

AUTOMOBILE ASSOCIATIONS

The **Automobile Club d'Italia** (ACI; www.aci.it, in Italian) is a driver's best resource in Italy. It has a dedicated 24-hour phone line for foreigners looking for emergency assistance, weather conditions or simply tourist information. To reach the ACI in a roadside emergency, dial ☎ 80 31 16 from a land line or ☎ 800 11 68 00 from a mobile phone. Foreigners do not have to join, but instead pay a fee per incident. Having a broken-down vehicle towed to the nearest mechanic's shop will set you back about €150.

FUEL & SPARE PARTS

Italy has a good network of petrol and repair stations. For fuel, you have three choices: *benzina* (petrol), *benzina senza piombo* (unleaded petrol) and *gasolio*

TRANSPORT

DISTANCE CHART (KM)   *Note: Distances between destinations are approximate*

	Arezzo	Assisi	Carrara	Cortona	Florence	Livorno	Lucca	Orbetello	Perugia	Pisa	Pistoia	Prato	Siena	Viareggio
Assisi	96													
Carrara	198	317												
Cortona	29	72	237											
Florence	80	172	122	109										
Livorno	195	266	72	224	115									
Lucca	155	243	56	184	74	45								
Orbetello	175	222	247	215	180	175	216							
Perugia	78	38	256	30	153	268	227	204						
Pisa	175	263	57	203	95	20	23	190	245					
Pistoia	115	208	92	143	35	85	45	215	190	65				
Prato	99	189	109	128	19	95	55	199	170	84	20			
Siena	65	124	153	99	70	130	140	116	109	110	105	81		
Viareggio	180	266	30	206	97	41	25	195	247	21	69	89	123	
Volterra	111	175	135	151	75	69	74	168	161	65	108	88	50	86

TRANSPORT

PASSING

You might call it passing or overtaking, but Italians call it a national pastime. On first glance, it seems as if the overtaker will soon be introduced to an undertaker, but there are actually a few rules in place.

The major hard-and-fast rule is: stay in the right lane unless you're passing or going Italian-driver-on-three-espressos fast!

Italians joke that they don't use their rear-view mirrors when driving. This means that you don't have to either. When a driver is on your tail at 160km/h, it's not your responsibility to pull over or slow down. If they want to pass, they will have to wait until it is safe (or not seriously dangerous) to do so. If they pass when another car is passing on the opposite side of the road, you can manoeuvre gently to the right with a turn signal indicator to allow the cars not to careen into each other, but that's your only choice.

When you pass, make sure you have your left-turn signal on. Wait until the solid yellow middle line turns into dots or dashes. Don't even think about passing on a curve. Oh, yes, and make sure there isn't a car coming from the opposite direction.

(diesel). Petrol costs around €1.30 per litre and diesel a little less, at about €1.15.

For spare parts, check with a repair shop or call the 24-hour ACI motorist assistance number ☎ 803 116. You'll probably be connected to an operator who speaks English.

HIRE

Tourist offices and most hotels can provide information about car or motorcycle rental. To hire a car or motorcycle you need to produce your driving licence.

Car

To rent a car you must be at least 25 years old and have a credit card. Many car-rental agencies expect you to bring the car back with a full tank of petrol and will charge astronomically if you don't. Make sure you understand what is included in the price (unlimited kilometres, tax, insurance, collision damage waiver and so on).

Consider vehicle size carefully. With the extremely narrow streets and limited, tight parking conditions in Italy, smaller is always better.

Following are among the most competitive multinational and Italian car-hire agencies:

Avis (☎ 199 10 01 33; www.avis.com)
Budget (☎ 800 472 33 25; www.budget.com)
Europcar (☎ 199 30 70 30; www.europcar.com)
Hertz (☎ 199 11 22 11; www.hertz.com)
Italy by Car (☎ 091 639 31 20; www.italybycar.it) Partners with Thrifty.
Maggiore (☎ 199 15 11 20; www.maggiore.it) Partners with Alamo and National.

A fun way to get around Italy is by renting a camper van. If you are travelling for more than a few weeks, it can be more cost-effective to buy, then sell the vehicle when you're finished. Check **IdeaMerge** (www.ideamerge.com), where you can lease or buy vehicles.

Motorcycle

You'll have no trouble hiring a small Vespa or scooter. There are numerous rental agencies in cities, where you'll also be able to hire larger motorcycles for touring. The average rental cost for a 50cc scooter is around €20/150 per day/week.

Most agencies will not rent motorcycles to people aged under 18. Many require a sizeable deposit, and you could be responsible for reimbursing part of the cost of the bike if it is stolen.

You don't need a licence to ride a scooter under 50cc. The speed limit is 40km/h, you must be 14 or over and you can't carry passengers. To ride a motorcycle or scooter between 50cc and 125cc, you must be aged 16 or over and have a licence (a car licence will do). For motorcycles over 125cc you will need a motorcycle licence. Helmets are compulsory for motorcyclists and their passengers, whatever the size of the bike.

On a motorcycle, you can ride freely in the heart of cities such as Florence that have restricted traffic areas. Traffic police generally turn a blind eye to motorcycles or scooters parked on footpaths. There is no lights-on requirement for motorcycles in daylight hours.

PARKING

Parking spaces outlined in blue are designated for paid parking. White or yellow outlines almost always indicate reserved parking or that residential permits are needed. You buy your ticket at a machine that's usually a few metres from wherever you've parked and display it in the front window.

ROAD RULES

Italians, like all mainland Europeans, drive on the right-hand side of the road and overtake on the left. On three-lane roads, the middle lane is reserved for overtaking. Unless otherwise indicated, you must always give way to cars entering an intersection from a road on your right.

The driver and all passengers must wear a seatbelt, wherever fitted. If you're caught with it unbuckled, you're in for a hefty, on-the-spot, non-negotiable fine. Children under 12 must travel in the back seat, and those under four must use child seats.

A warning triangle (to be used if you have a breakdown) is also compulsory. Recommended accessories are a first-aid kit, spare-bulb kit and fire extinguisher. If your car breaks down at night, take great care if you get out of the vehicle. You could be fined steeply unless you wear an approved yellow or orange safety vest (available at bicycle shops and outdoor stores).

Traffic police conduct random breath tests and the blood-alcohol limit is 0.05%. If you are involved in an accident while you are under the influence of alcohol, the penalties are severe. Speeding fines are determined by how many kilometres you are caught driving over the speed limit – they can reach up to €260.

Drivers usually travel at high speeds in the left-hand fast lane on the autostradas, so use that lane only if you need to pass other cars. Motoring organisations in various countries have publications that detail road rules for foreign countries. If you get an IDP, it should also include a road rules booklet. The website www.drivingabroad.co.uk has some useful tips and background information for driving in Italy.

SPEED LIMITS

- ★ Urban areas: 50km/h
- ★ Secondary roads: 90km/h
- ★ Main roads: cars 110km/h; caravans 80km/h
- ★ Autostradas: cars 130km/h; caravans 100km/h

TRANSPORT

TOLL ROADS

They're easy to avoid and the scenery is comparatively dire, but traversing parts of Tuscany can be done quickly on toll roads. The A1 (Milan to Rome) passes through Florence and Arezzo (€3.20). The A11 races through the Florence–Lucca (€3.10) and Lucca–Pisa corridor (€0.90). Finally, the A12 connects Pisa and Livorno (€1.30). Tolls vary depending on trip distance – the handy trip calculator at www.viamichelin.com provides prices. For up-to-date information on road tolls and passes, call the **Società Autostrade** (☎ 840 04 21 21; www.autostrade.it) or consult its comprehensive website.

TAXI

You can usually find taxi ranks at train and bus stations, or you can telephone for taxis. It's best to go to a designated taxi stand, as it's illegal for taxis to stop in the street if hailed. If you phone a taxi, bear in mind that the meter starts running from the moment of your call rather than when it picks you up.

TRAIN

The train network throughout Tuscany and Umbria is widespread so you can get to most tourist areas by train, with relatively few exceptions (such as the Chianti region in Tuscany and Monti Sibillini in Umbria). A Regionale or Interregionale train stops at nearly all stations, while faster trains such as the Intercity (IC), call only at major towns and cities.

Reservations are not essential but without one you may not be able to find a seat. They can be made when you buy your ticket, and usually cost an extra €3. You can book at most travel agen-

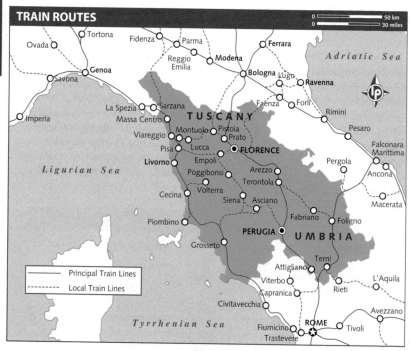

TRAIN ROUTES

0 _____ 50 km
0 _____ 30 miles

Principal Train Lines
Local Train Lines

cies and, in many cases, on the internet. Alternatively, you can buy your ticket on arrival at the station. Most have automatic machines that accept cash and credit cards.

Trenitalia (☎ 800 89 20 21 Italian speaking; www.trenitalia.com) is the partially privatised state train system, which runs most of the services in Italy. We indicate the few other private Italian train lines within relevant destination sections of this book.

In Umbria, there's an extremely helpful free **information source** (☎ 800 53 03 32; www.trasporti.regione.umbria.it) for regional train, bus and ferry details. You will rarely be connected to someone who speaks English, but usually, if you can understand numbers in Italian and tell them the city, they'll patiently tell you the prices and departure times.

CLASSES & COSTS

There are 1st and 2nd classes on most Italian trains; a 1st-class ticket costs just less than double the price of a 2nd-class one. There are special deals for families and group travel.

If you are simply travelling to a town a stop or two up the line, check the difference between the regular and Intercity train prices – you might arrive 10 minutes earlier, but pay €5 or more for the privilege. Check up-to-date prices of routes on www.trenitalia.com.

LEFT LUGGAGE

Most Italian train stations have either a guarded left-luggage office or self-service lockers. The guarded offices are usually open 24 hours or 6am to midnight and charge around €3 per 12 hours for each piece of luggage. In Florence, it's €4 for the first five hours and then €0.60 per hour from six to 12 hours.

VALIDATE!

Almost all train (and several bus) journeys require passengers to validate their tickets *before* boarding – just punch them in the yellow *convalida* machines installed at the entrance to all train platforms. On FCU trains in Umbria, and on local buses and trains run by some private railway companies, you validate your ticket on the bus or train itself. Getting caught freeloading or with a ticket that hasn't been validated risks a fine of up to €50. It's paid on the spot to an inspector who will be kind enough to escort you to an ATM if you don't have the cash on you. Don't even think about trying the *'Ma sono turista!'* line; it won't wash.

TRAIN PASSES

If you're just travelling within Tuscany and Umbria, train travel is inexpensive and a train pass doesn't make financial sense.

If you are planning to travel more widely, Trenitalia offers a variety of passes, including the free **Cartaviaggio Smart**. Armed with this, those aged from 12 to 26 can then buy a **Ticket Sconto Smart**, which has a 10% discount (25% discount for international tickets). If you get the free **Cartaviaggo Relax** and are over 60, you can buy a **Ticket Sconto Relax** (€30, over 75 years free), which entitles you to discounts of 15% on 1st- and 2nd-class tickets and 20% on couchettes. Children aged between four and 12 years are entitled to receive a 50% discount; those who are under four travel free.

The **Trenitalia Pass** (4/6/8/10 days of 2nd-class travel €174/210/246/282) must be used within a two-month period. Only available to nonresidents, it's on sale at all major train stations or through a travel agent in your home country.

LANGUAGE

Italian is a Romance language related to French, Spanish, Portuguese and Romanian. The Romance languages belong to the Indo-European group of languages, which includes English, so you might spot some similarities between English and Italian. In addition, as English has borrowed many words from Romance languages, you will recognise many Italian words.

Modern literary Italian began to develop in the 13th and 14th centuries, predominantly through the works of Dante, Petrarch and Boccaccio – all Tuscans – who wrote chiefly in the Florentine dialect. The language drew on its Latin heritage and many dialects to develop into the standard Italian of today. Although many dialects are spoken in everyday conversation, standard Italian is the national language of schools, media and literature, and is understood throughout the country.

While standard Italian was essentially born out of the Florentine dialect, anyone who has learned Italian sufficiently well will find many Florentines surprisingly hard to understand, at least at first. Whether or not they have their own localised nonstandard vocabulary you could argue about at length, but no one can deny the peculiarity of the local accent. Here, and in other parts of Tuscany, you are bound to hear the hard 'c' pronounced as a heavily aspirated 'h'. *Voglio una cannuccia per la Coca Cola* (I want a straw for my Coca Cola) in Florence sounds more like *Voglio una hannuccia per la Hoha Hola.* Over the regional border in Umbria, you'll be spared the peculiarities of Tuscan pronunciation, and understanding the local accent should be a lot easier.

GRAMMAR

You need to be aware that many older Italians still expect to be addressed in the third-person polite form, *Lei,* instead of *tu.* (Using *Lei* is a bit like in royal dramas in English where a king or queen is addressed directly as 'he/she', 'his/her majesty' etc, rather than 'you', 'your majesty', etc.) It is also not good form to use the greeting *ciao* when addressing strangers, unless they use it first; it's better to say *buongiorno* (or *buonasera*, as the case may be) and *arrivederci* (or the more polite form, *arrivederla*). We've used the polite address for most of the phrases in this guide. Use of the informal address is indicated by (inf).

Like other Latin-based languages, Italian has both masculine and feminine forms (in the singular they often end in 'o' and 'a' respectively). Where both forms are given in this guide, they are separated by a slash, with the masculine form first.

If you'd like a more comprehensive guide to the language, pick up a copy of Lonely Planet's *Italian Phrasebook*.

PRONUNCIATION

VOWELS

Vowel are pronounced shorter in unstressed syllables; longer, in stressed, open syllables:

a	as in 'art', eg *caro* (dear); sometimes short, eg *amico* (friend)
e	short, as in 'let', eg *mettere* (to put); long, as in 'there', eg *vero* (true)
i	short, as in 'it', eg *inizio* (start); long, as in 'marine', eg *vino* (wine)
o	short, as in 'dot', eg *donna* (woman); long, as in 'port', eg *ora* (hour)
u	as the 'oo' in 'book', eg *puro* (pure)

CONSONANTS

The pronunciation of many Italian consonants is similar to that of their English counterparts. Pronunciation of some consonants depends on certain rules.

c	as the 'k' in 'kit' before a, o, u and h; as the 'ch' in 'choose' before e and i
g	as the 'g' in 'get' before a, o, u and h; as the 'j' in 'jet' before e and i
gli	as the 'lli' in 'million'
gn	as the 'ny' in 'canyon'
h	always silent (ie not pronounced)
r	a rolled 'r' sound
sc	as 'sk' before a, o, u and h; as the 'sh' in 'sheep' before e and i
z	at the beginning of a word, as the 'dz' in 'adze'; elsewhere, as the 'ts' in 'its'

Note that when *ci*, *gi* and *sci* are followed by a, o or u, the 'i' is not pronounced unless the accent falls on the 'i'. Thus the name 'Giovanni' is pronounced jo·*va*·nee.

A double consonant is pronounced as a longer, more forceful sound than a single consonant. This can directly affect the meaning of a word, eg *sono* (I am), *sonno* (sleep).

WORD STRESS

Stress is indicated in our pronunciation guide by italics. Word stress generally falls on the second-last syllable, as in *spaghetti* (spa·*ge*·tee), but when a word has an accent, the stress falls on that syllable, as in *città* (chee·*ta*), meaning 'city'.

ACCOMMODATION

I'm looking for a ...	*Cerco ...*	cher·ko ...
guest house	*una pensione*	oo·na pen·*syo*·ne
hotel	*un albergo*	oon al·*ber*·go
youth hostel	*un ostello per la gioventù*	oon os·*te*·lo per la jo·ven·*too*

Where is a cheap hotel?
Dov'è un albergo a buon prezzo? — do·*ve* oon al·*ber*·go a bwon *pre*·tso
What is the address?
Qual'è l'indirizzo? — kwa·*le* leen·dee·*ree*·tso

Could you write the address, please?
Può scrivere l'indirizzo,   pwo skree·ve·re leen·dee·ree·tso
per favore?   per fa·vo·re
Do you have any rooms available?
Avete camere libere?   a·ve·te ka·me·re lee·be·re

I'd like (a) …	Vorrei …	vo·ray …
bed	un letto	oon le·to
single room	una camera	oo·na ka·me·ra
	singola	seen·go·la
room with two	una camera	oo·na ka·me·ra
beds	doppia	do·pya
double room	una camera	oo·na ka·me·ra
	matrimoniale	ma·tree·mo·nya·le
room with a	una camera	oo·na ka·me·ra
bathroom	con bagno	kon ba·nyo
to share a	un letto in	oon le·to een
dorm	dormitorio	dor·mee·to·ryo

How much is it …?	Quanto costa …?	kwan·to ko·sta …
per night	per la notte	per la no·te
per person	per persona	per per·so·na

May I see it?
Posso vederla?   po·so ve·der·la
Where is the bathroom?
Dov'è il bagno?   do·ve eel ba·nyo
I'm/We're leaving today.
Parto/Partiamo oggi.   par·to/par·tya·mo o·jee

CONVERSATION & ESSENTIALS

Hello.	Buongiorno.	bwon·jor·no
	Ciao. (inf)	chow
Goodbye.	Arrivederci.	a·ree·ve·der·chee
	Ciao. (inf)	chow
Good evening.	Buonasera.	bwo·na·se·ra
(from early afternoon onwards)		
Good night.	Buonanotte.	bwo·na·no·te
Yes.	Sì.	see
No.	No.	no
Please.	Per favore.	per fa·vo·re
	Per piacere.	per pya·chay·re
Excuse me.	Mi scusi.	mee skoo·zee
Thank you.	Grazie.	gra·tsye

LANGUAGE

MAKING A RESERVATION

Use these expressions in letters, faxes and emails:

To …	A …
From …	Da …
Date	Data
I'd like to book …	Vorrei prenotare …
in the name of …	in nome di …
for the night(s) of …	per la/le notte/i di …
credit card (…)	(…) carta di credito
number	numero della
expiry date	data di scadenza della
Please confirm availability and price.	Prego confirmare disponibilità e prezzo.

That's fine./ You're welcome.	Prego.	pre·go
Sorry (forgive me).	Mi scusi./ Mi perdoni.	mee skoo·zee/ mee per·do·nee

What's your name?
Come si chiama?   ko·me see kya·ma
Come ti chiami? (inf)   ko·me tee kya·mee
My name is …
Mi chiamo …   mee kya·mo …
Where are you from?
Da dove viene?   da do·ve vye·ne
Di dove sei? (inf)   dee do·ve se·ee
I'm from …
Vengo da …   ven·go da …
I (don't) like …
(Non) Mi piace …   (non) mee pya·che …
Just a minute.
Un momento.   oon mo·men·to

DIRECTIONS

Where is …?
Dov'è …?   do·ve …
Go straight ahead.
Si va sempre diritto.   see va sem·pre dee·ree·to
Vai sempre diritto. (inf)   vai sem·pre dee·ree·to
Turn left.
Giri a sinistra.   jee·ree a see·nee·stra

Turn right.
Giri a destra.   *jee·ree a de·stra*
at the next corner
al prossimo angolo   *al pro·see·mo an·go·lo*
at the traffic lights
al semaforo   *al se·ma·fo·ro*

behind	*dietro*	*dye·tro*
in front of	*davanti*	*da·van·tee*
far (from)	*lontano (da)*	*lon·ta·no (da)*
near (to)	*vicino (di)*	*vee·chee·no (dee)*
opposite	*di fronte a*	*dee fron·te a*
beach	*la spiaggia*	*la spya·ja*
bridge	*il ponte*	*eel pon·te*
castle	*il castello*	*eel kas·te·lo*
cathedral	*il duomo*	*eel dwo·mo*
island	*l'isola*	*lee·so·la*
(main) square	*la piazza*	*la pya·tsa*
	(principale)	*(preen·chee·pa·le)*
market	*il mercato*	*eel mer·ka·to*
old city	*il centro*	*eel chen·tro*
	storico	*sto·ree·ko*
palace	*il palazzo*	*eel pa·la·tso*
ruins	*le rovine*	*le ro·vee·ne*
sea	*il mare*	*eel ma·re*
tower	*la torre*	*la to·re*

EATING OUT

I'd like …, please.
Vorrei . . . , per favore.   *vo·ray … per fa·vo·re*
That was delicious!
Era squisito!   *e·ra skwee·zee·to*
I don't eat (fish).
Non mangio (pesce).   *non man·jo (pe·she)*
Please bring the bill.
Mi porta il conto,   *mee por·ta eel kon·to*
per favore?   *per fa·vo·re*

I'm allergic to …	*Sono allergico/a*	*so·no a·ler·jee·ko/a*
	… (m/f)	*…*
dairy produce	*ai latticini*	*ai la·tee·chee·nee*
eggs	*alle uova*	*a·le wo·va*
nuts	*alle noci*	*a·le no·chee*
seafood	*ai frutti di*	*ai froo·tee dee*
	mare	*ma·re*

SIGNS	
Aperto	Open
Chiuso	Closed
Gabinetti/Bagni	Toilets
Uomini	Men
Donne	Women
Informazione	Information
Ingresso/Entrata	Entrance
Polizia/Carabinieri	Police
Proibito/Vietato	Prohibited
Questura	Police Station
Uscita	Exit

HEALTH

I'm ill.
Mi sento male.   *mee sen·to ma·le*
It hurts here.
Mi fa male qui.   *mee fa ma·le kwee*
I need a doctor who speaks English.
Ho bisogno di un medico   *o bee·zo·nyo dee oon me·dee·ko*
(che parli inglese).   *(ke par·lee een·gle·ze)*

I'm …	*Sono …*	*so·no …*
asthmatic	*asmatico/a* (m/f)	*az·ma·tee·ko/a*
diabetic	*diabetico/a* (m/f)	*dee·a·be·tee·ko/a*
epileptic	*epilettico/a* (m/f)	*e·pee·le·tee·ko/a*
I'm allergic …	*Sono*	*so·no*
	allergico/a … (m/f)	*a·ler·jee·ko/a …*
to antibiotics	*agli antibiotici*	*a·lyee an·tee·bee·o·tee·chee*
to aspirin	*all'aspirina*	*a·la·spe·ree·na*
to penicillin	*alla penicillina*	*a·la pe·nee·see·lee·na*
antiseptic	*antisettico*	*an·tee·se·tee·ko*
aspirin	*aspirina*	*as·pee·ree·na*
condoms	*preservativi*	*pre·zer·va·tee·vee*
contraceptive	*contraccetivo*	*kon·tra·che·tee·vo*
diarrhoea	*diarrea*	*dee·a·re·a*
medicine	*medicina*	*me·dee·chee·na*
sunblock cream	*crema solare*	*kre·ma so·la·re*
tampons	*tamponi*	*tam·po·nee*

LANGUAGE

LANGUAGE DIFFICULTIES

Do you speak English?

Parla inglese? — par·la een·gle·ze

Does anyone here speak English?

C'è qualcuno che — che kwal·koo·no ke
parla inglese? — par·la een·gle·ze

How do you say ... in Italian?

Come si dice ... — ko·me see dee·che ...
in italiano? — een ee·ta·lya·no

What does ... mean?

Che vuol dire ...? — ke vwol dee·re ...

I understand.

Capisco. — ka·pee·sko

I don't understand.

Non capisco. — non ka·pee·sko

Please write it down.

Può scriverlo, per — pwo skree·ver·lo per
favore. — fa·vo·re

Can you show me (on the map)?

Può mostrarmelo — pwo mos·trar·me·lo
(sulla pianta)? — (soo·la pyan·ta)

NUMBERS

0	zero	dze·ro
1	uno	oo·no
2	due	doo·e
3	tre	tre
4	quattro	kwa·tro
5	cinque	cheen·kwe
6	sei	say
7	sette	se·te
8	otto	o·to
9	nove	no·ve
10	dieci	dye·chee
11	undici	oon·dee·chee
12	dodici	do·dee·chee
13	tredici	tre·dee·chee
14	quattordici	kwa·tor·dee·chee
15	quindici	kween·dee·chee
16	sedici	se·dee·chee
17	diciassette	dee·cha·se·te
18	diciotto	dee·cho·to

LANGUAGE

EMERGENCIES

Help!

Aiuto! — a·yoo·to

There's been an accident!

C'è stato un — che sta·to oon
incidente! — een·chee·den·te

I'm lost.

Mi sono perso/a. (m/f) — mee so·no per·so/a

Go away!

Lasciami in pace! — la·sha·mi een pa·che
Vai via! (inf) — vai vee·a

Call ...!	Chiami ...!	kee·ya·mee ...
	Chiama ...! (inf)	kee·ya·ma ...
a doctor	un dottore/	oon do·to·re/
	un medico	oon me·dee·ko
the police	la polizia	la po·lee·tsee·ya

19	diciannove	dee·cha·no·ve
20	venti	ven·tee
21	ventuno	ven·too·no
22	ventidue	ven·tee·doo·e
30	trenta	tren·ta
40	quaranta	kwa·ran·ta
50	cinquanta	cheen·kwan·ta
60	sessanta	se·san·ta
70	settanta	se·tan·ta
80	ottanta	o·tan·ta
90	novanta	no·van·ta
100	cento	chen·to
1000	mille	mee·le

PAPERWORK

name	nome	no·me
nationality	nazionalità	na·tsyo·na·lee·ta
date of birth	data di	da·ta dee
	nascita	na·shee·ta
place of birth	luogo di	lwo·go dee
	nascita	na·shee·ta
sex (gender)	sesso	se·so
passport	passaporto	pa·sa·por·to
visa	visto	vee·sto

QUESTION WORDS

Who?	Chi?	kee
What?	Che?	ke
When?	Quando?	kwan·do
Where?	Dove?	do·ve
How?	Come?	ko·me

SHOPPING & SERVICES

I'd like to buy …
Vorrei comprare … vo·ray kom·pra·re …
How much is it?
Quanto costa? kwan·to ko·sta
I don't like it.
Non mi piace. non mee pya·che
May I look at it?
Posso dare un'occhiata? po·so da·re oo·no·kya·ta
I'm just looking.
Sto solo guardando. sto so·lo gwar·dan·do
It's cheap.
Non è caro/a. (m/f) non e ka·ro/a
It's too expensive.
È troppo caro/a. (m/f) e tro·po ka·ro/a
I'll take it.
Lo/La compro. (m/f) lo/la kom·pro
Do you accept credit cards?
Accettate carte a·che·ta·te kar·te
di credito? dee kre·dee·to

more	più	pyoo
less	meno	me·no
smaller	più piccolo/a (m/f)	pyoo pee·ko·lo/a
bigger	più grande	pyoo gran·de

I'm looking for … *Cerco …* cher·ko …
an ATM	un Bancomat	oon ban·ko·mat
a bank	un banco	oon ban·ko
the church	la chiesa	la kye·za
the city centre	il centro	eel chen·tro
the market	il mercato	eel mer·ka·to
the museum	il museo	eel moo·ze·o
the post office	la posta	la po·sta
a public toilet	un gabinetto	oon ga·bee·ne·to
the tourist office	l'ufficio di turismo	loo·fee·cho dee too·reez·mo

I want to change … *Voglio cambiare …* vo·lyo kam·bya·re …
money	del denaro	del de·na·ro
travellers cheques	assegni dee viaggio	a·se·nyee dee vee·a·jo

TIME & DATES

What time is it?
Che ore sono? ke o·re so·no
It's (one o'clock).
È (l'una). e (loo·na)
It's (eight o'clock).
Sono (le otto). so·no (le o·to)
Half past (one).
(L'una) e mezza. (loo·na) e me·dza

today	oggi	o·jee
tomorrow	domani	do·ma·nee
yesterday	ieri	ye·ree
in the morning	di mattina	dee ma·tee·na
in the afternoon	di pomeriggio	dee po·me·ree·jo
in the evening	di sera	dee se·ra
Monday	lunedì	loo·ne·dee
Tuesday	martedì	mar·te·dee
Wednesday	mercoledì	mer·ko·le·dee
Thursday	giovedì	jo·ve·dee
Friday	venerdì	ve·ner·dee
Saturday	sabato	sa·ba·to
Sunday	domenica	do·me·nee·ka
January	gennaio	je·na·yo
February	febbraio	fe·bra·yo
March	marzo	mar·tso
April	aprile	a·pree·le
May	maggio	ma·jo
June	giugno	joo·nyo
July	luglio	loo·lyo
August	agosto	a·gos·to
September	settembre	se·tem·bre
October	ottobre	o·to·bre
November	novembre	no·vem·bre
December	dicembre	dee·chem·bre

LANGUAGE

TRANSPORT

PUBLIC TRANSPORT

What time does the ... leave/ arrive?	*A che ora parte/ arriva ...?*	a ke o·ra par·te/ a·ree·va ...
(city) bus	*l'autobus*	low·to·boos
(intercity) bus	*il pullman*	eel pool·man
plane	*l'aereo*	la·e·re·o
train	*il treno*	eel tre·no

I'd like a ... ticket.	*Vorrei un biglietto ...*	vo·ray oon bee·lye·to ...
one way	*di solo andata*	dee so·lo an·da·ta
return	*di andata e ritorno*	dee an·da·ta e ree·toor·no
1st class	*di prima classe*	dee pree·ma kla·se
2nd class	*di seconda classe*	dee se·kon·da kla·se

I want to go to ...
Voglio andare a ...   vo·lyo an·da·re a ...
The train has been cancelled/delayed.
Il treno è soppresso/   eel tre·no e so·pre·so/
in ritardo.   een ree·tar·do

the first	*il primo*	eel pree·mo
the last	*l'ultimo*	lool·tee·mo
platform (2)	*binario (due)*	bee·na·ryo (doo·e)
ticket office	*biglietteria*	bee·lye·te·ree·a
timetable	*orario*	o·ra·ryo
train station	*stazione*	sta·tsyo·ne

PRIVATE TRANSPORT

I'd like to hire a/an ...	*Vorrei noleggiare ...*	vo·ray no·le·ja·re ...
car	*una macchina*	oo·na ma·kee·na
4WD	*un fuoristrada*	oon fwo·ree·stra·da
motorbike	*una moto*	oo·na mo·to
bicycle	*una bici(cletta)*	oo·na bee·chee·(kle·ta)

diesel	*gasolio/diesel*	ga·zo·lyo/dee·zel
petrol	*benzina*	ben·dzee·na

ROAD SIGNS

Dare la Precedenza	Give Way
Deviazione	Detour
Divieto di Accesso	No Entry
Divieto di Sorpasso	No Overtaking
Divieto di Sosta	No Parking
Entrata	Entrance
Incrocio	Intersection/ Crossroads
Lavori in Corso	Roadworks Ahead
Parcheggio	Car Park
Passaggio a Livello	Level Crossing
Passo Carrabile/Carraio	Keep Clear
Pedaggio	Toll
Pericolo	Danger
Rallentare	Slow Down
Senso Unico	One Way
Senso Vietato	No Entry
Sosta Autorizzata	Parking Permitted (during times displayed)
Sosta Vietata	No Stopping/Parking
Svolta	Bend
Tutte le Direzioni	All Directions (useful when trying to find a way out of town)
Uscita	Exit

Where's a service station?
Dov'è una stazione   do·ve oo·na sta·tsyo·ne
di servizio?   dee ser·vee·tsyo
Please fill it up.
Il pieno, per favore.   eel pye·no per fa·vo·re
I'd like (30) litres.
Vorrei (trenta) litri.   vo·ray (tren·ta) lee·tree
Is this the road to ...?
Questa strada porta   kwe·sta stra·da por·ta
a ...?   a ...
What's the speed limit?
Qual'è il limite di   kwa·le eel lee·mee·te dee
velocità?   ve·lo·chee·ta
(How long) Can I park here?
(Per quanto tempo)   (per kwan·to tem·po)
Posso parcheggiare qui?   po·so par·ke·ja·re kwee

Where do I pay?

Dove si paga? do·ve see pa·ga

I need a mechanic.

Ho bisogno di un o bee·zo·nyo dee oon

meccanico. me·ka·nee·ko

The car/motorbike has broken down (at …).

La macchina/moto la ma·kee·na/mo·to

si è guastata (a …). see e gwas·ta·ta (a …)

The car/motorbike won't start.

La macchina/moto la ma·kee·na/mo·to

non parte. non par·te

I have a flat tyre.

Ho una gomma bucata. o oo·na go·ma boo·ka·ta

I've run out of petrol.

Ho esaurito la benzina. o e·zo·ree·to la ben·dzee·na

I've had an accident.

Ho avuto un incidente. o a·voo·to oon een·chee·den·te

	formula (infant milk)	*latte in polvere*	la·te in pol·ve·re
an (English-speaking) babysitter	*un/una*	oon/oo·na	
	baby-sitter (che parli inglese) (m/f)	be·bee·see·ter (ke par·lee een·gle·ze)	
a highchair	*un seggiolone*	oon se·jo·lo·ne	
a potty	*un vasino*	oon va·zee·no	
a stroller	*un passeggino*	oon pa·se·jee·no	

Do you mind if I breastfeed here?

Le dispiace se allatto le dees·pya·che se a·la·to

il/la bimbo/a qui? (m/f) eel/la beem·bo/a kwee

Are children allowed?

I bambini sono ee bam·bee·nee so·no

ammessi? a·me·see

TRAVEL WITH CHILDREN

Is there …?

C'è …? che …

I need …

Ho bisogno di … o bee·zo·nyo dee …

a baby change room	*un bagno con fasciatoio*	oon ba·nyo kon fa·sha·to·yo
a car baby seat	*un seggiolino per bambini*	oon se·jo·lee·no per bam·bee·nee
a child-minding service	*un servizio di baby-sitter*	oon ser·vee·tsyo dee be·bee·see·ter
a children's menu	*un menù per bambini*	oon me·noo per bam·bee·nee
(disposable) nappies/diapers	*pannolini (usa e getta)*	pa·no·lee·nee (oo·sa e je·ta)

Also available from Lonely Planet:

Italian phrasebook

LANGUAGE

GLOSSARY

abbazia – abbey
aeroporto – airport
affittacamere – rooms for rent in private houses (relatively inexpensive and not part of the classification system)
agriturismo – farm-stay accommodation
albergo – hotel
alimentari – grocery shop
alloggio – lodging (relatively inexpensive and not part of the classification system)
alto – high
ambulanza – ambulance
anfiteatro – amphitheatre
antipasto – preliminary course
aperitivo – predinner drink, often accompanied by snacks
appartamento – apartment, flat
arco – arch
autobus – local bus
autostazione – bus station/terminal
autostop – hitching
autostrada – motorway, highway

baldacchino – canopy supported by columns over the altar in a church

basilica – Christian church with a rectangular hall, aisles and an apse at the end
battistero – baptistry
benzina – petrol
biblioteca – library
bicicletta – bicycle
biglietteria – ticket office
biglietto – ticket
biglietto cumulativo – combined ticket that allows entrance to a number of associated sights
binario – platform
borgo – ancient town or village

cabinovia – two-seater cable car
caffetiera – cafeteria
calcio – football
camera doppia – room with twin beds
camera matrimoniale – double room with a double bed
camera singola – single room
campanile – bell tower
campeggio – camping
campo – field
cantinetta – small cellar where wine is served

cappella – chapel
carabinieri – military police
carnevale – carnival period between Epiphany and Lent
carta d'identità – identity card
carta telefonica – phonecard (also *scheda telefonica*)
cartolina (postale) – postcard
casa – house, home
castello – castle
cattedrale – cathedral
cava – quarry
cena – evening meal
centesimi – cents
centro – city centre
centro storico – (literally, 'historical centre') old town
chiaroscuro – (literally, 'light-dark') artistic distribution of light and dark areas in a painting
chiesa – church
chiostro – cloister; a covered walkway around a quadrangle, which is usually enclosed by columns
circo – oval or circular arena
colle – hill
colonna – column
comune – equivalent to a municipality; town or city council; historically, a commune (self-governing town or city)
contado – district around a major town (the area surrounding Florence was known as the *contado di Firenze*)
contrada – town district
convalida – ticket-stamping machine
coperto – cover charge
corso – main street, avenue
cortile – courtyard
cupola – dome

deposito bagagli – left luggage
distributore di benzina – petrol pump (see also *stazione di servizio*)
dolce – sweet; also dessert course
duomo – cathedral

enoteca – wine bar (see also *fiaschetteria* and *vinaino*)

farmacia – pharmacy
fattoria – farmhouse
ferrovia – train station
festa – festival
fiaschetteria – small tavern serving wine and snacks (see also *enoteca* and *vinaino*)
fiore – flower
fiume – river
fontana – fountain
forno – bakery
foro – forum
francobollo – postage stamp
fresco – painting method in which watercolour paint is applied to wet plaster
funicolare – funicular railway
funivia – cable car

gabinetto – toilet, WC
gelateria – ice-cream shop
golfo – gulf
grisaille – technique of monochrome painting in shades of grey
grotta – cave
guardia di finanza – fiscal police

HI – Hostelling International

intarsio – inlaid wood, marble or metal
isola – island

lago – lake
largo – (small) square
lavanderia – laundrette
lavasecco – dry-cleaning
lettera – letter
libreria – bookshop
lido – beach
locanda – inn, small hotel (relatively inexpensive and not part of the classification system)

loggia – covered area on the side of a building; porch
lungomare – seafront road, promenade

macchia – scrub, bush
macelleria – butcher shop
mare – sea
mausoleo – mausoleum; stately and magnificent tomb
mercato – market
monte – mountain, mount
motorino – scooter
municipio – town hall
museo – museum

navata centrale – nave; central part of a church
navata laterale – aisle of a church
nave – ship
necropoli – (ancient) cemetery, burial site

oggetti smarriti – lost property
ostello per la gioventù – youth hostel
osteria – casual tavern or eatery presided over by a host

palazzo – palace; a large building of any type, including an apartment block
parcheggio – car park
parco – park
passaggio ponte – deck class
passeggiata – traditional evening stroll
pasticceria – shop selling cakes and pastries
pensione – small hotel
permesso di lavoro – work permit
permesso di soggiorno – residence permit
piazza – square
piazzale – (large) open square
pietà – (literally, 'pity' or 'compassion') sculpture, drawing or painting of the dead Christ supported by Madonna

pietra serena – Greenish-grey 'serene stone'
pinacoteca – art gallery
piscina – pool
poltrona – (literally, 'armchair') airline-type chair on a ferry
polyptych – altarpiece consisting of more than three panels (see also *triptych*)
ponte – bridge
porta – door, city gate
portico – walkway, often on the outside of buildings
porto – port
presepio – nativity scene
primo – first course
profumeria – perfumery
pronto soccorso – first aid

questura – police station

rifugio – mountain hut, alpine refuge
rocca – fort
rustica – rural

sacristy – room in church where the sacred vessels, vestments etc are kept
sagra – festival (usually with a culinary theme)
sala – room in a museum or a gallery
santuario – sanctuary
scalinata – flight of stairs
scavi – excavations
scheda telefonica – phonecard
secondo – second course
servizio – service fee
sfumato – shading built up with layers of translucent colour instead of hard lines; used in painting
sgraffito – a surface covered with plaster, then scratched away to create a three-dimensional trompe-l'oeil effect of carved stone or brick
spiaggia – beach
spiaggia libera – public beach

spolia – creative reuse of old monuments in new structures
stazione – station
stazione di servizio – service/petrol station (see also *distributore di benzina*)
stazione marittima – ferry terminal
strada – street, road
superstrada – expressway; highway with divided lanes (but no tolls)

tabaccheria/tabaccaio – tobacconist's shop/tobacconist
teatro – theatre
telefonino – mobile phone
tempio – temple
terme – thermal bath
tesoro – treasury
torre – tower
torrente – stream
traghetto – ferry
trattoria – simple restaurant
triptych – painting or carving over three panels, hinged so that the outer panels fold over the middle one, often used as an altarpiece (see also *polyptych*)

ufficio postale – post office
ufficio stranieri – (police) foreigners' bureau
uffizi – offices

via – street, road
via aerea – airmail
vicoli – alley, alleyway
vigili urbani – traffic police, local police
vinaino – wine bar (see also *enoteca* and *fiaschetteria*)

ZTL – (Zona a Traffico Limitato) Limited Traffic Zone

BEHIND THE SCENES

THIS BOOK

This 6th edition was updated by Virginia Maxwell, Alex Leviton and Leif Pettersen. The previous edition was updated by Nicola Williams, Alison Bing, Alex Leviton, Leif Pettersen and Miles Roddis. This guidebook was commissioned in Lonely Planet's London office, and produced in Melbourne by the following:

Commissioning Editor Paula Hardy
Coordinating Editor Susan Paterson
Coordinating Cartographer Andrew Smith
Coordinating Layout Designer Carol Jackson
Managing Editors Imogen Bannister, Laura Stansfeld
Managing Cartographers Alison Lyall, Herman So
Managing Layout Designer Sally Darmody
Assisting Editors Jackey Coyle, Barbara Delissen, Melissa Faulkner, Charlotte Harrison, Sally O'Brien, Kirsten Rawlings, Gabrielle Stefanos
Assisting Cartographers Ross Butler, Alex Leung, Ross Macaw, Amanda Sierp
Cover Research Marika Mercer, lonelyplanetimages.com
Internal Image Research Aude Vauconsant, lonelyplanetimages.com
Language Content Robyn Loughnane
Project Manager Rachel Imeson
Thanks to Mark Adams, Lucy Birchley, Yvonne Bischofberger, Jessica Boland, Eoin Dunlevy, Janine Eberle, Owen

THE LONELY PLANET STORY

Fresh from an epic journey across Europe, Asia and Australia in 1972, Tony and Maureen Wheeler sat at their kitchen table stapling together notes. The first Lonely Planet guidebook, *Across Asia on the Cheap*, was born.

Travellers snapped up the guides. Inspired by their success, the Wheelers began publishing books to Southeast Asia, India and beyond. Demand was prodigious, and the Wheelers expanded the business rapidly to keep up. Over the years, Lonely Planet extended its coverage to every country and into the virtual world via lonelyplanet.com and the Thorn Tree message board.

As Lonely Planet became a globally loved brand, Tony and Maureen received several offers for the company. But it wasn't until 2007 that they found a partner whom they trusted to remain true to the company's principles of travelling widely, treading lightly and giving sustainably. In October of that year, BBC Worldwide acquired a 75% share in the company, pledging to uphold Lonely Planet's commitment to independent travel, trustworthy advice and editorial independence.

Today, Lonely Planet has offices in Melbourne, London and Oakland, with over 500 staff members and 300 authors. Tony and Maureen are still actively involved with Lonely Planet. They're travelling more often than ever, and they're devoting their spare time to charitable projects. And the company is still driven by the philosophy of *Across Asia on the Cheap*: 'All you've got to do is decide to go and the hardest part is over. So go!'

Eszeki, Ryan Evans, Mark Germanchis, Michelle Glynn, Imogen Hall, James Hardy, Aomi Hongo, Lauren Hunt, Paul Iacono, Laura Jane, Nic Lehman, John Mazzocchi, Annelies Mertens, Lucy Monie, Wayne Murphy, Darren O'Connell, Naomi Parker, Trent Paton, Julie Sheridan, John Taufa, Glenn van der Knijff, Juan Winata

THANKS

VIRGINIA MAXWELL

Greatest thanks and much love go to Max, who once again accompanied me on an Italy jaunt for Lonely Planet. And thanks and love to Peter for looking after things at home in Australia. Thanks to my fellow authors Leif Pettersen and Alex Leviton, who shared their expertise and contacts with great generosity. In Italy, many thanks to the extraordinarily helpful Ilaria Crescioli at Toscana Promozione, Roberta Berni from APT Florence, Giuseppe Magni, Marco Secci, Freya Middleton and Filippo Giabboni, Jane Morrow, Anna Rita Merlini from APT Pistoia, Antonella Giusti from APT Lucca, Linda Secoli from APT Massa-Carrara, Nadia Ferrini, Tania Pasquinelli from APT Montecatini Terme, Michele and Christa Giuttari, Fabrizio Quochi and Ilaria Antolini from APT Pisa, Carlo in Lucca, Vincenzo Riolo, Martin Rothweiler, Marzia Vaccaro from San Miniato Promozione, and Sandra and Letizia from APT Versilia. At Lonely Planet London, many thanks to Paula Hardy. At Lonely Planet Melbourne, thanks to the expert and unflappable team of Rachel Imeson, Herman So, Susan Paterson and Andrew Smith.

ALEX LEVITON

Alex would like to thank her fabulous travel companions/sherpas Lenny 'Il Muffino' Amaral (Lonely Planet assignment seven-timer) and fellow Lonely Planeteer Becca Blond. Jennifer Brunson and Scott Leviton deserve kudos as the kick-ass support team. Alex would also like to thank her wonderful friends and impromptu tour guides Carlo Rocchi Bilancini, Zach Nowak, Federico Bibi and Jennifer McIlvaine, Mario, Santoro and the folks at CSB. Thanks to the tourist offices that aren't horrendous – Spoleto, Assisi and Deruta. Fellow authors Leif Pettersen and Virginia Maxwell stun me with their innate helpfulness, and Susan Paterson and Kirsten Rawlings were the icing on the editorial cake. Plus, a huge debt of gratitude goes to Julia Pond for reining me in. *Tante grazie!*

LEIF PETTERSEN

Heartfelt thanks goes to all the Toscana Promozione folks that met with me and lent their considerable help: Ilaria Crescioli in Florence, Giovanni d'Agliano in Livorno, Cecilia Rosa in Massa Marittima, and Carlo Eugeni in Portoferraio. Paul Brady for his exhaustive proofing and editorial consulting. My *Tuscany & Umbria* cohorts Virginia Maxwell and Alex Leviton. Katie Mardis for the company and letting me taste all her food, despite the very real fear of cooties. Paula Hardy in London. Both of the people that complimented me on my Italian skills. Whoever invented wi-fi and the Blackberry Curve.

OUR READERS

Many thanks to the travellers who used the last edition and wrote to us with helpful hints, useful advice and interesting anecdotes:
Margo Armishaw, Larry Bieber, Nicolas Combremont, Guus Dekking,

SEND US YOUR FEEDBACK

We love to hear from travellers – your comments keep us on our toes and help make our books better. Our well-travelled team reads every word on what you loved or loathed about this book. Although we cannot reply individually to postal submissions, we always guarantee that your feedback goes straight to the appropriate authors, in time for the next edition. Each person who sends us information is thanked in the next edition – and the most useful submissions are rewarded with a free book.

To send us your updates – and find out about Lonely Planet events, newsletters and travel news – visit our award-winning website: **lonelyplanet.com/contact**.

Note: We may edit, reproduce and incorporate your comments in Lonely Planet products such as guidebooks, websites and digital products, so let us know if you don't want your comments reproduced or your name acknowledged. For a copy of our privacy policy visit lonelyplanet.com/privacy.

Manfred Horn, Ori Kalid, Kristine Lawton, Catherine Markey, Weia Reinboud, Daniel Rodríguez San José, Toon Van Geet

ACKNOWLEDGMENTS

All images are the copyright of the photographers unless otherwise indicated. Many of the images in this guide are available for licensing from Lonely Planet Images: lonelyplanetimages.com.

INDEX

INDEX

INDEX

INDEX

O

P

000 MAP PAGES
000 PHOTOGRAPH PAGES

INDEX

000 MAP PAGES
000 PHOTOGRAPH PAGES

INDEX

MAP LEGEND

Note Not all symbols displayed below appear in this guide.

ROUTES

- Tollway
- Freeway
- Primary Road
- Secondary Road
- Tertiary Road
- Lane
- Unsealed Road
- Under Construction
- Tunnel
- Pedestrian Mall
- Steps
- Walking Track
- Walking Path
- Walking Tour
- Walking Tour Detour
- Pedestrian Overpass

TRANSPORT

- Ferry Route & Terminal
- Metro Line & Station
- Monorail & Stop
- Bus Route & Stop
- Train Line & Station
- Underground Rail Line
- Tram Line & Stop
- Cable Car, Funicular

AREA FEATURES

- Airport
- Beach
- Building
- Campus
- Cemetery, Christian
- Cemetery, Other
- Land
- Mall, Plaza
- Market
- Park
- Sportsground
- Urban

HYDROGRAPHY

- River, Creek
- Canal
- Water
- Swamp
- Lake (Dry)

BOUNDARIES

- International
- State, Provincial
- Suburb
- City Wall
- Cliff

SYMBOLS IN THE KEY

Essential Information
- Tourist Office
- Police Station

Exploring
- Beach
- Buddhist
- Castle, Fort
- Christian
- Diving, Snorkelling
- Garden
- Hindu
- Islamic
- Jewish
- Monument
- Museum, Gallery
- Place of Interest
- Snow Skiing
- Swimming Pool
- Ruin
- Tomb
- Winery, Vineyard
- Zoo, Bird Sanctuary

Gastronomic Highlights
- Eating
- Cafe

Nightlife
- Drinking
- Entertainment

Recommended Shops
- Shopping

Accommodation
- Sleeping
- Camping

Transport
- Airport, Airfield
- Cycling, Bicycle Path
- Border Crossing
- Bus Station
- Ferry
- General Transport
- Train Station
- Taxi Rank

Parking
- Parking

OTHER MAP SYMBOLS

Information
- Bank, ATM
- Embassy, Consulate
- Hospital, Medical
- Internet Facilities
- Post Office
- Telephone

Geographic
- Cave
- Lighthouse
- Lookout
- Mountain, Volcano
- National Park
- Picnic Area

LONELY PLANET OFFICES

AUSTRALIA
Head Office
Locked Bag 1, Footscray, Victoria 3011
☎ 03 8379 8000, fax 03 8379 8111
talk2us@lonelyplanet.com.au

USA
150 Linden St, Oakland, CA 94607
☎ 510 250 6400, toll free 800 275 8555
fax 510 893 8572
info@lonelyplanet.com

UK
2nd fl, 186 City Road, London EC1V 2NT
☎ 020 7106 2100, fax 020 7106 2101
go@lonelyplanet.co.uk

Published by Lonely Planet Publications Pty Ltd
ABN 36 005 607 983
© Lonely Planet 2010
© photographers as indicated 2010
Cover photograph Farmhouse set among rolling
hills in Val d'Orcia, Tuscany, David Tomlinson/
Lonely Planet Images. **Internal title-page
photograph** Cypress trees, near Montalcino,
Tuscany, David Tomlinson/Lonely Planet Images.

Many of the images in this guide are available
for licensing from Lonely Planet Images:
lonelyplanetimages.com.

All rights reserved. No part of this publication
may be copied, stored in a retrieval system, or
transmitted in any form by any means, electronic,
mechanical, recording or otherwise, except brief
extracts for the purpose of review, and no part of
this publication may be sold or hired, without the
written permission of the publisher.

Printed by Fabulous Printers Pte Ltd
Printed in Singapore

Lonely Planet and the Lonely Planet logo are
trademarks of Lonely Planet and are registered
in the US Patent and Trademark Office and in
other countries.

Lonely Planet does not allow its name or logo to be
appropriated by commercial establishments, such as
retailers, restaurants or hotels. Please let us know of
any misuses: lonelyplanet.com/ip.

Mixed Sources
Product group from well-managed
forests and other controlled sources
www.fsc.org Cert no. SGS-COC-005002
© 1996 Forest Stewardship Council
FSC

Although the authors and Lonely Planet have taken all reasonable care in preparing this book, we make no warranty about the
accuracy or completeness of its content and, to the maximum extent permitted, disclaim all liability arising from its use.